Century
of Innovation

Century of Innovation

*A History of
European and American
Theatre and Drama
Since the Late Nineteenth Century*

SECOND EDITION

Oscar G. Brockett
University of Texas

Robert Findlay
University of Kansas

ALLYN AND BACON

Boston   London   Toronto   Sydney   Tokyo   Singapore

Series Editor: Steve Hull
Series Editorial Assistant: Amy Capute
Production Coordinator: Marjorie Payne
Production Editor: Anne Marie Fleming
Text Designer: Anne Marie Fleming
Cover Administrator: Linda K. Dickinson
Cover Designer: Suzanne Harbison
Composition Buyer: Louise Richardson
Manufacturing Buyer: Louise Richardson

Copyright © 1991 by Allyn and Bacon
A Division of Simon & Schuster, Inc.
160 Gould Street
Needham Heights, Massachusetts 02194

Copyright © 1973 by Prentice-Hall, Inc.

Library of Congress Cataloging-in-Publication Data

Brockett, Oscar Gross
    Century of innovation : a history of European and American theatre and drama since the late nineteenth century / by Oscar G. Brockett and Robert Findlay.
      p.   cm.
    Includes bibliographical references (p.) and index.
    ISBN 0–205–12878–5
    1. Theater—History—20th century.   2. Drama—20th century—History and criticism.   I.   Findlay, Robert
II. Title.
PN2189.B64   1990
792′.094—dc20   90–14452
                                                 CIP

Printed in the United States of America

10 9 8 7 6 5 4 3 2   95 94

Contents

Preface

As a "century of innovation," the twentieth has been precisely that—a century grounded in new ways of doing things and new ways of perceiving art and reality. It has been a century continually exploding with new discoveries, perspectives, and theories: relativity and nuclear energy, the twelve-tone scale and cubism, the atomic bomb and the computer, the motion picture image and television. And within this climate of change, theatre persistently has found ways of redefining and reinventing itself.

The first edition of *Century of Innovation: A History of European and American Theatre and Drama Since 1870* was published in January 1973. Like any history, it was a product of its time: a "reading" of events in the period 1870–1970 from the vantage point of the turbulent mid- to late-1960s and early 1970s. The second edition of *Century of Innovation*, now subtitled "A History of European and American Theatre and Drama Since the Late Nineteenth Century," is also inevitably a product of its time—a "reading" of theatrical history in chiefly the twentieth century from the vantage point of the close of that century. A number of contemporary terms not coined at the time of the first edition appear in the second: poststructuralism, deconstruction, postmodernism, theatre anthropology, feminist theatre, performance art, *glasnost, perestroika,* etc.

Twenty years' difference brings a different perspective of theatre history, and what follows is greatly reorganized, revised, and compressed from the first edition. The book is now approximately one-quarter smaller, though discussion covers events up to approximately January 1, 1990. Some photographic illustrations have been eliminated, but many new ones have been added, particularly of productions during the past twenty years.

As before, we acknowledge our great indebtedness to the work of many others, only imperfectly indicated by the bibliography at the end of the text. Again our gratitude is extended to those, named specifically in the first edition, who assisted in the realization of that book. In writing this updated second edition, we would like to thank specifically the following people for their awareness and assistance: Ronald Willis, William Kuhlke, Halina Filipowicz, Alma Law, Delbert Unruh, Yvonne Shafer, Uta Hoffmann, and Ellen Walterscheid, and the reviewers of the second edition, Marvin Carlson, City University of New York; Spencer Golub, Brown University; Bela Kiralyfalvi, Wichita State University; and Felicia Londré, University of Missouri-Kansas City. In addition, we would like to thank our many students over the years for their intellectual perceptivity and challenge in numerous classes and seminars. Credits for photographs are acknowledged in the captions accompanying the illustrations.

Oscar G. Brockett
University of Texas

Robert Findlay
University of Kansas

Century
of Innovation

Chapter 1

Challenging the Status Quo

Many contemporary critics and historians have argued that the late nineteenth century brought the most profound ideational changes in the entire history of Western civilization. Certainly a new—often called *modern*—era was ushered in. During the century that has passed since this new era began, the significance of the "modern" has become increasingly apparent, in part because of its diverse manifestations—realism, naturalism, symbolism, expressionism, surrealism, absurdism, to name only some of the most prominent.

In studying this modern era, some cultural historians have ignored realistic and representational art forms as mere extensions of previous practices, reserving the labels *modernist* and *modernism* for those ideas and works that reject realistic representation both as mode and goal. But any comprehensive overview of theatre and drama during the past century

1

must take into account the variant strains. Thus, both representational and nonrepresentational forms are considered here, and not solely for the sake of comprehensiveness. The realistic strain played an essential role in the evolution of modernism, especially in undermining the near-absolutist assumptions about truth, morality, and acceptable subject matter that had undergirded artistic practice during earlier centuries. Through its questioning of humanistic values and stereotypical "truths," the realistic strain played a crucial part in creating those relativist standards that infuriated conservative audiences and made almost everyone aware that something new was underway in the arts. These forces, first evident in the movement called *realism,* paved the way for the more innovative nonrepresentational modes that were to come. The representational and the nonrepresentational were merely two sides of the same coin: one reexamining the seemingly objective world, the other rejecting objective appearance for subjective vision. Both of these basic strains have continued throughout the past century, and both have an honorable place within it.

THE CULTURAL CONTEXT

Awareness that a new era was in the making came only gradually during the nineteenth century. It came in part from socioeconomic and political forces, especially those associated with the Industrial Revolution. One of the most important changes involved the creation of factories, made possible by a series of inventions, perhaps most notably the steam engine (1769) which, with its potential as a motive force, prompted so many others, among them the steamboat (1807) and the locomotive (1812), which made the transportation of raw materials and completed products increasingly efficient. The establishment of factories, in turn, required the displacement of large numbers of persons, since workers had to live close to their workplaces. Thus, one major consequence of industrialization was urbanization, bringing with it a host of problems, evident primarily in the slums that industrial towns spawned.

Unfortunately, the problems created by industrialization and urbanization came just at the time when governments were least disposed to deal with them, for memories of the Reign of Terror that had followed the French Revolution haunted Europe throughout the nineteenth century and made governments wary of any agitation among the masses. Following the defeat of Napoleon in 1815, most European countries sought to restore the conditions of pre-revolutionary times. But the American and French Revolutions had left a strong legacy—belief in the natural equality of all persons—which posed a serious challenge to the centuries-old tradition of monarchical rule over a society organized heirarchically into a small privileged and hereditary nobility, a somewhat large politically underprivileged but economically favored middle class, and a socially, economically, and politically deprived working class (by far the majority). Those in power argued that this organization represented God's will, and that those who opposed it not only flouted secular but also divine rule. Most countries reserved voting rights for property owners, thereby effectively disenfranchising most of the working class. Thus, despite the problems created by industrialization, those in power were suspicious of any proposal for reform on the ground that concessions to workers would only encourage new demands and ultimately rebellion.

Not surprisingly, rebellions did come, since violence was seemingly the only instrument of reform open to the workers. Scarcely a country in Europe escaped. The first wave of uprisings came in 1830, and a second, more intense one in

1848. Although most revolts were put down, by 1850 it was evident that more democratic political systems were desirable (although resistance to them was to remain strong) and that a host of pressing problems demanded solutions.

It is not mere coincidence that one of the most influential attacks on accepted ideas about religion, economics, and social norms—*The Communist Manifesto* by Karl Marx (1818–1883) and Friedrich Engels (1820–1895)—was published in 1848. It depicted all history as a struggle between classes over social, economic, and political advantage determined by control over the prevailing mode of production. Thus, Marx and Engels saw capitalism as a mode that systematically impoverished and exploited workers, and they predicted the inevitable overthrow of capitalism by the proletariat and, ultimately, the elimination of class distinctions. They also described religion as the "opiate of the people," under the influence of which workers were led to accept oppression in this life in return for promises of rewards in some future life. Marx's attacks on the existing social, economic, political, and religious systems became a rallying point for many of those dissatisfied with the status quo. While Marx's views are most clearly related to the rise of communism, they are also pertinent to other goals of the nineteenth century, such as the formation of trade unions and demands for universal suffrage. Here they are perhaps most important for their role in undermining and altering orthodox views of social, economic, political, and religious "truths."

By the mid-nineteenth century, then, there was a growing sympathetic audience for radically new ideas. Prominent among these new ideas was the belief that social problems could be solved if approached scientifically. This position was set forth most persuasively by Auguste Comte (1798–1857) in his *Positive Philosophy* (5 volumes, 1830–1842) and *Positive Polity* (4 volumes, 1851–1854). Comte sought to establish a "science of society"—later called *sociology*—which would be the apex of all the sciences, since knowledge was to be valued only insofar as it contributed to the good of society. Comte proclaimed the great task of his age to be the application of precise observation, hypothesis, and analysis (the scientific method) to social phenomena so that the causes of problems might be determined and the effects controlled.

Comte's positivism was reinforced by Charles Darwin's *The Origin of Species* (1859), often called the most important book of the nineteenth century. Darwin set out to explain how the various species came into existence and how and why they changed. His explanation had two essential parts. First, he argued that all life forms have evolved from a common ancestry. This idea was not original, having often been suggested since the time of the Greeks, but Darwin, unlike his predecessors, supplied much evidence to support his hypothesis. Second, he argued that evolution is to be explained by a process of natural selection (the ability of a particular species to adapt to environmental circumstances, leading to the "survival of the fittest"). Reduced to its essentials, Darwin's theory explains all biological phenomena in terms of heredity (factors transmitted to an individual at birth) and environment (forces to which the individual is subjected after birth).

The implications of Darwin's theories are many, although he may not have seen all of them himself. Darwin reduces (perhaps eliminates) the role of God or Divine Providence (the most crucial element in previous thought). The story of creation as given in the Bible (at least if interpreted literally) is called into question by Darwin's view that all life forms have evolved from a common ancestry. Furthermore, if causality can be reduced to heredity and environment, the intervention in human affairs by Divine Providence seems unlikely or indirect. Insofar as God retains a place in the Darwinian universe, it is as the original creator of matter, everything having evolved through a natural process in which divine intervention apparently was unnecessary.

If all causality is natural and can be explained by hereditary and environmental factors, then it can be apprehended through the five senses. Any "sixth" sense is to be distrusted unless its intuitions can be verified by scientific observation. Attention is therefore diverted from the metaphysical or supernatural to the natural realm and to those things which can be directly observed here and now.

In such a scheme, the place of humans in the universe is seriously altered, for they become evolutionary products of a natural process and a species to be studied scientifically like any other biological phenomenon. As several critics of the late nineteenth century observed, *homo sapiens* had been absorbed into nature as just another animal rather than, as in earlier views, treated as somehow superior, or as an exception to animalistic nature. More important, the scheme of causality summed up in "heredity and environment" makes humanity a victim of circumstances rather than the architect of its own fate, since individuals have no control over their heredity or their early environment. The implications of this view (perhaps the most far-reaching of all) are enormous for morality. Can people be blamed for actions determined by forces over which they have no control? Taken to its logical extreme, this view means that whatever people do, they *must* do. Many changes in legal doctrine and moral values during the following century can be traced to the gradual acceptance of these views. In drama they opened the possibility (even the necessity) of treating sympathetically behavior formerly considered willful villainy.

The inevitability of change suggested by Darwin's theory reinforced the idea of progress.

If all life forms, including human, have evolved from some infinitesimal grain of matter, movement from simplicity to complexity and from lower to higher forms seems inevitable. This encourages the notion that progress is also inevitable. Darwin's purely biological study was subsequently applied to cultural change. Consequently, beginning in the late nineteenth century, cultural phenomena were also frequently viewed as subject to an evolutionary process ("cultural Darwinism") in which simplicity inevitably precedes and leads to complexity. This idea was reinforced by Marx's belief in the ongoing and inevitable evolution of socioeconomic systems toward utopian communism. And, in the twentieth century, it would contribute to the avant garde's insatiable interest in innovation—in "newness." The idea of progress also contributed significantly to optimism about the ability of science to speed progress. The desire to apply scientific method to specific problems led to enormous advances in technology, upon which so much of modern life was to depend, and this in turn further reinforced faith in the ability of science to speed progress.

But it was not only technology that developed rapidly. The desire for more precise knowledge led to enormous gains in the physical, biological, and social sciences, and to the subdivision of fields into ever more specialized areas. Psychology was separated from philosophy, of which it had always been considered a branch, to become a field of inquiry in its own right. Anthropology, archeology, and geology were transformed by knowledge gained through field studies. More important here, the knowledge accumulated by these three fields destroyed the traditional belief that the world was only 6,000 years old (a figure arrived at by counting backward from the birth of Christ through all the generations named in the Bible). Combined with Darwin's theory, it called into question the account of creation as given in the Bible. Thus, a conflict between science and religion, one never fully resolved, was generated. Gradually science was cast in the role of skeptic or blasphemer, challenging all received knowledge and the accumulated beliefs of centuries. But the newly emerging sciences, while they uncovered much new evidence and answered many questions, also opened up new mysteries which made it seem unlikely that humans could fully comprehend, synthesize, and utilize all the knowledge needed to solve human problems. Thus, alongside optimism over scientific potential, there developed a sense of unknowability and mystery that would contribute to nonrealistic art forms.

These developments had enormous implications for moral standards and social mores. Pragmatists argued that nothing could be considered true unless it could be verified by scientific investigation. But attempts to apply scientific method to moral principle merely demonstrate that values are inevitably based on unverifiable cultural assumptions. Because Western morality since the early Christian era had based its claim to validity on the authority of the Bible, to question the truthfulness of the Bible (as much scientific evidence seemed to) was to undermine its moral authority as well. The concept of moral absolutes, which had held a dominant position in Western thought and which had undergirded social mores, was called into serious doubt. More than any other single change, it is the shift away from absolutist to relativist values during the late nineteenth century that made the modern era possible. As the faith that undergirded the old morality waned, no new faith appeared to replace it. The continuing search for a set of values capable of commanding widespread commitment and of serving as a basis for action is one of the major characteristics of the modern era and one of the most pervasive themes of modern drama. The struggle over

absolutist versus relativist values has also been an ongoing one, epitomized most obviously in late twentieth century society by controversies between religious fundamentalists and secular humanists.

New ideas and values did not replace old ones quickly or completely. Changes were gradual, and were first made evident in theatre and drama between 1850 and 1875 by the emergence of a new artistic movement called *realism*.

THE DEVELOPMENT OF REALISTIC SPECTACLE

Realism was first proclaimed a distinct style in a letter published in 1853 by Jules-Husson Champfleury (1821–1889), a novelist and critic. By the early 1860s, the theoretical bases of realism had been debated in such periodicals as *Réalisme* (founded in 1856), *Le Présent, L'Artiste,* and elsewhere. The proponents of realism agreed upon the following points: (1) realism provides a truthful representation of the real world; (2) it is based upon direct observation of contemporary life and manners; and (3) artists must be impersonal and objective in their attitudes toward subject matter. Opponents of realism responded that (1) in avoiding the ideal, realism limits itself to the ugly and trivial; (2) it emphasizes external detail only; (3) it is completely materialistic; and (4) it emphasizes sensualism and fatalism, and is morally indifferent or even immoral in its outlook. The conflict ultimately turned on opposing views of the nature and function of art. The detractors obviously believed that art should, either directly or implicitly, idealize human experience and provide a positive and moral picture of human destiny. The supporters saw art as a reflection of life as seen through direct observation and without being judgmental. To the charge of immorality, they answered that truth is the highest form of morality, that idealization only falsifies, and that such distortion is truly immoral. They further responded that, if the audience did not like what was represented in art, it should blame the society that had created the conditions portrayed rather than the author who had been fearless in reporting them.

It was almost entirely the "moral tone" of realistic plays that aroused hostility in the late nineteenth century, for even the most conservative critics accepted and admired the reproduction on stage of external reality—so long as it was not sordid or ugly. Ever since the picture-frame stage was introduced during the Renaissance, the theatre had sought to create the illusion of place. But, until the eighteenth century, place was usually generalized. That is, settings were not meant to show a specific location so much as to capture the essence of a type of place—a garden, a prison, a palace—since at that time art was thought to be concerned with universals rather than particulars, and time and place to be secondary to

FIG. 1.1
Elaborate setting for Byron's *Sardanapalus,* "The Hall of Nimrod," designed by E. Lloyds for Charles Kean in the 1850s. (Courtesy Victoria and Albert Museum.)

human nature, which was said to be the same in all times and all places. Scenic practice was a reflection of an absolutist and unchanging truth. This universalizing approach to settings, while illusionistic in the sense that it used representational means to depict idealized backgrounds, led to the use of stock settings which could be employed in many plays. Seldom were steps, platforms, and other three-dimensional units used. Furthermore, furniture was not brought onto the stage unless absolutely required by the action.

In the late eighteenth century, as local color and historical change began to be valued, elements of particularity were introduced, innovations which marked the beginning of a belief that events are determined in part by when and where they occur. This concern for historical accuracy developed gradually, but by the 1850s Charles Kean (1811–1868) at the Princess' Theatre in London was providing his audiences with a printed list of all the sources he had consulted in his search for absolute authenticity.

This growing demand for authenticity also extended to special effects. By the mid-nineteenth century, the plays of Dion Boucicault were exploiting all the possibilities of the stage in such effects as ghosts rising and disappearing through the floor, the destruction of houses by fire and of steamboats by explosions, and a host of others designed to create a maximum of sensation and suspense. In addition, moving panoramas and dioramas—scenes painted on continuous lengths of cloth and moved across the stage by turning spools—made it possible to present episodes in which characters or objects (such as boats or carriages) seemed to travel great distances without leaving the stage. By the late nineteenth century, this type of moving scenery was to be coupled with treadmills set into the stage floor so that such events as the chariot race in *Ben Hur* could be produced convincingly.

Similarly, the desire to depict everyday interiors led to the development of the box set with three walls and a ceiling. Box sets were to be found in most European countries by the

FIG. 1.2
Cross-section of a stage, showing the treadmills and moving panorama used in staging a horse race. The man at the upper right controls the speed of the treadmills. (From *L'Illustration*, March 14, 1891.)

1820s, although they were not fully exploited until the last quarter of the century. Once the box set was introduced, an increasing number of realistic touches were inevitable. Mme. Vestris (1797–1856), working in London in the 1830s and 1840s, furnished her settings as though they were real rooms.

The introduction of gas lighting around 1820 also made illusion more complete. Gas made it possible to put as much light on the stage as desired, difficult earlier when lighting had depended entirely on oil lamps and candles. Furthermore, intensity could be controlled by regulating the supply of gas. By 1850, the *gas table,* an early type of controlboard, made it possible for one person to control all lights from one central location. The limelight and the carbon arc, both in use by the 1840s, projected strong beams of light onto the stage to simulate moonlight, sunlight, rainbows, and other special lighting effects.

By 1850, then, illusionism was highly developed and accepted as a standard for which theatrical production should aim. Thus, the realists' demands that closely observed detail be reproduced on stage could be met. Still, the illusionism typical of theatres in 1850 had many limitations as far as the realists were concerned. First, spectacle was often extraneous to the dramas it accompanied. It provided picturesque and often sensational backgrounds, but the events and characters were not integrally related to it. The addition of historically accurate costumes, realistic sound effects, and elaborate settings do not make *King Lear,* for example, realistic; these elements merely add illusionistic embellishments. Second, spectacle was almost never sordid. The unpleasant was glossed over or transformed into painless picturesqueness. The seamy side of life was firmly concealed.

The primary distinction between this scenic realism and dramatic realism involves the relationship of character and event to environment. In true realism, agents act as they do because they are in part products of specific hereditary and environmental influences. Once this relationship is accepted, setting is treated as a major cause of action because of the influence of environment on character and event. In this way, setting becomes an environment and not merely picturesque background.

By 1850, then, the theatre was equipped to stage realistic dramas, and the demand for truly realistic plays was beginning to be felt. Still, it would be a long time before a fully developed realistic drama would emerge.

THE DEVELOPMENT OF REALISTIC DRAMA

Although there had been realistic plays before the 1850s—including such recent works as Georg Büchner's *Woyzeck* (1836) and Friedrich Hebbel's *Maria Magdalena* (1844)—they were isolated from a clearly defined realistic movement. On the other hand, in France in the 1850s playwrights were seeking to embrace realism even as its tenets were being promulgated. The first playwright to make a serious impact was Alexandre Dumas *fils* (1824–1895). His *The Lady of the Camellias* (often called *Camille),* written in 1849, was denied production until 1852, in large part because it treated sympathetically the heroine, Marguerite Gautier, modelled on a well-known kept woman of the time. Even though many earlier plays had included the prostitute with a "heart of gold," they had usually laid the scene in some distant past and further removed the story through poetic diction and other devices. Dumas, however, had set his story in contemporary Paris and had simulated everyday conversation. Consequently, both the subject and its handling were considered scandalous, although today they appear contrived and conventionally moralistic.

The Lady of the Camellias is the least characteristic of Dumas' plays. It remained for The Demi-Monde (1855) to establish the path he was to take thereafter. In The Demi-Monde, Dumas treats the same kind of characters and the same milieu as in The Lady of the Camellias but now unsympathetically. Whereas The Lady of the Camellias shows the kept woman falling in love and nobly renouncing her lover when her past threatens his family, The Demi-Monde depicts a kept woman, Suzanne, coldly seeking to conceal her past and gain respectability by marrying an unsuspecting dupe. Olivier is her friend, but when he discovers her intentions he shows no mercy in thwarting her. Today Olivier seems self-righteous in his rigid application of a double standard, for though he has participated as fully as Suzanne in the demimonde, he feels perfectly comfortable in returning to the world of respectability which he

so firmly denies her. (Few plays embody so clearly nineteenth-century attitudes about women.) The Demi-Monde established the thrust of Dumas' later work: the serious treatment of contemporary issues.

In dramatizing his subjects, Dumas created characters reasonably like those in real life, made them speak dialogue which simulated the conversational mode, and placed them in drawing rooms furnished like those of the day. Thus, on the surface his plays fulfilled most of the demands of the realists. If they fell short, it was because of two characteristic elements: didacticism and ingenuity. About his work, Dumas wrote: "if . . . I can exercise some influence over society; if, instead of treating effects I can treat causes; if, for example, while I satirize and describe and dramatize adultery, I can find means to force people to discuss the problem, and the law-maker to revise the law, I shall have done more than my part as a poet, I shall have done my duty as a man. . . . We need invent nothing; we have only to observe,

FIG 1.3
Final scene from The Lady of the Camellias by Dumas fils, first performed in 1852. (From Le Théâtre Contemporain Illustré, 1867.)

remember, feel, coordinate, restore.... As for basis, the real; as for facts, what is possible; for means, what is ingenious; that is all that can rightfully be asked of us."

Dumas' didacticism often overcame his stated goal of objectivity, since he structured his plays to demonstrate the correctness of his own views about the social problems he treated. Therefore, critics came to label his works "thesis plays." Dumas was no rebel against prevailing moral norms. He sought better social conditions by inculcating higher moral standards and by remedying social injustices. The sanctity of the home and family was his constant theme, and his position on most issues was beyond reproach. Thus, Dumas seldom offended conventional moralists and, except for *The Lady of the Camellias,* he did not create the storms of protest that Ibsen's plays were to raise.

Dumas' ingenuity in handling his subjects also causes his plays to fall short of the realistic ideal, for they all too clearly rely on the kinds of complications, fortunate discoveries, and other devices inherited from the "well-made" play as perfected by Eugène Scribe (1791–1861) earlier in the century. Dumas' Scribean ingenuity in plotting and in building suspense made his plays seem contrived and led to the charge that he subordinated issues to dramatic effect. Nevertheless, it was probably Dumas' didacticism and ingenuity that made him so successful with audiences, for although the plays brought "bold" subjects to the stage, they were always resolved in ways considered morally acceptable.

A more orthodox practitioner of the realistic mode was Emile Augier (1820–1889). His first play in the realistic vein was a comedy of manners, *The Son-in-Law of M. Poirier* (1854), written in collaboration with Jules Sandeau. It reflects the contemporary conflict between the aristocracy and the newly rich bourgeoisie. Representatives of each class are treated both

sympathetically and satirically, for each is certain that his own class is superior. In a somewhat sentimental resolution, the wife is able to reconcile her noble husband and her bourgeois father. Augier continued to write plays about contemporary problems—among them *Youth* (1858), *Giboyer's Son* (1862), and *Madame Caverlet* (1876)—and in all he adopted a balanced, commonsense view of the issues and was always careful to represent all sides fairly. Still, Augier succeeded with contemporary audiences because he remained within the bounds of conventional morality and because his technical brilliance kept his plays entertaining.

Thus, it was through the plays of Dumas and Augier that realism first made an impact. Not only were the plays popular in France, they became mainstays of theatres throughout Europe and the United States.

The French experience was repeated in miniature in England in the works of Thomas William Robertson (1829-1871), among them *Society* (1865), *Ours* (1866), and *Caste* (1867). In these plays, Robertson developed the action as much through detailed stage business as through dialogue. So carefully did he integrate setting, costumes, and properties with character and action that his plays scarcely exist without their stage environment. In printing, the stage directions consume as much space as the dialogue. Unfortunately, Robertson had no successors in England, and twenty years were to pass before the direction in which he pointed was followed by other English authors.

Other dramatists might be cited as incipient realists, but the basic picture would be altered little. It is merely important to note that between 1850 and 1870 a few dramatists took the first conscious steps toward realism. The dominant dramatic mode remained melodrama, the most popular form of the nineteenth century, perhaps because it reinforced the belief that right will always win out even

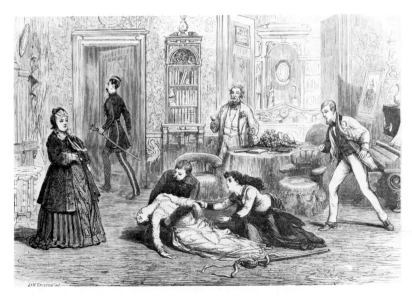

FIG. 1.4
Scene from Robertson's *Caste* at the Prince of Wales's Theatre in 1879. (Courtesy Enthoven Collection. By courtesy of the Board of Trustees of the Victoria and Albert Museum.)

against villains who are rich and powerful. It affirmed that absolutist faith which the next generation of realists was to destroy.

ALTERATIONS IN THEATRICAL TRADITIONS

The socioeconomic and ideational changes of the nineteenth century also led to alterations in theatrical practice which, when fully developed, would be typical of the modern era. One consequence of urbanization was the gradual decline of the repertory system. Until the nineteenth century, the number of theatres was small, even in cities. During most of the eighteenth century, for example, two theatres devoted to drama were sufficient to meet the demand in London. In addition, to keep the small potential audiences returning, theatres changed their offerings almost nightly. As audiences began to increase in the nineteenth century, theatre buildings were enlarged and the evening's bill extended in order to attract a cross-section of the population. A typical evening's offerings included a full-length play followed by a short farce, musical drama, or pantomime; between the acts of the long play incidental entertainment was presented. These *entr'acte* pieces ranged through songs and dances, trained animals, acrobats, and freaks. By 1850 such calculated appeal to mass tastes had led many critics to declare that the theatre had ceased to be a medium for serious ideas. By this time, the number of theatres in London had also increased to thirty.

Around 1850 theatre owners in large urban centers began to realize that they could survive by appealing to patrons from one segment of the population rather than seeking to please everyone. Consequently, they began to cater to specialized tastes by restricting their offerings to a specific type of entertainment. Most dramatic theatres dropped incidental entertainment, leaving music halls to specialize in variety and vaudeville. By 1900, most theatres offering drama were presenting one full-length play as the total evening's program.

Increased audiences also gradually led to the long run, which in turn reduced the number of plays in the active repertory. In the eighteenth century, when it was usual to change the bill nightly, a theatre usually had from fifty to seventy-five plays in its active repertory. As audiences increased in the nineteenth century, popular pieces had to be played for extended runs in order to meet the demand. By 1830 some productions were being presented for more than 150 consecutive performances, and the length of runs continued to increase through the remainder of the century. Such runs obviously reduced the number of plays needed to fill a season.

These changes probably affected actors most. From the beginning of the commercial theatre in the sixteenth century, actors had normally been employed by the season. So long as the bill had been rotated nightly, the workload was evened out over a period of time. But when productions began to be played consecutively more than 100 times, some actors were idle while others were working, although all had to be paid. As this problem increased, seasonal contracts were replaced by run-of-the-play contracts, thus leaving actors to find new employment when a production closed.

The long run was also encouraged by increased production costs, since demand for historical accuracy made it necessary to provide specially designed settings and costumes and thereby increased costs far beyond those of the eighteenth century when most productions used stock scenery and contemporary clothing. The greatly increased cost of mounting a production in the nineteenth century made it necessary to run the production longer if the original investment was to be recovered.

The theatre was also affected by the improvements in transportation that came with the development of the railroad. By the 1860s a network of railroads was sufficiently extensive that full productions, complete with actors, scenery, costumes, and properties, were beginning to tour. Such productions, usually mounted with considerable care, made it increasingly difficult for local companies to survive. Before the end of the nineteenth century, the provinces were largely dependent on touring companies for theatrical productions.

The growing complexity of society and ideas also created conditions out of which the modern director was to emerge as the dominant force in theatrical production. It is inaccurate to say, as many have, that the director is of modern origin. Someone has always taken responsibility for transferring scripts to the stage. The greater importance of directors in modern times is attributable to their increased authority and responsibility, direct outcomes of other changes.

Prior to the modern era, plays were normally staged by the manager or an actor in the company, usually called the *acting manager* or *stage manager*. This manager's authority and responsibility, however, were limited, largely because the goal, style, and methods of production were taken to be self-evident, and all participants in a production were considered to know their responsibilities and to need little supervision. Actors were employed according to "lines of business" (that is, a particular type of role), such as the heroines of comedies or tragedies, low-comedy roles, old men, and so on. Casting, then, was largely a matter of matching the line of business with the character type. Companies were assembled according to lines of business, often before the repertory was chosen. Once a role was assigned, it remained the actor's, and each actor was expected to play any role in his or her repertory on twenty-four hours' notice. Actors were assumed to be competent and to need little help beyond establishing where exits and entrances were to be made or with difficult stage business (such as duels). Because, until gas was introduced, lighting was poor, actors played most scenes near the front of the stage, where movement was largely restricted to trading off the most emphatic position, and, since virtually no furniture was used, actors usually stood in a semicircle. Actors considered this stage deportment to be their responsibility, and they resented interference as a reflection on their competence. Similarly, costumes, scenery, and properties were each the responsibility of personnel who were considered competent. While the director usually consulted with design personnel, he acted primarily as advisor.

The need for more centralized and autocratic control over production began to be evident during the early nineteenth century as concern for historical accuracy and realistic special effects increased. Theatrical personnel were loathe to give up authority to anyone, however, and so directors were able to extend their power only slowly.

A few pioneers of change in directing stand out because they deviated from the typical practices of their time and because they were able, through their prestige or exceptional power, to make demands most directors could not. Among these are Johann Wolfgang von Goethe (1749–1832) and Ludwig Tieck (1773–1853) in Germany, both of whom were able to exert control over productions largely because the rulers of the states in which they worked gave them the authority to work as they desired. In France, Guilbert de Pixérécourt (1773–1844), Victor Hugo (1802-1885), and Alexandre Dumas *père* (1802–1870) often demanded complete control over production as a condition for letting their plays be produced. In England, W. C. Macready (1793–1873) and Charles Kean (1811–1868), major actor-directors, were able to exert considerable authority

because of their prestige. All of these pioneers were concerned primarily with the classics or gentlemanly melodrama.

A fewer number of pioneers were concerned with plays of contemporary life. Dumas *fils* credits Adolphe Montigny (1805–1880), director of the Gymnase Théâtre in Paris, with taking the first significant steps toward realism in directing. Beginning around 1853, Montigny placed a table downstage center in order to prevent the actors from forming themselves into the traditional semicircle. Next, he put chairs around the table, seated the actors, and made them speak to each other, rather than to the audience, as had been typical. Finally, he furnished his box sets like real rooms and placed items, such as cigar boxes and handkerchiefs, about the stage to motivate movement from one place to another. His success encouraged others to adopt his methods. In this way, directing began to progress along lines suggested by realistic doctrine.

In England, such realism is most associated with the company headed by Squire Bancroft (1841–1926) and his wife Marie Bancroft (1839–1921) at the Prince of Wales's Theatre between 1865 and 1871. Their principal playwright was Tom Robertson, who also directed his own plays. Robertson worked with the actors on every detail of their performance, seeking to substitute understatement for bravura and to emphasize ensemble playing. The settings were fitted out like real rooms, and characters were asked to do such ordinary tasks as lighting fires, heating water, making tea, serving, and drinking it. This detailed attention to business led critics to dub the Robertson-Bancroft approach the "cup-and-saucer" school of acting.

By the 1870s, the position of the director was in a state of transition. The full potential of the director was seldom realized because several practices thwarted the desire for unified production. Among these, perhaps the most important was the star system. Most theatres built their productions around popular performers, who were able to defy a director in various ways. Many refused to wear anything they considered unflattering; most insisted on supplying their own costumes. Many refused to subordinate themselves to ensemble effects, arguing that the public wanted them to stand out. Another practice that militated against unity was the almost universal practice of recruiting supernumeraries off the streets as needed. A member of the company was paid to find extras, rehearse them, see that they were costumed, and that they appeared on stage as needed. Often a different group appeared each night. This impromptu handling of crowd scenes jarred harshly with the polish of the stars' scenes. Such difficulties had to be overcome before directors could assume the role they were to play in the modern theatre.

ON THE THRESHOLD OF CHANGE

By 1875, challenging ideas, new technology, and altered practices had paved the way for a new era in theatre and drama. It is doubtful, however, that many theatregoers were aware of imminent change since more than another decade would pass before truly realistic writing would be meshed with truly realistic stagecraft. During that time, Ibsen and the naturalists would so shock the general public that their plays would be denied production. At the same time, Wagner and Saxe-Meiningen were rethinking theatrical practice. But not until the late 1880s would the new drama and the new theatre be brought together to achieve their combined effect.

Chapter 2

A New Drama and a New Theatre

Between 1875 and 1890 the public became aware of striking innovations both in drama and in theatrical production. In drama, the key figures were Henrik Ibsen, "the Father of Modern Drama," and Emile Zola, the principal advocate of *naturalism*. At the time, both gained notoriety through plays that challenged prevailing notions of acceptable subject matter, social conventions, and moral values. The resulting controversy brought public awareness that a new era in drama had arrived. Meanwhile, Richard Wagner had set forth the theoretical bases for a fully integrated theatre art, and Saxe-Meiningen was demonstrating the enormous artistic gains to be achieved by an all-powerful director. Together, they brought awareness of a new approach to theatre. Nevertheless, the new drama and the new theatre remained separated from each other, thereby postponing the full realization of their potential.

IBSEN

Henrik Ibsen (1828–1906) began his playwriting career in 1850 with *Cataline,* a work about the ancient Roman rebel but clearly reflecting the European rebellions of 1848. Ibsen's friends, much impressed by the work, paid to have it published when it failed to win production. Ibsen's next play, *The Warrior's Barrow* (1850), a one-act drama about the Vikings' encounter with Christianity, fared somewhat better, being presented at the Christiania Theatre for three performances.

These plays, and some essays and poems, brought Ibsen to the attention of Ole Bull, a world-famous violinist, who was then promoting nationalism in Norway, where artistic life was still largely Danish, even though Norway had seceded from Denmark in 1814. In an attempt to counter this situation, Bull established a Norwegian theatre at Bergen, on the west coast of Norway, and in 1851 Ibsen obtained the position of stage manager there and later became the resident playwright. In 1857, Ibsen accepted the post of artistic director of the Christiania Norwegian Theatre (established in 1852), which was already in severe financial straits and which closed in 1862. Ibsen then served as literary advisor to the Christiania Theatre until 1864, when he left Norway for a long self-imposed exile.

A few points about Ibsen's early career are worth note. From this considerable practical experience as stage manager, director, and playwright, Ibsen gained first-hand knowledge of the theatre. He also learned much about playwriting, for although the Bergen theatre was designed to encourage Norwegian nationalism, the repertory was largely foreign. During Ibsen's six years there, 145 plays were produced of which 75 were by French authors, 21 by Scribe. From these works Ibsen absorbed the techniques of the well-made play, which he was later to adapt to his own ends. By the time he left Norway, Ibsen had completed his apprenticeship as a dramatist, having written nine plays.

Since Ibsen had been employed primarily in self-consciously Norwegian theatres, it is not surprising that all but two of his first nine dramas were based on Norwegian history or legend. Among the best of these Norwegian plays are *The Vikings at Helgeland* (1858) and *The Pretenders* (1864). These early works, most of which are in verse, already develop a theme that would remain dominant in Ibsen's work throughout his career: conflict between duty to self and duty to others. In the early, as in most of the late, plays, the characters pursue goals that are sometimes personal, sometimes public; but happiness usually escapes them because in their strivings they either sacrifice integrity or tread others underfoot. Consequently, even if the immediate goal is gained, the sense of fulfillment is missing.

By the time Ibsen left Norway, he had tired of nationalism and was turning to more philosophical subjects. Between 1864 and 1868, while living in Rome, he wrote two of his most important early dramas, *Brand* (1866) and *Peer Gynt* (1867). Originally conceived as an epic poem, *Brand* became a virtually unstageable, five-act tragedy in verse. The protagonist, Pastor Brand, believing himself to be God's chosen instrument for moral regeneration, devotes himself to his task with unflinching piety, making no concessions to human weakness. Like Kierkegaard, Brand takes as his creed "All or Nothing." His God is not the merciful, benevolent deity of Christianity but the wrathful, stern Jehovah of the Old Testament, and in His name Brand demands that human love, comfort, and weakness be suppressed. His own wife and young son eventually die because of his unwillingness to accept their human needs. Nevertheless, Brand steadily gains followers, and his growing power leads the civil authorities to offer assistance in building him a great new church. But, on the day of the church's dedication, Brand concludes that he has compromised his principles and leads his faithful followers into the icy mountains. When he is unable to feed them, they stone and desert him. A vision asks Brand to turn to God's mercy, and, as an avalanche sweeps down on him, a voice cries, "He is the God of Love." Thus, Brand dies a victim of his own sterile perfectionism. The ending has been called inconsistent, since it seems to void most of the criticism of society and human behavior voiced by Brand in the early parts of the work, but Ibsen's contemporaries did not find it so. It was Ibsen's first truly popular work, and the income from it (along with a small state grant) made it possible for him to work as he wished thereafter.

Peer Gynt depicted the opposite side of the coin. Unlike Brand, Peer is the eternal compromiser, always self-indulgent and accepting of life. He tries many vocations, travels throughout the world, and meets with many strange adventures, always moving on when he encounters difficulties, never staying to fight. Eventually, he returns to Norway, where the Button Moulder threatens to melt him down for buttons as a person who has failed to realize his potential. When Peer protests that he has not been truly bad, the Button Moulder replies, "Why, that's precisely the rub; you're no true sinner at all in the higher sense." Peer has failed because of his very mediocrity, for, never having committed himself to anything, he has never discovered his true self. Threatened with extinction, he is saved at the last moment by his childhood sweetheart, Solveig, who has grown old waiting faithfully for his return. Thus, as in *Brand,* love seems to be the great redeemer. The play aroused considerable hostility, since it was seen by many as a satire on the Norwegian character. Eventually, it was to become one of Ibsen's most popular and most frequently produced works.

Ibsen's last work in the romantic mode was *Emperor and Galilean* (1873), a two-part, ten-act philosophical work about the conflict between Christianity and paganism in the fourth-century Byzantine Empire. The protagonist, the emperor Julian, caught between two antithetical philosophies of life, seeks a synthesis that will be worthy of his full dedication. Unable to achieve it, he chooses paganism out of conviction that it will hasten the ruin of both Christianity and paganism, out of which will come a fusion of the two (the spirit and the flesh) since their mutual acceptance and reconciliation are necessary to the full realization of human potential. Ibsen always considered this play his masterpiece, in which he had presented "a positive theory of life." Few critics have agreed, but it was nevertheless a watershed play. As the thirteenth of Ibsen's twenty-five plays, it marks the midpoint of his writing career in several ways. It is the last of Ibsen's obviously philosophical works, the last of his romantic plays, the end of his poetic vein. From this time on, Ibsen was to write in prose and about contemporary subjects.

The plays that immediately followed are Ibsen's most consciously realistic dramas. Of these, two—*A Doll's House* and *Ghosts*—did more than any other plays of their era to call attention to innovations then underway, largely because both were viewed as attacks on the very foundation of society. *A Doll's House* (1879) explores the plight of a woman caught in the hypocrisy of a respectable marriage. Before the play opens, Nora Helmer, unaware of the law, has forged her father's signature in order to borrow money from the disreputable Nils Krogstad so she may take her husband to Italy where he can recover his seriously threatened health. When the play opens, her husband, Torvald, has recovered and is about to become manager of a bank. The family, which includes three small children, outwardly seems the epitome of happiness and respectability.

FIG. 2.1
Gabrielle Réjane as Nora in Ibsen's *A Doll's House* in the 1890s at the Théâtre du Vaudeville, Paris. (From *Le Théâtre*, 1900.)

Scarcely has the play begun, however, when Krogstad threatens to expose Nora as a forger unless he is assured a job in Torvald's bank. Frightened, Nora tries to keep the truth from Torvald, but she is convinced that, should he find out, he would take the blame on himself and praise her for her initiative in saving his life. But when he does learn the truth, Torvald, concerned only about his own reputation, denounces Nora as a criminal and declares her unfit to rear his children. Horrified, Nora realizes that she has always been treated as a doll, deliberately and condescendingly kept ignorant of the world; and although Krogstad withdraws his threat, Nora leaves her husband and children so she can find out about the world and become a fully functioning and responsible person in society.

A Doll's House was greeted as a scandalous attack on motherhood and the family, the bedrocks of society. Most theatres refused to produce it, and some did, but only after altering the ending to make Nora reconsider her decision. Because copyright laws of the day did not protect the play outside of Norway, Ibsen himself even supplied one alternate ending to prevent others from doing so.

The storm raised by *A Doll's House* paled in comparison to that created by *Ghosts* (1881) into which Ibsen introduced the taboo subject of syphilis. It is often said that Ibsen wrote *Ghosts* in response to the critics of *A Doll's House* to show the results of a marriage maintained for the sake of appearance. Many years before the play begins, the protagonist has married Captain Alving to escape her oppressive upbringing. This is her initial error, for her inability to provide love and sympathetic companionship causes him to turn to others and eventually to a life of debauchery. She then decides to leave him, but is dissuaded by Pastor Manders, who thinks only of maintaining the appearance of respectability. It is implied that Mrs. Alving is in love with Manders and that he could not face the scandal should she leave her husband for him. Mrs. Alving remains with the Captain and thereafter devotes her life to covering up his misadventures—she buys off a servant who is pregnant by the Captain and sends her only son, Oswald, away so that he will not know about his father's conduct. When Alving dies of syphilis, she builds an orphanage in his honor to allay any gossip. All of this has occurred before the curtain rises.

When the play begins, Oswald has returned home for the dedication of the just-completed orphanage, Mrs. Alving's attempt to put the past behind her before embarking on a new life of fulfillment with her son. But "ghosts" cannot so easily be laid to rest, and a series of events destroys her plan. Oswald begins to display signs of the disease from which his father had died. He also forms a liaison with the servant girl, Regina, who in actuality is the Captain's illegitimate daughter and Oswald's half-sister. Furthermore, on Pastor Mander's advice, Mrs. Alving has not insured the orphanage, since it might be interpreted as a lack of faith in God, and when the orphanage burns, there are no funds to rebuild it. Oswald's efforts in fighting the fire bring on a new attack; fearing that he will lose his mind, he

asks his mother to give him poison which he has provided her should he go mad. Seeking to quiet him, she promises. At the end of the play, he is little more than a babbling idiot, begging his mother for the sun. As the curtain falls, Mrs. Alving stands over him, indecisive about whether to give him the poison.

Everything that happens in the play comes about because of ghosts from Mrs. Alving's past. When the play opens, Mrs. Alving considers herself an emancipated woman who now understands the past and has come to terms with it. Thus, her sense of confidence at the start contrasts sharply with her dilemma at the end. Whether or not she gives Oswald poison, her world is destroyed—by the ghosts she has sought so valiantly to escape.

In *Ghosts*, Ibsen has suppressed most of the obvious contrivances of the well-made play. The action is almost entirely internal, composed of a series of psychological discoveries by Mrs. Alving. Almost every line is significant, but its economy and lack of obvious theatricality made many nineteenth-century readers conclude that it was totally lacking in dramatic action. The moral aspects of the play, however,

FIG. 2.2
Scene between Regina and Engstrand in Ibsen's *Ghosts*, produced in 1890 by Den Nationale Scene, Bergen, Norway. (From Bergens Teatermuseum.)

were what raised public ire. Ibsen was denounced for dragging drama into the sewer. In almost no country could *Ghosts* be licensed for production. Probably because no license was required, the first production was presented in America in 1882 by a Dano-Norwegian company touring midwestern states.

Through *A Doll's House* and *Ghosts* Ibsen established the pattern he was to follow thereafter. He limits the scope of the action, concentrating on a few characters caught in crisis. He carefully lays out the past so that character and environment are major determinants of the incidents. Each play treats only the end of a long chain of events, all interconnected but whose significance is unclear until the past recoils on the present and creates crisis and catastrophe. Most of the plays occur in a single room. Above all, the emphasis is on psychological conflict, external action serving only as response to or stimulus for internal struggle. The dialogue is a very precise prose which seems realistic, even though each speech is carefully tailored. Economy is the key. The overall effect is naturalness. Many of these characteristics are also typical of the work of other dramatists of this period, among them Dumas and Augier. Where Ibsen differed most and stirred up most controversy, however, was in the resolutions of his plays. Other dramatists ended their plays in reaffirmations of the accepted values of the day; thus, they might titillate audiences by treating daring topics, but they reassured viewers that their world remained intact. Ibsen offered no such comfort, Instead, he suggested that it was distorted social and moral values that created personal disasters. It was not a message that conservative audiences wanted to hear, and it was their storms of protest, along with the defenses offered by Ibsen's supporters, that created public awareness of Ibsen and dramatic innovation in general, which otherwise might have made little impression.

Ibsen soon moved on from emphasis on social import. In *The Wild Duck* (1884), he is concerned with the conflict between those who demand that everyone face unpleasant truths and those who construct illusions to make life bearable; he seems to come down on the side of illusions. In the play, one of the characters states: "Rob the average man of his life-illusion, and you rob him of his happiness at one stroke." In *Hedda Gabler* (1890), the chief interest lies in the central character, an emancipated woman who, rather than using her potential, hides under the mask of respectability as the wife of a pedantic academic. Unable to adjust, she stands outside the life around her, observing it ironically and destructively. When Eilert Lövborg, with whom she might have found happiness, returns, she manipulates him into attempting suicide with one of her duelling pistols, once the property of her father and used in the play as a symbol of Hedda's revolt. Judge Brack discovers Hedda's role in Lövborg's suicide and attempts to blackmail her sexually. Rather than submit, Hedda kills herself with the remaining pistol.

In several of Ibsen's late plays, a mystical or visionary element is apparent. It is first fully evident in *Rosmersholm* (1886) in which the image of white horses serves as a mysterious force related to guilt and retribution. This force became even more evident in *The Master Builder* (1892) and *When We Dead Awaken* (1899). The title character of *The Master Builder* is Halvard Solness, who has risen from humble beginnings to preeminence in his field. He realizes that he has paid dearly for his success, not only with his own happiness but with that of others, particularly that of his wife, Aline. His success has been made possible in part by the destruction of his wife's family home by fire, but to Aline the loss was so great that she became ill and, while she was incapacitated, her children died. According to Solness, Aline was meant to build human beings just as he was

FIG. 2.3

A production of *Rosmersholm* at the Schiller-Theater, Berlin, in 1901. (From the Deutsche Akademie der Künste zu Berlin.)

meant to build houses; now she is little more than a living corpse. Solness has come to believe that "the troll within" has willed the fire and that he is responsible for his wife's condition. This is the situation when the play opens. Then, Hilda Wangel, a charming and mysterious young woman, arrives and reminds Solness that ten years earlier he had promised to come and take her away. Since he has not come for her, she has come to him to collect "either my kingdom or your life." She urges him to regain once more the spirit she knew when he climbed to the top of a church steeple to crown with a wreath his completed building. When Solness completes a house for Aline (to which he has added a spire), Hilda persuades him to crown it. As she stands below, he falls to his death while Hilda ecstatically cries out, "My master builder."

On the literal level, the play concerns an aging man who falls in love with a young woman and, in attempting to assert his virility, dies. But on the symbolic level, it is extremely complex and not always clear. The deeper, inner drama concerns Solness' despair over his "sickly conscience," while Hilda seems to represent some higher power who leads him to retribution. Both Solness and Hilda speak of the "trolls" within themselves, and Solness sees himself at war with God, who he says has decreed his success and has taken away his children and his wife's love so that nothing can distract him from building churches; but Solness has defied God and has given up building churches in favor of homes. His final act, the crowning of a human dwelling equipped with something like a church spire, may be his supreme defiance, and death his punishment.

Although the irrational forces of which Solness speaks may be mere figments of his mind, in the drama they become active forces. In this play, human destiny has become far more complex than in *Ghosts*.

In Ibsen's final play. *When We Dead Awaken* (1899), Arnold Rubek, a world-famous sculptor, feels that his powers are gone. In a sanitorium, where he has come to rest, he encounters Irene, who years before had posed for the work that made him famous and who now believes she has been spiritually dead ever since he rejected her love. Rubek sees in her the possibility of his own artistic resurrection, but Irene tells him, "There is no resurrection. . . . . When we dead awaken we realize that we have never lived." He is determined to disprove her statement, but when he sets out with her to climb a mountain, they are both swallowed up by an avalanche. Nevertheless, in physical death they experience a spiritual release from the pains of a living death.

Shortly after completing *When We Dead Awaken,* Ibsen suffered a stroke from which he never fully recovered. He lived another six years but never wrote again. He died in May 1906, honored the world over as the principal architect of modern drama.

No dramatist after Ibsen exerted so wide an influence, perhaps because his work contained so many seeds later cultivated by others. At first, he was honored primarily as a realistic dramatist and was usually evaluated in one of two ways: as a writer whose works are exercises in moral persuasion (championed by George Bernard Shaw), or as a writer whose ideas are repulsive but whose technical skill is great (most conservative critics and audiences). In both cases, the plays of the 1870s and 1880s were considered to represent the "real Ibsen," while both the early and late plays were viewed as aberrant. For this reason, Ibsen came after a time to seem old-fashioned because his social problem plays lost their original bite.

But that group of plays make up only about one-quarter of his total output, and even they are not entirely realistic. *Ghosts,* for example, uses symbols as complex as those in many later works. The titles of the plays are in themselves symbolic, suggesting deeper meanings. Moreover, this symbolic element connects even the realistic works with Ibsen's poetic dramas, for, though Ibsen gave up writing in verse, he never gave up his search for a "poetry of the theatre." Through symbolism and the careful juxtaposition of contrasting elements, he implied relationships among seemingly unlike objects and actions so as to create the equivalent of metaphor.

Ibsen's late plays were especially attractive to dramatists of the symbolist movement, perhaps because they are so ambiguous and encourage a multitude of interpretations. They suggest that human destiny is influenced by forces that extend beyond heredity and environment, and that the analysis and control sought by the naturalists were doomed to failure because they were based on a too-restrictive view of causality. Perhaps Ibsen's greatest influence stemmed from his unflinching belief that drama is a medium of serious ideas and a search for truth. He always insisted on cutting through taboos and hypocrisies. Even if he could not find the answers he sought, he insisted on asking the questions, often embarrassing and disturbing ones. To him, drama was not mere entertainment but a confrontation with human behavior. The stylistic modes in which he presented this confrontation varied, but both the modes and the questions were to shape drama for many years to come.

ZOLA AND NATURALISM

While Ibsen was writing his realistic works, a new movement—*naturalism*—was underway in France. Although not very productive in significant plays, it was very self-conscious about the theoretical bases of drama. The primary theorist was Emile Zola (1840–1902), a disciple of Comte.

Although Zola's main interest was the novel, he sought to reform the theatre, which he declared to be fifty years behind the novel. To Zola, the theatre seemed a victim of worn-out conventions—the "last citadel of falsehood." In the prefaces to his plays and in his essays (collected in 1881 under the title *Naturalism in the Theatre*), Zola declared the traditional theatre an exemplar of untruth, an institution dying of pomposity, unreality, and platitudes. He proclaimed, "Either the theatre will die or it will become modern and naturalistic."

Zola's ideas about the proper approach to art were heavily influenced by Claude Bernard's *Introduction to Experimental Medicine* (1865), a study of the effects of environment on the functioning of the bodily organs and of changes in body chemistry upon behavior. In *The Experimental Novel* (1881), Zola sought to apply Bernard's method to literature. He compared the writer to the doctor, who seeks the causes of a disease so that it may be cured, not glossing over infection but bringing it out into the open where it can be examined. Similarly, the writer should seek out social ills and reveal them so they may be corrected. It was probably this analogy between pathology and art that led the naturalists so often to choose subjects from the more sordid aspects of human behavior. It also led Zola to demand that the writer be as objective as the scientist: "There should not be any school or formula anymore; there is only life itself, a great field where each may study and create as he wishes."

Nevertheless, Zola recognized that subjectivity is inevitable. He once defined art as "a corner of life seen through a temperament," by which he probably meant that the artist's personality dictates in part what subjects he chooses to treat. But he did not allow subjectivity much scope. For him, the subject and characters represented something akin to a scientific hypothesis; once established, these elements should be permitted to interact according to "the inevitable laws of heredity and environment," and the results should demonstrate the truth of scientific observation.

It was in the techniques then being used by dramatists such as Dumas and Augier that Zola saw the greatest danger to truth, for they tended to distort life for the sake of theatrical effect: "The word *art* displeases me: it contains I know not what ideas of necessary arrangement." He argued that truth is not revealed in a series of complications leading to crisis and resolution but in a more haphazard collection of events that create texture and a sense of direction. He suggested that a play should be "a fragment of existence" without apparent beginning, middle, or end: "Instead of imagining an adventure, complicating it, preparing stage surprises, which from scene to scene will bring it to a final conclusion, one simply takes from life the history of a being, or a group of beings, whose acts one faithfully records."

The application of naturalistic theory to literature had many results. Its emphasis on heredity and environment made humans victims of forces beyond their control; even "will" became merely an impulse dictated by earlier influences. Naturalists avoided concern for beauty and instead usually concentrated on human beings in the throes of greed, lust, fear, and anger. They sought to record social conditions without passing judgment. Nevertheless, naturalistic works included implied criticism by suggesting that social ills required that changes be made in society.

Many of the naturalists' demands seem excessive for plays of normal length. But Zola thought the theatre especially well suited to naturalism if properly used. He argued that descriptive passages, which are so important in novels, were unnecessary in plays because settings, costumes, properties, and stage business constitute "a continual description more exact and more striking than the descriptions of any novel." Spectacle provides a visible environment that illuminates character and action: "scenery is, in short, the surroundings where the characters are born, live, and die." Nevertheless, naturalism proved much more compatible with the novel than with drama, probably because in the novel hereditary and environmental forces can be explored at much greater length than on the stage, where time and scope are limited.

Naturalistic tendencies had been evident in the French novel since early in the nineteenth century, especially in the works of Honoré de Balzac, Stendhal, Gustave Flaubert, and the Goncourt brothers (Edmond and Jules). Zola built on this tradition and wrote a cycle of twenty novels, the Rougon-Macquarts, in which he traced the history of a single family over several generations, thereby creating a startlingly detailed picture of nineteenth-century life. Several tentative attempts at naturalistic effects had also been made in French drama prior to Zola. Balzac had written two plays, *The Stepmother* (1848) and *Mercadet* (1851); the Goncourt brothers had written *Henriette Maréchal* (1863), and *The Country in Danger* (1873); and Alphonse Daudet had written *L'Arlésienne* (1872). None of these plays, however, had made any lasting impression. In assessing the progress toward naturalism in drama, Zola praised Dumas *fils* for his treatment of social problems but declared that the preacher had killed the observer. He also praised Victorien Sardou for his minute recreations of specific milieus but labeled his subjects and dramatic structure false. Since no one had yet fully realized the demands of naturalism, Zola took on the task by dramatizing his own novel *Thérèse Raquin*. This play, the first important landmark of naturalistic drama, received a chilly reception from both critics

and audiences when it was produced in 1873. It was withdrawn after nine performances.

Thérèse Raquin is not the loosely structured "fragment of existence" that Zola champions in his essays. Part of the problem may come from reducing a novel to stage length, since what in the novel had been developed leisurely becomes in the drama hasty and melodramatic. The first act shows the environment—the world of lower-middle-class shopkeepers—in which Thérèse lives with her sickly husband Camille and his mother. Life is tolerable until Thérèse falls in love with the painter Laurent, a friend of Camille. When the second act opens, Thérèse and Laurent have murdered Camille during a boating excursion and made it appear to be an accident. In the third act, the lovers are married with the blessing of Mme. Raquin, with whom they will live. Not until their wedding night does the cold-bloodedness of the murder affect them. Their mutual recriminations are overheard by Mme. Raquin, who suffers a paralytic stroke. Throughout the fourth act, she glares at them as they go about their barely tolerable lives. In the fifth act, the old woman regains the use of one hand and, after beginning to write out a message, suddenly stops. Near the end of the play she regains her speech and says to Thérèse and Laurent: "I want to watch you pay for your crime.... I want to watch remorse tearing you like beasts." Thérèse and Laurent, now hating each other, take poison and die at the old woman's feet.

Zola has managed to rid the play of much that is typical of Dumas *fils'* works. No thesis is expounded, and the characters are neither glamorous nor villainous. But the play abounds in coincidences and contrivances not unlike those of melodrama. For example, Mme. Raquin is at just the right place at the right moment to overhear the couple admit their guilt, while her stroke prevents her from revealing her knowledge; her recovery also seems contrived for theatrical effect. The poetic justice of the ending is scarcely what one would expect from an author who decried conventional resolutions. Zola is most successful in creating an environment—a lower-middle-class room that serves as parlor, shop, and kitchen. Hung with drab wallpaper and cluttered with cardboard haberdasher's boxes, it is, according to Zola, "a setting in perfect accord with the occupation" of the characters, one in which "they might not play but live."

Zola wrote four other plays, none of them successful. In addition, a number of his novels and short stories were adapted for the stage. The best of these are the five attributed to William Busnach (although Zola seems to have taken an unacknowledged hand in them). Especially noteworthy are *The Dram Shop* (which ran for 300 performances in 1879–1880) and *Nana* (given 100 times in 1881). A number of other adaptations were made without Zola's cooperation. These include Léon Hennique's version of the short story, *Jacques Damour,* produced by Antoine in 1887, and Raoul de

Saint-Arroman and Charles Hugot's adaptation of the novel *Earth* (1902). For the most part, both Zola's own plays and the adaptations made by others are characterized by melodramatic action and inadequate characterizations. Consequently, they almost always seem inconsistent with Zola's expressed ideas. Their primary contributions were made through spectacle—painstaking recreations of specific environments.

By the 1880s, it was clear that, while Zola might provide leadership as a theorist, effective naturalistic drama would have to come from another source. Nevertheless, Zola remained naturalism's strongest advocate, so much so that even today it is impossible to discuss the movement without thinking first of him.

Ironically, it was Henri Becque (1837–1899), always contemptuous of Zola, who accomplished the most with naturalistic drama in France. Perhaps because he refused to align himself with the movement, his achievement is often overlooked. Becque's output was small—six full-length plays and approximately

FIG. 2.4
Production of the adaptation of Zola's novel, *The Dram Shop,* at the Porte-Saint-Martin, Paris, in 1900. Despite the naturalistic detail, note that much of the setting is painted rather than three-dimensional. (From *Le Théâtre,* 1900.)

the same number of short pieces—and of these only two can be considered significant. His masterpiece is *The Vultures,* produced by the Comédie Française in 1882 after having been refused by several other theatres. That this conservative company accepted the play is surprising; it apparently assumed that Becque would revise the piece as requested, and when he refused to do so, it was given only three performances.

The Vultures shows few traces of the well-made play. The first act serves as a prologue in which the characters and environment are presented with scarcely a hint of what is to come. It shows the prosperous and happy Vigneron family: the father; his wife; and their four children, Blanche (engaged to a man of good family), Judith (who studies music and is much praised by her teacher), Marie (the most intelligent of the three daughters), and Gaston (the overindulged son). Several persons arrive for a party: Mme. de Saint-Genis and her son (engaged to Blanche), Merckens (Judith's music teacher), Teissier (Vigneron's business partner), and Bourdon (Vigneron's lawyer). In the midst of the party, a doctor arrives and announces that Vigneron, who had been called away earlier, has died of a stroke. Becque has done

FIG. 2.5
Scene from Becque's *The Vultures,* as it was produced in 1903 at the Kleines Theater, Berlin. (From Deutsche Akademie der Künste zu Berlin.)

nothing to prepare for this occurrence; as it often does in life, death has come without warning. The remainder of the play shows the effects of this death on the family as the "vultures" prey upon them. Teissier and Bourdon connive to get as much of the fortune as possible; the music teacher laughs at Judith when she suggests she might teach music to support the family; Mme. de Saint-Genis breaks off her son's engagement to Blanche, even though she knows that Blanche is pregnant by him; Gaston joins the army in order to escape the family's problems. Ultimately Marie sacrifices herself by marrying Teissier, more than forty years her senior, who first proposes that she become his mistress. Bourdon then connives with the family against Teissier to see that half the old man's fortune is settled on Marie. There is no denouement in the usual sense. The final episode shows a creditor trying to collect a debt already paid. Teissier, after exposing him, remarks to Marie: "You have been surrounded by rascals since your father's death." Here is Darwin's survival of the fittest worked out in economic terms. Becque's victims awaken sympathy but are not drawn sentimentally. There is no hero or heroine. The vultures are not so much villainous as amoral. They believe it their duty to look after their own interests. The overall effect is pessimistic. *The Vultures* was not revived until 1897 and even then provoked protests against its cynicism.

Becque's *The Woman of Paris* (1885) is a mordant comedy of worldly individuals who have accepted without question the materialistic values of their society. The opening scene sets the tone. A woman is arguing with a man, who is accusing her of being unfaithful to him. At the height of the scene, she cautions him, "Take care, here comes my husband." The wife is a frivolous, extravagant, amoral young society woman who sins with complete freedom of conscience and subsequently enters into another affair in order to secure for her husband a political appointment. There is no moment of reproof for the wife. She is treated neither as heroine nor as villain. Overall, the play constitutes a strong comment on the

FIG. 2.6
Becque's *The Woman of Paris* at the Théâtre Antoine in 1904. Réjane, at center; Antoine, at right. (From *Le Théâtre*, 1904.)

society of the time, but it is not made overtly within the play.

Becque and Zola disagreed on two major points. In his *Souvenirs,* Becque describes drama as "the art of elimination." In this he recognized what Zola never fully grasped: that art is by nature selective, even when it seeks to create the impression of photographic reality. For Becque, elimination meant reducing a work to its absolute essentials, whereas for Zola there is no fundamental difference between what happens in life and what should be put on the stage. The second point of disagreement is related. Zola made scenic environment essential. Becque included only what was essential to the action. His sets are salons like those found in the plays of Dumas and Augier. But if Zola did not recognize Becque's importance, the second wave of naturalists did. Those dramatists who came to the fore around 1890 tended to honor Becque along with Zola. But in the 1880s, naturalism in drama remained for Zola a still-to-be-realized ideal, while Becque, frustrated by his failure to win recognition, ceased to be productive.

WAGNER AND UNIFIED PRODUCTION

During the 1870s and 1880s, the theoretical and practical bases of theatrical production were also being refined in ways that made the public aware of significant change. In this, Wagner takes precedence in theory and Saxe-Meiningen in practice.

Richard Wagner (1813–1883) composed his first opera when he was only eighteen, and by the age of twenty-one was conductor at the Magdeburg Opera. His first wide recognition as a composer came with *Rienzi* (1842) and was quickly extended by *The Flying Dutchman* (1843), *Tannhäuser* (1845), and *Lohengrin* (1850).

Much of Wagner's life was devoted to violent controversy—political, personal, and artistic. Because of his part in the revolutions of 1848, he was forced to live in exile for twelve years, and throughout his life he voiced revolutionary ideas. He was a man of contradictions, his democratic sentiments contrasting sharply with his autocratic treatment of others, his strong personal attachments alternating with betrayal of friends, and his taste for illusionism subverting his idealistic vision of drama. To many, Wagner was an egomaniac and conscienceless monster; to others, an artistic messiah.

Wagner's influence on the modern theatre stems largely from his theoretical writings, especially *Opera and Drama* (1852) and *The Purpose of Opera* (1871). Much of what he wrote was provoked by his opposition to Italian composers, who had dominated the operatic form since its origins in the late sixteenth century. Italian domination was so extensive that until the early nineteenth century most opera houses of Europe imported Italian singers and designers. The Napoleonic conquests in the early nineteenth century, however, aroused strong nationalistic sentiments, and local traditions began to be prized over foreign imports. In Germany, the Teutonic past and the concept of Germany as a nation held strong attraction. Folktales, legends, and histories were compiled and used as the basis for literary and dramatic works. In 1871 the Germanic states were at last united. As these changes occurred, the Italian opera troupes were gradually dismissed (the last at Dresden in 1832) and replaced by German personnel.

Wagner's concern for the Teutonic past is seen clearly in such operas as *Die Meistersinger* (1867) and *Der Ring des Nibelungen* (in four parts, 1869–1876). Not only did he use Teutonic subjects but he also sought to replace the Italianate operatic form with one more suited to German tastes. When Wagner began writing, opera was essentially a collection of showpiece arias separated by passages of recitative. Wagner obliterated the distinction between aria and recitative, making the melodic line continuous and eliminating the elaborate songs that focused attention on the singer's virtuosity at the expense of overall dramatic effect.

In addition to Italianate opera, Wagner disliked realism in drama. He argued that the poet is a mythmaker rather than a retailer of domestic intrigues—that, while drama must be a reflection of life, it should portray an ideal world through the expression of the inner impulses and aspirations of a people as embodied in its racial myths and so unite them as a "folk." (It was this element in Wagner's thought that later so endeared him to the Nazis.) To Wagner, the ideal realm is left behind as soon as spoken dialogue begins to replace sung lyrics; therefore, his ideal work consisted of Teutonic myth (or a mythlike story) embodied in a union of drama and music—a blending of Shakespeare and Beethoven, in which drama is "dipped in the magic fountain of music" to create and preserve ideality. This aspect of his theory was to be especially attractive to the symbolist dramatists of the late nineteenth century.

More important for modern theatrical practice were Wagner's ideas about production. His objection to spoken drama was based in part on its impreciseness—its vulnerability to the whim of actors. He considered musical drama much superior because the dramatist-composer could control performance through a score that prescribed melody, tempo, volume, and rhythm, whereas the writer of spoken drama had to depend on actors to make these important interpretive decisions.

Wagner is also important for his conception of the *Gesamtkunstwerk* (total art work) in which all the arts are synthesized through the sensibilities of a single master artist. Above all, it is from this demand for artistic unity and its corollary—the all-powerful director—that Wagner's enormous influence on the modern theatre stems.

Wagner was not content to be a theoretician, and throughout his life he sought to implement his ideas. While his operas might exemplify his conception of music-drama, without production they were only partial embodiments of the master work he envisioned. Wagner sought a theatre of his own, since he believed that conditions in opera houses of the day made it impossible to achieve his ideal. His dream was realized in the Bayreuth Festspielhaus.

Plans for this theatre took shape over many years and were reworked many times. When the theatre was built, primary credit went to Otto Bruckwald as architect and to Karl Brandt as stage machinist. It was originally intended for Munich but dissension led to its construction at nearby Bayreuth. The cornerstone was laid in 1872 and the theatre was formally opened in 1876. The annual festival at Bayreuth soon became famous throughout the world; it was to be the fountainhead of all those festivals that have enriched the artistic scene during the past century.

The innovations of the theatre building also were to revolutionize twentieth-century theatre architecture, especially auditorium design. Wagner's democratic sentiments led him to build a "classless" theatre which departed markedly from traditional theatres with their tiers of boxes and the consequent segregation of audiences. The auditorium was fan-shaped (about 100 feet deep, narrowing from 115 feet at the rear to about 50 feet at the front) with thirty rows of stepped seats rising rather sharply from front to back. The rows were not broken by aisles, each row giving onto an exit at either end. The main auditorium seated 1,345 persons, while a small box at the rear (intended for Wagner and his friends) seated about 100 and a balcony above it about 300. A uniform price was charged since all seats were considered equally good for seeing and hearing.

FIG. 2.7
The auditorium and stage of the Festspielhaus at Bayreuth. The setting is for *Parsifal,* as designed by Max Bruckne. (From *Le Théâtre,* 1899.)

If the auditorium was innovative, the stage was traditional. The floor raked upward toward the back and had provisions for seven sets of wings on either side shifted by chariot-and-pole machinery under the stage, the traditional European method since the seventeenth century. The major innovation was jets which permitted the use of steam to serve as a curtain to mask scene changes or to provide atmospheric effects, such as fog and mist. Several workshops, storage rooms, and rehearsal rooms were also included.

Two features of the theatre are of special significance to Wagner's approach to production: a hidden orchestra pit and double proscenium arches. The pit was sunken, and a part of it extended under the stage a distance of 17 feet. A curved wall at the front reflected sound toward the stage and hid the pit (including the conductor) from the spectators. (Wagner argued that seeing the conductor was as destructive of illusion as viewing a performance from backstage.) This pit and the two proscenium arches, according to Wagner, created a "mystic chasm" between the world of reality

(the auditorium) and the world of ideality (the stage).

The limitations of Wagner's vision are most evident in the productions staged at Bayreuth during his lifetime, for visually they differed little from those seen elsewhere. Although Wagner wished to raise his audience to the ideal plane, he sought to do so by creating a total illusion. To increase this illusion, he enforced several innovations. He would not permit musicians to tune their instruments in the pit; he discouraged applause during the performance and did not permit curtain calls at the end. To emphasize the distinction between the real and ideal worlds, he darkened the auditorium during performances, concentrating attention on the stage. (It had been usual since the Renaissance to leave the lights on in the auditorium during performances.) Wagner's scenery and costumes were also realistic and historically accurate, differing in no significant way from those in use elsewhere. He used such devices as moving panoramas to depict journeys and a dragon with scales, movable eyes, a mouth that opened, and nostrils that breathed fire. Thus, despite his antirealistic theories, Wagner aimed at total illusion.

Wagner's reliance on illusion stemmed from his ultimate concern—the audience experience. For Wagner, the purpose of art was to unify and give meaning to a whole culture through a communal experience. By creating total illusion on the stage, he hoped to provide a sensual experience so overpowering that it would induce in the audience "that spiritualized state of clairvoyance wherein the scenic representation becomes the perfect image of real life." Thus, Wagner sought to arouse an irresistible empathic response. From this aim came one of Wagner's greatest influences on the modern stage: the notion that the success of a production is determined by its ability to engage the audience's emotions and draw it fully into the world of the play. It was against Wagner's conception of desirable audience response and its dependence on illusionism that Bertolt Brecht was later to rebel.

During the first half of the twentieth century most directors would accept Wagner's notion that the finest theatrical art results from a synthesis of all the arts in a totally unified work. This view was reinforced by Adolphe Appia (whose inspiration came from Wagner) and Gordon Craig (whose writings repeat many of Wagner's concepts), the two major theoreticians of the early twentieth century. Wagner was also to influence those who sought to make of art a substitute for religion, for his ideal theatre was intended to provide a mystical vision of human destiny capable of bringing meaning to an otherwise limited existence. As religious faith declined under the impact of relativism, it became common to seek a substitute in art. The symbolists, expressionists, Artaudians, and others in the modern era have all viewed the theatre as an instrument for saving mankind.

Wagner was also to be a source of inspiration for those in the late nineteenth century who sought to counteract the growing influence of realism and naturalism, for on the surface his ideas run directly counter to realistic doctrine. Still his own productions fall clearly into the mainstream of illusionistic romanticism, and his most influential ideas—the need for unity and the master artist—could be applied to any artistic mode. Thus, Wagner's theories were eventually assimilated by many movements without regard for his own stylistic preferences.

SAXE-MEININGEN AND THE MODERN DIRECTOR

While the Bayreuth Festival Theater was under construction, another troupe destined to exert a strong influence—the Meiningen Players—came to public attention. Virtually unknown prior to 1874, when it played a six-week season in Berlin, this company from the small duchy of Saxe-Meiningen soon became world-famous for its productions which demonstrated forcefully the validity of Wagner's demand for unity.

The Meiningen Players was not a new organization in 1874. Theatrical performances had been given in Meiningen as early as 1781, and the Court Theater, home of the troupe, had been opened in 1831. The company was insignificant, however, until Georg II (1826–1914), the duke of Saxe-Meiningen, assumed control over it in 1866. Before becoming ruler, Georg II had received a broad education and had traveled widely. He had studied at the universities of Bonn and Leipzig, had received extensive art training, and had seen Charles Kean's productions in London, Ludwig Tieck's productions in Berlin, and the finest companies of Paris, Vienna, and elsewhere. He was also much involved in the political and social life of the time. Unlike his father, Georg II was much in favor of German unification; it was this difference that motivated Prussia (chief advocate of unification) to invade Saxe-Meiningen and force Bernhard II (who favored alliance with Austria) to abdicate in favor of his son. When Germany was united in 1871, Georg II, like other rulers of German territories, retained his position as head of his state.

As ruler of the duchy of Saxe-Meiningen, Georg II had control of the Court Theater, a state-supported institution. When he came to power in 1866, he set out to improve the theatre's repertory and the quality of its productions. Until 1870 his direct participation in production was limited, and primary responsibility fell to Friedrich von Bodenstedt (1819–1892) as *Intendant* (administrator). From 1870 until 1895, Saxe-Meiningen held the title of Intendant and employed a director (*régisseur*) to work under him and to implement his plans. From 1870 until 1873, Karl Grabowski served as director but eventually proved unsatisfactory. The great period of the Meiningen Players came during the years 1873–1891 when Ludwig Chronegk (1837–1891) was director. He worked extremely well with the duke, who, though excellent in his conceptions, was largely ignorant of stage terminology and precise means to achieve his plans. The eminently practical Chronegk was able to translate the duke's ideas into concrete terms. Both were strict disciplinarians and indefatigable workers. The company was actually presided over by a directorate which, in addition to the duke and Chronegk, included Ellen Franz (1839–1923), the duke's third wife, an actress in the company before their marriage in 1873. (As the morganatic wife of the duke she held the title, Helene, Baroness von Heldburg.) The baroness served as dramaturg, assuming primary responsibility for the repertory, proposing plays and adapting texts as required. She also took special interest in the actors' speech.

It was Chronegk who convinced the duke that the company should perform outside of Meiningen. The first essay came in 1874, when

a four-week season was planned for Berlin; it was so successful that the run was extended to six weeks. The company returned to Berlin in 1875 and 1876 and then began to perform in other cities. Gradually the tours became longer, eventually extending from six to eight months. The last tour was made in 1890. By that time the company had played in thirty-eight cities in Germany, Austria, Czechoslovakia, Holland, England, Switzerland, Russia, Poland, Belgium, Denmark, and Sweden. A tour of the U.S. was planned but cancelled because of Chronegk's illness. The tours were almost entirely under Chronegk's supervision. He made all arrangements and traveled with the troupe. The duke saw only three of the performances outside of Meiningen. When Chronegk died, the tours were discontinued and thereafter the troupe played only in its home theatre.

Between 1874 and 1890 the Meiningen Players became the most admired company in the world. Its success, however, was not attributable to any new aim, for the duke, like most producers of his day, sought to create a perfect illusion of reality. Furthermore, his repertory differed little from that of other companies. Outside of Meiningen, the company performed forty-one plays, the majority being either classics or recent poetic dramas. It had its greatest successes with Shakespeare's *Julius Caesar. The Winter's Tale* and *Twelfth Night* also figured prominently in the repertory. Next to Shakespeare's, Schiller's plays—*Wilhelm Tell, The Maid of Orleans, Fiesko, The Robbers,* and the Wallenstein trilogy—were the most popular. Saxe-Meiningen also championed the works of Heinrich von Kleist (1777-1811)—*The Battle of Arminius, Katchen of Heilbronn,* and *The Prince of Homburg*—outstanding plays of the early nineteenth century but little appreciated prior to the Meiningen productions. The company gave only minor attention to plays in the realistic vein. The most daring production came in 1886–1887 with Ibsen's *Ghosts*, a play Saxe-Meiningen admired and for which he decorated Ibsen. But he never attempted to perform the play outside his own duchy. Overall, it seems clear that the duke's tastes ran to drama in the romantic vein.

At Meiningen, exhaustive research preceded the designing of costumes, settings, and properties. Although by this time Jakob Weiss' monumental history of costume (published between 1856 and 1872) had been completed, Saxe-Meiningen found it only partially satisfactory. Weiss had divided each century into thirds and defined the characteristic features of dress within those divisions; Saxe-Meiningen insisted upon distinguishing national differences within Weiss' time segments. Consequently, his costumes were the most historically accurate yet seen on the German stage. Accuracy in costume was further insured by forbidding actors to tamper with their costumes. In most theatres of the day, stars assumed the right to alter their garments if unflattering, and actresses insisted on wearing crinoline petticoats under dresses of all periods. In his dual capacity as ruler of the country and manager of the company, Saxe-Meiningen could demand and gain obedience. To avoid misunderstandings, he gave all actors drawings of their costumes and detailed instructions about how each article was to be worn.

Georg II also insisted on authentic materials rather than the usual cheap substitutes, which were available only in a limited range of colors and patterns. If he could not find satisfactory materials locally, he imported them and often had them manufactured to his specifications. Furthermore, he insisted upon authentic chain mail, armor, and weapons (such as swords, halberds, and axes). This demand for accuracy extended to furniture and properties as well, and often led to having articles manufactured. As the influence of the Meiningen troupe increased, a number of theatrical supply houses were founded in Germany to meet the new demand for authentic costumes, armor, furniture, and properties.

The duke designed all of the costumes, scenery, and properties. In scenery he attempted to make both the overhead masking and the stage floor integral parts of the picture. Most designers had ignored the stage floor, leaving the boards clearly visible even in exterior settings. Saxe-Meiningen used fallen trees, rocks, hillocks, steps, platforms, and even a stuffed horse to disguise the stage floor. He abandoned sky borders in favor of foliage, banners, arches, beams, or other illusionistic devices to mask the overhead space. Since he believed that symmetrical balance appeared contrived, he favored irregularly shaped and asymmetrical settings. Saxe-Meiningen's settings illustrate well the then-current movement away from painted to actualistic detail.

The duke's enormous care for detail extended to the acting. The company was composed primarily of young performers or those who had not achieved fame. There were no stars. Saxe-Meiningen abandoned the practice of using as supernumeraries persons not regularly employed by the company. It is partially for this reason that the Meiningen company came to be known above all for its effective crowd scenes. Any actor not cast in a major role was required to appear as a supernumerary. In rehearsing mob scenes, Saxe-Meiningen divided the performers into small groups, each under the charge of an experienced actor, who was partially responsible for training those assigned him. Each member of the crowd was treated as an individual and given specific actions and lines. The small groups were rehearsed individually and then as a unit. Thus, both enormous variety and unusual unity were achieved. Crowds were also made to appear larger than they were by the effective use of space. Saxe-Meiningen typically forced his crowds into restricted spaces with some members seemingly

FIG. 2.8

Sketch by the Duke for a scene in Schiller's *Maria Stuart*. (From *Theatre Arts*, 1930.)

pushed into the wings, thereby creating the effect of a crowd so large that all its members could not be seen. He also used diagonal, hesitating, and conflicting movement to achieve effects of agitation and confusion. The contrast with the usual crowd scenes of the time was both startling and impressive.

Perhaps above all the success of the company can be attributed to its rehearsal methods. The duke rehearsed a play until he considered it ready, and refused to set a performance date until he was satisfied. This approach was possible because the duke's position as ruler of the state gave him firm control over both the actors and the company's finances. In addition, the company had much more rehearsal time than most companies, for the town of Meiningen was so small (about 8,000 people) that the theatre was only open two nights a week during a season of six months. Rehearsals were normally held in the evening after the duke's state duties were over. They began about 5 or 6 P.M. and lasted until midnight. Each play was rehearsed from the beginning with full settings, furniture, and properties, and with costumes simulating those to be worn in performance. From the beginning, actors were required to act and not merely walk through their parts. Blocking was worked out as they went along. If there were problems, various solutions were tried, even if it meant rearranging the scenery and furniture. Although time-consuming, such practices permitted the actors an active part in every decision. The final result was a remarkable ensemble effect. Once a production was ready, a promptbook was made. Chronegk edited twenty-eight and published them as *The Repertory of the Saxe-Meiningen Court Theater, Official Edition.*

The enormous impact of the Meiningen troupe stemmed in large part from its ability to realize more fully than any previous company the then-current ideal of absolute illusion. It became obvious that the Meiningen Players' power was ultimately attributable to its director's assumption of absolute control over all elements of production. Thus, the Meiningen troupe validated Wagner's demand for unity of production. Because of his methods, Saxe-Meiningen has come to be considered the first director in the modern sense and one of the pioneers of the modern theatre. Through its example, the Meiningen company became an inspiration to a new generation of theatrical innovators, among them André Antoine and Constantin Stanislavsky, both of whom acknowledged their debt.

Most producers did not have the authority, time, or financial resources to adopt completely Saxe-Meiningen's methods. Nevertheless, he established an ideal toward which to strive. Perhaps as important, his productions attracted sufficient attention to gain acceptance for his innovations.

OTHER INNOVATORS

Although Saxe-Meiningen was more successful than most producers of his day in achieving the illusion of reality through centralized control, he was by no means the only practitioner of unified production. Several directors were working along parallel lines, some in ignorance of Saxe-Meiningen. Many instances could be cited, but among the most important were Henry Irving in England, Victorien Sardou in France, and Augustin Daly in the United States. The failure of these men to make as great an impact as Saxe-Meiningen may be explained by the conditions under which they worked and by their divided appeal: Irving was better known as an actor, and both Sardou and Daly were among the most successful playwrights of their time.

Henry Irving (1839–1905) was, from the 1870s until his death, considered to be England's finest serious actor. His position as head of his profession was recognized in 1895 when he became the first English actor to be knighted. Irving was also manager of the Lyceum Theatre from 1878 to 1898, where he directed his company's productions and starred in most along with his leading lady, Ellen Terry (1847–1928), mother of Gordon Craig (who for a time was an actor in Irving's company before becoming a major theoretician of the modern theatre). Irving also took his company on international tours (including eight to the U.S. after 1883), thereby extending its influence.

Irving's practices paralleled in many ways those of Saxe-Meiningen. His repertory was made up almost entirely of classics, poetic drama, and melodramas. He was concerned with historical accuracy in scenery and costumes (often employing archeologists as consultants or designers), although he deviated from accuracy whenever he thought it interfered with theatrical effectiveness. He liberally employed three-dimensional elements in settings. In 1881 he remodeled his stage, removed the grooves, and leveled the stage floor so as to achieve greater freedom in handling scenery. Thereafter, he made increased use of steps, platforms, and practical elements. Irving is also said to be the first English director to make an art of stage lighting by manipulating color and intensity to achieve beauty, mood, and atmosphere. In addition, he was the first English producer regularly to darken the auditorium during

FIG. 2.9
Irving's production of *Romeo and Juliet*, influenced by his seeing the work of Saxe-Meiningen. Note the extensive use of three-dimensional units. (From *The Illustrated London News*, 1882.)

performances. Irving himself controlled and coordinated all elements of a production to create a unified effect. If Irving's productions did not achieve the impact of Saxe-Meiningen's, several reasons may be offered. As manager of a commercial theatre, Irving could not devote unlimited time to rehearsals. Furthermore, his productions were built around stars, and scripts were often reshaped to emphasize these leading performers. And, like most producers of the day, he used many untrained supernumeraries in his crowd scenes.

In France, unified production was most fully realized in the historical dramas written and staged by Victorien Sardou (1831–1908). Sardou wrote some seventy plays (ranging through vaudevilles, melodramas, comedies, and historical dramas) which became so popular throughout Europe that Bernard Shaw feared the theatre had succumbed entirely to "Sardoodledom." For his *Patrie!* (1869), *Hatred* (1874), and *Theodora* (1884), Sardou worked out every aspect of setting, properties, and costumes to create such vivid past milieus that even Zola applauded their accuracy. Nevertheless, Sardou failed to make a deep impact on the French theatre because he did not control a company and confined his directing to his own plays.

In the U.S., Augustin Daly (1836–1899) came closest to implementing unified production. Daly is credited with writing some ninety plays, many of them adaptations of French works by Dumas, Augier, and Sardou. From 1867 until his death, Daly was also the manager of a series of theatres where he directed the plays in the repertory, primarily recent comedies and melodramas but with occasional classics mixed in. Daly assumed control over every element of production and insisted on his right to coach actors in their interpretations, stage business, and blocking. Like Saxe-Meiningen, Daly demanded on accuracy in settings, properties, and costumes. Every detail was worked out with care and

FIG. 2.10

Scene from Sardou's *Patrie!* as staged by the author in 1869. The settings were by Cambon. (From a contemporary engraving.)

were all coordinated for maximum effect. Although he voiced dislike for stars, he eventually built his best-known productions around four principal performers: Ada Rehan, John Drew II, James Lewis, and Mrs. G. H. Gilbert. Rehan especially won international fame and is still considered by many to have been the greatest of all Katherines (in Shakespeare's *Taming of the Shrew*). Daly toured several of his productions in England and on the Continent and eventually had his own theatre in London. Along with Irving and Sardou, Daly helped to establish the validity of Saxe-Meiningen's methods.

THE SEPARATE PATHS OF PLAYWRITING AND THEATRICAL PRODUCTION

The years between 1875 and 1890, then, brought major innovations in playwriting and production. For the most part, the contributions in both fall into the realistic or naturalistic modes, although other movements were foreshadowed. The innovations did not gain full acceptance immediately. The new drama was appreciated and supported by a relatively small group, while the majority most often denounced it as depraved or undramatic. What most struck the popular mind was the seeming attack on traditional morality and standards of decency. No play epitomized this as well as *Ghosts*. Many plays could not be presented because they were considered too immoral to be licensed. Thus, some of the most significant of the new plays were denied a hearing. Furthermore, many of the plays that were produced did not fare well because they were produced as if they were romantic dramas or melodramas.

The new drama demanded new approaches to production. The approach of Saxe-Meiningen, Irving, Sardou, or Daly was perhaps the one most appropriate to the new drama, but it was applied almost entirely to poetic drama or recent plays that followed accepted conventions. Until the late 1880s, the new drama and the new production approaches were to develop along parallel lines but without merging in any significant way. It remained for the *independent* theatre movement to mesh the two.

Chapter 3

The Independent Theatre Movement

By the late 1880s, both a new drama and innovative theatrical theory were evident. But the new drama, though widely read, was being performed only rarely, while the innovative theatrical practices were being applied primarily to traditional plays. Thus, the potential of neither had been fully realized. It remained for André Antoine to merge the two in an "independent theatre," which was to become the inspiration for others throughout Europe.

ANTOINE AND THE THEATRE LIBRE

In 1887 André Antoine (1858–1943) must have appeared an unlikely candidate for the role of theatrical reformer. A clerk at the Paris Gas Company, he had no formal education to speak

37, Passage de l'Elysée des Beaux-Arts **(Place Pigalle)**

MERCREDI 30 MARS 1887

à 8 heures très-précises du soir

Première Représentation

Jacques Damour

Pièce en 1 acte, en prose
Tirée de la nouvelle de M. Emile ZOLA
par M. Léon HENNIQUE

La Cocarde

Comédie en 1 acte, en prose
par M. Jules VIDAL.

Mademoiselle Pomme

Comédie-Farce en 1 acte, en prose
par DURANTY
et M. Paul ALEXIS

Un Préfet

Drame en 1 acte, en prose
par M. Arthur BYL

NOTA. — Cette invitation étant **rigoureusement personnelle,**
prière de vouloir bien retourner, avant la représentation, les places dont on
ne disposerait pas.   A. ANTOINE.

FIG. 3.1
Invitation and program for the first bill of plays presented by Antoine on March 30, 1887. (From a contemporary program)

of, and his theatrical background was confined to having served occasionally as a supernumerary at the Comédie Française, after attempting unsuccessfully to gain admission to the Conservatoire (France's major training school for actors), and working in an amateur theatre.

That Antoine founded the Théâtre Libre was largely accidental. In 1886 he had joined the Cercle Gaulois, one of the many amateur theatrical groups in Paris. Seeking to enliven the group, Antoine in early 1887 suggested that it produce a bill of plays by new playwrights. Unenthusiastically the group agreed to do so if Antoine would make all the arrangements. He acquired four short plays: *A Prefect* by Arthur Byl; *The Cockade* by Jules Vidal; *Mademoiselle Pomme* by Paul Alexis; and *Jacques Damour,* an adaptation by Leon Hénnique of Zola's story. The Cercle became increasingly reluctant about being involved, especially because Zola was so controversial, and eventually withdrew its sponsorship. Antoine, refusing to give up,

rented the Cercle's theatre for one performance. All the work of the production fell on Antoine. He even borrowed furniture from his mother and transported it to the theatre by handcart.

Since he could not use the Cercle Gaulois' name, Antoine had to find another. He eventually settled on Théâtre Libre (or Free Theatre, borrowed from a Victor Hugo epigraph, "A Theatre Set Free"). Paul Alexis, who wrote a daily column for a Parisian newspaper, publicized the program, and other journals printed notices of the production. Zola, who attended the dress rehearsal, was sufficiently impressed to return for the single public performance (on March 30, 1887) with a group of friends and critics. The audience was lukewarm to two of the plays, hissed one, and responded favorably only to *Jacques Damour,* in which Antoine played the title role. Nevertheless, the total effort received considerable favorable attention from the press.

Antoine had not intended to continue the Théâtre Libre, but, encouraged by his friends and the critics, he decided to prepare another bill, presented in May 1887: Emile Bergerat's *Bergamasque Night,* a long verse play written to be performed in *commedia dell'arte* style; and Oscar Méténier's *In the Family,* a one-act naturalistic piece. Although not all critics liked the plays, almost all were impressed by the productions. On the strength of the response, Antoine resigned his position with the gas company and set out to make the Théâtre Libre permanent.

The Théâtre Libre began its first full season in the fall of 1887. It was at this time that Antoine decided to run the theatre by subscription, primarily because he needed to raise capital. This arrangement was ultimately to be of greater importance because it made the theatre a private organization open only to members, thereby permitting the presentation of plays that otherwise might have been refused a license from the censor. This ploy, adopted by later imitators throughout Europe, gained a hearing for many previously banned plays. During its existence, the Théâtre Libre, roughly comparable to today's off-off-Broadway theatres, presented 62 programs composed of 184 plays. At least 69 authors, several of whom went on to become important in the French theatre, had their initial productions there. Antoine's actors were for the most part amateurs, although many aspired to professional status. Several became sufficiently accomplished to be hired by other theatres. In fact, the Théâtre Libre became a victim of its own success, for it was progressively weakened by the defection of authors and performers to established theatres.

During its existence, the Théâtre Libre occupied three different out-of-the-way theatres, all small (ranging from 343 to about 800 seats). Each season it gave a series of bills (an average of seven each year), most composed of short plays, although some were full length. Until 1890-1891 each bill was given only one performance; even at the height of the company's popularity no bill received more than

FIG. 3.2
Scene from Méténier's *In the Family,* as it was produced on the second bill of plays offered by the Théâtre Libre, May 1887. (From a contemporary photo.)

three performances, and one of those was for an invited, nonpaying audience. Consequently, income was always inadequate. Nevertheless, Antoine insisted on the highest standards of production, and debts steadily increased. When Antoine left the Théâtre Libre in 1894, he owed more than 100,000 francs. The group struggled on until April 1896 (under the direction of Paul Larochelle) and then closed permanently.

Antoine exerted untold influence on the theatre both in France and elsewhere through articles about his work and through his company's performances in Paris and on tour. In 1888 he played in Brussels, and later in Germany, Holland, Italy, and England. Antoine's influence came from three sources: the independent theatre concept; Antoine's production methods; and the theatre's plays and authors.

It is difficult to overestimate the importance of the independent theatre concept. Although many realistic and naturalistic plays had been written by 1887, they had not received an adequate hearing because of opposition from conservative producers, censors, and audiences. It was Antoine who showed others how to skirt the censor by playing for "private" audiences. He also demonstrated that it was possible to make an enormous impact by playing for an audience too small in numbers to interest commercial producers. When the significance of his innovations became apparent, other independent theatres were formed in France and elsewhere. As a result, by 1900 audiences almost everywhere had become aware of the new drama and in many places were becoming sufficiently tolerant to accept it in the repertory of mainstream theatres. Since Antoine's time, the independent theatre, or some variation on it, has remained the major venue for significant innovations in writing and production. Practically all alternative the-atres are lineal descendants of the Théâtre Libre.

Antoine was also instrumental in reshaping staging practices, although like many reformers, Antoine invented little. In many respects his methods differed little from those of Saxe-Meiningen, Irving, or Daly, but he applied them to plays that truly needed actualistic staging. From the very beginning, Antoine was concerned with realism, but his concern seems to have increased after the summer of 1888, when he witnessed performances of Irving's company in London and Saxe-Meiningen's in Brussels. He admired Irving's use of three-dimensional scenic pieces and came back to Paris determined to abandon the practice of painting objects (often even furniture) on the walls and to adopt the "free plantation" system of positioning and changing scenery. He was even more impressed by the Meiningen troupe, especially its ensemble effects and crowd scenes. Thus, after 1888 the goal of complete illusion influenced every aspect of his productions.

For scenery, Antoine insisted on new flats for each new production, since the sagging canvas on old ones destroyed illusion. He also insisted on specially designed settings for each play because he considered the setting to be an environment necessarily different for each play. In creating sets, Antoine sought first to imagine the locale as it would be in real life. He furnished rooms completely, including bric-a-brac. According to his own testimony, it was only after he was satisfied with every detail that he decided which wall to remove for stage use. Sometimes furniture remained along the curtain line, which was always treated as an invisible—and inviolable—fourth wall. The properties were numerous and as real as Antoine could obtain. The most famous example is the real carcasses of beef used in Fernand Icre's *The Butchers* in 1888. (It is only fair to note that Antoine later declared the carcasses to have been a last-minute addition because the set looked too bare.) For *Old Heidelberg* Antoine bought the contents of a student's room and transferred them to the stage. In lighting, Antoine sought to approximate the direction of the supposed source: sun, moon, lamps, windows, doors, and so on. He objected to footlights because of their unnatural direction and shadows. Perhaps the most famous example of realistic lighting was a council of war in Hennique's *Death of the Duc d'Enghein* (1888), lighted entirely by lanterns on the table around which the actors sat.

The same care extended to acting. In his booklet, *The Théâtre Libre* (1890), Antoine severely criticized the training of actors given at the Conservatoire because students were taught that the stage voice must be quite different from that used in real life. He also charged that all students were trained to use the same basic gestures and movements. He declared this training wholly inappropriate to realistic plays of present-day life and suggested that actors should seek "to live" rather than "to act" on stage. To discourage playing to the audience, he required actors often to turn their backs to the auditorium; he also asked them to speak in a conversational tone. Antoine's aim was to create the impression of real people in real places taking part in real actions—seemingly unaware of the audience's presence.

Antoine worked hard to achieve the kind of ensemble he had seen in the Meiningen troupe. He produced few plays that included crowds, but these he staged with extreme care. By his own account, he was able to assemble a crowd of 500 for J. H. Rosny's *Nell Horn* in 1891. According to Antoine, the storming of the employer's home in Hauptmann's *The Weavers* (in 1893) was so convincing that the spectators rose from their seats in alarm.

Antoine's efforts to reform the stage ex-

tended to the audience as well. He believed that spectators should forget that they are in a theatre and be affected as though watching a real event. To encourage this response, he darkened the auditorium and discouraged both actors and audience from acknowledging the presence of the other during performances. The proscenium always served as a fourth wall. As Jean Jullien put it: "The front of the stage must be a fourth wall, transparent to the public, opaque for the player."

Antoine was not always successful in achieving his aims. He was often criticized for making it difficult to see all of the action because of obstructions (furniture along the curtain line, the backs of the actors, crowds obscuring major characters). Sometimes the audience could not hear actors who faced upstage or were drowned out by sound effects. At times, actors were unintelligible because they were too intent on being natural. Furthermore, Antoine sought to make almost all plays equally realistic regardless of literary style. Thus, although Antoine perceived that realistic plays demanded a new production style, he was not fully aware that this style was not suited to all new plays.

Nevertheless, Antoine's influence was tonic. His methods made audiences aware of shortcomings in other theatres, and by 1900 his approach had become usual in most theatres. When Jacques Copeau set out to found his theatre in 1913, it was against Antoine that he felt it necessary to rebel. Almost all historians acknowledge that Antoine set the tone for the French theatre from the 1890s until World War I.

Antoine also exerted considerable influence on French drama by nurturing new talent. Eclectic in taste, he presented plays of many types, although perhaps because of his production style he has come to be associated primarily with naturalistic works. There are probably many reasons for this association. First, it seems clear that Antoine considered illusionism the goal of production. Second, most of the plays he presented were those that could not find other outlets; since poetic plays seldom ran into trouble with the censor, Antoine felt a special obligation to the naturalists; the resulting notoriety tended to attract other writers of the same school. Third, after 1890 a number of other independent theatres were founded in Paris, many of them opposed to realism and naturalism.

Not only did Antoine introduce new French plays, he began in 1888 to present significant foreign works not previously seen in France. The first was Leo Tolstoy's *The Power of Darkness,* a play forbidden production in Russia and which Dumas, Augier, and Sardou thought unsuitable for French audiences. It outraged conservative theatregoers because in it a small child, born of adulterous parents, is murdered onstage. (A variant version in which the murder takes place offstage is now better known.) Antoine also presented Ibsen's *Ghosts* and *The Wild Duck,* Hauptmann's *The Weavers,* and Strindberg's *The Father.* The production of *Ghosts* prompted the French Senate to investigate the need for stricter censorship (fortunately not acted upon). Such productions served to acquaint the Parisian public with significant trends in other countries.

The Théâtre Libre was associated in the public mind with *comédie rosse,* a type introduced in 1887 by *The Serenade* by Jean Jullien (1854–1919). *Rosserie* became a descriptive term for naturalistic plays which treat amoral characters who hide behind a facade of respectability. The critic Filon defined it as "a sort of vicious ingenuousness, the state of soul of people who never had any moral sense and who live in impurity and injustice like a fish in water." In *The Serenade,* a young tutor, Maxime, carries on an affair with Nathalie, the wife of a rich Parisian, Cottin. Confronted by Cottin,

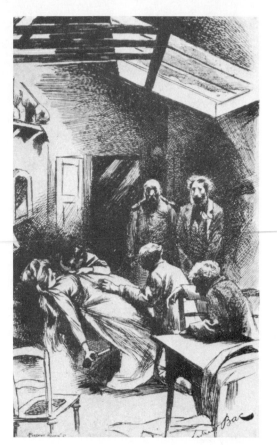

FIG. 3.3

The final scene from Antoine's production of Ibsen's *The Wild Duck* at the Théâtre Libre. (From a contemporary lithograph.)

Maxime readily admits the truth, but it also comes out that he has been having an affair with Cottin's daughter Geneviève, who is pregnant by him. When Cottin insists that he marry Geneviève, Maxime reluctantly agrees. The problem seemingly resolved, the family goes in to lunch as Nathalie whispers insinuatingly to Maxime, "Sit by me—son-in-law." While the situation is potentially comic, Jullien tends to make it distasteful because Cottin is basically a good man who is deeply injured by the indiscretions of his wife and daughter. The result is a kind of perverse humor in which traditional poetic justice is reversed. Many of the *comédies rosses* were too strong even for the Théâtre Libre's tolerant audiences. Perhaps the play that most outraged them was August Linert's *Christmas Story* in which a child is killed and his body thrown to the pigs as Christmas carols play in the background.

Not all of Antoine's dramatists wrote *comédies rosses* (or what critics came to call the *genre Théâtre Libre*). In fact, the three who were to win greatest renown—Porto-Riche, Curel, and Brieux—never wrote this type, being considerably more conservative than the writers of *comédie rosse*. Perhaps for this reason, all eventually were courted by mainstream theatres.

Georges de Porto-Riche (1849–1930) was given his first production when in 1888 Antoine presented *Françoise's Luck*. The play revolves around Marcel, a husband approaching middle age, who, bored with married life, seeks to renew an old affair; but his wife, Françoise, delicately and subtly wins him back. This play introduces what was thereafter to be Porto-Riche's main concern: the power of love. He later published a collection of his works under the general title *Theatre of Love*. In almost all his plays, the characters are tormented by emotions, centering around love, that they do not fully understand. Restraint was Porto-Riche's hallmark.

François de Curel (1854–1929) made his debut as a playwright at the Théâtre Libre in 1892 with *The Other Side of a Saint*. In this play, Julie returns after nineteen years from a convent which she entered because in a fit of jealousy she had attempted to kill Jeanne, who had married her lover. Now the lover has died and Julie seeks to alienate Jeanne's daughter from her mother. But when Julie learns that the dead man has left an affectionate note addressed to her, she decides that she must return to the

convent, the only place where she can find peace. The interest resides almost entirely in the psychological portrait of the protagonist. Curel's most famous play, *The Fossils* (1892), combines deep psychological analysis with the theme of a decaying aristocracy (to which Curel himself belonged). Of Curel's later plays, one of the most interesting is *The Dance Before the Mirror* (1914), in which a man kills himself at the moment when he sees true love mirrored in his beloved's eyes, for he prefers to die at the peak of happiness rather than risk the death of love. Curel's plays won mixed response, for he seemed to care little about pleasing audiences. His work, devoid of sensationalism, combined qualities often considered antipathetic: the real and the unreal, the poetic and the prosaic, the straightforward and the near-allegorical.

The best known of this trio of writers is Eugène Brieux (1858–1932), in part because in 1911 he was declared by Shaw to be the most important dramatist then living in Europe. Brieux gained his first recognition in 1892 when Antoine presented *Blanchette*. Brieux seems a successor to Dumas, since he was concerned with specific social problems and wrote from a clear point of view. His targets were many. In *The Three Daughters of M. Dupont* (1897) he treats loveless, arranged marriages; in *The Red Robe* (1900) he indicts the judicial system under which public prosecutors are more interested in convictions for the sake of promotion than in seeing justice done, and in *Maternity* (1903) he launched a bitter attack on a society that refuses to permit birth control. In *Damaged Goods* (1902), a man discovers on the eve of his marriage that he has syphilis; after being treated by an incompetent doctor, he believes he is cured and marries; a child (infected by the disease) is born; when the wife discovers the truth she is saved only by a doctor who suggests that a cure may be possible. Perhaps no other play demonstrates so clearly how much

FIG. 3.4
Scene from Act II of the original production of Brieux's *The Red Robe*, performed in 1900 at the Théâtre du Vaudeville, Paris. (From *Le Théâtre*, 1900.)

public tolerance had changed since *Ghosts* was written some twenty years earlier. Brieux's play treats venereal disease much more explicitly than Ibsen did, yet it failed to raise public ire (although perhaps only because of the upbeat ending). Jullien, Porto-Riche, Curel, and Brieux are only a few of the many dramatists introduced by Antoine, but they are sufficient to suggest the crucial role he played.

In 1894, Antoine left the Théâtre Libre. After touring South America, he returned to Paris, where in 1897 he established his own professional company, the Théâtre Antoine. There he worked until 1906, when he was named head of the Odéon, France's second state theatre. This appointment signals the full acceptance of Antoine's methods, for it gave semiofficial recognition to his leadership. (His work at the Odéon will be treated later.)

Antoine is clearly one of the most important figures of his day. Scarcely a significant theatrical leader of the next generation remained unaffected by him (although several who had begun work with him became antirealists). Among the most important were Lugné-Poë, Gémier, and Dullin. The most immediate influence, however, was the lesson learned about the potential of independent theatres to reshape standards and practices.

BRAHM AND THE FREIE BÜHNE

In Germany in the late 1880s, drama was also ripe for change. No significant new playwrights had appeared since the death of Hebbel in 1863, and for the most part new works had been poetic plays influenced by Schiller, chauvinistic dramas provoked by German unification in 1871, or imitations of Dumas and Augier.

During the 1880s, dissatisfaction with this situation gave rise to agitation by young people, most of them ideologically allied with the growing socialist movement in Germany. One group, Youngest Germany, found an outlet for its position in a short-lived periodical, *Waffengange,* under the editorship of Julius and Heinrich Hart in Berlin. In Munich the Modern Life Society, under the leadership of Michael Georg Conrad, inaugurated a journal, *Munich*

Art, devoted to naturalism. Karl Bliebtreu also championed naturalism in his widely read pamphlet, *Revolution in Literature.* All demanded a new art based upon reality, with subjects chosen from peasant or working class life. More influential was another loosely organized society, Through, founded in Berlin in 1886 by Conrad Custer. Arno Holz, the chief spokesman, reflected Zola's ideas but was even more stringent in his demands for objectivity. For Holz the greatest artist is inferior to the poorest photographer, since the writer's major task is to overcome the limitations of "art" so as to attain "truth." In collaboration with Johannes Schlaf, Holz wrote a series of narrative pieces, under the title of *Papa Hamlet,* about life in the Berlin slums. Later they turned to drama with *The Happy Family* (1890), in which a drunken father returns home laden with Christmas gifts and falls into a stupor as his youngest child dies in the same room. But the greatest influence on these groups was Ibsen, by the 1880s the most controversial dramatist in Europe, although his plays, like theirs, were seldom seen in the theatre.

Like its drama, Germany's theatre was also conservative. Wagner's and Saxe-Meiningen's work was admired and imitated, but their influence was felt primarily in the staging of the standard repertory. In Berlin, Saxe-Meiningen's methods were being applied at the Deutsches Theater, founded in 1883 by Adolf L'Arronge (1838–1908) and Ludwig Barnay (1842–1924). Its acting company included Josef Kainz (1858–1940) and Agnes Sorma (1865–1927), destined to become two of Germany's leading performers. Both Barnay and Kainz had worked in the Meiningen company but, perhaps because of strict censorship, they had shown little adventurousness in repertory.

In Germany, then, there had been no significant meshing of new dramatic modes with new theatrical practices. As in France, change came only with the establishment of an independent theatre, the Freie Bühne (Free Theatre), founded in Berlin in 1889, two years after the opening of the Théâtre Libre.

Though inspired by the Théâtre Libre, the Freie Bühne differed from it in several respects. First, it was founded by design rather than by accident. Second, it was run by a group. Its elected president and dominant figure was Otto Brahm (1856–1912), a drama critic, but he was assisted by a governing council of ten members. Third, it employed professional actors exclusively. Consequently, it worked around the schedules of other Berlin theatres and presented its offerings on Sunday afternoons at the well-equipped Lessing Theater with actors who were otherwise employed at the Lessing, Deutsches, and Berliner Theaters (the last headed by Barnay after he left the Deutsches in 1887). Fourth, major emphasis was on plays with much less concern for production. The Freie Bühne resembled the Théâtre Libre most in being organized as a private theatre club to avoid censorship. Subscribers numbered 360 even before the first production was given, and that number tripled by the end of the first year. Each subscriber received a copy of the society's periodical, *Free Stage,* which contained critical discussions of the plays produced by the group, the texts of other new plays, and essays on various dramatic, literary, and philosophical issues.

The Freie Bühne's principal work was done between 1889 and 1891. It opened in September 1889 with *Ghosts,* chosen because Brahm believed Ibsen's play to be the "pathfinder of the new dramatic art." The play also set the adventurous tone of the new enterprise, which went on to produce the Goncourts' *Henriette Maréchal,* Tolstoy's *The Power of Darkness,* Zola's *Thérèse Raquin,* Becque's *The Vultures,* and Strindberg's *The Father* and *Miss Julie.* Among the German works were Holz and Schlaf's *The Happy Family.*

The Freie Bühne's one great discovery was

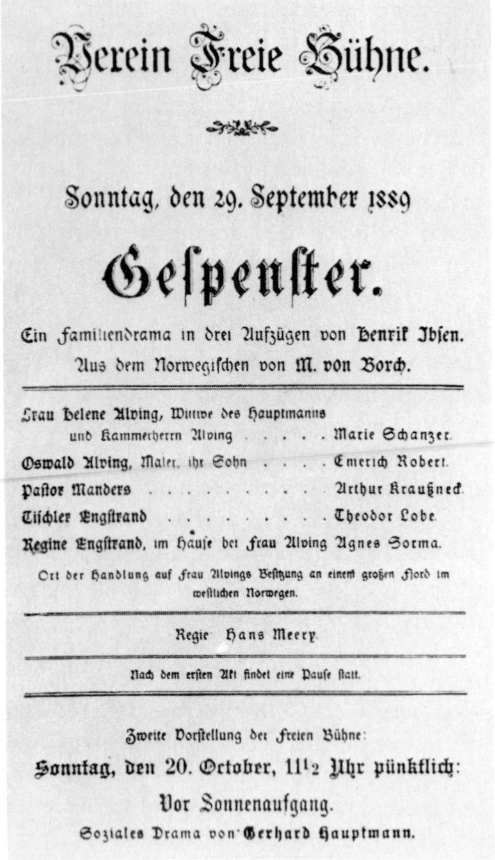

Verein Freie Bühne.

Sonntag, den 29. September 1889

Gespenster.

Ein Familiendrama in drei Aufzügen von Henrik Ibsen.
Aus dem Norwegischen von M. von Borch.

Frau Helene Alving, Wittwe des Hauptmanns
    und Kammerherrn Alving . . . . . Marie Schanzer.
Oswald Alving, Maler, ihr Sohn . . . . Emerich Robert.
Pastor Manders . . . . Arthur Kraußneck.
Tischler Engstrand . . . . Theodor Lobe.
Regine Engstrand, im Hause der Frau Alving Agnes Sorma.

Ort der Handlung auf Frau Alvings Besitzung an einem großen Fjord im
westlichen Norwegen.

Regie: Hans Meery.

Nach dem ersten Akt findet eine Pause statt.

Zweite Vorstellung der Freien Bühne:
Sonntag, den 20. October, 11½ Uhr pünktlich:
Vor Sonnenaufgang.
Soziales Drama von Gerhard Hauptmann.

FIG. 3.5
Program for Ibsen's *Ghosts*, the first production of the Freie Bühne, 1889. Also announced is the forthcoming production of Hauptmann's first play, *Vor Sonnenaufgang (Before Sunrise)*, the following month. (From the Deutsche Akademie der Künste zu Berlin.)

Gerhart Hauptmann (1862–1946). Like Ibsen's, Hauptmann's career spanned a period of approximately fifty years and was extremely diverse. He wrote approximately thirty plays, in addition to novels, epic poems, lyric poetry, and autobiographical and travel works. By the early twentieth century, he was Germany's most respected dramatist (in 1912 he was awarded the Nobel Prize in literature), although toward the end of his life he fell into disfavor because of his acceptance of Naziism. Hauptmann began his career as a naturalist but soon began to oscillate between realistic and symbolic works, a pattern he continued through the rest of his life. He first won recognition, however, with naturalistic works, especially *Before Sunrise* and *The Weavers*.

Before Sunrise, presented by the Freie Bühne in 1889, is usually considered the first important modern German drama. In it, Hauptmann deals with a Silesian peasant family that has become wealthy from the coal discovered under its land. Its new wealth, however, leads only to drunkenness and debauchery, except in the daughter Helene, who falls in love with a young social worker and is eventually rejected by him because he doubts that she can escape her heredity. Helene then commits suicide. The play is simple in structure, free from any of the typical devices of the well-made play. It is admired especially for exactness of dialect and usage according to social level. To many, this play appeared the redeemer of German drama, but to others, all that was odious in the new trends.

Hauptmann's most famous play, *The Weavers* (1892), is considered by many critics to be the finest of all naturalistic dramas. It deals with the futile uprising (in which Hauptmann's own family had participated) of Silesian weavers in 1844. The background is the Industrial Revolution at the time when machine weaving was destroying cottage industry. The weavers in Hauptmann's play are those who work at home, securing thread from an employer and then selling the finished cloth back to him. One of the most striking features of *The Weavers* is the absence of an individual protagonist. The focus shifts from act to act so that the weavers as a group become the protagonist. In the opening act, the near-starving weavers stand in line to show their week's work and are bullied

FIG. 3.6
Poster for Hauptmann's *The Weavers*. (From the Deutsche Akademie der Künste zu Berlin.)

into accepting whatever they are offered. The second act, set in the household of Old Baumert, shows the conditions under which the weavers live; Old Baumert becomes physically ill after eating flesh (a dog's) for the first time in two years. In the third act, a returning soldier puts courage into the weavers, and in the fourth act they loot the elegant home of their employer. The final act takes place in the room of another weaver, Old Hilse, who refuses to join the revolt. The weavers set out to destroy the power looms, but are met by soldiers; they drive the soldiers back, but a stray bullet kills Old Hilse at his loom, suggesting the ultimate outcome. Throughout the play, it is clear that Hauptmann's sympathies lie with the weavers, almost all of whom are depicted as decent people who have been degraded to the level of animals. He tends to make heroes of the workers and villains of the employers, although economic conditions have entrapped both groups. Hauptmann is not objective in Zola's sense. Nevertheless, he effectively meets another demand of naturalism—that art be a weapon for social change. The play makes the need for economic and social planning emotionally convincing, and its compelling human interest has kept the play, unlike most naturalistic drama of that time, fresh and powerful.

Hauptmann's difficulties with the censors may have prompted him to write *The Beaver*

Coat (1893), one of the few comedies to come out of the singularly humorless naturalist movement. *The Beaver Coat* is a satiric thrust at entrenched bureaucracy, showing its defeat by seeming compliance. In it, Frau Wolff, an amoral washerwoman, steals a beaver coat and then so befuddles the judge, von Wehrhahn, that he ends by lauding her honesty.

In 1893, Hauptmann wrote his first nonrealistic play—*The Assumption of Hannele*—though the departure from naturalism is only partial. It treats a wretched, neglected, and mistreated girl, whose death becomes almost euphoric through her visions of heaven. Although it does not imply that the visions are to be accepted as objective phenomena, the play's emphasis has shifted toward the poetic. Soon thereafter Hauptmann began to alternate realistic and symbolic works, and his defection from realism increased as time went by. With the possible exceptions of *Rose Bernd* (1903) and *The Rats* (1911), Hauptmann never regained the strength of his early works. Most of his late drama is mediocre. Much of it, such as his tetralogy on the house of Atreus (1940–1944), is a reinterpretation of classical mythology.

Two basic qualities remained constant throughout Hauptmann's work—great compassion and sensitivity to human suffering. Unlike Ibsen's, Hauptmann's protagonists are almost always passive; they fall not because of mistakes so much as from external circumstances. Thus, they are more pitiable than heroic. Nevertheless, it was Hauptmann who heralded the rejuvenation of German drama in the 1890s, and with his plays the Freie Bühne made its greatest impact. The Freie Bühne succeeded so well that it discontinued regular programs at the end of its second season (1890–1891). When the need arose, as it did in the case of *The Weavers* in 1892, it was temporarily revived.

In 1894, when L'Arronge retired as head of the Deutsches Theater, Brahm was appointed to that post, where he remained until 1904. While director of his own troupe, he staged not only recent plays but also classics. He sought to reform the traditional staging of classics through making them "come to life by utilizing . . . the new naturalistic art of acting," and by proving that realism and "the style of classical drama are not mutually exclusive." Unfortunately, most of the classics he staged in this manner were failures, and the considerable reputation of the theatre was based almost entirely on modern realistic works. Still, Brahm was instrumental in ridding the German stage of artificiality.

The Freie Bühne inspired a number of other independent theatres in Germany and Austria, among them the Deutsches Bühne and Fresko-Bühne in Berlin, Max Halbe's Intimes Theater in Munich, and a large number of student groups in Berlin, Munich, and Vienna. The most significant offshoot of the independent theatre movement was the *people's theatres* (*Volksbühnen*) initiated in the 1890s. Most of these were established by socialist parties, whose leaders were concerned with increasing cultural opportunities for the working classes. The most important of these theatres were founded in Berlin. The first, the Freie Volksbühne, was organized in 1890 by Bruno Wille, Julius Turk, and Wilhelm Bolsche. A second, the Neue Freie Volksbühne, was founded in 1892 by Wille when he came into conflict with members of the original organization.

The Freie Volksbühne began with a membership of 600. Like the Freie Bühne, its performances were given on Sunday afternoons at regular theatres. Its repertory consisted of plays considered especially relevant to the working classes: Ibsen's *Ghosts*, Hauptmann's *Before Sunrise*, Zola's *Thérèse Raquin*, and similar dramas. Season tickets were distributed by lot and at a nominal cost. This scheme was so successful that by 1908 the membership had grown to 12,000. When it became clear that there was a large potential audience, a number of mainstream theatres began to give their own Sunday matinees for workers, making it difficult for the Volksbühnen to assemble strong casts for their own productions. To combat this competition, the Neue Freie Volksbühne began in 1905 to make arrangements for its members to see certain productions in mainstream theatres at a slight additional cost over its regular subscription fee. Soon it was possible for members to choose among large numbers of special Sunday matinees. By 1914 the two Volksbühnen had amalgamated and had a combined membership of 50,000. They decided to build their own theatre and maintain their own company. Opened in 1915, the new theatre, with its advanced machinery, was one of the best equipped in the world.

Perhaps the greatest contribution of the people's theatres came from their encouragement of persons who did not normally attend the theatre to take an interest in thoughtful and entertaining plays, both old and new. Their repertories included works by Shakespeare, Goethe, Schiller, Ibsen, and Hauptmann, as well as those of lesser authors. The Volksbühnen did much to broaden audiences in Germany.

GREIN AND THE INDEPENDENT THEATRE

In England, as in France and Germany, the independent theatre was crucial in rescuing drama from stagnation. Although the theatre was flourishing, with Irving's company in the vanguard, no significant new playwrights had appeared after Robertson's death in 1871. The theatre was given over to revivals of standard dramas of the past, foreign adaptations (especially of Sardou's plays), and inconsequential new English plays. In the 1880s several critics, among them William Archer, Frank Harris, and George Moore, voiced their unhappiness

with the situation. The first response was a series of dramas that paralleled the work of Dumas and Augier.

England's equivalent of the two French authors were Henry Arthur Jones (1851–1929) and Arthur Wing Pinero (1885–1934), who, though often labeled followers of Ibsen, were highly successful adapters of the well-made play's techniques and conventional moralists in the resolutions of their dramas. They served to pave the way for a new drama by titillating audiences with provocative subjects while never seriously questioning accepted values. Before becoming serious playwrights, both Jones and Pinero had achieved success with popular forms—Jones with melodrama and Pinero with farce.

Jones' pioneering effort in social drama came in 1884 with *Saints and Sinners,* a work about the disparity between a man's religious profession and his actual deeds. Jones went on to write a great many serious plays, including *The Dancing Girl* (1891), *The Liars* (1897), and *Mrs. Dane's Defense* (1900). His best play, although not his most popular, is *Michael and His Lost Angel* (1896), in which he treats an illicit sexual relationship between a minister and one of his parishioners. Ultimately the play is partially unsatisfactory because he distorts character in order to preserve a conventionally moral position. Although Jones sincerely desired to write thoughtful drama, he was not a rigorous thinker, and his analysis of problems was grounded in the conventional views of his day. Nevertheless, his plays and his endorsement of Ibsen in *The Renascense of English Drama* (1895) did much to win over the public to a new type of drama.

Pinero's first major success came in 1885 with *The Magistrate,* a farce which is still played with success. After writing more farces, Pinero turned to serious drama in 1889 with *The Profligate.* But *The Second Mrs. Tanqueray* (1893) was to be Pinero's most famous work and the

FIG. 3.7
George Alexander and Mrs. Patrick Campbell in the original production of Pinero's *The Second Mrs. Tanqueray*, 1893. (Courtesy Enthoven Collection. By courtesy of the Board of Trustees of the Victoria and Albert Museum.)

one that made the new type a commercial success. In it, Paula Ray, a "woman with a past," has married Aubrey Tanqueray, a middle-aged widower with a grown daughter, Eileen. When Eileen's suitor arrives, he turns out to be a man with whom Paula has had an affair. When Eileen learns why the suitor has left so discreetly, Paula, realizing that her hopes for happiness are gone, commits suicide. Thus, although there is an air of sophistication throughout, the ending conveys the message that no woman who has strayed can hope to find happiness. The play is clearly in the well-made play tradition, depending as it does on concealed information, fortunate arrivals, and

startling reversals. Although the action depends almost entirely on coincidence, to London audiences it seemed startingly new and shockingly daring. The play was produced by George Alexander (1858–1918) who, as manager and star actor of St. James' Theatre, sought to encourage English dramatists. He also presented plays by Oscar Wilde and several other new playwrights. The role of Paula Tanqueray also did much to establish Mrs. Patrick Campbell (1865–1940) as one of England's leading actresses.

Pinero continued to write plays until 1932, but his reputation declined steadily after World War I. Between 1890 and 1915, Pinero was often called a disciple of Ibsen, a label that infuriated Shaw, who rightly saw that Pinero was more concerned with theatrical effect than with ideas.

The significance of Jones and Pinero lies in their paving the way for the acceptance of Ibsen and Shaw. By casting seemingly shocking subjects in a mold palatable to Victorian audiences, they gradually prepared spectators to accept a more strenuous drama.

Ibsen was the rallying point for champions of a truly serious drama. He was first mentioned in England in an article by Edmund Gosse in 1873. *Emperor and Galilean* was the first of Ibsen's works to be translated into English—by Catherine Ray in 1876. Shortly afterwards, William Archer began his series of translations of Ibsen's plays, the standard English versions until the mid-twentieth century. Significant productions of Ibsen's plays were lacking until 1889. In that year Janet Achurch (1864–1916) and her husband Charles Charrington presented *A Doll's House* at a private showing, the first of several productions of Ibsen's plays by Achurch. In 1889 Elizabeth Robins also inaugurated a series of Ibsen productions, beginning with *The Pillars of Society*. During the 1890s she would appear in seven of the plays, for most of which she held the English stage rights. In 1891 Shaw published his pamphlet *The Quintessence of Ibsenism,* in which he defined Ibsenism as a critique, in dramatic form, of conventional morality. Nevertheless, progress was slow toward winning acceptance for Ibsenesque drama until the Independent Theatre was founded in 1891.

The motive force behind the Independent Theatre was J. T. Grein (1862–1935), a Dutchman then residing in London. The stated purpose of the theatre was "to give special performances of plays which have a literary and artistic rather than a commercial value." Like its Continental counterparts, the Independent Theatre was organized on a subscription basis and thus was able to avoid censorship by the Lord Chamberlain, who licensed all plays for public performance. The group did little about mounting the plays, being concerned primarily with providing a hearing for otherwise unproduced plays. Like the Freie Bühne, it performed on Sundays so as to use regular theatres and the services of professional actors. Its first production (on March 13, 1891) was of Ibsen's *Ghosts,* a play that had been refused a license for public performance. It provoked a critical storm of almost unbelievable ferocity and brought the organization and Ibsen's play publicity far beyond what they could ever have achieved through normal means. The second program, Zola's *Thérèse Raquin,* was greeted with almost as much abuse. The theatre continued until 1897, presenting a total of twenty-six programs, mostly of foreign works.

While the Independent Theatre was extremely successful in making the English public aware of new trends in drama, it had not been founded primarily to present Continental plays. Grein believed that the low state of English drama was attributable to the conservatism of producers and was convinced that he would be deluged with plays by frustrated English dramatists. He soon discovered, however, that no significant unproduced English plays were available. It was in response to Grein's desperate appeal that George Bernard Shaw (1856–1950) began his playwriting career. Shaw was to be the only major playwright launched by the Independent Theatre, but his discovery alone justifies the existence of the organization.

By the time Shaw began to write plays he was almost forty years old. Born in Ireland, he had moved to London in 1876, where he began his literary career with five novels. After 1885 he turned primarily to criticism—of music, art, and theatre—which he wrote for *The Pall Mall Gazette, The Star,* and *The Saturday Review.* He also became a firm believer in socialism and in 1884 was a founding member of the Fabian Society, whose goal was socialism through gradual reform. Shaw's commitment to Fabianism heavily influenced his drama.

Shaw believed that to be significant, drama must lead the audience to right action. It was this belief that made him praise Brieux so fulsomely and downgrade Shakespeare (on the grounds that he did not demand social and ethical improvement). He also disliked the well-made play because it sacrificed truth to dramatic effect. He championed Ibsen because he was not a "mere artist" (Shaw's favorite pejorative), but a practical man seeking to reform the world through drama. Despite Shaw's demands for utilitarianism, his own plays do not provide practical solutions to specific problems—they merely illuminate the problems and expose the paradoxes. His fundamental revelations tend to be more philosophical than practical.

A few concepts tend to dominate Shaw's work. One set of ideas involves the *life force* and the *superman* (both concepts developed by the French philosopher Henri Bergson, who argued that through man an inscrutable "life force" is instinctively working to evolve the "superman"). This moral evolution is a counterpart to Darwin's biological evolution and Marx's economic evolution. It is also related to Fabianism, one tenet of which was that leadership should be determined by intelligence and common sense rather than by birth, wealth, social position, or popularity. Shaw championed the gradual solution of human problems, which he thought would be eliminated once the superman had fully evolved. For the moment, Shaw saw the prospect for limited progress only, but he believed that better living conditions and education could free people from immediate petty concerns and hasten achievement of the ultimate goal. Thus, through his plays Shaw sought to correct wrongheaded notions, shake prejudices, and arouse skepticism. Fortunately, Shaw had as keen an eye for what is entertaining as he did for what is philosophically striking. He was firmly rooted in the nineteenth-century tradition of melodrama and the well-made play, and, despite his denunciations of that tradition, he utilized it to great effect.

The play that launched Shaw's career as a dramatist, *Widower's Houses* (1892), allegedly was begun in 1885 in collaboration with William Archer. Abandoned for a time, it was completed by Shaw at Grein's urging. It ostensibly attacks slum landlordism but actually explodes the self-righteous and romantic notions of the protagonist by showing that his own funds are ultimately derived from slum property. Shaw is obviously most interested in exposing the unthinking philistinism of respectable people who condemn others without acknowledging their own involvement in exploiting the weak and poor.

Shaw's later plays, more than fifty, continued to puncture popular prejudice. *Arms and the Man* (1894) attacks romantic notions of war and love; *Major Barbara* (1905) argues that a munitions manufacturer is a greater force for good than the Salvation Army, since the former, through the material rewards he gives his workers, makes it possible for them to better themselves, whereas the Salvation Army prolongs misery by dispensing charity without doing anything to better humanity's lot. In *Pygmalion* (1913), Shaw is concerned with dialects as instruments of class distinctions and illustrates his concern with the story of a flower girl who, after speech training, passes as a duchess. This Cinderella story is probably Shaw's most popular work, in part because of its adaptation into the musical *My Fair Lady* (1956).

Several of Shaw's plays are concerned with creative evolution through the life force. This subject is most effectively developed in *Man and Superman* (1903), which shows how its heroine instinctively chooses and wins the man best suited to be her mate for the evolution of the superman. It also includes a dream interlude, usually called "Don Juan in Hell," essentially a philosophical dialogue about creative evolution. Shaw later wrote five plays under the collective title *Back to Methuselah* (1919–1920), which argues the necessity for creative evolution if mankind is not to perish.

Between 1900 and 1910 Shaw wrote a number of plays which he labeled "disquisitory" because each explored varying views of a problem. The best-known of these are *Getting Married* (1908), on marriage and divorce, and *Misalliance* (1910), on the relationship of parents and children.

Among Shaw's later works, the most important are *Heartbreak House* (1919), a symbolic drama about Europe and the conditions that led to World War I, and *Saint Joan* (1923), written at the time Joan of Arc was finally canonized, in which Shaw argues that saints are always so upsetting to their own age that they must be destroyed and that it is possible to confer sainthood on Joan now only because she no longer represents any threat. All of Shaw's best work had been done by 1923. He continued to write until the time of his death, but the late works are pale reflections of his former vitality.

Few dramatists have believed so firmly as Shaw in the power of dialectic to bring about progress. This commitment probably prevented him from emphasizing the darker side of human nature and obstacles to change. It is fortunate, therefore, that he chose comedy as his medium, since optimism is inherent in the comic form; in more serious plays, his optimism might have appeared shallow. His dramatic actions are most usually constructed by establishing the prejudices about his subject then prevalent in society (typically treated sympathetically in the opening scenes) and then undermining them and proving them false; since the new perceptions remove the bases of conflict, the action can be resolved harmoniously. Thus, Shaw's works differ considerably from those of most of the realists with whom he allied himself, since most treated problems in a deadly serious, often gloomy light. Shaw usually wrote with the "fourth wall" in mind and rarely permitted his characters to transgress it, but he had no patience with attempts to transfer nature directly to the stage or to recreate milieus in all their details. His own statement about Dickens applies equally well to himself: he combined a "mirror-like exactness of character-drawing with the wildest extravagance of humorous expression and grotesque situation." In writing dialogue, Shaw was never hobbled by any theory that it must approximate real conversation. Although his characters are distinguishable by peculiarities of speech, all are articulate and most are masters of the witty, well-turned phrase. Thus, Shaw's is a hyperrealism in which the essence of life is captured by sharpening and exaggerating chosen elements. Shaw always billed himself as a thinker. He cultivated this role by writing numerous essays and by prefacing many of his dramas with lengthy discussions

developing ideas parallel to those dramatized in the plays they accompany. Still, it is not as a thinker but as a dramatist that Shaw will be remembered.

In the 1890s Shaw's drama was still sufficiently unusual that to many spectators it was either puzzling or outrageous. Furthermore, many of his subjects and ideas were considered dangerous or unsuitable for public consumption. Several of the plays were denied licenses for production. Shortly after 1900, however, the plays began to be accepted in the theatre, and by World War I Shaw's position was secure. He is still recognized as perhaps the dominant figure in modern English drama.

After the demise of the Independent Theatre in 1897, a new organization was founded to

FIG. 3.8
Scene from Shaw's *Mrs. Warren's Profession* in its original production in 1902 at the New Lyric Club, by the Incorporated Stage Society. (Courtesy Enthoven Collection. By courtesy of the Board of Trustees of the Victoria and Albert Museum.)

carry on its mission. The Incorporated Stage Society was founded in 1899 to produce recent and experimental British and foreign plays not otherwise likely to receive public performances. Its productions were given on Sundays so that professional actors could appear in them. Its first presentation was Shaw's *You Never Can Tell,* and eventually it first produced ten of his plays, among them *Candida, Mrs. Warren's Profession,* and *Man and Superman.* It also gave first hearings to plays by Harley Granville Barker, Somerset Maugham, and many others. In addition, it presented plays by such foreign writers as Tolstoy, Chekhov, Brieux, and Hauptmann. By 1914 the membership had grown to 1,500 and Monday matinees had been added. The organization continued until 1939, by which time it had presented more than 200 programs.

THE MOSCOW ART THEATRE

In Russia, the establishment of the Moscow Art Theatre (in 1898) may also be seen as an extension of the independent theatre movement. Inspired by Saxe-Meiningen and Antoine, the Moscow Art Theatre was motivated by dissatisfaction with the established theatre. It differed from the other independent theatres in being from the beginning a fully professional theatre and in having as its principal concern improved theatrical production rather than dissatisfaction with repertory. These differences are explained by the prevailing theatrical conditions in Russia in the late nineteenth century.

Realism in drama had arrived in Russia even before it had in France. In 1850, Ivan Turgenev (1818–1883) had completed *A Month in the Country,* just as Ibsen was writing *Cataline* and before Dumas and Augier had written any of their realistic works. Like Chekhov's major works, Turgenev's is set on a remote country estate and emphasizes psychological relation-

ships and inner struggles. A play of cross-purposes without villains, it treats people who are essentially good but who are led into questionable deeds by feelings over which they have no control.

Realism was more consistently developed by Alexander Ostrovsky (1823-1886), Russia's first fully professional playwright, who wrote some seventy-five plays after 1846. His works are considered the essence of Russian realism and the cornerstone of the Russian repertory. He is often said to be the most Russian of playwrights, since his work is so deeply rooted in the speech, thought, and actions of small tradesmen and civil servants of his time. His better-known plays include *Diary of a Scoundrel* (1868) and *The Forest* (1871). His most popular play outside of Russia has been *The Thunderstorm* (1860), in which a young wife, caught in a loveless marriage, commits adultery and then, out of a sense of guilt, kills herself. Ostrovsky was also much involved in the theatre of his day—in improving the dramatist's lot, in training actors, and in directing. Ostrovsky was probably the most important single individual in the Russian theatre of the nineteenth century.

Leo Tolstoy (1828–1910), the great Russian novelist, is often associated with naturalistic playwriting through his first important drama, *The Power of Darkness* (1886). Denied a license in Russia, it had its premiere at Antoine's Théâtre Libre in 1888. In it, the farmhand Nikita carries on an affair with Anisya, the wife of his employer, Petr, and assists her in murdering him. After marrying Anisya, Nikita, feeling guilty, takes to drink. When he seduces the mentally retarded Akulina and she bears a child, Nikita, at the urging of Anisya and his own mother, kills the child. Later, overcome by guilt and at the urging of his father, Nikita confesses his crimes.

Through these and other plays, Russia, despite many obstacles, the greatest of which was probably censorship, had by the late nineteenth century established a strong dramatic tradition. Next to censorship, the greatest problem was antiquated theatrical conditions. Rehearsal practices discouraged ensemble performance and encouraged individual virtuosity. Plays often received no more than three rehearsals and frequently neither the director nor the actors knew what scenery would be used until opening night. Furthermore, until 1882 the state-owned theatres held monopolies on theatrical production in Moscow and St. Petersburg. Since they were headed by political appointees who had few qualifications for their jobs beyond loyalty to the state, the managers showed little concern for artistic excellence. After the monopolies were abolished in 1882, private theatres brought some improvement. The visits of the Meiningen troupe in 1885 and 1890 were also significant. These fitful and uncoordinated efforts, however, made little impression on the Russian theatre as a whole. The general dissatisfaction came to a focus in the First All-Russian Conference of Theatre Personnel in 1897. There the sorry state of the Russian theatre was blamed on the commercial motive, the inadequate training of performers, conventionalized staging, and other factors. All agreed that reform was needed. The crucial step toward reform was taken the following year with the formation of the Moscow Art Theatre.

The Moscow Art Theatre (MAT) was the creation of Vladimir Nemirovich-Danchenko (1858–1943) and Constantin Stanislavsky (1863–1938). Born into the aristocracy, Nemirovich-Danchenko had been educated at Moscow University and was an established dramatist and journalist when in 1891 he became a teacher of acting at the Moscow Philharmonic Society. He soon came to feel that no training would be effective unless the theatres in which students were to work changed their methods. Stanislavsky (born

Constantin Alexeyev), the educated son of a wealthy industrialist, early developed an interest in theatre and took advantage of a stay in Paris to attend classes at the Conservatoire. He also assumed the stage name Stanislavsky. Returning to Russia, he in 1888 became chairman of the Moscow Society for Arts and Letters, an organization that offered theatrical productions as a part of its program. By 1898, Stanislavsky had had approximately ten years of experience as an actor and director with a company that included both amateurs and professionals.

Out of a meeting between Nemerovich-Danchenko and Stanislavsky in 1897 came the decision to found the Moscow Art Theatre. Nemerovich-Danchenko was to be literary advisor and Stanislavsky production director. Eventually both men directed plays, and Stanislavsky became one of the company's leading actors, while Nemerovich-Danchenko performed many of the managerial tasks. The original company was composed of thirty-nine persons, many chosen from among Nemirovich-Danchenko's students and from Stanislavsky's Society for Arts and Letters. The best-known of the actors were to be Ivan Moskvin (1874–1946), Vassily Kachalov (1875–1948), Olga Knipper (1870–1959), and Maria Ghermanova (1884–1945). Rehearsals got underway in the summer of 1898 in a village about thirty miles outside Moscow, where the company lived and worked on a rigorous schedule.

The first season of the MAT opened on October 14, 1898, with Alexey Tolstoy's historical drama, *Tsar Fyodor,* mounted with infinite care for its sixteenth-century milieu. Director, designer, and actors had visited monasteries, provincial villages, and museums to acquire a sense of the period. The public response was enthusiastic, although some claimed that the production was merely an imitation of the Meiningen's methods. The company next performed Sophocles' *Antigone*

FIG 3.9
Scene from *Tsar Fyodor*, the first production of the Moscow Art Theatre, 1898. Victor Simov designed the setting, one of several used in the production.

and Shakespeare's *The Merchant of Venice* in the same antiquarian mode. Interest in the company began to wane because it seemed merely to be repeating what the Meiningen company had shown Russians some ten years earlier.

The turning point came with the fourth offering, Chekhov's *The Sea Gull.* With this production, the group brought to bear on a contemporary play all the care it had lavished on classics. The result was mutually beneficial, for in Chekhov the MAT found a dramatist whose plays were attuned to its own aspirations, while Chekhov for the first time found actors who were willing to discover and project the nuances of his drama. The collaboration was so fruitful that eventually the MAT adopted the sea gull as its emblem and called itself "The House of Chekhov."

Despite its successes, the MAT ended its first season with a sizable deficit. Saved by the generosity of a wealthy financier, Savva Morozov, and his friends, the company thereafter was able to support itself primarily from box-office receipts. In 1902 it was able to build its own theatre, designed by F. O. Schechtel,

seating 1,200 and with all the latest stage machinery and facilities for scenery, lighting, and costumes. At this time, the company was enlarged to 100, and it settled into the pattern that was to be typical until the revolution of 1917: the majority of performances were proved successes, to which were added three to five new productions each year. The repertory, therefore, had considerable stability and permitted new productions to be mounted leisurely and with great care, somewhat in the manner of the Meiningen Company.

Of the MAT's early playwrights, the most important were Chekhov and Gorky. Anton Chekhov (1860–1904), son of a grocer and grandson of a serf, turned to writing in 1880 as a means of supporting himself and his family while he attended medical school. These early works were sketches, topical commentaries, parodies, and short comic pieces. Upon receiving his medical degree in 1884, he decided to devote himself entirely to literature and soon attained considerable renown as a short story writer. His first long play, *Ivanov* (1887), was presented successfully in 1889, and his short

FIG. 3.10
Chekhov's *The Cherry Orchard,* originally produced at the Moscow Art Theatre in 1904.

farces, among them *The Boor* (1888), *The Proposal* (1888–1889), and *The Wedding* (1889–1890), were widely performed as curtain raisers. But when *The Sea Gull* was presented in 1896, it was a miserable failure. Chekhov resolved to give up playwriting, but the MAT's resounding success with *The Sea Gull* led him to permit the company to produce *Uncle Vanya* (1897). He then went on to write two new works, *The Three Sisters* (1901) and *The Cherry Orchard* (1904), for the company. His ties with the company were further cemented in 1901 when he married Olga Knipper, one of its leading actresses.

Chekhov's reputation rests primarily on the four plays produced by the MAT. Each is set in rural Russia and treats the boredom and monotony of life among the landowning class; all show the vast gulf between desire and fulfillment. *The Three Sisters* may be taken as typical. In it, Chekhov deals with the Prozoroff family, the children of a deceased officer in a provincial army post far from the gaiety and culture of Moscow, which for them symbolizes all that is missing from their lives. The sisters—Olga, Masha, and Irina—and their brother, Andrey, have been equipped by education and upbringing for sophisticated city life and feel useless in their present surroundings. Olga has become a teacher; Masha, married to a dull schoolmaster, enters into an affair with Colonel Vershinin; Irina, after trying a civil service post, agrees to marry Tusenbach, a man she does not love. Their plight is intensified by Andrey's marriage to the insensitive Natasha, who gradually displaces them from their home. In the last act, the army garrison, their one shield against the provincialism that surrounds them, is transferred, and Tusenbach is killed in a duel. Now more isolated than ever, the sisters, somewhat unconvincingly, resolve to find real purpose in their lives.

Although on the surface seemingly simple, Chekhov's plays are among the most complex in the modern repertory. In them, most violent deeds and emotional climaxes occur offstage. Thus, the action is muted. In the foreground, the onstage action is a plethora of seemingly trivial, commonplace occurrences chosen and arranged with enormous care to give the effect of randomness while they constantly reveal character, mood, and idea. Attention is concentrated not on events but on the texture of life that surrounds and shapes the characters and upon their psychological responses. Since the characters do not fully understand their own feelings and motives and since they seek to conceal more than to express their emotions, the dramatic action is revealed somewhat indirectly through the seeming trivia, nuances, and subtext that underlie the dialogue.

All of Chekhov's characters are victims of conflicting forces; most try to act decently. As a play progresses, Chekhov gradually strips his characters of their illusions and reveals the anxieties and inadequacies that have been concealed. In the process, he shows that character and fate are essentially one. In all his revelations there is tolerance and compassion. At the same time, he distances the characters sufficiently to permit the audience to see them as both sympathetic and ridiculous. Thus, the pathetic and the comic are inextricably intertwined. Chekhov also creates an extraordinary sense of atmosphere and environment. The dominant impression is one of indolence and moral inertia. One simultaneously feels sympathy for the characters because of their pointless lives and impatience with their inability to act. Thus, although Chekhov never comments directly on the society of his time, he implies much.

Despite their surface naturalness, Chekhov's four major plays make considerable use of symbolism to enlarge meaning and to comment indirectly on the action. In *The Cherry Orchard,* for example, the orchard, once productive and useful, is now merely decorative and destined to be cut down to make way for villas for the middle class. As a symbol of the aristocracy, the orchard is used to suggest much about the Russian society of Chekhov's time.

Just as Chekhov's mosaic-like technique was realized in performance through the MAT's concern for detail, the company found in Chekhov the kind of drama that gave full scope to its working methods. Through the productions, both the playwright and the company attained deserved recognition.

Maxim Gorky (Alexei Peshkov, 1868–1936), son of a paperhanger, was orphaned at eight, had only five months of schooling, and earned his living as an errand boy, baker, shipworker, and at other odd jobs. His voracious reading made him aware of the wide gap between the idealistic literary world and his own harsh existence. His first writing was published in 1892, and fame came with the publication of his collected stories in 1898. His first play, *Smug Citizens,* was produced by the MAT in 1902. His greatest success as a playwright came with the production by the MAT later that year of *The Lower Depths.*

The Lower Depths, a naturalistic play set in a flophouse, is peopled with human derelicts, victims of social conditions. For a time, a pilgrim rekindles their illusions, but after he leaves, nothing has changed. While staging the play, Stanislavsky made his actors visit flophouses in Moscow and study the behavior, surroundings, and dress. These elements were re-created on stage with such care that spectators in the first few rows were said to fear being infested with lice. Before the revolution of 1917, Gorky had written eight plays, most denied production because Gorky had participated in the abortive revolution of 1905. Of these, the best known are *Summer Folk* (1904) and *Enemies* (1907). From the beginning, Gorky was a strong supporter of communism, and

FIG. 3.11
The Lower Depths, by Gorky, produced originally by the Moscow Art Theatre in 1902. (From *Moscow Art Theatre, 1898–1917,* 1955.)

after the revolution of 1917 he eventually became head of the writers union. (This final stage of his career will be discussed in a later chapter.)

By the time Chekhov died in 1904, the MAT was a secure and thriving institution. But the stability of its repertory, which meant that actors had to play the same roles over and over, led Stanislavsky to be increasingly concerned over how to keep performances fresh and vital. It was through his attempts to analyze and solve the actors' problems that he was to arrive at that system which was to exert untold influence on twentieth-century theatre. When the MAT was founded in 1898, there was no system, and Stanislavsky did not give it serious attention until 1906. He wrote down his first sketch of a system in 1909, the year in which he first attempted to apply it in a production of Turgenev's *A Month in the Country.* He did not gain the company's acceptance of his approach until 1911 in a production of Tolstoy's *Redemption.* It was then decided that a studio should be formed to train students in the system and work out problems as they arose.

Called the First Studio, this workshop was founded in 1911 under the direction of Leopold Sulerzhitsky (1872–1916), who embraced the new system fully and had taught it at another school even before it was fully accepted at the MAT. In the Studio were a number of young actors who would achieve considerable importance, among them Yevgeny Vakhtangov, Mikhail Chekhov, and Richard Boleslavsky. The Studio's small theatre had neither footlights nor an orchestra pit to separate actors and audience. It was designed to encourage actors to be natural and to avoid any forcing of voice or gesture. The Studio's first triumph came in 1914 with Sulerzhitsky's adaptation of *The Cricket on the Hearth.* When Sulerzhitsky died, leadership passed to Vakhtangov, who after the revolution was to be one of the most significant figures of the Soviet theatre.

Thus, before the revolution Stanislavsky's system had been formulated and tested. It was to undergo many revisions thereafter, but the basic features were clear. The system's broad outline was first published in Stanislavsky's *My Life in Art* (1924), but details had to wait for *An Actor Prepares* (1936), and were not extensively revealed in the West until after World War II through *Building a Character* (1949) and

FIG. 3.12 Sulerzhitsky's production of *The Cricket on the Hearth* at the First Studio in 1914. It was with this and similar productions at the First Studio that Sulerzhitsky and the younger members of the Moscow Art Theatre first experimented in depth with the Stanislavsky system.

Creating a Role (1961). It is now acknowledged that neither the English-language nor the Russian version of Stanislavsky's writings is accurate. Since Russia did not subscribe to the International Copyright Agreement when Stanislavsky's works were published in the West, they were copyrighted under the name of Stanislavsky's American translator, Elizabeth Reynolds Hapgood; thus, she, and subsequently her estate, controlled the international publication rights to his works. Unfortunately, her English-language versions considerably distorted Stanislavsky both through many mistranslations and through considerable cutting and rearrangement. The Soviet versions, on the other hand, altered the texts to make them conform to official doctrine. Only recently have agreements between the Hapgood estate and Soviet officials made possible plans for an accurate, complete edition of Stanislavsky's works. Implementation of these plans will take many years.

It is difficult to give a brief summary of Stanislavsky's system, even as it has come down to us. Still, the main outlines can be sketched. Stanislavsky assumed that the actor's body and voice should be so well trained that they could respond efficiently to demands made on them and that actors would be schooled in stage techniques so they might project their characterizations to an audience without any sense of contrivance. These basics have often been downgraded by Stanislavsky's American disciples, perhaps because they were less innovative than his insistence that actors find an inner justification for whatever they do in order to avoid the appearance of insecurity or artificiality.

Many exercises created by Stanislavsky were designed to help actors discover inner justification. His "circle of attention" asks actors to draw an imaginary circle around themselves and to shut out all distractions so they may concentrate wholly upon entering the world of the play. Actors can also use the "magic if" by saying, "If I were this character in this situation, I would. . . ." In this way the truth of life is transposed to the truth of art so as to provide meaningful motivation. "Memory of emotion" is a further aid to be used if actors have difficulty in developing appropriate and sincere emotional responses to dramatic situations. Using this device, actors recall some analogous situation from their own lives which they then re-create until the emotional response is evoked.

If actors are not merely to play themselves, however, they must be thoroughly aware of the "given circumstances" of the production, discovered through detailed analysis of the play, the role, the directorial concept, the setting, costumes, and other limitations under which they must work. In this process, actors also become aware of each character's "objective" in each scene and in the play as a whole. They must be aware of the play's major lines of action so they can determine the "through line" around which all else is built. By understanding the function of their own roles and those of their fellow actors in each scene, they can contribute effectively to the overall ensemble effect, for they must seek to serve the dramatic action rather than to stand out from their fellow players. Above all, Stanislavsky demanded absolute dedication and the desire for continued improvement.

These are Stanislavsky's basic points, although he made many others. Various parts of the system have been emphasized by Stanislavsky's disciples who have argued strenuously among themselves about conflicting interpretations. In the U.S., the inner psychological aspects were to be emphasized at the expense of technical facility. It seems clear, nevertheless, that Stanislavsky sought to analyze and find a solution for each of the actor's problems, and that he was concerned with everything from basic training through finished performance. He was never fully satisfied with his answers and often cautioned others against trying to use his system without allowing for differences in artistic need or cultural background. Despite all deficiencies or misunderstandings, Stanislavsky's system has undoubtedly

been the most influential approach to acting in the twentieth century.

By the time Stanislavsky began to give serious thought to his system, he was already concerned about the MAT's problems in dealing with nonrealistic drama. He was to seek solutions throughout the remainder of his life. How he and the MAT addressed this issue will be discussed later. The early years of the MAT, however, contributed most fully to the triumph of realistic drama and theatrical production.

THE LEGACY OF THE INDEPENDENT THEATRE MOVEMENT AND NATURALISM

By 1900 the major battles over a new drama and new approaches to theatrical production had been fought and won. Many of the gains were only of immediate importance but others provided ongoing lessons. The independent theatre concept has been used down to the present under such labels as *art, little, avant-garde, off-Broadway, fringe,* and others. Whenever established theatres have become unresponsive to innovation, in dramatic writing or in production, the answer has been some variation on Antoine's Théâtre Libre.

It was also in the independent theatres that naturalistic production techniques were first consistently applied to create a unified style for naturalistic plays. Unfortunately, these theatres tended to use the same basic style for all plays. It may be for this reason that the 1890s saw both the peak and decline of naturalism, for once naturalistic methods were applied to plays of various styles its limitations became readily evident. Furthermore, many of the plays given their first hearing were so extreme as to set off a reaction against naturalism even among its former supporters. Even Zola underwent a change during the last decade of his life. Though he never gave up his faith in science, he found the techniques he had formerly advocated in art no longer adequate to express the growing idealism of his final works. Just before he died, Zola turned once more to dramatic composition but now he composed six opera librettos—set to music by Alfred Bruneau. In this final phase, Zola seems more nearly related to Wagner than to Becque. By 1900 naturalism as a conscious movement was largely over. Thereafter it was absorbed into the more acceptable realistic mode, which was to remain a major stream of twentieth-century drama.

Naturalism left a powerful legacy nevertheless. Its concern for concrete environment established the idea that each play should be performed in a setting designed especially for it. Even those who rejected naturalism came to expect an appropriate artistic environment for each play. Furthermore, many twentieth-century plays have continued to emphasize the integral relationship of character and action to heredity and environment. In addition, naturalism's concern for social ills has remained a significant ingredient of much drama.

In any case, by 1900 what had seemed innovative in 1875 had become acceptable, even commonplace. But by this time, another stream of drama and production, consciously opposed to realism and naturalism, was making itself felt.

Chapter 4

Antirealism and the Modernist Temperament

By the time the independent theatre movement got underway in the late 1880s, another strand of drama—antipathetic to realism and representationalism—was becoming evident. Some critics, considering this new strand to be the first true manifestation of the modern spirit, reserve the term *modernist* for it. Nevertheless, this new strand can be viewed as an alternative development growing out of many of the same impulses that had led to realism and naturalism. Both developments questioned long-standing views of the universe and the economic, political, social, and moral values based on them. The skepticism of the realists and naturalists was manifested in their insistence on seeking "truth"—usually conceived in scientific terms—and then representing it "objectively" without concern for conventional morality. While their search was motivated by the desire to discover more truthful values, its results undermined that humanist ideal (which posited a set of universal, unchanging values as the very basis of civilization) which had dominated Western thought and art since the Renaissance. During the late nineteenth century, values began to be treated as relative and changeable, and the naturalists' attempt to reduce all truth to what is scientifically knowable merely underscored how much of human experience involves the ultimately unknowable.

The unknowable and relative were the bedrocks of antirealism (and, for many critics, modernism). The antirealists' awareness of perpetual uncertainty (as William Butler Yeats put it: "Things fall apart; the center cannot hold") rendered traditional artistic forms unacceptable, since they had been devised to represent humanist perceptions of reality. The belief that truth is knowable and that it should be depicted representationally—that there should be a direct relationship between reality as normatively perceived and its artistic representation—had dominated artistic theory and practice since the Renaissance, but modernists refused to accept these premises and substituted their own subjective visions and esthetic modes (usually involving abstraction and distortion) for the traditional approach that had allowed the audience to compare the subject with its artistic rendering. This rejection of the long-accepted relationship between perception and representation is often considered the true beginning of the modernist temperament. Sets of related dichotomies serve to distinguish key aspects of the old and new approaches: tradition/novelty; convention/innovation; rules/freedom; nature/artificiality. Artists, no longer shackled to the natural world, could now be valued for novelty and formal innovation rather than for accurate renditions of recognizable subjects.

ANTECEDENTS OF SYMBOLISM

As with realism, antirealism found its first conscious expression in France. It took its inspiration from various sources, but especially the works of Poe, Baudelaire, and Wagner. Edgar Allan Poe (1809–1849) came to French attention during the 1850s through translations made by Charles-Pierre Baudelaire (1821–1867). Poe's influence was exerted in several ways. First, it came through his critical writings, in which he declared it a heresy to demand that literature be didactic; he argued that poetry is valuable in itself without any need to justify itself as moral teaching or social message. Second, it was exerted by his poetry, with its exactness of language, meter, and structure, and its musicality—qualities epitomized in such poems as "The Bells," in which sound is manipulated to create near-musical impressions. Third, Poe's influence was exerted through his macabre fiction in which mysterious forces beyond heredity and environment seem to control destiny. Fourth, it was exerted through his essay, "The Philosophy of Composition," in which Poe argued that the desired effect (rather than realistic representation) should determine the structure of a piece as well as all other choices made by the writer. Because of his influence, Poe became something of a patron saint to those French writers opposed to realism.

It was as the translator of Poe that Baudelaire first became widely known. (He was to begin several plays but finish none.) His first article on Poe appeared in 1852, just as realism was coming to the fore. Between 1852 and 1865, Baudelaire translated a number of Poe's stories and essays. His fame as the translator of Poe led to the publication of some of his own poems and to overnight notoriety. When his collection *The Flowers of Evil,* now among the most admired poems of the nineteenth century, was published in 1857, he and the publisher were prosecuted for obscenity, were heavily fined, and six of the poems were suppressed. For several generations, *The Flowers of Evil* was a by-word for depravity, morbidity, and obscenity in literature. Baudelaire's remaining years were spent in growing pessimism, and in 1867 he died in obscurity.

Baudelaire was fascinated by the irrational forces that distort and destroy people; he affronted many readers by flouting "evil" and making it a judgment on humanity. The symbolists were attracted to his depiction of human nature as mysterious and irrational, by his impeccable literary style, and by his rebellion against accepted standards of decency and poetic utilitarianism. His critical ideas were also influential. He believed that the writer works through an irrational and mystical grasp of intuitive truths which can never be expressed directly—the writer enters a "forest of symbols" which speak a language that cannot be fully understood and can be communicated only through a system of "correspondences" which suggest, but never fully express, the intuitions.

Baudelaire was also the first (in 1861) to call attention in France to Wagner's theories. But it was the outpouring of eulogies following Wagner's death in 1883 that made the greatest impact. The *Revue Wagnérienne* (published from 1884 to 1888) was to serve both as a major outlet for writing about Wagner and about the emerging symbolist movement. Wagner's most attractive ideas to the French were his rejection of realism, advocacy of myth as subject, fusion of music and poetry, synthesis of all the arts, and a quasi-religious vision for art.

Diverse antirealist strands converged in the mid-1880s in *symbolism,* a self-conscious movement launched in 1885 with a manifesto written by Jean Moréas and claiming as adherents Stéphane Mallarmé, Paul Valéry,

Claude Debussy, and many others. Mallarmé (1842–1898) soon became the acknowledged leader of the symbolists. Early in his career, Mallarmé wrote two dramas, *Hérodiade* (begun in 1864 and later rewritten as a poem) and *The Faun* (1865), later reshaped into the poem "The Afternoon of a Faun," which became the basis for the Ballets Russes' controversial ballet in 1912. Although Mallarmé abandoned the dramatic form, he never abandoned his interest in drama. As critic for *La Dernière Mode* in the 1870s, he commented on almost every play seen in Paris, including those of Dumas, Augier, Sardou, and Zola. He deplored the dominance of realism and championed the need for a "higher form." His ideas on drama found their fullest expression in the criticism he wrote for *La Revue Indépendante* in the 1880s and in his essays of the 1890s.

For Mallarmé, drama was essentially a sacred and mysterious rite which, through dream, reverie, allusion, and musicality, evokes the hidden spiritual meaning of existence. To him, the theatre was a kind of secular religious experience in which both actor and audience participate and in which the mystery of the universe is suggested and celebrated; it is concerned with humanity rather than particular people. Like Baudelaire, Mallarmé believed that the poet can only evoke intuitions of a mysterious reality which forever remains beyond human understanding.

For Mallarmé, poetic language, with its images and symbols, took precedence over all else. He objected to Wagner's elevation of music above poetry and argued that music must be incorporated into poetic structure. He also objected to Wagner's conception of the theatre as a synthesis of all the arts, declaring instead that, although the constituent arts should interact and reinforce each other, all should remain under the dominance of the word. Such views were reinforced by his dissatisfaction with the overemphasis on detailed, representational spectacle in the theatre of his day. To counteract these tendencies, Mallarmé called for the "detheatricalization of the theatre" and a "dematerialized" stage which would include only those elements absolutely essential to support the spoken word. Perhaps because the established theatres of his day catered to a popular audience who favored spectacular representationalism, Mallarmé favored an esthetically elite audience capable of appreciating the kind of theatre he advocated. He once proposed a theatre in which there would be only one actor who would recite works for an audience of not more than twenty-four people.

Not all symbolists agreed with Mallarmé's ideas, but nearly all were affected by them. His view of drama—as an evocation of the mystery of existence through poetic and allusive language, performed with only the most essential and atmospherically appropriate theatrical aids, for the purpose of creating a mystical experience—was to dominate the symbolist movement.

Although symbolist playwrights were numerous, only two—Maeterlinck and Claudel—are of major importance. Between 1890 and 1910, Maeterlinck was considered the leading symbolist writer, while Claudel was virtually unknown. But as Maeterlinck's reputation declined, Claudel's grew. Maurice Maeterlinck (1862–1949) was born in Belgium but moved to Paris in 1886 and soon came under the influence of the symbolists. His first play, *Princess Maleine* (1889), based on a fairy tale, tells of the destruction of Maleine by the wicked queen. Octave Mirbeau, one of the most influential critics of the day, praised it as more tragic and significant than *Hamlet.*

During the 1890s Maeterlinck was looked upon as the major dramatist of the symbolist school, since his plays—especially *The Intruder* (1890), *The Blind* (1890), and *Pelléas and Mélisande*

(1892)—most nearly embodied the symbolist ideal. Maeterlinck also wrote theoretical essays that illuminate his dramatic practice. In one, he states that the most important element in a play, "enveloping the whole work and creating the atmosphere proper to it," is "the idea which the poet forms of the unknown in which float about the beings and things which he evokes, the mystery which dominates them, judges them, and presides over their destinies." He also championed a "static theatre," in which the surface dialogue and action is unimportant but in which the unspoken addresses the soul: "I have grown to believe that an old man, seated in his armchair, waiting patiently, . . . giving unconscious ear to all the eternal laws that reign about his house . . . does yet live in reality a deeper, more human, and more universal life than the lover who strangles his mistress, the captain who conquers in battle, or 'the husband who avenges his honor.'" Maeterlinck's *The Intruder* embodies this statement, for in it an old blind man sits quietly throughout the play, sensing what is lost on others who are unaware that death is approaching to take his daughter, who has given birth in an adjoining room.

By far the most famous symbolist play of the 1890s was *Pelléas and Mélisande,* in which Golaud brings home his new bride Mélisande, only to have her and his brother Pelléas fall unwillingly in love; eventually Golaud kills Pelléas, and Mélisande dies after giving birth. But the primary emphasis is not on this story but on the mood of mystery and fate that envelops it. The action develops through a set of loosely related symbols, the significance of which can only be suggested. Water plays some part in almost every scene: Mélisande is first discovered by a pool in the forest; later, she and Pelléas play by a fountain, in which she loses her wedding ring, by which they declare their love, and by which Pelléas is killed; they search for her lost ring in a grotto which can only be approached by a narrow path between two lakes; the sea is the only open space visible from the castle. Light and darkness is another recurring motif: the castle is surrounded by dark and impenetrable forests (in contrast with the open sea and light); the characters often sit in darkness or anxiously seek pools of light; lamps refuse to stay lit. Height and depth are also imbued with significance: Mélisande sits in a tower and combs her hair, which falls down to engulf Pelléas standing below as doves fly away from the tower never to return; Pelléas and Golaud go into the bowels of the castle to investigate the stench that arises from there; the numerous pools and fountains are described as bottomless. Several scenes in the play are connected with the dramatic action only symbolically. In the opening scene, women try unsuccessfully to wash away stains from the castle steps; in a later scene, sheep are driven to slaughter and the boy Yniold seeks unsuccessfully to remove a golden ball from beneath an enormous boulder. Such scenes are almost allegorical in their comment on the human condition. Although it is impossible to assign definite meanings to the complex web of symbols, it is clear that with it Maeterlinck seeks to suggest the struggle of the characters as their desires for love, happiness, and openness are pitted against deceit, misery, and fate. The recurring symbols are reinforced by the dialogue, which is extremely simple and repetitive.

Characterization is also minimal. All the characters desire good but are overcome by mysterious forces more powerful than themselves. At the end, the old king Arkel says of Mélisande: "She was a little being quiet and fearful, a poor mysterious being like us all. I shall never understand it." And of the newborn child, he adds: "It is the poor little one's turn," thereby suggesting that the pattern applies not just to this group of people but is typical of all persons. Maeterlinck's characters are victims of forces much more mysterious than Zola's

FIG. 4.1

Maeterlinck's *The Blue Bird* at the Théâtre Réjane, Paris, in 1911. The scenery by V. E. Egerov was loaned by the Moscow Art Theatre, for which it was originally designed. (From *Le Théâtre*, 1911.)

heredity and environment. His world is both unknowable and unremediable.

Maeterlinck eventually tired of this rather abstruse symbolism. Of his later works, by far the most famous is *The Blue Bird* (1908), an allegory about two children searching for a blue bird (a symbol of happiness) who, after numerous adventures, discover it in their own backyard. Despite its overwhelming scenic demands, it has been Maeterlinck's most enduring play in the theatre. Although the late plays are much more accessible for audiences, they are generally considered far less important than the plays he wrote in the 1890s.

Paul Claudel (1868–1955) began his career as a poet in Mallarmé's circle, but he came to consider Mallarmé's views spiritually empty. Nevertheless, from Mallarmé Claudel had absorbed the notion that drama is a revelation of the hidden wonder of the universe, that it links the visible and invisible planes of existence, and that language has the power to evoke intuitive perceptions; out of these convictions, Claudel fashioned a Christian version of symbolism. Claudel ignored the physical limitations of theatrical production more fully than any of his contemporaries. It is probably for this reason that none of his works was staged in the 1890s and that he is often passed over in discussions of symbolist drama. His first work to reach the stage (in 1912) was *The Tidings Brought to Mary* (written in 1892 as *The Maid Violane*). Set in the Middle Ages, it shows the beautiful Violane encountering a leprous architect on his way to Rheims to build a cathedral; she kisses him, thereby taking the curse upon herself, and lives the rest of her life as an outcast. The focus is upon the effect of her saintliness upon others. Like Claudel's other plays, this one illustrates that the value of life can only be realized in giving it away, that in submitting to God's will one finds fulfillment.

Claudel's theological message is cloaked in language of great beauty, powerful moods, and symbolic indirection (so much so that the religious message often escapes the casual reader). The play also projects Claudel's view of humanity caught in a spiritual wasteland seeking some meaning in life. Nevertheless, Claudel was not an ascetic. For him, physical passion is a primary means of discovering divine love, which can best be comprehended as an extension of human love. This aspect of Claudel's work is perhaps most clearly evident in *Break of Noon* (1905).

Although Claudel's plays began to appear in the theatre sporadically from 1912 onward, it was only after Jean-Louis Barrault's production in 1943 of *The Satin Slipper* (1919–1924) that Claudel's theatricality was fully acknowledged. This play, like others by Claudel, is not concerned with illusion or with psychological and sociological problems so much as with the symbolic exploration of those spiritual states which can best be expressed through visions,

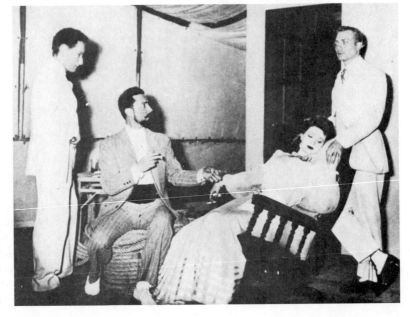

FIG. 4.2
Claudel's *Break of Noon*, produced at the Théâtre Marigny in 1948. Jean-Louis Barrault, at left, had much to do with the revival of Claudel's works after World War II. (Photo by Bernand.)

often reaching out to encompass enormous spaces and leaps across time. The events in *The Satin Slipper* span a century and occur in Spain, Italy, Africa, America, and at sea. At one point, the hemispheres converse, and at another the earth is represented as one bead on a rosary. Thus, it requires more than ordinary means and more than ordinary imagination to do Claudel's plays justice in the theatre.

SYMBOLIST INDEPENDENT THEATRES

Like their realist and naturalist counterparts, the symbolists did not find a sympathetic theatrical platform until, taking their cue from Antoine, they adopted the independent theatre concept. The first important symbolist producer was Paul Fort (1872–1960), who in 1890 at the age of seventeen founded the Théâtre Mixte, which metamorphosed into the Théâtre d'Art (the theatre usually associated with Fort's work). At the Théâtre d'Art, Fort produced seven bills between November 1890 and March 1892. After a lapse of several months, Fort, in cooperation with Lugné-Poë, began work on *Pelléas and Mélisande* but withdrew before the play was presented. Thus, in 1893 the Théâtre d'Art came to an end and Fort retired permanently from the theatre at the age of twenty-one.

According to Fort, he founded his theatre to present works not intended for the stage. His first program was composed entirely of recited poems (perhaps influenced by Mallarmé's concept of the ideal theatre), but he later added drama, although almost all bills included some nondramatic poetry. His repertory ranged through selections from the Bible and the *Iliad,* poems by Mallarmé, Poe, and Rimbaud, and plays by Shelley, Marlowe, and various symbolist dramatists. Most bills included several contrasting items. As a result, the evenings often seemed interminable; one program is said to have lasted until 5 A.M.

Fort was encouraged by Mallarmé and Verlaine, whose portraits graced *The Book of Art,* the symbolist review that served as a program for the productions. The theatre was always so financially shaky that Fort was never able to pay any of his authors, actors, or designers. For the most part, his actors were amateurs considerably out of their depth, but he also recruited a number of professionals, among them Marguerite Moreno, Suzanne Desprès, and Berthe Bady. The settings were by leading symbolist painters—Paul Gauguin, Edouard Vuillard, Maurice Denis, and Paul Sérusier.

It is difficult to overstate the importance of the Théâtre d'Art's approach to staging. It was the first to reject, consciously and as artistic principle, representationalism. The motto of the Théâtre d'Art was "the word creates the decor." As Pierre Quillard put it: "The decor ought to be a pure ornamental fiction which completes the illusion by color and line analogous with the drama. Most often some mobile draperies will suffice to give the impression of the infinite multiplicity of time and place. . . . the theatre . . . ought to be: *a pretext for dream.*" The Théâtre d'Art's sets were extremely simple—ornamental and atmospheric rather than illusionistic. They were influenced by the impressionists' use of clean color and by the careful geometry of Japanese prints. For a recitation of Rimbaud's "The Drunken Boat," a four-leafed folding screen, on which was painted a Japanese-style underwater garden, was used. For *The Girl With Severed Hands,* Denis used three scrims and a gold-colored backdrop on which angels and other figures were depicted in icon fashion. On the forestage, in front of the scrims, a reciter spoke (in a monotonous voice) passages that explained the drama, while behind the scrims, as in a vision, the silhouetted actors moved slowly. For de Gourmont's *Théodat,* a play about a Christian martyr in Rome, the setting was composed of a single gold backdrop on which were glued a large number of red, cut-out lions. For some productions, the background was wholly unadorned. The scrim was especially popular with the symbolists, perhaps because more than any other scenic device it "dematerialized" the actors and the settings by converting them into shadowy images.

Fort and his associates were more enthusiastic than accomplished, more ambitious in planning than scrupulous in execution. Much of the work was outrageously amateurish, and what had been intended often remained unclear. Audiences tended to be divided into two camps: ardent supporters, who overlooked all shortcomings; and deriders, who found every production outrageous or hilarious. Of Fort's supporters, Jules Lemaître wrote: "A scattered insanity floats in the air. . . . The very young heads of schoolboys, ecstatic and illuminated, listen to the words of Maeterlinck. . . . [There is] an undercurrent of perversion and craziness." Francisque Sarcey, Paris' most influential critic, was often in a state of uncontrollable laughter. Fort also received numerous letters threatening him with violence if he did not cease productions. Today, when novelty is so common as to have lost much of its power, it is difficult to appreciate how revolutionary these productions were and how shocking they must have been to some and how tonic for others. Fort is the precursor of all modern departures from representational staging.

Still, there was always an element of preciosity and dilletantism in Fort's work, and it remained for Aurélien-Marie Lugné-Poë (1869–1940) to solidify what Fort had begun. Lugné-Poë had been present at Antoine's first production at the Théâtre Libre and had performed in productions there between 1888 and 1890 while still a student at the Conservatoire. But he shared an apartment with Pierre Bonnard, Maurice Denis, and Edouard Vuillard—all destined to become leading figures in painting, and all involved in the work of the Théâtre d'Art—and through them Lugné-Poë was introduced to Fort, for whom he acted in and directed a number of plays.

In 1893, Fort and Lugné-Poë decided to cooperate on the premiere of *Pelléas and Mélisande;* when Fort withdrew, Lugné-Poë became the principal purveyor of symbolist theatre in Paris. The opening of *Pelléas and Mélisande* (May 1893) is usually considered the birth of the Théâtre de l'Oeuvre, although that name was not chosen until later and elevated to a credo (the theatre as a work of art). Lugné-Poë was assisted by Camille Mauclair, poet and critic, and Edouard Vuillard, who oversaw design. The original Théâtre de l'Oeuvre continued until 1899 (Lugné-Poë later revived it), by which time it had presented fifty-one bills, most for two or three performances but some for as many as twenty (though not consecutively). The company considerably extended its influence by playing in Belgium, Holland, Denmark, Norway, and England.

Lugné-Poë stated two goals for the Théâtre de l'Oeuvre: to familiarize the public with great foreign dramas; and to perform the plays of young symbolist playwrights. Among foreign authors, Ibsen was favored, nine of his plays being presented. It was Lugné-Poë who made Ibsen acceptable to the French, and he was rewarded by being named Ibsen's agent in France. Other foreign playwrights included Hauptmann, Oscar Wilde, Thomas Otway, and Marlowe, as well as two Sanskrit dramatists. Among the native writers were Maeterlinck, Pierre Quillard, Mme. Rachilde, Judith Cladel, Emile Verhaeren, and Alfred Jarry. Each program was preceded by a lecture intended to increase understanding of the plays on that bill.

Lugné-Poë, following the Théâtre d'Art's creed that the word creates the decor, used simplified settings designed to evoke the appropriate atmosphere through color, line, and light. For *Pelléas and Mélisande* there were no furniture or properties; the backdrops were painted in grayed tones; all light came from overhead; the action, all behind a scrim, appeared to be enveloped in mist; costumes reflected the paintings of the fifteenth-century artist Memling; the actors used a singsong delivery (or chant) and angular, stylized gestures. It is difficult to envision a production more unlike those then being staged by Antoine.

A similar style seems to have been used for most symbolist productions. In 1894, a critic wrote: "The most simple and sensible things take on a different appearance in passing through the mouth and gestures of the l'Oeuvre actors under the direction of Lugné-Poë. They have a continual ecstatic air of perpetually being visionaries. As if hallucinatory, they stare before them far, very far, vaguely, very vaguely. Their voices are cavernous, their diction choppy. They seem to be attempting to give the air that they are fools." Despite such criticism, Lugné-Poë remained firm in his conviction about the appropriate style for symbolist plays, since he felt it necessary to divert attention from external reality to mysterious inner and outer forces that control destiny and since he thought of the actors and settings as generalized, depersonalized signs.

It is difficult to judge the effectiveness of the productions. The symbolist mode was clearly incomprehensible to many. Officials were prone to consider the symbolists to be anarchists and often sent undercover agents to productions looking for known subversives. Some critics, such as Octave Mirbeau and Catulle Mendes, supported the symbolists, but many, like Sarcey, derided them. Nevertheless, familiarity bred indulgence, and after a time Sarcey wrote: "There was a time when I was overcome with laughter when the curtain went up to discover that green scrim behind which were the mute

puppets of a vast marionette show. But we have come to the point where we are no longer astonished by the most nonsensical eccentricities."

Lugné-Poë eventually came to doubt the value of symbolism, and in 1897 he stated that since, with the exception of Maeterlinck, no significant dramatist had come out of the movement, henceforth he intended to choose plays without reference to their origin. It seems likely that Lugné-Poë had also come to perceive that his production style was not suited to Ibsen's plays, for as he stated: "l'Oeuvre has found itself engulfed by this movement [symbolism] despite the evident contradiction which exists between Ibsen's theatre and the Symbolist theories." Lugné-Poë was bitterly attacked by the symbolists. The resulting controversy signalled the disintegration of the symbolist movement. Maeterlinck was already turning in new directions, and in 1898 Mallarmé died. The Théâtre de l'Oeuvre was discontinued in 1899. Thus, by 1900 symbolism as a conscious movement was virtually over in France.

JARRY

In addition to the symbolist playwrights, another dramatist of the 1890s—Alfred Jarry (1873–1907)—was eventually to win an enviable reputation, although his work was not fully appreciated until after World War II. Jarry's drama is related to that of the symbolists in being antirealistic and in being produced at the Théâtre de l'Oeuvre. But Jarry's vision of humanity was quite unlike that of his symbolist contemporaries. The moral topsyturvydom of his world more nearly resembles that of the *comédies rosses,* although it completely disregards naturalism's scientific bias and concern for specific environments.

Jarry's reputation is based primarily on one

play, *Ubu Roi* (1896), a work begun in 1888 by Jarry and his schoolmates for puppets in their Théâtre des Phynances. *Ubu Roi* is a grotesque and bitter comedy about which Jarry stated: "Once the curtain went up, I wanted the stage . . . to become like that mirror in the stories of Mme. Leprince de Baumont in which the vicious see themselves with bull's horns and a dragon's body. . . . [The public] is made up, as Catulle Mendes has so well expressed it, 'of eternal human imbecility, eternal lust, eternal gluttony, baseness of instinct which takes over completely; of decorum, virtue, patriotism, and the ideal of people who have dined well.' The comic element must at the most be the macabre comedy of an English clown or a dance of the dead." Jarry depicts a grotesque world without human decency. The central figure, Ubu, is violent and totally devoid of

moral scruple; he is the epitome of all that Jarry found monstrous and stupid in human beings. The action of the play shows Ubu seizing power to become king of Poland and retaining his position by killing and torturing all those who oppose him; eventually he is chased from the country but promises to continue his exploits elsewhere.

At about the time this play was published, Jarry went to work for the Théâtre de l'Oeuvre, where he was in charge of publicity. Jarry urged the production of his two favorite dramas—*Peer Gynt* and *Ubu Roi*—and did an adaptation of Ibsen's play (which was presented with minor success). Eventually Lugné-Poë also agreed to produce *Ubu Roi*.

On opening night, every literary faction in Paris was represented. Jarry himself—dressed in baggy black suit and in grotesque makeup—

FIG. 4.3
Sketch for the production of *Ubu Roi* at the Théâtre Antoine in 1908. (From *Le Figaro*, February 16, 1908.)

delivered the lecture that preceded the play. The setting was by Jarry, assisted by Bonnard, Vuillard, Toulouse-Lautrec, and Sérusier. Arthur Symons wrote this description of it: "The scenery was painted to represent by a child's convention, indoors and out of doors, and even the torrid, temperate and arctic zones at once . . . at the back of the stage, you saw . . . against the sky a small closed window and a fireplace . . . through . . . which . . . trooped in and out those clamorous and sanguinary figures of the drama. On the left was painted a bed, and at the foot of the bed a bare tree, and snow falling. On the right were palm trees, about one of which coiled a boa constrictor. . . . Changes of scene were announced by . . . placard. A venerable gentleman in evening dress . . . trotted across the stage on the points of his toes between every scene and hung the new placard on a nail." In the battle scenes, two men represented the opposing armies, but for the slaughters Jarry had bought forty life-sized wicker mannequins which were beheaded. To indicate that he was on horseback, Ubu wore a cut-out of a horse's head around his neck.

Firmin Gémier, an actor at the Odéon, played Ubu. At a loss about how to play such a role, Gémier was advised by Lugné-Poë to imitate Jarry's own speech and gestures (no inflection and equal stress on every syllable, even silent ones, and a few monotonous, jerky gestures). Gémier's costume made him appear pear-shaped and swollen; Jarry had designed a mask for the character (which included a nose like an elephant's trunk) but Gémier did not wear it. Accounts of the opening night have become legendary. One account states that when Gémier spoke the opening line—"*Merdre*" (the French *merde* with an extra syllable, in English "shit-e")—the audience was thrown into an uproar that lasted for fifteen minutes, since such an obscenity on the stage was

unknown. This account also maintains that many spectators walked out, while the rest quickly divided themselves into supporters and opponents of the play, even to the point of fist fights; and that this pattern continued throughout the evening being renewed with each *merdre*. Other accounts suggest that the uproar developed only gradually and was not extreme until well into the performance. The play received only two performances. Of the production, William Butler Yeats (who attended the premiere) wrote: "After S. Mallarmé, . . . after our own verse, . . . what more is possible? After us the Savage God." This remark was later considered prophetic, for as the twentieth century progressed, symbolism's mysterious universe gave way increasingly to Jarry's grotesque "savage" vision.

Jarry went on to write two more plays about Ubu, *Ubu Bound* (1900) and *Ubu the Cuckold* (published 1944), but they were not produced during his lifetime. Jarry also wrote about the theatre. He advocated eliminating settings (since they are neither natural nor entirely artificial), and he preferred the mask to the actor's face because it captures the eternal qualities of a character.

Jarry's own life was as bizarre as his work. He deliberately flouted every standard of his day and turned himself into a character not unlike those about whom he wrote. When he died in 1907, Gémier revived *Ubu Roi* briefly at the Théâtre Antoine. Following World War I, the surrealists proclaimed Jarry one of their progenitors, and in 1927 Antonin Artaud and Roger Vitrac founded their short-lived Théâtre Alfred Jarry. In 1945, Cyril Connolly dubbed Jarry "the Santa Claus of the Atomic Age," and shortly thereafter Eugène Ionesco and several others paid homage to Jarry by founding the College of Pataphysics to explore the "science of imaginary solutions" which Jarry had proclaimed at the beginning of the twentieth century. Jarry was to be something of a patron saint for the absurdists.

ENGLISH AESTHETICISM

England produced little antirealistic drama in the late nineteenth century, but several critics championed ideas similar to those of the French symbolists. In England, the movement was usually called *art-for-art's-sake* or *aestheticism* because of its insistence on art as valuable in itself without concern for its usefulness.

A key figure in the English movement was Walter Pater (1839–1894) who, in the conclusion to his *Studies in the History of the Renaissance* (1873), declared: "Not the fruit of experience, but experience itself, is the end. A counted number of pulses only is given to us of a variegated, dramatic life. How may we see in them all that is to be seen in them by the finest senses? How shall we pass most swiftly from point to point, and be present always at the focus where the greatest number of vital forces unite in their purest energy? To burn always with this hard, gemlike flame, to maintain this ecstasy, is success in life." To Pater, then, that person is most successful who lives life most intensely, and it is art that most thoroughly distills human experience and makes it most nearly possible to "maintain this ecstasy," for "art comes to you professing frankly to give nothing but the highest quality to your moments as they pass, and simply for those moments' sake." Pater (like many of the French symbolists) wished to turn life itself into a work of art. By 1880, Pater had attracted a number of disciples who sought to implement this creed in their own lives. They adopted a kind of dandyism in dress and proudly proclaimed their indifference to the opinion of the masses. That they had captured the public's attention is attested by the extensive satire of them found in Gilbert and Sullivan's *Patience* (1881).

Oscar Wilde (1856–1900) soon became the movement's best known spokesman. He declared: "As a method, Realism is a complete failure." He added: "The only beautiful things . . . are the things that do not concern us. As long as a thing is useful or necessary to us, or affects us in any way, either for pain or pleasure . . . it is outside the proper sphere of art." Wilde praised purely decorative art for its "deliberate rejection of Nature as the ideal of beauty, as well as of the imitative method." Such views would eventually lead to the rejection of recognizable subjects so that the artistic medium might be explored for its own intrinsic values rather than for its ability to reproduce likeness faithfully.

Wilde's theoretical views are not always evident in his dramas. Only *Salome* (1893) links him to the French symbolists, perhaps because, according to Fort, it was written with the Théâtre d'Art in mind. It treats the perverse passion of Salome for John the Baptist, whose life she demands of her stepfather Herod, who in turn is so revolted when she makes love to the severed head that he has her crushed to death. Banned in England, it was first produced in Paris in 1894, and was to hold the stage primarily in Richard Strauss' operatic setting. Others of Wilde's plays—*Lady Windermere's Fan* (1892), *A Woman of No Importance* (1893), and *An Ideal Husband* (1895)—remind one of Jones and Pinero. By far his most successful work is *The Importance of Being Earnest* (1895), a play that both calls attention to and makes innovative use of the shopworn stories, sentiments, and devices of traditional comedy. Its epigrammatic inversion of ordinary sentiments creates a world not unlike that of Gilbert and Sullivan operettas.

Aestheticism did not make a deep impact on English drama. Its force was largely negated when in 1895 Wilde was sentenced to prison (for perjury, although behind this lay charges of sodomy). His conviction served as a kind of

FIG. 4.4
As early as 1906, the British designer Charles Ricketts experimented innovatively with stage space in this design for Wilde's *Salome*, produced at King's Hall, Covent Garden.

public revenge on aesthetes and their elitist conception of art and disdain for conventional behavior and ordinary people.

GERMAN ANTIREALISM

Several Germanic writers also espoused many of the ideals voiced by the French symbolists and English aesthetes. In Germany and Austria, the movement, often called *neoromanticism,* denounced the ugliness, dullness, and utilitarianism of naturalism and championed "beauty" and "life." Like Pater, the neoromantics suggested that one should live for beauty, and that the highest value is to be truly alive and aware of vital forces at their most intense. Intuition was placed above reason; dogma, conventions, and middle-class values were proclaimed false. Baudelaire, Mallarmé,

Maeterlinck, Wilde, and Ibsen were significant influences.

Neoromanticism probably found its fullest Germanic expression in the work of Hugo von Hofmannsthal (1873–1929). As a dramatist, Hofmannsthal's career may be divided into two parts—before and after 1900. Before 1900, he wrote short pieces primarily—among them *The Fool and Death* (1893) and *The Adventurer and the Singing Girl* (1899). In the first of these, an aristocratic young aesthete who has lived entirely for art protests when summoned by Death that he has not yet lived. A number of those who have known him are summoned to show that he has not lived because he has never committed himself fully to life. Around 1900 Hofmannsthal underwent a crisis during which he came to suspect that all language is meaningless. Although he overcame much of this doubt, his work was never the same afterwards.

Most of his subsequent effort went into librettos for Richard Strauss' operas—among them *Die Rosenkavalier* (1911) and *Ariadne auf Naxos* (1912)—or reworkings of plays from the past—among them *Everyman* (1912) and *The Great World Theatre* (1922), both of which became mainstays of the Salzburg Festival. In all of his work, Hofmannsthal proved himself to be an excellent poet. Much of his drama shows a rather pessimistic outlook, but throughout he upheld basic human values. More so than most of his contemporaries, Hofmannsthal seemed caught between affirmation and doubt.

In general, however, Germanic writers were inclined to treat the rational and the irrational in oppositional terms or even to intermingle them. This pattern was established in part by Friedrich Nietzsche (1844–1900), one of the nineteenth century's major philosophers. Nietzsche wrote his first important work, *The Birth of Tragedy* (1872), under the influence of Wagner. In it, Nietzsche explores the origin of Greek tragedy, not through historical evidence but through human impulses and the role of myth in Greek society. He concludes that tragedy united two conflicting human impulses: for clarity and order, and for irrationality and disorder. He finds these two impulses personified in two Greek art deities, Apollo and Dionysus. The Apollonian (the rational) shields humans from the terror of reality by creating illusions and giving them form; the Dionysian (the intuitive) tears away the veil of illusion and forces humans to recognize their oneness with all nature. "Dionysiac art . . . makes us realize that everything that is generated must be prepared to face its painful dissolution . . . we become one with the immense lust for life . . . we realize our great good fortune in having life—not as individuals, but as part of the life force with whose procreative lust we have become one." According to Nietzsche, tragedy came into existence when the Apollonian impulse imposed order and harmony on this Dionysian wisdom. He argues that great art—such as that of classical Greece—depends on perfect balance between the Apollonian and the Dionysian. When the Apollonian dominates—as it did in postclassical Greece—tragedy declines because rationalism denigrates the Dionysian element. Similarly, he attributed the low state of drama in the 1870s to reverence for scientific rationalism.

The Birth of Tragedy has influenced almost all modern artistic movements. Its argument for the ritual origin of tragedy has informed all subsequent discussions about the origins of theatre and the mythic bases of drama and art. Its denunciation of scientism and its insistence on looking behind physical phenomena for more profound insights have been important in all subsequent antirealist movements. Its conception of the Dionysian and Apollonian foreshadows Freud's conceptions of the human psyche (with the Dionysian roughly equivalent to the id and subconscious, and the Apollonian to the conscious mind with its tendencies to suppress unpleasant truths). Nietzsche's description of the Dionysian element—its dark, tortured, subterranean wisdom—was also to be echoed by many later writers, perhaps most notably by Strindberg and Artaud.

Nietzsche's later writings were also to be very influential. He radically reevaluated all of Western philosophy, questioning the validity of its truths: "truths are illusions of which one has forgotten that they *are* illusions." In *Thus Spake Zarathustra* (1883–1885), he made his famous declaration: "God is dead," by which he meant that Christianity has lost its potency and can no longer serve as an authoritative basis for moral values, a position already implied by much nineteenth-century science. It was the precursor of twentieth-century arguments that all systems of value are equally groundless. In *Beyond Good and Evil* (1886) and

The *Genealogy of Morals* (1887), Nietzsche called for the "re-evaluation of all values." He charged that Christianity has created a "slave morality" by teaching people to accept debasement in this world in return for rewards in the next. As a countermeasure, he proclaimed the need to give up any hope for an individual afterlife and instead to work toward developing the superman, one who is able to gain power over himself and use that mastery creatively. This struggle to create the superman is the true Dionysian state, the opposite of Christianity. "The God on the Cross is a curse on life, a pointer to seek redemption from it. Dionysus cut to pieces is a *promise* of life: it is eternally reborn and comes back from destruction." Nietzsche called for not only emancipation of human beings from traditional values but also for the emancipation of art from realistic representationalism rooted in a rationalism that determinedly ignores the irrational and intuitive aspects of being.

Much of the Germanic writing that mingled the realistic and nonrealistic was concerned with sexual repression. The most notorious of these works is *The Council of Love* (1894) by Oskar Panizza (1853–1921), a satire on the papal court and the holy family in which God is shown as a tottering old man, Christ as a weakling (because of his worshippers' addiction to his flesh and blood), Mary as proud and erotic, and the papal court as a scene of sexual orgy. Having lost control over the world, God asks the devil to assist him by devising a punishment that will destroy the body but leave the soul; the devil's solution is syphilis, with which the pope, along with others, becomes infected. This grotesque play, closer to Jarry than to the symbolists, earned Panizza a year in prison. The play is an expression of Panizza's convictions that the individual need for freedom is ultimately irreconcilable with the institutional demand of church or state for conformity, and that when restraints become

too great, violence results. Panizza argued that the purpose of art is not "to give a nearly exact illusion" of nature, but through "a subjective metamorphosis of nature . . . through exaggeration, . . . overstatement, . . . distortion and twisting, to bring us . . . out of our equilibrium, to upset, interest, and amuse us." Because of the publicity surrounding his trial, Panizza made a far greater impact on the public consciousness than the play alone would ever have done. Following his trial, Panizza became increasingly paranoid, and the final years of his life (from 1904 on) were spent in an insane asylum.

Benjamin Franklin Wedekind (1864–1918)— so named by a father who had spent sixteen years in the U.S. following the revolution of 1848—shared many of Panizza's ideas but fared somewhat better. His first major drama, *Spring Awakening: A Children's Tragedy* (1891), is a play about adolescent trauma and suicide provoked by the unwillingness of adults (parents, teachers, clergy) to deal with sexuality. Because her mother is too ashamed to explain sex to her, the pubescent Wendla becomes pregnant and then dies when her mother insists that she have a surreptitious abortion. Another adolescent, Moritz, commits suicide because of his anxieties over sex; and his friend Melchior, expelled from school, disowned by his family because of books and drawings found in his possession, and sent to a reformatory, is on the verge of suicide urged on by Moritz's ghost (who appears carrying his head under his arm), when he is saved by the Man With a Mask, who revives Melchior's desire to live. *Spring Awakening* is a strange mixture of naturalistic, grotesque, and symbolic scenes, although the impression made on Wedekind's contemporaries was a determined antirealism. The play was not produced until 1906 (by Max Reinhardt and with Wedekind in the role of the Man With a Mask), and even then only in a heavily censored version. Not only was the play considered obscene but also subversive in its mingling of various styles, collapsing of accepted genre distinctions, and questioning of social mores.

In *Earth Spirit* (first version 1895), the principal character is Lulu, the "earth spirit" whose age and origin are unknown and who is introduced in the prologue in the guise of a snake, the eternal temptress. A series of characters seek, each through some artistic medium, to impose a limiting vision on Lulu and die when they fail. In *Pandora's Box* (1895), Lulu has been imprisoned for the death of her last husband; she then becomes a prostitute in Paris, and eventually is murdered by Jack the Ripper in London. In these two plays, Wedekind suggests a relationship between the commercialization of art and the commercialization of sex, for just as the men in *Earth Spirit* seek to shape Lulu by placing her within various artistic media because they cannot deal with her directly on her own terms, the German

public can deal with sex only through the titillating but nonexplicit commercial theatre of the time. Thus, unfiltered truth becomes the equivalent of prostitution in life, while art that caters to the public's desire for disguised sexuality is itself a disguised form of prostitution. Like *Spring Awakening,* the Lulu plays also intermingle various styles, although not so extremely.

Wedekind eventually completed twenty-one quite uneven plays, among them *The Marquis of Keith* (1900), *Death and the Devil* (1906), and *Bismarck* (1916). Because of their subjects and eccentric style, the plays did not easily win acceptance. After 1900, opposition to them gradually lessened; by 1903–1904 there had been 149 performances of his plays in German theatres, and thereafter productions became more numerous, especially as his influence on German expressionism was acknowledged. After 1905, Wedekind also acted frequently in his own plays and performed

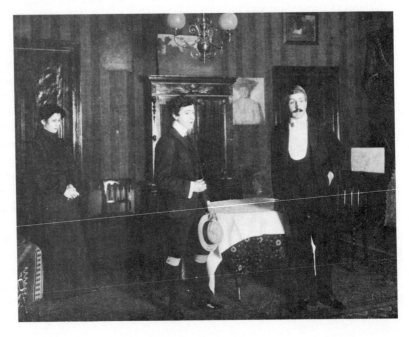

FIG. 4.5
Scene from the Kleines Theater production of Wedekind's *The Marquis of Keith* in 1905. The playwright himself, at right, played the title role. (From *Le Théâtre,* 1906.)

in cabarets. Brecht was to acknowledge the strong influence of Wedekind's cabaret songs (and Wedekind's cabaret performance style) on his own work. Overall, Wedekind must be considered one of the seminal figures of modern German theatre.

FREUD

Many late nineteenth-century trends in thought—both realistic and antirealistic—were to come together in the revolutionary views of human psychology set forth by Sigmund Freud (1856–1939) and eventually influence most twentieth-century drama.

During the last quarter of the nineteenth century, psychology for the first time was separated from philosophy and recognized as an autonomous discipline. A decisive step came in 1879 when Wilhelm Wundt set up a laboratory in Leipzig for psychological experimentation. At about the same time, Jean-Martin Charcot in France was investigating hypnosis and the power of suggestion over human behavior. This pioneering work attracted the interest of Freud who, after completing his medical studies in Vienna in 1881, had specialized in diseases of the nervous system. He went to study with Charcot and then returned to Vienna to work with Josef Breuer on the use of hypnosis in the treatment of hysteria. With Breuer, Freud published his first important work, *Studies in Hysteria* (1895). Thereafter, Freud extended his theories in such books as *The Interpretation of Dreams* (1900), *Three Contributions to the Theory of Sex* (1905), and *Civilization and Its Discontents* (1930). Freud's ideas took shape over a long period and many underwent considerable revision. Thus, a summary of his ideas can only be approximate.

Freud saw the mind as composed of three parts. The *id,* an unconscious level that seeks to enhance pleasure and reduce pain by giving full scope to elemental impulses, is devoted to the pleasure principle. The *ego,* concerned with facing up to the demands of the real world and with impulses from both the id and the superego, is devoted to the reality principle. The *superego,* the censor or conscience, is largely unconscious but manifests itself in conscious feelings of guilt and shame. Psychological conflict—competition among these three parts—plays a central role in personalities, both the healthy and neurotic. The normal mind finds a satisfying solution to the conflicts, whereas the abnormal mind does not. In all cases, unconscious processes exert pressure on consciousness and action. Freud's principal concern was to discover the causes of and remedies for abnormal behavior. Out of this work grew psychoanalysis, an attempt to bring unconscious motives and repressed memories to the level of consciousness so that psychological disorders might be alleviated.

As a diagnostic tool, Freud found dreams of primary help, since in dreams conscious control is lulled, and suppressed urges and memories come to the surface, though most often in disguised form or symbols (for example, a stick or knife may signify the phallus). He also found that in dreams events widely separated by time or place were often merged and that one person often metamorphosed into another.

Freud's ideas were to become so fully assimilated that it is difficult to appreciate how revolutionary they seemed at the turn of the century. Previous views had usually idealized rationality. Impulse and intuition were looked upon as urges that needed to be carefully controlled by reason. Freud argued that not only is a large percentage of behavior motivated by impulses we do not fully understand but also that the basic instincts are sexuality and aggression (topics avoided whenever possible in Freud's day). These instincts are those involved in the preservation and propagation of life and in pleasure. (Later, Freud would expand on the destructive aspect of aggression as the death instinct.) Furthermore, conscience, which earlier periods had considered an innate gift from God, was described by Freud as a censoring faculty (the superego) built up during childhood through punishments and rewards from family and society. Conscience, then, according to Freud, is culturally induced, not inborn.

Freud's theories were to have enormous significance for twentieth-century drama. First, his conception of the id and superego located within the human mind much of what in earlier periods had been considered supernatural or demonic. Thus, he provided a "scientific" explanation for what had previously been considered suprahuman; this, in turn, made it possible to bridge realistic and antirealistic modes in drama, since the rational and the irrational blended into each other. Second, motivation in drama became more complex. In part, Freud's views reinforced Darwin's, since both explained causality in terms of heredity and environment. But Freud saw these forces as much more individualized than Darwin had, and he also assigned a large role to the unconscious. Third, the superego as censor created by environmental influences (familial and cultural) made morality relative and mutable. In addition, the idea that culturally unacceptable instincts, feelings, and behavior are sublimated and buried in the subconscious mind opened up infinite possibilities for disparities between surface appearance and suppressed realities (between "mask" and "face"). Consequently, truth became enormously complex (perhaps ultimately unknowable), since it is difficult to penetrate not only the masks of others but our own as well. Almost nothing could be taken any longer at face value. The unspoken and unacknowledged (the subtext) acquired significance equal to that of the openly stated and recognized (the text). Probably no other of Freud's ideas has so permeated

modern drama. Fourth, the fundamental role of sex and aggression in human behavior became increasingly important as subjects of drama. Furthermore, Freud's view that failure to find satisfying outlets or substitutions for sexuality and aggression leads to deviant behavior and violence are evident in much modern drama. Fifth, Freud's emphasis on the subconscious and dreams was to influence almost all nonrealistic drama. The surrealists were to argue that fundamental truths can only be intuited during dreamlike states freed from conscious control. Furthermore, many of the characteristics of dreams were adopted as technical devices in nonrealistic drama—telescoping or rapid shifts in time and place; disjuncture; flashbacks; symbolic substitutions; transformations in the identity or appearance of persons, places, or objects; structure through association; and so on.

Freud was certainly not wholly original; many playwrights who were his contemporaries reached many of the same conclusions without being aware of his work. But it was Freud who formulated the unified conception of human personality that was to dominate much of twentieth-century psychology. Subsequent psychologists have attacked various aspects of his theory, but most have felt it necessary to begin with his work.

Among the playwrights of the day, Arthur Schnitzler (1862–1931) was the one who most fully reflected Freud's views. Like Freud, Schnitzler was a doctor in Vienna, and like Freud he was interested in hypnosis, the treatment of neuroses, and the power of the unconscious. His interests are most readily apparent in his novels and short stories. His novella *Lieutenant Gustl* (1901) was one of the first literary works to make use of stream of consciousness, while in his short story "Fraulein Else," the title character, having disrobed in the lobby of a hotel, gradually and unconsciously reveals what lies behind this act.

Among Schnitzler's plays, *Anatol* (1893) and *Reigen* (or *La Ronde,* 1903) are the best known. *Anatol* is composed of seven sketches, each dealing with a different love affair. The title character is always haunted by the ephemeral nature of happiness, but rather than seeking to make it last he unconsciously destroys every potentially meaningful relationship. *Reigen* is divided into ten scenes that show a series of sexual encounters among characters who represent a cross-section of society: prostitute, soldier, housemaid, young gentleman, wife, husband, young girl, poet, actress, and count. It suggests that sexual drives are universal, and that there is an enormous difference between lust and love.

Schnitzler's preoccupation with sexual themes made him suspect to conservative critics, while to others his irony and wit seemed mere cynicism, since he failed to condemn the imperfections he saw. Though fully aware of human flaws, he was content to record them with compassion and a resignation that convey a sense of worldweariness. Within the narrow range he chose, Schnitzler has seldom been surpassed.

STRINDBERG

The most effective use of those devices Freud associated with dreams was made by the Swedish playwright August Strindberg (1849–1912), one of the most influential writers of the twentieth century. Like Ibsen's, Strindberg's career may be divided into several phases—historical-romantic, realistic-naturalistic, and visionary-expressionistic. He began writing plays around 1870 and for the next dozen years treated subjects drawn primarily from Swedish history, as in *Master Olaf* (1872) and *Sir Bengt's Wife* (1882). In the 1880s he first attracted international attention with a series of plays in the realistic-naturalistic vein. Zola's essays

were a crucial influence on *The Father* (1887) and *Miss Julie* (1888), the best known of Strindberg's realistic plays.

In *The Father,* the Captain wages a battle with his wife over the upbringing of their only child; just as he seems about to win, his wife implies that he is not the child's father, and thereafter deliberately provokes him into acts which she uses to have him declared insane. The play is not naturalistic in Zola's sense; it lacks objectivity (Strindberg clearly favors the Captain), and there is no concern for heredity and environment. But Strindberg considered it naturalistic because it reflected the psychological work then being done by Charcot. In an essay, "The Battle of the Brains" (1887), Strindberg argues that he has made discoveries beyond those of the French psychologist: ". . . suggestion is only the stronger brain's struggle with and victory over the weak. . . . this procedure is applied unconsciously in everyday life." In another essay, "Psychic Murder," Strindberg wrote: "The struggle for power has, from being purely physical (prison, torture, death), gradually developed into a more psychological battle, but a no less cruel one." It is probably for this reason that Strindberg's so-called naturalistic plays seem poised on the edge of irrationality.

Miss Julie adheres more closely to Zola's ideas. It dramatizes the struggle between two wills, but it also develops complex characters shaped by hereditary and environmental forces. Miss Julie, the daughter of an aristocratic father and a man-hating mother, allows herself to be seduced by the valet, with whom she plans to run away; but when the father returns unexpectedly, the valet reverts to his subservient role and declares that the only path open to Miss Julie is suicide, which she accepts. In his preface to the play, Strindberg also set down his ideas about its staging, most of them innovations that Antoine was then carrying out at the Théâtre Libre. Strindberg wrote a few other realistic plays, but by 1890 he was already losing interest in realism and naturalism.

Between 1892 and 1898, Strindberg underwent a psychological crisis, during which he wrote no plays, although he did write extensively about this "inferno" itself. During this time, he turned increasingly to Oriental religions and the philosophy of Schopenhauer and Nietzsche. In 1898, he returned with renewed energy to dramatic writing and during the next dozen years composed thirty new plays. Many of these reflect his pre-inferno interests. More than one-third of the late plays treat historical subjects ranging from the thirteenth to the nineteenth centuries. They include *Erik XIV* (1899), *Charles XII* (1901), and *Queen Christina* (1903). Despite their considerable power, they have seldom been performed outside of Sweden. Strindberg also returned to the vein of *The Father* in the two-part *Dance of Death* (1901), which traces the struggle for dominance between husband and wife in what was to be one of the recurring themes of his work, the male-female, love-hate relationship.

But his expressionistic works—the *dream* and *chamber plays*—were what set Strindberg's plays apart most from those of other writers of the period. This new direction is seen first in *The Road to Damascus* (parts 1 and 2, 1898; part 3, 1901), an autobiographical work in which, as the title suggests, Strindberg relates his own search to that of Saul of Tarsus. Here as in most of his late works, Strindberg treats with great compassion alienated humanity, lost and rootless, seeking meaning in an incomprehensible universe, trying to reconcile disparate elements: lust and love, body and spirit, filth and beauty.

Of all the late plays, the best known is *A Dream Play* (1902), which both sums up Strindberg's preoccupations and introduces the dramatic devices that were to exert such powerful influence on later dramatists, especially the German expressionists. In his preface to the play, Strindberg wrote: "The author has tried to imitate the disconnected but seemingly logical form of a dream. Anything may happen; everything is possible and probable. Time and space do not exist. On an insignificant background of reality, imagination designs and embroiders novel patterns, free fancies, absurdities and improvisations. The characters split, double, multiply, vanish, solidify, blur,

FIG. 4.6
Scene from Strindberg's *The Dance of Death*, produced at the Intimate Theatre in 1909. Strindberg's associate in founding the Intimate Theatre, August Falck, is at right, in the role of Edgar. (Courtesy Drottningholms Teatermuseum.)

clarify. But one consciousness reigns above them all—that of the dreamer; and before it there are no secrets, no incongruities, no scruples, no laws." Here Freud's conception of dream is converted into dramatic form.

Like Goethe's *Faust, A Dream Play* begins with a prologue in Heaven. Because of the wails from earth, the god Indra decides to send his Daughter down to find out why humans are so unhappy. When she arrives, she finds the Captain imprisoned in a castle which rests on a dunghill but has a chrysanthemum bud on top (a symbol of the human condition, with feet mired in filth but aspiring to beauty and happiness). She frees the Captain and they set out on the search to discover why humans suffer. The identities of these characters change often, but in all guises there is only anguish and disillusionment. At last the Poet offers an explanation: the world is eternally caught in a conflict between the spirit and the flesh. When the Daughter returns to the castle, it bursts into flames, and she and the other characters throw all material things that symbolize their cares into the fire; as the flames rise, the bud atop the castle opens into full flower. Thus, Strindberg suggests that happiness can only be achieved by freeing the spirit from material claims. The major source of unity in *A Dream Play* is thought—a near-allegorical view of the human condition—rather than cause-to-effect arrangement of incidents. But the most innovative feature was the techniques used to achieve fluidity of time and space, identity and appearance, idea and image.

It was not easy for Strindberg to find producers for this new type of play. Consequently, when he was approached by the young actor and director August Falck (1882–1938) about a theatre to be devoted entirely to his plays, Strindberg eagerly assented. The Intimate Theatre, with a company of only 13 actors and seating for only 161 spectators, was launched in 1907. At last, Strindberg had the theatre he had sought since the 1880s and which he himself had tried to found more than once.

FIG. 4.7
Interior of Strindberg's and Falck's Intimate Theatre in Stockholm, opened in 1907. The theatre seated only 161. It was here that Strindberg produced his chamber plays. (From Esswein, *August Strindberg,* 1909.)

By the time it closed in 1910, the Intimate Theatre had presented twenty-four of Strindberg's plays for a total of 1,025 performances in Stockholm, and had toured Sweden, Norway, and Denmark. For this theatre, Strindberg wrote five *chamber plays,* composed with the company's strengths and limitations in mind. Of these, *The Ghost Sonata* (1907) is representative and by far the best known.

As its title suggests, *The Ghost Sonata* is conceived musically: the first act allegro, the second largo, and the third andante. The action represents a search for the mystery of life. The action begins in front of a house and then moves inside from one room to another just as it successively strips away the characters' masks. A seeming benefactor turns out to be a murderer; a nobleman is revealed to be a servant in disguise; a once-beautiful woman is now a mummy confined to a closet. In the final act, young love seems about to triumph over this deceit, but the young woman dies when the hero tries to help her face the truth. He concludes that the only hope lies in repentance. "No deed that we have wrought in anger can find in evil its atonement. . . . Good is to be innocent." As the play ends, the room dissolves into a vision of the peaceful Isle of the Dead. In many ways, *The Ghost Sonata* resembles *A Dream Play,* but in deference to the Intimate Theatre's limitations, Strindberg avoided the earlier play's numerous shifts in time and space and its large cast. The view of the human condition, however, and the air of surreality and magically charged events found in *A Dream Play* remained intact.

By the time Strindberg died in 1912, his position as one of the major dramatists of the age was secure, even though opinion was still divided as to whether he was a madman or a visionary. As the twentieth century progressed and the vision of humanity as alienated increased, Strindberg's work came to seem prophetic. His technical devices also served as lessons about how psychological states, intuitions, and the unconscious could be externalized. Although the status of his plays in the active repertory has usually been precarious, he has continually commanded attention and respect.

GAINING ACCEPTANCE FOR ANTIREALISM

By the early twentieth century, an antirealistic theatre and drama had emerged in many countries. Since it departed drastically from the modes of writing and staging that had prevailed for centuries, antirealism encountered much more resistance than realism and naturalism had. Not only was it stylistically strange, it seemed to many an artistic equivalent of political anarchy. At first antirealism appealed primarily to coterie audiences, especially those who despised bourgeois standards of thought, morality, mores, and art.

By 1900, self-conscious symbolists and aesthetes were disappearing. The public had become tired of a general air of insubstantiality, ineffable mystery, and death or decay (preoccupations that led many critics to label the antirealists *decadents*). But the strain of antirealism represented by Wedekind, Strindberg, and Freud was gaining strength, probably because it was rooted in the everyday world, even though it treated subjects (sex, politics, education, and morals) in ways often considered scandalous. Despite all objections or shortcomings, antirealism had firmly established a modernist alternative to realism and naturalism.

Chapter 5

Tradition and Assimilation

Although by the early twentieth century, innovations, both realistic and antirealistic, had been numerous, the majority of playwrights and producers either continued in the older, accepted vein or embraced the new cautiously and partially. Thus, the popular theatre in the years between 1890 and 1915 tended to remain conservative.

UNITED STATES

In the United States, playwriting prior to 1915 was little influenced by foreign developments, although a tentative realism was evident in a few works. The best-known example is *Margaret Fleming* (1891) by James A. Herne (1839–1901). In it, a young businessman has an extramarital affair with a girl who dies giving birth to his child. When the man's wife,

Margaret Fleming, learns the truth, the shock causes her to lose her already weakened eyesight. Nevertheless, she takes the illegitimate child into her home to rear with her own children, although she refuses to live with her husband. Ultimately, there is a reconciliation, but at the end happiness has yet to be regained. Herne avoided sensationalism, but the play was still considered by commercial producers too daring for public performance, and Herne had to present the play himself. Although acclaimed by many leading realists, the production was so unsuccessful that Herne was ruined financially. Thereafter, Herne returned to the kind of play—exemplified in his *Shore Acres* (1892)—that was long to dominate the American stage, a sentimental story embedded in naturalistic detail.

It was this type of realism that William Gillette (1855–1937) exploited so successfully in such plays as *Secret Service* (1895) and *Sherlock Holmes* (1899). In the most famous scene in *Secret Service* (concerning a Union spy among Confederate forces during the Civil War), the actors tapped out messages in accurate Morse code on a working telegraph key. Such care for minutiae provided a sense of reality far in excess of that demanded by the action. One of the finest actors of his day, Gillette approached performance much as he did writing—building up a character out of many small concrete details. Gillette's was a realism of surface detail applied to melodramatic subjects.

Clyde Fitch (1865–1909), author of some fifty plays, is remembered primarily for three works: *The Girl With the Green Eyes* (1902), about the evil effects of jealousy on a marriage; *The Truth* (1906), about the unhappiness created by a congenital liar; and *The City* (1909), about the effect of city life on a family from a small town. All demonstrate a gift for characterization and compelling dramatic situation, but all degenerate into melodramatic devices and imposed happy endings.

Two other American playwrights of the early twentieth century failed to realize their early promise. *The Great Divide* (1906) by William Vaughn Moody (1869–1910) treats the conflict between the reserved, puritanical East (represented by Ruth Jordan) and the

FIG. 5.1
Moody's *The Great Divide*, with Margaret Anglin as Ruth Jordan, at the Princess Theatre, New York, 1906. (From *The Theatre Magazine*, 1906.)

impulsive, lusty West (represented by Stephen Ghent). The strength of the play lies in its characterization, dialogue, and symbolic treatment of the American consciousness. Edward Sheldon (1886–1946) wrote about potentially powerful subjects in *Salvation Nell* (1908), about a scullery maid turned Salvation Army worker; *The Nigger* (1909), about a Southern governor who discovers that his grandmother was a slave; and *The Boss* (1911), about a ruthless political leader. But all were ultimately sentimentalized in happy endings.

As these examples illustrate, many American playwrights prior to 1915 adopted lifelike dialogue and characterization and set their plays in actualistic locales. But their addiction to melodrama, sentiment, and conventional morality undermined all attempts at true realism.

The low state of American playwriting can be explained in part by theatrical conditions. After 1870, the touring company gradually undermined local resident companies until New York became the only important theatrical center. Booking touring productions soon posed major problems, since local managers had to go to New York and deal with many different producers in order to secure a season of traveling productions. The failure of many producers to live up to their agreements, leaving local managers without attractions, prompted the creation of booking agencies to serve as middlemen between local managers and New York producers. Circuits covering limited geographical areas soon emerged. In 1896 a group of booking agents and theatre owners (Sam Nixon, Fred Zimmerman, Charles Frohman, Al Hayman, Marc Klaw, and Abraham Erlanger) conceived a plan to gain control over the entire American theatre, since among them they controlled circuits throughout the country. They agreed to pool their assets in what came to be called the Syndicate. In the beginning they offered a full season of star

attractions to any manager who would book exclusively through them, a welcome development to many local managers. Next, the Syndicate set out to eliminate all competition by gaining control over key routes, since rival productions could not afford to tour if they were unable to perform in towns between major cities. In towns where they could not gain control over existing theatres, they encouraged the building of rival houses into which they booked their most outstanding productions at reduced prices until competing houses were eliminated. New York producers who would not book exclusively through the Syndicate were denied all engagements in Syndicate theatres, and actors who opposed them were "blackballed" (that is, the Syndicate would accept no productions for touring in which they appeared). Through such means, the Syndicate had by 1900 gained virtual control over the American theatre. Now in a position to influence (if not dictate) play selection, it refused to book any production it thought incapable of attracting a mass audience. Furthermore, it favored productions featuring stars with large personal followings. Thus, the Syndicate forced the American theatre to remain in the premodern mold.

Of the Syndicate's members, Charles Frohman (1854–1915) was especially important, for he was the only member directly involved in theatrical production. Not only did he maintain a company in New York but also eventually controlled five theatres in London—from which plays were often imported to the United States—thereby extending the conservative influence of the Syndicate into the British theatre.

The Syndicate did not go unopposed. Some of America's best actors, including Minnie Maddern Fiske, James A. Herne, and James O'Neill, refused to work through it and were reduced to performing in minor theatres or makeshift quarters. Its most effective opponent was David Belasco (c. 1854–1931), who in the first decade of the twentieth century became the most popular producer-dramatist in the United States.

Born in San Francisco, Belasco had gained considerable practical experience before coming to New York in 1882. For a time he served as a stage manager and was coauthor (with Henry C. DeMille) of several successful plays. After 1890 he continued his successful playwriting career with such works as *Madame Butterfly* (1900) and *Girl of the Golden West* (1905), both adapted into librettos for operas by Puccini. In 1902, Belasco acquired his own theatre, where until 1928 he was to be one of America's most successful producers and directors.

Belasco is remembered above all for his naturalistic staging of melodramatic plays. With him, actualistic staging reached its peak in America. For *The Governor's Lady* (1912), he recreated a Childs Restaurant on stage, and the Childs chain stocked it daily with food which was served and consumed on stage. For *The Easiest Way* (1909), he bought the contents of a boarding-house room, including the wallpaper, and transferred them to the stage. The blizzard in *Girl of the Golden West* seemed absolutely authentic, and the twelve-minute silent sequence in *Madame Butterfly* during which the passage of night was shown was considered a marvel of stage lighting. Belasco controlled every element of his productions, working in the tradition of Saxe-Meiningen and Daly. Whatever one might think of Belasco's choice of plays, no one ever accused him of careless staging. Although Belasco achieved all the qualities most admired by the Syndicate, he refused to sign an exclusive contract with it. By 1909, Belasco was so popular and his productions in such demand that the Syndicate finally accepted Belasco on his own terms, the first significant break in the Syndicate's power.

The Syndicate's willingness to make such concessions, however, was probably more fully motivated by the rise of the Shuberts (Sam, Lee, and Jacob J.) who, when the Syndicate closed its theatres to their productions in 1905, began a rival organization. Unlike the

FIG. 5.2
Belasco's *Girl of the Golden West*, with Blanche Bates and Frank Keenan, in 1905. (From *The Theatre Magazine*, 1906.)

Syndicate (which was always merely a cooperative arrangement among independent businessmen), the Shuberts created a corporation (a new organizational form at that time) and used its financial base to outmaneuver the Syndicate by building or buying its own theatres throughout the country. After Frohman's death in 1915, the Syndicate ceased to be a major force, but unfortunately the Shuberts soon became as dictatorial as the Syndicate and were able to retain effective control over the road until 1956, when the federal government, acting under the antitrust act, ordered them to sell many of their theatres.

Although most U.S. theatre remained firmly within the nineteenth-century mold, a few attempts were made to introduce European innovations. A few short-lived independent theatres were founded—among them New York's Criterion Independent Theatre (1897–1900) and Chicago's New Theatre (1906–1907)—but none made a strong or lasting impression. Between 1900 and 1910, a few producers not associated with the Syndicate introduced the work of European dramatists. Among these, Minnie Maddern Fiske (1865–1932) and her husband Harrison Grey Fiske (1861–1942) are especially noteworthy for their productions of Ibsen's plays (including *A Doll's House, Hedda Gabler,* and *Rosmersholm)* and for their carefully staged productions at the Manhattan Theatre between 1901 and 1907. Mrs. Fiske was also instrumental in replacing bravura performance with psychologically realistic portraiture.

Ibsen's reputation, as well as realistic acting, were also enhanced by Alla Nazimova (1879–1945), a Russian actress who in 1906 presented a repertory that included *A Doll's House* and *Hedda Gabler.* For many years, her name was virtually synonymous in the U.S. with great acting. Similarly, Arnold Daly (1875–1927) did much to establish Shaw's reputation in the U.S. In 1903, he presented *Candida* and in 1905 a two-month repertory devoted entirely to Shaw. But *Mrs. Warren's Profession* led to Daly's prosecution for immorality and, though acquitted, he was forced by adverse publicity to return to a more conventional repertory. Overall, then, American drama and production remained firmly within past traditions, while innovations were few.

ITALY

In Italy, there was little vitality in playwriting during the nineteenth century, perhaps because of the preoccupation with political and territorial unification, goals finally achieved between 1861 and 1870. But unification did not end factionalism over the role of the church, monarchy, and economic organization. Furthermore, each region clung to its own dialect and customs, making the development of a national drama difficult. The most important regional centers were Milan, Turin, and Naples, in each of which a school of dramatists developed. Most of these playwrights were exponents of realism (*verismo*).

In Milan, Marco Praga (1862–1929) was the most admired playwright. He usually focused on the conflict between men and women and especially on the subordination of women to male values. His plays include *The Ideal Wife* (1890) and *The Closed Door* (1913), but perhaps the best known of his works is *The Virgins* (1889), the story of Paolina, whose mother, while posing as respectable, urges her daughters to give themselves to wealthy admirers in return for gifts. Paolina resists and is ecstatic when she becomes engaged; wishing to be honest, she tells her fiancé about her family, and he responds by suggesting that she become his mistress rather than his wife. Deeply hurt, she refuses but is doomed to be a hopeless victim of the moral hypocrisy with which she is surrounded.

The most important of the Turin play-wrights, Guiseppe Giacosa (1847–1906), now remembered as Puccini's librettist for *La Bohème, Tosca,* and *Madame Butterfly,* was considered a disciple of Ibsen. His indebtedness to *A Doll's House* is clear in his *Rights of the Soul* (1894), in which a wife, though attracted to another man, renounces him only to be ordered out of her home when her husband discovers that she has even been tempted. Although the husband relents, the wife remains firm in her decision to leave. Others of Giacosa's plays, among them *Like Falling Leaves* (1900) and *The Stronger* (1904), more nearly resemble the works of Dumas than Ibsen.

In Naples, the most important dramatist was Roberto Bracco (1862–1943), whose plays, including *A Woman* (1892), *The End of Love* (1896), and *Maternity* (1903), mingle thorough-going realism with deep compassion. A characteristic work is *Don Pietro Caruso* (1895), in which a man is determined to shield his daughter from harsh reality only to discover that she has become the mistress of his best friend.

The Sicilian writer, Giovanni Verga (1840–1922), achieved international renown with his *Cavalleria Rusticana* (1884), although primarily through its use as a libretto for Mascagni's opera. A tale of illicit love affairs, jealousy, and honor, the action culminates in a duel fought offstage while Easter festivities are celebrated onstage. The counterpoint between death and resurrection, between the demands of "rustic chivalry" and Christian forgiveness, creates a near-mythic quality.

As these examples indicate, the *veristi* writers were concerned primarily with the effects of social mores and custom on personal relationships. They tended to depict victims without suggesting the need for changes that might save others from similar fates. Despite the sizable output, Italy never offered a sympathetic home to veristic drama.

Neoromanticism was welcomed much more enthusiastically, although few of the playwrights are now remembered. By far the most popular was Gabriele D'Annunzio (1863–1938), whose reputation depended as much on his flamboyant amoral personal life as upon his

FIG. 5.3
Bracco's *The End of Love* at the Bouffes-Parisiens, in 1904. (From *Le Théâtre,* 1904.)

literary works. In his plays, among them *The Dead City* (1898), *Francesca da Rimini* (1902), and *La Piave* (1918), the central character is controlled by a single, almost elemental urge, although the incidents are swept along by powerful poetic diction and passionate commitment. Many of his subjects seemed almost perverse, therefore daring or scandalous. His most characteristic work is *La Giaconda* (1898), in which a sculptor finds inspiration in his model (Giaconda) rather than his wife (Silvia). During a confrontation between wife and model, the model seeks to destroy the sculptor's masterpiece, which is saved by Silvia, although her hands are crushed in doing so. Nevertheless, the sculptor leaves his wife because the call of art overrides everything else. As time passed, both D'Annunzio and his plays lost their appeal and today seem more pretentious than significant. But between 1900 and 1920, D'Annunzio was considered one of the world's major playwrights.

A major deterrent to Italian playwriting was the Italian theatre which offered little incentive to serious dramatists. Since the only form that commanded wide public support was opera, most dramatic troupes could maintain themselves only through constant touring. Standards of production were low, everything being subordinated to starring performers, whose bravura style perpetuated earlier practices. Unlike other countries, Italy had no reformer capable of bringing about significant change.

The nearest equivalent to a reformer was Eleanora Duse (1859–1924), the finest Italian actress of her age. On stage from the age of four, she had by the age of nineteen become leading lady to Ernesto Rossi, one of Italy's major stars, with whom she toured widely. In 1885, she formed her own company, with which she appeared throughout the world until 1900. In 1897 she met D'Annunzio with whom she fell in love and whose fame she did much to

establish through the plays (including *La Giaconda* and *Francesca da Rimini*) he wrote with her in mind. But it was as Ibsen's heroines—among them Nora, Mrs. Alving, and Hedda Gabler—that Duse's acting was seen to best advantage. To all these she brought enormous psychological insight and the capacity to seem completely different in each role. All critics remarked on her subtlety and praised her for avoiding the heroic diction and flamboyance typical of starring performers in her day.

Like most stars of the time, Duse mounted

FIG. 5.4
Duse in the title role of D'Annunzio's *Francesca da Rimini*. This is the original production of 1902 at the Constanzi Theatre, Rome. (From *Le Théâtre*, 1902.)

her own productions. Her interest in updating theatrical practices is indicated by her invitation in 1906 to Gordon Craig to work with her on a production of Ibsen's *Rosmersholm*. Craig designed a drawing-room setting with a 30-foot-square window looking out on a red, green, and yellow landscape; shafts of light through the window enveloped the actors in an atmosphere of mystery. Duse sought to adapt her acting style to the setting but soon gave up. Thereafter she relied on her own taste in staging. In 1913 ill health led Duse to retire, but financial reverses forced her to return in the 1920s. She died in Pittsburgh while on a tour of the United States. Duse probably did more than any other actress of her time to demonstrate the strength of a quiet, subtle, realistic style of acting. But the Italian theatre as a whole remained essentially derivative.

SPAIN

Much the same pattern is found in Spain, which in the nineteenth century was still an agricultural nation dominated by the church and the aristocracy. Nowhere was its conservatism more evident than in drama, since until 1850 its theatres, continuing practices begun in the sixteenth century, were exploited as means of raising funds for charity. Around 1850 this practice finally ceased, and a national theatre was created. The nation's theatres were divided into categories, each restricted to a stated range of dramatic types. In 1870, Madrid had thirty-two theatres, only eight of which were devoted to regular drama. The others were offering an evening's bill made up of four distinct entertainments, any part of which could be paid for and seen separately. This flexibility made it difficult for the major theatres to compete with full-length serious plays. Under these conditions, it is not surpris-

ing that Spanish drama did not reach a high level. Still, it followed major European trends at a distance.

Spain's first modern playwright, José Echegaray (1832–1916), was much influenced by Ibsen, as is evident in *The Son of Don Juan* (1892), which like *Ghosts* ends with a young man calling for the sun as his mind deteriorates from a hereditary disease. Unlike Ibsen's play, however, it focuses on the libertine father. Echegaray is now remembered primarily for *The Great Galeoto* (1881), in which gossip and the Spanish sense of honor combine to destroy the happiness of three persons.

Of Echegaray's contemporaries, the most famous was Benito Pérez Galdós (1843–1920), although his subjects were usually so Spanish that they did not export well. Among his best works are *The Duchess of San Quintin* (1894), in which a young noblewoman, much to the horror of her relatives, chooses to marry a vital commoner rather than a member of her own class; and *Electra* (1900), in which a girl is driven into convent life, for which she is wholly unsuited.

In 1896, the independent theatre movement arrived with the formation of the Teatre Independent in Barcelona and its opening production, *Ghosts*. Still more influential was the Teatre Intim, founded in 1898 by Adria Gual (1872–1943), who for the next thirty years presented a cross-section of world drama. But the most crucial influence of the 1890s was Spain's humiliating defeat in the Spanish-American War. It spawned a new movement, the Generation of '98, which began to agitate for reform in every aspect of life.

The major playwright of this new movement was Jácinto Benavente y Martinez (1866–1954), one of the world's most prolific dramatists. Author of more than 300 works, he kept the Spanish stage supplied with new plays of all types—short and long; romantic, realistic, sentimental; farce, comedy, drama, and history. Of Benavente's realistic works, the most famous is *Passion Flower* (1913), which treats the growing passion of a man for his stepdaughter and the tragic consequences. Benavente's international fame rests above all on *Bonds of Interest* (1907), in which the conflict between love and materialistic interests are embodied in a story making use of *commedia dell'arte* characters and conventions. Its blend of convention, fantasy, high spirits, and social criticism found a ready audience almost everywhere and was long considered one of the modern theatre's major works.

Next to Benavente, Spain's best-known playwright of the post-1898 era was Gregorio Martínez Sierra (1881–1947), although it has been revealed that many of the works attributed to him were written by his wife. The best of these plays is *Cradle Song* (1911), which, set in a convent, shows the impact of a foundling on the life of the nuns. After 1916, Martínez Sierra also directed the Teatro Eslava in Madrid, where he maintained a fine company and produced the works of major European dramatists.

Somewhat similar in tone were the works of Serafín Alvarez Quintero (1871–1938) and Joaquín Alvarez Quintero (1873–1944), joint authors of some 150 plays. A typical work is *The Merry Heart* (1906), in which the austere world of Doña Sacramento is gradually changed after the arrival of her orphaned niece. Only rarely did they write about darker subjects, as in *Malvaloca* (1912), in which a young man tries to right the wrong done by his brother in seducing a young girl. Even in their darker moments, the Alvarez Quinteros celebrated the essential goodness of human beings.

As this brief account suggests, Spanish dramatists in the years after 1880 were aware of foreign developments and for the first time in almost 200 years began to win international recognition (both Echegaray and Benavente were awarded Nobel Prizes). But for the most part their work was marred by sentimentality and conventionally moral endings. Like the Italian, Spanish drama and theatre seemed more derivative than original.

FRANCE

In France, a number of lesser writers reinforced the trends begun by their more innovative contemporaries. Among the writers of the realistic school, the best known were Lavedan, Hervieu, and Donnay. The most characteristic works of Henri Lavedan (1859–1940) are rather jaundiced pictures of fashionable life in Paris. In one of the most successful, *The Rakes* (1895), a couturier's studio and a well-known Parisian restaurant serve as backgrounds for the intrigues of decadent but fashionable pleasure seekers. As in all of Lavedan's work, a moral attitude can be perceived, but it is always subordinated to sensational elements. Paul Hervieu (1857–1915) wrote often about family life and divorce. In *The Pincers* (1895), a woman's request for a divorce is refused; then, several years later her husband proposes divorce but the wife now refuses, wishing to protect her child, actually the son of the man for whom she had sought a divorce in order to marry. In *Man-Made Law* (1897), a woman discovers that her husband is having an affair with the mother of her son's fiancé, but she is forced by her husband to remain silent so as not to create scandal and break off the marriage. Hervieu enjoyed an enormous following during his lifetime, but his plays now seem monotonously similar. Maurice Donnay (1859–1945) was concerned primarily with the power of love over human behavior. In *Lovers* (1895), two young people, despite their mutual love, are forced to marry others, and in *The Other Danger* (1902), a woman finds happiness for the first time but renounces it when her daughter falls in love with the same man. Donnay suggests that happiness is fleeting but that life does not end merely because joy goes.

Of the nonrealistic writers, the most popular was Edmond Rostand (1868–1918), who began his playwriting career in 1894 with *The Romancers,* a delightful satire on young love. (It is now known primarily in its adaptation, the popular American musical, *The Fantasticks.*) But Rostand's lasting reputation rests on *Cyrano de Bergerac* (1897), written as a vehicle for Constant Coquelin, one of France's greatest actors. It tells the story of Cyrano: poet, lover, and faithful friend, whose noble spirit seems mocked by his enormous nose. Feeling that his love for Roxane is hopeless, he aids the handsome but limited Christian to win her. He dies, with his love unspoken but conscious that Roxane has come to perceive his true spirit. The overall tone is one of courage and integrity, of joy gained through unselfishness. The many-sided Cyrano has remained a role coveted by actors. The success of *Cyrano* led Sarah Bernhardt, the most famous French actress of her day, to commission a play from Rostand, *The Eaglet* (1900), about Napoleon's

FIG. 5.5
Coquelin in Rostand's *Cyrano de Bergerac* at the Porte-Saint-Martin shortly before the turn of the century. (From *Le Théâtre,* 1900.)

adolescent son. Some of Rostand's work is related to that of the symbolists but, by writing about compelling characters and actions, he was successful in creating a popular poetic drama where they failed to do so.

France's most popular plays were farces. Georges Courteline (1861–1929) wrote often about the vagaries of army life, as in *High Spirits in the Squadron* (1895), or of the law, as in *Article 330* (1901). His best play is *Boubouroche* (1893), a mixture of wit and brutality not unlike medieval farce. Behind his humor there is always a rather cynical commentary on humanity. Georges Feydeau (1862–1921) seems to have been content to extract the greatest possible humor from masterfully engineered misunderstandings and deceptions underlined by incongruous repartee. His masterpieces, *Hotel Paradiso* (1894), *A Flea in Her Ear* (1907), and *Look After Emily* (1908), have continued to delight audiences.

Among the playwrights who kept the popular theatres supplied, the most successful was Sacha Guitry (1885–1957) who, as dramatist, director, and actor, was from 1910 to 1940 the undisputed master of popular (or boulevard) theatre. His ninety plays include *The Illusionist* (1917) and *When Do We Begin the Play?* (1935). He also composed a number of plays—such as *Deburau* (1918) and *Pasteur* (1919)—as vehicles for his father, Lucien Guitry (1860–1925), one of the most popular actors of the period.

In France, the emphasis on tradition was strong, in part because of the Comédie Française's prestige as the world's oldest national theatre with the mission of keeping the best in French drama alive. Although it produced many new plays, the Comédie Française's repertory had as its mainstay French classics performed by France's leading actors, most of whom were little interested in innovation. Its company included Mounet-Sully, Paul Mounet,

FIG. 5.6
Feydeau's *A Flea in Her Ear* in its original production at the Théâtre des Nouveautés in 1907. (From *Le Théâtre*, 1907.)

Eugène Silvain, Julia Bartet, and Eugénie Segond-Weber—major stars of the day. But the performers with the greatest international reputations were Coquelin and Bernhardt. Constant-Benoît Coquelin (1841–1909) was a member of the Comédie Française from 1860 to 1886; he then toured widely in Europe and the U.S. and managed his own company in Paris. He was noted for his superb technique, seen at its best in Cyrano, a role created especially for him. Sarah Bernhardt (1845–1923) was probably the best-known actress in the world from 1870 until her death. After 1862 she appeared sporadically at the Comédie Française, but as her fame grew she toured increasingly and managed her own companies. Among her finest roles were Phaedra, Camille, and the roles written especially for her by Sardou—Fedora, Theodora, and Tosca. She came to epitomize the "great actress."

Between 1900 and 1915, France did not produce many dramatists of the first rank, but it maintained a strong theatrical tradition. France also remained relatively unaware of significant innovations then underway elsewhere until shaken out of its complacency around 1910 (developments that will be discussed later).

CENTRAL EUROPE

In Central Europe, as elsewhere, dramatists assimilated and popularized the new trends. Among those who did so in Germany, some of the most popular were Sudermann, Halbe, and Hirschfeld.

Hermann Sudermann (1857–1928), author of numerous plays, was considered Hauptmann's greatest rival. His *Honor* (1889) was produced just before Hauptmann's *Before Sunrise* and to far greater praise. It voices superficial social protest but, in the vein of Dumas and Augier, remained acceptable to conservative audiences. In Sudermann's most popular work, *Die Heimat* (*Home,* usually translated as *Magda,* 1893), the protagonist flees her puritanical home and makes a career as a singer; when she gives birth to an illegitimate child, her father insists that she marry her lover and, when she refuses, he dies of a stroke. The play was a favorite with actresses, including Bernhardt, Duse, and Mrs. Patrick Campbell.

Max Halbe (1865–1944) sought a stringent naturalism. His most famous play, *Youth* (1893), concerns Annchen, an illegitimate child, and her mentally retarded half-brother, who are dominated by their puritanical uncle. When Annchen falls in love, the half-brother tries to kill her lover but kills Annchen instead when she throws herself between them. Halbe also championed the rights of the poor in such plays as *The Just World* (1897), which contrasts the misery of one family with the prosperity of another.

Georg Hirschfeld (1873–1935) was especially adept at capturing the texture of contemporary life. His most famous play is *The Mothers* (1896), in which a would-be composer, opposed by his wealthy father, goes to live in the slums with a working-class girl; when his father dies, the composer returns with the girl who, realizing that she will never fit in, leaves without telling him that she is pregnant.

In Austria, Schönherr and Bahr were leading playwrights. Karl Schönherr (1867–1943) was fascinated by the bitter side of life, which he sometimes treated seriously and sometimes comically. In *Carnival Folk* (1904), hunger drives a young boy to betray his father for a loaf of bread, and in *The Children's Tragedy* (1919), a mother's love affair ruins the lives of her three children. His more comic side is seen in *Earth* (1908), in which an aging innkeeper keeps his son of fifty under his thumb, neither permitting him to marry nor take over the business; thinking that he is near death, he watches for months as his son is fought over by two women; eventually he rises from his bed and dashes the hopes of the others.

Among European dramatists, one of those most adept at recognizing and capitalizing on new trends was Hermann Bahr (1663–1934). Originally attracted to naturalism, Bahr edited the Freie Bühne's journal. He next embraced symbolism, and thereafter tried almost every mode, eventually writing some eighty plays of various types and in various styles. Ironically, his most famous work was a flimsy light comedy, *The Concert* (1909), in which a married pianist, who has indulged in numerous affairs, is momentarily recalled to faithfulness when his wife pretends to be involved in an affair of her own; the reform is temporary, and as the play ends he is embarking on a new affair. Bahr's major contribution was probably as a popularizer of new trends.

ENGLAND

In England, several dramatists tended to follow in the footsteps of Pinero and Jones or to be disciples of Shaw. Among the best of these were Barker and Galsworthy. Harley Granville Barker (1877–1946), originally an actor and eventually one of England's most important directors, began his playwriting career in 1902 with *The Marrying of Ann Leete,* in which an upper-class woman, much to the chagrin of her family, chooses to marry a gardener rather than a dull aristocrat. Perhaps Barker's best play is *The Madras House* (1910) which presents a cross-section of English society seen against the background of the business world. The main character, Philip Madras, seeing beyond his drapery firm to the suffering in the world, eventually decides to go into politics, even though he recognizes that one man alone can do little to alter the entrenched customs and attitudes against which he rebels. Like Shaw's, Barker's plays progress more through dis-

cussion than physical action. He was praised for his subtle dialogue and psychologically sound characterizations but faulted for lack of emotional intensity. Nevertheless, after years of neglect, Barker's plays have recently returned to the active repertory.

John Galsworthy (1867–1933) turned to playwriting in 1906 after establishing his reputation as a socially conscious novelist. His first play, *The Silver Box,* treats the inequities of the judicial system by showing the differences in punishment for the same crime by men from different social classes, a theme to which he returned in *Justice* (1910) and *Loyalties* (1922). *Strife* (1909) is concerned with the struggle between labor and management, in which the leader of each side is blind to any position but his own and persists until workers are starving and the company is on the point of collapse. All of Galsworthy's dramas are concerned with principle (perhaps more so than with human beings) and depict characters as victims of the social system. He strove to remain objective and to let the audience draw its own conclusions. He was long considered one of England's most significant dramatists.

A quite different outlook animated the plays of James M. Barrie (1860–1937), whose closely observed pictures of life are filtered through whimsy, sentiment, and optimism. Though often satirical, he was never bitter. These qualities won him a following far more extensive than that of his more pessimistic contemporaries. Most of his works are rooted in character. *The Admirable Crichton* (1902) begins in an aristocratic household where the butler Crichton fulfills his function admirably but aloofly. Then, when the family is shipwrecked, Crichton emerges as the leader and is about to marry one of the family's daughters when they are rescued. Back in England, the characters resume their old roles, accepting the necessity of social convention. Several of Barrie's plays center around women. *What*

Every Woman Knows (1908) shows how the quiet but forceful Maggie advances her husband's career so subtly that he is unaware of her assistance until he leaves her for another woman. Barrie is now remembered above all for *Peter Pan* (1904), his glorification of childhood make-believe as seen in adventures involving pirates, fairies, and Indians.

It was also between 1890 and 1915 that musical comedy was established as a separate genre, primarily by George Edwardes (1852–1915), manager of the Gaiety Theatre in London, where beginning in 1892 he presented such prototypical works as *In Town, The Shop Girl,* and *San Toy.* In them, a sketchy plot provides excuses for songs, elaborate production numbers performed by beautiful chorus girls, and specialty acts like those seen in music halls and variety theatres. Many of Edwardes' productions were exported to New York and provided a basis on which Americans would later build.

Between 1890 and 1915, the British theatre remained in familiar paths, since it was dominated either by commercial producers or by actor-managers seeking to maintain the traditions of Charles Kean and Henry Irving. The dominant figure after 1900 was Herbert Beer-

FIG. 5.7
Barrie's *Peter Pan* at the Duke of York's Theatre in 1904. (Courtesy Enthoven Collection. By courtesy of the Board of Trustees of the Victoria and Albert Museum.)

Dream featured a forest of three-dimensional trees, carpets of grass, real flowers, and live rabbits. It was the most popular production of a Shakespearean play seen in London up to that time. Tree is also remembered for founding England's first important acting school (in 1904), which was to become the still-prestigious Royal Academy of Dramatic Art.

Tree was merely the most prominent of many actor-managers of his day: John Hare, Charles Wyndham, Madge and William Hunter Kendal, John Martin-Harvey, and others. They were the last of their breed, since during World War I the actor-manager system, which had dominated English theatre for more than 200 years, virtually ended. Until that time, these twentieth-century actor-managers preserved the traditions of the past but did little to support new trends.

THE IRISH RENAISSANCE

One of the most important developments of the years between 1900 and 1915 was the Irish Renaissance, a manifestation of growing nationalism in Ireland, which had been under English domination for centuries. Since the seventeenth century, Ireland had played an important part in the theatrical life of the British Isles: Dublin was second only to London as a theatrical center, and many of Britain's most famous playwrights (among them Congreve, Sheridan, Wilde, and Shaw) were born in Ireland. Thus, the theatre in Ireland was essentially an English theatre. Then, in the late nineteenth century, as Ireland began to glorify its Celtic heritage, the demand grew that it create its own native literature and theatre.

A major step toward a native Irish theatre was taken in 1899 with the formation of the Irish Literary Theatre by William Butler

FIG. 5.8
Edwardes' production of *San Toy* at Daly's Theatre, London, in 1899, with Topsy Sinden. (Courtesy Enthoven Collection. By courtesy of the Board of Trustees of the Victoria and Albert Museum.)

bohm Tree (1853–1917), who in 1897 built Her Majesty's Theatre which, with its repertory of Shakespeare and melodrama, rapidly became the leading theatre of its day. With Tree, spectacular realism reached its peak in England. In 1900, his production of *A Midsummer Night's*

FIG. 5.9

Scene from Tree's production of *A Midsummer Night's Dream* at Her Majesty's Theatre in 1900. (Courtesy Enthoven Collection. By courtesy of the Board of Trustees of the Victoria and Albert Museum.)

Yeats, Lady Augusta Gregory, George Moore, and Edward Martyn. Between 1899 and 1902, this group presented three programs consisting of seven plays, all of them Irish in subject and sentiment although only one in Gaelic. It also published a periodical, *Beltaine,* to advance its goals. In 1902 the theatre was dissolved following dissension over repertory (whether to confine its offerings to Irish plays) and personnel (all of the productions except one had been performed by English actors).

In 1899, still another theatre—the Ormond Dramatic Society—had been founded by W. G. Fay (1872–1947) and his brother Frank Fay (1870–1931). Using amateur actors, it presented at irregular intervals programs composed primarily of farces. In 1901, however, after becoming aware of Ole Bull's Norwegian theatre, the Fays decided to work toward the creation of an Irish national theatre. They began actively to seek Irish plays, and in 1902 gave their first Irish program. In early 1903, the

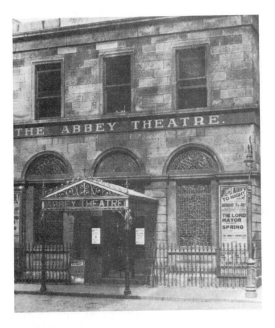

FIG. 5.10
Exterior of the Abbey Theatre, Dublin, in the early twentieth century.

group was renamed the Irish National Theatre Society, and Yeats was elected its president. Invited to perform in London, the group so impressed Miss A. E. F. Horniman that she took a lease on the Mechanics' Institute Theatre in Dublin, had it remodeled, and gave it to the Irish players free of charge for six years along with an annual subsidy. Thus, in 1904 the Abbey Theatre came into being, the first endowed theatre in the English-speaking world. Opposition from existing theatres caused the Abbey to be restricted to works written by Irishmen or on Irish subjects and foreign plays originally written in languages other than English. The Abbey seated only 562, and its stage was only 15 feet deep. The first bill was made up prophetically of plays by Yeats, Lady Gregory, and Synge, the writers who were to be its mainstays.

William Butler Yeats (1865–1939), thoroughly familiar with recent literary trends, was most attuned to the symbolists, much of whose drama he had seen performed in Paris. He disliked modern realism, believing that ordinary people are not fit subjects for drama. He favored ritualistic actions capable of arousing a sense of community among spectators and enlarging their capacities for exalted experience—to make them "temporary aristocrats." According to Yeats, "tragedy must always be a drowning and breaking of the dykes that separate man from man." The Yeatsian hero is a spiritual aristocrat who acts according to a code independent of time and place, custom, or law. Most of his plays are in blank verse with imagery of great emotional intensity. Yeats' playwriting career extended over more than forty years (1892 to 1938), during which he wrote about thirty plays. Prior to 1910, many of the plays were written especially for theatres with which he was associated. These include *Cathleen ni Houlihan* (1902), *The Hour Glass* (1903), *On Baile's Strand* (1904), and *Dierdre* (1906). Of the early plays, one of the most characteristic is *The King's Threshold* (1903), in which the master musician, Seanchan, ousted from the King's council by "Bishops, Soldiers and Makers of the Law," sits at the King's threshold without food or drink. His pupils serve as a chorus, tracing his spiritual ordeal and growth. Finally the King relents, acknowledging that poetry is more enduring than earthly power, and gives his crown to Seanchan, who refuses it because it is the poet's function to sing of greatness rather than to wield the scepter. (In 1922, a revised version shows Seanchan dying at the end.)

After 1910 Yeats ceased to write specifically for the Abbey, and soon afterwards he came under the influence of Japanese Noh drama.

FIG. 5.11

Costume design by Charles Ricketts for Yeats' *The King's Threshold* in 1904. A set of ancient costumes was built first for this play but used later for all of Yeats' and other ancient Irish pieces.

Consequently, his later plays—which include *The Only Jealousy of Emer* (1918), *Calvary* (1920), *A Full Moon in March* (1935), and *Purgatory* (1938)—differ considerably from the earlier ones. They are much more concentrated, using two principal characters representative of polar choices, and reducing each element to its essentials. Among the late plays, one of the best is *At the Hawk's Well* (1917), in which musicians act as a chorus and describe the action of the characters at the Hawk's Well, whose waters confer immortality but appear only for an instant. The play is set on a lonely promontory between sea and land and earth and sky; the action occurs at twilight (between day and night). Two men wait, determined not to miss the water. But the older man falls asleep and the attention of the younger is distracted at the crucial moment. The play suggests that immortality is not to be won by standing and waiting but through deeds that can restore the broken bond between the natural and supernatural realms.

Yeats never won a wide following in the theatre, perhaps because his plays require a special sensibility in the spectator. Over the years he worked to find appropriate means for staging his plays, experimenting with acting styles and consulting on design with such outstanding artists as Charles Ricketts and Gordon Craig. Eventually Yeats resigned himself to his limited popular appeal. Nevertheless, he won the respect of virtually all major critics and came to be recognized as one of the greatest of modern poets. His work was to be central in practically all subsequent attempts to revive and reshape poetic drama.

The Irish Renaissance encompassed both the realistic and nonrealistic. From the beginning two dramatic modes were evident: the poetic-mythic and the realistic-domestic. Yeats most fully embodied the first, while the second was best exemplified by Lady Augusta Gregory (1852–1932) who, like Yeats, was one of the Abbey's managing directors. She continued to be intimately involved with the Abbey until she was almost eighty years old. Prior to 1915 she assumed primary responsibility for raising money, reading scripts, and encouraging new writers. Between 1908 and 1915 she also frequently supervised production and directed a few plays.

Lady Gregory was in many ways as devoted to legend as Yeats was. She translated several of the ancient sagas and myths that Yeats used as subjects. Most of her dramatic writing was done between 1902 and 1912 but she did not cease altogether until 1926. She was most at home in the one-act play and especially peasant comedy. *The Spreading of the News* (1904), in which a passing remark is inflated as it passes from mouth to mouth, has remained a favorite. Irish daily life is also depicted in *The Rising of the Moon* (1907), *The Workhouse Ward* (1907), and many others. Lady Gregory virtually invented the Irish folk-history play based primarily on oral tradition. They include *Kincora* (1905), an epic drama about a figure comparable to the English King Alfred, and *The White Cockade* (1905), a comedy about James II's escape from Ireland. Only rarely did Lady Gregory venture into serious writing, and then the effect was usually more pathetic than tragic. Toward the end of her career, she wrote a few religious plays. Although she cannot be ranked with Yeats, Lady Gregory was far more successful than he with the Abbey's audiences. Overall, she was probably the major stabilizing force of the Abbey.

It remained for John Millington Synge (1871–1909), who, from 1905 until his death, served with Yeats and Lady Gregory as directors of the Abbey, to bridge the gap between the two principal streams of writing as represented by Yeats and Lady Gregory. After completing a university education and living in Paris for a time, Synge developed an interest in the Irish past. Yeats convinced him that he should go and live for a time among the peasants of western Ireland, and his extended visits there ultimately informed all of his dramatic writing.

Synge's plays are typically concerned with one of two issues: the struggle of joyous, elemental urges to escape the repression imposed by religion; or the struggle against (or acceptance of) mortality. As appropriate diction, Synge considered a near-Elizabethan dialect (which he found still used in some parts of Ireland) combined with Gaelic constructions and figures of speech to be that most suited to his needs; from these elements he fashioned his own distinctive, lilting, poetic prose.

The first of Synge's plays to be produced, *In the Shadow of the Glen* (1903) made him notorious. It shows a peasant, seeking to punish his wife for flirting with a tramp (who represents for her all that lies beyond her narrow world), pretending to die, watching his wife make plans for the future with the tramp, and then rising up to order her from his house. Unrepentant, she goes, happy to escape her repressive life. The play infuriated many, who declared Irish women incapable of adultery. *Riders to the Sea* (produced in 1904) illustrates Synge's interest in humanity faced by its own mortality. Many critics consider it the finest short play in the English language. Set in a cottage on the Aran islands, it focuses on a woman who has lost her husband and five of her six sons to the sea. Despite her pleas, her

FIG. 5.12
Scene from the 1906 production of Synge's *Riders to the Sea* with, left to right, Brigit O'Dempsey, Sara Allgood, and Maire O'Neill.

last son sets off on a journey and he, too, is lost. This play illustrates Synge's methods and helps to explain why he was more successful than Yeats with audiences. Typically, Synge presents concrete contemporary situations treated in such a way as to make them seem timeless, thereby infusing the immediate world with mythic qualities and universal significance. Contrarily, Yeats presents a remote past through which he seeks to suggest ideals for the present; his plays achieve mythic grandeur but often remain obscure as to their contemporary relevance.

Of Synge's later works—which include *The Well of the Saints* (1905), *The Tinker's Wedding* (1909), and *Dierdre of the Sorrows* (produced 1910)—the best-known is *The Playboy of the Western World* (1907). The central character of this play is Christy Mahon, a shy young man who thinks that he has killed his brutal father. Arriving at a strange village, he exaggerates his deed and wins the admiration of the villagers and the love of Pegeen Mike. When the supposedly dead father arrives, Christy is denounced by the villagers, and to regain their esteem he attacks his father once more. But the villagers' repressions will not allow them to accept in actuality what they have so romanticized in the telling, and Christy is treated as a criminal. When the father revives once more, now with new-found respect for his son, he takes Christy away, promising to tell the whole world about the villagers' perfidy. Pegeen is left to bemoan the loss of the only "playboy of the western world." Few plays have elicited so stormy a response from audiences. Riots greeted the comedy nightly in Ireland (and later in the U.S. when the Abbey Theatre toured). Yeats and Lady Gregory defended Synge, although Lady Gregory thoroughly disliked the play's amorality. Many years had to pass before Synge's worth was fully acknowledged. Synge's reputation has continued to be strong.

He is now considered by most critics to be the finest playwright of the Irish Renaissance.

While Irish drama was gaining in stature, the Abbey Theatre was developing an ensemble of note. Nevertheless, its history was stormy. Originally, the company chose its repertory by democratic vote, being considered an actors' theatre. After 1905, when the theatre was reorganized as a corporation with Yeats, Lady Gregory, and Synge as its directors, it became a playwrights' theatre. Several actors resigned. In 1907, Miss Horniman, believing W. G. Fay (who had directed most of the productions) incapable of staging Yeats' plays satisfactorily, insisted that B. Iden Payne be employed as artistic director. Payne lasted only six months, and shortly afterwards Fay left. Continued controversy led Miss Horniman to withdraw her support in 1910. Under such circumstances, it is surprising that the company was able to win such an enviable reputation. Nevertheless, not only did it become a major force in Ireland, it also toured extensively in England and paid three trips to the U.S. (in 1911, 1912, and 1914), where it provided significant impetus in the emergence of the *little theatre* movement.

By the time the Abbey Theatre visited the U.S., however, it was already faltering. Many of its finest actors had left, and its major writers had died, defected, or ceased to be productive. (Synge died in 1909; several writers withdrew their plays during the controversy over *The Playboy of the Western World;* Yeats ceased to write for the Abbey after 1910; and Lady Gregory wrote few plays after 1912.) Much of the credit for holding the Abbey together thereafter must go to Lennox Robinson (1886–1958), who became the company's principal director and leading playwright. The company would regain some of its vitality in the 1920s, but its existence became especially precarious after the struggle for Ireland's independence flared into open rebellion in 1916.

THE PEOPLE'S THEATRE, PAGEANTRY, AND OUTDOOR THEATRES

The intertwining of tradition and innovation was especially apparent in the work of those theatrical reformers who looked to the past for inspiration. Of all the demands made in the years between 1890 and 1915 perhaps none was more persistent than the call for a theatre that would engender a sense of community like that of ancient Greece and medieval Europe.

The notion of a *people's theatre* first took shape in France, where in 1895 at Bussang (a small village in eastern France) Maurice Pottecher, an actor and dramatist who had worked with the Théâtre Libre, initiated his Théâtre du Peuple. Annually thereafter until World War I the residents of Bussang, under Pottecher's guidance, mounted a new production each summer and eventually built their own outdoor theatre. Most of the plays were written by Pottecher, while the actors and other personnel were drawn from the community. As the fame of this endeavor grew, other communities followed its example. In 1899, a number of prominent writers proposed the formation of a people's theatre in Paris. Although not implemented, this idea did not die, and in 1903 Romain Rolland (1866–1944) proposed in his *The People's Theatre* that each community perform dramatizations of local and national history so as to inspire the people of the present.

These ideas soon spread to other countries. In England they were put into practice by Louis N. Parker (1852–1944) when at Sherbourne in 1905 he staged a pageant about the community's past. Soon similar works were being written and performed elsewhere throughout England. The pageant movement was to be especially strong in the U.S. One of the first examples was the masque staged in 1905 at Cornish, New Hampshire, to celebrate the twentieth anniversary of Augustus Saint-Gaudens' art colony. Hundreds of others were to follow, most of them dramatizing local history. Others were more remote, and some required enormous casts. Perhaps the most ambitious was the *Pageant and Masque of Saint Louis* (1914) with a cast of 7,500 and a stage 1,000 feet long and 200 feet deep. In 1915, the American Pageant Association recorded sixty-three productions in twenty-three states. The major champion of these community efforts was Percy Mackaye (1875–1956) who touted their merits in such books as *The Civic Theatre* (1912) and *Community Drama* (1917), and wrote a number of pageants and masques.

Intertwined with the people's theatre movement was another that championed outdoor playing. Many critics, arguing that the deterioration of drama had begun when performances moved indoors, considered the return to outdoors a prerequisite for the renovation of drama. Consequently, outdoor theatres began to be built throughout the world. By 1918, when he published *The Open-Air Theatre*, Sheldon Cheney could distinguish three types of recent outdoor structures: architectural (based on ancient Greek models); natural (capitalizing on some existing natural setting); and garden (formal arrangements of shrubbery and hedges). He described theatres ranging from the Hearst Greek Theatre (1903) in California, to the Harz Mountain Theatre (1903) in Germany, to the Klampenborg Woods Theatre (1910) in Demark. Most of these outdoor theatres were used by amateur groups, but occasionally professionals played there. During the early twentieth century, Ben Greet made a career of presenting Shakespearean drama and other classics outdoors for school, college, and community audiences. The ancient Roman theatres were also refurbished and used. In France, the theatre at Orange was

FIG. 5.13
The ancient Roman theatre at Orange in 1911 during a rehearsal of Gluck's *Orpheus*. Reopened in 1894, this theatre influenced the development of festivals at Nîmes, Arles, and Béziers. (From *Le Théâtre*, 1911.)

reopened in 1894, and soon there were annual festivals at Nîmes, Arles, and Béziers. Such theatres encouraged the modern vogue for summer festivals.

Wagner's festival at Bayreuth, like the people's theatres, was intended to generate a sense of community, and its success influenced the foundation of the Shakespeare Festival at Stratford-on-Avon (instituted in 1879). At first a different company was invited to present a short season there annually, but from 1886 until World War I almost all of the festival's productions were provided by Frank Benson (1858–1939), who headed a touring company devoted primarily to Shakespeare's plays mounted in a simplified version of nineteenth-century realism. Above all, Benson was noted for his strenuously athletic productions. As the provincial theatre shrank, Benson became virtually the only purveyor of Shakespeare outside of London, and his company became the primary training ground for a whole generation of actors (usually referred to as the *Bensonians*).

Also embedded in the demand for a people's theatre was the idea that drama should be available to everyone and not merely an elite. It was partially out of this conviction that the German *Volksbühnen* had emerged. In France, the person most concerned with making theatre accessible to everyone was Firmin Gémier (1869–1933) who, after beginning his career in 1892, had gone on to perform the title role in *Ubu Roi* at its premiere before becoming director of the Théâtre Antoine from 1906 until 1922. In 1902, Gémier directed *The Fourteenth of July,* one of the plays Rolland wrote to demonstrate his idea of appropriate community plays, and in 1903 he staged the Festival of Vaud, a pageant (with a cast of 2,400) tracing the history of that Swiss canton. In 1911, he founded the Théâtre Ambulant to bring to people throughout France productions he had staged in Paris. Using thirty-seven trailers pulled by eight steam-driven tractors, he traveled over the inadequate roads of outlying areas and at each stop erected an enormous tent within which he set up a stage on which to perform his realistically mounted, spectacular productions. He was able to continue this venture for only two seasons, but after World War I he would conceive still other plans for a people's theatre.

For the most part, the people's theatre movement was brought to an end by World War I, not only because that war disrupted daily life but also because it undermined the idealism that had informed the movement. After the war, the movement gradually metamorphosed into that form of community theatre in which local amateur actors perform recent commercial hits for local audiences.

In the late nineteenth century, tradition and innovation also merged in the work of several directors who were seeking more effective modes of staging the classics. Much of this effort centered around Shakespeare's plays, which by the nineteenth century were weighed down by multiple elaborate pictorial settings, the shifting of which disrupted the flow of dramatic action and destroyed a play's rhythmic structure.

Interest in reforming Shakespearean staging was especially strong in Germany. In 1840 Karl Immermann, working in Dusseldorf, devised a setting the main feature of which was an unchanging architectural facade with doors at either side and, at the rear, an opening behind which pictorialized decors could be changed. A somewhat similar arrangement was adopted at the Hoftheater in Munich in 1889 by Karl von Perfall and Jocza Savits, and still another variation was devised at the same theatre in 1909–1910 by Julius Klein and Eugen Kilian. All of these arrangements had the virtue of permitting uninterrupted playing (the action could proceed downstage while pictorial elements were changed behind a curtain which masked the inner stage), but all suffered from the anachronistic intermingling of formal elements downstage with representational scenery upstage. Nevertheless, they were widely publicized, admired, and imitated.

Meanwhile, in England a far more drastic solution was being championed by William Poel (1852–1934). As early as 1881, Poel had staged the first-quarto *Hamlet* on a bare stage. His major experiments, however, date from

FIG. 5.14
Immermann's Shakespearebühne, Dusseldorf. (From a contemporary print.)

FIG. 5.15
Klein's and Kilian's
Shakespearebühne at
the Munich
Hoftheater in 1909–
1910. The production
is of *Hamlet;* the
design by Klein.
(From *Stage
Yearbook*, 1913.)

1893, when he staged *Measure for Measure* at the Royalty Theatre in London on a reconstructed Elizabethan public stage. A large forestage was backed by a two-leveled facade equipped with curtains which could reveal or conceal the interior, while two posts on the forestage supported the heavens. Actors costumed in Elizabethan garments were seated on stools at either side to simulate the audience of Shakespeare's day. Between 1894 and 1905 Poel was supported by the Elizabethan Stage Society, and under its aegis Poel in 1895 presented A *Comedy of Errors* at Gray's Inn which, with its large hall built in Tudor times, permitted a much more authentic relationship between audience and performers than was possible in a picture-frame theatre. Similarly, in 1896 Poel mounted *Two Gentlemen of Verona* in the Merchant Taylors' Hall and *Twelfth Night* in the hall of the Middle Temple. In addition to Shakespeare's plays, Poel presented other English classics, among them Marlowe's *Doctor Faustus* and the first production in modern times of *Everyman.* He was to continue similar staging throughout his life.

Although he did not always use the same approach, Poel is now remembered entirely for his attempts to reconstruct the Elizabethan public stage. He also popularized several conventions: dressing the actors in Elizabethan garments to reflect Shakespeare's own day rather than the historical era of the action; using costumed pages to draw the curtains of the inner stage and to arrange properties and furniture; and having an onstage audience. But Poel's main emphasis was on continuity of action, without any interruptions for scene shifting or intermissions. Although his productions did not generate widespread enthusiasm, they demonstrated the advantages of unbroken playing and concentrating attention on the characters rather than on the background spectacle. Poel's methods were taken to the U.S. by his associate in the Elizabethan Stage Society, Ben Greet (1857–1936), who toured extensively in the United States between 1903 and 1914, although Greet usually performed out of doors. They were also taken to France by Lugné-Poë in 1898 when, in imitation of Poel's production, he mounted *Measure for*

FIG. 5.16

Poel's reconstruction of an Elizabethan theatre for his production in 1893 of *Measure for Measure* at the Royalty Theatre. (Courtesy Enthoven Collection. By courtesy of the Board of Trustees of the Victoria and Albert Museum.)

Measure in the Cirque d'Eté in Paris. It attracted little attention and spawned no imitators.

Interest in reviving the staging conventions of past eras extended beyond the Elizabethan. Edward Godwin, father of Gordon Craig, simulated a Greek theatre in 1886 when he staged John Todhunter's *Helen of Troy* at Hengler's Circus in London. The French stage of the seventeenth century was also reconstructed, most notably by Antoine at the Odéon. Believing that French classical drama is rooted in its era, Antoine ignored the period of the dramatic action and mounted the plays in seventeenth-century milieus. In 1907 for

Corneille's *Le Cid* he sought to recreate the original production of 1636. Corneille's text became a play within a play as Antoine surrounded it with the invented action of an onstage audience. Similarly, in 1909 Antoine staged Racine's *Andromaque* in a setting which simulated a seventeenth-century drawing room with a courtier audience on either side.

Such attempts were another form of antiquarianism in which the historical accuracy of architecture and dress were replaced with accuracy of past theatrical traditions. Nevertheless, they showed an awareness of the integral relationship between the theatre and the society in which it appears. In addition, they showed clearly how tradition and innovation often merged in the years between 1890 and 1915.

THE ASSIMILATION OF INNOVATIONS

Between 1890 and 1915, both realism and antirealism came to be accepted as dramatic modes. Both attracted many adherents and, as these modes became familiar and gained acceptance, both were assimilated into the mainstream of drama and production. Nevertheless, those traditions inherited from the nineteenth century continued to dominate both writing and production, even though they had been somewhat altered by the assimilation of new modes. At the same time, other innovations were underway that would eventually undermine premodern traditions.

Chapter 6

Forging
a New Art
of the Theatre

Although in every period its leading practitioners have considered the theatre an art (and often a business as well), a new wave of directors, designers, and playwrights at the end of the nineteenth century had begun to denounce their predecessors as misguided or tasteless perverters of the theatre's true mission. They proclaimed their intention of transforming the theatre into an art worthy of its rightful place among the other arts. They discussed at length the theatre's nature, function, and elements, and through both theory and practice sought to revitalize it. In almost every country there was a self-conscious attempt to define, and realize in practice, the "art of the theatre."

APPIA AND CRAIG

The number of would-be reformers in the years between 1890 and 1915 was indeed large,

113

but the most crucial among them were Adolphe Appia and Gordon Craig, the most important theorists of the early twentieth-century stage. Although neither was extensively involved in theatrical production nor markedly successful when he was, together they formulated the theoretical bases on which others would build. Working independently, they drew many of the same conclusions, although each had many distinctive ideas. Their careers also followed quite different paths.

Born in Geneva, Adolphe Appia (1862–1928) came to his interest in theatre through Wagner's operas. But when he went to Bayreuth, he was deeply disappointed, for he considered the productions there completely misguided, and from the early 1880s he struggled to resolve the disparity between Wagner's theoretical statements and his staging. Almost all of Appia's early writing, beginning about 1891, was addressed to this problem.

Appia's first important work, *The Staging of Wagnerian Music Drama* (1895), attracted little attention. Undaunted, Appia elaborated his ideas in a longer work, *Music and the Art of the Theatre* (1899), which included nineteen of Appia's own designs for Wagnerian operas. Since his next major book did not appear until 1921, Appia's ideas were long known primarily through these two early works.

The problem Appia first addressed was the causes of disunity in the productions at Bayreuth. He concluded that the primary cause was the disparity between the three-dimensional actor and the two-dimensional stage settings. Since he believed that the performer is the intermediary between dramatist and audience and that "scenic illusion is the presence of the living actor," Appia sought to harmonize all other elements with the performer. Like Wagner, Appia believed that the goal of production is to create an ideal realm into which the spectator is drawn by an overpowering empathic experience. He also accepted the need for a unifying artistic force—the director—to control all of the elements of production. But Appia believed that Wagner had violated his own theory when he used realistic spectacle to

FIG. 6.1
Setting for Wagner's *Parsifal* at Bayreuth shortly after the turn of the century. The attempt at illusionism is still apparent in this setting of two-dimensional cutouts. (From *Le Théâtre*, 1911.)

FIG. 6.2
Appia's design for
Wagner's *Parsifal,*
1895. (From Fondation
Adolphe Appia,
Berne.)

express his idealized vision. It seemed to Appia
that ideality could only be created through
simplicity and suggestion harmonized with the
three-dimensional actor. He established a hierarchy of means, with the actor first, followed
by spatial arrangement, lighting, and painted
flats.

The essential problem for Appia, then, lay
in the relationship among the moving actor,
the horizontal floor, and the vertical scenery.
In past practice, the three had normally been
treated as unrelated elements, since the flat,
two-dimensional scenery usually stopped
abruptly at the stage floor and was designed
without adequate concern for the presence of
the living actor. Contrarily, Appia conceived
his designs in terms of space, volume, and mass,
and he used platforms, steps, and ramps to
create transitions between scenery and floor
(thereby providing opportunities for the actor
to move both horizontally and vertically) and
to serve rhythmical functions in the visual
composition. Other typical scenic elements (in
addition to steps and platforms) were pillars,

drapes, and walls—all free of nonessential
details and all three-dimensional.

Appia's designs were rendered in shadings
of black and white, for he thought in terms of
light and shadow. He also recognized that even
three-dimensional elements may appear flat
under general illumination. Consequently, he
called for multidirectional lighting with strong
contrasts to emphasize mass, shape, and plasticity. For Appia, light was the visual element
most analogous to music, since it is capable of
reflecting moment-by-moment changes in
mood, tonality, and rhythm. Thus, he considered light the primary means of unifying
and blending all the other visual elements into a
harmonious whole. Because of these ideas,
Appia is usually considered the originator of
modern stage lighting theory.

Ultimately, Appia sought to create an
absolute beauty through idealized elements.
He completed the scheme that Wagner had
envisioned but had failed to realize. He hoped
that his work would be read and heeded by
Wagner's widow, who controlled the Bayreuth

Festival, but she steadfastly ignored it. His first opportunity to implement his ideas did not come until 1903, when the Countess de Béarn invited him to mount a production in her private theatre in Paris. He planned to present portions of Wagner's *Tristan and Isolde* but had to settle for scenes from Bizet's *Carmen* and Schumann's musical setting of Byron's *Manfred*. Although the response was highly favorable, no new commissions came his way.

In 1906 a new phase in Appia's life began when he met Emile Jaques Dalcroze (1865–1950), next to Wagner the greatest influence on Appia. Dalcroze had by the 1890s achieved considerable fame as a composer and as a teacher at the Geneva conservatory. Increasingly concerned about the inability of his students to master rhythm, he began experiments from which he evolved *eurythmics*, a system under which students were led to experience music kinesthetically by moving to the rhythms of musical compositions. After becoming acquainted with Appia, Dalcroze expanded his system to include emotional values. Much of Dalcroze's work would be assimilated into modern dance and actor training.

In 1910 two wealthy German manufacturers offered to build Dalcroze a school at Hellerau, a suburb of Dresden. For it, Appia, in collaboration with Alexander von Salzmann and Heinrich Tessenow, designed the auditorium, stage, and lighting. This was the first theatre in modern times to be built without a proscenium arch—that is, the first completely open stage. There was no separation (other than a sunken orchestra pit) of stage from auditorium, the walls and ceiling being continuous. Furthermore, the walls and ceiling were covered with transparent canvas behind which about 3,000 lamps were installed to give indirect light. The auditorium held about 600 people on steeply raked banks of seats. The major collaboration between Appia and Dalcroze at Hellerau came in 1913 when Gluck's *Orpheus and Eurydice* was staged. The sets, among the most abstract of the period, had no representational details beyond those of a formal arrangement of steps, platforms, and draperies.

When the war began in 1914, the school at Hellerau was closed and the intimate association between Appia and Dalcroze ceased. Still, the years with Dalcroze permanently influenced Appia, and in *The Work of Living Art* (1921), the fullest expression of Appia's ideas, rhythm plays the key role. His hierarchy of elements and his ideas about light and three-dimensionality remained unchanged, but his notions about how elements were to be fused had been refined. Placing much greater emphasis on movement and rhythm, he declared, "Our body is the expression of space in time and time in space," and "movement brings about the meeting of Space and Time." He had also come to believe that the rhythm embedded in

FIG. 6.3
Appia's design for Schiller's *The Diver*, 1910, a demonstration of what Appia referred to as "Rhythmic Space." (From Fondation Adolphe Appia, Berne.)

FIG. 6.4
Design by Appia for
*Orpheus and
Eurydice.* (From
Fondation Adolphe
Appia, Berne.)

FIG. 6.5
Photograph of the
staging by Appia and
Dalcroze of *Orpheus
and Eurydice* at
Hellerau in 1913. (A
contemporary photo.)

the text provides the key to every gesture and movement on the stage, and that the proper mastery of rhythm will unify all the spatial and temporal elements of a production into a harmonious and satisfying whole. He wrote of the theatre as a "cathedral" in which a union of body and soul creates an experience "lived in common with others."

By the 1920s Appia began to gain his long-delayed recognition. In 1922 an International Theatre Exhibition in Amsterdam made his and Craig's work the focus of designs from all over the world. He also began to receive commissions. The most important of these came from La Scala in Milan, where he assisted Arturo Toscanini in staging *Tristan and Isolde* in 1923. The results were disillusioning, for Appia's simple, expressive settings were disliked by patrons used to sumptuous mountings in the Italianate style. Furthermore, the stage personnel, rooted in traditional practices, resisted the techniques needed to do Appia's scenery and lighting justice. Still, Appia was almost immediately invited to Basel to stage Wagner's *Ring* cycle, his lifetime ambition. In 1924 *The Rhinegold* was favorably received, but in 1925 *The Valkyrie* led to such a virulent campaign against Appia that the rest of the cycle was abandoned. In its place, Appia was asked to mount *Prometheus*, and, though well received, it was little comfort to the thwarted Wagnerite.

This was the end of Appia's practical work in the theatre, and three years later he died, still not fully appreciated.

Gordon Craig (1872–1966) was as flamboyant as Appia was retiring, and he achieved notoriety throughout Europe long before Appia's work was widely known. Thus, prior to 1914 Craig often received sole credit for many of their shared ideas. The illegitimate son of Ellen Terry and Edward Godwin, he was given the name "Craig" because Terry liked its strength. In 1889, Craig joined Irving's company and during the next nine years acted a number of roles, by far the most significant being Hamlet. Around 1890 Craig became interested in scenic design. His early designs were in the spectacular realistic vein favored by Irving, and not until around 1900 did he adopt a more stylized mode. The first of his settings to reach the stage was for the Purcell Operatic Society's *Dido and Aeneas* in 1900. By 1903 he had designed seven productions (among them Ibsen's *The Vikings at Helgeland* and

FIG. 6.6
Craig's design for the production of Ibsen's *The Pretenders*, staged in Copenhagen in 1926. (From *Theatre Arts*, 1929.)

Shakespeare's *Much Ado About Nothing* for the company his mother had founded after Irving had left the Lyceum), more than he was to do during the remainder of his life. After 1903 he was involved in only five productions: *Venice Preserved* (in von Hofmannsthal's version) at Otto Brahm's Deutsches Theater in Berlin (1904); *Rosmersholm* for Eleanora Duse in Florence (1906); *Hamlet* at the Moscow Art Theatre (1912); *The Pretenders* at the Theatre Royal, Copenhagen (1926); and *Macbeth* in New York (1928). Thus, most of Craig's practical work had been done before he turned to writing.

Craig's influence was exerted primarily through his writings—*The Art of the Theatre* (1905, translated into German in 1905 and into Dutch and Russian in 1906), *On the Art of the Theatre* (1911), *Towards a New Theatre* (1913), *The Theatre Advancing* (1919), and his periodical *The Mask* (published sporadically from 1908 to 1929)—and his drawings, most of which were not intended as designs for actual productions. He was continually involved in controversy, partially because he accused practically every major theatrical figure in Europe of plagiarizing his ideas.

A disciple of Walter Pater, Craig advocated art-for-art's-sake and the theatre as an independent art. He rebelled against Wagner's conception of the theatre as a union of all the arts, declaring: "the Art of the Theatre is neither acting nor the play, it is not scene nor dance, but it consists of all the elements of which these things are composed: action, which is the very spirit of acting; words, which are the body of the play; line and colour, which are the very heart of the scene; rhythm, which is the very essence of dance." He refused to assign any hierarchy to these elements, arguing instead that the theatre artist uses them all in his work, which is as pure and autonomous as that of the painter, sculptor, composer, or poet. Craig acknowledged that in most past

theatrical production a craftsman-director had coordinated the work of several other craftsmen, but he was seeking a higher form in which a master-artist, without the medium of a literary text, would create every element of a wholly autonomous art. The purpose of this new theatre was to express absolute beauty unconcerned with everyday appearance—realism—and reveal the mysterious, interior, and secret planes of being that make up the "spiritual universe of the imagination." Like the symbolists, Craig believed that this ideal

FIG. 6.7

Design for *Electra* by Craig, 1905. (From City of Manchester Art Gallery, *Exhibition of Drawings and Models . . . by Edward Gordon Craig*, 1912.)

beauty could not be expressed directly but could only be suggested through the symbol—"the visible sign of the idea." He rejected realism and historical accuracy in favor of color, line, mass, light, movement, gesture and sound—all chosen for their evocative (rather than their representational) power.

Craig's influence was to be felt most in design, perhaps because he conceived of the theatre primarily in visual terms. He argued that the public goes to see rather than to hear a play and that it is through sight that the imagination and intelligence are most fully stimulated. His drawings show a marked preference for right angles—strong vertical and horizontal lines—and almost an obsession with parallelism. Their most notable feature, however, is height, resulting in a sense of grandeur. (Critics have argued that, if built, most of Craig's sets would be eight stories tall.) Like Appia, Craig was concerned with volume and space (created by a few strong lines and devoid of realistic detail) which emphasize the three-dimensionality and plasticity of stage and actor. Also like Appia, Craig used light both as compositional element and as atmospheric effect. Unlike Appia, who thought in terms of light and shadow, Craig relied heavily on color to evoke the dramatic quality of a scene. He also made considerable use of textures, often ones (such as heavy woven fabrics and metal) not normally used for scenery.

Perhaps Craig's favorite project was the mobile setting. Most of his predecessors had conceived of scenery as static. (One set might replace another, but it did not itself move.) Craig experimented with screens, out of which he hoped to create settings which, by means unseen by the audience, could move in ways analogous to the actor and the lighting. He began these experiments in 1907, authorized Yeats to try them at the Abbey Theatre in 1911, and used them himself in his production of *Hamlet* at the Moscow Art Theatre in 1912. Craig's screens were neutral in color so their appearance might be altered almost infinitely by light. In Moscow they were cream and gold; they were to have been covered in different natural materials, such as metal and cork, but, out of concern for weight and mobility, the materials and textures were simulated by paint. They also were supposed to glide from one position to another in full view of the audience, but so many difficulties arose that the curtain was closed between scenes to mask changes. Craig continued to experiment with screens into the 1920s. Although he never found a satisfactory solution, he did inspire the unit set (using the same pieces recombined in various ways to create various locales), which was widely used after World War I.

Although Craig influenced visual elements most, he affected other aspects as well. He blamed most of the theatre's shortcomings on the predominance of one or another element—playwriting, acting, or spectacle. He often denounced the dramatist for overemphasis on the spoken word and for creating a theatre of sermons and moral lessons. Similarly, he often blamed starring actors for the low state of theatre. To counteract the influence of actors, perhaps the dominant force in Craig's youth, he made some of his most controversial pronouncements. He argued that acting is not an art, since it is impossible to mold human beings into an artistic product and because the actor is forever seeking to aggrandize himself and to interpose his own ideas between those of the master artist and the audience. As a remedy, he suggested that the actor be replaced by an *Uebermarionette,* a superpuppet without an ego but capable of carrying out demands efficiently. No idea voiced by Craig aroused a greater storm. A less controversial proposal was the adoption of the conventionalized movement

FIG. 6.8

Craig's screens, as used in the production of *Hamlet* at the Moscow Art Theatre in 1912. (From *Moscow Art Theatre, 1898–1917*, 1955.)

and gestures of Oriental theatre to express ideas, attitudes, and emotions. Occasionally, he also advocated the revival of masks.

Appia and Craig arrived at many of the same conceptions. Both considered the theatre an autonomous art and sought to redefine its elements and sources of unity. Both rejected realism in favor of suggestion, selectivity, and synthesis. Both sought three-dimensional plasticity and demanded an artist capable of welding the theatre's diverse elements into a harmonious whole. Both were idealists who through the theatre desired to create a pure

beauty—for Appia one almost religious, for Craig one more nearly sensuous.

But there were also important differences. Appia's artist was to be primarily an interpreter of the composer-dramatist's work; Craig's was an autonomous artist. Appia assigned a hierarchy to the theatrical elements; Craig refused to do so. Appia thought in terms of successive settings; Craig sought a single (preferably mobile) setting capable of expressing the spirit of the entire work.

Appia and Craig were often denounced as impractical men who knew little of the workaday theatre. In actuality, they were visionaries who championed ideals and goals that practitioners of the theatre did not perceive. Together they forced their contemporaries to reconsider the nature and function of the theatre as an art. They encouraged the trend toward simplified decor, plasticity of space, and atmospheric lighting—toward evocation rather than actualistic representation. Theirs was a theatre of ideal beauty addressed to the imagination and spirit. At first highly controversial, their theories were to prevail after World War I and were to dominate both theory and practice until after World War II. Even today, their influence is still great, although considerably diminished by such later theorists as Brecht and Artaud.

FUCHS AND REINHARDT

Between 1900 and 1910 a number of groups began to follow the path sketched by Appia and Craig. Of these, one was the Munich Art Theater. Although this theatre was the creation of many persons, it is associated primarily with its principal spokesman, Georg Fuchs (1868–1949), a critic whose theoretical writings for a time ranked with those of Appia and Craig. Before the theatre opened, Fuchs had already published *The Stage of the Future* (1905) and at the end of its first season he published *Revolution in the Theater* (1909).

Arguing that auditorium design was still mired in the past (the box, pit, and gallery arrangement), Fuchs proposed to reform it along lines already adopted by Wagner at Bayreuth. Like Wagner, Fuchs wanted to obliterate class distinctions and achieve a communal experience. Also like Wagner, he rejected the realistic (and most other) drama of his time. Unlike Wagner, he rejected the realistic scenic conventions of the picture-frame stage and championed a shallow "relief"

stage backed by two-dimensional scenery, an arrangement intended to focus attention on the stylized acting favored by Fuchs. He argued that his practices would "retheatricalize the theatre" along ancient Greek lines but through modern means.

In designing the Munich Art Theater, Fuchs worked with Max Littmann (1862–1931), who had already designed two theatres heavily influenced by Wagner's Festspielhaus—the Prinzregenten in Munich (1901) and the Schiller in Berlin (1906). The auditorium of the Art Theater, seating 642, was steeply raked and without a central aisle or side boxes (although, like Wagner's theatre, there were some boxes at the rear). A sunken orchestra pit (which was partially under the stage) could be covered over to create a forestage. The stage itself differed markedly from that at Bayreuth. An inner proscenium was sufficiently thick to contain a door below and a window or balcony above at either side. These side structures, coordinated with an overhead bridge, could be moved on or off stage to alter the size of the proscenium opening or to serve as scenic elements. The stage, deeper than Fuchs had proposed, was broken into sections, each mounted on an elevator that could be lowered into the basement to change scenic elements or raised above the stage floor to create levels of varying heights. It was also backed by four cloth cycloramas that could be changed electronically.

The most controversial aspect of the productions was the acting, which for the most part was confined to the plane outlined by the inner proscenium, the area back of this plane being reserved primarily for scenery. Fuchs thought this arrangement would create a sense of communion with the spectator. But in crowd scenes, the actors often seemed in danger of toppling into the auditorium. Like Appia, Fuchs believed that rhythm fuses all the elements of production, but unlike Appia, he placed the actor in front of the setting rather than within it.

The theatre's principal designer was Fritz Erler (1868–1940) who, believing that the theatre is based in convention, favored stylized decor. At times he used the adjustable proscenium as the principal scenic elements; at others he used it in combination with other pieces, but Erler's effects were achieved primarily through simple forms, painted drops, and especially the play of colored light (the production element most consistently praised).

The theatre opened in 1908 (Munich's 750th anniversary) with Goethe's *Faust, Part I* directed by Fuchs and designed by Erler. This was the only production under Fuchs' management that gained much attention, and none was judged truly effective by Munich's critics. After one season Fuchs was replaced as manager. Nevertheless, Fuchs' *Revolution in the Theater* (1909) treated the Munich Art Theater as an unqualified success, and people outside of Germany tended to accept Fuchs' version. Largely because of this book, Fuchs' influence was for a time second only to that of Appia and Craig.

Ironically, in 1909 the Munich Art Theater was turned over to Max Reinhardt (1873–1943), a director for whom Fuchs had little respect. Nevertheless, Reinhardt was the di-

FIG. 6.9
Setting for the throne room in Ibsen's *The Pretenders,* staged by Reinhardt at the Neues Theater, Berlin, c. 1905. (From Deutsche Akademie der Künste zu Berlin.)

rector most responsible for synthesizing all the new trends that had become evident since the 1870s. Born in Austria, Reinhardt began his career as an actor there before joining Otto Brahm's troupe at the Deutsches Theater in Berlin in 1894. From Brahm he learned much about ensemble playing, respect for the script, and care for the details of production. But he was not wedded to Brahm's naturalistic approach. His first step away from naturalism came when he and several friends founded a cabaret, Sound and Smoke, where after theatre hours they presented vaudeville sketches and other kinds of popular entertainment, along with short plays. In 1902 this cabaret was transformed into the Kleines Theater (Little Theater), where Reinhardt presented such works as Wilde's *Salome,* Wedekind's *Earth Spirit,* and Gorky's *The Lower Depths.* In 1903, Reinhardt left Brahm to become director of the Neues Theater, a large house which he ran in conjunction with the Kleines Theater. Here he presented Maeterlinck's *Pelléas and Mélisande* and *Sister Beatrice,* Euripides' *Medea,* Shakespeare's *A Midsummer Night's Dream,* and Shaw's *Candida.*

When Brahm retired in 1905, Reinhardt became director of the Deutsches Theater, where he was to remain until the 1930s. By 1906 he had given up the Neues and Kleines theatres, but in the same year he converted a dance hall next door to the Deutsches into a small theatre, the Kammerspiele (chamber theatre), seating 300 persons and with a stage only three feet from the first row. The Deutsches Theater seated around 1,000 and, with its revolving stage, plaster skydome, and elaborate lighting system, was one of the best-equipped theatres in the world. Reinhardt was the first major producer to use this combination of small and large theatres. Prior to Reinhardt, most experimentation had been done in the independent theatres, whereas he created a place for experimentation within an established

theatre by providing a small house for productions not likely to attract a large audience. This arrangement was eventually adopted by most of the state theatres in Germany, by the Moscow Art Theatre, and by educational theatres in the United States. Within a few years, Reinhardt had won an international reputation. He was frequently asked to direct not only at other theatres in Germany (including the Munich Art Theater from 1909 to 1911) but also in other European countries.

Reinhardt's major contribution was his recognition that no single approach is appropriate to the staging of all plays. Until the twentieth century, directors in each era staged all plays in much the same style. Despite widespread experimentation in the late nineteenth century, each director had adopted a distinctive approach and then applied it to all plays. Reinhardt was the first to proclaim that each play represents a new problem demanding its own solution. Thus, unlike his predecessors, he could embrace realism without denying antirealism. To him it was not a question of choosing sides but of finding the approach most appropriate to a particular production of a particular play for a particular audience. Consequently, Reinhardt developed eclecticism into an artistic creed. Because he did not champion any particular school and because he seldom used extreme departures from realism, he was often accused of vulgarizing other people's ideas. Even if the charge were true, he should still be credited with establishing eclecticism, which was to become the norm for most twentieth-century directing.

Reinhardt presented plays ranging through almost every period, form, and style. In all, he was concerned with establishing a community among spectators through shared emotion. Consequently, the major problem became how to make a play emotionally moving for a contemporary audience. He did not consider the theatre a literary or moral institution designed to educate or indoctrinate humanity. Rather, he considered his theatre to be apolitical and nonideological. He was more interested in helping the audience forget the misery of everyday existence than in making it confront problems. Therefore, for each production, Reinhardt sought to establish a powerful psychological relationship between performers and spectators. Sometimes this led to recreating the spatial arrangement for which the play was originally written. He staged *Oedipus Rex* (1910) and the *Oresteia* (1911) in the Circus Schumann in Berlin, believing that such an amphitheatre offered the closest modern equivalent to the Greek theatre. For a production of *Hamlet* at the Deutsches Theater in 1910 he removed several rows of seats and extended a forestage into the auditorium to simulate the Elizabethan stage. For *Sumurun* (1910), a pantomime based on the *Arabian Nights,* he bor-

rowed devices from the Oriental theatre, including the *hanamichi,* along which entrances were made through the auditorium. For *The Miracle,* a pantomime based on a medieval legend about a nun whose place is taken by the Virgin, he converted the vast Olympia Hall in London into the nave of a cathedral so that the audience seemed to be watching a ritualized religious spectacle.

Recreations of audience-actor spatial relationships were one among many of Reinhardt's approaches to texts. Several of his Shakespearean productions—*A Midsummer Night's Dream, The Merchant of Venice, Othello,* and *Henry IV*—used "sculptural" settings mounted on a revolving stage. In this way, Reinhardt succeeded where the experiments with *Shakespearebühnen* had failed: he provided an uninterrupted flow of scenes in appropriate locales while avoiding the disparity between formalism

FIG. 6.10
Reinhardt's production of *Oedipus Rex* at the Circus Schumann in Berlin, 1910. (From *Theatre Arts,* 1924.)

FIG. 6.11
Model by Ernst Stern, showing the revolving stage for one of Reinhardt's earliest productions of *A Midsummer Night's Dream* at the Neues Theater in 1905. Reinhardt staged the play at least four times. (From Österreichische Nationalbibliothek.)

and representationalism. In other productions, Reinhardt chose visual motifs as a stylistic focus. The settings and costumes for Gozzi's *Turandot* (an eighteenth-century *commedia dell'arte* script set in China) used motifs taken from eighteenth-century European *chinoiserie,* to emphasize that the Oriental aspects of the script were exotic embellishments seen through the European consciousness of Gozzi's time. Such an approach not only made for visual unity but also created a perspective through which the audience might better experience the spirit of the piece.

In choosing his approach to each production, Reinhardt seems to have been guided in part by his designers. In the early years he used such painters as Arnold Bocklin (noted for his atmospheric effects) and Emil Orlik (addicted to Japanese composition and coloration). His most important productions were done in collaboration with Ernst Stern (1876–1954), who was not only sensitive to actor-audience spatial relationships but also noted for his bold use of color, line, and mass to suggest the dominant mood of a play. Though he always used recognizable pictorial elements in his settings, Stern simplified and stylized them so as to evoke a powerful emotional response in the audience.

Much of Reinhardt's success came from his working methods, which in many respects echoed those of Saxe-Meiningen. Each department of his theatre was headed by a trusted associate who was responsible for its efficiency, and all supervisory personnel conferred regularly to ensure coordination of the theatre's work with Reinhardt's desires. Thus, Reinhardt delegated authority but remained the undisputed master. Like Saxe-Meiningen, Reinhardt made his mark in large part because of his care for detail and the integration of all elements into a unified whole. Unlike Saxe-Meiningen, Reinhardt was an entrepreneur who often controlled several theatres simultaneously and often restaged essentially the same production in different cities.

As a director, Reinhardt created a prompt-book (*Regiebuch*) for each production, in which he worked out every detail before rehearsals began. He was often accused of using actors as mere puppets since he had decided in advance precisely what he wanted from each. His actors—among them Gertrude Eysolt (1870–1955), Alexander Moissi (1880–1935), Friedrich Kayssler (1874–1945), Max Pallenberg (1859–1934), Albert Bassermann (1867–1952), Werner Krauss (1884–1959), and Emil Jannings (1887–1950)—were among the best of the time. In conjunction with the Deutsches Theater, Reinhardt also maintained an acting school where students were trained in voice and speech, movement, dance, and characterization.

By 1915, Reinhardt's working methods were well established. By today's standards many of his departures from realism would seem slight, but they were sufficient to accustom audiences to stylistic approaches that previously would have been found unacceptable. He had also made eclecticism the favored approach for directors not addicted to some specific ideology. After World War I, Reinhardt would continue his work, but his basic approach would remain unchanged.

GRANVILLE BARKER

In England, the eclectic ideal was best exemplified by Harley Granville Barker (1877–1946) who, after beginning his career in 1891 as an actor, had worked with Poel, had served as both director and actor with the Incorporated Stage Society, and had gained considerable prominence as a playwright. As a director, his important work began in 1904 when he was invited by the Royal Court Theatre in London to assist John Vedrenne (1863–1930) with a production of *Two Gentlemen of Verona*. Barker accepted on the condition that he be permitted to stage Shaw's *Candida* for a series of six matinees. The collaboration was so successful that Barker and Vedrenne soon took full control of the Royal Court.

The Barker-Vedrenne company was to be of major significance to the English theatre. It virtually established George Bernard Shaw's reputation in the theatre. Prior to this time, Shaw's plays had been seen primarily in private performances, and he was known as a polemicist more than as a dramatist. In 1904, the overwhelming success of *John Bull's Other Island* at the Royal Court immediately created a demand for Shaw's plays in the theatre. But Shaw remained faithful to Barker and Vedrenne, who eventually produced eleven of his works. Of the 946 performances given at the Royal Court under Barker and Vedrenne, 701 were of Shaw's works. By 1907 (when Barker and Vedrenne gave up the Royal Court), Shaw's theatrical reputation was fully established. Since Shaw directed his own plays, he had also become the company's principal director. Furthermore, the controversy that surrounded Shaw's plays kept the Royal Court in the public eye.

In addition to Shaw, the Royal Court presented works by Euripides, Ibsen, Hauptmann, Maeterlinck, Schnitzler, Galsworthy, and others. It also built an excellent ensemble company, made up mostly of young, dedicated performers (including Louis Calvert, Lillah McCarthy, Lewis Casson, Matheson Lang, Harcourt Williams, and Nigel Playfair) who were to be among England's most respected actors in years to come. Barker also appeared in practically every production, and occasionally such stars as Ellen Terry, Mrs. Patrick Campbell, and Johnston Forbes-Robertson made guest appearances. The mounting of plays was always simple, with no more than 200 pounds spent on any. Thus, major attention was concentrated on the acting.

The Royal Court's success as a repertory theatre dedicated to high artistic principles stimulated the revival of repertory companies outside of London. The first of the new groups was formed in 1908 by Miss A.E.F. Horniman in Manchester, and a second soon followed in Glasgow in 1909. In 1911 the Liverpool Repertory Theatre, under the leadership of Basil Dean, was founded, and in 1913 Barry Jackson founded the Birmingham Repertory Company. These were pioneers in the effort to rescue the English provinces from dependence on touring companies from London.

Despite their critical success, Barker and Vedrenne were constantly under financial stress. Convinced that their dilemma was attributable to the inconvenient location of the Royal Court and its small size (614 seats), they gave up the theatre in 1907 and moved to the Savoy, a much larger house in a more central location. But they soon discovered that there was not yet an audience of sufficient size to support their kind of theatre, and they had to abandon their new venture. In 1910 an attempt was made to salvage the company when Charles Frohman (with a guarantee from J. M. Barrie) installed it in his Duke of York's Theatre. After seventeen weeks it was discontinued. In 1911, the Barker-Vedrenne partnership was dissolved and Shaw paid its debts.

Barker did not give up directing. Between 1912 and 1914 he mounted at the Savoy Theatre three Shakespearean productions—*A Winter's Tale, Twelfth Night,* and *A Midsummer Night's Dream*—that outraged conservatives and delighted the avant-garde. Through these productions, Barker synthesized much of the experimentation in Shakespearean staging of the preceding two decades. He divided his stage into three parts: a wide forestage forward of the proscenium, a middle plane upstage of the proscenium, and a slightly raised inner stage. Like Poel's, Barker's stage permitted continuous playing, but it avoided the sense of archeological reconstruction that had plagued Poel's work. Like the German *Shakespeare-bühnen,* it provided for scenery, but it avoided the disparity between the formal and pictorial by using highly stylized decor and by making the frame of the inner stage (which repeated the architectural details of the proscenium arch) seem a part of the theatre rather than a scenic element. The extent of the innovations can be seen in relation to *A Midsummer Night's Dream,* which in 1900 had been presented in London by Beerbohm Tree in settings that featured seemingly real trees and flowers, grass carpets, and live rabbits. In sharp contrast, Barker's scene designers, Norman Wilkinson (1882–1934) and Albert Rutherston (1884–1953), represented the forest with stylized trees painted on draperies that hung in folds, and they formed Titania's bower from lengths of brightly colored gauze suspended from a garland of flowers. The fairies, to distinguish them from mortals, were bronzed and restricted to puppetlike movements. With these Shakespearean productions, Barker provided a major lesson in how to synthesize diverse trends from the theatre of his time.

TENTATIVE AMERICAN INNOVATIONS

Barker was to take the same lesson to the U.S. in 1915, when, at the invitation of the New York Stage Society, he mounted a season of plays (including *A Midsummer Night's Dream* and plays by Shaw) which were to be landmarks in American theatre. Shortly afterwards, Barker retired from active work in the theatre and thereafter confined himself to translating plays and writing criticism.

Barker's work in New York had been preceded by other attempts to make Americans aware of European developments. In 1911–1912 the Abbey Theatre toured the country to

FIG. 6.12
Barker's production of *A Midsummer Night's Dream* at the Savoy Theatre in 1914. (Courtesy Enthoven Collection. By courtesy of the Board of Trustees of the Victoria and Albert Museum.)

high critical praise amid the furor created by riots precipitated by *The Playboy of the Western World*. In 1912, Reinhardt's production of *Sumurun* was imported, and in 1914 Sam Hume mounted the first exhibit of the *new stagecraft* (as the European trends were called) seen in the United States. Besides designs by Appia, Craig, and several of Reinhardt's artists, the exhibit also featured models of European theatres and stage machinery. After opening in Cambridge, Massachusetts, it moved to New York, Chicago, Detroit, and Cleveland. In 1915, Barker, in addition to bringing several of his productions, also mounted a new production of Anatole France's *The Man Who Married a Dumb Wife,* for which he commissioned designs from Robert Edmond Jones, which are now considered the first important native expression in the United States of the new stagecraft.

These developments were accompanied by other indications that innovative European ideas were being felt in the U. S. By 1912,

little or art theatres began to be founded, and by 1917 there were about fifty groups dedicated to presenting a series of plays for limited runs for subscribers (much in the manner of European independent theatres). Among the most important of these groups were the Chicago Little Theatre (headed by Maurice Browne and his wife Ellen Van Volkenburg), the Toy Theatre in Boston (under the direction of Mrs. Lyman Gale), the Neighborhood Playhouse in New York (established by Irene and Alice Lewisohn), the Washington Square Players in New York, the Provincetown Players (founded in Provincetown, Massachusetts, but soon moved to New York), and the Detroit Arts and Crafts Theatre.

The new spirit was also nurtured by colleges and universities. Although plays had been presented by college students since colonial days, course work in theatre was rare until 1903, when George Pierce Baker (1866–1935) initiated a class in playwriting at Radcliffe

College. This course was later opened to students at Harvard, and in 1913 a workshop for producing plays was added. To these courses came several persons—among them Eugene O'Neill, S. N. Behrman, Sidney Howard, Robert Edmond Jones, Lee Simonson, Winthrop Ames, Samuel Hume, and Hallie Flanagan—who would be leaders in postwar American theatre. In 1914, the Carnegie Institute of Technology inaugurated the first degree-granting program in theatre under the leadership of Thomas Wood Stevens (1880–1942). After the war, educational theatre would burgeon.

After 1900, many schemes for establishing a fully professional repertory company like those on the European continent were set forth in the U.S., and in 1909 the goal seemed possible when the New Theatre was opened in New York under the direction of Winthrop Ames (1871–1937). But the theatre was too large, and its affluent board and supporters insisted on employing the well-established stars E. H. Sothern and Julia Marlowe rather than seeking to develop an ensemble. The company lasted only two seasons. In 1912, Ames opened his own Little Theatre where he presented a repertory of meticulously mounted plays. But the 300-seat house proved too small to sustain itself in midtown Manhattan and had to be abandoned. Despite these setbacks, Ames was to remain one of the most progressive of producers both before and after World War I. Overall, the American theatre remained far behind that of Europe, but by 1915 the foundations for a vital postwar theatre had been laid.

RUSSIAN EXPERIMENTS

In Russia, the Moscow Art Theatre, although highly successful with actualistically mounted productions, almost immediately found itself under attack from nonrealists. In 1902, Valery Briussov (1873–1924), a leading symbolist, denounced the company for its "faithfulness to life," and argued that, since the stage is based on aesthetic conventions, conscious stylization rather than realistic imitation is needed. Another symbolist, Vyacheslav Ivanov (1866–1949), argued for a "theatre of congregate action" which, through myth-like drama in a "temple theatre," would unite spectators and performers in a "common ecstasy." Sologub (Fyodor Teternikov, 1863–1927) demanded that all barriers between the stage and auditorium be removed so that an "active audience" might assist in a "collective creation." For these and other reasons, Stanislavsky began to feel the necessity of finding a place for nonrealistic drama in the Moscow Art Theatre's repertory. In the season of 1904–1905, he presented a bill of Maeterlinck's one-act plays, but finding the results unsatisfactory, he decided it was necessary to explore, outside the confines of the theatre's repertory, methods of staging nonrealistic plays.

To direct this new studio, Stanislavsky turned to Vsevolod Meyerhold (1874–1940), who had studied acting with Nemirovich-Danchenko before becoming one of the original actors in the Moscow Art Theatre. After playing some eighteen roles, including Treplev in *The Sea Gull*, Meyerhold left the company in 1902 to form his own company, which, in the beginning, staged plays in much the same manner as the Moscow Art Theatre. Around 1903, Meyerhold became intensely interested in nonrealistic modes, and when Stanislavsky heard of these experiments, he invited Meyerhold to take charge of the new studio in 1905.

From the beginning, Stanislavsky and Meyerhold had differing views of the studio's goals. Stanislavsky seems to have envisioned an evolutionary process in which new means would gradually enlarge the old, whereas Meyerhold envisioned a complete break with past practices. Meyerhold was encouraged by

Briussov, who had been appointed literary advisor to the studio. Meyerhold began work on Maeterlinck's *The Death of Tintagiles,* but Stanislavsky became increasingly disturbed by what he considered Meyerhold's tendency to subordinate the actors to his directorial concept. The revolution of 1905 delayed the scheduled opening, and both the production and the studio were then abandoned. Work in the studio had begun on several projects, and surviving scenic designs indicate the direction Meyerhold was taking. In Hauptmann's *Schluck and Jau,* an artist's studio was represented by a huge easel canvas; in another scene, several identically costumed women embroidered in perfect unison on a single broad ribbon which was long enough to encircle the stage. Of the studio, Briussov declared that the director's and designer's work was entirely successful but that the actors were unable to break away from the training they had received in the parent company.

This studio drew the battle lines, epitomized by the work of Meyerhold and Stanislavsky, that were to shape the Russian theatre until World War II. In 1922 Yevgeny Vakhtangov explained the polarities: "For Meyerhold a performance is theatrical when the spectator does not forget for a second that he is in a theatre, and is conscious all the time of the actor as a craftsman who plays a role. Stanislavsky demands the opposite: that the spectator become oblivious to the fact that he is in a theatre and that he be immersed in the atmosphere in which the protagonists of a play exist." Throughout his career, Stanislavsky was to seek satisfying means for staging nonrealistic plays, but he seldom was content with the results, since all tended to subvert the sense of actuality and the kind of audience response he sought. Thus, although he closed the studio in 1905, he did not abandon his search for new methods.

Stanislavsky went on to stage Ibsen's *Brand,* Maeterlinck's *The Blue Bird,* and several other nonrealistic plays. One of his most interesting experiments came in 1907 with Leonid Andreyev's (1871–1919) *The Life of Man.*

FIG. 6.13
Andreyev's *The Life of Man* as staged by Stanislavsky at the Moscow Art Theatre. Setting by V. E. Egerov. (From *Moscow Art Theatre, 1898–1917,* 1955.)

Originally a realistic writer, Andreyev after 1906 wrote some thirty plays in the symbolist vein. For a time, he was the most popular of all Russian dramatists, but after the revolution his reputation declined rapidly. *The Life of Man* is more allegorical than symbolic. The characters have generic names (such as The Man and The Wife). At one side of the stage, Someone in Gray sits and by the light of a candle reads aloud the story of Man's life as the scenes unfold on the stage. For this production, Stanislavsky's designer, V. E. Egerov, hung the stage in black velvet and on it outlined doors, windows, and other details in white rope. The characters were also dressed in black and white. Against the black background, the characters seemed isolated in space and at times became almost invisible. The actors spoke as though making reports. Although the production was very popular, it was soon removed from the repertory because of Stanislavsky's unhappiness over the impossibility of his actors to create living characters in such an abstract play.

Around 1908, Stanislavsky became interested in Gordon Craig and invited him to stage *Hamlet* at the Moscow Art Theatre. (It was finally performed in 1912.) The association was not entirely happy. Craig designed three-dimensional screens intended to move quickly into new configurations to create different locales, but to Stanislavsky they seemed overly abstract. In addition, Craig's attempt to minimize many personal and subjective elements in the actors' characterizations led to disagreements. Ultimately, Craig would exert greater influence on Russian nonrealists than on the Moscow Art Theatre.

By 1917, the Moscow Art Theatre had undertaken a great many experiments with fragmentary scenery, directional lighting, and stylized acting. But Stanislavsky tended to be unhappy with deviations from illusionism, and few nonrealistic productions remained in the repertory. He found it difficult to reconcile stylization with his conviction that great acting is synonymous with realistic characterization and that the finest productions make the audience forget that it is in a theatre.

Most of the prerevolutionary innovative directors were linked to Vera Komissarzhevskaya (1864–1910), who had begun her enormously successful acting career in 1891 and had founded her own company in St. Petersburg in 1904. She declared realism "uninteresting and unnecessary" and sought to replace it with a "theatre of the spirit." Seeking a sympathetic director, she employed Meyerhold in 1906 after he had been dismissed by Stanislavsky. Their association was short-lived (it ended in 1907) for they proved incompatible. Meyerhold had recently read Fuchs' *The Stage of the Future,* and it apparently prompted him to adopt the relief stage. For Maeterlinck's *Sister Beatrice,* he used a platform only seven feet deep backed by a decorative screen. On this shallow stage, he created a production analogous to a bas-relief frieze in a Gothic cathedral. *Hedda Gabler,* usually staged with thoroughgoing realism, was mounted on a stage 33 feet wide and 12 feet deep. The walls and much of the furniture were blue-green; other furniture was white. (One large chair covered in white fur served as a kind of throne for Hedda.) Each character was costumed in a distinctive color and had a characteristic pose to which he or she always returned. In their most intimate scene, Hedda and Lövborg looked straight ahead at all times.

Meyerhold soon found this two-dimensionality unsatisfying and sought new inspiration in Alexander Blok's (1880–1921) *The Fairground Booth* (1906), a presentational combination of *commedia dell'arte* and the grotesque, to which Meyerhold would return often throughout his career. Meyerhold tried still another approach in 1907 with Wedekind's *Spring Awakening,* for which he placed all the scenic elements for the eighteen scenes on stage at the same time and used lighting to isolate that part of the stage needed for each scene. Today this solution may seem commonplace, but it was original at the time and only later was widely adopted by other directors for episodic plays requiring rapid transitions among locales. In his work with Komissarzhevskaya, Meyerhold privileged directorial concept over acting, virtually ignoring Komissarzhevskaya's great talent, around which the company had been built. Thus, it is not surprising that they soon parted.

Meyerhold was employed almost immediately as a director in St. Petersburg's imperial theatres, veritable strongholds of tradition, where he was to remain until 1917. Although many of his productions there were relatively conventional, others were not. One of the most innovative and popular was of Molière's *Don Juan* at the Alexandrinsky Theatre in 1910. For it, he removed the front curtain and footlights and extended the stage into the auditorium. For lighting, he used candles extensively and left the lights on in the auditorium. Much interested in Oriental theatre, Meyerhold borrowed from it the convention of using stage attendants to arrange the scene and carry properties on and off as needed. On either side of the stage, visible costumed prompters sat behind screens. Much of the actors' balletic movement was set to Lully's music.

At the imperial theatres, Meyerhold staged both plays and operas. His production of *Tristan and Isolde* in 1909 offered him the occasion to become thoroughly acquainted with the writings of both Wagner and Appia. Between 1908 and 1910 Meyerhold also published articles on Reinhardt and Craig, translated a Kabuki play, and staged one of Calderón's *autos*. Thus, his interests and knowledge continued to grow.

Between 1908 and 1917, Meyerhold was also associated with a number of studios, where he did most of his major experimentation with staging. At first, he was associated with Interlude House, a theatre converted into a cabaret by linking the stage and auditorium with steps and by replacing theatre seating with restaurant tables and chairs. Here he staged *Columbine's Scarf*, a pantomime adapted from Schnitzler's *The Veil of Pierrette*, in which Meyerhold once more returned to *commedia* and the grotesque. The whole production seemed to be controlled by the insistent rhythms of the orchestra, an impression enhanced when the conductor fled through the auditorium after Columbine committed suicide.

From 1913 to 1917, Meyerhold controlled his own studio, where he experimented and published a journal, *The Love for Three Oranges*. Here he explored patterned movement based on squares, circles, rectangles, and other shapes; had his students improvise pantomimes to various musical rhythms; sought to utilize techniques borrowed from the theatres of Japan and China; experimented with wholly nonrepresentational settings; and adopted uniform clothing for the actors. This list could be considerably extended, but it is sufficient to suggest Meyerhold's restless search for new and expressive means. Without doubt, he was the most innovative and persistent experimenter in the Russian theatre between 1900 and 1917.

Meyerhold's was a director's theatre, the first to deny primacy to the text. Meyerhold believed in the director's right to use a script merely as material to be reshaped (like scenery, costumes, and acting) into his own creations. To enlarge the possibilities open to him as a director, he explored older forms, other cultures, and contemporary sources, as well as experimenting with spatial relationships (both among actors on stage and between actor and audience) and with technical means (including speech, movement, and rhythm). His search would continue and intensify after the revolution of 1917.

Theodore Komissarzhevsky (1882–1954) grew up around the theatre (his father was an opera star) and had studied architecture before becoming scenic director for his sister's theatre at about the same time Meyerhold came to work there. He soon came into conflict with Meyerhold who, he charged, fitted actors into scenery instead of fitting scenery to the actors. When Meyerhold left, Komissarzhevsky became artistic director of the theatre and shared directorial duties with Nikolai Evreinov and A. Zonov, a former assistant to Meyerhold. The theatre was unable to survive its financial setbacks (many of them blamed on Meyerhold) and was closed in 1909. Komissarzhevskaya went on tour hoping to recover her fortunes and reopen her theatre, but in 1910 she contracted smallpox and died.

Between 1910 and 1919 (when he emigrated to the West), Komissarzhevsky was involved with many of Russia's major theatres. During his last year in Russia, he was running four theatres and a school. Like Meyerhold, Komissarzhevsky was opposed to realism and was much interested in *commedia dell'arte* and in reinterpreting the classics. But he disapproved of Meyerhold's subordination of the actor to visual elements just as he did of Stanislavsky's emphasis on realistic detail. Above all, he thought the director should serve the author but, because each author differs, the director must adapt his approach accordingly. He was the most eclectic of Russian directors.

Komissarzhevsky's eclecticism extended beyond Reinhardt's into a working method best described as *internal eclecticism*. Rather than choosing a style for a production and remaining consistently within it, Komissarzhevsky believed that each character and action has its own qualities for which the director must find some visual equivalent that will immediately set up

the right association for contemporary audiences. Thus, his productions combined elements from many periods and styles (all blended by Komissarzhevsky's impeccable visual sense)—thereby anticipating an approach now associated with postmodernism. In his productions, always heavily influenced by music, he sought for each scene and character an appropriate rhythm and tempo, which would allow him to orchestrate speech, pause, gesture, movement, and lighting like a musical score to create strong moods and emotionally charged dramatic action. Komissarzhevsky directed plays and operas from an extremely wide range of periods and forms. Gorchakov called him "the most profound thinker of all the prerevolutionary innovators." His influence can be seen especially in the work of Tairov and Vakhtangov.

For a time Komissarzhevsky shared directorial duties at his sister's theatre with Nikolai Evreinov (1879–1953), and later the two ran a theatre together. Evreinov's basic outlook was set forth in a famous essay, "Apology for Theatricality" (1908), in which he argued that there is an innate human instinct for transformation which makes each person wish to be someone else and to transform life into something more desirable. "To make a theatre of life is the duty of every artist. . . . The stage must not borrow so much from life as life borrows from the stage." Through highly controlled acting, masks, nonrealistic scenery, and lighting, the stage should reveal a life worth imitating. Out of these views, Evreinov shaped his concept of *monodrama,* through which he sought to transport spectators inside the play as direct participants by making them see everything from the viewpoint of the protagonist, the spectator's alter ego. These theories were most fully developed in Evreinov's *Monodrama* (1909) and *Theatre for Oneself* (1915–1917). His ideas about the power of theatre to transform society were to exert considerable influence on the Soviets, although they would use them to quite different ends.

Evreinov declared that the whole nineteenth century and its concern for realism had been erroneous, since it had sought to imitate rather than transform life and had separated audience and stage completely. To provide a basis for returning the theatre to its rightful path, Evreinov staged two seasons of plays, the first in 1907–1908 devoted to works from the Middle Ages and the second in 1911–1912 devoted to the Spanish Golden Age. For each production in these seasons, he attempted to recreate not only the stage conventions of the play's time but the entire milieu, including the incidental entertainments and the spatial relationships of audiences and performers. These productions were extremely successful; not only did they arouse interest in the theatre of other times but they also reintroduced many theatrical conventions from the past onto the contemporary stage.

Evreinov was also associated with two cabaret theatres, the Crooked Mirror and the Happy Theatre for Grown-up Children. Most of his cabaret pieces were short parodies of things he disliked in plays, operas, directing, and acting. One famous piece showed various directorial approaches to *The Inspector General*. His cabaret work set a standard for sophisticated revues for many years.

Alexander Tairov (1885–1950) joined Komissarzhevskaya's company in 1905, but left after becoming disillusioned with Meyerhold's subordination of acting to directorial concept. In 1913 he married Alice Koonen (1899–1974), who was to be his leading actress thereafter, and in 1914 he founded the Kamerny (Chamber) Theatre, which he was to direct until 1949. By the time of the revolution in 1917, he had staged fourteen works of widely varying types.

Tairov believed that the theatre should be kept free of all tendentiousness so that it could fulfill its role as an activity roughly analogous to the sacred dances of an ancient temple. He placed primary emphasis on emotion-charged gesture, which he considered the true art of theatre, and thought the ideal production would be one based on a scenario worked out collectively with the actors and filled out improvisationally in performance. But since few actors who could work in this way had yet appeared, he considered it necessary to reshape existing means as thoroughly as possible to achieve his goals.

Tairov believed that settings should resemble architecture rather than painting and that, above all, they should be functional for movement. Most of his sets were composed of steps, levels, and "sculptural" elements that changed appearance under skillfully manipulated lighting. His designers included Natalie Goncharova, Alexander Yakovlev, and Alexandra Ekster. Tairov, considering music to be the purest art, sought to approximate it in his productions by fusing all the elements through rhythm. Dialogue was intoned, and movement tended toward dance. His was an antiliterary theatre—polished, refined, and sensual—that sought to arouse a sense of deeply experienced beauty.

The Kamerny opened in 1914 with a production of the Sanskrit drama *Shakuntala,* transformed by Tairov into something resembling an opera-ballet. The brilliant compositions, half-naked bodies, processions, pantomimes, and subtle rhythms were greatly admired. The theatre's most famous prerevolutionary production was *Famira Kifared* by Innokenty Annensky, in which the Greek mythological theme was developed around a clash between the Dionysian and Apollonian—the ecstatic and the calm—with two distinctive rhythms dominating all the elements. As in all his productions, Tairov executed every detail faultlessly. He would

FIG. 6.14
Tairov's production of *Famira Kifared* by the symbolist poet Annensky at the Kamerny Theatre in 1914. The cubist settings and costumes were by Alexandra Ekster. (From *The Art of the Kamerny Theatre, 1914–1934*, Moscow, 1935.)

continue and extend this work in the post-revolutionary era.

THE BALLETS RUSSES

Still another Russian company—the Ballets Russes—was to exert great influence, especially in Western Europe. The Ballets Russes developed out of the World of Art group, which advocated the artistic principles and trends associated with Russian symbolism. The group took its name from the lavishly illustrated periodical, *World of Art,* launched in St. Petersburg in 1898 by Sergei Diaghilev (1872–1929). Each issue included reports from correspondents in Paris, Rome, Munich, and other European cities about literature, the visual arts, theatre, and music. It also began to explore the Russian past, especially icons and other forms that eschewed realism, and issued a number of monographs on Russian art which were to influence scenic design. Although the magazine ceased publication in 1904, the positions it had championed long continued to provide a focus for modernist tendencies.

The World of Art group promoted the arts in many ways. It organized exhibitions in Russia of paintings by such French artists as Degas, Renoir, and the late impressionists. (The interest these exhibitions stimulated are partially responsible for the excellent collection of modern painting now held by the Hermitage in Leningrad.) It also arranged "Evenings of Contemporary Music," which included works by Strauss, Debussy, Ravel, Scriabin, Stravinsky, and Prokofiev. Diaghilev also brought Russian art to the West. In Paris he mounted an exhibition of Russian painting in 1906, concerts of Russian music in 1907, and productions of Russian opera in 1908. But by far the greatest impact was made with a six-week season of ballet in 1909. An overnight sensation, the Ballets Russes reawakened intense interest in ballet and introduced a new type of stage decoration.

The ballets that made such a deep impression in the West were also new in Russia. During the last part of the nineteenth century, Russian ballet had been dominated by Marius Petipa (1822–1910), who placed great emphasis not only on technical excellence (which came to set the standard for the rest of the world) but also on long story-telling works with elaborate pantomime, scenery, and costumes in the pictorial-realistic mode. Typical of these were *Sleeping Beauty, Swan Lake,* and *The Nutcracker* with music by Peter Ilyich Tchaikovsky (1840–1893). After Petipa retired in 1903, leadership passed to Mikhail Fokine (1880–1942), who disliked the Petipa style and chose instead shorter subjects, which through innovative choreography he invested with a great sense of vitality. The dancers with whom he worked— among them Vaslav Nijinsky, Anna Pavlova, Ida Rubenstein, and Tamara Karsavina—and who went to Western Europe with Diaghilev,

were perhaps the best in the world. When the Ballets Russes first appeared in Paris, it was called the "Diaghilev miracle."

The effect was not created by dance alone. Of equal importance were the scenery and costumes. The major designers for the Ballets Russes were Leon Bakst (1866–1924) and Alexandre Benois (1876–1960). Bakst's work was characterized by a kind of oriental and barbaric splendor in which startling color combinations and decorative motifs blended to create an overpowering sensual effect. Benois was praised for his delicate handling of period motifs, but he was equally adept at creating the Chinese background for *Le Rossignol* and the Russian folk setting for *Petrouchka.* Other major designers were Alexander Golovin, Nicolas Roerich, Mstislav Dobuzhinshky, and Natalie Goncharova. There was nothing new in the technical means used for the scenic designs, since they relied on wings and drops.

FIG. 6.15
Bakst's design for *Tamar* at the Ballets Russes, 1912. (From the souvenir program.)

FIG. 6.16

Costume design, "The Beautiful Princess," by Bakst, for the Ballets Russes production in 1910 of Stravinsky's *The Firebird.* (From the Museum of Modern Art, New York.)

The novelty lay in the stylization achieved through unusual coloration, compositions, and decorative motifs. Many of the settings made considerable use of perspective painting, but it was a forced perspective that did not seek to give a sense of reality or to cheat the eye. Other settings deliberately avoided perspective and adopted the flatness typical of primitive painting, icons, and folk art. No doubt this convention was also influenced by the then-popular *art nouveau,* with its posterlike flatness. Mikhail Larionov and Natalie Goncharova

were especially fond of this technique. The stylization, deliberate avoidance of illusionism, riotous color, and exotic detail made a profound impression on Parisian audiences in 1909.

The effect was probably owing also to the care with which spectacle, music, and choreography were coordinated. The creators of the Ballets Russes were conscious of working to develop a *Gesamtkunstwerk* in the Wagnerian sense. All of those involved in a ballet worked together from the beginning. Not only did Bakst, Benois, and other designers provide settings, they often conceived the scenarios. For example, Bakst supplied the scenarios for *Scheherazade, Tamar,* and *The Afternoon of a Faun* (based on Mallarmé's poem), while Benois conceived *Armide's Pavilion.* Stravinsky collaborated with Benois on *Petrouchka* and with Roerich on *The Rite of Spring.* In several instances, composers worked directly with the choreographers and the designers.

The impact made by the Ballets Russes in 1909 was so great that Diaghilev soon formed a permanent company to tour the major cities of western Europe. It was to exert unprecedented influence both on ballet and scenic design until Diaghilev's death in 1929.

THE FRENCH REVIVAL

The appearance of the Ballets Russes in Paris signaled a theatrical reawakening there, for after the feverish activity in the 1890s France had virtually abandoned experimentation and had remained largely indifferent to developments elsewhere. The Ballets Russes forced the French to recognize how far behind the rest of Europe they had fallen. This impression was confirmed in 1910 when Jacques Rouché (1862-1957) published *Modern Theatre Art,* a description of the work of Reinhardt, Fuchs, and Erler in Germany; Stanislavsky, Komissarzhevskaya, and Meyerhold in Russia; and the theories of Appia and Craig. Rouché also set forth a program of reform.

Rouché decided to implement his recommendations by establishing the Théâtre des Arts, which he headed from 1910 to 1913. In imitation of the Ballets Russes, he appointed a committee of artists (including Maurice Denis, Xavier Roussel, Maxime Dethomas, and Edouard Vuillard) to design settings, costumes and properties, to advise on gesture and movement, and to assist in achieving visual unity. All of the artists he chose had matured during the 1890s; he ignored the more contemporaneous fauvists and cubists. Thus, the visual style of the Théâtre des Arts reflected the tastes of somewhat older artists, especially Maxime Dethomas (1867–1929), the most successful of Rouché's designers. Rather than extreme stylization, they favored simplicity of line, elimination of nonessential detail, and subtle coloration.

Rouché was more responsible than anyone else for the renewed interest in experimentation in the French theatre. In 1913 he gave up the Théâtre des Arts to assume the direction of the Opéra, where he remained until 1936 and where, with the assistance of Dethomas and the choreographer Serfe Lifar, he revitalized the repertory.

By 1913, Rouché had inspired others to take up the task of renovation. In 1912, Lugné-Poë revived his Théâtre de l'Oeuvre (which he was to direct until 1929) and presented *The Tidings Brought to Mary,* the first of Claudel's plays to reach the stage. Jean Variot, the designer, acknowledged his indebtedness to the Munich Art Theater. On either side of the stage he erected a fixed structure (to simulate the Art Theater's inner proscenium), and behind it he used a series of extremely stylized painted drops in conjunction with essential properties and furniture. In 1913, for *Hamlet,* Variot used conventions borrowed from the *Shakespeare-bühnen.* The forward part of the stage was surrounded by a permanent unit with a door at either side and a large arch at the back; this neutral architectural unit, formalized further by a pattern of heraldic devices painted on it, was supplemented with simple, evocative properties and set pieces.

The most important event in the French theatre of the time occurred in 1913 when the Théâtre du Vieux Colombier was founded by Jacques Copeau (1879–1949), who would dominate the French theatre between the two world wars as thoroughly as Antoine had in the years before World War I. By 1913, Copeau had served as dramatic critic and editor of several journals and had been initiated into the theatre in 1911 when Rouché produced Copeau's adaptation of *The Brothers Karamazov.* In "An Essay on the Renovation of the Drama" published in 1913, Copeau acknowledged his admiration for Rouché (while deploring his overemphasis on decor) and his dissatisfaction with Antoine's realism. He proclaimed that the renovation of the stage required a return to the bare stage (*le tréteau nu*), since only then could attention be focused fully on the actor, the essence of the theatre as the "living presence" of the author. For Copeau, the director's ultimate task was the transformation of a written text, which the director has studied until he understands its every nuance, into a "poetry of the theatre," of which acting is the principal ingredient and in which decor should be reduced to absolute essentials.

With the financial assistance of several leading literary figures, Copeau acquired an out-of-the-way theatre and had it remodeled by Francis Jourdain into the Théâtre du Vieux Colombier. (After the war, it would be remodeled along somewhat different lines by Louis Jouvet.) It had a forestage forward of a proscenium but no machinery except for a set

FIG. 6.17
A Woman Killed With Kindness, the first production of the Vieux Colombier in October 1913. (From *Le Théâtre*, 1913.)

of curtains and asbestos hangings that could be moved on rods to effect rapid changes of locale. To these curtains, only the most essential furniture and set pieces were added as needed.

During the summer of 1913, Copeau assembled a company of young actors—including Charles Dullin, Louis Jouvet, Suzanne Bing, and Romain Bouquet—and took them to the country (following Stanislavsky's example) to rehearse a repertory of diverse plays. The theatre opened in October 1913 with Heywood's *A Woman Killed With Kindness* and later presented fifteen works by Molière, Shakespeare, and several modern playwrights before being forced to close by the start of war in 1914. It was not to reopen in Paris until 1919.

In some respects, Copeau's theatre resembled Poel's, but Copeau adopted the bare stage out of aesthetic conviction rather than from a desire to recreate the conditions of an earlier period. Furthermore, Copeau was dedicated to training actors, whereas Poel's performers were often second-rate and were not part of an ongoing company. Furthermore, Copeau was ultimately interested in the renovation of contemporary drama rather than in presenting the work of a long-dead writer. Above all, Copeau wished to serve the dramatist through the scrupulous rendering of his text. His was an ascetic—almost religious—approach requiring absolute dedication.

NEW TECHNOLOGY

The struggle to create a new art of the theatre was accompanied by another search—for the new technology capable of realizing that art. This search can be traced back to the beginning of the modern era, when realism was creating the need for devices capable of shifting three-dimensional settings efficiently. The need was strong, since during the last part of the nineteenth century the time required for scene changes sometimes added as much as an hour to the playing time. Edwin Booth (1833–1893), now remembered primarily as one of America's greatest actors, was among the first to devise new methods of scene shifting. In 1869 he opened his Booth's Theatre in New York, where he staged some of the most lavish productions then to be seen. This theatre apparently was the first in modern times to have a level stage floor. It also had a number of elevator traps powered by water-driven rams which allowed heavy, scenic pieces to be set up beneath the stage and then raised noiselessly to stage level in seconds. In addition, this theatre was the first in New York to have a stage house sufficiently tall to permit drops to be flown out of sight without being rolled or folded.

FIG. 6.19

Sectional plan of the Madison Square Theatre, opened by Mackaye in 1879. Note the two stages, one above the other, mounted in a large elevator shaft. (From *The Scientific American*, April 5, 1884.)

Booth's pioneering efforts were extended by Steele Mackaye (1842–1894), one of the most inventive men of the American theatre. At the Madison Square Theatre in 1879, Mackaye installed two stages, one above the other, inside an elevator shaft 114 feet deep. The stages, each 31 by 22 feet, could be moved to any of three locations—basement, stage level, or attic—permitting one set to be changed while another was in use at stage level. One stage could replace another in forty seconds. This is the first example of an entire stage mounted on an elevator. In 1884, the Budapest Opera House installed its Asphaleian stage (named for the Austrian Asphaleia company), which was divided into three sections (from front to back), each mounted on elevators, which could be raised, lowered, or

FIG. 6.18

Backstage at Booth's Theatre, New York, in 1870. Note the elevator traps. (From *Appleton's Journal*, 1870.)

tilted. After 1900 elevator stages of this type came into wide use in Europe. Such stages could be used to raise scenery to stage level or lower it into the basement, or sections could be raised above stage level to create platforms of the desired height. But, since the elevator stage had the disadvantage of being restricted to vertical movement, other still more versatile means were sought.

One of the most prolific inventors of the period was Karl Lautenschlager (1843–1906). With his interest in the potential of electricity as a technological force, he became a pioneer in the use of electric motors to operate heavy stage machinery. In 1882, for the International Exhibition of Electricity held in Munich, he created a theatre operated entirely by electricity. Perhaps his most important contribution was the introduction into western Europe of the revolving stage (a device invented in Japan), which in 1896 he installed in the Residenz Theater in Munich. After 1900, revolving stages were installed at the Deutsches Theater in Berlin, the Moscow Art Theatre, and many others.

A third solution was the rolling platform. At first, small wagons were mounted on casters to move heavy units on and off stage, but in 1900 at the Royal Opera House in Berlin, Fritz Brandt (1846–1927) introduced large platforms moved on and off stage by means of wheels set in tracks. This arrangement permitted entire settings to be mounted on platforms offstage and then moved onstage. It also required extensive wing space and created problems with noise as sets were changed just offstage while the performance proceeded. To overcome these difficulties, Adolf Linnebach (1876–1963), first at the Dresden Schauspielhaus in 1914, divided the stage floor into three sections, each of which could be raised to stage level by elevators; when lowered to the basement, they could move horizontally in tracks to an area where scenery was mounted;

at stage level, each could move up or down stage on tracks. Thus, while one set was in use, another could be raised behind it; when the scene ended, the setting in front could sink to the basement and the one that had been behind it could roll forward.

As Linnebach's invention demonstrates, solutions were sometimes combined. By 1915 almost every possible combination of elevator, revolving, and sliding stages had been attempted. The majority of such complex machinery was installed in Germany, since in countries without subsidized, resident companies the devices were suspect because productions often toured to theatres where such machinery was not available. Consequently, in most theatres shifting continued to be done manually, supplemented by such means as small wagons and overhead battens. When realism began to decline, many critics thought elaborate machinery would become obsolete (since its invention had been motivated by the need to shift actualistic settings), but it was soon evident that nonrealistic sets, such as abstract arrangements of steps and platforms, also benefited from mobility. Consequently, elevator, revolving, and sliding stages continued to play a prominent role in theatres equipped with such machinery.

Heavy machinery also encouraged the use of structural steel and concrete in theatre architecture. Such materials served still other purposes by making it possible for the first time to cantilever auditorium balconies and eliminate supports that had obstructed sightlines. Aisles were relocated to ensure seating at the spots most advantageous for seeing and hearing, and in most new theatres, boxes were eliminated, not only because they were badly located for seeing and hearing but also because of the growing concern for cultural democracy. Despite these changes, theatre architecture remained wedded to the proscenium arch. A few small theatres sought to bridge the barrier between auditorium and stage by adding forestages or steps, but with a few exceptions, most notably Appia's theatre at Hellerau, the proscenium remained intact.

Other innovations stemmed from increased concern for lighting. In 1879 Edison invented the incandescent lamp, and by 1881 the Savoy Theatre in London was lighted entirely by electricity. The Stadttheater in Brunn (Austria) installed electricity in 1882, as did the Bijou Theatre in Boston. Thereafter the switch from gas to electricity was rapid, especially after two disastrous fires attributed to gas—the Opéra Comique in Paris and the Exeter Theatre in England—took hundreds of lives in 1887. By 1900 almost every major theatre in the world had changed to electricity. Control-boards were available for use with electricity from the beginning. The board installed in the Residenztheater in Munich in 1883 had twenty-nine circuits, each of which could be set at twenty-five different grades of intensity, while several circuits could be coupled and controlled by a single lever.

Nevertheless, by 1900 there had been few advances over gas. Since the wattage of lamps was low (100 was the maximum), incandescent lamps were used primarily for footlights, borderlights, and striplights, or in groups of ten or twelve mounted in a single housing for floods (*bunchlights*). Bright beams of light still depended on the limelight or carbon arc. Then in 1907 the introduction of tungsten filaments made lamps up to 500 watts feasible, and in 1913 the replacement of gas-filled with vacuum lamps made 750–1,000 watt lamps available. In 1911, a concentrated filament made it possible to develop spotlights designed to use incandescent lamps in conjunction with lenses and reflectors. By 1915, single-source floodlights were replacing bunchlights, and spotlights were replacing arclights and limelights.

Equally important, the demand for three-dimensionality, plasticity, and atmospheric ef-

fects led to many experiments with distribution, direction, intensity, and color in lighting practice. Because of the unnatural shadows they created, footlights came under increasing attack, and many theatres eliminated them. This did not create serious problems so long as the action remained upstage of the proscenium, but when directors began to utilize the forestage, new lighting positions had to be found. As spotlights were developed, they came to be mounted on the front of balconies or in ceiling apertures, although this was still a novelty in 1915. Lighting from the side, rear, or from above (to emphasize shape and dimension or to create atmosphere) began to play a prominent role. Numerous methods of attaining color (dipped lamps, glass filters, silk reflectors) were also tried.

The most ambitious lighting system of the period was designed around 1903 by Mariano Fortuny (1871–1949), who thought an acceptable lighting system had to be able to simulate both direct and reflected light (as in nature). Direct light offered little challenge, since it could be supplied easily by the available instruments, but Fortuny found reflected light more difficult to simulate. Eventually he succeeded by projecting light onto panels of colored silk, from which it was reflected onto a neutral-toned, spherical cyclorama, from which it was in turn reflected onto the stage. Because of its inefficiency (and consequent high cost), the system was never fully developed. Nevertheless, Fortuny's division of light into direct and indirect (specific and general) and his analysis of the means to attain satisfactory results remained influential. Furthermore, his neutral-toned cyclorama became standard in most theatres. In Germany, it often took the form of a fixed plaster-dome (the *Kuppelhorizant*), but elsewhere it was more often made of cloth and mounted so it could be raised out of sight when unneeded. The cyclorama served many purposes: its shape and height encouraged theatres to dispense with obtrusive borders, it created a sense of infinite space, and it provided an ideal surface for lighting, including projections—which began to be used in the theatre in the 1890s. Appia wrote about the scenic possibilities of projections, but prior to 1915 projections were used primarily for clouds, nonrealistic shapes, and atmospheric effects.

A related development was the motion picture. The desire to record visual appearance had motivated the development of photography during the nineteenth century, but until the 1890s it lacked one important ingredient—movement. In 1894, Edison invented the kineto-scope, which permitted one person at a time to view moving pictures through a peephole, and in 1895, moving pictures were projected onto a screen for the first time. At first this novelty was exploited primarily for its ability to record everyday, actual events. Georges Méliès (1861-1938) first recognized film's potential for fantasy, transformation, dissolves, and other effects impossible to achieve in more concrete media, although the significance of his work between 1896 and 1914 was not fully appreciated until much later. Around 1903, films with connected plots began to be popular, and the first motion picture theatres were opened around 1905. The early movie houses usually were small, but in 1914 the Strand Theatre, seating 3,300, was opened in New York. Meanwhile films had been increasing in length

and sophistication, and with D. W. Griffith's *Birth of a Nation* in 1915, a new era of full-length works with great emotional appeal began. Technology had created a new art—one that at times seemed to threaten the very existence of theatre but one that also opened up new possibilities. The film's ability to record far more elaborate and convincing spectacle than the theatre could provide also was to motivate many practitioners to re-evaluate the theatre's strengths and limitations.

TOWARD A NEW ART OF THE THEATRE

By 1915 comprehensive new theories of the theatre had been voiced by Appia, Craig, and others, and had been partially realized by such directors as Reinhardt and Meyerhold. Intense concern for theatre as an art was evident in the widespread inclusion of *art* in the titles of organizations. High idealism, along with the invocation of culture, beauty, and communion, was omnipresent. But neither the theory nor the practice had won the battle. Commercial producers and the mass audience still clung to dramatic stereotypes and realistic spectacle inherited from the nineteenth century. Nevertheless, audiences were being made aware of new theories and practices and, if not yet fully accepted, the innovations were well on their way toward forging a new art of the theatre.

Chapter 7

New Modes of Perception

Expressionism, Futurism, Dada, and Surrealism

Few eras have provoked so diverse and relentless questioning as did the years between 1910 and 1925. The sources of discontent were many, but all seemed to suggest that the perceptions inherited from the past were mistaken or overly restrictive and should be reexamined. These explorations gave rise to countless artistic movements, of which even the names of some—such as *orphism, rayonnism,* and *suprematism*—are now largely unfamiliar. But others, among them *cubism, expressionism, futurism, dada,* and *surrealism,* not only won widespread recognition but set in motion forces that are still potent. On the surface, the diverse strands may seem distinct, at times even in conflict, but they were unified in their rejection of the past and their attempt to find new modes of perception and expression. Taken together, they constitute the third wave—of which realism-naturalism and symbolism were the first two—of that artistic experimentation that had begun in the nineteenth century. Some critics insist that this third wave constituted the only true avant-garde.

THE THEORETICAL CONTEXT

A common denominator among the movements that sprang up between 1910 and 1925 was skepticism about earlier modes of perception. Realism and naturalism had been based on the assumption that reality can be apprehended through systematic observation of objective phenomena. Contrarily, symbolism had sought truth in inexpressible intuitions. The realist-naturalist outlook came to seem overly materialistic; the symbolist view, overly vague. Both had located reality outside the human subject.

Many of the new movements placed considerable emphasis on the unconscious, especially after 1910 when Freud's theories were given a new dimension by Carl Jung (1875–1961). Originally a friend and disciple of Freud, Jung, beginning in *Psychology of the Unconscious* (1912), suggested significant emendations to Freud's views. Because he thought Freud's description of the mind was incomplete, he posited still another layer, the *collective unconscious.* He argued that the human brain has acquired its structure in part through dealing, generation after generation, with certain basic experiences, and that, because of this structure, the brain responds more fully to some stimuli (those Jung called *archetypal*) than to others.

According to Jung, the collective unconscious is "nothing but a possibility . . . which from primordial time has been handed down to us in the definite form of mnemonic images, or expressed in anatomical formations of the very structure of the brain." It incorporates "the psychic residua of numberless experiences of

the same type." Jung considered the collective unconscious to lie beyond the reach of psychoanalysis: "by no analytical technique can it be brought to conscious recollection, being neither repressed nor forgotten." Thus, Jung pushed concepts of the unconscious a step beyond Freud and suggested explanations other than those proposed by Freud for psychological responses.

Jung also described two basic types of personality—introverted and extroverted—and two kinds of art related to them, one grounded in the personal unconscious and the other in the collective unconscious. Since introverted art is limited by the author's personal vision, the second is more profound because it activates (through archetypes, symbols, or myths) the collective unconscious. "The moment when the mythological situation appears is always characterized by a peculiar emotional intensity; it is as though . . . forces were unloosed the very existence of which we had never even dreamed. . . . At such moments we are no longer individuals but the race."

Jung's ideas about myth, symbol, and archetype were reinforced by other ideas then being voiced by cultural anthropologists. The scientific revolution of the nineteenth century had given rise to several new disciplines, among them anthropology, one branch of which was concerned with the cultural patterns of earlier societies. Out of this interest came J. G. Frazer's (1854–1941) monumental *The Golden Bough,* a comparative study that traced how the same basic mythic patterns are found in almost all societies, despite lack of contact among them. His work was extended into the study of Greece and Rome by the Cambridge school of classical anthropologists—among them F. M. Cornford, who wrote on the ritual origins of comedy; Gilbert Murray, who studied the ritual bases of tragedy; and A. B. Cook, who traced the god-king as a ritual figure. This group, like Nietzsche, promoted the idea that all art and drama originated in ritual and that myth is merely the residue of rite (that is, that myths are stories that grew up around rites, either to explain or to mask them, and then survived the rites they accompanied). They also sought to uncover patterns and structures that secular art forms had inherited from myth.

Related developments were underway in linguistics. Ferdinand de Saussure (1857–1913), in his *Course in General Linguistics* (published posthumously, 1916), was concerned not so much with the individual act of speaking (*parole*) as with the structure of language or sets of relationships (*langue*) that undergird the individual speech act and make it possible. (Saussure's *structuralism* had little immediate influence outside linguistic circles, but following World War II, it would affect practically all fields of learning. It will be discussed again in a later chapter.) Thus, Saussure, the anthropologists, and Jung shared a concern for patterns (concealed archetypes, variants on the same myths, embedded structures) buried beneath seemingly uncomplicated surfaces but which, once unearthed, reveal significant new perceptions about the nature of language, social bonding, communication, and art. One implication was that the surface (the immediately observable) is less significant than the subterranean, universal pattern, of which an observable phenomenon is merely one manifestation. These ideas provoked renewed interest in myth, archetype, and symbol as keys to the unconscious and to art.

Developments in physics were also to influence, directly or indirectly, practically all twentieth-century thought. Albert Einstein (1879–1955) was the person most responsible for amending Newtonian physics, in which physical laws had been formulated in relation to fixed points of reference. Einstein, in articles and books published from 1905 onward, set forth his theory of relativity (eventually proven correct through experiments) that amended Newtonian concepts. This theory is too complex to pursue fully, but essentially it posited that variations in the perception of a phenomenon by observers located at different places or moving at different speeds demand that concepts of absolute space and absolute time be replaced by a four-dimensional continuum: space-time. Perhaps more important here, the general public rapidly transformed Einstein's theory of relativity into the concept of relativism, a result quite foreign to Einstein's goals, since he never doubted the orderliness of the universe or the possibility of formulating a theory that would harmonize all of the apparent variables. For most people, nevertheless, relativity came to mean that all perceptions (especially about morality and aesthetics) are subjective and unverifiable.

Most important here, the questions raised about time and space were to affect artistic practice profoundly. In painting, space had, since the Renaissance, been conceived as fixed, and objects had been depicted as viewed from a single eye-point at a specific moment in time. The entire logic of perspective painting was based on this convention. The first major break from this tradition came in the late nineteenth century when Paul Cézanne began to include in a single painting objects that could only have been seen from different eye-points. But it was cubism (usually dated from 1907) that first systematically introduced into a single painting several points of view, no one of which had more authority than the others. Pablo Picasso and Georges Braque, the leading cubists, broke down objects geometrically into cubes, spheres, cylinders, and cones, and provided several views of the same object simultaneously. Thus, cubism not only treated space analytically but also incorporated the dimension of time.

Similar innovations can be seen in drama. Whereas painting is essentially a space art, drama is primarily a time art (that is, composed of successive occurrences that are experienced in sequence). Traditionally in drama, time had been treated as linear (events occurring in orderly sequence from beginning to middle to end) rather than as simultaneous or random. Just as fixed space had governed painting, so orderly sequence of time had governed drama. Consequently, most plays were unified through a cause-to-effect arrangements of incidents. Using this approach, the playwright set up in the opening scenes all of the necessary conditions—the situation, the desires and motivations of the characters—out of which the later events developed. The story made sense because of the sequential and causal relationships among events. Less often, dramatists had used thought to unify incidents (as in Aristophanes' comedies and medieval morality plays). Here the logic of thesis and supporting evidence related the incidents to one another. It is a variation on this latter method that practically all nonrealistic dramatists have adopted, for most have organized their works around some central theme or motif. But the specific form that such organization takes depends in large part upon the assumptions about reality made by the playwright. Most dramatists prior to the modern period assumed that ours is a logical universe ruled over by a just God. Thus, behind any apparent chaos lay ultimate orderliness and justice. In such a world, the logic of cause and effect was fundamental. But beginning with symbolism, the world became merely mysterious. In *Pélleas and Mélisande,* the characters are led to slaughter like sheep, but for reasons that are never clear, either to them or to the audience. There is sequence but little causality (that is, one event follows another but is seldom caused by it).

Symbolist drama illustrates a characteristic feature of much modern art: the juxtaposition of elements whose relationships are uncertain. The effect is discontinuous—the audience is provided with fragments from which it must assemble a whole, and what the audience perceives depends upon its ability to supply missing connectives. This point can perhaps best be illustrated with a short poem by Guillaume Apollinaire, a leading theoretician, critic, poet, and dramatist of early twentieth-century France:

Three lit gas jets
The proprietor has lung trouble
When you're finished we'll have a game of
  backgammon
A conductor who has a sore throat
When you come to Tunis I'll have you smoke
  some kiff
It seems to rhyme.

These lines may evoke the experience of an outdoor cafe at night during which (perhaps) a streetcar passes, but the lines are independent, existing side by side. The sequence could be rearranged; all connectives are missing. The poem exhibits many of the qualities found in much modern art—abruptness, illogicality, discontinuity, obscurity—that in earlier periods would have been considered unfinished, inept, unacceptable. Much that is praised in the twentieth century would earlier have been considered pure amateurishness.

Between 1910 and 1925 such techniques as juxtaposition of disparate elements, discontinuity, multiple focus, and unity through theme or motif came into widespread use for the first time. Through such means, artists in all fields sought to express new modes of perception related to (though not necessarily accurately reflecting) the diverse, sometimes contradictory, ideas of Freud, Einstein, Jung, and others—about the unconscious, relativity, archetypal patterns, disruption, and chance.

EXPRESSIONISM

Among the movements that flourished between 1910 and 1925, the one most intimately connected with the theatre was *expressionism.*

Around 1901, expressionism gained currency as a label to distinguish the kind of painting done by Van Gogh and Gauguin from the works of impressionists, who sought to analyze and capture the appearance of objects as seen under a certain light at a particular moment. By contrast, expressionism was thought to project the painter's strong feelings into objects, often through distortion. Thus, in expressionism truth or beauty was said to reside in the mind rather than (as in impressionism) in the eye.

In Germany, expressionism was adopted as a label for tendencies already underway both in literature and the visual arts. Although those called expressionists varied widely in outlook and method, most agreed upon certain points. They were opposed to realism and naturalism because those movements glorified science and technology, which the expressionists associated with materialism. They also disliked naturalism's emphasis on external appearance. They were equally contemptuous of symbolism because of its flight from contemporary social problems. Thus, although they were willing to accept as valid truth the realists' concern for modern problems and the symbolists' antirealistic techniques, they found both movements unsatisfactory.

The expressionists believed that fundamental truth is to be found within humanity—its spirit, soul, desires, visions—and that external reality should be reshaped to make it possible for the human spirit to realize its highest aspirations. Subjective vision was given priority over objective appearance: "We expressionists . . . are overcome by visions. . . . We do not reproduce but create."

Some historians have divided expressionist dramatists into two basic groups: the mystics and the activists. The mystics tended to depict humans as struggling to free the spirit from the limitations of material existence. Much of their drama had a messianic tone, seeking as it did the "regeneration of humanity" and the

creation of the "new man." The activists often expressed their desire to destroy materialism and all the trappings of an industrial society. In 1917, Ludwig Rubiner stated both the utopian and the destructive goals: "We want to arouse by means of heart-shaking assaults, terrors, threats, the individual's awareness of his responsibility in the community! . . . We are the scum, the offal, the despised. We are the holy mob. We do not want to work because work is too slow. . . . We believe in miracles. . . . For us destroyer is a religious concept, inseparable for us today from creator." Overall, the expressionists sought a world free from war, hypocrisy, and hate, where social justice and love would reign, where the new man would be free from materialistic urges and live by humanitarian principles.

The drama written to embody this vision has a number of characteristics. First, because it is "message-centered," most expressionist drama is organized primarily through idea, theme, or motif rather than through cause-to-effect sequence. The action in many plays takes the form of a search, pilgrimage, or "stations" on the road to martyrdom. Second, the central character, most often a Christ-like figure, is usually sacrificed to the materialism, hypocrisy, or callousness of the other characters. The events are sometimes given a strongly subjective bent because they are seen through the eyes of the central figure. Third, dramatists typically seek to reduce each element to its essentials. Plots may be mere demonstrations of a thesis or argument, and characters entirely generic (Husband, Son, Soldier, Mother, Prostitute, Minister, and so on). Dialogue is frequently reduced to one-word or two-word sentences (the "telegraphic" style), and gesture and pantomime are usually chosen for their ability to evoke through succinctness some intense feeling. Fourth, distortion is evident in every element. Often events are bizarre (corpses rise from their graves, a man carries his head in a sack, characters are identical in appearance) in order to illuminate some point in the play's argument. Distortion is especially evident in the visual elements. Walls may lean inward to suggest oppression; trees may change into skeletons as precursors of death; characters may move mechanically to indicate dehumanization; color, shape, and size of objects may be distorted to emphasize departures from everyday reality. Light is often used to arouse a strong sense of mood, to give unusual coloration, or to isolate characters in a void. Fifth, sharp contrasts are omnipresent. Dialogue often alternates between poetry and prose, idyllic passages and obscenities, telegraphic speeches and lengthy monologues. Realistic scenes may fade into dream visions, and brutality into transcendental apotheoses. Sixth, the works are permeated with a sense of dreamlike fantasy and magic, sometimes ecstatic, sometimes frightening. Seventh, the overall impression is one of allegory clothed in nightmare or vision.

The influences on expressionist drama were numerous. They include the doctrine of democratic love and the free verse forms of Walt Whitman, the writings of Freud and Jung on the unconscious, and the dramas of Kleist, Grabbe, and Büchner. Another pervasive influence was Goethe's *Faust,* with its dramatization of the search for spiritual fulfillment. In fact, some critics have labeled the entire expressionist outlook *Faustian.* But the most immediate influences were the dramas of Wedekind (a cycle of whose plays were staged by Reinhardt in 1911) and Strindberg, especially *To Damascus* and *A Dream Play.* Between 1913 and 1915, more than 1,000 performances of Strindberg's plays were given in Germany.

Some critics consider the first true expressionist playwright to be Oskar Kokoschka (1886–1980), who in 1907 wrote two short pieces, *Sphinx and Strawman* and *Murderer, Hope of Women.* The first was staged by students at the Vienna School of Arts and Crafts in 1907 and was later enlarged into *Job* (1917). It translates inner states into visual symbols to create an allegory played out by masked marionettes with names such as Firdusi, Rubberman, Female Soul, and Death. Firdusi, an intellectual, poet, and idealist (represented as a gigantic, revolving straw head—that is, all head, a man of straw), is eventually destroyed by his wife's infidelity. Overall, the play is concerned with the destructive relationships of men and women and the struggle between passion and spirit. Similarly, *Murder, Hope of Women* gives a savage view of the relationship between the sexes.

Like Kokoschka, Vassily Kandinsky (1866–1944), was to be more famous as a visual artist than as a playwright. Between 1909 and 1914, Kandinsky wrote four plays—*The Yellow Sound, The Green Sound, Black and White,* and *Violet*—the titles of which suggest his elevation of visual elements over plot. It is difficult to give a reliable interpretation of these plays, but ultimately they seem concerned with the need to reconcile harmoniously the material and the spiritual. According to Peter Jelavich, Kandinsky sought a "counterpoint" of contradictions, in which sounds, sights, and movements express entirely different feelings and ideas simultaneously, but which in the end lead to a "mystic sensation of universal harmony." Kandinsky sought in his drama to embody his belief that, if people were uncorrupted by material civilization, they "would establish a community whose harmony, rooted in the spiritual [resonance] of common humanity, would encompass the seeming contradictions of personal differentiation." Kandinsky's dramas embody, almost in the extreme, the modernist characteristics of discontinuity, illogicality, obscurity, and disparateness. Perhaps for that reason, the plays have seldom been produced, although they have continued to present interpretational challenges for critics.

The plays of Kokoschka and Kandinsky are not typical of expressionist drama, which is more commonly all too clear in its messages. For that reason, some critics consider *The Beggar* (1912) by Reinhard Johannes Sorge (1892–1916) to be the first true expressionist play. In this piece, the primary conflict is between generations, the older represented by The Father (obsessed with machines and technology) and the younger by The Poet (who kills both of his parents and thereby is freed to devote himself to the ecstatic visions that come to him through his art). This allegorical play about the struggle of the new man to fulfill himself despite the obstacles of a materialistic, hypocritical society, dramatized a favorite theme of expressionist drama until about 1915. The same theme is found again in *The Son* (1914) by Walter Hasenclever (1890–1940), in which the protagonist threatens to kill his father (who as a result dies of a stroke) because his freedom to experience the full glory of life is restricted by his puritanical, materialistic parents.

With the coming of World War I, expressionism began to change, perhaps because the global conflict seemed the logical outgrowth of those mistaken values and outmoded social forms against which expressionists were in revolt. Several expressionist writers (among them Sorge) died in battle. Others, opposed to the war, fled to Switzerland, where they became involved with dada. Of those who remained in Germany, many suffered deep psychological trauma. Increasingly, expressionist dramatists abandoned personal concerns for warnings of impending catastrophe or pleas for the reformation of society. The change can be seen in the plays of Hasenclever, who abandoned themes of personal freedom to champion universal humanitarian values. His *Antigone* (1916) depicts a Kreon so obsessed with order and power that to maintain them he destroys everything, including the city. But Hasenclever does not permit the play to end on a wholly negative note. A Voice from the Grave cries out: "People, fall to your knees.

FIG. 7.1
A post-World War II production of Hasenclever's *The Son*, directed by Hans Schalla at the Schauspielhaus, Dusseldorf. (Photo by Liselotte Strelow.)

God has restored order." Now that Kreon's repressive power is destroyed, Antigone's regenerative love can flourish. In *Humanity* (1918), Hasenclever extended his indictment to include not only misguided rulers but humanity in general. Hasenclever seems to suggest that the regeneration of humanity itself is the prerequisite for a regenerated society. *Humanity* also utilizes many characteristic expressionistic devices in their most extreme form. At the beginning of the play, the protagonist rises from his grave and is handed his head in a sack. Later the head is used as evidence against him when he is accused, tried, and condemned as his own murderer. The dialogue is telegraphic; the scenes are brief, shifting in rapid, dreamlike fashion and lasting only long enough to make a point; everything is reduced to essentials. (The five acts take up only about thirty pages in print.)

Fritz von Unruh (1885–1970) underwent equally drastic changes. His prewar plays upheld militarism and obedience to authority but, after serving in the army, he had by late 1914 begun to denounce war. *One Race* (*Ein Geschlecht,* published in 1918) was written at the front and dedicated to his dead brother. The German title suggests several levels of meaning, not only one race (or humanity) but also a generation or a family, just as the play's family represents all humans. Eventually, the mother, understanding that her misguided values are what have brought destruction to her family, seizes the staff from an army officer as a symbolic rebellion. Only the Youngest Son survives, and he urges his comrades to storm "the barracks of violence."

In 1918, widespread revolution in Germany overthrew the government and brought an end to the war. For a time, optimism prevailed, as the expressionist vision seemed possible to achieve. Expressionism reached the peak of its popularity in 1919. In 1917 there were ten expressionist periodicals; in 1919 the number had increased to forty-four; by 1922 the number had declined to eight. This decline can be partially explained by the harshness of the Versailles treaty (and the economic hardship it imposed on the newly created Weimar Republic). Under these adverse conditions, postwar optimism gradually gave way to bitterness and the growing suspicion that human beings are beyond redemption. By 1924 expressionism had ceased to be a major force in German life.

Nowhere is the movement from optimism to pessimism more evident than in the work of the two major expressionist playwrights, Kaiser and Toller. Georg Kaiser (1878–1945), sometimes called the finest German dramatist between Hauptmann and Brecht, was the first German playwright to win acceptance abroad after the war. (Anti-German sentiments in large measure explain why expressionism remained essentially a German movement.) Kaiser wrote over sixty plays of various types. Most are dialectical demonstrations showing the awakening of the human will to act, or attempts to overcome mechanizing and dehumanizing forces. Today Kaiser is remembered primarily for *From Morn to Midnight,* (written in 1912) and the trilogy composed of *The Coral* (1917), *Gas I* (1918), and *Gas II* (1920). In *From Morn to Midnight,* the Cashier's pilgrimage or search unifies the play. In the opening scene, the Cashier is little more than an automaton, taking in and paying out money in a bank. Jarred out of his daily routine by the exotic, sensual Lady from Italy, he stuffs his pockets with money and follows her, thinking that, like everything else, she is for sale. Rejected by her, he cannot go back and consequently is forced to reassess his world. The remainder of the play is devoted to his search for something that will give meaning to his life: family, social forms, sensuality, religion. Finally, at a Salvation Army meeting, he recognizes that the road to fulfillment lies through the soul; but, when he flings away his stolen money, the supposedly repentant sinners fight for it like animals, and the Salvation Lass, in whom he had perceived his soul mate, betrays him for the reward. Thus, even religion has succumbed to the materialistic urge. When the police come to seize him, he backs into and is electrocuted on a neon cross. As with Christ, the world is not yet ready for the Cashier's message, although he has pointed the way.

From Morn to Midnight is a modern morality play for, as the title suggests, it uses a day to symbolize the length of human life, during which the Cashier-Everyman moves through the principal types of human experience. The characters are generic, and the situations are archetypal. The action takes place in a nightmarish atmosphere where, through distortion and condensation, everything is charged with strangeness. Kaiser's message is summed up in the final line of the play (spoken by the Policeman when the lights go out), "There must be a short-circuit in the main," which, though ostensibly referring to electricity, is a comment on a society that has short-circuited the human desire for spiritual fulfillment.

The Coral also follows a protagonist who gradually acknowledges the primacy of the soul. After a childhood of misery, the Billionaire has attained security through the enormous wealth he has accumulated at the expense of the poor. Led by his children to see his errors, he seeks to disrupt the materialistic forces of which he has become a part. This theme of the regenerated man is extended in *Gas I* to regenerated society. Its protagonist, the Billionaire's Son, enters into cooperative ownership with the workers in his gas plant (treated as a symbol of industrialization). When an explosion destroys the plant, the protagonist seeks to lead his workers back to a simpler, more fulfilling life. But the spokesman for industrialization, the Engineer, rallies the workers and, during the ensuing riot, the Billionaire's Son is killed. His daughter promises to carry on his fight.

Gas II has as its protagonist the Billionaire-Worker, to whom the daughter has given birth. All industry has now been placed under state control, and humans have become mere automatons in the service of a political machine. The Billionaire-Worker first seeks to stop the production of a deadly gas intended for use in war but, recognizing the futility, he sets off a cataclysmic explosion which will destroy the entire human race. The final stage direction reads: "In the mist-grey distance, sheaves of flaming bombs bursting together—vivid in self-extermination." Thus ended Kaiser's vision of regenerated man. Thereafter Kaiser abandoned expressionism. In 1933 his plays were banned in Germany, and in 1938 he fled to Switzerland. The most interesting of his later works is *The Raft of Medusa* (1943), which shows a group of English children adrift on a raft after their boat has been sunk by a German submarine. When they throw overboard the smallest and weakest child because he takes up space and food, Allan, one of the older children, is so disillusioned that, when a rescue plane arrives, he refuses to return to a civilization so lacking in human values. Left alone on the raft, he is strafed by a German airplane. Like Kaiser's earlier protagonists, Allan is a martyr to man's inhumanity, but Kaiser no longer holds out any hope for change.

The plays of Ernst Toller (1893–1939) reflect his own personal experiences. A university student at the outbreak of World War I, Toller volunteered for military duty and served for more than a year at the front before being released in 1916 following a breakdown. Now a confirmed pacifist, he took part in a strike of munitions workers and was imprisoned. While in prison he wrote *Transfiguration* (1918), his first major work. Alternating between realistic scenes and dream visions, the play shows events as seen through the eyes of Friedrich (easily identified with Toller) as he is transformed from a naive chauvinist into a

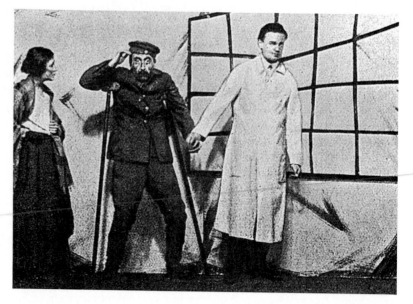

FIG. 7.2
Scene from a
production of Toller's
Transfiguration at the
Tribune Theater,
Berlin, in 1919,
directed by Karlheinz
Martin. (A
contemporary photo.)

militant rebel. Its dream sequences include one in which skeletons hanging on barbed wire in no-man's land perform a dance of death. At the end, Friedrich appeals to the masses to revolt against their leaders: "destroy them laughing, the false castles of illusion."

In 1918 a rebellion of workers did bring the abdication of Kaiser Wilhelm and the cessation of hostilities. In the following year, Toller was one of the leaders of a commune established in Munich following an uprising there. Upon its suppression, Toller was sent to prison again until 1924. While in prison he wrote one of his best-known plays, *Man and the Masses* (1920), in which the Woman seeks revolution through bloodless means, for she believes that people can be saved only by humanitarian principles. She is opposed by the Nameless One, who is interested only in overthrowing capitalism. He proclaims: "The masses count, not man. . . . Our cause comes first." The Woman replies: "People come first. You sacrifice to dogmas." The Nameless One fans the frustration of the

Masses into rebellion but, when it is put down, it is the Woman who is betrayed. Jailed and condemned to death, she is offered a chance to escape but refuses because it would mean killing her guard. As the title is meant to suggest, the Masses can be saved only when they recognize the value of Man; they cannot be transformed by adherence to a cause that merely substitutes one type of mechanization for another. The play ran in Berlin for two years and was produced throughout Europe and the United States.

Toller's last major work, *Hurrah, We Live!* (1927), is his most bitter. A revolutionary, released after several years of imprisonment, discovers that his old comrades have settled into comfortable lives and want to forget the ideals for which they had once fought. Believing that the world has gone mad, he commits suicide in despair. The play is prophetic: Toller, after fleeing the Nazis, committed suicide in 1939 when World War II broke out.

The disillusionment so evident in the works

FIG. 7.3
Design by Feuerstein
for a Czech
production in 1921 of
Karel Čapek's *R. U. R.*
(Courtesy Professor F.
Cerny, Charles
University, Prague.)

of Kaiser and Toller had by 1925 virtually brought the expressionist movement to an end, although residues persisted for a time, both in Germany and elsewhere. As late as 1930 the Austrian playwright Hans Chlumberg (1897–1930) achieved considerable success with *Miracle at Verdun,* in which 32 million war-dead rise from their graves in protest against the living who have learned nothing.

In Eastern Europe, expressionism reached its peak with *R.U.R.* (1921) by the Czechoslovakian Karel Čapek (1890–1938). It depicts an almost wholly mechanized world in which humans are served by Rossum's Universal Robots. (This play invented and popularized the word *robot.*) When the robots seize power, the world seems doomed to total dehumanization, but the unexpected stirring of love between two robots leads to an act of self-sacrifice and the hope of a new humanitarianism. Expressionism is inconsistently reflected in Čapek's other plays. *The Insect Comedy* (1921) explores various human philosophies

through such insect behavior as the butterflies' hedonism and the dung beetles' materialism. But, like the expressionists, Čapek seems to have become increasingly pessimistic. *Adam the Creator* (1927), written with his brother Josef (1887–1945), shows the protagonist blowing the world to pieces out of horror; forced by God to refashion it, Adam does so only to discover that his new world is precisely like the one he has destroyed.

A number of American playwrights borrowed techniques from expressionism, although none seems to have been committed to the expressionist vision. The most obvious examples are Elmer Rice's *The Adding Machine* (1923), Eugene O'Neill's *The Hairy Ape* (1922), and George S. Kaufman and Marc Connelly's *Beggar on Horseback* (1924). Indeed, expressionist techniques became the currency of nonrealist playwrights everywhere. The legacy of expressionism can be seen especially in the late 1960s when rebels against materialism and hypocrisy sought to discomfit the enemy through caricature and distortion, and proclaimed a vision of regenerated humanity.

EXPRESSIONIST PRODUCTION IN GERMANY

Expressionist drama was available to a reading public long before it was to theatre audiences, largely because the plays were denied licenses for production. The first public professional production of an expressionist drama did not come until 1916, when Hasenclever's *The Son* was presented at the German National Theatre in Prague (then part of the Austro-Hungarian Empire). The first public performances in Germany were given in 1917, but by the end of 1918 only eight theatres had presented expressionist plays. Most of these productions were

given for single or afternoon performances. Hasenclever's *Antigone* was banned after one showing. In addition to these public performances, a few private showings (to avoid censorship) had been given. In 1917–1918 Reinhardt instituted at the Deutsches Theater in Berlin a series of afternoon private performances of works by Sorge, Kaiser, Kokoschka, von Unruh, and others. He also published a magazine, *Das Junge Deutschland (Young Germany)* to accompany the plays. By the end of the war, then, only a few expressionist plays had been produced. Furthermore, most of them had been staged rather traditionally. Thus, both public presentation and the development of an appropriate performance style had to await the end of the war. Beginning in 1919, expressionist productions came into vogue, and a new approach developed rapidly.

FIG. 7.4
An example of expressionist design (by Ludwig Sievert for Brecht's *Drums in the Night*). Note that all vertical lines are distorted to diagonals and that the mood, thus, is tense and energetic. (From a contemporary design.)

The most common notion in expressionist drama is that the world of science and technology, established government, and traditional morality is a nightmare—that the external appearance depicted by realism and naturalism merely mask the horror that has distorted and is destroying the human spirit. Taking their clues from the plays, postwar directors and designers tended to emphasize the nightmarish through stylization and distortion.

In expressionist production, a subjective vision is simultaneously projected and commented on. To capture this double point of view, expressionist designers adopted a number of characteristic devices. Like the dramatists, they often reduced scenic elements to essentials. Black drapes or cycloramas were used to create a void in which characters and objects appeared and disappeared. This arrangement was especially useful in highly episodic plays with rapidly shifting locales. Light was an integral part of the design. It was used as a selecting device, since it permitted set pieces for several scenes to be placed on stage simultaneously and be picked out by light as needed. This was especially effective for plays in which one event faded into another as in stream of consciousness. Through selective lighting, the frame of vision could be narrowed to show only the face of one person or extended to include the entire stage. Light also created mood and atmosphere. Strongly contrasting light and shadow, extreme angles from the side, overhead, or the rear, intense or unusual coloration—all helped to arouse that nightmarish atmosphere in which the action passed. Probably no movement did so much to develop the expressive qualities of stage lighting.

Perhaps the most characteristic aspect of expressionist design was distortion—of line, color, mass, proportion, or balance. Diagonal lines, leaning walls, large blocks of bold color, enlarged furniture and properties, and other

exaggerations were used to project emotion into objects and to achieve a sense that the physical and the spiritual interpenetrate. Similarly, makeup and costume were more often used to reflect social roles, inner truth, or psychological state than to depict everyday appearance. The uniformity or mechanization of modern life was frequently suggested by dressing several characters identically. Caricature was common: the bloated capitalist, the general, the diseased seeker of carnal pleasure, the starving worker.

Acting was not based on everyday behavior. In the "Epilogue to the Actor" appended to his *The Seduction,* Paul Kornfeld advises: "Let him not be ashamed of the fact that he is acting.... The melody of a great gesture says more than the highest consummation of what is called naturalness. Let him think of the opera, in which the dying singer still gives forth a high C and with the sweetness of his melody tells more about death than if he were to crawl and writhe."

The triumph of expressionistic theatrical techniques is especially associated with two directors, Fehling and Jessner. Jurgen Fehling (1885–1968) did his most important work at the Berlin Volksbühne, which in 1915 had built one of the best-equipped theatres in Europe. Under the direction of Friedrich Kayssler, who had been one of Reinhardt's actors, the Volksbühne promoted expressionistic drama, perhaps because the theatre catered to the working class. (Volksbühnen flourished in Germany after 1918; by 1933 there were more than 300 separate groups.) In the years immediately following the war, the Berlin Volksbühne presented plays by Strindberg, Toller, Kaiser, and other expressionists.

Fehling was catapulted to fame in 1921 as the director of Toller's *Man and the Masses.* For this production, Hans Strobach designed an extremely simple setting, essentially a single unit composed of a platform and steps enclosed by black curtains within which light could be used to reveal or conceal sections of the stage. For the "dream visions," caricature and distortion were used extensively: perched on a fantastically high stool, a man recorded bids for war contracts in a giant ledger; when a new enterprise (a brothel disguised as a War Convalescents' Home) was created, the bankers fox-trotted to music suggesting jingling coins; when the Nameless One gained control over the Masses, he led them in a wild dance that gave the impression of a witches' sabbath. Throughout, the Masses were used to create striking effects through movement and sound. Fehling's production was considered revolutionary, in large part because, despite the many locales indicated in the script, virtually no scenery was used to indicate specific place. Major attention was paid to mood, created by shafts of light, music, and the chorus-like Masses. Although perhaps the most abstract staging yet seen in Germany, it elicited an overpowering emotional response. Because Fehling's reputation was made with expressionist drama, it is sometimes forgotten that he was one of Germany's most eclectic directors. His adaptability is perhaps best illustrated in his appointment under the Nazis to the directorship of the Berlin State Theater, the most prestigious of Germany's subsidized companies.

While Fehling was making his reputation as a director of expressionist plays, Leopold Jessner (1878–1945) was becoming even better known for his application of expressionist techniques to the plays of Shakespeare, Schiller, Hauptmann, and Wedekind. He is best known for his work while director of the Berlin State Theater between 1919 and 1925. Jessner used the same basic approach in nearly all his productions, on most of which he worked with the designer Emil Pirchan (1884–1957). His favorite scenic device was a permanent arrangement of steps and platforms, the appearance of which could be disguised or altered

through the addition of a few set pieces or properties and especially through curtains and light. Decorative detail was almost wholly abandoned. Perhaps his most famous production was of Shakespeare's *Richard III,* in which Richard's rise to power was indicated by his progress upward on the levels and by the growing intensity of the red costumes and background lighting. During the battle with Richmond, Richard was gradually forced to descend the stairs; as Richmond's strength grew, white diluted the red until, at Richard's death, it was entirely washed away.

Jessner's use of steps and levels became so well known that such an arrangement came to be called *Jessnertreppen* (Jessner steps), or alternatively *space staging*—suggesting an anonymous space that could be altered by the addition of set pieces and properties. This scheme not only provided a variety of playing areas but also could suggest varying levels of reality, serve as symbols of dominance and repression, or reinforce rhythmic and kinetic effects. Lighting also played an important role, not only to isolate scenes but to reflect the emotional states of the characters as well. Othello's jealousy might turn the entire cyclorama green and his rage change it to red. Costumes also reflected emotional states, and the actors' rapid speech and movement created a frenetic quality. Jessner's favorite actor was Fritz Kortner (1892–1970) who, after spending the Nazi years in exile, would be one of Germany's most respected directors following World War II. By 1925, Jessner's approach had come to seem monotonous. By the time he left Germany in 1933, his career was over.

Films also served to gain acceptance for expressionist techniques throughout the world. Perhaps the best-known of these films is *The Cabinet of Dr. Caligari* (1920), directed by Robert Weine. Several important theatrical directors also made films, among them Jessner, who directed Wedekind's *Earth Spirit* (1922),

FIG. 7.5
Setting for Jessner's production of *Richard III* at the Berlin State Theater in 1919. (From Bab, *Das Theater der Gegenwart.*)

and Karlheinz Martin, who filmed Kaiser's *From Morn to Midnight* (1920). Such films brought expressionism to audiences who otherwise would have remained ignorant of it.

Expressionism in the theatre seems to have reached its peak during 1923. After that time, audiences declined and critics began to find the plays repetitious. By the end of 1924, the movement was at a standstill. Nevertheless, its emphasis on inner vision and its production techniques made a lasting contribution, perhaps most easily traceable through the work of Brecht.

FUTURISM

Another movement—*futurism*—developed more or less simultaneously with expressionism. It was launched by the Italian poet Filippo Tommaso Marinetti (1876–1944) in an impassioned manifesto published in 1909. At first a literary movement, it was enlarged almost immediately to include the visual arts and music.

Like the expressionists, the futurists rejected the past and wished to transform society. But, whereas the expressionists associated the past with soul-destroying materialism and industrialization, the futurists deplored veneration of the past, perhaps because for the most part they were from an Italy that was not only industrially backward but also valued primarily for its artistic past. Consequently, the futurists glorified the energy and speed of the machine age and called for the destruction of all museums and libraries. In his manifesto, Marinetti wrote: "We declare that the world's splendor has been enriched by a new beauty: the beauty of speed. A racing motor car . . . is more beautiful than the *Victory of Samothrace.*" (In one of his best-known poems, "My Pegasus," Marinetti praised the racing car as the modern equivalent of the mythical winged horse). Their love of energy and aggression led the futurists to label war the supreme activity: "We wish to glorify

War—the only health giver of the world—militarism, patriotism, the destructive arm of the Anarchist, . . . the contempt for women.''

The futurists' pronouncements were publicized around the world. But the group was not content with such indirect contacts, and it sought direct confrontations with audiences. From 1910 onward, the futurists gave performances (*serate*), during which they read their manifestos, presented plays and concerts, exhibited visual art, and recited poems—sometimes several of these simultaneously. At times, they moved about among the spectators, using various parts of a hall sequentially or concurrently. Because of their militancy, they were soon considered the epitome of all that was new and dangerous. Welcomed by a few, they were more often greeted with barrages of fruit or physical violence. On several occasions, the evenings ended in true riots.

In their attempts to create art forms appropriate to a machine age, the futurists utilized various means. They created *picture-poems* (what today would be called *concrete poetry*) out of type of varying size arranged on the page in configurations designed to arouse sensations of movement, space, time, and sound. Their kinetic sculptures introduced the dimension of movement and energy into what had previously been a static form. Along with the cubists, the futurists invented collage, an ''assemblage'' of fragments torn from newspapers, cloth, or prints, thus making it possible to ''paint'' with any material. Some futurists also argued that modern utilitarian objects (such as wine racks and urinals) are more beautiful than the sculptures of old masters and entered such ''ready-mades'' in exhibitions.

In music, the futurists developed the notion of *bruitisme* or dynamic sound. They argued that, since every movement produces sound, noise is a reflection of the volcanic soul of life. Therefore, they orchestrated the sounds of everyday existence (along with abstract noise) to create musical works they thought more suitable to modern life than those created through traditional means. (Much of their work anticipates later developments in electronic and aleatoric music.) On one of their programs, the futurists included a ''noise symphony,'' using the sounds of pot lids, typewriters, and other machines to evoke the life of a modern city. *Bruitisme* was explained in *The Art of Noise* (1913) by Luigi Russolo (1885–1947), who also invented ''noise organs'' (*intonarumori*) upon which he and others gave concerts.

As in other areas, the futurists did not think conventionally about theatre and drama and, beginning in 1911, they published a series of manifestos demanding change. ''The Variety Theatre''(1913) proclaimed music halls, nightclubs, and circuses superior to traditional theatre as models for the drama of the future, and championed the variety theatre's carefree and unself-conscious atmosphere, rapid succession of disparate attractions, interaction of performers and spectators, mingling of elements from several media, and overall dynamism. It also suggested jarring spectators out of their conventional propriety through such practices as selling the same seat to more than one customer and leaving wet paint on some seats. ''The Futurist Synthetic Theatre'' (1915) condemned traditional drama for being lengthy, analytic, and static, and proposed to replace it with ''synthetic'' drama: ''That is, very brief. To compress into a few minutes, into a few words and gestures, innumerable situations, sensibilities, ideas, sensations, facts, and symbols.'' To promote their ideas, futurist writers published seventy-six short plays (*sintesi*) in 1915–1916, many of which were performed in several Italian cities. This was probably the futurists' most concerted effort to establish their presence in the theatre.

Sintesi varied widely in techniques and subjects. Some were distillations into a few lines of plays by Shakespeare and Alfieri. Most, however, sought to capture the essence of some mood, situation, condition, or sensation. One of the briefest is Francesco Canguillo's *Detonation* (1915): the curtain rises on a deserted road at night; silence; a gunshot, the curtain falls. Compression is exemplified in *Sempronio's Lunch* (1915) by Bruno Corra and Emilio Settimelli: in five short scenes Sempronio moves from the age of five to ninety as he eats lunch. Some plays seem to foreshadow those of Ionesco, as in Marinetti's *They Are Coming* (1915), in which furniture assumes more importance than people and eventually moves offstage by itself. Still others seek to involve the audience, as in Canguillo's *Lights* (1919): the curtain rises; total darkness which continues until the audience is provoked into shouting for light; sudden blinding light, the curtain falls. Some plays use simultaneity, as in Marinetti's *The Communicating Vases* (1916), in which three actions in three separate settings proceed concurrently.

As these examples indicate, *sintesi* used many innovative techniques: extreme brevity, discontinuity, abstraction, simultaneity. In many of the plays, the place of the action is the stage itself; time is indefinite or telescoped; nonverbal sound and symbolic lighting are common; several media are intermingled. In almost every instance, clear story, logical progression, and psychological characterization are minimized or ignored.

During World War I, the international influence of futurism waned, for the horrors of war made the glorification of aggression seem perverse. Nevertheless, futurism was to regain much of its prestige during the 1920s and remain a major artistic force in Italy until the 1930s. After World War I, Marinetti and his followers continued to champion innovations: a theatre of touch, a theatre of smells, a theatre of variable air temperatures, a *radiophonic* theatre. In 1918–1919, Fedele Azari proposed and gave a performance of *aerial* theatre, in which the performers were airplanes. Futurism was also promoted by Anton Bragaglia (1890–1960), one of Italy's most important postwar directors. Originally a member of the futurist movement, he left it in 1913 perhaps because he wished to support a number of modern movements, which he subsequently did in his periodical *Chronache d'Attualita* (1916–1922). He began directing plays around 1916, and from 1922 to 1936 ran the Teatro degli Independenti in Rome, where on a tiny stage he presented an eclectic program of plays by Strindberg, Schnitzler, Jarry, Apollinaire, Maeterlinck, and Pirandello, as well as the futurists.

Among the postwar futurists, the most important were Depero and Prampolini. Fortunato Depero (1892–1960) was especially interested in kinetic sculpture, which carried over into theatrical designs that underwent transformations during performance. To achieve unity of performer and background, he often distorted the human shape into mechanical, floral, or geometric forms. Most of his designs were done for ballet.

The most important postwar futurist scenographer was Enrico Prampolini (1894–1960) who, in addition to designing more than 100 productions, was a dramatist, director, and painter. In his manifestos, "Futurist Scenography" (1915) and "Futurist Scenic Atmosphere" (1924), Prampolini demanded that painted scenery be replaced with "dynamic stage architecture that will move." He proposed that, instead of the stage being lit, the stage space should incorporate luminous sources "coordinated analogically with the psyche of each scenic action." Furthermore, "human actors will no longer be tolerated. . . . Vibrations, luminous forms (produced by electric currents and colored gases) will wriggle and writhe dynamically, and . . . replace living actors. . . . The appearance of the human element on the stage shatters the mystery of the beyond that must reign in the theatre."

FIG. 7.6

The Merchant of Hearts, a pantomime staged by Enrico Prampolini at the Théâtre de la Pantomime Futuriste, Paris, in 1927. (From Moussinac, *New Movement in the Theatre.*)

FIG. 7.7
Scenery and costumes by Enrico Prampolini for the "mechanical ballet," *The Psychology of Machines* by Silvio Mix in the 1920s. (A contemporary photo.)

Prampolini called his stage "a center of spiritual attraction for the new religion of the future." In 1925 his model for a "Magnetic Theatre" won the Grand Prize in theatrical design at the International Exposition of Decorative Arts in Paris. His best-known work was done for his Théâtre de la Pantomime Futuriste in Paris in 1927, where he presented a series of dance-dramas, some of which combined living actors with abstract shapes and geometric marionettes, while others eliminated human actors altogether.

After 1930, interest in futurism declined. If it never became a major theatrical movement, it nevertheless pioneered innovations that would resurface forcefully once more in the 1960s: simultaneity and multiple focus; direct confrontation of audiences by performers; intermingling of actors and spectators; antiliterary and alogical biases; removal of theatre from a museumlike atmosphere; erasing the boundaries among the arts.

In addition to its long-range inheritors, futurism had more immediate heirs. In early Soviet Russia it came to be associated with the destruction of old social forms and creation of an art suited to a revolutionary society. Consequently, many Russian artistic experiments sailed under the banner of futurism, even when they had little in common with Marinetti's views. In Germany, many futurist innovations were extended by the Bauhaus. But the immediate heir to futurism was dada, though more so in techniques than in goals.

DADA

Although its antecedents remain controversial, *dada* as a movement was launched in Switzerland in 1916. In Zurich, a mecca for those seeking to escape the war, the Cabaret Voltaire, run by the German writer Hugo Ball (1886–1927), served as headquarters for the circle of artists and writers involved in dada. Other leading members were Emmy Hennings, a German actress and cabaret singer; Richard Hulsenbeck, a German medical student who later became a Jungian psychoanalyst; Hans Arp, a German painter; Marcel Janco, a Romanian artist who decorated the cabaret's interior and provided the settings for its programs; and Tristan Tzara (1896–1963), a Romanian poet usually considered the move-

ment's principal spokesman as author of its manifestos (seven between 1916 and 1920) and editor of the periodical *Dada* from 1917 to 1920. The name *dada,* supposedly chosen at random from the dictionary, has been explained in many ways but most often as French baby talk for anything having to do with horses.

Dada was grounded in disgust with a world that could produce a global war. Since insanity seemed the world's condition, the dadaists sought to replace logic and reason with calculated madness. Nevertheless, dada, though it wished to destroy outmoded and mistaken ideas and conventions, sought to replace them with spontaneity, freedom from constraint, and all-inclusiveness. Tzara wrote: "Freedom: Dada Dada Dada, a roaring of tense colors, an interlacing of opposites and of all contradictions, grotesques, inconsistencies, LIFE." To show their rejection of past restraints, the dadaists created "antiartistic" paintings and poems, deliberately illogical works, rubbish collages, and noise music.

Although they totally rejected the futurists' glorification of war, the dadaists borrowed much from the earlier movement. Hulsenbeck acknowledged that the dadaists borrowed *bruitisme,* simultaneity, and collage from futurism. In addition, the dadaists, like the futurists, engaged in direct confrontation with their public. At the Cabaret Voltaire (which seated thirty-five to fifty people at tables), every "manifestation" was something of a collage composed of lectures, readings, dances, concerts, visual art, and plays. In addition, more than one event was usually presented simultaneously. Ball was especially fond of *sound poems* (composed of nonverbal vocal sounds), whereas Tzara favored *chance poems* (created by cutting sentences from newspapers, mixing them up in a hat, drawing them out at random, and reciting them). Hulsenbeck was interested in African chants and dances, for which Janco created masks, often covering

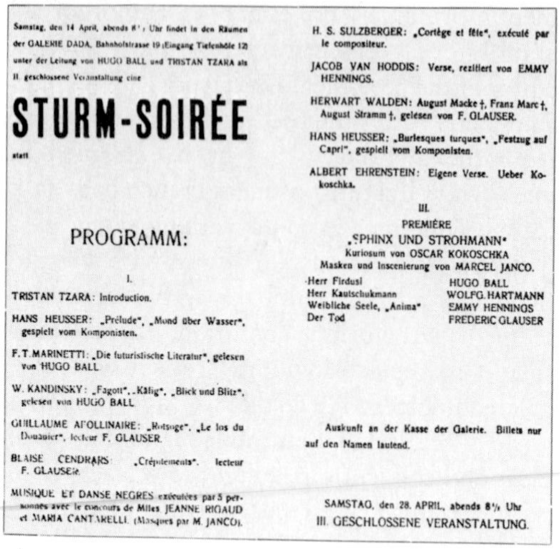

Samstag, den 14 April, abends 8½ Uhr findet in den Räumen der GALERIE DADA, Bahnhofstrasse 19 (Eingang Tiefenhöle 12) unter der Leitung von HUGO BALL und TRISTAN TZARA als II. geschlossene Veranstaltung eine

STURM-SOIRÉE

statt

PROGRAMM:

I.

TRISTAN TZARA: Introduction.

HANS HEUSSER: „Prélude", „Mond über Wasser", gespielt vom Komponisten.

F. T. MARINETTI: „Die futuristische Literatur", gelesen von HUGO BALL.

W. KANDINSKY: „Fagott", „Käfig", „Blick und Blitz", gelesen von HUGO BALL.

GUILLAUME APOLLINAIRE: „Rotsoge", „Le los du Douanier", lecteur F. GLAUSER.

BLAISE CENDRARS: „Crépitements", lecteur F. GLAUSER.

MUSIQUE ET DANSE NEGRES exécutées par 5 personnes avec le concours de Mlles JEANNE RIGAUD et MARIA CANTARELLI. (Masques par M. JANCO).

H. S. SULZBERGER: „Cortège et fête", exécuté par le compositeur.

JACOB VAN HODDIS: Verse, rezitiert von EMMY HENNINGS.

HERWART WALDEN: August Macke †, Franz Marc †, August Stramm †, gelesen von F. GLAUSER.

HANS HEUSSER: „Burlesques turques", „Festzug auf Capri", gespielt vom Komponisten.

ALBERT EHRENSTEIN: Eigene Verse. Ueber Kokoschka.

III.

PREMIÈRE

„SPHINX UND STROHMANN"

Kuriosum von OSCAR KOKOSCHKA

Masken und Inscenierung von MARCEL JANCO.

Herr Firdusi	HUGO BALL
Herr Kautschukmann	WOLFG. HARTMANN
Weibliche Seele, „Anima"	EMMY HENNINGS
Der Tod	FREDERIC GLAUSER

Auskunft an der Kasse der Galerie. Billets nur auf den Namen lautend.

SAMSTAG, den 28. APRIL, abends 8½ Uhr
III. GESCHLOSSENE VERANSTALTUNG.

FIG. 7.8
Program for the first dada soirée, on April 14, 1917, in Zurich. Oskar Kokoschka's *Sphinx and Strawman* was given its premiere performance. (From a contemporary program.)

much of the body. After the Cabaret Voltaire was abandoned, the group gave programs at the Dada Gallery between 1916 and 1919. Rudolf Laban, a pioneer of modern dance, had also moved his dance studio from Germany to Zurich in 1916 and his students, among them Mary Wigman, sometimes participated in the dada performances. The dadaists also presented plays, the first being Kokoschka's *Sphinx and Strawman.*

As the war drew to a close, the dadaists dispersed. For a brief time, dada thrived in Germany. Hulsenbeck returned to Berlin, where he, Georg Grosz, John Heartfeld, and others attacked the expressionists for being bourgeois in their values and romantic in their concern for the human spirit. In Berlin, dada had died out by 1922. In Cologne in 1920, Max Ernst, Hans Arp, and Johannes Theodor Baargeld arranged one of the most famous dadaist programs. For it, they rented a glassed-in court which could only be reached through a public urinal where a young girl, dressed as if for her first communion, recited obscene poems; one art work featured a skull emerging from a pool of blood-red liquid from which a hand projected; a wooden sculpture had a hatchet chained to it for the convenience of those who wished to attack it. The event was closed by the police. Cologne dada came to an end in 1922 when Ernst and Arp went to live elsewhere. The most famous version of German dada, the one promoted in Hamburg by Kurt Schwitters, was called *Merz,* supposedly from a word fragment (part of *Kommerziale*) that appeared in one of Schwitters' collages. None of these German versions contributed significantly to theatre.

In 1920, Tzara moved to Paris, having earlier corresponded with a group of young men there, including Louis Aragon, Philippe Soupault, and André Breton, who had founded the periodical *Littérature.* During the first half of 1920, *Littérature* sponsored a series of dadaist *manifestations.* The first theatrical program, given in March 1920 at Lugné-Poë's Théâtre de l'Oeuvre, was composed of Tzara's *The First Celestial Adventure of Mr. Fire-Extinguisher,* Breton and Soupault's *If You Please,* Francis Picabia's "Cannibal Manifesto" (read in total darkness), and Georges Ribemont-Dessaignes' *The Silent Canary* (in which a man who thinks himself to be Gounod teaches his compositions to a canary who is said to sing them "beautifully but silently"). It concluded in an exchange of mutual insults between audience and performers. Dada soon lost its vigor but continued for a time. In 1923, Tzara's *The Gas Heart,* in which actors impersonating parts of the body—the neck, mouth, nose, ear, eyebrow—spoke disconnected dialogue in the tones of polite conversation, was performed at the Théâtre Michel and provoked a pitched battle between supporters and detractors.

By this time dada had lost its momentum. In 1922, Breton had sought to convene an "Inter-

FIG. 7.9

A scene from the sketch by Breton and Soupault titled *You Would Have Forgotten Me* at the Salle Gaveau, Paris, 1920. Soupault is kneeling and Breton sits in the chair. (A contemporary photo.)

national Congress to establish directives for the modern spirit and to defend it," and, though it did not take place, it provoked a definitive break between Tzara and Breton, which led to the establishment of surrealism. By 1924, when Breton published the first "Manifesto of Surrealism," dada as a movement can be said to have ended.

To drama and theatre, dada contributed little. Its legacy was more one of spirit than of products. It questioned everything, thumbed its nose at conventional behavior and sacred cows, and privileged novelty and contradiction. Its spirit would reemerge in the 1960s.

SURREALISM

Although dada and surrealism were compatible in viewing existing conditions as unsatisfactory,

they parted ways on how to respond. Dada was content to ridicule anything that set limits on options, whereas surrealism concentrated on the capacity of the human mind to provide revelations. Surrealism resembled expressionism in locating its primary point of reference within the human being, although for the surrealists the unconscious was the key, whereas for the expressionists the human spirit (vague and undefined) was the focus. Surrealism looked inward (to a freed subconscious mind) whereas expressionism looked outward (to a reshaped nonmaterialistic society) in the search for transformation and fulfillment.

Given its emphasis on the unconscious, it is not surprising that surrealism should be grounded in Freudian concepts. Surrealism's principal spokesman (indeed he considered himself its near owner) was André Breton (1896–1966), who had been a medical student and had developed an interest in Freudian psychology while serving as an orderly in wards for victims of shell-shock during World War I. He is often said to be the first Frenchman to be well-acquainted with Freud's writings.

Breton defined surrealism as "pure psychic automatism, by which is intended to express, verbally in writing, or by other means, the real process of thought. Thought's dictation, in the absence of all control exercised by the reason and outside all esthetic or moral preoccupation." Thus, Breton made the unconscious mind the source of significant perception. Breton had been experimenting with automatic writing since 1919 and had come to believe that, although on the conscious level language is as corrupt as the social forces that distort reality, when freed by the unconscious from these "intellectual policemen," it can become a unifying force. As Breton wrote: "There is a certain point for the mind from which life and death, the real and the imaginary, the past and the future, the communicable and the incommunicable, the high and the low cease being perceived as contradictions." This unified-field concept (somewhat analogous to Jung's racial unconscious) probably explains Breton's subsequent insistence (expressed in the *Second Manifesto of Surrealism* in 1929) that there is a necessary relationship between surrealism and communism (which he saw as eliminating all social and political barriers among people).

The surrealists argued that humans would cease viewing the world as chaotic and discontinuous if they could recapture the ability to think metaphorically (that is, to see the connections among things normally thought to have nothing in common). They believed that this ability had once been universal but had subsequently been so suppressed by a materialist society as to be found only in primitive civilizations and in children, the insane, and certain artists—those in whom the imagination has not been shackled by the conscious, materialist world. Thus, for the surrealists, art, if adequately grounded in the unconscious, was the key to understanding and transforming the world.

Surrealist art (whether verbal or visual) is essentially metaphorical. In Salvador Dali's (1904–1989) paintings, probably the best-known examples of surrealist visual art, everyday objects are rendered with extreme care for ordinary detail but are placed in such unfamiliar surroundings or put to such unfamiliar uses (a detached arm supports a boulder, an eye grows from a tree), or perform in such unfamiliar ways (a watch bends as if made of rubber) as to be invested with an air of significance in which the animate and inanimate worlds interpenetrate. In drama, familiar characters are placed in unusual surroundings (the Greek mythical characters Orpheus and Eurydice live in modern suburbia) or seemingly unrelated scenes are juxtaposed. Such alogicality and discontinuity break the bonds of ordinary reality and create a

surreality in which associational patterns lead the mind to new perceptions. As Breton wrote: "The spirit is marvelously prompt to seize the faintest rapport that exists between two objects selected by chance. . . ."

As a descriptive term, surrealism seems to have been coined around 1917 (several years before Breton launched his movement) by Guillaume Apollinaire (1880–1918), who was in the forefront of every important artistic movement in France between 1900 and 1917. He did more than any other critic to win acceptance for the works of Jarry, the fauves, and the cubists, and was closely allied with the futurists, dadaists, and surrealists. It was as a subtitle (*drame surréaliste*) for his play *The Breasts of Tiresias* (begun, according to Apollinaire, under Jarry's influence in 1903 and completed in 1917) that surrealism was first used by an artist to describe his own work. Ostensibly set in Zanzibar, *The Breasts of Tiresias* purports to contain a serious message about the repopulation of the postwar world, but it can also be seen as a spoof of women's liberation. Early in the play, Thérèse, finding her life too confining, releases her breasts, which float away as balloons, and is transformed into Tiresias. Now forced to take over her functions, her husband discovers the means for creating children (sheer willpower) and becomes the parent of more than forty thousand offspring. In the prologue to the play, Apollinaire describes his ideal theatre: a circular structure with two stages, one in the middle of and one surrounding the audience. On these stages, as in life itself, "sounds, gestures, colors, cries, tumults, music, dancing, acrobatics, poetry, painting, choruses, actions, and multiple sets" join.

Apollinaire also used surrealist as a label for *Parade,* presented by the Ballets Russes in 1917, and for which he wrote the program notes. Jean Cocteau provided the scenario, Erik Satie

FIG. 7.10
The original production of Apollinaire's *The Breasts of Tiresias* in 1917. Scenery and costumes designed by M. Ferat. (A contemporary photo.)

the music, Pablo Picasso the settings and costumes, and Léonide Massine the choreography. It marks Diaghilev's first use of contemporary French painters as designers (a practice that brought new vitality to the Ballets Russes and made it as influential on postwar as it had been on prewar design through the work of Picasso, Henri Matisse, Georges Braque, Juan Gris, and Marie Laurencin). *Parade* marks the theatrical debut of Cocteau, who was to be the major surrealist playwright. In it, Cocteau draws on the eighteenth-century practice of using a short skit (a *parade*) outside to draw customers into the theatre. But in the ballet, the crowd mistakes the *parade* for the performance (suggesting the human tendency to mistake outer for inner reality). The ballet was divided into three parts, each featuring a different theatre manager. Picasso depicted the first as a ponderous cubist construction, the second (an American) as a skyscraper, and the third as a Chinese conjurer accompanied by a horse. Overall, the work seemed more nearly a collage of circus and music hall acts than a ballet. Satie's score was based on popular songs and jazz elaborated through such futurist instruments as typewriters, sirens, airplane propellers, and telegraph tickers. Many historians have credited this production with setting the tone for postwar experimentation in France.

Cocteau went on to write other ballet-dramas. *The Ox on the Roof* (1920), set in the "Nothing-Doing Bar" during prohibition in the U.S., was performed in part by the Fratellini family of circus clowns in settings by Raoul Dufy and to a score by Darius Milhaud. *The Wedding on the Eiffel Tower* (1921) was presented by the Ballets Suédois, which, under the direction of Rolf de Maré (1888–1964), between 1920 and 1925 served as a focus for innovative experimentation in Paris. The setting for *The Wedding on the Eiffel Tower* (a painted backdrop showing a stylized bird's-eye view of Paris as seen through the girders of the tower) was by Irène Lagut and the costumes by Jean Hugo. Two actors dressed as phonographs narrated

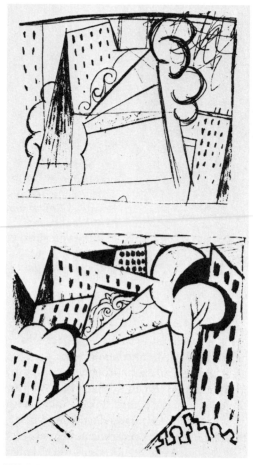

FIG. 7.11
Two variations by Pablo Picasso of the scene design for Cocteau's *Parade*, staged by the Ballets Russes in 1917. (From Editions Cercle d'Art, Paris.)

the story from the sides of the stage. The characters (an ostrich, a lion, a hunter, a bathing beauty, and the wedding party) emerged from a giant camera when the shutter was clicked.

In 1924, Maré presented another ballet of historical significance, *Relâche* (*No Performance*),

with scenario and designs by the dadaist Francis Picabia and music by Satie. The dancers smoked incessantly, a fireman poured water from one bucket to another, and two seemingly nude dancers posed as Cranach's Adam and Eve. The backdrop was composed of round metal discs that reflected bright light into the eyes of the spectators. Satie's opening melody, taken from an obscene song, provoked some spectators to sing the lyrics, thereby setting off heckling that continued throughout. This was the first live production to incorporate a film (René Clair's *Entr'acte,* made from Picabia's scenario).

Thus, by 1924, when surrealism was launched as a movement, many productions labeled surrealist (and sometimes futurist or dadaist) had already been seen in Paris. The self-conscious surrealists were not very active in drama, in large part because after 1925 Breton considered the theatre to be a hopelessly decadent, bourgeois form that catered to commercial instincts. Consequently, two of the most productive surrealists, Artaud and Vitrac, were expelled from the movement in 1927 when they founded (in association with Robert Aron) the Théâtre Alfred Jarry. Not only were they attacked in pamphlets but also their performances were disrupted.

Antonin Artaud (1896–1948) was drawn to surrealism by his preoccupation with the unconscious and dreams, and for a time he was the keeper of the surrealists' archive of dreams. During the 1920s, he wrote a few plays: *Spurt of Blood* (a short scene inserted into *The Umbilical Cord of Limbo,* 1925), *The Philosopher's Stone* (a speaking pantomime, 1926), and *The Burnt Belly* (1927). All used violent imagery and discontinuous action. They were virtually ignored at the time. Artaud was also involved with film and, in addition to acting in several (among them *Entr'acte*), wrote film scripts, of which only one, *The Seashell and the Clergyman* (1927), was produced. It is sometimes con-

FIG. 7.12
The original production in the 1920s by the Ballets Suédois of Cocteau's *The Wedding on the Eiffel Tower*. This scene shows the wedding feast, while in the background is a panorama of Paris and the Seine as seen through the girders of the Tower. (A contemporary photo.)

sidered the first true surrealist film. But Artaud is remembered primarily for those theoretical writings of the 1930s that eventually made him one of the most influential figures of the postwar theatre. (That aspect of his career will be discussed at length in a later chapter).

Roger Vitrac (1899–1952) wrote several surrealistic, vaudevillesque plays that brutally attack conformity. *The Mysteries of Love* (1924) treats the fantasies of a pair of lovers in situations where identities change rapidly. There is also considerable interchange between stage and auditorium, and eventually a character shoots a spectator. In *Victor, or Children in Power* (1928), Vitrac satirized the follies of society through a world of fantasy in which a seven-foot-tall child speaks and acts like an adult. In many ways Vitrac's work resembles Ionesco's, which may explain Vitrac's resurgent popularity in the 1960s.

Surrealism gained its greatest popularity in the theatre through the plays of Jean Cocteau (1892–1963), although he was never accepted by Breton as a member of the movement. After composing his ballet-dramas, Cocteau turned to classical myth. His first attempt, *Antigone* (1922), with music by Paul Honneger and settings by Picasso, was not successful, but with *Orpheus* (1926) he found firmer ground. Cocteau transposed the story of Orpheus and Eurydice to a modern domestic setting, but immediately added an element of magic through a talking horse, and compounded it by showing the glazier Heurtebise remain suspended in midair after a chair, on which he has been standing, is removed from beneath him. When Eurydice dies, Death, dressed as a beautiful woman, enters through a mirror, performs a ritual that resembles a surgical operation, and takes Eurydice away. Death forgets her glove, however, and Orpheus, on Heurtebise's advice, uses it to pass through the mirror. Eurydice is brought back but with the proviso that Orpheus never look at her again. During a domestic quarrel, Orpheus forgets his promise, and Eurydice dies again. Not caring to live, Orpheus goes to meet the Bacchantes who have been trying to kill him, and soon his severed head is thrown through the window. Heurtebise places it on a pedestal; when asked its name by the police inspector, it replies, "Jean Cocteau." After the inspector leaves, Orpheus, Eurydice, and Heurtebise enter through the mirror, now apparently in the world of the dead, and sit down happily to lunch. Through such intermingling, Cocteau made the everyday mythical and the mythical familiar, simultaneously commenting both on the myth and the present. As the first modern French dramatist to use myth in this way, Cocteau provided a lesson that his successors were to exploit.

Cocteau's best-known play is *The Infernal Machine* (1932), a retelling of the Oedipus story. The title refers to Fate, an instrument of the gods, which, like a time bomb, goes on ticking while humans behave as though free to determine their own destinies (a vision that recalls symbolism and clearly differentiates Cocteau's from mainstream surrealism). Cocteau's indebtedness to surrealism was not one of vision but of literary and visual devices. But if Cocteau was not a true surrealist, he did more than any other dramatist to popularize the movement both through his plays and through such films as *The Blood of a Poet* (1932), *Beauty and the Beast* (1945), and *Orpheus* (1950).

By 1930 surrealism as an organized movement was disintegrating, in part because it had become repetitious but also because Breton's insistence that only communists could be surrealists had politicized the movement and alienated many followers. Its lasting accomplishments, made clear by the definitive International Exhibition of Surrealist Art mounted in Paris in 1938, were above all in the visual arts. Its theatrical legacy would resurface after 1960 in happenings, performance art, and the work of such directors as Robert Wilson.

SPAIN

Surrealism was not confined to France, nor were all those whose works may be called surrealist even aware of Breton's views. In Spain, Ramón María del Valle-Inclán (1866–1936) was writing surrealist plays before that label had been invented. His early works, beginning in 1899, resembled those of the symbolists, but he soon adopted a method he called *esperpento* (which may be translated, perhaps too conveniently, as absurd) and described as a truthful vision arrived at "by a mathematics of concave mirrors" as in a fun house. He declared that the reality of Spanish life can only be conveyed through a systematic deformation "because Spain is a grotesque deformation of European civilization." Valle-Inclán's work is seen at its best in *Divine Words* (1913), in which a deformed idiot is the object of contention among several persons who want to display him as a sideshow attraction. The idiot dies and is left in a wheelbarrow where his face is eaten away by pigs while his female guardian is involved in an adulterous affair. Incensed by her sexual activities, neighbors taunt and strip her, but slink away when her husband, the church sexton, intones a Latin prayer. According to the final stage directions: "Led by her husband's hand, the adulteress takes refuge in the church, a sanctuary wreathed in a resplendent religious prestige which, in that superstitious world of rustic souls, is conjured up by the incomprehensible Latin of the DIVINE WORDS." The play suggests that under its beautiful exterior, Spain hides a callous and pagan soul kept in check by religious superstition.

During the 1920s several Spanish artists were to come under the direct influence of surrealism. Of the dramatists, the most important was Federico García Lorca (1898–1936). Coming to Madrid in 1919, he joined a circle which included Salvador Dali (who would become the best-known of surrealist painters) and Luis Buñuel (who was to be a pioneer of surrealist film). In 1925, Louis Aragon, one of Paris' leading surrealists, lectured in Madrid, and thereafter Lorca's group became increasingly interested in surrealism. But the key event of the decade was the celebration in 1927 of the 300th anniversary of the death of Gongora, which so effectively brought to focus the ideas of young Spanish artists that they came to be called the Generation of '27. Their hallmark was the combination of traditional native subjects with modernity of style. In 1927 Lorca founded a magazine, *Gallo,* in which he acknowledged his indebtedness to "Picasso, . . . Tristan Tzara, . . . Aragon, . . . Jean Cocteau, . . . André Breton, etc., etc."

Lorca began writing around 1919. His first play, *The Butterfly's Spell* (1920), written under the influence of symbolism, was a failure, and he avoided the dramatic form for some time. *Mariana Pineda* (1927) reflects the interests of the Generation of '27, being based on a traditional ballad but cast in determinedly modern form. It achieved a limited success when produced by Margarita Xirgu (one of Spain's leading actresses).

Lorca's major plays were written after he had worked closely with a theatrical troupe. The Spanish Republic, created in 1931, seeking to increase educational opportunities, established "cultural missions" to those areas devoid of artistic activities. As part of this mission, it created the Teatro Universitario (more commonly called La Barraca), headed by Lorca and Eduardo Ungarte. La Barraca performed plays of the Golden Age for rural audiences. The unabashed involvement of these unsophisticated spectators deeply impressed Lorca and motivated him to write the plays for which he is now best known: *Blood Wedding* (1933), *Yerma* (1934), and *The House of Bernarda Alba* (1936), in all of which he raises familiar situations to near-mythic status.

Blood Wedding may be taken as representative. It shows a girl who, after her lover has married another woman, agrees to an engagement. On the day of the wedding, Leonardo, her former lover, carries her away. Honor demands that the new husband kill Leonardo. This much of the play occurs on a realistic though intensified plane. The next section

FIG. 7.13
Lorca's *Yerma* at the Teatro Eslava, Madrid, in 1960, directed by Luis Escobar and designed by José Cabellero. (From *World Theatre.*)

becomes surrealistic through its chorus of woodcutters and the Moon, who comment on the action as the men kill each other. It develops a story of overpowering love, honor, revenge, and loss in which fate and blood are associated with the Spanish land itself. The characters embody elemental forces that cannot be denied, and the clash between them leads inescapably to destruction. The surface is sometimes realistic, but the conception is archetypal.

Lorca's career was cut short when he was executed by Falangist forces at the beginning of the Spanish Civil War. The manner of his death did much to spread his fame, for to many he became a symbol of a despised war. Lorca is now almost universally considered the finest Spanish dramatist of the twentieth century.

THE LEGACY OF EXPERIMENTATION

The years between 1910 and 1925, then, spawned numerous artistic movements which, though most soon disappeared, contained the seeds of innovations that continued to bear fruit. Brecht's epic theatre is the direct descendent of expressionism, just as Artaud's theatre of cruelty is the offspring of dada and surrealism. Futurism, dada, and surrealism introduced many of the techniques that would be exploited by happenings, environmental theatre, performance art, and the theatre of images. Thus, the attempts of such men as Jung and Einstein to refine perceptions of reality, and of theatre practitioners to find appropriate modes of expression, were to have lasting effects.

Chapter 8

The Interwar Years in the Soviet Union and Eastern Europe

Revolution in 1917 brought a new form of government to Russia and important changes in the theatre. The groundwork for theatrical innovation had been laid earlier by directors such as Stanislavsky, Meyerhold, and Tairov, who continued as leaders in the postrevolutionary era. Most theatrical workers welcomed the release from stringent tsarist restraints, and some, led by Meyerhold, saw the new state as a call to create comparable new artistic forms. At first, the theatres were left relatively free to make their own decisions, but during the 1930s, after Stalin began to demand that art be subordinated to the needs of the state, *socialist realism* became the only accepted style. Thus, by the beginning of World War II, the theatre had been almost completely subordinated to the will of the Communist party. During the 1920s, however, the Russian theatre was among the most innovative in the entire world, although its drama tended to be inferior to that of the West and even neighboring Eastern Europe. With the rise of totalitarianism in the Soviet Union, Spain, Italy, and Germany in the late 1920s and early 1930s, and the consequent suppression of theatrical experimentation in all these countries, the center of the avant-garde shifted in this period to Eastern Europe, particularly Czechoslovakia and Poland. But the outbreak of World War II led ultimately to the suspension of much experimental practice.

AFTERMATH OF THE REVOLUTION

In 1917, Russia underwent two revolutions, one in February and the other in October (actually March and November by the Western calendar, which was not adopted until after the revolution). The first revolt overthrew the tsarist regime and replaced it with a provisional government led by Alexander Kerensky. The second brought the Bolshevik branch of the Communist Party to power, ended the Russian involvement with World War I, and precipitated a civil war lasting until 1921.

During the eight months of the provisional government, the theatre underwent many changes. The strict censorship imposed by both the tsarist government and the Orthodox church was repealed. Many plays previously forbidden for their criticism of royalty (A. K. Tolstoy's *The Death of Ivan the Terrible,* for example) or for their questionable moral stance (such as Oscar Wilde's *Salome*) were allowed performance for the first time. Also the special privileges and subsidies given the five imperial theatres in Moscow and Petrograd (formerly St. Petersburg and eventually to become Leningrad) were canceled. Such changes were welcomed by the majority of theatre workers, who at the time saw the possibility of complete freedom for the arts.

The new political structure seemed to demand new organizational patterns in the theatre. It became common to associate all theatre managers with the former tsarist regime. Tairov, for example, noted the "class antagonism" between actors and managers in the regulations he drew up for the Union of Moscow Actors. In August 1917, this theme was pursued at length by the All-Russian Conference of Theatrical Trade Unions, over which Tairov presided. Even the general public became involved in the debate, and it was not uncommon for audience members to make public speeches about art and politics during intermissions. Some theatres were turned over to governing boards on which all personnel, ranging from janitors to starring actors, were represented. There was also much concern about making the theatre more appealing to the working class.

In a sense, the whole development of Soviet theatre has been determined by one question: what form should the theatre take in a socialist society? In the years between 1917 and 1927, most theatre personnel saw themselves as able to pursue whatever answer seemed best. Almost everyone seemed to have an answer, and almost everyone sought to make his or her plan prevail, a circumstance that ultimately led to fundamental conflicts in the new governmental system. It was this freedom to choose and this struggle for supremacy, however, that gave the Russian theatre of the 1920s its peculiar character and enormous versatility.

Much that happened in the Russian theatre after 1917 went contrary to the wishes of the government. Lenin, for example, deplored avant-garde experiments, preferring instead the continuation of an "understandable" theatre of realism, into which there would merely be poured new ideological content. But such artists as Meyerhold declared that a new society required wholly new theatrical forms and derided the very modes that Lenin and his friends supported. Still others wished to educate the masses through a classical repertory, and some declared that only those of working-class origins were capable of producing meaningful art for the proletariat.

Even though the governmental leadership had firm ideas about the appropriate theatrical form, it was not as yet in a strong enough position to enforce these ideas. Until 1923, the leadership was concerned primarily with its own survival. Not only was there military opposition from both without and within, and a civil war continuing until 1921, but also the economy was in shambles and the entire country on the verge of famine. Thus, close supervision of the theatre was not given high priority. Furthermore, the government was faced with a paradoxical situation: its most ardent supporters were members of the avant-garde, whereas the realists, whom the government favored, were at best neutral. Furthermore, the government itself had as yet formulated no clear program for the theatre. It wished to make art available to the masses and to have art assist in the socialization of Russian society, but it had no real plan for bringing about these aims. Thus, the theatres were left relatively free to deal with the question of what art would be in a socialist system.

Perhaps the most remarkable feature of the Russian theatre in the chaotic years between 1917 and 1921 was its universal appeal. Amateur groups sprang up everywhere—in factories, in military barracks, in villages. Even in the midst of famine and deprivation, the theatres, both amateur and professional, were filled nightly.

In many ways, the Russian theatre between 1917 and 1923 paralleled the people's theatre movement in the West before World War I. The Russians were conscious of the similarities, for they frequently quoted Rolland and compared their own productions with those of the French Revolution. Many enthusiasts spoke of transforming the theatre into an expression of all the people. For example, Andreyev, the major symbolist dramatist of the prerevolutionary era, declared that the old theatres would be replaced "by other theatres, perhaps theatres based on the entire nation . . . the walls of the theatres will fall, but the theatre will remain." Others argued that the theatre of the future would be entirely out-of-doors.

Such ideas reached their peak between 1919 and 1921 in a series of mass spectacles. The most ambitious, *The Taking of the Winter Palace,* was presented in November 1919 on the anniversary of the Revolution. Directed by Nikolai Evreinov, it required a cast of more than eight thousand soldiers, sailors, workers, and actors, and utilized the site of the original event. There was an orchestra of five hundred, and even the guns of battleships anchored nearby were brought into the action. At first glance, such a production might seem far removed from Evreinov's prerevolutionary work, but it is in keeping with his idealistic notions of the theatre as a tool for transforming life. It was the vision of a new era of humanitarian idealism that attracted practically all directors of the time, even if many were to become disillusioned later. But the mass spectacle as a form never developed as many had envisioned. By 1922, it had virtually been abandoned. Thereafter, the people's theatre was largely restricted to amateur theatrical clubs.

A large number of dramatic productions in this period were propagandistic. The mass spectacles were essentially melodramatic glorifications of the Revolution and denunciations of the past. Such an approach was even more prevalent in programs presented for peasants, soldiers, and factory workers, and in numerous street demonstrations. Immediate problems were treated in such skits as *The Fight Against Typhus, The Intrigues of Finance Capital,* and *The Plots of the Counterrevolution.* Mock trials— of the typhus louse, landowners, White Army

FIG. 8.1
Evreinov's spectacular,
*The Taking of the
Winter Palace,* in
November 1919, the
second anniversary of
the Revolution.

officers, and others—were popular, as were staged debates and reports in which opposing points of view were illustrated through pantomimes, songs, dramatic skits, and choruses. Eventually such productions gave rise to more ambitious documentary forms—the *literary montage* and the *living newspaper.* In the literary montage, some topic (such as the life of Lenin or Marx) or an historical event (the Revolution of 1905 or of 1917) was developed through selections culled from memoirs, letters, official documents, poetry, and songs. Usually a narrator and chorus bridged the selections, which were given variety through extensive use of pantomime, dance, dramatization, and comic episodes.

The living newspaper developed from the practice (which grew up immediately after the Revolution when newspapers were scarce) of reading from the stage actual news items. Soon such presentations were being supplemented by other devices designed to illustrate and interpret current events. Eventually the living newspaper was taken over by the *Blue Blouses* (named for the first professional living newspaper, which featured performers wearing the

workers' dress of the period). After a time, the form palled and disappeared around 1927. By far the most radical version of a people's theatre was that championed by the Central Committee of Proletarian Cultural and Educational Organizations (more commonly known as the Proletarian Culture Movement or simply Proletcult). Headed by Alexander Bogdanov, the Proletcult considered itself superior to both the Communist party and the government, since it was devoted to a "purely class organization of the proletariat." It was contemptuous of everything with bourgeois origins. In *Creative Theatre* (1919), Planton Kerzhentsev, Proletcult's major theoretician, declared: "Any effort to establish a socialist theatre with even the most brilliant bourgeois actors would be as fruitless as analogous efforts to organize, for example, a socialist magazine with the aid of bourgeois writers." He insisted that no distinctions should be made between proletarian artists and workers: "Only by standing at his machine, by remaining a worker, can the worker become the genuine creator of the proletarian theatre."

In 1918, the Proletcult began to establish its

own theatres, which it hoped would soon replace all others. But in 1923, Proletcult was suppressed because it sought to make the industrial worker the sole repository of truth and creativity, thus sowing discord between industrial workers and peasants.

Although the people's theatre movement never completely disappeared, it was of little importance after 1923. But in the years immediately following the Revolution, it was perhaps the greatest source of vigor, for the established theatres remained in old paths or were still wary of the new regime. For the most part, the major professional groups bided their time.

POSTREVOLUTIONARY THEATRICAL EXPERIMENTS

Unlike their predecessors, the Communists recognized the enormous potential of the theatre as a medium for education and propaganda. In an essentially prefilm and pretelevision culture, in which the majority of the population was illiterate, they also realized that it could easily work against them and consequently they sought to maintain surveillance of the theatre, if not full control. As part of their program to attain popular support, they sent hundreds of theatre troupes to perform for the armed forces, in factories, and on farms. Everywhere theatre was encouraged as a medium of national enlightenment and party propaganda.

In 1917, much of the responsibility for the theatre was assigned to the Commissariat of Education and Enlightenment, headed by Anatoli Lunacharsky (1875–1932), a critic and dramatist who in the early years of the new regime sought through advice and cajolery to set the theatre on the path advocated by the Party. His was not an easy task. In late 1917, he invited 120 leading artists to a conference devoted to reorganizing the arts. So cautious

were artists about the new regime that only five attended this meeting—among them Meyerhold, Alexander Blok (the symbolist poet, dramatist, and critic), and Vladimir Mayakovsky (1894–1930, leader of the Russian futurists). All three were prominent in the avant-garde. Thus Lunacharsky was forced to work primarily with opponents of the traditional realism he and the government favored. Consequently, when a Theatre Section was formed in early 1918, Meyerhold was appointed as Deputy Head under O. L. Kameneva, Trotsky's sister. Each of a number of subsections had its own chair. Blok, for example, was in charge of the subsection on repertory, and there he advocated that the theatre could best serve the needs of the people through an emphasis on the classics. Other subsections were devoted to theatre for workers, peasants, and young people. (The young people's subsection is a significant innovation, for Russia seems to have been the first country to give serious thought to children's theatre.) Another subsection for directors was headed by Yevgeny Vakhtangov, who, with Meyerhold, gave courses for directors.

To celebrate the first anniversary of the Revolution, Meyerhold staged the first Soviet play, Mayakovsky's *Mystery-Bouffe*, a parody of the biblical story of the ark, ending with the arrival of the survivors in a Communist promised land. Most theatre personnel were still so uncertain about the permanence of Bolshevism that they hesitated to participate in the production, and Meyerhold was forced to make a public appeal for actors. Lunacharsky also had reservations about the production, if not about the play, for before it was presented, he announced: "As a work of literature, it is most original, powerful, and beautiful. But what it will turn out like in production I don't yet know. I fear that the Futurist artists have made millions of mistakes." His fears were well-grounded, for the production was not popular, in part because the setting was composed of geometric designs painted on a backcloth, a few cubes to indicate the ark, and a huge blue globe to represent the world. This was to be Meyerhold's last production for almost two years, for in early 1919, he went south for "reasons of health."

The setting in question for *Mystery-Bouffe* was by leading avant-garde painter Kazimir Malevich (1878–1935), who belonged to a group of artists who in 1912 broke with the "World of Art" school and allied themselves with the cubists, futurists, and expressionists. Malevich launched his own movement, *suprematism,* which he defined as the primacy of "pure feeling or perception in pictorial art. . . . The object in itself means nothing. Sensibility is the only thing that counts." Malevich seems to have believed, as did the expressionists, in the supremacy of inner vision, but, unlike them, he favored pure abstractionism. In 1918, for example, he exhibited a series of paintings called "White on White," which created a sensation in the Soviet Union. The suprematists also had much in common with the constructivists, led by Vladimir Tatlin, Naum Gabo, and Antoine Pevsner, who also, like Malevich, were influenced by the cubists, expressionists, and futurists. Tatlin's sculptures, for example, were made of such industrial materials as glass, wire, and metal, and conceived of as objects in space (a series of intersecting planes in depth) rather than as volume and mass (as in traditional sculpture). Thus, the major Russian artists of this period were concerned with those same qualities sought by cubists and futurists (dynamism, geometric form, the sense of time) and by the expressionists (inner emotion and vision). To these schools belonged a number of artists who would make significant contributions to Soviet scenic design: Alexandra Ekster, Lyubov Popova, Ignaty Nivinsky, Nathan Altman, Georgy Yakulov, Marc Chagall, and Mikhail Larionov, among others.

Parallel attitudes and movements were underway in literature. The most important new outlook was futurism, which was strengthened by the Italian futurist Marinetti's visit to Russia in 1914. The Russian futurists declared: "Set words free, destroy all grammatical structure, cultivate speed and modernity, be aggressive, repudiate all tradition, search for startling forms of expression, and act as new barbarians in renovating creative life." The futurist manifesto, written in 1912 by Mayakovsky, was entitled "A Slap in the Face," and its signers sought to live up to the title. When the Revolution arrived, Mayakovsky declared that futurism was the form most suited to it, and he urged his fellow artists to take to "the barricades of souls and hearts." In the 1920s, Mayakovsky joined with artists from other fields to create an integrated movement, the Left Front (LEF), which stated that art is to be judged by its service to the state—its ability to educate the masses, to provide them with revolutionary songs, uplifting slogans, and a vision of the transformed society. There were, then, many strong parallels in the outlook, goals, and techniques of Soviet artists, German expressionists, and other avant-garde Western artists. The important difference among them lay in the Russian political situation.

While Meyerhold was away from Moscow for his health, several important changes occurred. The most significant was a reclassification of theatres, under which governmental financial support and protection were given a group of so-called "academic" theatres, while all others were required to be self-supporting and willing to submit to close scrutiny from the Party. Ironically, the theatres designated as academic were the five former imperial theatres, the Moscow Art Theatre, and Tairov's Kamerny Theatre, none of which actively supported the new regime and all of which emphasized a classical repertory and, with the exception of the Kamerny, realistic production methods. To Meyerhold and the so-called futurists, this decision seemed a negation of all that the Revolution stood for.

But in 1920, Meyerhold was invited by Lunacharsky to become head of the Theatre Section, a position which made him nominal head of the Russian theatre. Meyerhold accepted, no doubt believing that through this position he might carry out his intention to revolutionize the Soviet theatre. He took over the section's periodical, *The Theatre Herald,* where he launched bitter verbal attacks on the "academic" theatres and, conversely, wrote strongly supportive essays on the avant-garde. Inevitably the contradictory situation of the head of the Russian theatre attacking the theatrical policies of the government he represented caused much friction.

Meyerhold's difficulties were compounded when also in 1920 he took over direction of a troupe and renamed it RSFSR Theatre No. 1. After adding a number of actors and students, he prepared his first production, an adaptation of the Belgian symbolist Emile Verhaeren's *The Dawns.* While Verhaeren's play is a generalized treatment of imperialism and militarism in which the people are passive victims, Meyerhold reworked the original into a play about a worldwide proletarian revolution in which the masses are active participants. The auditorium and stage were stripped of all theatrical trappings to give the feeling of a political meeting hall. Actors onstage spoke as though delivering political orations; other actors in the auditorium asked questions and made speeches of their own. A chorus located in the orchestra pit also commented on the action, while leaflets were from time to time dropped on the audience. At one point, a messenger arrived to read actual news dispatches from the front (the civil war was still in progress). Despite the fact that the production ran for more than one hundred performances and seemed generally liked by

average theatregoers, critics attacked it as a distortion of political reality, and Lenin's wife in addition to other party officials publicly denounced it. Furthermore, Lunacharsky removed the so-called academic theatres from under Meyerhold's administration, and Meyerhold, recognizing the hopelessness of his desire for theatre reform, in February 1921 resigned his post as head of the Theatre Section. Later the same year, the RSFSR Theatre No. 1 was closed, ostensibly for overspending its budget, thus leaving Meyerhold without a theatre.

The year 1921 was important for several other reasons. The civil war was drawing to a close and reconstruction now began. Since the state was on the verge of bankruptcy and financial collapse, Lenin sought to encourage greater initiative through his New Economic Policy (NEP), under which many earlier decrees were rescinded and limited private enterprise was reinstated. Many theatres now reverted to private ownership, and Western plays began to find their way into the repertory. All theatres were to enjoy considerable freedom of repertory and productional style from 1921 until Stalin assumed full control around 1927. But by 1921, it also seemed clear that the Bolshevik regime was something more than a temporary phenomenon, and those theatres that previously had bided their time now began to make accommodations with the government and began to enlarge their programs. The next decade would be one of the most fruitful in all Russian theatrical history, perhaps even in world theatrical history of the twentieth century.

MEYERHOLD'S EXPERIMENTS IN THE 1920s

The strange divisions within the Soviet theatre at this time are well-illustrated by the appointment in 1921 of Meyerhold, despite his obvious disaffection from official policies, as director of the State Higher Theatrical Workshop, a major trainer of directors. In 1922, he also acquired a theatre of his own, where he now began his best-known experiments—those with biomechanics and constructivism.

Biomechanics, basically, was an attempt to deal quasi-scientifically with the motion of living bodies. Meyerhold, however, greatly complicated the matter—at least for the understanding of others—by mingling his ideas about biomechanics with a number of other issues and related techniques. From the beginning of his career, he had been concerned with movement, pantomime, and *commedia dell'arte* techniques, and in the years preceding the Revolution he had experimented at length with rhythm, patterned movement, acrobatics, and circus techniques. The new element added after the Revolution was the desire to forge an art suited to a proletarian society in which the actor would be merely one worker among many. Meyerhold began to think of the theatre as a kind of factory. At this time, he came under the influence of Taylorism (a name derived from the time-and-motion studies of the American Frederick Winslow Taylor), a theory of time and motion and efficiency that was beginning to have some influence in Soviet industry. Meyerhold declared that it was "essential to discover those movements in work which facilitate the maximum use of work time. If we observe a skilled worker in action, we notice the following in his movements: (1) an absence of superfluous, unproductive movements; (2) rhythm; (3) the correct positioning of the body's center of gravity; (4) stability." It was precisely those qualities that Meyerhold sought in his actors. His students were asked to study the economy of movement in cats and other animals. They were asked to study human behavior and, in rendering it, to eliminate everything superfluous. They studied dance, acrobatics, fencing, and other physical disciplines until their bodies were as responsive as a machine in fulfilling its tasks. This in essence was biomechanics—thorough physical efficiency and control.

What caused some confusion was Meyerhold's tying of biomechanics to other, more complex, concepts. In addition to Taylorism, Meyerhold also saw biomechanics coupled with a theory of psychological response. He suggested that Stanislavsky's and earlier systems of acting were mistaken because they asked the actor to base his stage behavior on internal psychological motivations, a waste of time and energy (thus anti-Taylorian), since the desired effects could be achieved more efficiently through purely physical means: "From a sequence of physical positions and situations there arise those 'points of excitation' which are informed with some particular emotion." Basically what Meyerhold proposes is a variation on the James-Lange theory: particular patterns of muscular activity elicit particular emotions. Consequently, the actors, to arouse within themselves or the audience a desired emotional response, need only enact an appropriate kinetic pattern; to go through a search for realistic internal motivations is not only wasteful of time but is wholly ineffective if it is not projected through appropriate muscular activity. To create a feeling of exuberant joy, for example, it may be more efficient for the actors to plummet down a slide, swing on a trapeze, or turn a somersault than to restrict themselves to behavior considered appropriate by realistic social standards.

Biomechanics was further mingled with two other elements: Meyerhold's long-standing interest in *commedia dell'arte* and popular entertainment techniques plus the futurists' concern with energy, speed, and vitality.

Constructivism was Meyerhold's attempt to achieve a setting that would be a "machine for acting" without any superfluous details, for he argued that the stage, like an industrial machine, should be efficient rather than decorative. In 1921, Meyerhold saw an exhibit of sculpture and painting by constructivists and invited one of the artists, Lyubov Popova, to join his teaching staff at the Theatrical Workshop and to design the setting for his first major production at his new theatre, *The Magnificent Cuckold* by the Belgian playwright Fernand Crommelynck. It was with this production in April 1922 that Meyerhold made his first important experiments with biomechanics and constructivism.

Crommelynck's cynical farce deals with the village miller Bruno, who believes every man in the village is in love with his beautiful wife. Believing his wife has a lover (he is mistaken), Bruno plots to find the culprit by forcing his wife to submit to the advances of all the men of the village. The previously virtuous wife, now disgusted with her jealous husband, eventually runs off with a younger man who seems more likely to trust her.

Crommelynck's slight plot was simply a jumping-off point for Meyerhold's experiments in biomechanics and constructivism. The stage and flies were stripped of all machinery and laid completely bare. Popova's setting consisted primarily of steps, platforms, slides, and two moving elements—a windmill and a large disk bearing the letters *CR ML NCK,* which

FIG. 8.2
Meyerhold's production of *The Magnificent Cuckold,* 1922.

turned at varying speeds depending on the emotional and rhythmic demands of a scene. Lighting instruments were exposed to view, and no color filters were used. Costumes were the same for all characters: blue coveralls varied only by small accessories such as a riding crop or eyeglasses. Igor Iliinsky, who played Bruno, is reported to have delivered his long speeches in a monotonous manner with set gestures. But in addition, he commented on the impassioned moments by performing acrobatic stunts, "belching and comically rolling his eyes while enduring the most dramatic anguish."

Although Meyerhold continued to experiment in subsequent productions, he sought continually to refine and perfect his techniques. Eventually, for example, he came to use captions projected on a screen. When in 1923, the centennial of Ostrovsky's birth, Lunacharsky declared a new Soviet realist policy of "Back to Ostrovsky," Meyerhold replied with a production of Ostrovsky's *The Forest,* which made a mockery of the government's position. Meyerhold stated what had long been his practice (and some fifty years later would become a commonplace with many Western directors): "A play is simply the excuse for the revelation of its theme on the level at which that revelation may appear vital today." He completely reworked Ostrovsky's original text, separating and rearranging episodes, inserting invented pantomimes, and giving each scene a title that was projected on a screen. As the lovers, for example, became enthusiastic about their plan to run away, they soared higher and higher in their swings. Another character's stupidity was revealed by his balancing on two chairs while conversing. There were innumerable acrobatic tricks and much singing and dancing. Overall, the production seemed an improvisation based on Ostrovsky's original. As might be expected, Meyerhold's *The Forest* was roundly denounced by traditionalists, but

it was popular with audiences and eventually was given more than fifteen hundred performances. Furthermore, it led to many imitations, a contributing factor in Meyerhold's ultimate downfall.

By 1925, Meyerhold seems to have tired of his constructivist experiments and turned in new directions. In Faiko's *Bubus the Teacher* (1925), rhythm was the governing element. Meyerhold suspended bamboo to create a semicircle and used a circular green rug to outline the acting area. These materials and their arrangement became part of an overall rhythmical pattern, almost orchestral in conception. Each scene was set to musical accompaniment, a few to jazz (particularly those involving decadent and frenetic capitalists), but most to works of Liszt and Chopin, played by a pianist placed in a visible alcove high above and at the rear of the stage. Each character also had its own individual rhythmic pattern. Perhaps the most controversial element in *Bubus the Teacher* was the "preacting"—long pauses between speeches during which pantomime was used to show transitions in thought and response and to prepare for what was to come.

By common consent, Meyerhold's finest production came in 1926 with his reworking (with Mikhail Korenev) of Gogol's *The Inspector General.* The classic text was considerably altered through insertions of material taken from others of Gogol's works, the adding of characters, and the invention of pantomimes and tableaux. The performance was divided into fifteen episodes, each with its own title. The provincial atmosphere of the original was abandoned in favor of the elegance, pomposity, and luxury more nearly that of St. Petersburg. In this way, the work was transformed into a judgment of the whole tsarist epoch.

The stage was surrounded by a semicircular arrangement of simulated mahogany screens in which there were fifteen doors. The back

FIG. 8.3

The "bribery" scene from Meyerhold's production of Gogol's *The Inspector General*, 1926.

opened to permit wagons (approximately 16 by 20 feet in size) to glide forward or back in tracks. The actors were dressed in elegant period costume and the furnishings were authentic early nineteenth-century period pieces. At the beginning of each scene, the wagon moved forward with the actors arranged in frozen wax-figure poses; at the end of scenes they froze once again as the wagon was rolled away. Meyerhold used the relatively small platforms often for scenes containing as many as thirty carefully though tightly arranged actors—a technique referred to as *crowd setting*. At the end of the performance, the actors froze in rigid, distorted poses. The lights went out. When they came up a few seconds later, the actors were gone, but in their place stood mannequins in exactly the same poses as the actors.

Again rhythm played an important role in the production. Most action was accompanied by music (much of it taken from nineteenth-century sources but the rest composed by Mikhail Gnesin). Characters often spoke and gestured in unison, one of the most famous moments being that in which eleven hands extended simultaneously from eleven doors to offer bribes to the bogus inspector, Khlestakov.

The production provoked a tempest and was widely discussed in the press. Some critics denounced the liberties taken with Gogol's classic text and the unorthodox political slant taken by the production. Nonetheless, *The Inspector General* was one of the most popular productions of the era and remained in Meyerhold's repertory until his theatre was closed in 1938. But while the work was perhaps Meyerhold's greatest accomplishment, it also marks the beginning of his decline. Increasingly, and especially after Stalin came to full power around 1927, Meyerhold was accused of being out of touch with the needs of the people, both in his choice of plays and in his production methods.

By 1928, attendance at Meyerhold's theatre began to fall off, partly because there had been so few recent additions to the repertory. Seeking to remedy the situation, Meyerhold in 1929 presented Mayakovsky's *The Bedbug,* a satire on the philistine Soviet society set fifty years into the future in 1979. Scenes set in 1929 were done in semirealistic costumes and settings, while those done in the future were done in constructivist style. The production was very popular with audiences, but Mayakovsky's *The Bath House* (1930), a satire on Soviet bureaucrats and red tape, seemed dangerously pointed. Here an inventor, held back by inefficient bureaucracy, goes forward in a time machine to the year 2030. He brings back the Phosphorescent Lady, who comments acidulously on the conditions of 1930. Among other topics, the realism of the Moscow Art Theatre and conformity in all the arts are ridiculed. Reminiscent of his earlier productions, Meyerhold clothed the inventor and his friends in workers' coveralls and had them perform with great vitality. The bureaucrats, however, were dressed in business suits and sat about languidly in overstuffed chairs. Stalin is said to have been deeply offended by *The Bath House,* and it was viciously attacked by Party spokesmen. Mayakovsky committed suicide shortly afterward.

These rebuffs were no doubt lessened somewhat for Meyerhold by the praise his company won on its foreign tour later that year. In Paris he received a standing ovation from an audience that included Cocteau, Picasso, Jouvet, Dullin, and Baty. But from then on, Meyerhold would fight a losing battle at home.

In the 1920s, Meyerhold was without doubt the dominant figure in the Russian theatre, a fact even recognized by the government. Not only was Meyerhold appointed to some of the country's most important training programs, but in 1923 he was the first director to be named "People's Artist of the Republic." In 1928, his and Vakhtangov's companies represented the Soviet Union at an international festival in Paris, where the performance of *The Inspector General* was well received. At home, Meyerhold's productions were especially popular with young audiences and young directors, who spread his influence throughout the country. But if *formalism* and *abstraction,* as opposed to *understandable realism,* were to be weeded out, Meyerhold necessarily became the foremost target.

Never a cautious man, Meyerhold supplied his enemies with plenty of ammunition to use against him. It was almost as if he were playing a kind of game with them, a course other directors and artists would take in the Communist bloc in the future, particularly in the closing decades of the twentieth century. It was a dangerous game nonetheless. Meyerhold had elevated his individual taste, ideas, and will above those of all the people with whom he worked. His actors and designers were expected to carry out his ideas rather than to contribute their own. He reshaped plays as he saw fit (even contemporary plays against the expressed wishes of their authors). Thus, he could easily be accused of fostering a cult of the individual over the collective. And he favored formalism, perhaps the most damning quality in Soviet eyes. The Soviet leaders wanted orthodox political ideas presented in understandable (that is, traditional) forms. It is probably true, as well, that Meyerhold's productions sometimes lacked polish (he often left detailed work to his assistants) and that he was more interested in exploring new ideas than in perfecting old ones. Nonetheless, Meyerhold's was one of the most inventive and fertile talents the theatre has known.

It is often suggested that Meyerhold's influence was not lasting because he created no school of followers as did Stanislavsky and Vakhtangov. This is at least partly true, for Meyerhold never developed a system that could be transmitted. His was a restless exploration of new means, and consequently if he taught anything it was that each artist must find his or her own creative approach.

But in the 1920s, Meyerhold was clearly an inspiration to many young directors, the most important of whom was Sergei Eisenstein (1898–1948), who worked as an assistant to Meyerhold before he was given in 1922 the directorship of Proletcult's Moscow theatre and later became one of the Soviet Union's most masterful film directors. Eisenstein developed a technique similar to film montage, partly based upon the influence of Meyerhold's rapid and sometimes abrupt scene transitions. Eisenstein's most famous theatrical production was based on Ostrovsky's *Enough Stupidity in Every Wise Man*. He treated the stage as an arena, with actors on tightropes exchanging dialogue. Part of the action was shown on film. Probably most interesting was Eisenstein's collage of seemingly unrelated events happening simultaneously, as in the quick-cut transitions of a filmic montage.

While Meyerhold and his followers were strong supporters of the Revolution (if not always Soviet policy), it is ironic that in the 1930s they should fall victims to a politicized theatre that they, at least theoretically, had helped create. But before considering such results, it is necessary to trace other developments prior to the 1930s.

TAIROV AND THE KAMERNY THEATRE

Next to Meyerhold, Alexander Tairov was the major antirealist of the 1920s, but, unlike Meyerhold, he sought to keep the theatre free of ideology. In *Proclamations of an Artist* (1917), Tairov declared art's independence of politics and stated that the current turmoil had nothing to do with the theatre. He criticized Meyerhold for presenting productions about contemporary social and political events. Tairov said this was "like eating mustard after a meal." Tairov believed that the theatre, through aesthetic and sensual experiences of great intensity, should lift audiences above the drabness of life. His policies at the Kamerny Theatre after 1917 remained essentially unchanged, though his major concern always was to show the beauty of art on the stage. This was keeping with the current trends in visual arts that were moving toward abstraction and almost mathematical precision. Tairov looked at the stage as if it were a painting.

Tairov's first production after the Revolution was of Wilde's *Salome* (previously banned as immoral), with settings and costumes by Alexandra Ekster, a leading cubist-expressionist artist. Ekster sought to find a basic rhythm for the costume of each character. She wrote of "delaying velvet, the speedy, agile silk, the heavy-paced brocade," and of "quieting and disquieting," "heavy and light" colors. She painted fabrics with pigment and fitted some costumes with rigid frameworks to ensure that they would "move" as she wished. Through the manipulation of fabric, texture, color, and line, she sought to create a "living, colorful sculpture" or "make-up for the body." Her basic setting was an architectural arrangement of columns, steps, and levels, but it was made "dynamic" by draperies and curtains of various materials, colors, and designs which were raised or lowered, piled up on the floor, or torn. At the beginning of Salome's dance, for example, the backdrop was torn to reveal a red curtain that seemed to bleed. The entire production was a masterful handling of color, rhythm, music, dance, and intoned speech.

Tairov's first opposition from party officials

FIG. 8.4
Tairov's production of Wilde's *Salome* in 1917. Costumes and setting are by Alexandra Ekster.

came shortly thereafter with his productions of Claudel's *The Exchange* and *The Tidings Brought to Mary*. Claudel's mystical Catholicism was denounced as "imperialist" and the author himself referred to as a "reactionary bourgeois." Undeterred, Tairov, in the midst of famine, disease, and civil war, presented Scribe's *Adrienne Lecouvreur* in 1919. Its refined, colorful, and lyrical atmosphere in Tairov's production was a startling contrast to the realities of the Russian moment. Nonetheless, the Kamerny was designated as an "academic" theatre and provided a subsidy by the new regime. Perhaps Tairov felt nonetheless a need to justify his work, for in 1921 he published *Notes of a Director,* which set forth his ideals and described his practice.

In presenting Racine's *Phaedra* in 1921 with settings and costumes by A. Visnin (also, like Ekster, a cubist-expressionist), Tairov sought to be monumental, archaic, and mythic. The actors wore *cothurnoi*, which increased their height but restricted their movement, and their costumes and gestures made them seem like animated stone statues. In 1922, in contrast, Tairov turned to comedy and operetta with E. T. A. Hoffmann's *Princess Brambilla* and Charles Lecocq's *Giroflé-Girofla*. Here he made use of the techniques of popular entertainment: music hall, harlequinade, and circus. *Giroflé-Girofla*

was particularly admired for its unrestrained gaiety and startling lighting effects.

In 1923, Tairov's Kamerny Theatre won outstanding critical acclaim during its first foreign tour. (It was to tour also in 1925 and 1930, and thus became one of the best-known internationally of all Russian troupes, a factor which may have restrained the Soviet government from taking overly harsh measures against it.) But Tairov at home was encountering increasing criticism for his seeming lack of commitment to the revolutionary cause. Perhaps as an attempt to comply with Lunacharsky's "Back to Ostrovsky" policy, Tairov mounted in 1924 a production of *The Thunderstorm*, the first clearly realist Russian drama he had ever staged. However, the single setting by the constructivist-expressionist Stenberg brothers was simply a wooden ramp and platform resembling a bridge. The costumes retained the basic lines of nineteenth-century garments, but all superfluous details were eliminated. The actors recited their lines in the characteristic Kamerny song-chant style. Thus, by avoiding both naturalism and extreme formalism, Tairov achieved a style later designated as *purism* or *neorealism,* one to which he would often return thereafter.

The year 1924 also marks the beginning of several new directions in Tairov's work. First

of all, his production of G. K. Chesterton's *The Man Who Was Thursday* was his first attempt to present a work about contemporary life. The play also signals Tairov's turn to the West in his repertory and to "urbanism" in his production style. The setting, designed by S. E. Krzhizhanovsky, outwardly resembled Meyer-hold's "constructions," for it was composed of girders, turning wheels, elevators, and flashing signs, thus allowing Tairov to create a rhythmical "symphony of the big city."

Through the remainder of the 1920s, Tairov's major productions were of Western plays. Some of the most outstanding were Shaw's

Saint Joan (1924), O'Neill's *The Hairy Ape* (1926), *Desire Under the Elms* (1926), and *All God's Chillun Got Wings* (1929), and Hasenclever's *Antigone* (1927). But by the late 1920s, Tairov was succumbing to the political pressures he had sought to resist, and both *The Hairy Ape* and *All God's Chillun Got Wings* were given strong anticapitalist treatments much in the manner of Meyerhold. One might argue that Tairov was only copying. Also Tairov capitulated to the demand that he include more contemporary Soviet plays in his repertory, though with unfortunate results. In 1928, for example, Bulgakov's *The Purple Island,* a satire on the propagandistic drama of the day and of party members who pass judgment on theatrical repertories, was viciously attacked and removed from the stage.

Tairov, like Meyerhold, was tolerated throughout the 1920s. Though he made many compromises with his desire to remain apolitical and thus true to his aesthetic ideals, he did not go far enough, according to party officials, who after 1930 stepped up their attacks against Tairov's formalism and his alienation from the needs of the state. For him, too, the 1930s would be traumatic.

VAKHTANGOV AND FANTASTIC REALISM

One of the most important of all Russian directors following the Revolution was Yevgeny Vakhtangov (1883–1922), whose career was cut short by his early and untimely death at thirty-nine. At the time of the Revolution, Vakhtangov already had established some reputation as a director and head of the Moscow Art Theatre's First Studio. He also had worked with an independent student group, the Mansurov Studio, which in 1917 became Vakhtangov's Studio and eventually in 1921 the Third Studio of the Moscow Art Theatre. (Stanislavsky had created the Second Studio in 1916 as a three-year actor-training course.)

Despite his strong connection to the Moscow Art Theatre, Vakhtangov's great significance lies in his successful blending of Stanislavsky's realism with Meyerhold's experimental stylization. In the attempt to find an effective means of staging nonrealistic drama without denying the actor's creativity and the inner reality of the characters, Vakhtangov succeeded where Stanislavsky had failed. Stanislavsky thoroughly approved of Vakhtangov's work and saw in the young director, because of his own experiments with nonrealist drama, his natural successor. Vakhtangov labeled his approach *fantastic realism,* but if, like Meyerhold and Tairov, he exaggerated and distorted reality, he did so with an eye to Stanislavskian "inner belief." Vakhtangov said that the director is fundamentally bound by the text of the playwright, but the director should "contemporize" the script. A production of a particular play should be pertinent to not only the specific audience for whom it will be performed but also precisely right for the actors performing it, the space in which it will be performed, and the time and circumstances in which it will be played. Vakhtangov suggested that each production is the expression of a "theatrical collective at the given stage of its creative development," and in his actors he sought partners who could fill form with content and find the necessary emotional and theatrical justification for what they did on the stage, even though this justification had to be found not in the psychological but in the theatrical plan of the spectacle. Thus, to Stanislavsky's motivational technique of inner belief, Vakhtangov added the purely theatrical technique of *theatrical belief*—that which would be appropriate, correct, and proper for a given theatrical moment between an audience and a group of actors.

In practice, Vakhtangov began by deciding how he wished the audience to respond at each moment of a performance, not precisely but at least generally. The actors, keeping in mind the desired results, then sought through improvisation both the appropriate means and hence theatrical justifications for those means. From these *études,* Vakhtangov eventually chose those means which seemed most theatrically effective. Unlike Meyerhold and Tairov, who essentially dictated to their actors precisely what they wanted, Vakhtangov avoided imposing his own preconceptions by making his actors collaborators at the most creative level. Nevertheless, it was Vakhtangov who made the crucial decisions—about which effects were desired and which of the many possible solutions would be used in performance—and it was his strong sense of fittingness that molded his actors' inventions into a unified production.

Although Vakhtangov's ultimate influence derived as much from his teaching as from his productions, his theatrical fame now rests primarily upon four productions done during the last two years of his life: *The Miracle of Saint Anthony, Erik XIV, The Dybbuk,* and *Turandot.* Vakhtangov had worked on Maeterlinck's *The Miracle of Saint Anthony* for almost four years before presenting it at the Third Studio in 1921 as a biting satire on bourgeois society. The play tells a simple story: upon the death of the rich Hortense, relatives and hangers-on assemble to claim her wealth; then the tramp-like Saint Anthony arrives and revives her, much to the chagrin of the relatives, who have him arrested; only the servant, Virginie, recognizes his saintliness. In Vakhtangov's production, all the would-be heirs were conceived of as a unit—dressed in black, they performed wooden gestures, and were treated as living corpses seen against the white background of the setting and furniture. On the other hand, Saint Anthony and Virginie, representatives of virtue,

were essentially realistically performed and were dressed in white and played with vitality. Hortense was costumed as a large doll. The whole production was rhythmically precise in a way that some critics described as geometric. Strindberg's late history play, *Erik XIV,* was performed at the First Studio in 1921. A near-pathological prince yearns for the simple life of his subjects and seeks to marry the daughter of a poor soldier. Vakhtangov emphasized the struggle between the dying world of the nobility and the vital world of the proletariat: the aristocrats were performed as soulless automatons; the proletarian characters were treated more colorfully and individually. The great revelation, however, was the performance of actor Mikhail Chekhov as Erik. Thereafter, he was considered one of the Soviet Union's foremost performers.

Vakhtangov directed *The Dybbuk* by Solomon Rappaport (S. An-sky) for the Habima Theatre in 1922. (Composed of Jewish actors and created in 1918 by Alexander Granovsky [1890–1937], the Habima toured widely, eventually settling in Israel, where it became the national theatre.) Although he understood neither Hebrew nor Yiddish, the languages used by the Habima, Vakhtangov worked with this company from its beginning and was largely responsible for establishing its experimental style. In *The Dybbuk* there are two lovers: Leah (daughter of the wealthy Sender) and Channon (a poor struggling student). When Sender demands that Leah marry a rich man, Channon dies and his spirit (or dybbuk) enters Leah's body and takes control of it. At the urging of Sender, holy men exorcise the dybbuk, but Leah's spirit also leaves and she dies. The setting, costumes, and makeup were by Nathan Altman, who painted the actors' faces to integrate them into the whole design. The vital and essentially realistic style of Leah and Channon was contrasted sharply with the stylized and grotesque figures of Sender and the elders. Sender's dark, stifling, and joyless house was underscored by the presence of the ten elders, who moved in unison and were dressed identically in grease-stained black robes. Even those who could not understand the language were greatly impressed by the production's nightmarish oppressiveness.

Vakhtangov's final production, Gozzi's *Turandot,* presented at the Third Studio in 1922, is considered his true masterpiece. Unlike the preceding serious productions, *Turandot* was a joyful, seemingly spontaneous improvisation, although all its details were worked out very precisely. Gozzi's play tells of the cruel Princess Turandot, who beheads any suitor who cannot answer her three riddles, and how she is ultimately conquered by Prince Calaf. It is a *commedia dell'arte* script, the action of which supposedly occurs in China.

The setting by Nivinsky was a cubist-constructivist arrangement of ramps, platforms, balconies, and leaning walls. As the performance opened, four *commedia* figures—Pantalone, Brighella, Truffaldino, and Tartaglia—came forward to tell the audience about the play, and while they spoke, the other actors, dressed in evening clothes, began to improvise their costumes. Prince Calaf made a turban from a towel; the Wise Man created a beard by tying a scarf about his chin; King Timur fashioned a scepter from a tennis racket. Music was improvised by the actors humming on combs and wax paper. Perhaps Vakhtangov's combination of inner realism and theatrical irony was best illustrated by the scene in which an actor cried real tears, only to have another come from the wings, collect the tears in a bowl, and exhibit them to the audience as proof of the actor's talent. Vakhtangov himself never saw a real performance of *Turandot,* having fallen ill during the period of dress rehearsals. He died three months later. Considering the director's view of "contemporizing" a given text for a performance here-and-now, it is ironic that his production of *Turandot* was retained in the repertory as a memorial to Vakhtangov's genius. On the fortieth anniversary of Vakhtangov's death in

FIG. 8.7
Design by Nivinsky for Vakhtangov's production of Gozzi's *Turandot* in 1922.

FIG. 8.8
The production of *Turandot*, directed by Vakhtangov shortly before his death, at the Third Studio, 1922.

1962, the production was faithfully recreated.

It is perhaps fortunate that Vakhtangov died early and did not live to suffer the fate of Meyerhold and Tairov, for like them, he was a formalist, and his major successes were with non-Soviet plays. But Vakhtangov did leave a school of followers, members of which became heads of important Soviet theatres: Yuri Zavadsky (1894–1977), who also taught Jerzy Grotowski; Boris Shchukin (1894–1939); Reuben Simonov (1899–1968); Boris Zakhava (1896–1976); Nikolai Akimov (1901–1968); and Alexei Popov (1892–1961).

After Vakhtangov's death, both the Third Studio and the First Studio were separated from the Moscow Art Theatre. In 1926, the Third Studio became the Vakhtangov Theatre and remains one of Moscow's leading companies. In 1924, the First Studio was renamed the Second Moscow Art Theatre and placed under the direction of Mikhail Chekhov (1891–1955), who had headed the studio since Vakhtangov's death. Chekhov soon established himself as one of the Soviet Union's leading innovators.

Nephew of the playwright, Chekhov became a member of the Moscow Art Theatre in 1910 at the age of nineteen and was one of the young actors chosen for the First Studio when it was founded in 1911. At the time, Chekhov was totally committed to Stanislavsky's system, but gradually he moved away from it, declaring his independence ultimately with his portrayal of Erik XIV.

Chekhov explored his developing ideas in his own studio and later described them in *The Actor's Path* (1929), *The Problem of the Actor* (1946), and *To the Actor* (1951). He argued that creativity is aroused by a vision of what can *be* rather than by what *is*. Thus he stressed imagination and inspiration over observation and psychological truth. He stressed use of the "psychological gesture," an archetypal gesture employing the whole body, one that captures the essence of a character being played. By repeating this gesture rhythmically offstage, the actor prepares his mind and body to play the character onstage. Chekhov was an extremely versatile performer, playing roles ranging from the comic and grotesque to the tragic. However, his seeming emphasis on the spiritual and fantastic eventually laid him open to charges of mysticism and lack of sympathy with the Bolshevik cause. Chekhov later chose to leave the Soviet Union, spending the remainder of his career acting in films and theatre in Austria, France, Germany, England, and the United States. In 1936, he established a school in England and later, when war broke out, moved it to the United States.

Chekhov's solution—flight to the West— had already been adopted by several others, among them Evreinov (who after his work with mass spectacles had gradually withdrawn from theatrical activities before departing in 1925 for Czechoslovakia and France) and Komissarzhevsky (who left in 1919 and thereafter worked in England, the United States, and France).

THE MOSCOW ART THEATRE AFTER THE REVOLUTION

Not all Soviet directors, of course, were interested in experimentation and innovation. Some theatres sought merely to maintain earlier standards and to educate the masses through realistic productions of the classics. Such groups more nearly represented the tastes of Soviet leaders than did the experimenters. The most conservative companies were those at the former imperial theatres. In Petrograd, for example, the Alexandrinsky at first performed a repertory that relied heavily on Ostrovsky, Fonvizin, and Turgenev. In Moscow, the Maly in some seasons devoted up to 98 percent of its performances to the classics. Its position was strengthened after 1923 when Lunacharsky proclaimed his "Back to Ostrovsky" campaign, for since the nineteenth century, the Maly had been known as the House of Ostrovsky. The company became deeply involved in the struggle between traditionalists and innovators. When, for example, Meyerhold launched his attack against the academic theatres in 1921 and called for their liquidation, he was vigorously answered by Alexander Yuzhin (1857–1927), the Maly's director, who accused Meyerhold of sterile formalism. This was one of the first skirmishes in the long battle between the two attitudes that would end in the triumph of socialist realism.

The Moscow Art Theatre also upheld tradition, although perhaps less rigidly. However, the group did not play a very active role for several years after 1917. For a time, it depended solely on its prerevolutionary repertory, and, in 1919, suffered a serious loss when a number of its actors, on tour in southern Russia, were cut off by the White Army and defected to the West. Between 1917 and 1924, the Moscow Art Theatre mounted only two new important productions, *Cain* and *The Inspector General,* the former of which was withdrawn after only eight performances. And the production of *The Inspector General,* which featured Mikhail Chekhov as Khlestakov, drew attacks from critics who called his performance near-pathological and grotesque.

By 1922, the Moscow Art Theatre was playing such a small role in Soviet theatrical life that no objections were raised when the company left on a two-year tour of Europe and the U.S. While the tour increased the company's considerable fame abroad, upon its return in 1924, the group probably was at its lowest popularity nationally. The company began to present Soviet plays, although before its foreign tour it had steadfastly refused to do so. It had taught the rest of the world about realistic acting, but it now had to find a way to get in touch with Soviet life. Among the works presented were Trenyov's *Pugachev's Rebellion* (1925), Bulgakov's *The Days of the Turbins* (1926), and Ivanov's *Armored Train 14-69* (1927). It was about this time also that other companies began to win recognition with Soviet drama. Although unrecognized at the time, a turning point had been reached. The prototypes of socialist realism had been created, and soon the campaign for its exclusive claims would begin. Thus, the fortunes of the Moscow Art Theatre now steadily improved. The question of what drama and theatre ought to be in a socialist society had, at least for the moment, been answered.

SOCIALIST REALISM AND THE BEGINNINGS OF ARTISTIC REPRESSION

The pressure to subordinate artistic to ideological ends was intensified around 1927. With the end of the New Economic Policy and the beginning of Stalin's first Five-Year Plan came the demand that everyone be dedicated to realizing the party's goals. The Russian Association of Proletarian Writers (RAPP) was given considerable latitude in its attacks on all nonproletarian art. It declared that no apolitical art should be tolerated and that the last remains of bourgeois art should be stamped out. All academic theatres were denounced for their bourgeois tendencies, and Meyerhold and Tairov were strongly criticized for their appeal to bohemians and symbolists. In 1927, RAPP helped found the Theatre of Working Young People (TRAM), which through amateur productions sought to indoctrinate and propagandize for governmental programs.

RAPP won many victories and thus much power. After 1927, party members were systematically trained and installed as theatre managers and given the task of building political orthodoxy among theatre companies. A more stringent censorship was instituted after 1930, and every production had to be licensed before it could be publicly performed. In 1931, RAPP proposed establishing its own theatres to replace all existing theatres, but by now both RAPP and TRAM, like Proletcult, had made the error of elevating their views above those of the Communist Party. Consequently, in 1932, RAPP and TRAM were suppressed, and the somewhat more liberal Union of Soviet Writers was created to insure that literary and dramatic artists be ideologically "correct" in their attitudes toward socialist goals.

Nonetheless, the first truly repressive measure came in 1934 when the Union of Soviet Writers proclaimed *socialist realism* to be the appropriate style for all writing: "Socialist realism, being the basic method of Soviet literature and criticism, requires from the artists truthful, historically concrete representations of reality in its revolutionary development. Moreover, truth and historical completeness of artistic representation must be combined with the task of ideological transformation and education of the working man in the spirit of Socialism."

The official support of socialist realism was to last until the 1950s. Under it, not only were writers expected to reflect contemporary political realities but to include a positive hero or heroine who pointed the way toward the total triumph of Communism.

In the theatre, socialist realism in effect required that all artists be subordinated to the dramatist, since it was the script that provided the primary ideological content. Unfortunately, playwriting was the Soviet theatre's weakest element, and few of the plays produced under the period of socialist realism merit very much attention. Most are melodramatic and fundamentally sentimental: characters who support the Communist ideal are presented as heroes, and those who oppose it are treated as villains; resolutions always point toward the ultimate triumph of Communism and the discomfiture of its enemies. While it is an exaggeration to say that socialist realism produced only "boy-meets-tractor" plots, few examples of socialist realism go beyond these simplicities. Several "important" dramas of the period suggest the basic pattern.

In 1926, Constantin Trenyov (1884–1945) achieved enormous success with *Lyubov Yarovaya,* the story of a schoolteacher whose husband has disappeared during the civil war. When the White Army comes to Lyubov's region seeking to root out Reds, whom she fully supports, she recognizes a White officer to be her missing husband. Though she still loves him, she eventually betrays him because of their political differences.

Another successful playwright was Alexander Afinogenov (1904–1941), whose *Far Taiga* (1934) deals with a dying Red Army officer who is on his way home to Moscow and is forced to stay for a few days in a small village. There he becomes involved in local problems and convinces the people that all of them are important to the huge collective that is the Soviet state.

Alexander Korniechuk (1905–1972), a Party official, was part of the group of Soviet playwrights who sought to glorify Lenin. His play *Truth* (1937) tells how a Ukrainian peasant in search of truth comes to Petrograd and encounters Lenin (thus finding truth) just as the October revolution begins. Another such dramatist was Nikolai Pogodin (1900–1962), whose most popular play, *Man With a Gun* (1937), deals with a soldier who guards the corridors of the Kremlin after the October Revolution. There he meets Lenin and Stalin before he goes to fight at the front. Pogodin's *The Kremlin Chimes* (1942), set in 1920, shows Lenin hunting, talking to old people and children, and in general demonstrating his concern for the common people even as he deals with the most pressing problems of state. Still later Pogodin wrote *The Third, Pathetic* (1955), which treats Lenin's death and his great faith in the future.

Vsevolod Vishnevsky (1900–1951) wrote *Final and Decisive* (1931), a play intended to counteract the romanticized versions of sailor

FIG. 8.9
Korniechuk's *The Front* at the Moscow Art Theatre during World War II. (From Komissarzhevsky, *Moscow Theatres,* 1959.)

FIG. 8.10
Pogodin's *The Kremlin Chimes* at the Moscow Art Theatre. (From Komissarzhevsky, *Moscow Theatres,* 1959.)

FIG. 8.11
Vishnevsky's *Final and Decisive,* directed by Meyerhold in the early 1930s. (From Komissarzhevsky, *Moscow Theatres,* 1959.)

life then prevalent on the Russian stage. (Vishnevsky himself had been a sailor.) The early scenes show the rather crude and immoral life of the sailors, but when war breaks out they prove their devotion to the Soviet Union. Twenty-seven defend their posts to the end, and when the last is wounded, he dies only after scrawling 162,000,000 (the population of the Soviet Union) minus 27—to show how many more will have to be killed before the Soviets will capitulate.

Certainly in another category and clearly one of the very best playwrights of the period was Mikhail Bulgakov (1891–1940), author of thirty-six plays, but nevertheless a writer unable to please authorities. *The Days of the Turbins* (1926) treats the civil war from the viewpoint of the Whites. It was the first (and perhaps last) Soviet play to give a sympathetic portrait of the enemy, and, although the protagonist acknowledges the defeat of his cause and declares his willingness to serve Russia's new leaders, Bulgakov was severely denounced. Opposition grew stronger with *Zoya's Apartment* (1926) and *The Purple Island* (1928), satires on contemporary Soviet problems. The latter play was especially disliked, for it was directed against the committee on theatrical repertories and the propaganda plays it favored. Bulgakov's *Molière* (1931) is a veiled attack on Communist Party hypocrisy and artistic suppression. Treating the seventeenth-century objections to Molière's *Tartuffe* by the religious "cabal," the *Compagnie du Saint-Sacrament,* Bulgakov intended the play as an analogue to the Soviet present. Of his thirty-six plays, only five were permitted on the stage, and these for only very short periods.

Many other playwrights could be mentioned, but they would add little to the overall picture of Stalinist suppression and manipulation of the arts. Almost all dramatists who won favor did so by writing on ideologically acceptable subjects and only in the realist mode. During the 1930s, the classics were "Sovietized" by interpreting them as supporting Communist positions or as showing the necessity of the Revolution because of the decadence of tsarist society. Many pre-revolutionary playwrights (among them Chekhov) who had been downgraded were now "rehabilitated" and brought back into the repertory. But like the work of the living, the plays of dead writers had to be made conformable to Soviet ideology.

STAMPING OUT FORMALISM

It was to such drama that theatrical production was subordinated during the 1930s, and even stricter controls were in the offing. In 1936, the Central Direction of Theatres was created to concentrate in a single agency authority over all troupes (approximately nine hundred). In 1938, a policy of "stabilizing companies" was proclaimed, an edict under which the size and personnel of all troupes were fixed, making it extremely difficult for any theatre worker in the Soviet Union to change jobs.

Furthermore, around 1936 the campaign to stamp out formalism was intensified. Tairov and Meyerhold were the major victims, even though both had compromised their earlier ideals extensively. While in the 1930s Tairov had declared his allegiance to socialist realism and in 1934 had been named a National Artist of the USSR, his position was undermined continually. In 1936 his company was merged with that of the Realistic Theatre. Though he regained control of the Kamerny in 1939, the group was evacuated to Siberia because of the war. While in 1945 he was awarded the Order of Lenin for his wartime services, he nonetheless continued to be charged with formalism. In 1950 his theatre was liquidated, and Tairov died the same year.

Meyerhold's downfall was more rapid and final. During the 1930s, Meyerhold seems to have sought a production style more acceptable to his critics, but with such apolitical stagings as Dumas *fils' Camille* in 1934, which featured Meyerhold's wife, Zinaida Raikh, the campaign against his work intensified. In 1938, his theatre was closed. After this, Meyerhold was offered a position in the Moscow Art Theatre's

Opera Studio. When Stanislavsky died the same year, Meyerhold was named artistic director of the studio. Then in June 1939 came the All-Union Conference of Stage Directors, at which Meyerhold was scheduled to speak (on the assumption, it is said, that he would make a public confession of his artistic errors). It was reported, contrary to expectation, that Meyerhold roundly denounced socialist realism as the ruin of theatrical art. Although his alleged speech has been widely circulated, there is no fully clear indication of what actually occurred. (Some scholars even have questioned whether the speech attributed to him is authentic.) Whatever the case, Meyer-

hold was arrested immediately afterward and was probably executed in 1940. Shortly after his arrest, Zinaida Raikh's mutilated body was discovered in their apartment. Almost twenty years would pass before Meyerhold would be rehabilitated and his pioneering work acknowledged once more in the Soviet Union.

But experimentation was not wholly missing from the Soviet theatre in the 1930s. The most significant work was done by Nikolai Okhlopkov (1900–1966). Okhlopkov began his career as a disciple of Mayakovsky and as a dramatist-actor-producer of mass spectacles. In the mid-1920s, he studied under Meyerhold, and in 1932 became director of the Realistic

FIG. 8.12

Okhlopkov's Realistic Theatre in 1932. Note the various playing levels in relation to audience seating.

Theatre (until 1927 the Moscow Art Theatre's Fourth Studio). Here Okhlopkov applied many of Meyerhold's theories and adapted Eisenstein's technique of having several different actions occurring simultaneously.

Okhlopkov's major innovation was the elimination of the proscenium stage and the relocation of multiple acting areas in the auditorium in close proximity to the audience. Okhlopkov favored scripts, many adapted from novels, which moved rapidly from one episode to another as in film. Although his work enjoyed enormous popularity with audiences, who were attracted to its intimacy, Okhlopkov was denounced by Soviet critics as anarchistic. In 1936, he publicly confessed his errors, and in 1937, his theatre was merged with Tairov's. Unable to work with the older director, Okhlopkov left in 1938 to join the Vakhtangov Theatre, where he directed until he was named head of the Theatre of the Revolution in 1943.

Obviously the official policies of the 1930s tended to favor the traditional companies, for they found it easier than others to adjust to the demands of socialist realism. Above all, it was the Moscow Art Theatre that most gained under the system. In 1932, both Nemirovich-Danchenko and Stanislavsky denounced formalism and declared realism to be the only healthy approach. That same year they announced that henceforth their theatre would be called the House of Gorky (thus renouncing Chekhov) and that they intended to stage a cycle of Gorky's work. (Gorky had just been named head of the Union of Soviet Writers.) In 1937, the Moscow Art Theatre was awarded the Order of Lenin and after Stanislavsky's death in 1938, his system became virtually the only acceptable one for training actors.

By the beginning of World War II, the Russian theatre had lost its independence and had become an instrument of the state. Its great creative urge was spent.

CZECH THEATRE BETWEEN THE WARS

In the 1930s, as Germany and the Soviet Union yielded to totalitarianism and hence artistic suppression, the innovative theatres and dramatic traditions of Czechoslovakia and Poland came to prominence, though not a prominence that was widely recognized in the West, partly owing to the complexity and diversity of Slavic languages. (Just as Ibsen and Strindberg, writing in the minor languages of Dano-Norwegian and Swedish, had had difficulty at first in disseminating their work, so too with the Czechs and Poles.) It was only with the Cold War after World War II that the West truly became interested in Slavic culture. The prominence of Czech and Polish theatre and drama in the interwar years was only short-lived. By 1939, both countries had been invaded by the Nazis. The rich theatrical discoveries of particularly the Czechs and Poles in Eastern Europe in the interwar period were major for the future, even if the fruits of those discoveries had to be postponed until after World War II.

Until World War I, Czechoslovakia had been part of the Austro-Hungarian Empire and had had little opportunity to develop its theatrical resources, although some progress had been made after 1883 when a Czech National Theatre was established in Prague with funds raised through national subscription. After 1900, the general level of production at the National Theatre was raised by Jaroslav Kvapil (1868–1950), who introduced plays by Tolstoy, Ibsen, Chekhov, Wilde, Claudel, and others. In 1906, he sponsored performances given in Prague by the Moscow Art Theatre and thereafter did much to implant Stanislavsky's ideals in his own country. Consequently, he is usually credited with creating a Czech school of psychological acting.

After Czech independence was gained in

1918, the direction of the National Theatre passed to K. H. Hilar (1885–1935), who was attuned to all the new artistic movements occurring in the rest of Europe. His productions, usually designed by Vlatislav Hofman or A. Heythum, reflected the influences of expressionism, futurism, dada, surrealism, neorealism, and other trends. Thus through the work of Hilar, Hofman, the Čapeks, and others, the Czech theatre in the 1920s and 1930s became an up-to-date and vital force.

Alongside the major theatres there grew up a number of experimental studios, among them being Gamza's, the Dada, the Proletkult, the Devetsil, and the Liberated. It was out of these experimental companies that E. F. Burian (1904–1959) came just at that point when experimentation was being suppressed in the Soviet Union. In 1934, he founded the Theatre D34 (the name changed with the year), in which he sought to establish a creative partnership among writers, directors, actors, designers, and other stage personnel. Here with his principal designer Miroslav Kouril (1911–

), he laid the foundations for experimental work that continues even today in Czechoslovakian theatre.

Burian worked in a small concert hall that seated only 383 people and which had a stage only 20 by 12 feet. Perhaps because of these limited facilities, Burian placed special emphasis on light and music, out of which evolved three significant multimedia productions: Wedekind's *Spring Awakening* in 1936; Pushkin's *Yevgeny Onegin* in 1937; and *The Sorrows of Young Werther* in 1938, based on the novel by Goethe. Burian seldom produced texts written for the stage, preferring to make his own adaptations.

Even Wedekind's drama was significantly altered in Burian's production. Kouril made the stage a black void surrounded by black velvet drapes hung so as to permit characters to appear as if by magic. The acting area was composed of two connected platforms on which furniture and properties were placed as needed. The main feature of the stage was a narrow screen at the back, on which slides

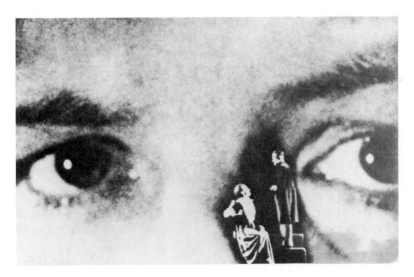

FIG. 8.13
Burian's production of Wedekind's *Spring Awakening* at Theatre D37 in 1936. Setting by Kouril. (Courtesy Professor F. Cerny, Charles University, Prague.)

could be projected from the wings. More important, the entire proscenium opening was covered with a scrim through which the action could be seen and on which slides and films were projected from the front. Thus, the entire acting area was left free for use by the performers, and the scenic elements (except for properties) were created with projections and light.

Burian used light to emphasize his actors' three-dimensionality, to isolate them in space, to reveal a hand or a face, or to make actors appear or disappear. The lighting also changed in color and intensity to reflect emotional and atmospheric qualities or to shift emphasis from one character to another.

The most remarkable feature of the production, however, was the overlapping of projected images with actors, for the performers were perceived within and through projections. Most of the slides showed enlarged or selective details. A schoolroom was created, for example, by projecting on the scrim images of stuffed birds from the school museum; a meadow was revealed through closeup projections of daisies in blossom; Melchoir's room was simply a projection of a window; and a projection of prison bars represented a reformatory. Often the actors related themselves directly to the projections: in the meadow, the girl seemed to caress the daisies; in his room, Melchoir stared out the window; later in the reformatory, he sought to break the bars.

A still more dynamic use was made of film. In the scene in which the girl is seduced, the entire action took place on film. Beginning with a closeup of the girl's face, the scene continued by showing the boy's hand tearing away her dress to expose a breast. Then the whole screen was covered with lily buds, which slowly opened to full flower. Similarly the girl's death was conveyed by the filmed speeded-up fading of a rose. In some scenes, films of the actors were projected on the scrim while the microphoned actors' voices from backstage were heard over loudspeakers. Occasionally the picture of an absent person was projected on a screen while he or she was discussed by onstage characters. For example, as Melchoir's parents discussed the girl, her face appeared and moved closer and closer until only her accusing eyes were seen.

Burian was extremely successful in blending his various media. The film and slides were always subordinated to the dramatic action and were meaningless without it. Thus, such elements did not compete with the main action, as was the case often in Piscator's use of film and slides. The overall impression was summed up well by a critic: "The rapid succession of images and settings, together with the use of light to model the characters on the stage, and the accompaniment of subdued music, accomplish true wonders here. The action seems to go on in a vision of budding, pulsing, blossoming spring, in waves of blossoms through apparitions of accusing, terrifying eyes and faces, in alternation of light and darkness, out of which scenes and images emerge one by one." Burian's were probably the most skillful multimedia productions seen prior to World War II.

When the Nazis came, the Czech theatre was soon reduced to mediocrity. In 1941, Burian's theatre was closed and he was confined to a concentration camp. Nevertheless, it is from the work of Burian and Kouril that the more recent Czech interest in multimedia have come, best represented by the work of Josef Svoboda. In the 1950s, Kouril, with Svoboda, founded the Scenographic Institute in Prague. But in the 1930s, the Czech experiments, particularly of Burian and Kouril, seemed but one of the last flickers of originality before the Holocaust of World War II engulfed all of Europe.

THE POLISH THEATRE TRADITION AND THE INTERWAR PERIOD

During the interwar years, the theatre in Poland also came to maturity. Although the Polish dramatic tradition can be traced back to the Middle Ages, its first significant expression came in the romantic period at the beginning of the nineteenth century. Poland's three major romantic poet/playwrights—Adam Mickiewicz (1798–1855), Juliusz Słowacki (1809–1849), and Zygmunt Krasiński (1812–1859)—all wrote and published their plays in exile. Though Poland since the Renaissance had been a large kingdom, by 1795 the country was totally eliminated by partition, being divided among Prussia, Austria, and Russia. Like Czechoslovakia, Poland did not once again achieve independence until 1918, following World War I. Thus the "dramatic poems" of Mickiewicz, Słowacki, and Krasiński were not staged until the early twentieth century. Since that time, however, their work has become the backbone of the Polish national repertory, and the influence of this romantic tradition permeates all that has happened in Polish theatre to the present.

Of the three writers, Mickiewicz is usually considered the most significant, being accorded a position in Polish art and culture not unlike that of Goethe in Germany. His most important play, *Forefather's Eve* (in four parts, 1823–1832), like Goethe's *Faust,* Parts I and II, written over a long period, uses as its framework an ancient folk ritual performed on All Saints Day when peasants come to remote chapels and call forth the dead, offering them food. The heart of the lengthy drama is Part III, in which the hero, Gustaw-Konrad, confined to a Russian prison, gradually moves beyond his self-preoccupation and personal concerns to identification with the struggle of his partitioned nation and its people. Eventually he assumes a moral stance superior even to that of God, for God sees misery in the world and allows it to continue, whereas Gustaw-Konrad resolves to oppose misery. Like many of the Polish plays that emerge in the romantic period, *Forefather's Eve* is a series of fragments unified by dream-visions.

Mickiewicz also influenced Polish thought in the twentieth century through a series of lectures on Slavic literature delivered in Paris in the 1840s. He declared that Slavic drama continues the only valid theatrical tradition—that of ancient Greece and medieval religious drama, in which heroes and saints are brought to life. Mickiewicz argued that through the Slavic gift for grasping the supernatural, Polish dramatists blend a concern for current problems with historical and spiritual awareness. Mickiewicz recognized that the type of play he wrote and championed was impossible to stage in his day, but his call for a new, more resourceful theatre has gained many Polish listeners in the present.

The plays of Słowacki and Krasiński, like those of Mickiewicz, require theatrical means beyond those in vogue at the time they were written. The hero of Słowacki's *Kordian* (1834) is similar to Mickiewicz's Gustaw-Konrad, in that his progressive search for personal fulfillment ultimately leads to his commitment to the national cause of partitioned Poland. After an unsuccessful attempt to assassinate the tsar (foiled by Kordian's moral scruples), the hero is confined to an insane asylum. Though Kordian passes a test of valor to gain his release, ultimately the tsar issues the order for his execution anyway. But an outline such as this cannot suggest the enormous scope of the action nor the monumental visual effects of Słowacki's play.

Krasiński's *The Undivine Comedy* (1833) depicts the struggle between an entrenched aristocracy and a revolutionary proletariat. The hero, Count Henry, an aristocrat like

Krasiński himself, resembles both Mickiewicz's Gustaw-Konrad and Słowacki's Kordian in that he changes from a man of self-absorption to one identifying with the larger concerns of his countrymen. Count Henry views revolution as inevitable and foresees his own destruction, but at the moment when his premonitions prove true, a cross appears in the sky, signaling that the ultimate answer may lie in a synthesis of the old aristocratic view of Christianity and the new spirit of revolution.

Unlike the rest of Europe, Poland never experienced a truly significant period of theatrical realism following the romantic movement. Only Gabriela Zapolska (1857–1921), an actress, playwright, and novelist, who worked for a time in Paris with Antoine, produced plays in the realist style. Her most famous work, *The Morality of Mrs. Dulska* (1907), develops an action similar to that of Shaw's *Mrs. Warren's Profession*.

The playwright usually considered the founder of modern Polish drama was Stanisław Wyspiański (1869–1907), a man of many artistic talents. A painter, poet, dramatist, and theatre director, Wyspiański was well-educated and widely traveled. His plays include classical tragedies on patriotic themes, dramas of peasant life, pieces based on contemporary events, and (above all) symbolic dramas about the national character and destiny. In the last type, he was the direct heir of Mickiewicz, Słowacki, and Krasiński.

Wyspiański's most famous work is *The Wedding* (1901), often said to have begun a new era in Polish drama. In it Wyspiański uses a country wedding between a peasant girl and an aristocrat (based on his own experience of an aristocratic friend who married a peasant girl) to bring together representatives of all levels of society to discuss literature, business, and politics. The characters come onstage one or two at a time and then return to the noisy festivities in an adjoining room. But as time

passes and drink flows more freely and music weaves a spell, characters of a quite different sort begin to appear. Some of them are historical or fictional personages; others, such as a personified straw rosebush mulch, are fantastic creatures. At the end, all the characters join in a somnambulistic dance led by the straw creature and his fiddle. Thus Wyspiański mingles real persons and embodied dreams to create a cross-section of Polish society and mythology. Throughout there is a hint of some great revelation in the offing, but it never comes. At the end Wyspiański seems to suggest that the will of the Polish people is paralyzed— that they are men of straw with no power to throw off their oppressors. Thus, Wyspianski continues the tradition of the exiled Polish romantic artist whose homeland is paralyzed by invaders.

Wyspiański's *Akropolis* (1904) is also of considerable interest, in part because it served as the basis for a famous production by Jerzy Grotowski in the 1960s. The play is set in Cracow, the center of Polish art and culture— the Polish Acropolis. During the action, biblical and classical figures from the statues and tapestries of Cracow cathedral and castle come to life and enact scenes relevant to the contemporary situation. (Grotowski, incidentally, set his production in the concentration camp at Auschwitz, some thirty miles from Cracow, a site he viewed ironically as the new Polish Acropolis.)

In addition to writing plays, Wyspiański also was concerned with reforming the theatre. Like Wagner, he believed that the theatre should be a unified work of art composed of word, color, music, and movement. His plays were more nearly librettos for a director than self-contained literary works, and his stage directions call for effects beyond the theatre technology of his time. He staged many plays himself and was the first to perform the works of Mickiewicz, Słowacki, and Krasiński. Despite his imaginative genius, however, Wyspiański failed to conceive of an abstract stage. Like most directors at the turn of the century, he believed it necessary to have a different setting for each scene indicated, thus making it overly difficult to stage not only the works of the earlier romantics but his own works as well.

A more significant director was Arnold Szyfman (1882–1967). If Wyspiański signals the beginning of modern Polish drama, Szyfman marks the beginning of the modern Polish theatre. In 1913, he opened the Polski Theatre in Warsaw. Equipped with all the latest technical devices (including a revolving stage), the Polski was the first theatre in Poland consistently to use specially designed settings and costumes for each new production. The two principal designers, Karol Frycz and Wincenty Drabik, among the best in Europe, were sympathetic to cubism, expressionism, and constructivism, and both emphasized a polydimensional space which could be transformed endlessly through light. After Poland became independent in 1918, the Polski Theatre, named a state company, continued to champion innovative techniques.

After independence, the attempt to create a

FIG. 8.14
Szyfman's production of *Romeo and Juliet* at the Polski Theatre, Warsaw, in 1931. Scenery and costumes by Karol Frycz. (From Lorentowicz, *Teatr Polski w Warszawie, 1913–1938*, 1938.)

truly national form of theatre was avidly pursued by a host of talented directors and designers. Among them, by far the most important was Leon Schiller (1887–1954), for it was he who synthesized the major trends and gave them their most characteristic expression. As a music student, Schiller had studied and traveled widely in Europe before turning his attention to theatre after meeting Gordon Craig. He then came under the influence of Wyspiański and eventually evolved his own outlook during the time he served as literary advisor to the Polski Theatre. Schiller championed what he called *monumental theatre* (based on the ideas of Mickiewicz, Wyspiański, and Craig, in addition to his own). He favored works with a large number of plots and with moods and ideas that he could shape to give

interpretations compatible with his own artistic, social, and political views. He did not hesitate to alter texts. Furthermore, he wholly ignored stage directions, seeking instead to utilize modern technology (machinery, lighting, projections, and sound), carefully orchestrated movement, and polydimensional, flexible space to achieve effects comparable to those suggested by the authors but more compatible with modern sensibilities.

Schiller did not begin to work as an independent director until 1924, when he founded his own theatre—the Bogusławski—in collaboration with Wilam Horzyca. After his troupe was disbanded in 1926, he directed at the Polski Theatre and later in Lvov. He made his greatest impressions with productions of plays from the romantic tradition and also

FIG. 8.15

Leon Schiller's production of Mickiewicz's *Forefather's Eve* at the Polski Theatre in 1934. Design by A. Pronaszko. (From Lorentowicz, *Teatr Polski w Warszawie, 1913–1938*, 1938.)

adaptations of novels. Among his most important productions were Krasiński's *Undivine Comedy,* Słowacki's *Kordian,* Wyspiański's *Achilles,* an adaptation of Żeromski's novel *The Story of Sin* (in forty-three scenes), and Mickiewicz's *Forefather's Eve.* For Mickiewicz's play, Andrzej Pronaszko designed a permanent setting with three levels surmounted by three crosses which remained visible through most of the action to symbolize the Polish Calvary. There were no interior settings; instead, generalized architectural forms and lighting were used in conjunction to define playing areas for the multiple locales of the ever-shifting action. Ghosts, rather than being played by actors, were depicted by such devices as a flame or pillar of smoke from which disembodied voices seemed to emanate. It was through his work with such "unstageable" plays that Schiller most firmly set his stamp on the theatre of his time.

During the 1930s, Schiller became increasingly interested in politics and moved in the direction of German neorealism. He called his work of this period *composed realism.* During World War II, he survived Auschwitz, and from 1945 to 1949 he once again became the most important director in Poland. When, under Soviet domination, socialist realism became the only accepted mode, Schiller lost his privileged position. Nevertheless, there are few directors in the postwar Polish theatre who were not influenced by Schiller, not only through his productions but through his teaching (at the State Theatre Institute) and writings (more than two hundred essays). During the interwar years, the Polish theatre probably reached its peak with Schiller's work, which both technologically and artistically equaled that to be seen anywhere in the world.

During this period one playwright—Stanisław Ignacy Witkiewicz (1885–1939), or Witkacy, as he called himself—could also claim true originality. Although his plays were virtually ignored until after World War II—most had been produced only by amateurs during his lifetime—Witkiewicz's approximately thirty plays today are continually produced in Poland. His works, almost all of which were written between 1918 and 1926, predate the Theatre of the Absurd by almost a quarter of a century. To his contemporaries, however, Witkiewicz seemed little more than a madman or prankster.

Son of a famous artist, Witkiewicz made his living as a talented though unconventional portrait painter. By 1914, he had traveled widely in Europe (becoming familiar with cubism and futurism) and in Asia, Australia, and New Guinea (where unfamiliar cultural patterns made a deep impression on him). During World War I, he served as an officer in the Russian army and was elected political commissar of his regiment following the Revolution. By the time he returned to Poland in 1918, he had arrived at that vision of the world that was to inform his work thereafter. He considered Western civilization to be on the verge of collapse, and about it he had mixed feelings: on the one hand, he saw revolution as essential to social equity, but, on the other, he was convinced that the aftermath would produce a leveling in which all individuality would be lost. About this he observed gloomily, "From a herd we came and to a herd we shall return."

To Witkiewicz, art was the only means of expressing and soothing the anxiety which results from the "metaphysical strangeness of existence." He suggested that when religion and philosophy were still potent forces they gave to art an harmonious order no longer possible. The contemporary artist must seek unity out of increasingly disparate and dissonant elements, for modern art tends toward perversity compounded of the strident, the ugly, and the jarring.

Witkiewicz wrote three books on aesthetic

questions, of which the most important here is *An Introduction to the Theory of Pure Form in the Theatre* (1923). He proposed the need for a theatre which, rather than seeking to imitate life, would manipulate the theatrical elements for purely formal ends, as in abstract painting or music. He wrote: "Our aim is not programmatic nonsense; we rather try to enlarge the possibilities of composition by abandoning lifelike logic in art, by introducing a fantastic psychology and fantastic action, in order to win complete freedom for formal elements." About the ultimate effect he sought, Witkiewicz wrote: "When leaving the theatre, one should have the impression that one wakes up from a strange dream in which the most trite things have the elusive, deep charm characteristic of dreams, not comparable to anything."

Witkiewicz felt it necessary to move beyond the realm of objective reality into the inner world of the unconscious, and he often used drugs to assist him in subverting his intellect. (In the lower right-hand corners of his portraits and drawings, for example, he wrote the precise chemical formulas for the drugs he used in the process of creating the portrait or drawing, and he described his experiences in *Nicotine, Alcohol, Cocaine, Peyote, Morphine, and Ether,* published in 1932.) In this realm beyond logic (comparable to that described by the surrealists), he was able to juxtapose several levels of reality and elements from various genres and styles. His pessimism about the future led him to write most often about madmen and misfits as specimens of a doomed world. They engage, often comically, in violent actions in which sex and murder are the most common ingredients, although those killed usually come back to life. Witkiewicz's characters are motivated by a fantastic psychology and speak a language bearing little resemblance to everyday speech. Even the least educated are apt to discourse learnedly about literature and philosophy and to create esoteric treatises. The plays, which Witkiewicz sometimes called "comedies with corpses," may be grouped with those of Strindberg, Jarry, Artaud, Ghelderode, the surrealists, and the later absurdists.

His best-known works include *They* (1920), *The Water Hen* (1921), *The Madman and the Nun* (1923), *The Crazy Locomotive* (1923), and *The Mother* (1924). All are difficult to describe because they are composed of disparate elements and much that defies logical explication. *The Madman and the Nun,* however, is representative. The basic situation is that of a young "madman" poet, Alexander Walpurg, confined to the cell of a lunatic asylum. Surrounded by even more "insane" psychiatric doctors and a matronly Mother Superior, Walpurg wins the confidence and passion of the beautiful young nun, Sister Anna, who has been placed in Walpurg's cell to find out more about his "complex." Sister Anna, however, releases Walpurg nightly from his strait-jacket into a euphoric world of sexual passion. Meanwhile, Walpurg kills one of his doctors with a pencil stab to the temple while another calmly rationalizes his action as "a wonderful lesson for the old psychiatric school." The doctor will write a monograph about Walpurg's act and become world famous, so he says. Eventually, however, Walpurg and Sister Anna's romantic trysts are discovered, but instead of a conventional denouement, Witkiewicz tricks expectancy. Walpurg hangs himself but a moment later enters impeccably dressed in a stylish cutaway accompanied by the doctor he has killed. The two carry a stylish dress and hat for Sister Anna. Doctor, Walpurg, and Sister Anna leave the cell together, locking in the rest of the asylum doctors and staff and the Mother Superior. As the play ends, those left in the cell are seen wrestling furiously under blue lights with a dummy representing Walpurg's corpse in "a rough-and-tumble, hand-to-hand free-for-all in the Russian manner."

After 1926, Witkiewicz's interests turned away from theatre, and thereafter he wrote only one important work, *The Shoemakers* (1934), his most conventional play. Shortly after the beginning of World War II, Witkiewicz committed suicide, like Ernst Toller, as an act of protest.

After 1939, the theatre in Poland suffered much the same fate as that in Czechoslovakia. No country in Europe was more devastated by World War II. But the Polish spirit was not broken, and after the war some of its theatre artists would gain worldwide recognition and acclaim.

experiments, particularly of Meyerhold, Tairov, Vakhtangov, Eisenstein, and Okhlopkov, provided stimulation for numerous directors internationally following World War II. Socialist realism, the official style of Soviet production and playwriting, maintained its stranglehold until the so-called thaw in the mid-1950s following the death of Stalin. After the war came the Soviet political domination of the whole of Eastern Europe, and the rich theatrical and dramatic discoveries of individuals such as Burian and Witkiewicz were held in abeyance until the denunciations of Stalinism. In the 1960s, however, the theatre and drama, particularly of Czechoslovakia and Poland, were to become of great importance internationally.

PREWAR INNOVATIONS HELD IN ABEYANCE

Even though theatre in the Soviet Union ceased to be innovative in the 1930s, the

Chapter 9

Italian, French, and Belgian Theatre and Drama Between the Wars

Though its theatrical and dramatic output was small during the interwar years, Italy made a major contribution to modern drama through the work of Pirandello, whose preoccupation with "seeming" and "being" influenced virtually all subsequent Western playwrights. France, on the other hand, made its major impact through its "studio" theatres, most of which took their cue from the Vieux Colombier and Copeau, a director who sought to establish the highest artistic standards in both production and playwriting. At the same time, however, quite contrary ideals—epitomized in the theories of Artaud—were gathering force. Similarly, playwriting in France was dominated by Giraudoux, who emphasized literary merit, even as the dominant role of language was being challenged by the Belgian playwright Ghelderode.

PIRANDELLO AND
HIS CONTEMPORARIES

During those years when the futurists were seeking to transform the theatre in Italy, other equally powerful (but not wholly antipathetic) forces were at work in drama. They first became evident in the *theatre of the grotesque,* a type of play that took its name from Luigi Chiarelli's (1884–1947) *The Mask and the Face* (1916), subtitled "a grotesque in three acts," which made such an impact that it was considered the pioneering work in a new school of writing. The protagonist of *The Mask and the Face,* Paolo, wishes to live by his country's code of honor but is faced with a dilemma when he thinks his wife Savina has been unfaithful. Not wanting to kill her but unable to face possible ridicule, he sends Savina away and then declares he has killed her and thrown her body into a lake. At his sensational trial, Paolo depicts himself as a husband acting to protect his honor; acquitted, he is given a civic welcome and receives many proposals of marriage. Then the public insists that a suitable funeral service be arranged for Savina, who unable to resist attending, appears veiled in black. Paolo recognizes her, takes her home, and locks her in a room. Faced with rampant gossip, he realizes Savina is necessary to his happiness and decides to reinstate her as his wife regardless of what is said.

By 1920, critics were conscious of a school of "grotesque" dramatists, which included in its ranks such writers as Luigi Antonelli (1882–1942) and Piermaria Rosso di San Secondo (1887–1956). Among this group, critics at first also placed Luigi Pirandello (1867–1936), although the resemblance was largely superficial, for, although he too was concerned with appearance and reality, unlike the others he questioned whether a more reliable truth is to be seen when the mask is stripped away. Thus, even though he employed some of the same

means, he differed considerably from his contemporaries in his philosophical concerns. The plays that expressed his views were to have a profound effect on subsequent Western drama.

By birth a Sicilian, Pirandello had already earned an enviable reputation as novelist and short story writer before turning to drama, first in short plays in 1910 and to full-length works in 1915. Thereafter, he devoted himself almost entirely to the theatre. But if Pirandello wrote many plays, in all of them he developed the same related issues. Unlike the dramatists who wrote in the grotesque vein and treated reality as clearly discernible behind the mask, Pirandello denied that reality can be grasped. He declared: "Each of us believes himself to be one, but that is a false assumption: each of us is so many, . . . as many as are all the potentialities of being that are in us. . . . We ourselves know only one part of ourselves, and in all likelihood the least significant." Thus, for Pirandello, it is impossible to distinguish the mask from the face not only in others but in ourselves as well.

Pirandello believed that each person constructs a personality out of the innumerable roles one is asked to play in various realms (family, society, religion, business, etc.) but that no one of these roles is the entire person, for each is like a separate mask for a separate occasion. Thus, it is virtually impossible to know the full truth about anyone. Furthermore, people become so accustomed to playing a role that they forget they are doing so. Pirandello thought of his plays as mirrors in which people would be forced to view themselves. Like Shaw, Pirandello was much influenced by Bergson's concept of creative evolution, according to which an instinctive urge within human beings moves them toward a higher state of being. Thus, to be vital means to be forever changing. On the other hand, human beings also desire order, which can be gained only through fixity. Consequently, each human being is confronted with a fundamental conflict, and society at large is subject to the same conflict.

The search for fixity in a world of constant flux undergirds all of Pirandello's plays, which dramatize the evanescence of truth and proclaim that "the certainty of today . . . is not the certainty it was yesterday, and will not be the certainty of tomorrow." Though Pirandello's specific situations change from play to play, his philosophical concerns remain constant.

Pirandello's outlook and dramatic method were first clearly evidenced in *Right You Are—*

FIG. 9.1

Scene from Pirandello's *Right You Are—If You Think You Are,* produced at the Teatro Quirino, Rome, by the Emma Gramatica Company in 1957. (From *World Theatre.*)

If You Think You Are (1917), in which Signor Ponsa and his mother-in-law Signora Frola argue over the identity of Ponsa's wife. The wife, the only person who could resolve the issue, refuses to do so: "I am she whom you believe me to be." Thus, Pirandello establishes his thesis that truth varies according to the point of view. He is most successful in meshing idea and action in *Henry IV* (1922). Twenty years before the play opens, the protagonist, while impersonating the eleventh-century Holy Roman Emperor Henry IV in a pageant, falls from his horse (goaded by Tito Belcredi, we later learn) and thereafter believes himself to be the emperor. When the play opens, he has regained his senses and recognizes that life has completely passed him by. Overcome by rage at his wasted life, Henry kills Belcredi. He now realizes that his deed has condemned him to go on playing the role of a madman for the rest of his life.

Pirandello's concern for multileveled reality found its most complete and complex expression in three plays about the theatre: *Six Characters in Search of an Author* (1921), *Each in His Own Way* (1924), and *Tonight We Improvise* (1930). Here his affinity with the futurists was most evident, for Pirandello deliberately broke the fourth-wall convention to explore varying levels of illusion. By focusing on the theatre, he was able to depict self-conscious attempts to create an illusion of reality, which is itself already compounded of illusions. Also in these plays, Pirandello explored another of his obsessions—the relationship of art to nature. Since truth means continual change and since "a finished work of art is fixed forever in immutable form," the theatre is the most satisfying form of art. Since the theatre ultimately depends on the actor (who can only partially assume the mask of a character and whose impersonation differs at each performance), theatre is "not enduring creation. [It is a] thing of the moment. A miracle. A statue that moves." Pirandello suggests how inadequate is realism, which can only produce a travesty of truth, and suggests that the only remedy lies in writing philosophical plays that show reality as ever-changing. One cannot capture reality even on the stage.

In *Six Characters in Search of an Author*, fictional characters interrupt a rehearsal and plead to have their stories played out so that they as characters may take on full being. But when the actors seek to do just that, they present mere lifeless stereotypes. Even the characters cannot agree among themselves about the details of their essentially melodramatic story. But, because they are imbedded in an art work, their fates are already sealed by the author; they may struggle against the inevitable but they are doomed by the artistic form. By using the device of a rehearsal, Pirandello is able to explore reality on at least three different levels: in a written text, on the stage, and in life. *Each in His Own Way* takes the process one step further, for here the drama

being presented in the theatre (the play-within-the-play) supposedly treats real events and persons, some of whom are in the audience watching. Furthermore, some scenes are set in the lobby, where spectators discuss both the play and its real-life counterparts. In *Tonight We Improvise*, Pirandello makes the Director announce that, in order that art may more nearly approximate life, the actors will improvise a play from a brief scenario. The performers then move in and out of the drama, commenting on it, the theatre, and life, but eventually they get so caught up in their roles that they play out a conclusion contrary to their wishes. Despite Pirandello's attempts in these plays to present various levels of reality, one ultimately recognizes that it is the playwright himself who has created all the levels and consequently that all is simply dramatic illusion.

Though Pirandello's philosophical outlook was unusual for his day, most of his dramatic techniques were not. He made use of extreme

FIG. 9.2
Pirandello's *Tonight We Improvise*, directed by Silvio D'Amico at the Royal Academy of Dramatic Art, Rome. (From *World Theatre*.)

situations—adultery, murder, mistaken identity, and betrayals—and devices inherited from melodrama and the well-made play. Thus he clothed his philosophy in conventional dramatic forms. His principal departure from tradition lay in breaking down the convention of the fourth wall in order to involve the audience more directly in the conflict of ideas.

During the interwar years both Pirandello's ideas and theatrical techniques, particularly in his theatre trilogy, were sufficiently novel to baffle audiences and occasionally create minor scandals. When *Six Characters in Search of an Author* was performed in Rome in 1921, for example, there was a near-riot at the Teatro Valle, and when *Tonight We Improvise* was produced in Berlin in 1930, members of the audience became so unruly that the enraged director, Hans Hartung, shouted insults at them from the stage.

In 1924, Pirandello formed his own company, the Art Theatre of Rome, of which he was the director and Marta Abba (1906–1988) the principal actress. Between 1925 and 1927 the troupe toured widely in Europe and South America. By the time it dissolved in 1928, it had done much to spread Pirandello's fame throughout the world. After this, Pirandello had little to do with dramatic production and lived abroad much of the time. In 1934 he was awarded the Nobel Prize. If Pirandello's plays no longer seem as remarkable as they once did, it is because the ideas he championed have since gained such wide currency that they no longer startle. But probably no other writer was to be so influential in establishing the philosophical view espoused by dramatists of the post-World War II period.

GEMIER, LUGNE-POE, HEBERTOT, AND COPEAU

In France, the years between 1914 and 1918 were extremely difficult ones for the theatre, since virtually every able-bodied man was conscripted. Many theatres closed altogether, and even the august Comédie Française was reduced to using students from the Conservatoire in some of its productions. Most theatres that remained open concentrated on productions designed to boost morale or to provide escapist entertainment. But when hostilities ceased, the theatres rapidly regained vitality. In the revival, four people—Gémier, Lugné-Poë, Hébertot, and Copeau—were most important.

During the war, Gémier continued to operate the Théâtre Antoine, though on a reduced scale. At this time, he made only few innovations, the most important of which was the removal of footlights and the installation of steps to bridge the stage and auditorium, thus breaking down barriers between performers and spectators.

When the war ended, however, Gémier resumed his prewar efforts to create a people's theatre. He turned to a circus-theatre, the Cirque d'Hiver, which he saw as a modern equivalent to the ancient Greek theatre. In 1919–1920, Gémier mounted at the Cirque d'Hiver productions of *Oedipus, King of Thebes* by Saint-Georges de Bouhélier and *The Great Pastoral,* a Provençal nativity play adapted by Charles Hellem and Pol d'Estoc. In the former, the most striking scene occurred when two hundred supernumeraries, many of them trained gymnasts, javelin throwers, and jumpers, staged an olympic contest.

In 1920, Gémier won a small victory in his effort to establish a people's theatre when the government created the Théâtre National Populaire (TNP) and named him its director. The government scheme, however, was merely to take established productions from the national theatres and perform them at the Trocadero, a large exhibition hall, at reduced prices for popular audiences. The TNP was given only token financial support, had no troupe of its

FIG. 9.3

Gémier's production of *Oedipus, King of Thebes* at the Cirque d'Hiver, Paris, in 1919. (From *L'Eclair*, 1919.)

own, and could not produce its own plays. It was partially Gémier's desire to serve the TNP that brought him in 1922 to take over directorship of the Odéon, France's second state theatre. Though he led the TNP until 1933, he was never able to develop it beyond the embryonic stage. But to Gémier goes credit for sustaining the organization and laying the groundwork for later developments. After 1951, when Jean Vilar became its head, the TNP at last would become the force Gémier had envisioned.

Gémier sought to make the Odéon (which he headed until 1930) an experimental theatre capable of appealing to a wider audience than its traditional one, composed primarily of students and families. In his efforts, he was assisted by Austrian designer René Fuerst, who was attuned to Appia's theories and recent theatre experiments in Germany. Under

Gémier, the Odéon became truly eclectic, reflecting all recent trends, including cubism, surrealism, and expressionism. Gémier was the French director who most nearly approximated Reinhardt's wide-ranging eclecticism. A further example of this eclectic talent is evidenced in Gémier's interest in the studio theatres so characteristic of postwar Paris. The studios were based almost exclusively on artistic rather than commercial principles, and their directors, like dedicated painters, believed that art should never be sacrificed in order to attract an audience. In 1920 with one of the studies of the Comédie Montaigne, which he placed under the direction of Gaston Baty, Gémier developed a season which featured works by Lenormand, Crommelynck, Shaw, Claudel, and Shakespeare, starring both Charles Dullin and Gémier himself as actors. The season was a considerable critical success but a financial failure, and consequently the enterprise was abandoned in 1921. Gémier also developed a school, the Conservatoire Syndical de Gémier, headed for a time by Dullin. Thus, Gémier's involvement in many and varied activities made him a major force in the postwar theatre. His career, extending from the 1890s to the 1930s, also represented a major link with the past.

Lugné-Poë provided a similar link, but he played a less prominent role than did Gémier in the theatre of the 1920s. With the coming of war in 1914, Lugné-Poë closed the Théâtre de l'Oeuvre, but in 1919 he reopened it and continued to lead it until 1929, when he turned it over to Paulette Pax and Lucien Berr. Lugné-Poë saw his theatre as serving the special function of encouraging young playwrights, and he often derided Copeau's efforts by suggesting that Copeau had a predilection for authors who had taken up playwriting in middle age. Lugné-Poë's programs were devoted to new or unrecognized writers, among them being Crommelynck, Salacrou, Achard, and Passeur. He was also the only producer in Paris to open his theatre to the dadaists, and, in addition to encouraging new writers, Lugné-Poë sought to familiarize the French public with plays by foreign writers such as Strindberg, Shaw, Chekhov, Kaiser, and D'Annunzio. He also published the *Revue de l'Oeuvre,* in which appeared essays on dramatists, ballet, architecture, and related subjects, thus seeking to keep audiences abreast of new developments.

But Lugné-Poë became increasingly independent and irascible. He reserved the right to select his own subscribers, and, though critics were admitted, they were not invited to the Oeuvre. He launched frequent and bitter attacks on Copeau's choice of plays and his austere productions. Though he came to be considered something of an eccentric, Lugné-Poë in the years between 1919 and 1929 nonetheless played an important role in the French theatre.

FIG. 9.4

Lugné-Poë's production of Crommelynck's *The Magnificent Cuckold,* Théâtre de l'Oeuvre, Paris, 1920. (From *Le Théâtre,* 1920.)

Jacques Hébertot (1886–1971) contributed to the postwar theatre primarily as an entrepreneur. A poet, critic, and editor, Hébertot ran two adjacent theatres, the Théâtre des Champs-Elysées and the Comédie des Champs-Elysées, from 1920 to 1926; in 1923, in response to the growing interest in studios, he added the Studio des Champs-Elysées. For these houses, he sought the best directors, plays, and companies and was remarkably astute in recognizing talent. In 1922, he invited Georges Pitoëff to form a company, in the same year employed Jouvet as a director, and, when he established his studio, secured Baty to lead it. He also employed Theodor Komissarzhevsky as a director. Furthermore, Hébertot sponsored many foreign troupes, among them the Moscow

Art and Kamerny theatres, and it was in his theatres that the Ballets Suédois performed between 1920 and 1925. Hébertot gave up management in 1926 and thereafter edited a series of theatrical magazines. In 1940, he returned to directing, working in a theatre that later bore his name.

Above all, however, it was Jacques Copeau who set his stamp on French theatre between the wars. After the Vieux Colombier was closed in 1914, he visited Gordon Craig in Florence (he had earlier gone to Switzerland to see Dalcroze and Appia) and with Suzanne Bing in 1915 opened a school for young amateurs, children, and professionals. In 1917, Copeau was sent by the French government on a cultural mission to New York, where he gave lectures and play readings. Otto Kahn, a banker and patron of the arts, was so impressed with Copeau that he offered to subsidize Copeau's company in America. Consequently, with the blessing of the French government, Copeau reconstituted his company and from 1917 to 1919 performed a repertory of plays in French at the Garrick Theatre. It is difficult to assess Copeau's impact on the American theatre, but undoubtedly the presence of his company in New York served along with several other forces to hasten the acceptance in America of new techniques.

In 1919 Copeau returned to Paris and to the Vieux Colombier, which was now remodeled by Jouvet along lines slightly different from those used in 1913–1914. Forward of the proscenium was an apron with three semicircular steps leading to a lower level and then into the auditorium itself. There were no footlights. Back of the proscenium there was virtually no wing space, and access to acting areas could be gained only from stage right. At the rear of the stage, Jouvet erected a permanent structure which included an alcove below and a playing level above, reached by a series of curved stairs. The entire structure could be

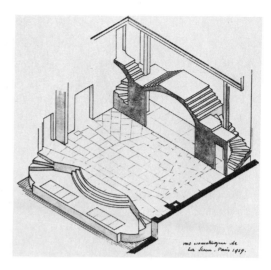

FIG. 9.5

Interior of the Vieux Colombier in 1919. (From Moussinac, *New Movement in the Theatre.*)

masked or altered in various ways. On this stage only the simplest, most necessary, and expressive set pieces and properties were used, and its appearance was only slightly altered from one production to the next. The theatre's one luxury was its lighting, which was used to create mood and to give emphasis to the three-dimensionality of the performers and the space in which they played. Thus, the Vieux Colombier was an architectural stage intended to enhance but never to detract from the actor.

When the company returned to France in 1919, Copeau's aesthetic attitudes had changed little since founding his company in 1913. His ultimate aim was to renovate dramatic literature, although his choice of plays sometimes appeared inconsistent with that goal. Although his repertory included Shakespeare and Molière, Copeau increasingly came to select works influenced by *commedia dell'arte* (the plays of Marivaux, Gozzi, and Musset, for example). Some critics accused him of wishing to renovate the drama by reducing it to farce, pantomime, and improvisation. The contemporary plays

FIG. 9.6
The Winter's Tale as produced by Copeau at the Vieux Colombier in 1920. Note the bareness of the stage. (From *Le Théâtre,* 1920.)

Copeau chose were by writers such as André Gide, Georges Duhamel, Jean Schlumberger, and Charles Vildrac, in whom it is difficult to perceive the seeds of a newly forming, vital, dramatic tradition.

Copeau continued to demand complete respect for the text and unflinching integrity in production. But his interests gradually shifted from drama to acting, perhaps in the belief that a renovation of performance had to precede a renaissance in writing. Thus, in 1924 he announced the closing of his theatre so that he might concentrate on his school. The theatre itself had never been financially profitable and had been supported in part by an organization of patrons, The Friends of the Vieux Colombier. Copeau's decision grew from his perception of the fundamental incompatibility between a schedule of regular performances and the pursuit of high artistic standards. Perfectionism was Copeau's strongest trait, and it often led to attacks on his work for its elitism, asceticism, and austerity. Thus, to pursue perfection without distraction, he transferred his school to the small Burgundian village of Pernand-Vergelesses, where from 1924 to 1929 he devoted his full energies.

It was primarily as teacher-theoretician-reformer that Copeau made his greatest impact on the French theatre. Indeed, his whole mission depended upon education—of writers, actors, the public—and from the beginning he considered a school necessary. When the Vieux Colombier had returned to France, Copeau had established such a school, which he had placed under the direction of Jules Romains. But with the move to Burgundy, Copeau himself became the school's director and principal teacher.

In Burgundy, the heart of Copeau's teaching continued to be thorough understanding of the text, its milieu, and the techniques that would permit the actor to transpose to the stage what he found in the text. What seemed most remarkable about the training in the 1920s was its emphasis (then new) on the expressive power of mime and gesture. In Paris, the school's teachers had included the Fratellini family of circus clowns and the mime Jean Dorcy. In Burgundy, Copeau focused on

FIG. 9.7

Molière's *Misanthrope* at the Vieux Colombier in 1922 with Valentine Tessier as Célimène and Copeau as Alceste. (From *Le Théâtre,* 1922.)

improvisation, with much of the work centered on a group of approximately ten type-characters which Copeau saw as epitomizing the basic aspects of human behavior. Students learned to make masks that captured the essence of these types and, wearing the masks as actors, they sought to eliminate all actions, gestures, and motivations foreign to that particular type. Students also improvised scenes based on such archetypal situations as war, famine, and lust. As the culmination of their student work, they evolved scenarios, which were performed at village festivals in Burgundy. Through such means, the students, known as Les Copiaux, learned artistic discipline and selfless devotion to ensemble playing.

In 1929, Copeau closed his school at the point when a powerful campaign was launched to have him named head of the Comédie Française. Though unsuccessful, the campaign brought Copeau back to theatrical production in Paris and elsewhere. Some of his most ambitious work in this period resembled that done by the people's theatres. In Florence in 1933, he staged *The Miracle of Saint Uliva* in the cloister of Santa Croce; in 1935, he produced Rino Alessi's *Savonarola* in the Piazza della Signoria; and in 1943, he staged his own religious spectacle, *The Miracle of the Golden Bread,* in a courtyard in Beaune.

In 1936, another effort was made to have Copeau named as head of the Comédie Française when Emile Fabré resigned. Once more, however, Copeau was passed over in favor of the successful Boulevard dramatist Edouard Bourdet (1887–1945). Bourdet, however, recognized Copeau's worth and invited him to serve as his advisor. As a result, after 1936 Copeau (along with Jouvet, Dullin, and Baty) directed a number of productions at the Comédie Française. Finally in May 1940 Copeau was named head of the company but was forced to resign in less than a year because of his son's participation in the Resistance movement. Once more Copeau retired to the country, where he died in 1949.

THE CARTEL: JOUVET, DULLIN, BATY, PITOEFF

Although Copeau had left Paris for Burgundy in 1924, his influence in the capitol remained, for the most prestigious companies were the studios he had inspired. None was as austere as the Vieux Colombier, but all placed artistic above commercial concerns even though this stance often meant playing to small audiences. Among Copeau's successors in the 1920s, the most important were Jouvet, Dullin, Baty, and

Pitoëff, who constituted the *Cartel des Quatre* (Coalition of Four—so called because of an agreement they made in 1926 to advise and assist one another). In the period after Copeau left for Burgundy until the beginning of World War II, these directors became the artistic leaders of the French theatre.

Of the four, Louis Jouvet (1887–1951) seems to have been the one most closely attuned to Copeau's ideals. In 1913, Jouvet joined the Vieux Colombier to play minor roles and to serve as technical director of the company. In 1917, after Copeau returned to France, Jouvet rejoined the company and remained with it until 1922, when he went to work for Hébertot. Jouvet's first major success came in 1923 with Romains' *Knock,* a play that he would revive fourteen times during the next twenty-five years. (Some critics maintain that there was something of the character of Knock, a quack who assumes the role of a medical doctor, in every role Jouvet played.) In 1924, Jouvet formed his own company, but at first it had to rely for financial assistance on the Society of the Théâtre Louis Jouvet, formed in 1925 by Romains. The turning point in Jouvet's career came in 1928 when he staged Giraudoux's *Siegfried.* With this production, both director and playwright found his ideal collaborator, and thereafter Jouvet devoted much of his energy to staging Giraudoux's works.

When he produced Cocteau's *The Infernal Machine* in 1934, he employed, at Cocteau's suggestion, Christian Bérard (1902–1949) as designer, and thereafter retained him. In the same year, Jouvet saw that he now could command a larger audience and thus leased a Boulevard theatre, the Athenée, where he remained. Bérard's designs contributed significantly to Jouvet's success. In 1934, Jouvet was named to a teaching post at the Conservatoire, and after 1936 he mounted a number of productions at the Comédie Française.

In 1940, the occupation government forbade Jouvet to perform the works of both Giraudoux and Romains, and in protest he closed his theatre. From 1941 to 1945 he toured South America, but when the war ended, he returned to the Athenée, where he presented Jean Genet's *The Maids* and Sartre's *The Devil and the Good Lord.* Most of Jouvet's postwar productions, however, were of the classics. He died in 1951.

Like Copeau, Jouvet was a staunch believer

FIG. 9.8
Jouvet as Knock in the play by Jules Romains. (A contemporary photo.)

in the sanctity of the text. He saw directors as of two types: those who expect everything from the play and those who expect everything from themselves. The first type seeks to illuminate the text; the second type uses the play as a pretext for his own creation. The first type admits spectacle only sparingly and never lets it intrude; with the second type "the work is swathed in personal contributions and inventions." Jouvet sought to be a director of the first type. In his productions, movement was restricted and vocal delivery slow so that every subtlety of idea and emotion in the text could be projected. His productions were noted for their lucidity, no doubt made possible by his devoted actors, namely Lucienne Bogaert, Valentine Tessier, Madeleine Ozeray, Romain Bouquet, and Pierre Renoir. Except with Molière's works, Jouvet seldom ventured into the classics or into plays by foreign writers. Contemporary French playwrights such as Romains, Achard, Cocteau, and Giraudoux provided him with his repertory. And he gave them impeccable productions, for perfect finish was always Jouvet's trademark.

Charles Dullin (1885–1949), like Jouvet, was a member of Copeau's company before establishing his own troupe. Dullin came to Paris in 1903 and played in many minor theatres and at the Odéon under Antoine before appearing in Copeau's adaptation of *The Brothers Karamazov* in 1911 and joining the Vieux Colombier in 1913. During the war he served in the army but was released after being wounded and went with Copeau to New York. After a misunderstanding with Copeau, Dullin went to work for Gémier, for whom he ran an acting school and performed at the Cirque d'Hiver and at the Comédie Montaigne. But Dullin wanted his own company and in 1919 created the Atelier, housed in a small theatre in the Montmartre district of Paris. There he remained for sixteen years.

Dullin was little concerned with theory, but, like his associates in the Cartel, he was opposed to naturalism. Deeply interested in

FIG. 9.9
Dullin's production of Cocteau's adaptation of *Antigone* at the Atelier in 1922. (From *Le Théâtre*, 1923.)

Oriental theatre and the *commedia dell'arte,* he sought in his work to achieve a synthesis of dance, music, and plastic expression, qualities he associated with these forms. Like both Copeau and Jouvet, he believed in the primacy of the text, and his preferences in art—Picasso in painting, Schoenberg in music, and Joyce in literature—tell much about his theatrical proclivities. He combined modernity of visual expression with almost melodramatic intensity of acting. Thus, though emphasizing the text, Dullin never neglected the other elements that would support it. His designers—Jean Hugo, Picasso, Michel Duran, Lucien Coutaud, Louis Touchagues, Georges Valmier, and André Barsacq—were among the finest of the day, and he often commissioned music from such composers as Milhaud, Auric, Delannoy, and Sauguet. Dullin's practice of combining music, dance, and mimed spectacle is perhaps best exemplified in his production of *Richard III,* in which the battle scenes were mimed and danced to the rhythms of a drum and the clashing of weapons. It is significant that Dullin admired Meyerhold above all foreign directors.

Dullin was perhaps the most eclectic of the Cartel in his choice of repertory. Not only did he produce the works of Aristophanes (*The Birds, Peace,* and *Plutus*) and Shakespeare (*Richard III* and *Julius Caesar*) but also *Volpone* by Ben Jonson, *'Tis Pity She's a Whore* by John Ford, *Life is a Dream* by Calderón, and *Right You Are—If You Think You Are* by Pirandello. Among the French writers whose work he produced were Molière, Cocteau, Achard, Salacrou, Romains, and Passeur. He ranged from farce to tragedy but showed a predilection for the great classics. Performing in all of his own productions, he was especially effective in ambitious, cynical, and restless roles. Among the actors who worked with Dullin were Julien Bertheau, Raymond Rouleau, Tania

FIG. 9.10
Dullin as Richard III, one of his most important roles. (A contemporary photo.)

Balachova, Madeliene Robinson, Jean Marchat, and the mime Etienne Decroux.

Like Copeau, Dullin made a lasting contribution through his school. His students studied ballet, music-hall techniques, circus clowning, acrobatics, *commedia dell'arte,* music, and, above all, the text and its milieu. Though little formally educated himself, Dullin had a profound respect for knowledge and great contempt for the anti-intellectualism of commercial producers (whom he called "grocers"). His legacy was most fully extended through the work of two students, Jean-Louis Barrault and Jean Vilar, who after World War II would play dominant roles in the French theatre.

Dullin always longed for a larger audience than he could attract to the Atelier, and, perhaps seduced by the success of his productions at the Comédie Française after 1936, he gave up the Atelier just before the beginning of World War II. After 1941 he headed the large Théâtre de la Cité, which was subsidized by the city of Paris. Although his old audience remained faithful, he failed to attract a sufficiently large new one and could not remain financially solvent. After considerable conflict with city authorities, Dullin gave up the theatre in 1947 and ended his career as director of the theatre section of the Maison des Arts in Geneva.

Neither of the other members of the Cartel, Baty and Pitoëff, ever worked with Copeau, but they nonetheless shared his uncompromising devotion to theatre as an art. Gaston Baty (1885–1952), the only member of the Cartel who was not an actor, was highly educated, having studied in Lyon, his home city, and Munich, where he became familiar with the work of Fuchs and Erler. At first, though he wrote plays and criticism, he had no outlet for his interests in theatrical production. But in 1918, during the bombardment of Paris, Gémier came to Lyon to work, met Baty, and put him under contract for five years as his assistant. Thus, in 1919, at the age of thirty-four, Baty entered the Parisian theatrical world as Gémier's apprentice at the Cirque d'Hiver. In 1920, he made his theatrical debut as director of *The Great Pastoral,* and that same year Gémier put Baty in charge of the Théâtre Montaigne, where he directed plays by Lenormand, Crommelynck, Shaw, Claudel, and Shakespeare. In these early projects, Baty worked with both Gémier and Dullin.

But Baty wished to be independent, and in 1921 he founded the Chimère, a group with which he produced plays irregularly while completing his contract with Gémier. In 1924, his apprenticeship over, Baty was employed by Hébertot to take charge of his newly created Studio des Champs-Elysées. In 1928, he left the Studio and, after playing in temporary locations, settled in 1930 at the Théâtre Montparnasse, where he remained until he turned it over in 1947 to Marguerite Jamois.

Baty was the most philosophically inclined of the Cartel, and it is difficult to understand his work without being aware of his views. He argued that since the Renaissance the French theatre had been primarily Cartesian and Jansenist in its orientation, for it had emphasized rationality and had reduced drama to almost total dependence on the word. Thus Baty placed great emphasis on the visual aspects of production, so much so that he was often accused of subordinating everything to what was seen.

Baty's outlook encompassed aspects of both naturalism and symbolism, for he recognized the importance of heredity and environment but also the mysterious powers that lie beyond the material realm. Although his settings were always three-dimensional, they were imbued with symbolic implications, achieved through the careful composition of scenic elements and the masterful handling of lighting and color, thus creating all-pervasive moods and strong emotional stimuli. So skillful was Baty's work that he came to be called "the magician of the mise-en-scène."

Baty's repertory was comprised chiefly of modern works, although occasionally he ventured into the classics. His greatest successes were achieved through the adaptation of novels, the most significant of which was his famous production in 1936 of his own adaptation of Flaubert's *Madame Bovary.* Although the original work is usually considered a master-

FIG. 9.11

Baty's production of his own adaptation of Flaubert's *Madame Bovary* in 1936. The performers are Lucien Nat and Marguerite Jamois. (From *Theatre Arts*, 1936.)

piece of realistic writing, Baty was concerned primarily in showing a woman tortured by romantic dreams. Many expressionistic touches were added, such as a chorus of girls who reveal the heroine's romantic attitudes. Also in an early scene, Emma Bovary is happy with her lover in an arbor covered with flowers and flooded with sunlight, while later, deserted and ready to commit suicide, she is seen in the arbor, the flowers now dead and the lighting grey and harsh. Baty seems also a descendant of the symbolists, and, like them, there was always an edging toward the sentimental in his work, though rarely did he fall over that edge.

After 1930, Baty became increasingly interested in marionettes, and his productions, especially in the gestures and movements of his actors, began to reflect this preoccupation. He eventually gave up his theatre so as to concentrate more fully on such experiments. In 1951, he became director of the newly created state-sponsored dramatic center in Aix-en-Provence, but he died before his work made any impact there. Of all French directors between the wars, Baty was most committed to what eventually came to be called *total theatre*. His attack on the word and his concern for the expressive powers of nonverbal means form a bridge between the Cartel and Artaud's *theatre of cruelty*.

Similarly, Georges Pitoëff (1884–1939) provided a bridge between the Parisian stage and foreign drama. Son of a theatre manager, Pitoëff was born in Russia and for a time lived in Moscow, where he became familiar with Stanislavsky's work. Following the Revolution of 1905, his family emigrated to Paris, but he returned to Russia shortly afterward and entered Vera Komissarzhevskaya's company, in which he worked under Meyerhold. Caught up in the ferment of Russian theatre, he moved away from Stanislavsky's views toward those of the symbolists. In 1911, Pitoëff met Dalcroze, a great influence upon his work, and it may have been this meeting that led him to move to Switzerland in 1914.

It was in Paris during the war that Pitoëff met his future wife, Ludmilla (1896–1951), a Russian student at the Conservatoire. When she completed her course, they were married and in 1918 formed their first company. This troupe, based in Switzerland, played short engagements in Paris each year, and in 1922 Hébertot invited Pitoëff to form a company and to play regularly at his Théâtre des Champs-Elysées. After Hébertot gave up his theatre, Pitoëff's group performed in a number of theatres in Paris and toured abroad before settling in the Théâtre des Mathurins in 1934, where the group remained until Pitoëff's death in 1939. During the war, Ludmilla Pitoëff performed in the United States and after 1946 in Paris until her death in 1951.

Pitoëff was known best for his productions of foreign plays, which comprised about two-thirds of his repertory. His was an important contribution, for the French were notoriously ill-informed about the drama of other countries and complacently convinced of their own superiority. Pitoëff favored plays which emphasized strong internal struggles and won his

FIG. 9.12

The Pitoëffs in a production of Claudel's *The Exchange* in 1937. (From *Le Théâtre*.)

greatest successes with plays by Chekhov, Pirandello, Ibsen, Schnitzler, Shaw, and O'Neill. His productions of Pirandello's *Six Characters in Search of an Author* and Shaw's *Saint Joan,* for example, were especially admired.

Like Dullin, Pitoëff was little given to theorizing, but he placed primary emphasis upon the text and above all sought to isolate those elements most capable of communicating with a contemporary audience. His settings, which he designed himself, suggest a marked leaning toward cubism and expressionism. Most were strongly geometrical with a dominant central focus, often created by concentric circles or radiating lines. His means varied from one production to another—simple curtains, simultaneous settings, cross-sections of houses, a revolving stage, set pieces changed within a basic unit—but all were characterized by a radical simplicity in which only the most essential and expressive elements were retained. Pitoëff also paid close attention to groupings and lighting but, in particular, to rhythm, which he saw as the linking element to all that made up a production.

Pitoëff's acting was hampered by his strong accent, but he was effective in ironic and bitter roles. His wife, much superior to him as a performer, was noted for her spirituality, musical voice, and precise inflections. Despite Pitoëff's remarkable abilities as a director, as a foreigner he was, as Hébertot once remarked, the last of the Cartel to be honored.

Around 1930 there emerged a new wave of activity, also owing much to Copeau. Most directly related to Copeau was the Compagnie des Quinze (Company of Fifteen), composed of students from his school, who were led by Michel Saint-Denis (1897–1971), Copeau's nephew and his assistant after 1919. Saint-Denis directed all productions and acted in most as well. At the Vieux Colombier, the group presented eight plays, four of them by André Obey, between 1931 and 1934. At this time, the Vieux Colombier was redesigned by André Barsacq toward even greater simplification; it now became only an unadorned large room with visible ceiling and walls, and only essential set pieces were permitted. The company's considerable impact was made through its ensemble playing, stylized gesture and movement, and near incantatory diction.

In 1934, the troupe made an enormous impression in London, and, when it dissolved for lack of finances, Tyrone Guthrie persuaded Saint-Denis to establish an acting school there. With the assistance of George Devine and the support of Laurence Olivier, John Gielgud, Edith Evans, Michael Redgrave, and others, Saint-Denis operated the London Theatre Studio from 1935 to 1939 and directed plays at the Old Vic and for Gielgud's company. After the war, Saint-Denis would establish and operate an acting school for the Old Vic. Thus, the methods of Copeau were brought to England.

Those who were part of the legacy of Copeau were numerous. A conservative partial list would include the director Léon Chancerel (1886–1965), who more than anyone else was responsible for establishing a tradition of children's theatre in France; the playwright Henri Ghéon (1875–1944), whose conversion to Catholicism caused him to found Les Compagnons de Notre Dame, a troupe of about thirty amateurs who performed a repertory of medieval-like religious plays written by modern authors; André Barsacq (1909–1973), who became director of the Atelier after Dullin and was instrumental in producing the plays of Anouilh; Jean Dasté (Copeau's son-in-law), who worked with Barsacq at the Atelier and then founded his own company in 1947 at St. Etienne; Maurice Jacquemont (1910–   ), who from 1944 to 1960 was the director of the Studio des Champs-Elysées; the actors Marcel Herrand (1897–1953) and Jean Marchat (1902–1966); and Etienne Decroux (1898–   ), who was acclaimed internationally as a teacher of mime, his most famous pupil and disciple being Marcel Marceau (1923–   ).

ARTAUD AND THE THEATRE OF CRUELTY

Although it was Copeau who dominated theatrical art between the wars, another theorist and sometimes practitioner—Artaud—little heeded in his own time, would surpass Copeau in international fame after World War II. Born in Marseilles, Antonin Artaud (1895–1948) had by 1915 already experienced his first bout with that mental disturbance that would often plague him through the remainder of his life. In 1920, he came to Paris, where Lugné-

Poë gave him his first role. In 1921, he joined Dullin and designed the settings for the Atelier's first production, Calderón's *Life Is a Dream.* Later Artaud acted for Pitoëff, Jouvet, and in films, his most famous role being that in Carl Dreyer's *The Passion of Joan of Arc,* in which Artaud played the young monk who defended Joan. Between 1924 and 1926, he was deeply involved in the surrealist movement, but, along with many others, he was expelled from the movement by Breton. Nevertheless, the surrealist influence remained strong in Artaud's work. In 1926, he founded, in association with Roger Vitrac and Robert Aron, the Théâtre Alfred Jarry and presented four programs before the group was disbanded in 1929. Not until 1931, when he was deeply impressed by a troupe of Balinese dancers at the Colonial Exposition in Paris, did Artaud begin to formulate the theories upon which his fame now rests. Between 1931 and 1936, he wrote a series of essays and manifestoes, thirteen of which were collected in 1938 to form *The Theatre and Its Double.* In 1935, Artaud staged the only production on which he worked after formulating his theories, his own play *The Cenci* (based on works by Shelley and Stendhal). Not well received, it closed after seventeen performances.

In 1936, Artaud went to Mexico hoping to find there an authentic primitive culture which would provide him with clues to the relationship between art and ritual. Experimenting in Mexico with the drug peyote, used in rituals by the Indians, Artaud came to believe that "international dark forces" were seeking to destroy him, and he thus returned to France. In 1937, he was committed to a psychiatric hospital, where he remained until 1946. In 1947, he gave a lecture at the Vieux Colombier and recorded a work for radio, "To Have Done With the Judgment of God." In 1948, he died of cancer.

According to Artaud, Western theatre has been devoted to a very narrow range of human experience, primarily the psychological problems of individuals or the social problems of groups (in other words, the kinds of experiences that can be dealt with by the conscious mind). To Artaud, the more important elements of existence are those submerged in the unconscious. Like the futurists, Artaud declared that Western theatre typically is seen as a preserver of culture, more like a museum than a place which provides the kind of living experiences found in ritual. Thus, the theatre has become the property of an elite group cut off from the masses. Artaud considered all that is normally called "civilization" to be a numbing overlay of a deeper, more elemental culture. He argued that this form of civilization would eventually pass into oblivion "and that spaceless, timeless culture which is contained in our nervous capacities will reappear with an increased energy." What is needed is a theatre "which does not numb us with ideas for the intellect but stirs us to feeling by stirring up pain."

The human being's important problems, according to Artaud, are those buried in the subterranean reaches of the mind, which cause divisions within and between human beings and lead to hatred, violence, and disaster. For Artaud, then, the theatre should serve a near-psychiatric function, but for the whole society, not merely the individual. The goal is something similar to religious experience and ritual, in which a true communion—the elimination of all divisions—is achieved.

If the theatre Artaud envisioned is akin to ritual, its subject matter tends toward the mythic. But his vision of myth is quite unlike that of Wagner, who tended to see myth as uplifting and idealized. Artaud said: "The great myths are dark, so much so that one cannot imagine, save in an atmosphere of carnage, torture, and bloodshed, all the magnificent fables which recount to the multitudes the first sexual division and the first carnage . . . in creation." Artaud also suggested that we cannot return to the myths of the past (those of the ancient Greeks and early Christians), for these have lost their power to affect us sufficiently. Rather, new myths will arise out of something similar to a plague, which destroys repressive social forms. "Order collapses, authority evaporates, anarchy prevails and man gives vent to all the disordered impulses which lie buried in his soul." But Artaud saw all this happening in the theatre rather than outside it. His proposed theatre would serve the function of cleansing society: "For impelling men to see themselves as they are, [the theatre] causes the mask to fall, reveals the lie, the slackness, baseness, and hypocrisy of the world. . . [T]he theatre has been created to drain abscesses collectively."

Artaud often referred to his as a *theatre of cruelty,* since in order to achieve its ends it would have to force the audience to confront itself and its deepest taboos. The theatre, as Artaud saw it, is a force similar to the plague: "In the theatre as in the plague there is something both triumphant and vengeful." But the cruelty Artaud advocated is not physical but moral. "Cruelty is rigor," he said. "We are not talking about that cruelty which we can exert upon one another by cutting up each other's bodies, by sawing on our personal anatomies. Rather, it is an extramoral identification which will take hold of us physically, kinesthetically." About his production of *The Cenci,* which dealt with the Renaissance story of a forced incest by a father upon his daughter and the daughter's murdering revenge, Artaud wrote that it is not a question of a "purely corporal cruelty but a moral one; it goes to the extremity of instinct and forces the actor to plunge right to the roots of his being so that he leaves the stage exhausted. A cruelty which acts as well upon the spectator and should not

allow him to leave the theatre intact, but exhausted, involved, perhaps transformed."

To achieve this transformation, Artaud sought what he called a "new language of the theatre." He was much impressed by Eastern art with its symbolic, ritualistic elements, and he argued that Western theatre could be transformed only by the use of comparable means, though he recognized that Eastern devices could not be taken over directly. Much of his interest in Eastern theatre stemmed from his discontent with the West's emphasis on language and its almost exclusive appeal to the rational mind: "Whereas most people remain impervious to the subtle discourse whose intellectual development escapes them, they cannot resist effects of physical surprise, the dynamism of cries and violent movements, visual explosions, the aggregate tetanizing effects called up on cue and used to act in a direct manner on the physical sensitivity of the spectators."

Artaud's intention to operate directly on the nervous system led him to suggest many new devices for the theatre. Among these was the replacement of the traditional theatre building with remodeled barns, factories, or aircraft hangers, a cue taken very seriously by avant-garde directors of the 1960s. He wanted to locate acting areas in corners, on overhead catwalks, along the walls. Spectators, surrounded by the action, would sit in swivel chairs, allowing them to turn in any direction. Artaud states: "There will be no decor. That will be adequately taken care of by hieroglyphic actors, ritualistic costumes, puppets thirty feet tall . . . , musical instruments as tall as a man, objects of unheard of form and purpose."

In lighting, he sought a "vibrating, shredded" effect. He called for "flashes of light whose nature changes, goes from red to crude pink, from silver to green, then turns white, with suddenly an immense opaque yellow light the color of dirty fog and dust storms." Sound is treated in much the same way: it should feature shrillness, staccato effects, abruptness in volume. In his script for *The Cenci,* he suggests that a scene set in a torture chamber should "give off the noise of a factory at peak production." When he staged the play, he used a screeching wheel that produced an almost intolerable sound. He also employed an electronic device (a forerunner of the Moog Synthesizer) that could vary volume from the softest tones to those louder than could be produced by a full symphony orchestra. There was also a great deal of vocal, nonverbal sound. Artaud used the human voice not so much as an instrument of discursive speech but more for tonalities, prolonged modulations and yelps, barks, in order to create harmonies and dissonances. About language, Artaud asked: "Why is it that in the

theatre, at least the theatre as we know it in . . . the West, everything that is specifically theatrical, namely everything that . . . is not contained in dialogue, . . . is left in the background? . . . I say that the stage is a physical and concrete place that demands to be filled, and demands that one make it speak its own concrete language." This language should be "addressed first of all to the senses rather than to the mind, as is the case with the language of words," for "the public thinks first of all with its senses."

Thus, Artaud wanted to assault the audience with sights and sounds that would break down its resistance and purge it morally and spiritually. Like Appia and Craig, Artaud was a visionary rather than a wholly practical man, and like them he was at first little appreciated. Many of their ideas are similar, yet Artaud differed drastically in his conception of the theatre's ultimate purpose. Appia and Craig (as well as Copeau and his followers) tended to value art for its own sake, whereas Artaud saw in the theatre a kind of salvation of the human species. Thus, as the post-World War II view of human beings darkened, the influence of Appia, Craig, and Copeau declined and that of Artaud increased.

It is difficult to isolate immediate and certain influences from Artaud, although in the period of the 1960s, his writings in *The Theatre and Its Double* came to be viewed internationally as a kind of bible by the theatrical avant-garde. But two French directors, Jean-Louis Barrault and Roger Blin, who worked with Artaud on *The Cenci,* later declared their indebtedness to him. Blin's work would not be important until after the war, particularly in productions of the absurdist plays. But Barrault (1910–   ) had served his apprenticeship and had won widespread fame before the war began.

Barrault had worked at several odd jobs by 1931 when he auditioned for Dullin, who was

FIG. 9.13
Scene from Artaud's *The Cenci* at the Folies-Wagram, Paris, 1935. (A contemporary photo.)

sufficiently impressed to admit him to his school without charge and let him sleep in the theatre. Not only did he perform in Dullin's troupe, but he studied with Decroux and appeared in Decroux's first independent production in 1931. In 1935, Barrault acted in Artaud's *The Cenci* and came under his influence. (Barrault suggests that *The Theatre and Its Double* is the most important book written about the theatre in the twentieth century.) Shortly afterward, he presented at the Atelier his own first production, a mime drama based on Faulkner's *As I Lay Dying*. After leaving Dullin, Barrault adapted and staged Cervantes' *The Siege of Numancia* (1937) and Knut Hamsun's *Hunger* (1939). By this time he had also made a number of films and had married Madeleine Renaud (1903–   ), a leading actress at the Comédie Française. When the war began, he served in the army but was demobilized when France surrendered. In 1940, he joined his wife as a member of the Comédie Française. Soon afterward he would begin the series of productions that would make him the best known of postwar French directors.

FRENCH PLAYWRIGHTS BETWEEN THE WARS

A number of French playwrights between the wars were highly regarded but few have withstood the test of time. One of the more controversial was Henri-René Lenormand (1882–1951), for he emphasized the power of the unconscious and the relativity of time and space, ideas then still novel. Lenormand explored many of the same themes as the surrealists, but his work was more accessible, chiefly because it was framed, like Pirandello's, in essentially conventional forms. Although he began writing in 1905, he attained little success until 1919, when Pitoëff presented *Time Is a Dream*, still his best-known work. In it, the young woman Romée has a "waking dream" in which a young man drowns in a lake. Then Nico, just returned from the Orient, enters, and Romée discovers that he is the drowning man. Later they become engaged and he commits suicide exactly as she has foreseen. This clairvoyance and relativity of time is mingled with the psychoanalytic. Nico has been deeply affected by the climate and Eastern thought, and his return to Holland and its mists precipitates a psychological and moral disintegration that leads to his death. The play combines most of the interests that Lenormand would develop thereafter in plays such as *The Simoun*, directed by Baty at the Comédie Montaigne in 1920, *The Eater of Dreams*, staged by Pitoëff in 1922, and *Asia*, based on the Medea-Jason legend.

Interest in the unconscious was reflected in a somewhat different way by *the school of silence*, best seen in the work of Bernard and Vildrac. Jean-Jacques Bernard summed up the outlook in an article published in 1922 in Baty's bulletin for the Chimère, when he suggested that literary drama misrepresented truth by making characters openly express their inner feelings, whereas in reality people neither consciously analyze nor openly state their responses. Rather, in moments of crisis, inner emotion is more apt to take the form of a cliché, gesture, or glance than a well-articulated statement. This approach is well-illustrated in Bernard's *Martine*, presented by Baty in 1922, about a young peasant girl who loves and suffers but who is unable to tell anyone. She sees the young man she loves marry someone else, while she is forced to wed an obtuse husband. Her feelings are revealed almost entirely through indirection—small gestures, oblique remarks, looks—and at the end she resigns herself to a dull existence.

Charles Vildrac (1882–1971) fits the same mold as Bernard, although he was less interested in theory and had written his most significant play, *The Steamship Tenacity* (1920), before Bernard had articulated the view that underlies the practice. The work was presented by Copeau at the Vieux Colombier and was the most successful of all contemporary works staged there. Two French workers, Bastien and Ségard, decide to emigrate to Canada aboard the Tenacity, but before they leave they meet Thérèse, who prefers Ségard but goes with the direct and outspoken Bastien. Ségard goes to Canada alone, though he had only consented at Bastien's urging. There is no surface conflict, only the subtleties of looks, gestures, and clichés. Bernard and Vildrac, though never making a deep impression dramatically, are in the French tradition of revealing subtle internal psychological states, more profoundly revealed in the plays of Racine, Marivaux, Musset, and in the films of Truffaut.

Several other French playwrights of the interwar period deserve at least brief notice, particularly for their comedies and satires. Jules Romains (1885–1972) is primarily remembered for his play *Knock, or, The Triumph of Medicine* (1923), Jouvet's first major success; but Romains' somewhat similar work, *Musse, or, The School of Hypocrisy* (1930) is an excellent comic treatment of the situation of an insignificant man who wishes to be honest but discovers that the only way he can achieve true freedom is by joining others in hypocrisy.

Steve Passeur (1899–1966) also wrote in the satirical mode, but his work most nearly resembles post-World War II "black comedy." His is a world turned upside down: parents fear their children, husbands their wives, and love is only truly passionate when it is not returned. Most of his plays focus on duels between men and women, with one dominant (usually the woman) and the other dominated, often humiliated. His most characteristic work is *The Buyer* (1930), in which a spinster buys a young husband by paying off his debts. Her love turns to hatred almost immediately, for following the wedding her husband attempts to run off with his mistress. Torturing her husband with a thousand small cruelties, which he seems to delight in, she finally commits suicide when her husband is freed by his father.

Marcel Achard (1899–1974) is almost opposite to Passeur in outlook, for his plays usually begin in a cynical atmosphere and end in romantic reconciliation. Achard is noteworthy for capitalizing on the interest among 1920s French intelligentsia in *commedia dell'arte* and popular entertainments. For the Fratellini family of circus clowns, for example, he wrote *Will You Play With Me?*, which achieved great success under Dullin's direction at the Atelier in 1923. Perhaps his best work before World War II is *Jean de la Lune* (1929), in which Jef, a Pierrot figure, is married to a coquette who eternally flirts with other men. Eventually, however, his seeming ardent belief in her fidelity charms her into being the faithful woman he has always imagined.

Armand Salacrou wrote in a wide variety of styles from surrealist fantasy, comedy ballet, and satirical comedy to historical and psychological dramas. Many of his plays are concerned with the suffering of innocents and the absurdity of the human condition. (He used the term *absurd* long before Camus did.) Some of his works resemble those of Pirandello in their insistence that each human being differs from one day to the next and cannot be judged today for past deeds. One of his most interesting experiments in technique is *The Unknown Woman of Arras* (1935), which begins and ends with the same suicidal gunshot. The entire action occurs in the split second between the firing of the bullet and the reaching of its target, as the man committing suicide relives incidents from his past. Perhaps Salacrou's best play, however, is *The World Is Round* (1938), set in Florence in the time of Savonarola, who has established a virtual dictatorship out of his

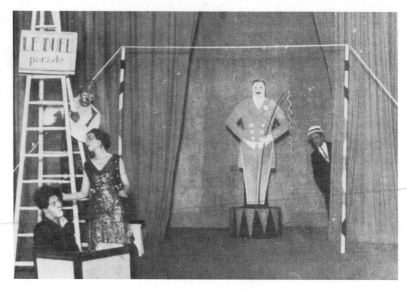

FIG. 9.14
Achard's *Will You Play With Me?* at the Atelier in 1923. (From *Le Théâtre*, 1924.)

desire to serve an ascetic God in a debauched age. The then-revolutionary discovery that the world is round calls Savonarola's absolutism into question. The people demand a miracle (that Savonarola submit to a trial by fire), and his refusal thus seals his doom.

André Obey's (1892–1975) best-known play is *Noah* (1931), based on the biblical story of the flood and the ark. The play is composed of a series of episodes ranging from domestic comedy to scenes of epic grandeur. The animals, wiser than humans, come to the ark of their own accord and ally themselves sympathetically with Noah during the trials and petty bickerings that plague him. When the waters recede, the animals and Noah's own children desert him. At first discouraged, he regains his faith and sets about rebuilding the world.

GIRAUDOUX

Of all French playwrights between the wars, however, it is now generally agreed that Jean Giraudoux (1882–1944) was the most impor-

tant. Educated in France and Germany, Giraudoux served as a tutor in the household of the Duke of Saxe-Meiningen and later taught at Harvard University before entering the foreign service in 1910. Following World War I, he wrote a series of novels, and it was with the adaptation of one of these, *Siegfried* (1928), that he made his debut as a dramatist at age forty-six. Jouvet directed the first productions of almost all Giraudoux's dramatic works. Their ideal collaboration resulted from both author and director placing primary emphasis on language.

Most of Giraudoux's plays are based on well-known myths or legends, and only *Siegfried*, *Intermezzo* (1933), and *The Madwoman of Chaillot* (1944) use stories of his own invention. His plays are essentially dramas of ideas that turn on the reconciliation of antitheses: peace and war, fidelity and infidelity, life and death, liberty and destiny, the absolute and the ephemeral. The dramas occur at those moments when human beings are faced with a choice between contradictory positions, and, in his exploration of his characters' seeming dilemmas, Giraudoux often suggests the means whereby the contradictions can be reconciled. Thus, though the physical outcome of the actions often seem fated (the use of myths and legends in part dictate the outcome), the protagonists still insist upon their intellectual independence from facts: "Nothing is true except what you accept as such; only logic is absurd and, since I am a man, I am god in my arbitrary rule."

Despite his interest in ideas, Giraudoux did not engage his characters in direct arguments about philosophical questions. Rather, he sought to work by indirection and to let new perceptions insinuate themselves into the mind through feelings and imagination. Language is Giraudoux's primary means, and he considered it to be the highest expression of human reason and a major tool for escaping chaos. His dialogue is euphonious and highly expressive, at times overly subtle, almost precious; yet through his language, the playwright reveals his marked disposition toward fantasy, irony,

and humor. Among Giraudoux's best-known works are *Amphitryon 38*, *The Trojan War Shall Not Take Place*, and *The Madwoman of Chaillot*.

Amphitryon 38 (1929), so called because Giraudoux considered it the thirty-eighth dramatic treatment of the myth, shows that true love is impervious even to the machinations of the gods. Jupiter desires Alcmene, wife of Amphitryon, and uses all his wiles to trick her into an affair. Only when he transforms himself into the complete image of her husband is his quest successful. Thus, since Jupiter never shakes Alcmene's love for Amphitryon nor her belief in marital fidelity, he ultimately feels a certain emptiness in his seduction.

The Trojan War Shall Not Take Place (1935, played in English as *Tiger at the Gates*) is one of Giraudoux's darker works. It shows the Trojan Hector's desperate attempt to avoid war—for he knows its horrors—in the face of a war party, who see in Helen a symbol of love and beauty for which men must be willing to die. All seems to go Hector's way until in a quarrel

FIG. 9.15
Giraudoux's *The Trojan War Shall Not Take Place*, directed by Jouvet at the Théâtre Athenée in 1934. (From *Theatre Arts*, 1938.)

he wounds the leader of the war party, who, as he dies, declares that he has been treacherously killed by the Greeks. Despite Hector's protests, the Trojans swear to avenge the killing. As the play ends, war is inevitable.

FIG. 9.16
Madeleine Ozeray and Louis Jouvet in the 1938 production of Giraudoux's *Ondine*. (Photo by Lipnitzki.)

The Madwoman of Chaillot is Giraudoux's least characteristic work. Written during the German occupation of France, it reflects Giraudoux's hope for the liberation of Paris, the symbol of all Western civilization. The barbarians, here represented by materialistic exploiters, are lured into a pit and entombed there by the Madwoman's tale of oil beneath her cellar. At this moment, all the benevolent forces of nature are released and the world's beauty is renewed. The play seems to suggest that human welfare is closely linked to nature and that whatever is humanitarian should be elevated above that which is simply materialist.

While Giraudoux's fame has declined, it has not been eclipsed. He was, between the wars, the most respected of French playwrights, and his influence on such successors as Anouilh, Montherlant, Sartre, and Camus was significant.

BELGIAN PLAYWRIGHTS: CROMMELYNCK AND GHELDERODE

Two Belgian dramatists—Crommelynck and Ghelderode—are closely linked with the French theatre, for both wrote in French and owe their fame to French productions. Fernand Crommelynck (1888–1970), born in Brussels, began writing at an early age, two of his works being staged in Brussels before he went to Paris in 1911. Though he wrote little after 1934, he was prolific in the period of the 1920s. His fame dates from 1921, when his most popular work, *The Magnificent Cuckold*, was produced at the Théâtre de l'Oeuvre and his next play, *The Childish Lovers*, won production at the Comédie Montaigne. As already noted in connection with Meyerhold's famous production, *The Magnificent Cuckold* pushes a banal situation to the edge of absurdity. *Hot and Cold* (1934) is similar in that it deals with a wife who is completely indifferent to her husband and takes on a series of lovers so casually that she cannot even remember their names. But when her husband dies, she learns that he has been adored by his young mistress, of whose existence the wife had been completely unaware. The widowed wife now becomes obsessed with her dead husband's virtues and schemes to have her husband's mistress take a new lover. Only then can she claim her dead husband entirely for herself.

Ultimately more important as a playwright was Michel de Ghelderode (1898–1962), who was virtually unknown outside Belgium until 1949, when *Chronicles of Hell*, directed by Barrault, became the sensation and scandal of the Parisian season. Thereafter Ghelderode's fame spread rapidly. Before he died, his works were being performed throughout the world. But if Ghelderode's fame is postwar, the plays are not, for virtually all were written between 1918 and 1937. Their popularity undoubtedly stems from their affinity with absurdist drama and the theories of Artaud.

Although the plays are in French, they are distinctively Flemish in flavor, often likened in spirit to the paintings of Bosch, Brueghel, and Ensor. Indeed, Ghelderode based some of his plays on the works of these painters. Throughout his some thirty plays, both short and full length, runs the vision of human beings as creatures whose flesh overpowers their spirit. Corruption, death, and cruelty are always near the surface, although underneath lurks an implied criticism of degradation and materialism and a call to repentance. Yet Ghelderode avoids didacticism. Faith is apt to be approached through blasphemy, and suffering through ludicrous farce. As one critic puts it, "Where most authors . . . attempt to discover rational explanations, Ghelderode discovers the demon."

Like Artaud, Ghelderode downgrades language in favor of spectacle. He has said, "I discovered the world of shapes before discovering the world of ideas." His visions are revealed through images, sound, color, light and shadow, and atmosphere. Place is apt to shift rapidly and unexpectedly; characters are exaggerated and frequently descendants of clowns from the music hall, circus, and carnival.

While his earliest works are little more than brief developments of a single episode, his first full-length play, *The Death of Doctor Faust* (1926), exhibits almost all the qualities that characterize his later work. Faust emerges from his medieval study into a modern-day carnival, during which a performance of *Faust* is given in a tavern. Faust meets a young girl (Marguerite), seduces her, and then refuses to marry her on grounds that he is both too old and from another age. Threatened by the crowd, Faust is saved by the Devil, who transforms the scene into a poster advertising the performance of *Faust*. When Marguerite commits suicide, the actors of *Faust* are accused of murder, and, seeking to escape, they enter the study of the real Faust, where they come face to face with their real-life counterparts. The characters merge so fully that when Faust seeks to kill his impersonator, he murders himself.

In *Hop Signor!* (1935), Marguerite, the chaste wife of Jureal, finds herself attracted to the handsome young executioner Larose. She is fascinated by the public killings he performs and gradually begins to intermingle this fascination with sexual fantasies. Ultimately she can only be satisfied by her own public execution by Larose on the headsman's block. Here, as in several others of Ghelderode's plays, sexual desire is not far removed from the lust for death.

Like the plays of Witkiewicz in Poland, Ghelderode's work seems distinctly prophetic of later experiments. He used, for example, the technique of simultaneity—the mingling of sixteenth-century and twentieth-century contexts as in *The Death of Doctor Faust*—and multiple playing areas for concurrent scenes. While Ghelderode pursues the Pirandellian themes of appearance and reality and multiple levels of illusion, unlike Pirandello, Ghelderode's dramaturgy is not traditional. Furthermore, his scripts call for such Brechtian technical devices as projections and titles flashed on a screen.

THE SIGNIFICANCE OF THE INTERWAR YEARS

The plays of Pirandello, though conventional in form, were perhaps the most advanced of those written on the continent during the interwar period, chiefly because they focused on themes of truth and illusion. In France, the standard was set by the prominence of language in the plays of Giraudoux and the dominance of text in the productions of Copeau and the Cartel. Nonetheless, the theories of Artaud and the plays of Ghelderode pointed to the imminent challenge of language as the primal element of theatre, a trend that would become of great significance after World War II.

Chapter 10

German and Austrian Theatre and Drama Between the Wars

Until approximately 1924, expressionism dominated drama in Germany and Austria, but, as national disillusionment grew over inflation and unemployment, a new style of neorealism (*Neue Sachlichkeit*) emerged. At the same time, significant innovations were being made in production by Piscator and Brecht and at the Bauhaus.

In 1918, the German Empire had collapsed. Strict censorship was lifted, and the previously suspect expressionist drama began to flood the stage. Before 1919, expressionism had been an essentially literary movement, since few of the plays written before this time had been produced, but from 1919 to 1924 expressionism was the dominant mode both in German theatrical writing and production. In addition, the former royal theatres were reconstituted to suit the new form of government that emerged with the Weimar Republic. Thus freed from former restrictions, a number of these state-subsidized theatres took the lead in developing an expressionist style of production.

The private theatres perhaps suffered most from the chaotic economic situation, and many turned to a repertory of wide popular appeal in order to subsist. In this period also the upsurge of interest in theatre among the working classes was so great that by 1933 when Hitler came to power there were more than 300 such groups in Germany.

REINHARDT BETWEEN THE WARS

The dominant postwar director was Max Reinhardt, who continued his eclecticism both in choosing and producing plays. Beginning in 1917, he directed a number of expressionist dramas, among them Sorge's *The Beggar*, Hasenclever's *The Son*, and works by both Toller and Kaiser. While Reinhardt for the most part continued his prewar practices, a few of his postwar activities deserve special attention.

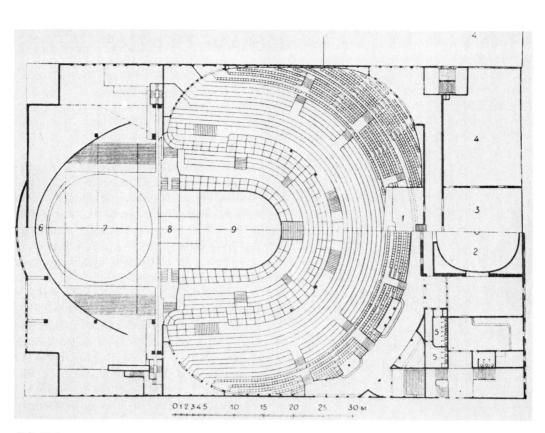

FIG. 10.1

Floorplan of Reinhardt's Grosses Schauspielhaus, converted from the Circus Schumann in 1919. (From Barkhin, *Teatra Architectura*, Moscow, 1947.)

In 1919, Reinhardt converted Berlin's Circus Schumann into the Grosses Schauspielhaus (sometimes called the "Theatre of Five Thousand," although in actuality it seated about thirty-five hundred). As remodeled by Hans Poelzig, the Grosses Schauspielhaus retained some of its circus qualities, for seating rose in tiers around three sides of the former ring, which now simulated the orchestra of an ancient Greek theatre. There were three acting areas: the orchestra; a raised platform forward of the proscenium and connected to

the orchestra by steps; and, back of a proscenium arch, a fully equipped stage with an enormous revolving stage and plaster skydome. Here between 1919 and 1922, Reinhardt produced such works as Aeschylus' *Oresteia*, Aristophanes' *Lysistrata*, Sophocles' *Oedipus Rex*, Shakespeare's *Julius Caesar*, Goethe's *Goetz von Berlichingen*, Rolland's *Danton*, Hauptmann's *The Weavers*, Hasenclever's *Antigone*, and Toller's *The Machine Wreckers*.

With such productions, Reinhardt made an effort to break down barriers between audience

FIG. 10.2
Interior of Reinhardt's Grosses Schauspielhaus, converted from the Circus Schumann in 1919. (From Barkhin, *Teatra Architectura*, Moscow, 1947.)

and performers. (In *Danton*, for example, he planted actors in the audience to increase the spectators' sense of involvement.) He also sought to attract a wider audience to the Grosses Schauspielhaus by setting ticket prices at approximately one-half those charged by other major theatres. Although his enterprise was successful for a time, gradually the theatre's popularity waned, and in 1922, he abandoned the operation. The problem probably was that the house was too enormous, a fact that encouraged dependence upon spectacle, since acoustics were so poor that subtlety was virtually impossible.

Like other private theatre owners, Reinhardt was caught in the economic squeeze of the time, and in 1920 he gave over the Deutsches Theater to Felix Hollander. Between 1920 and 1924, aside from the Grosses Schauspielhaus, Reinhardt's major enterprises were Austrian. With Hugo von Hofmannsthal, he founded the Salzburg Festival with the expressed aim of restoring Austria's cultural prestige and of preserving the best in Austrian dramatic and musical heritage. Like other manifestations of the people's theatre movement, the Salzburg Festival sought to coalesce the sentiments of a nation in an artistic endeavor. Hofmannsthal's adaptation of *Everyman,* staged in front of Salzburg Cathedral, became and remains the centerpiece of the festival. In 1922, Hofmannsthal's adaptation of Calderón's *The Great World Theatre,* performed inside a church, used medieval mansions as the basic scenic convention. Soon the Salzburg Festival was world famous, and, except for wartime interruptions, it has continued to be a major annual artistic event.

In Vienna in 1922, Reinhardt created the Redoutensaal theatre in the ballroom of an eighteenth-century palace. The Redoutensaal, owing to its elegant intimacy, was almost the opposite of the Grosses Schauspielhaus. Since the palace was considered a national treasure, no major alterations were permitted. Thus, there was no proscenium arch or front curtain. A platform backed by a curving screen and balcony reached by stairways constituted the

FIG. 10.3
Hofmannsthal's adaptation of Calderón's *The Great World Theatre,* produced by Reinhardt at the Salzburg Festival in 1922. (From Österreichische Nationalbibliothek.)

FIG. 10.4
Reinhardt's Redoutensaal theatre, Vienna, in 1922, created in the ballroom of an eighteenth-century palace. (From *Le Théâtre*, 1922.)

stage. For the most part, scenery, designed by Alfred Roller, was restricted to screens and small set pieces. The effect was somewhat similar to the architectural stage of the Vieux Colombier. Appropriate to the environment, Reinhardt produced at the Redoutensaal plays and chamber operas by Goethe, Beaumarchais, Molière, and Mozart. After 1924, Reinhardt also controlled Vienna's Josefstadt Theater, where he mounted a diverse repertory with his principal designer, Oskar Strnad.

After some economic stability returned to Germany, Reinhardt resumed his Berlin operations (after 1924 he sometimes managed as many as three different theatres in the city) but also continued his Austrian activities. In addition, he staged a number of productions elsewhere. Perhaps the most significant was Vollmoeller's *The Miracle*, which he staged in a number of European cities and eventually in New York at the Century Theatre, which designer Norman Bel Geddes transformed into a simulated cathedral, by far the most effective of the settings devised for Reinhardt's various versions of the pantomime. Reinhardt also

staged a season of plays (including *A Midsummer Night's Dream, Everyman,* and *Danton's Death*) in New York in 1927–1928 and several plays in England in 1932–1933.

When Hitler came to power, Reinhardt, as a Jew, was forced to give up his theatres and leave Germany. Most of his final years were spent in the United States, where he headed an acting school in Hollywood and directed films and plays. His last major stage production was Werfel's *The Eternal Road* in New York in 1936.

By 1933, Reinhardt had produced 452 plays in Berlin for a total of 23,374 performances. But it was quality and variety more than volume that made him the dominant German director from 1905 to 1933. Still, by the time he left Germany, Reinhardt was being accused of subordinating a script's meaning to some unifying visual motif or limited directorial concept and was being dismissed by some as a "mere popularizer." Even if the charges are true, he still performed a significant service, for he kept audiences abreast of new movements and directed their attention to significant dramatists and production techniques that had appeared strange and obscure in other theatres.

THE NEUE SACHLICHKEIT

As expressionism declined after 1923, a new outlook became evident. Usually labeled Neue Sachlichkeit (literally, "New Matter-of-factness") or neorealism, this new trend was characterized by a return to more conventional dramatic techniques both in writing and production and by subjects dealing with ordinary people in everyday situations and settings. As at the end of nearly every romantic era, there arose a demand that idealistic visions be abandoned in favor of down-to-earth fact. Indeed, some of the most rhapsodic of expressionists now fervently embraced neorealism. In *The Great Dream* (1923), for example, former expressionist Paul Kornfeld ridiculed the utopian ideal of the expressionists. In 1924, he demanded: "No more about war, revolution and salvation of the world! Let us be modest and turn our attention to other and smaller things. Let us ponder on a human being, or a soul, or a fool."

But the neorealism of the 1920s differed considerably from the realism of the nineteenth century. The techniques were never as objective as those used by the realists and naturalists, for antirealism and interest in the subconscious had left their mark. The Neue Sachlichkeit also lacked the essential optimism of nineteenth-century realism and naturalism which, despite the degraded images of life and cities in the 1880s, always implied the possible perfectibility of human beings and society. The Neue Sachlichkeit was more pessimistic and disillusioned about the possibilities of remedying the ills of the human condition and of society in general.

Unfortunately, the movement lacked dramatists sufficiently strong to embody its goals effectively. It remained a diverse collection of secondary and third-rate figures. Typical subjects included a wide variety of contemporary problems: returning soldiers, adjustment to peacetime life, an overly rigid legal system, the traumas of adolescence and school life. Of the

FIG. 10.5
Zuckmayer's *The Devil's General*, directed by Heinz Hilpert and designed by Caspar Neher, at the Schauspielhaus, Zurich, in 1946. (From *World Theatre*.)

many playwrights involved, three were most important at the time: Wolf, Bruckner, and Zuckmayer, although another, Horvath, gained belated fame.

Friedrich Wolf (1888–1953) began as an expressionist but in the early 1920s turned to realism. His most characteristic play is *Cyanide* (1929), an attack on antiabortion laws, showing a young girl dying because she is forced to seek help outside legitimate channels. *The Sailors of Cattaro* (1930) is a leftist-oriented documentary about an uprising in the Austro-Hungarian navy during World War I. When Hitler came to power, Wolf fled Germany but continued to write. In *Professor Mamlock* (1933), he tells the story of a Jewish doctor who becomes a victim of the Nazis.

Ferdinand Bruckner (1891–1958), an Austrian, had been an expressionist poet and the director of a theatre in Berlin. His first play, *The Malady of Youth* (1926), created an overnight sensation because of its treatment of the disillusionment of young people. Its characters, mostly medical students, come to believe that the only alternative to corruption is death. As one sums it up: "Either one turns into a philistine, or one commits suicide. There is no other way out." Eventually Bruckner turned to history for his subjects, and his play *Elizabeth of England* (1930) gained some fame outside Germany. Tracing Elizabeth's conflict with Philip of Spain, one of the play's most striking scenes shows Elizabeth at church in England and Philip at church in Spain, each praying to God for assistance against the other. Ultimately Bruckner suggests that the principal conflict is between fanaticism (Philip and the Catholic Church) and reason (Elizabeth and especially Sir Francis Bacon). Like Wolf, Bruckner spent the Nazi era in exile.

Carl Zuckmayer (1896–1977), like many of his contemporaries, entered military service during World War I as a confirmed patriot and ended the war as a rebel. At first he, too, wrote as an expressionist but later turned to neorealism. His most famous play is *The Captain of Kopenick* (1931), a satirical treatment of Prussian bureaucracy and militarism. Based on a true incident, it shows how a cobbler who needs official documents in order to obtain work is frustrated by bureaucrats. By accident, a captain's uniform falls into his hands, and, now desperate, he dons the uniform, commandeers a company of soldiers, takes over the town hall, arrests the mayor, and attains the documents he needs. When the Nazis came to power, Zuckmayer also left Germany and eventually settled in the United States. Of his late work, *The Devil's General* (1946) is perhaps his best. Set in Germany at the height of Hitler's power, the play's protagonist is a charming man who, through political naiveté and misguided patriotism, has risen to become a general in the Luftwaffe. He learns that saboteurs are at work in the airplane factory he supervises, and he seeks out the culprits, discovering that the principal saboteur is his own chief engineer. Through the engineer, the general comes to self-awareness about the horrors of Nazism and seeks to protect the saboteurs. But when the Gestapo closes in, the general takes to the air in one of the defective planes and dies.

Another playwright, now usually associated with the Neue Sachlichkeit, deserves mention because of his postwar reputation. Odon von Horvath (1901–1938), born in Hungary but considered an Austrian, did not gain true recognition until many years after his death by accident in Paris after fleeing from the Nazi takeover. (He was killed there by a tree struck by lightning.) His seventeen plays, which include *Tales of the Vienna Woods* (1931) and *Don Juan Comes Back From the War* (1936), are essentially realistic yet touched by a quality of lyricism reminiscent of the differences between the Austrian Schnitzler and the rest of the so-called realist/naturalists of the late nineteenth century. One of his best plays is his first, *Italian Night* (1930), a satire set in the beer garden of a small town in southern Germany. Here a group of complacent republicans drinks and mingles with a group of Nazis. While Horvath satirically reveals the crudeness and vulgarity of the Nazis, he also underscores the numbed naiveté of the republicans. Under the surface, however, is a prophetic awareness of the impending catastrophic circumstances soon to be unleashed in Hitler's Germany. Horvath's reputation began to grow in the 1950s and increased thereafter, perhaps because his views of societal hypocrisy and evasion of responsibility fit so well with the postwar vision.

THE BEGINNINGS OF EPIC THEATRE: MARTIN AND PISCATOR

Though the Neue Sachlichkeit or neorealism was the dominant mode after 1923, another movement—*epic theatre*—was also taking shape and would eventually surpass it in critical estimation, even though prior to World War II it would be considered a minor strain. Epic theatre combined features of both expressionism and neorealism, and added distinctive theatrical touches all its own.

In part, epic theatre grew out of the intense political awareness of the period. In some respects, German theatre between 1918 and 1923 resembled its Russian counterpart, for in both many attempts were made to use drama as a weapon for social change. In 1919, a Workers' Theatre League was formed in Germany to assist in winning acceptance for working-class causes. Troupes of amateurs, for example, performed propaganda skits at meetings and in the streets, while in several cities mass spectacles were mounted. Epic theatre had its roots in such social and political

ferment, and, in its early stages, the form owes most to Martin and Piscator.

In 1919, Karlheinz Martin (1888–1948), upon organizing a theatre called The Tribune, declared: "The urgent revolution of the theatre must start with a transformation of the stage.... We do not ask [for] an audience, but a community, not a stage, but a pulpit." During strikes, for example, The Tribune actors appeared at gatherings to read poems and perform skits, but the group also presented full-length works, the most important of which was Toller's expressionist play, *Transfiguration*. The Tribune was run as a collective in which all members of the company had a voice. No names were given in the program, for Martin sought to discourage all tendencies toward stardom. Later Martin abandoned The Tribune for a new group, the Proletarian Theater, which was less communal and partisan in its approach, and it was here that he first met Piscator, who soon gained control of the company. In 1920, Martin went to work for Reinhardt and thereafter had little to do with the emerging epic theatre.

Erwin Piscator (1893–1966) began his career in 1913 as an apprentice actor in Munich and eventually during military service in World War I came to the strong political and social beliefs he held throughout the rest of his life. After the war, Piscator went to Berlin for a time, but then in 1919–1920, he established a theatre in Königsberg, which, like Martin's, was called The Tribune. When it failed financially, partly from political pressure, Piscator returned to Berlin, where he met Martin and soon assumed control of the Proletarian Theater.

Piscator's early attitudes paralleled somewhat the outlook of the Russian Proletcult movement. In the October 1920 issue of *The Antagonist*, for example, he suggested that drama must be subordinated to revolutionary ends, even if it meant altering scripts, and that productions should represent a collective effort of all workers. Actors should be recruited from the working class rather than from professionals. Though Piscator thereafter would move increasingly toward greater professionalism, his political attitudes changed little.

While Piscator admired the expressionists' desire to transform society, he considered their work overly idealistic and abstract. The naturalism of the nineteenth century, though concerned with social problems, seemed to Piscator too confining in its attempt to be objective. Finally, he believed the *Volksbühnen* movement ultimately had only produced middle-class plays for the proletariat. Piscator eventually stated that it was through accident and necessity that he discovered the principle of "epic" scenery, for unable to provide traditional settings, he had to rely on demonstration and explanation rather than representation. For example, instead of a painted backdrop depicting a street, a map might be used to show the location of the town in which an action

occurs. But such theatrical innovation has always been supported by intellectuals rather than the working-class audience to whom it is directed—an audience that prefers to be entertained rather than harangued—and, no exception, Piscator's Proletarian Theater eventually failed with his intended audience.

It was the Berlin Volksbühne, ironically, that in 1924 gave Piscator his first real opportunity to experiment. Here, for the first time, Piscator had a first-rate stage and professional company at his disposal in addition to a potential audience of 30,000 subscribers. His first production was of Alfons Paquet's *The Flags,* based on the trial of the Chicago anarchists in 1888. Labeled "epic" by Piscator, the production showed through extratextual materials, added by means of projections on screens, the social and economic background of the action. In 1926, Piscator developed an even more spectacular production of Paquet's *Tidal Wave* (or *Sturmflut*), concerned with the Russian October Revolution. Here he used filmed sequences behind live actors, the most

FIG. 10.6
Scene from Piscator's production of Paquet's *Tidal Wave,* produced in 1926. The ships are part of a motion picture projected in the background. (A contemporary photo.)

impressive being one in which battleships in the harbor of St. Petersburg fire on live actors in the foreground. But Piscator's most controversial work at the Volksbühne was Ehm Welk's *Storm Over Gothland* in 1927, which caused his resignation. Although the play deals with Swedish fishermen in the Middle Ages, Piscator contemporized the work to recall the Russian Revolution. The actors playing the leaders of the fishermen were made to look like Lenin and Trotsky.

By 1927, Piscator had built up a considerable following among the intelligentsia and many younger members of the working class, and he now decided to open his own theatre. He obviously had been contemplating this move, for he had commissioned Walter Gropius to design a theatre for him. (Gropius' plans will be discussed later in this chapter.) Unfortunately, he was unable to obtain the financial backing needed to realize the theatre Gropius had designed for him and he thus leased the Theater-am-Nollendorfplatz and renamed it the Piscator Theater. It is for three productions there—*Hurrah, We Live!, Rasputin,* and *The Good Soldier Schweik*—all presented in the season 1927–1928, that Piscator is most famous.

The Piscator Theater opened in 1927 with Toller's *Hurrah, We Live!,* the story of a revolutionary political prisoner released after ten years only to discover that his former comrades have settled into comfortable lives. To Karl Thomas the world (on the eve of National Socialism) seems so bent on destruction that he commits suicide. The major feature of the production was the use of newsreel excerpts to review events of the period 1917–1927 during which the protagonist had been in jail: the Russian Revolution, the entry of the United States into World War I, the end of the war, the founding of the League of Nations, the beginning of Prohibition in the United States, Mussolini's assumption of power, Hitler's beer-hall *Putsch,* the Scopes trial,

Lindbergh's flight, the execution of Sacco and Vanzetti, and Trotsky's expulsion from the Communist party. It was the most extensive attempt yet made to integrate film and live performance.

In Alexey Tolstoy's *Rasputin,* Piscator erected a structure symbolically shaped like a globe, within which were several acting areas. The structure could turn or open to reveal the interior, or its exterior white surface could serve as a screen for projections. Six thousand feet of film, assembled from libraries and archives, were projected on several surfaces. At times, as many as three different events were shown on screens simultaneously while a dramatic episode was in progress on the globular stage.

But Piscator's most famous production during this season was *The Good Soldier Schweik,* based on an uncompleted novel by the Czech author Jaroslav Haček. Its protagonist is that familiar comic figure, the seeming fool, who, through naive acceptance, shows up the pomposity and madness of the world. In Haček's book, the peasant Schweik, wishing to serve his country, accepts unquestioningly whatever happens, always rising above difficulties and never losing his enthusiasm. His experiences and comments constitute a devastating satire on bureaucracy, militarism, and war in general.

The text used by Piscator was the work of Bertolt Brecht, Leo Lania, and Felix Gasbarra. The setting owed most to George Grosz, who made innumerable cartoonlike sketches that were enlarged and integrated into the action. The other principal scenic ingredients were two treadmills that moved in opposite directions. Thus Schweik (on one of the treadmills) seemed always on the move although he never left the stage; the treadmill was stopped while brief episodes were performed. On the other treadmill were mounted the various moving set pieces (mostly cutouts of Grosz cartoons). In addition, Piscator used film sequences of real

FIG. 10.7
Production of
Tolstoy's *Rasputin* at
the Piscator Theater
in 1927. (From
Moussinac, *New
Movement in the
Theatre.*)

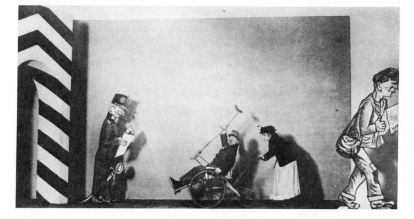

FIG. 10.8
*The Good Soldier
Schweik* in 1927 at
the Piscator Theater.
The cartoon figures
are by George Grosz.
(A contemporary
photo.)

places and events. But after much satirical laughter for the audience, the play ended soberly with Schweik's death. Then projections of row upon row of burial crosses seemed to move ever nearer the audience itself. The production was a great triumph, for Piscator as well as for Max Pallenberg, the masterful actor who played Schweik.

Despite the critical success of this season, Piscator lost his theatre because he was unable to pay the taxes due on it. Thereafter he worked in a number of places before leaving Germany when Hitler came to power. Eventually he went to the United States where from 1939 to 1951 he headed the Dramatic Workshop at the New School for Social Research in New York and directed a number of works on Broadway and elsewhere.

Thus it was Piscator who laid the foundations upon which Brecht built his version of epic theatre. But though their ideas are similar in several respects, they also differ on major points. Both stated their desire to make the spectator think and act in the world, but they differed on the proper approach. Brecht sought to "historify" or "distance" his subjects in order to induce objectivity. Piscator, as in *Storm Over Gothland,* sought to contemporize historical events—to make them closer to the audience's own experience. Piscator also sought to involve his audience emotionally in the action—to make the audience "feel" the plight of the group protagonists. Brecht sought to keep his audience from full emotional involvement, using techniques for a certain distancing so that audience members could think about the action portrayed. Admirers of Brecht, in contrasting the two artists, would suggest that the catharsis of Piscator's productions occurred inside the theatre rather, as in Brecht's, outside it.

BRECHT AND EPIC THEATRE

In pre-World War II Germany, Piscator was the best-known practitioner of epic theatre, for only later did Brecht overshadow him and come to be the major exponent of the epic approach. Bertolt Brecht (1898–1956), after studying medicine and serving as an orderly in a military hospital during the war, began his playwriting career in 1918 with *Baal,* an expressionist piece displaying a decidedly nihilistic vision of the world. Composed of twenty-two short scenes, the play focuses on the exploits of Baal, an ugly, sensually insatiable, bohemian poet who defies all of society's restraints. The work includes a great amount of drunken revelry, sexual conquest, and bawdry, but these elements are intermingled with intimations of idealism, for Baal is a poet as well as a criminal.

In the years immediately following the war,

Brecht worked as a free-lance writer, critic, and cabaret performer before winning the Kleist Prize in 1922 for *Drums in the Night,* his first play to be produced. In the following year, *In the Jungle of Cities* was produced in Munich, and Brecht worked for a time in this city at the Pocket Theater as a director. In 1924, he moved to Berlin, where until 1926 he served (along with Zuckmayer) as an assistant dramaturg in Reinhardt's Deutsches Theater.

The first phase of Brecht's career as a playwright ended in 1926. All the plays to that time are seemingly anarchistic rejections of society and are indebted to the techniques of expressionism. In these works, Brecht seems dissatisfied with the world, but his discontent is without direction. A major turning point came with *Man Is Man* (1926). Here are found the seeds of that social consciousness and didacticism that would characterize his work thereafter. It is probably also significant that by this time expressionism had declined and the agenda of the Neue Sachlichkeit had begun to proclaim the need for a greater concreteness and sharper awareness of social realities. The protagonist of *Man Is Man* is Galy Gay, a meek dockworker in the Indian port of Kilkoa, who is gradually transformed by three British soldiers into a "human fighting machine" through a kind of inversion of Kipling's imperialistic outlook. Brecht's earlier nihilism has here been replaced by a dawning interest, still not fully articulated, in the exploitation of the working classes and in antimilitarism. It was also in 1926 that Brecht began his Marxist studies at the Berlin Workers' School. Thereafter his concern with social and political thought increased and his plays reflected a Marxist view, though not always sharply defined.

The years between 1927 and 1933 were productive ones for Brecht. In 1927–1928, he worked with Piscator on *The Good Soldier Schweik* and became thoroughly familiar with Piscator's views and methods (having seen

FIG. 10.9
A production of Brecht's *Baal* as performed by the Berliner Ensemble. Directed by Alejandro Quintana, design and costumes by Manfred Grund. (Photo by Vera Tenschert, courtesy Berliner Ensemble.)

most of Piscator's earlier work as well). In 1928, Brecht achieved his first real fame with *The Threepenny Opera,* which ran for 400 performances. Thereafter until 1933, he had a theatre available to him. In 1928, he also married Helene Weigel (1900–1971), the performer with whom he worked closely thereafter. He now completed a number of works in rapid succession, including *St. Joan of the Stockyards* (1928), *The Rise and Fall of the City of Mahagonny* (1930), and a number of *Lehrstücke* or didactic plays.

To understand Brecht's work in this period, one needs to know something of contemporary music, for his contacts with composers influerced him greatly. Just as there was a movement toward a new matter-of-factness in drama, so, too, was there a similar trend in music. It arose during World War I when such composers as Stravinsky and Satie began to rebel against the complexities of Wagner, Richard Strauss, and Gustav Mahler, who had written music that could only be played by highly accomplished professionals, thus relegating it to recital halls and opera houses divorced from daily life. The revolt began in approximately 1915 when Stravinsky wrote *Renard,* a chamber opera intended "to be played by clowns, dancers or acrobats, preferably on a trestle stage with the orchestra placed behind it." The intention was to bring music down from its pedestal and to encourage the kind of simplicity already evident in the visual arts. Stravinsky followed *Renard* with *The History of a Soldier* (1918), which required only seven musicians, narrators, dancers, and the simplest of stages. In 1917, Satie turned to popular and jazz music for themes in *Parade,* and later he introduced what he called "furniture music"—a background for other activities and only to be half-listened to. A number of Satie's associates, most notably Darius Milhaud, joined this movement.

The trend toward simplicity soon reached Germany (where it was called *Neue Musik*). In 1921, its adherents founded an annual festival at Donaueschingen to promote the Neue Musik, and here Stravinsky appeared annually after 1925. It was here too that Kurt Weill presented many of his early works. In 1927, the festival was moved to Baden-Baden, where Brecht was asked to stage some of the productions and later to present a number of his own works.

The leading spokesman for the Neue Musik in Germany was Paul Hindemith, who ran the festival. Hindemith believed that composers had gone astray by losing sight of how music is to be used. Thus, he tended to promote compositions of two kinds: functional music, which included scores for films and dances and settings for poems and other texts; and music written for amateur performers. Hindemith sought to restore music in society by promoting works that could be played by nonprofessionals; he was especially interested in compositions written for performance in schools. Out of this grew a number of "school" operas and *Lehrstücke,* or didactic musical plays, often likened to the school plays of the sixteenth-century humanists. The festivals at Baden-Baden and a

Neue Musik festival held in Berlin in 1930 promoted such *Lehrstücke* as a didactic medium. It was among the adherents of Neue Musik that Brecht found all the composers with whom he worked thereafter: Weill, Hindemith, Hanns Eisler, Paul Dessau, and Rudolf Wagner-Regeny.

Music played an important role in Brecht's drama from the very beginning. For the early works, he composed his own music, and only after 1927 did he collaborate with others. The first collaborative results were *The Threepenny Opera* and *The Rise and Fall of the City of Mahagonny,* with music by Kurt Weill. Of all

FIG. 10.10
Brecht's *The Threepenny Opera* as first performed in 1928 at the Theater am Schiffbauerdamm, Berlin. Directed by Erich Engel, design by Caspar Neher. (Courtesy Deutsches Theatermuseum, Munich.)

Brecht's pre-Hitlerian works, *The Threepenny Opera* is the best known. It was motivated in part by, in 1928, the two-hundredth anniversary of John Gay's *Beggar's Opera* but also Gay's satire on grand opera and the ruling classes. Brecht relocated the action in nineteenth-century rather than eighteenth-century England. In *The Threepenny Opera*, he sought to denounce the hypocrisy and resignation of the lower classes and through his thieves and whores to caricature middle-class values, although most audiences have tended to see the play merely as entertaining rather than as cautionary.

The Rise and Fall of the City of Mahagonny approaches opera in its use of musical accompaniment throughout and in its score for forty instruments plus a stage orchestra of twenty-one pieces. (*The Threepenny Opera* uses only eight instruments.) The play begins with the decision of three criminals to found the city of Mahagonny and enrich themselves by appealing to human vices—the propensity to seek happiness in alcohol, sex, drugs, and money. Ultimately the protagonist concludes that everything bought with money is worthless and that anything gotten through force is ephemeral. Brecht seems to suggest that a society built upon the principles of Mahagonny will eventually die of its own contradictions, yet he offers no positive alternatives.

In the various *Lehrstücke*, Brecht was consciously didactic, although even here he did not escape ambiguities. Perhaps the best of the *Lehrstücke* is *The Measures Taken* (1930). It uses four soloists and a chorus to tell the story of Four Agitators who have returned from a mission to China, where they have liquidated a fifth agitator, the Young Comrade. The Control Chorus, representing the Communist party, asks the agitators to act out what has happened. They show how the Young Comrade, by following his humanitarian instincts, has helped others and thereby delayed the revolution.

When he comes to see the errors of his ways, the Young Comrade asks to be executed. The Control Chorus weighs the evidence and approves "the measures taken"—the unfortunate necessity of sacrificing the individual for the good of the collective. The piece aroused a storm of controversy, especially within the Communist party (most orthodox members strenuously rejected it), and Brecht eventually forbade its presentation.

In 1933, Brecht fled Germany and for years led a nomadic existence—in Austria, Switzerland, France, Denmark, Finland, the Soviet Union—before settling in the United States between 1941 and 1947. Practically all of Brecht's pre-Hitlerian work had been damned by critics, who generally considered him a minor though controversial writer. It was during this exile that he wrote those works upon which his reputation rests. Practically all that went into them had been sketched out by 1933, but it remained to be translated into mature accomplishment.

BRECHTIAN THEORY

After 1933, Brecht matured both as dramatist and theoretician, and since his drama is illuminated by his theory, it is helpful to examine the theoretical views first. While his views evolved slowly, by 1933 the basic outlines were discernible in postscripts and notes to various plays, especially those for *The Threepenny Opera, Mahagonny,* and the revised version of *Man Is Man.* Still, he did not use the term *alienation* until 1936 (although the concept is adumbrated in earlier writings), and he did not publish a fully integrated theory until 1948, when "Little Organon for the Theatre" appeared. Even then, he continued to modify his views up to the time of his death, and toward the end of his life declared his unhappiness at ever having written theoretical works at all.

He suggested that "dialectic" might better describe his work than "epic," and he came to favor a Hegelian approach in which thesis and antithesis are resolved in a new synthesis. Regardless of its evolutionary nature, there is a core of Brechtian theory that, for better or worse, has come to be called epic, and that has precipitated arguments among Brecht's disciples not unlike those that have raged among Stanislavsky's admirers.

Brecht's theory has many antecedents, both artistic and political. Among the artistic, the most important are the *Sturm und Drang* writers, Büchner, Hegel, the expressionists, Piscator, and the Neue Sachlichkeit, while clearly the most significant political influence was Marxism. Much of Brecht's theory amounts to a rebuttal of the Wagnerian (or "dramatic," "Aristotelian") outlook, which through the work of Appia and Craig had come to dominate European and thus American thought about theatrical practice. Brecht begins with the assumption that the hypnotic effect sought by Wagner is fundamentally mistaken, since it reduces the audience to a role of complete passivity. Thus, Wagner's spectator is unable to translate theatrical experience into practical action outside the theatre. Brecht wished a quite different relationship among spectator, theatre, and society. He therefore adopted the term *epic* to distinguish his work from the *dramatic* or Aristotelian approach, which he believed had outlived its usefulness. Not only did this theatre make the spectator passive but it also suggested the fixity and unchangeability of events. Furthermore, Brecht believed that the dramatic theatre's illusionistic staging methods gave stability to traditional values and modes of behavior. Since everything appears fixed, spectators can only watch, for nothing is left for them to do.

Brecht saw his epic theatre as one in which the spectator would play a vital and active role. While he believed in entertaining the spectator, he wanted to keep the spectator critical and objective. The means of achieving this critical and objective state is, as Brecht suggested, through *alienation* (*Verfremdung*)—a process of making events, actions, and characters strange, of sufficiently distancing spectators from the play so that they can watch it critically. Whereas Wagner wanted a total empathic response, Brecht sought to short-circuit empathy by breaking illusion and overtly reminding the audience that it is in a theatre watching a reflection of reality, not reality itself—that the real societal problems lie outside the theatre, not on the stage. At times Brecht approached alienation through "historification," a process in which the "pastness" of events is emphasized so that the audience can not only judge them but also be led to recognize that, since things have changed, present conditions may also be altered.

Some have interpreted Brecht's concept of alienation to mean that the audience should be in a continuous state of objective detachment. In actuality, Brecht manipulated aesthetic distance so as to involve spectators emotionally and then to jar them out of their empathic responses, thus forcing them to contemplate and judge the experience. Consequently, in a Brechtian performance, there is a perpetual shifting, dynamic relationship between empathy and alienation.

All elements of dramatic structure and theatrical production are used by Brecht to achieve this constantly shifting relationship. Plays are divided into a series of carefully separated episodes. Usually the episodes are separated by songs, brief speeches, or visual devices that suspend the action so that the spectator can contemplate the implications of what has been seen. Like the structure of an epic poem, a Brechtian play often alternates dialogue with narration, and time and place shift rapidly.

Brecht conceived of drama primarily as a

FIG. 10.13
Bauhaus Dance by
Oskar Schlemmer.
(Courtesy Tut
Schlemmer.)

could be altered dynamically by abstract and colored light from front or back.

Out of his experiments with space, shapes, motion, light, and color, Schlemmer evolved a number of stage productions ranging in tone from the comic to the mystic. The best-known is *The Triadic Ballet*, which he first conceived in 1912 and refined thereafter. The work was first seen in its entirety in 1922 and was later repeated at the Neue Musik festival at Donaueschingen with music by Hindemith. *The Triadic Ballet* was in three parts: a burlesque section set against lemon-yellow curtains; a serious and festive part in a rose-colored setting; and a heroic and mystical finale played against a black background. The entire work was subdivided into twelve parts, each danced by three performers whose shapes were altered by three-dimensional costumes made of rigid frameworks and padded fabrics. Schlemmer stated that the costumes were conceived first; next the music was chosen to fit the shapes; then movement was evolved. Schlemmer also developed a number of nonhuman "figural cabinets" in which mechanical figures were

programmed to move into different configurations to act out a strange, grotesque drama.

The Bauhaus stage work made its greatest impact through the Stage Workshop's tour of several German and Swiss cities in 1929. The program was composed of several short pieces, the titles of which give some indication of their sources of inspiration: "Dance in Metal," "Dance of Hoops," "Game With Building Blocks," "Chorus of Masks." Some pieces were humorous, others surrealistic, mysterious, or frightening. One reviewer wrote: "No feelings are 'expressed,' rather, feelings are evoked. . . . Pure absolute form."

When Schlemmer left the Bauhaus in 1929, the Stage Workshop came to an end. After Hitler came to power, Schlemmer was barred from all teaching posts and had to subsist thereafter on odd jobs. His work at the Bauhaus had little immediate influence on the theatre, but interest in it revived in the 1950s, when the idea of total design in dance became popular. Like much of the Bauhaus' work, Schlemmer's can probably best be viewed as "basic research," the possible applications of which are almost infinite.

Paralleling the interests of Schlemmer were those of László Moholy-Nagy (1895–1946) in light and motion. Moholy-Nagy joined the Bauhaus in 1923 as head of the Metal Workshop, but he became increasingly interested in the problems of mobile, three-dimensional works of art, in the role of light, and in spatial interrelationships. He was to make important contributions to kinetic sculpture, photography, film, and advertising. His "Light-Space Modulator," moved by electricity and using electric light to project ever-changing patterns, is considered a major pioneering work of art.

In 1925, Moholy-Nagy published a statement on *total theatre* (one upon which Gropius and Piscator would build and which preceded Artaud's theories by many years). He first noted the characteristics of the traditional theatre but also recognized the contributions of the futurists, dadaists, and the Bauhaus, all of which he found partial. His belief was that all such approaches could be absorbed into a new totality. Moholy-Nagy suggested that the problem of the theatre is more complex than the other arts because of the living actor: ". . . how can we integrate a sequence of human movements and thoughts on an equal footing with the controlled 'absolute' elements of sound, light (color), form, and motion?" The means suggested by Moholy-Nagy include the amplification of voices and characters, inner thoughts, close-up images of faces and gestures, recordings, and films. He speaks of directional sound and multiple projections. Of lighting, he says: "We have not yet begun to realize the potential of light for sudden or blinding illumination, for flare effects, for phosphorescent effects, for bathing the auditorium in light synchronized with climaxes or with total extinguishing of lights on the stage." He recommended that the barriers between stage and auditorium be removed and that bridges be suspended overhead horizontally, diagonally, and vertically, or that stages be extended far into the auditorium. Unlike many theorists of the time, Moholy-Nagy did not want to eliminate the text; he merely sought to place the other elements of theatre on an equal footing with the spoken word. Moholy-Nagy's ideas are of considerable importance as one of the earliest manifestoes for total theatre and multimedia productions. His influence on the theatre Gropius designed for Piscator shortly afterward is clear. After leaving the Bauhaus in 1928, Moholy-Nagy worked for Piscator and eventually designed many highly inventive settings for operas in Berlin.

In theatre architecture, the Bauhaus' most important work was done by Gropius, who in 1927 designed a total theatre for Piscator. According to Gropius, there are only three basic stage forms—the arena, thrust, and proscenium—and in his total theatre he sought to incorporate all three. In his design, he mounted a segment of seats and an acting area on a large revolvable circle forward of the proscenium. When the acting area was moved to a position contiguous with the proscenium, it formed a thrust stage, and when rotated 180 degrees it became an arena. Seats could also be mounted on the acting area when the proscenium stage was to be used alone. From the wings of the proscenium stage ran an open platform that completely surrounded the audience. Upon this platform, scenery could be shifted by means of wagons. A translucent cyclorama at the rear of the proscenium stage also provided a surface for projections as did panels between columns around the auditorium and screens overhead. Thus the audience could be surrounded by the action.

Gropius wanted to achieve a "unity of the scene of action with the spectator," and to use all available means to overwhelm the viewers, to "stun them, and to force them to participate in experiencing the play." Thus, through the

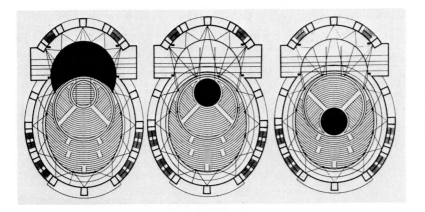

FIG. 10.14
Gropius' Total
Theatre. Floorplans
show arrangements
for, left to right,
proscenium, thrust,
and arena stagings.
(Courtesy Walter
Gropius.)

work of Gropius, Moholy-Nagy, and Piscator, the ideals of the Bauhaus and of epic theatre met. Unfortunately, Piscator never found the funds to build Gropius' theatre. Nevertheless, Gropius' plans have remained an inspiration to others.

When Hitler came to power, the members of the Bauhaus dispersed, many to the United States. Gropius became head of the department of architecture at Harvard University and a partner in some of the most influential architectural firms of the world. Moholy-Nagy served as head of the New Bauhaus, founded in Chicago in 1937, and, when it was dissolved the following year, his own Institute of Design until his death. Mies van der Rohe became head of the department of architecture at the Illinois Institute of Technology in Chicago. The list of Bauhaus exiles could be extended many times. Scarcely an element of Western contemporary life has failed to be influenced by the Bauhaus, often in unsuspected ways.

THE RISE OF NAZISM

When the Nazis came to power in 1933, they effectively silenced liberalism in thought and experimentation in the arts. Many theatre artists and playwrights had little choice except to go into exile, some because they were Jews, others because their ideas made them targets of the Gestapo. In exile many committed suicide, among them Toller and Hasenclever. After Austria was taken over in 1938, there remained no German-speaking areas except Switzerland to which exiles could go. Consequently, most exiled Germans were forced into an alienation from their own language. Cut off, many were unable to work, although a few, such as Brecht and Zuckmayer, were remarkably productive. Hauptmann, by then more than seventy years old, was the only major dramatist to remain in Germany under Hitler, and his seeming acquiescence did much to destroy his reputation.

The plight of many artists and writers who remained in Germany was not unlike that of their Russian counterparts in the same period. Playwrights in both countries were either compliant or they were silenced. Several German authors underwent what has been called an "inner emigration" by writing historical works or by deliberately distancing their work from the contemporary scene. In Germany, as in the Soviet Union, an official style of variations on realism was enforced. In Germany, the glorification of the Teutonic past and the Nietzschean superman (as interpreted by the Nazis) produced numerous sterile dramas that featured grandiose, larger-than-life evocations of an all-powerful, all-Nordic world.

The Nazis considered everything that had occurred since 1918, such as expressionism, to be a mistake, and they set out to eliminate all vestiges of those years and to recapture the glories of the First Reich (the Holy Roman Empire) and the Second Reich (1870–1918) in their own Third Reich. Some playwrights such as Eberhard Wolfgang Möller (1906–1972) and Hanns Johst (1890–1978) indeed accepted the Hitlerian ideal, but it is significant that no play written in Germany between 1933 and 1945 is now considered at all worthwhile. During the Third Reich, however, the theatre remained highly active, particularly as a medium of Nazi propaganda, and the government poured huge funds into its showcase of Teutonic culture. But when conditions in Germany began to worsen around 1942, less support was possible, and in 1944, all theatres were closed. Thus ended the Nazi era.

THE SIGNIFICANCE OF THE INTERWAR YEARS

In German-speaking countries, the matter-of-factness of the Neue Sachlichkeit pointed away from the emotionalism of the expressionists, while the epic theatres of Piscator and Brecht echoed with leftist political and social engagement. As the forces of Nazism took power, however, the theatre was transformed into a source of extreme rightist propaganda, and it would not be until after the most devastating war in world history that new forms would be found to pose tentative answers to new theatrical questions.

Chapter 11

British, Irish, and American Theatre and Drama Between the Wars

During World War I, the figure of the actor-manager, who had dominated the English theatre for nearly two hundred years, was superseded by commercial producers, more concerned with profit than artistic excellence. Fortunately, a few groups in London and the provinces followed a different path. Perhaps because the English seldom have been strongly influenced by artistic movements elsewhere, the style of most playwriting and production in the interwar years remained in the realistic mode. In general, English drama of the period was not outstanding, although a few writers gained some notoriety in their time. In Ireland, the theatre regained some of its former glory with the plays of O'Casey and the productions of the Dublin Gate Theatre.

With World War I, the United States became a major global power, and soon afterward its theatre and drama for the first

259

time began to win international recognition. In the 1920s and 1930s, significant contributions were made by such groups as the Theatre Guild, the Provincetown Players, the Group Theatre, and the Federal Theatre. Playwrights such as O'Neill and Wilder won high praise both at home and abroad. As in England, the major stylistic mode was realism in playwriting and production, although the Americans were somewhat more responsive to the experiments of continental Europe and the Soviet Union. By the time the United States entered World War II in 1941, its theatre and drama had reached maturity, even if its accomplishments were not great in comparison with those of most European countries.

THE STRUGGLE AGAINST COMMERCIALISM

World War I marked the end of the actor-manager system in England. The change is summed up at His Majesty's Theatre, which under Herbert Beerbohm Tree had been the home of Shakespeare. After Tree's retirement in 1915, the theatre was given over to 2,238 consecutive performances of Oscar Asche's *Chu-Chin-Chow*, a musical extravaganza based on *Ali Baba and the Forty Thieves*. *Chu-Chin-Chow*, with its emphasis upon escapist entertainment, set the tone for the war years as well as those that followed. While some actor-managers such as Fred Terry and Ben Greet

FIG. 11.1

Chu-Chin-Chow at His Majesty's Theatre in 1916. This is the slave market scene. Oscar Asche, the author, is seated under the umbrella at right. (Courtesy Enthoven Collection. By courtesy of the Board of Trustees of the Victoria and Albert Museum.)

continued to maintain companies, they were forced to spend most of their time on the road and thus made little impact on London's West End, now dominated by businessmen like those who had gained control of the American theatre in the early twentieth century. Actors were hired for the run of a play, and scripts were chosen primarily for their potential to attract a mass audience. While there was no decline in the number of productions, quality suffered in the major houses. As in France, however, a few out-of-the-way theatres brightened an otherwise gloomy picture. The most important of these groups were the Lyric Theatre, the Gate Theatre, the Barnes Theatre, and the Old Vic.

The Lyric Theatre, Hammersmith, was founded in 1918 by Nigel Playfair (1874–1934), who had been a secondary performer with Benson, Tree, and Barker. Playfair remodeled an old western suburban theatre into an elegant resort. The group featured a number of young actors who would later become stars— among them Herbert Marshall, Hermione Baddeley, and Leslie Banks. Several successful productions led to the company's real triumph in 1920 with John Gay's *The Beggar's Opera*. By the time its run of 1,463 performances had ended, the Lyric had become London's most fashionable theatre.

In addition, *The Beggar's Opera* reawakened interest in the drama of the Restoration and

FIG. 11.2

The Beggar's Opera at the Lyric Theatre, Hammersmith, in 1920. Setting by Claud Lovat Fraser. The arch unit remained throughout, while pieces were changed behind it. (Courtesy Enthoven Collection. By courtesy of the Board of Trustees of the Victoria and Albert Museum.)

eighteenth century, which, with the exception of Sheridan's works, had long been dormant. Thereafter, the majority of Playfair's repertory was chosen from that era. Among his most significant productions were *The Way of the World*, *The Beaux' Stratagem*, *Love in a Village*, *Lionel and Clarissa*, *She Stoops to Conquer*, *The Critic*, *The Duenna*, and *The Rivals*.

Playfair's productions muted all harshness and sexual innuendo (even in *The Beggar's Opera* and *The Way of the World*) and made of the scripts playful entertainments verging on caricature. Nevertheless, the productions were completely unlike anything to be seen in the English theatre and therefore did much to create a sense of style in production. Always characterized by colorful costumes and settings, formalized compositions and stylized gestures, a liberal use of music and dance, the Lyric's productions were inevitably elegant and modish. Because of its narrow range, however, the Lyric's appeal eventually declined and in 1932 Playfair relinquished its direction. But its influence was lasting, for here such major English performers as John Gielgud and Edith Evans gained an appreciation for the importance of style in acting.

The Gate Theatre was as dilapidated as the Lyric was elegant. It was the creation of Peter Godfrey (1899–1971), who had been a magician in music halls as a child, a circus clown, a member of Ben Greet's Shakespearean troupe, and an actor in a number of repertory companies. Godfrey became interested in expressionist drama, a form that had found no outlet in England before Godfrey opened the Gate in 1925 as a private club in a loft near Covent Garden. The space held only eighty audience members and had a tiny stage. A production of Kaiser's *From Morn to Midnight* inspired a laudatory review by James Agate, one of London's most influential critics, and the demand to see the play became so great that the production was moved to a West End theatre.

Godfrey eventually presented a large number of plays by such authors as Strindberg, Wedekind, Toller, Evreinov, Čapek, Hauptmann, Ibsen, Maeterlinck, and Rice. While not all were expressionist pieces, expressionism was the dominant mode. For most productions, the stage was surrounded with black drapes in front of which were erected set pieces, often painted in distorted perspective and nonrealistic color. Major emphasis was placed upon lighting and rhythmical effects. In 1927, however, the Gate moved to a building measuring 55 by 30 feet, which Godfrey remodeled to suit his needs. Despite the small size, he reserved a generous space for the stage, which was raised only 18 inches above the auditorium floor. The theatre's intimacy encouraged sincerity in acting, and here Godfrey presented plays by such authors as Pirandello, Cocteau, O'Neill, and others. Because of the quality of the plays, Godfrey attracted a number of fine performers who were willing to work a few weeks at minimal pay. Among others, Flora Robson, Robert Speaight, Eric Portman, Hermione Gingold, Elsa Lanchester, and Jean Forbes-Robertson appeared at the Gate, which continued to produce plays until 1934.

Another venture of some importance was the Barnes Theatre, housed in a converted cinema in a suburb of London. Here in 1925–1926, Theodore Komissarzhevsky, who had left the Soviet Union in 1919 and had worked in Paris for Hébertot, staged a season of plays that included Chekhov's *Uncle Vanya*, *The Three Sisters*, *The Cherry Orchard*, and *Ivanov*. These were the first effective presentations of Chekhov's work in England. Komissarzhevsky's productions were considered revelations, for the plays were for the first time not merely understandable but deeply moving. Furthermore, his subtle handling of tempo,

FIG. 11.3
Peter Godfrey's
production of Kaiser's
*From Morn to
Midnight* at the Gate
Theatre in 1928.
(Courtesy Enthoven
Collection. By
courtesy of the Board
of Trustees of the
Victoria and Albert
Museum.)

pause, modulation, sculptural lighting, and simple but imaginative settings gave a badly needed lesson to the English in what directing at its best could achieve. Among the company for this season were Charles Laughton, Claude Rains, Martita Hunt, Jean Forbes-Robertson, and John Gielgud.

Ultimately the most significant London theatre of this period was the Old Vic. Built in 1818, the theatre eventually called the Old Vic was a very minor music hall. In the early twentieth century the theatre came under the control of Lilian Baylis (1874–1937), who began to present operas, and, by the time of World War I, productions of Shakespeare. With its presentation of *Troilus and Cressida* in

1923, directed by Robert Atkins (1886–1972), the Old Vic became the first theatre in England to have produced all of Shakespeare's plays.

GUTHRIE, GIELGUD, AND SAINT-DENIS

In the 1930s, gradually the principles demonstrated by Barker, especially in his Shakespearean productions of 1912–1914, triumphed in the theatres of London. After Barker's retirement, the West End theatre had settled once again into the style of photographic realism advocated by Irving and Tree (indeed, except for Barker's work, it had never departed from this style). Despite the work of Playfair and Godfrey, there was no marked change in the commercial theatre until the 1930s. The direction then taken owed most to a few people: Tyrone Guthrie (and the Old Vic), John Gielgud, Michel Saint-Denis, and the circle of actors who worked with them.

Most of the innovations at the Old Vic in the 1930s are attributable to Tyrone Guthrie, who first worked for Baylis in 1933–1934. Baylis had always insisted that Shakespeare be performed in a straightforward manner that stressed the human and humorous qualities. She also spent very little in mounting the plays and was legendary for her penurious treatment of directors and actors. Nonetheless, she was greatly admired for her dedication to a mission—to bring the best of drama and opera to an otherwise deprived audience. Over the years, however, her protectiveness had tended to keep productions in a very narrow path. Thus there was something of a struggle between her and Guthrie from the beginning. She fired him after one season only to bring him back in 1936. When Baylis died the next year, it was Guthrie who became head of the Old Vic and Sadler's Wells (which Baylis had acquired in 1931).

Until Guthrie's time, the acting company of the Old Vic had been composed almost entirely of competent but relatively unknown performers. But in 1933–1934, four well-known actors—Charles Laughton, Flora Robson, Athene Seyler, and Ursula Jeans—were employed. Indeed, under Guthrie, almost every English performer of note passed through the Old Vic troupe. For the first time, because of the improvement in the acting company, the Old Vic began to draw West End audiences, thus alienating many of the older patrons who had become something of a coterie contemptuous of, or aloof from, the commercial theatre. Until Guthrie's leadership, each Old Vic production was offered for three weeks, no matter what its popularity. Now the run might extend up to eight weeks if demand justified it. In 1939, Guthrie devised a true repertory system under which a permanent company would alternate plays in regular rotation, a novelty at the time. But before the new system could be fully tested, the war caused the company to move its headquarters to Burnley, where it remained until 1944, making only occasional forays into London. But by the time the war began, the Old Vic was looked upon by many as England's nearest equivalent to a national theatre.

Tyrone Guthrie (1900–1971) had made his debut as an actor in 1924 in the Oxford Repertory Company but soon gave up acting in favor of directing. Thereafter he was a director for the Scottish National Theatre and the Cambridge Festival Theatre. His debut in London, at the Westminster Theatre with Bridie's *The Anatomist,* was a considerable hit, and thereafter he was much in demand. But his finest work before World War II was at the Old Vic or with Gielgud's company.

In London, Guthrie rapidly became known for those qualities which thereafter characterized his work: his boldness in giving plays new and startling (sometimes bizarre) interpretations, his disregard for tradition, his inventive and novel stage business, and restless, sometimes near-frenetic movement. His productions were often controversial because of novel directorial conceptions, but they were seldom boring. He made the director a major force in the theatre and perhaps did more than anyone in the 1930s to provoke the common complaint among critics that directors were more concerned with novel than with sound interpretations of plays.

As important as the work was of Guthrie and the Old Vic, it did not at the time seem as significant as that of John Gielgud (1904–   ), for he prevailed in the West End while the Old Vic remained on the fringe, outside the mainstream of commercial theatre. A grandnephew of Ellen Terry and cousin to Gordon Craig, Gielgud made his acting debut at the Old Vic in 1921 and then performed with the Oxford Repertory Company, Komissarzhevsky, Playfair, and in various London productions, including two seasons under Harcourt Williams at the Old Vic. Nevertheless, in 1930 he was still considered merely a promising actor. The turning point came in 1932–1933 when he directed and starred in Gordon Daviot's play about Richard II, *Richard of Bordeaux.* From this time on, he was deemed to be both a major actor and the finest director of the new school. It was Gielgud who made Barker's principles acceptable to the English public, and with his work the English commercial theatre began to catch up with practices that had been common in most European countries since the beginning of World War I.

Gielgud's acceptance probably was aided by his belief in the integrity of the text. Unlike Guthrie, who tended to impose interpretations on most plays, Gielgud sought to develop what he believed to be a script's inherent meanings. His productions in the 1930s favored simplified settings that captured appropriate mood and atmosphere through line, color, and composition, and his acting and directing stressed inner psychological appropriateness. His successes in the 1930s were numerous, but in 1934, he directed and starred in *Hamlet,* certainly the most honored staging of Shakespeare's play during the decade. The production was designed by Motley—a firm composed of Sophia Harris (1901–1966), Margaret F. Harris, and Elizabeth Montgomery—which also played a significant role in altering public taste. The setting was a semipermanent arrangement of steps and platforms that could be revolved, the appearance of which was altered with curtains, a few set pieces, and lighting. The costumes, inspired by the paintings of Cranach, were made of canvas trimmed with silk and velvet and sprayed with paint. In 1935, Gielgud directed *Romeo and Juliet,* in which he alternated the roles of Romeo and Mercutio with Laurence Olivier and in which Edith Evans played the Nurse and Peggy Ashcroft played Juliet. In 1936, he starred in *The Sea Gull,* which, as designed and directed by Komissarzhevsky, was one of the finest productions of Chekhov ever to be seen in the West End.

Gielgud's prewar work reached its climax in 1937–1938 at the Queen's Theatre, where the season included *Richard II,* directed by Gielgud; *The School for Scandal,* directed by Guthrie; *The Three Sisters,* directed by Saint-Denis; and *The Merchant of Venice,* directed by Gielgud and Glen Byam Shaw. All were designed by Motley, and the company included Peggy Ashcroft, Alec Guinness, Michael Redgrave, Anthony Quayle, Harcourt Williams, Glen Byam Shaw, and Athene Seyler. In quality and artistry, this season has seldom been surpassed in the English theatre. It set a standard for a whole era.

In 1936, Michel Saint-Denis (whose early career was discussed in Chapter 9) at the urging of Guthrie and others opened the London Theatre Studio as a training school for actors. He also directed at the Old Vic and for Gielgud. Consequently, after 1936 there was an alliance among Guthrie, Gielgud, and Saint-Denis, around whom gathered a whole new school of performers that included Edith Evans, Flora Robson, Peggy Ashcroft, Laurence Olivier, Maurice Evans, Michael Redgrave, Alec Guinness, Ralph Richardson, and Anthony Quayle. But many other outstanding actors, of

FIG. 11.5
Olivier as Romeo, Edith Evans as the Nurse, and Gielgud as Mercutio in *Romeo and Juliet* at the New Theatre in 1935. (Courtesy Debenham Collection, British Theatre Museum, London.)

course, were not associated with Gielgud and Guthrie in these years, among them Sybil Thorndike, Lewis Casson, Cedric Hardwicke, and Donald Wolfit. While England produced no marked schools of acting, the younger performers, particularly those associated with Gielgud, tended to be more concerned with inner psychology than were their older counterparts. For the most part, however, all major English actors of the period were devoted to a common ideal: convincing, life-like impersonation. There was little argument about methods or techniques.

Thus, though the London theatre improved in the 1930s, it remained unimpressive in comparison to theatre in other European capitals. It was clearly a conservative institution to which change came slowly. It was almost wholly devoid of the extreme experiments so common in Germany, France, the Soviet Union, and Eastern Europe between the wars.

PROVINCIAL REPERTORY COMPANIES AND FESTIVALS

Among the brightest elements in the British theatre between the wars were several resident companies in the provinces. The most important was the Birmingham Repertory Theatre, founded by Barry Jackson (1879–1961) in 1913. Heir to a fortune and trained as an architect, Jackson became involved with the Pilgrim Players, a group of amateurs. But he soon became convinced of the need for a fully professional organization and in 1913 built a modern theatre with plaster skydome, advanced lighting system, apron stage, and a steeply raked auditorium which offered a good view from each of its five hundred seats. Here between 1913 and 1935, Jackson produced approximately four hundred plays and operas. His taste was eclectic and his repertory extremely varied. He valued good acting and had

a flair for recognizing young talent. Among those who passed through his company were Laurence Olivier, Ralph Richardson, John Gielgud, and Cedric Hardwicke. His settings and costumes, most of them by Paul Shelving, were among the best to be seen in England.

Despite the high level of his work, Jackson received such little support that in 1924 he announced his intention of closing the theatre. Birmingham now seemed to feel its reputation was at stake, and the Civic Society guaranteed him sufficient subscribers to keep the theatre open. During the next ten years, Jackson provided perhaps the finest repertory in all of England. (His was the first theatre, for example, to present Shaw's *Back to Methuselah*.) But in 1934, the theatre was in trouble again, and Jackson refused to continue as the sole financier of the company, for by this time he had lost 100,000 pounds. Thus in 1935, when he gave the building to the city of Birmingham, it became the first civic theatre in England. While Jackson continued as the company's director, civic control forced a loss of adventurousness. Thereafter the Birmingham Repertory Theatre declined in importance.

Jackson did not confine his activities to Birmingham. Between 1922 and 1934, he produced forty-two plays in London, many of them transferred from Birmingham. In London, he had the reputation for winning success with plays that commercial producers avoided, among them Pirandello's *Six Characters in Search of an Author,* Ibsen's *Rosmersholm,* and Rice's *The Adding Machine.* Perhaps his most influential productions were modern-dress stagings of Shakespeare, such as *Hamlet* (1925) and *Macbeth* (1928). Jackson also founded the Malvern Festival in 1929 with a season of two weeks devoted entirely to works by Shaw. In the seasons from 1931 through 1933, each three weeks in length, Jackson staged a survey of five hundred years of English drama, ranging from

FIG. 11.6
Birmingham
Repertory production
of Shaw's *Back to
Methuselah* in 1924.
(From *Le Théâtre*,
1924.)

FIG. 11.7
Modern dress
production of
Macbeth at the
Birmingham
Repertory Theatre in
1928. Olivier is at far
right. (Courtesy
Mander and
Mitchenson Theatre
Collection.)

medieval plays to new original works. By the end of the 1930s, the Malvern Festival had become one of the most popular annual events in England, and its success did much to promote the idea of summer festivals, which were to flourish after the war.

The Malvern Festival was not England's first, for at Stratford-on-Avon a festival had been in operation since 1879. During World War I, however, the festival was interrupted for two years, and this brought an end to Frank Benson's domination. (He had staged every festival except three since the 1880s.) When productions resumed in 1919, they were placed under the direction of W. Bridges-Adams (1889–1965), who also designed settings and costumes for each production. In 1926, the Stratford theatre, an inadequate Gothic structure erected in 1879, was destroyed by fire. Bernard Shaw cabled the festival governors: "Congratulations. You must be delighted." While a motion picture house served as the festival's home from 1926 to 1931, funds were raised to build a new theatre that would seat 1,000, with an unraked stage 50 feet deep. Elizabeth Scott won the design competition, and the new building was opened in 1932. While many of the structure's features were praised, the stage was very unsatisfactory. The elevator stages could not be sufficiently lowered below or raised above stage level to be useful, and the wing space was too small to permit the rolling platforms to be used effectively. There was insufficient rehearsal, dressing room, and greenroom space. As a result, the theatre has had to be remodeled several times.

When Bridges-Adams resigned from the Stratford Festival in 1934, he was succeeded by B. Iden Payne (1881–1976), whose most characteristic productions followed the scheme popularized by William Poel: an acting area simulating that of the Elizabethan public theatre; costumed page boys to draw curtains and move furniture and properties; and actors dressed in Elizabethan costumes. The major change that came with the opening of the new theatre was the employment of one or more guest directors each season. Among them were Robert Atkins, Tyrone Guthrie, E. Martin Browne, and Theodore Komissarzhevsky. Of these, Komissarzhevsky created the greatest controversy, for even before Guthrie won a reputation for eccentric productions, Komissarzhevsky was outraging traditionalists and delighting the avant-garde with novelties. His most controversial production was of *Macbeth* (1934), from which he completely eliminated the supernatural element. His setting, an arrangement of aluminum steps and platforms and entangled wire, gave the impression of a modern battlefield or of a modernistic building (depending on the lighting). He treated the witches as battlefield scavengers who, when accosted by Macbeth, pose as fortune-tellers. Later scenes in which they appear were staged as Macbeth's nightmares. On the whole, Komissarzhevsky's work at Stratford on such productions as *Macbeth, The Merry Wives of Windsor, The Merchant of Venice,* and *King Lear* was little appreciated because it was so much in advance of its time. After the war, he would be recognized as one of the pioneers of modern Shakespearean production in England.

The Cambridge Festival Theatre, operated by Terence Gray from 1926 to 1933, was the most determinedly antirealistic company in England. Independently wealthy and trained as an Egyptologist, Gray early became interested in the theatre but found typical English practices unsatisfactory compared with those he observed on his frequent visits to the Continent. Deciding to open an alternative to traditional practice, he acquired the Theatre Royal Barnwell near Cambridge and converted the structure into a house unlike any to be seen in England. He removed the proscenium arch and linked the auditorium and stage with a broad flight of

FIG. 11.8

Komissarzhevsky's production of *The Comedy of Errors* at Stratford in 1939. (From the Royal Shakespeare Theatre, Stratford-on-Avon.)

steps running the full length of the house. Several actors' entrances were provided forward of the old proscenium, and on the stage, he erected a 40-foot plaster skydome plus a turntable 15 feet in diameter. The theatre probably had the best lighting system in England, designed by Harold Ridge, Gray's partner during the first season and later one of England's major authorities on stage lighting. Seating was extremely comfortable, and there was a restaurant of the highest quality.

Gray's repertory of plays represented every period from the ancient Greeks to the present, and his audience was drawn largely from the university. His season followed the Cambridge term, and each year Gray presented twenty-four plays, directing approximately one-half of them, while the others were staged by two assistant directors. He declared that the audience is weary of "the old game of illusion, glamour, and all the rest of the nineteenth century hocus pocus and bamboozle. . . . We are the theatre theatrical. . . . We think the stage should be a raised platform . . . the levels and angles of which fulfill a function of emphasizing dramatic relations. Beyond this platform all that is called for is a background against which the actors can be seen." Practically every production was staged on an arrangement of steps and levels which could be turned or altered through lighting (though never for the sake of illusion). His settings were solid and decorative versions of Meyerhold's "machines for acting." Few properties were used, and actors often pantomimed stage business involving objects. This worked well for some plays, but in a production such as *The Wild Duck,* it was merely confusing. Entrances and exits sometimes were made through the auditorium, and sometimes scenes were played there.

Gray's productions of Greek tragedy were outstanding, but his interpretations of other plays often were unorthodox. Sometimes he sought to draw modern parallels, as in *As You Like It,* when he dressed Rosalind as a boy scout and Celia as a girl scout when they went into the forest, or as in *Twelfth Night,* when he placed Sir Toby Belch and Sir Andrew Aguecheek on roller skates. In the trial scene of *The Merchant of Venice,* the judge played with a yo-yo during Portia's oration. One of his best productions was of Shakespeare's *Henry VIII,* which Gray viewed as transparent flattery of the English monarchy. He dressed most of the characters as playing card figures, and raised Cardinal Wolsey on *cothurnoi* to indicate his dominant role. In one scene, the cardinal moved listlessly back and forth in a swing as he delivered malicious speeches. Such touches delighted Cambridge students but outraged conservative theatregoers.

BRITISH PLAYWRIGHTS OF THE INTERWAR PERIOD

Today English drama of the interwar years seems hardly distinguished, although at the time it appeared impressive, perhaps more because of its civilized tone, wit, or skill than for its lasting values. Much of the best work was done by older dramatists who continued to write during and after the war. Shaw contributed such outstanding works as *Heartbreak House* (1919), *Back to Methuselah* (1919–1920), and *Saint Joan* (1923) before writing a series of minor works that include *The Apple Cart* (1929), *The Millionairess* (1935), and *Good King Charles' Golden Days* (1939). Barrie wrote *Dear Brutus* (1917) and *The Boy David* (1936), and Galsworthy wrote *Escape* (1926) and *Exiled* (1929). These writers added little to their reputations with such post-World War I work, although their plays, both old and new, gave distinction to theatrical repertories at the time.

Perhaps the most characteristic form of the period was a worldly-wise satirical comedy, though by present-day standards it no longer

FIG. 11.9
Terence Gray's production of *Henry VIII* at the Festival Theatre, Cambridge, in 1931. (From Moussinac, *New Movement in the Theatre.*)

seems as cynical as it once did. The most representative writer was Noel Coward (1899-1973), who, after beginning his career as an actor, turned also to writing in the 1920s. Interestingly enough, his first success came with a serious work, *Vortex* (1924), concerned with a mother who loses her young lover to the fiancée of her son. The play was especially noted for its scene of confrontation between mother and son, played by Lilian Braithwaite and Coward himself, during which, after mutual recriminations, they are reconciled. A great popular success, the play began the vogue for Coward's work, which reached its peak the following year, 1925, when five of his plays were being performed simultaneously in the West End.

Coward's best work is probably *Private Lives* (1930), in which a divorced couple meet accidentally while on honeymoon with new mates and discover that they are still in love. It is a well-constructed, sophisticated, and witty comedy, although it seldom probes beneath the surface. *Design for Living* (1933) is somewhat more daring, for it treats a love triangle among a woman and two men, who finally agree to a ménage à trois. Such plays won Coward the reputation for being a spokesman for the new generation of disillusioned men and unshockable women. Of his later works, the most popular is *Blithe Spirit* (1941), in which a medium creates havoc in a married man's life by inadvertently calling up the spirit of his former wife.

The post-World War I comedy of manners is perhaps seen at its best in the plays of W. Somerset Maugham (1874–1965). A novelist and short story writer, Maugham turned to drama shortly after the turn of the century, devoting himself primarily to light comedy deliberately designed to attract a wide audience. In 1908, for example, he had four plays running simultaneously in London. But it is for his later

FIG. 11.10
Original production of Coward's *Private Lives* at the Phoenix Theatre in 1930. Left to right are Adrienne Allen as Sybil, Coward as Elyot, Gertrude Lawrence as Amanda, and Laurence Olivier as Victor. (Courtesy Mander and Mitchenson Theatre Collection.)

work, particularly plays such as *The Circle* (1921), that he is now remembered. The title refers to the recurrence of behavioral patterns in successive generations. Thirty years before the play opens, Mrs. Champion-Cheney has deserted her husband and small son to run away with Lord Porteus. Now back in England for the first time, they are invited to the home of Mrs. Champion-Cheney's son, whose wife is considering running away with another man. The young wife is so disturbed by the unconscious vulgarity of the older couple that she almost changes her mind, despite her husband's insensitivity and her own lack of affection for him. Ultimately she does run away, however, when her lover says: "I don't offer you happiness; I offer you love."

Among serious writers, the best were probably Priestley, Bridie, and Eliot. J. B. Priestley (1894–1984) began his career in the early 1930s, establishing his reputation with *Dangerous Corner* (1932), directed by Guthrie and acted by Flora Robson. *Time and the Conways* (1937) begins shortly after World War I during a birthday party, then switches forward twenty years to show what has happened to the characters since. Finally the play returns to the original time to point to the great disparity between the characters' ambitions and their accomplishments. In *Johnson Over Jordan,* Priestly treats a businessman, a contemporary Everyman, with whom the author wishes his audience to identify. The action takes place after Johnson has died and while his spirit still lingers between life and death, in "a prolonged dreamlike state, in what may be called the fourth dimension of space, filled with hallucinatory visions." Time and place shift rapidly as Johnson recalls various incidents from his life, and the play ends on a poignant note, for Johnson concludes as he walks off into the unknown, "The earth is nobler than the world we have built on it." Typical West End playgoers found it all very puzzling. In the 1930s, when Einsteinian conceptions of time and space were still novel, Priestley's plays seemed very "intellectual."

James Bridie (Osborne Henry Mavor, 1881–1951), a Glasgow physician who continued to practice medicine throughout his playwriting career, achieved his first critical success in 1931 with *The Anatomist,* directed by Guthrie. Set in the nineteenth century, the play focuses on Professor Knox, who for his experiments purchases cadavers from two men later discovered to be murderers. In spite of his double career, Bridie was extremely prolific as a playwright, turning out thirty-four full-length plays in twenty years in addition to adaptations, one-acts, and radio plays. His works range from serious to comic and from historical and biblical to modern. Almost all his plays begin with striking dramatic situations, but Bridie's principal fault was his inability to develop the potential suggested by his opening scenes.

The period saw many attempts to revive poetic drama, which since the romantic era (and earlier) had languished. In the twentieth century, William Butler Yeats had written outstanding lyric dramas, but they had failed to find a receptive audience. In England, a number of playwrights such as Stephen Phillips (1868–1915), John Masefield (1875–1968), Louis MacNeice (1907–1963), and Stephen Spender (1907–   ) had gained some notoriety through their poetic dramas. Of particular interest is the collaboration of W. H. Auden (1907–1973) and Christopher Isherwood (1904–1986) on a series of poetic plays: *The Dog Beneath the Skin* (1935), *The Ascent of F6* (1936), and *On the Frontier* (1938). By far the most successful was *The Ascent of F6,* in which the British government sends out an expedition to scale and lay claim to a mountain, designated on maps simply as F6. The protagonist, Michael Ransom, heads the mission, even though he is deeply opposed to England's imperialism, for the mountain also represents a challenge to gain

spiritual control over himself. Another related theme treats Ransom's relationship to his mother. After many trials, he at last meets his spiritual daemon on the mountain, only to discover that it is his own mother, on whom he has had a fixation throughout his life.

The most impressive achievement in poetic drama, however, was that of T. S. Eliot (1888–1965). Born in America, Eliot settled in London in 1914 and became a British citizen in 1927. After 1920, he was considered a major poet, but he wrote no complete play until 1934, when he expanded an outline supplied by E. Martin Browne for a religious pageant, *The Rock*. Following this, he was commissioned to write a play for the Canterbury Festival. The result was *Murder in the Cathedral*, first performed in the Chapter House at Canterbury in 1935 and subsequently produced in London to great critical acclaim. (All the productions were directed by Browne and starred Robert Speaight as Becket.) Eliot's protagonist is a

man beset by tempters, who, although real, also symbolize his own inner torment. The play is little concerned with Becket's past life but concentrates instead upon his moment of decision, caught between his duty to Church and State. Thus, the principal emphasis is upon Becket's spiritual growth, while the context is supplied almost entirely by a chorus of Canterbury Women.

Murder in the Cathedral remains Eliot's finest drama, in part because in it he gave his lyric gift considerable scope. In a work such as *The Family Reunion* (1939), a contemporary recasting of the Orestes myth, Eliot seems to have been overly influenced by those who, attuned to realism, attacked his poetic diction. In this play and those that came after World War II (to be discussed in a later chapter), Eliot steadily pared down his verse until it was virtually indistinguishable from prose. Since he was not an accomplished constructer of plots, Eliot had given up his greatest gift (poetic diction) to depend upon other skills he had not fully mastered.

O'CASEY AND THE IRISH DRAMA

Fortunately, the English-language dramatists of Ireland helped alter the rather disappointing record of British playwrights of the interwar period. Like many other parts of Europe, Ireland became embroiled in civil conflict during World War I, when the desire for national independence, increasingly evident since the nineteenth century, burst into rebellion in 1916. Put down, the fighting broke out again in 1919 when Ireland declared itself free. In 1921, Great Britain offered Ireland dominion status within the empire and the Irish Free State came into being, although internal strife continued until 1923. These years of unrest seriously interrupted theatrical life, but, when peace came, activities were quickly resumed. The Abbey Theatre, now provided with a subsidy by the state, became Ireland's national theatre. But with support came pressure to respect conventional taste and morality.

Nevertheless, with O'Casey's plays the Abbey for a time regained some of its old vigor. Sean O'Casey (1880–1964), reared in the Dublin slums, was virtually illiterate until he was fourteen. He then read voraciously, especially the works of Shakespeare, and attended the Abbey Theatre whenever he could. Although he soon began to write plays of his own, he was over forty before his first play was produced. Nonetheless, with *The Shadow of a Gunman* (1923), it was evident that a major new talent had emerged. Set in the Dublin slums in the midst of civil war, the play centers on a braggart whose pose as a revolutionary leads to the death of a young girl. The portraits of Dubliners caught up in the atmosphere of anxiety and violence are masterful and sympathetic.

The promise of his first play was more than fulfilled in *Juno and the Paycock* (1924), considered by many to be his masterpiece. Also set in Dublin during the civil strife, it focuses on the Boyle family. Captain Boyle, the "paycock" father, is a lazy braggart who spends his days in drunken carousing with his likable, ne'er-do-well friend Joxer, while his wife, Juno, works to support the family. There are also two children. A son, Johnny, who skulks about the house anxiously, is eventually killed by men who accuse him of having betrayed a comrade, while the daughter, Mary (perhaps symbolizing Ireland itself), is seduced and betrayed by an Englishman. Juno emerges as the dominant figure—a heroic woman fighting against overwhelming odds to keep the family going and refusing even to capitulate to the problems the family heaps upon her. She finally leaves the drunken Boyle to make a decent life for her daughter and the unborn child. Despite the grimness of the surroundings and the pathos aroused by several characters, there is much humor.

The action of *The Plough and the Stars* (1926) occurs during the Easter Rebellion of 1916, and recalls that week of fighting as it affects the dwellers of a tenement. Although again the characters are developed with great insight and sensitivity, O'Casey glorifies none of them and shows ultimately the destructiveness of all war. The opening night audience considered the play an insult to Irish patriotism, and a riot resulted the like of which had not been seen since the premiere of John Millington Synge's *The Playboy of the Western World* in 1907.

With *The Plough and the Stars*, O'Casey's realistic period came to an end. In these early works, O'Casey is less interested in story than he is in developing a texture of true and lifelike characters, brought into close contact by their meager living conditions. It is the social unit—the family, the inhabitants of a tene-

FIG. 11.12

O'Casey's *The Plough and the Stars,* produced by the Abbey Theatre in 1926. Sara Allgood is at left. (From *Theatre Arts,* 1928.)

ment—that presents in a human context (not devoid of implied symbols) a microcosm of contemporary Irish attitudes. His men usually talk about (and sometimes die for) ideals, whereas the women cope with the realities of daily life. The conflicts that result from juxtaposing contrasting individuals, ideals, and priorities lead both to humor and violence. The tone of the plays shifts often and abruptly, and this quality creates a compelling theatrical excitement when they are staged.

The Silver Tassie (1929) marked O'Casey's break with realism as well as with the Abbey Theatre, which refused the work. As a result of the rebuff, O'Casey moved to England and thereafter remained aloof for many years from the Irish scene. In this play, O'Casey began to move toward expressionism, although the new approach was only partially adopted. Harry Heegan, a man of powerful physical physique, is acclaimed by his friends for winning the "silver tassie," a football trophy, on the eve of his entrance into the army. The realistic atmosphere is followed by an expressionistic evocation of life in the trenches and the horrors of war. (There is a chorus of chanting soldiers, for example.) The final act returns once more to realism and to Heegan, now incapacitated forever by wounds received in action. Forsaken by his girlfriend and others, an embittered Heegan is a useless, living symbol of the horrors of war.

Among O'Casey's later plays, the best are *Purple Dust* (1940), in which an Irish peasant bests an Englishman, and *Red Roses for Me* (1943), about a poet who is killed and the misery and courage of the unemployed. Even later plays such as *Cock-a-Doodle-Dandy* (1949) and *The Drums of Father Ned* (1956) move further away from the realist style. In his last years, O'Casey devoted little time to writing drama but focused instead on the volumes that make up his excellent autobiography. No playwright of his time had a finer ear for language, a sharper sense for character, or greater human compassion. He was probably the best of all interwar dramatists writing in the British Isles.

With its rejection of O'Casey, the Abbey Theatre lost much of its vitality and settled into its comfortable role as a national theatre. Although it continued to encourage new writing among Irish authors, few outstanding playwrights emerged. The conservatism of the Abbey motivated Micheál MacLiammóir (1899–1978) and Hilton Edwards (1903–1982) to found the Dublin Gate Theatre in 1928. Unlike the Abbey, which continued to emphasize plays of Irish life, the Gate sought to include works from all periods and countries and to establish a standard of production comparable to that found on the Continent. In both goals it was very successful, and when it toured abroad during the 1930s the Gate won universal praise. Most of the credit belongs to MacLiammóir, who, after being a child actor in London, had studied art and had had his work exhibited widely in Europe, where his travels acquainted him with contemporary theatrical practices. His outstanding talents as designer, director, and actor resulted in a high artistic standard at the Gate, where he continued to work until 1956.

The Gate also developed new playwrights, among whom the most accomplished was Denis Johnston (1901–1984), whose best play is *The Moon in the Yellow River* (1931). The action centers on an idealistic young revolutionary who has fought for Ireland's liberation and now seeks to keep his country free from the blight of industrialism, symbolized by the plan to build a power plant near Dublin. Here Johnston captures the mood of the 1920s with its conflict between conservatives and liberals. A free-wheeling mixture of zany humor and philosophical inquiry, its strong characterizations capture the contrast of those who are irresponsible and those who are idealistic.

Thus, the Irish theatre between the wars was lively but lacked the ferment that made the early years of the Abbey Theatre (from 1904 until World War I) so memorable. Except for the plays of O'Casey, no strong impact was made by Irish playwrights internationally, and in theatrical production the Irish simply co-opted trends already established elsewhere.

POSTWAR CHANGES IN THE AMERICAN THEATRE

Despite some American experiments with nonrealistic forms, the realist style that had dominated European theatres in the late nineteenth century remained almost universally accepted by American producers. Nonetheless, by 1915, various incentives for change were emerging from foreign sources. American critics such as Hiram Moderwell, Clayton Hamilton, Kenneth Macgowan, Oliver Sayler, and Sheldon Cheney wrote voluminously of the work going on in Europe and the artistic principles upon which it was based. In 1917,

Cheney founded *Theatre Arts Magazine,* which between the wars was a focal point for the new movement and a disseminator of new ideas. While much of the writing of these men now seems vague and near-precious in its invocation of beauty, art, spirit, and the ideal, it was nonetheless inspirational in its incitement to develop a theatre antithetical to that of Broadway.

Foreign visitors also were a major inspiration for American theatre workers as concrete examples, and the New York Stage Society played a major role in their importation. In addition to the visits of Barker in 1915 and Copeau in 1917–1919, the Ballets Russes arrived in 1916, the Moscow Art Theatre in 1923–1924 (with performances of thirteen plays in twelve cities), the Habima in 1926–1927 (playing, among others works, Vakhtangov's production of *The Dybbuk*), and Reinhardt showed his production of *The Miracle* in 1924 and a season of plays in 1927–1928.

But all this had to be translated into native effort if the American theatre was to change.

A major step already had been taken around 1912, when "little theatres" began to appear in several cities. Taking their cue from European independent theatres, these groups offered subscribers seasons of plays mounted with care for artistic principles. By 1917, there were approximately fifty such organizations. It was out of a few of these—namely the Provincetown Players, the Neighborhood Playhouse, and the Washington Square Players—that the major impulse for change came.

The Provincetown Players was founded in the summer of 1915 by artists and writers vacationing in Provincetown, Massachusetts. At first they staged short plays on the porches of their homes, but in 1916 they remodeled a wharf into a theatre seating 100 to 200 spectators. The group produced the first plays of Eugene O'Neill, thus making a major contribution to American theatre. Also in 1916, the group decided to continue its work in New York during the winter, acquiring a theatre in Greenwich Village, where it continued under various guises until 1929.

FIG. 11.13
O'Neill's *All God's Chillun Got Wings,* produced by the Provincetown Playhouse, New York, in 1924. (From *Stage Yearbook,* 1925.)

The Provincetown differed from most other little theatres in that it sought to encourage new American dramatists. Most other groups tended to present European works or classics, being interested chiefly in new production methods. While the Provincetown also sought to assist actors, designers, directors, and technicians in new experiments, it believed that "[e]laborate settings are unnecessary to bring out the essential qualities of a good play." Under the inspirational leadership of George Cram Cook, the Provincetown presented programs of three or four one-act plays, although occasionally a full-length work was offered. By 1925, ninety-three new plays by forty-seven writers had been presented.

Like several other little theatres, the Provincetown soon encountered difficulties. Novelty and enthusiasm had been enough at first, but soon both members and public were demanding higher standards. Professionalism thus began to replace the camaraderie that had originally characterized the group, and in 1920, when O'Neill's *The Emperor Jones* became a hit and was moved to Broadway, the trend was crystallized. In the flush of success, the Provincetown faltered, and in 1922–1923, Cook declared a year of rest to reevaluate the group's purpose.

In 1923, a new phase began with the reorganization of the group as the Experimental Theatre, Inc., led by the triumvirate of O'Neill, Robert Edmond Jones (1887-1954), and Kenneth Macgowan (1888–1963). In addition to engendering greater professionalism, the repertory began to include works by Strindberg, Gozzi, Molière, and other Continental playwrights, as well as those works by O'Neill that Broadway producers would not accept. Jones had the chance to develop settings not likely to be used on Broadway in addition to being able to direct occasionally. New American playwrights were not ignored, but they ceased to be the group's major

concern. Although 1925 brought still another reorganization, the original spark was dimming. Union problems and production costs made survival difficult, and with the coming of the Depression in 1929, the group folded. Perhaps the Provincetown's most significant contribution was to build an audience for plays not normally acceptable to the commercial theatre.

The Neighborhood Playhouse, also founded in 1915, performed at the Henry Street Settlement House in New York. It too contributed to the new spirit, though less significantly than the Provincetown. The founders, Irene and Alice Lewisohn, were wealthy, well-educated, and widely traveled sisters who first taught dancing at the settlement house and eventually built and endowed one of the best-equipped small theatres in America (the first to have a plaster skydome, for example). The technical director, Agnes Morgan, had been one of George Pierce Baker's students, and under her guidance, the productions were noted for their variety of approach and artistic unity of all elements.

The pattern was similar to the Provincetown, for at first the actors were unpaid amateurs. The Neighborhood Playhouse, too, eventually transferred successful productions to Broadway. By 1920 there was a demand for higher quality, and eventually ten professionals were added. The Neighborhood Playhouse also took a season's rest in 1922–1923. In 1923–1924, Richard Boleslavsky (prominent in the Moscow Art Theatre's First Studio before he emigrated) was engaged to direct some of the productions. But rising costs, difficulties with unions, and other problems led to the closing in 1927. In 1928, the Neighborhood School of Theatre was formed and soon became and has long remained one of the major professional schools in the United States.

The third major group founded in 1915 was the Washington Square Players, which came into being after a group of artists, writers, and theatre enthusiasts staged Dunsany's *The Glittering Gate* in the back room of a bookstore. This led to the renting of the Bandbox Theatre in Greenwich Village, and the group began to give weekend performances of one-act plays. Eventually the members began performing four times per week and moved to the Comedy Theatre in the Broadway area. Now competing with commercial productions, the group began to hire professional actors, but numerous difficulties led to dissolution in 1918. Nonetheless, the Washington Square Players had presented sixty-two short and six long plays, and had provided valuable experience for such young actors as Katherine Cornell, Rollo Peters, and Roland Young while encouraging designer Lee Simonson.

The experience of the Provincetown Players, the Neighborhood Playhouse, and the Washington Square Players demonstrated that enthusiasm and high ideals were not enough. Although none of these companies made the transition to professionalism successfully, all pointed toward theatrical change in the U.S., and out of the ashes of the Washington Square players emerged the first successful new group, the Theatre Guild.

THE THEATRE GUILD, HAMPDEN, AND LE GALLIENNE

The Theatre Guild was the cooperative creation of several people who made up its board of directors: Lawrence Langner, Helen Westley, Rollo Peters, Philip Moeller, Lee Simonson, and Justus Sheffield. To this list Theresa Helburn and Maurice Wertheim were soon added. In a statement of purpose, the group declared its intention "to produce plays of artistic merit not ordinarily produced by the commercial managers." Drawing inspiration from Continental models, the group sought to attract that audience which had been ignored by commercial producers in their attempts to win mass popularity, a familiar American pattern that would emerge again in the 1950s with off-Broadway.

The Theatre Guild rented the Garrick Theatre in New York (just vacated by Copeau's

FIG. 11.14
Andreyev's *The Life of Man* as produced by the Washington Square Players. (From *Stage Yearbook*, 1918.)

Vieux Colombier) and opened in April 1919 with Benavente's *The Bonds of Interest.* The production was not well received by audiences or critics, and the Guild was on the verge of financial collapse when it offered St. John Ervine's *John Ferguson,* which was successful and restored the group's stability. During the early years, the Guild depended almost entirely on foreign plays, giving world premieres to Shaw's *Heartbreak House, Back to Methuselah,* and *Saint Joan,* and presenting plays by writers such as Kaiser, Lenormand, Claudel, Andreyev, Toller, Pirandello, Gorky, Ibsen, Strindberg, Goethe, Schnitzler, Turgenev, Tolstoy, and many others. Although its first notable production of an American piece was Rice's *The Adding Machine,* it was not until the season 1927–1928, when it began its association with O'Neill, that it paid much attention to native authors.

In 1925, the Guild built its own 930-seat theatre in the Broadway area, and in 1926–1927 employed a permanent nucleus of ten actors: Helen Westley, Alfred Lunt, Lynne Fontanne, Dudley Digges, Henry Travers, Claire Eames, Margalo Gillmore, Edward G. Robinson, Earle Larimore, and Philip Loeb. (It hired other actors as needed to fill out casts.) While briefly the Guild rented a second theatre and mounted four plays at a time, alternating them weekly, the great success in 1927–1928 of O'Neill's *Marco Millions* and *Strange Interlude* convinced group members of the financial feasibility of longer runs. This choice in favor of commercialism may have signaled the eventual death of the Guild.

By 1926–1927, the Guild had 23,000 subscribers and began to extend its work to other cities. In 1928–1929, it offered subscription series not only in New York but also in Baltimore, Boston, Cleveland, Pittsburgh, Philadelphia, and Chicago, employing 200 actors who played before 75,000 subscribers. The increasing number of productions placed a

strain on the Guild's resources, and quality began to suffer. With the coming of the Depression, the Guild's fortunes declined, and it had to abandon its seasons in other cities. Soon it also departed from the adventurousness that had marked its early work. Eventually, of the founders, only Langner and Helburn remained. The theatre building, now a liability, was lost around 1935, although the Guild continued to rent it until approximately 1943. By the time of World War II, the Theatre Guild was scarcely distinguishable from the commercial producers against which it had originally rebelled.

Between 1919 and 1935, the Guild set a high standard of artistic excellence. The majority of plays was directed by Philip Moeller (1880–1958), but such outstanding European directors as Copeau and Komissarzhevsky occasionally were employed. The usual designer was Lee Simonson (1888–1967), who, aware of what the Europeans were doing, was one of the principal naturalizers of the *new stagecraft.* His most characteristic settings utilized basic units within which smaller pieces could quickly transform the appearance of the whole. His design solutions not only achieved simplicity but also reduced production expenses. Despite the Guild's ultimate failure, it was an example to the entire American theatre that it was possible to compete, at least for a time, with the commercial theatre and still maintain high artistic standards.

During the 1920s, two other producers—Hampden and Le Gallienne, both distinguished actors—sought like the Theatre Guild to develop permanent organizations that would provide productions of high quality. Walter Hampden (1879–1955) was born in the U.S. but trained in England, where he worked with both Benson and Barker before returning to the United States in 1907. He was Alla Nazimova's leading man and worked for Henry Miller, the Shuberts, and several other producers.

Hampden's ideals were formed in the actor-manager British tradition, and by 1919 he had created Walter Hampden, Inc., an acting company with which he toured widely in a repertory of Shakespearean plays. In 1923, he added *Cyrano de Bergerac* to the repertory and won considerable acclaim over the next ten years for his productions. Leasing the Colonial Theatre in New York in 1925, he rechristened it Hampden's Theatre and performed there until 1930, adding to the repertory such works as *An Enemy of the People* and *The Bonds of Interest*. Like groups already mentioned, Hampden's troupe was not able to survive the Depression. Thereafter he played in other companies and in films. He was a member of Le Gallienne's American Repertory Theatre in the mid-1940s and made his last Broadway appearance in 1953 in Arthur Miller's *The Crucible*. Essentially Hampden was more backward-looking than forward-looking, since his example was a revival of the old actor-manager system. Most of his productions were in the romantic vein, the only significant modern work in his repertory being Ibsen's *An Enemy of the People,* which probably appealed to him because of Dr. Stockmann's quasi-romantic rebellion against great odds.

Eva Le Gallienne (1899–   ) was born in England and studied at the Royal Academy of Dramatic Art before coming to the U.S. and gaining considerable notice in early productions of the Theatre Guild. In 1926, she formed her own company—the Civic Repertory Theatre—with which she hoped to attract an audience of students, workers, and low-income playgoers. She rented the rundown, out-of-the-way Fourteenth Street Theatre (which seated about one thousand) and established a price range of fifty cents to $1.50. With a company of thirty-three mostly young actors (but also Nazimova), she developed a true repertory system under which the bill was changed from three to five times each week

and productions of merit were retained for several seasons. She also instituted an apprentice program which included from thirty to fifty students.

The theatre opened in 1926 with Benavente's *Saturday Night* and Chekhov's *The Three Sisters.* The operation continued for seven seasons (until 1933) with thirty-four plays by authors such as Shakespeare, Molière, Goldoni, Ibsen, Tolstoy, Dumas, Schnitzler, and Chekhov for a total of 1,581 performances. Some productions accumulated impressive records over the years: Martínez Sierra's *Cradle Song,* for example, was played 164 times and Chekhov's *The Cherry Orchard,* 108 times. Though attendance was excellent, the prices were so low that financial difficulties never

FIG. 11.15

Eva Le Gallienne as Masha in Chekhov's *The Three Sisters* at her own Civic Repertory Theatre in 1926. (From Theatre Arts, 1927.)

disappeared. Le Gallienne was often rescued by Otto Kahn, and in 1928–1929 she sought to raise an endowment fund for her operation. Nonetheless, like many other groups of the period, the Civic Repertory Theatre was a victim of the Depression and closed in 1933.

HOPKINS

Not all progressive work was done by those working in repertory theatre. Arthur Hopkins (1878–1950) perhaps did as much as anyone to introduce European practices into the American theatre. After a period of working as a reporter, vaudeville press agent, talent scout, producer of vaudeville acts, and eventually theatre director, Hopkins went to Europe around 1913 to visit the major theatres of England, France, and Germany. Greatly impressed by Reinhardt's work, he determined to apply in his own productions what he had seen in Europe. Upon his return to New York, he produced Elmer Rice's first play, another work starring Mrs. Fiske, and a series of Ibsen's plays featuring Nazimova.

In 1918, Hopkins leased the Plymouth Theatre from the Shuberts, intending to produce there at least two new works each year and gradually to build a repertory. He engaged John Barrymore (1882–1942) as his principal actor and Robert Edmond Jones as his designer. The first production was Tolstoy's *The Living Corpse* (retitled *Redemption*), which at first was not well received. At the point when it began to attract audiences, the production closed in order to offer the second production, Sem Benelli's *The Jest,* in which Lionel Barrymore (1878–1954) starred with his brother. After this successful run came *Richard III*, which established John Barrymore's reputation as a classical actor. Unfortunately Barrymore suffered a breakdown in the course of the run, and Hopkins' original scheme had to be abandoned.

Nonetheless, these three productions established Hopkins as a major force in the Broadway theatre. Much of the credit belongs to Jones' simple but imaginative designs. His setting for *Richard III* employed a single unit (the Tower of London), while changes were suggested by lighting and curtains or small pieces placed within or in front of the main structure.

In 1921, Hopkins presented *Macbeth* with Lionel Barrymore, who made the protagonist a tortured, near-mad creature. Jones' settings added to the nightmarish quality by emphasizing the all-pervasive power of witch-craft. Jones had recently returned from Europe, having seen the work of Jessner and Fehling, and the setting for *Macbeth* reflected the influence of expressionism. Characters seemed to appear from and disappear into a black void. The basic architectural units were a series of Gothic arches that tilted ever more precariously as the action progressed. During some scenes, three large masks symbolizing the witches and fate were suspended above the stage. The production was so controversial that it seems to have turned Jones and Hopkins (and the rest of Broadway) away from further experimentation with expressionist techniques. Barrymore was so disturbed by the reaction that he soon left the stage for films.

In 1922, Hopkins presented John Barrymore in *Hamlet* (perhaps the first actor to make the Oedipus complex integral to his performance). Jones' settings were reminiscent of those by Craig, and, perhaps as much as any other production, Hopkins' *Hamlet* signaled that a new era had arrived. Nevertheless, it was a very uneven production, for Barrymore was an erratic performer and like his brother soon deserted the stage. Hopkins also presented Ethel Barrymore (1879–1959) in a series of plays that included Pinero's *The Second Mrs. Tanqueray* and *Romeo and Juliet*. He took over O'Neill's *The Hairy Ape* from the Provincetown and then directed *Anna Christie*. He also

FIG. 11.16
Robert Edmond Jones'
design for Hopkins'
production of
Macbeth in 1921.
(From *Theatre Arts*,
1921.)

directed Stallings' and Anderson's *What Price Glory?*, the first modern serious play on war to win wide popular success, and went on to produce plays by Sidney Howard, Robert E. Sherwood, George S. Kaufman, and Philip Barry. In addition, Hopkins promoted the careers of such actors as Pauline Lord, Katherine Hepburn, Barbara Stanwyck, Louis Wolheim, and Clark Gable.

Although Hopkins continued to direct until World War II, his most significant work was done between 1918 and 1925. Placing primary emphasis on the text, he sought to make actors and settings unobtrusive so that the inner meaning of the play might emerge without interference. He sought creative actors, of whose feelings he was always very considerate, never criticizing them in the presence of others and only offering suggestions when absolutely necessary. Because he permitted so much freedom to the actor, some detractors have suggested he did little as a director. Nonethe-

less, Hopkins often achieved results comparable to some of the best work seen in Europe.

THE NEW STAGECRAFT

Much of the credit for the triumph in the U.S. of the new stagecraft (that followed the example of European production styles and methods) belongs to American designers, for the most readily apparent changes were visual. The major leaders in the interwar years were Jones, Simonson, and Norman Bel Geddes (1893–1958). Geddes' designs often resembled Appia's, but they were conceived on the grand scale of Craig's. Geddes' unproduced project for staging Dante's *Divine Comedy* (1921) was one of the most remarkable works of its age. Composed of a series of concentric levels, the appearance of which was changed through skillful lighting, it was too monumental for an ordinary stage but awe-inspiring in its grandeur.

FIG. 11.17
Norman Bel Geddes' project for staging Dante's *The Divine Comedy*. (Courtesy Hoblitzelle Theatre Arts Library, University of Texas.)

Later he staged plays such as *Lysistrata* and *Hamlet* on unadorned steps and platforms, and used actors with hand-carried properties (such as banners and weapons) to create changes through "living scenery" and light. But Geddes could also work effectively in the realistic mode, as demonstrated by his setting for Kingsley's *Dead End,* for which he designed a naturalistically detailed East River pier, complete with water in the orchestra pit. Though perhaps the most inventive of all American designers, Geddes seems to have been the most atypical, for he had few followers. After 1943, he gave up the stage for industrial design.

Other important designers included Cleon Throckmorton (1897–1965), who won recognition with his designs for O'Neill's *The Emperor Jones* and *The Hairy Ape;* Mordecai Gorelik (1899–1990), who was especially noted in the 1920s and 1930s for designing social-problem plays and left-wing drama; and Jo Mielziner (1901–1976) who began as Jones' assistant, became an independent designer in 1924, won great acclaim through his poetically realistic settings for works such as *Winterset,* and eventually was recognized as the most influential American designer of the post-World War II period because of his settings for such works as *A Streetcar Named Desire* and *Death of a Salesman*.

THE AMERICAN LABORATORY THEATRE AND THE GROUP THEATRE

A number of talented actors performed during the interwar period in the U.S., among them Helen Hayes, Katherine Cornell, Jane Cowl, Pauline Lord, Laurette Taylor, Ina Claire, Ruth Gordon, Lynne Fontanne, Alfred Lunt, the Barrymores, Frederic March, Florence Eldridge, Tallulah Bankhead, Walter Huston, Winifred Lenihan, and Alice Brady. Like their English counterparts, these actors belonged to no particular school, although most tended to place greater emphasis upon inner motivation than had their predecessors. On the other hand, two groups, the American Laboratory Theatre

and the Group Theatre, were seriously committed to a particular approach, the Stanislavsky system, which they sought to introduce into the American theatre.

The American Laboratory Theatre came into being in the wake of the enthusiasm aroused by the visit of the Moscow Art Theatre, when two former members of the troupe—Richard Boleslavsky (1889–1937) and Maria Ouspenskaya (1881–1949)—were persuaded to head the school. Opened in 1923, the American Laboratory Theatre offered training in ballet, interpretive dance, eurythmics, improvisation, fencing, mime, phonetics, diction, voice production, theatre history, art, music, and literature. The training sought to enhance the imagination and memory of the actor, through which the development of characterization would occur. Beginning in 1923, Boleslavsky published a series of essays in *Theatre Arts Magazine* (collected in 1933 as *Acting: The First Six Lessons*), which constituted the first,

FIG. 11.18 American Laboratory Theatre production of Bernard's *Martine* in 1928. Setting by Robert Edmond Jones. (Courtesy Ronald A. Willis.)

and perhaps most accurate, American version of the Stanislavsky system.

The American Laboratory Theatre also included a performing company, in connection with which some students studied directing. As time passed, Boleslavsky became increasingly concerned with staging and Ouspenskaya with actor training. Among the plays presented were *Twelfth Night, Much Ado About Nothing, Martine, The Three Sisters, Dr. Knock,* Cocteau's *Antigone,* Scribe's *A Glass of Water,* and Thornton Wilder's first full-length play, *The Trumpet Shall Sound.* But like so many other theatrical groups already noted, the American Laboratory Theatre was forced by the Depression to close in 1930. Fortunately, such former students as Harold Clurman, Lee Strasberg, and Stella Adler were to carry on its work in the Group Theatre.

The Group Theatre evolved slowly. In 1928, several actors, among them Harold Clurman (1901–1980), Lee Strasberg (1901–1982), Morris Carnovsky (1898–   ), and Sanford Meisner (1905–   ), had begun to rehearse plays in their spare time and to perform them for invited audiences. In 1929, several future members of the Group participated in a studio project at the Theatre Guild, for which Cheryl Crawford (1902–1986) was then casting director and Clurman a play reader—a production of Kirshon's *Red Dust.* In part, members of the Group were protesting against the Guild itself, which they saw as having no program other than rather vague "cultural" and "artistic" aims. The Group, on the other hand, was committed to the Stanislavsky acting system and to leftist politics. Ironically, it was the Guild that gave the budding organization support: not only did it contribute $1,000, it released Clurman, Crawford, Carnovsky, and Franchot Tone from their contracts and gave up its option on Paul Green's *The House of Connelly,* which was to be the Group's first production.

In the summer of 1931, the three directors—Clurman, Strasberg, and Crawford—took twenty-eight actors to the country to study and rehearse, and in the fall, with further assistance from the Theatre Guild, opened their first season. For the next ten years the Group Theatre was to be one of America's most influential companies. It was a close-knit unit that lived and worked together, seeking to develop an ensemble from the example of the Moscow Art Theatre. Among its actors were Carnovsky, Tone, Meisner, Stella Adler (1904–   ), Luther Adler (1903–1984), J. Edward Bromberg (1903–1951), Elia Kazan (1909–   ), Alexander Kirkland (1908–   ), John Garfield (1913–1952), and Lee J. Cobb (1911–1976). Its principal designer was Mordecai Gorelik, whose work was supplemented by that of Donald Oenslager and Boris Aronson.

In the early years, Strasberg was the dominant figure, but his authority was challenged in 1934 by Stella Adler and Clurman, who had spent some time with Stanislavsky in France, and returned with the message that Strasberg had placed too much emphasis on "emotion memory" and not enough on "given circumstances" and the "magic if." In 1935, Clurman and Crawford went to the Soviet Union and saw many productions. They visited with Meyerhold, whose work impressed them greatly. By this time, Mikhail Chekhov also was appearing in America, and many members of the Group were interested in his variations on Stanislavsky's work. The shift away from Strasberg was hastened when Odets' *Awake and Sing!* (1935) was produced with resounding success but over Strasberg's strong objections. From that time on, Clurman became dominant in the Group Theatre. In these early years can be found the seeds of that endless American debate over the proper interpretation of the Stanislavsky system.

Other factors also contributed to rifts within the company. While there was the desire to maintain a permanent troupe, finances eventually made that impossible. Many members lived in virtual poverty for many years. Franchot Tone was the first to give in to the lure of Hollywood, but he was not to be the last. In 1937–1938, Clurman reorganized the Group and changed many of its earlier policies. A decision was made not to pay members who were not working in a current production, and eventually the operation differed little from other New York commercial theatres. After the failure of Odets' *Night Music* in 1940, Clurman was so dissatisfied with the rapidly disintegrating troupe that he threatened to cast outside the membership in the future. This provoked a revolt, and in 1941 Strasberg returned to direct Odets' *Clash by Night,* which he suggested was an attempt to revive the original spirit of the company. But the Group Theatre was now doomed, and it ceased to exist when Odets' play closed.

Despite its problems, the Group Theatre was the most important artistic force in the American theatre during the ten years of its existence. It emphasized socially conscious plays by writers such as Paul Green, John Howard Lawson, Sidney Kingsley, Irwin Shaw, Robert Ardrey, and above all Clifford Odets. The Group's emphasis on Stanislavskian methods and techniques was its chief legacy to acting and directing in the United States, and even today this legacy still has its strong reverberations.

THE FEDERAL THEATRE PROJECT

The social consciousness evident in much of the Group Theatre's work was widespread during the 1930s, for the U.S. was in the depths of economic depression. One significant result was the Federal Theatre Project, inaugurated

FIG. 11.19
Odets' *Awake and Sing!* as produced by the Group Theatre in 1935. (Courtesy Alfredo Valente.)

in 1935 as part of the Works Progress Administration (WPA) program to provide jobs for the unemployed. The project was headed by Hallie Flanagan (1890–1969), one of George Pierce Baker's students who after 1925 had won a considerable reputation for her experimental productions at Vassar College. Flanagan saw in the Federal Theatre an opportunity to create something like a national theatre with five regional centers and numerous sub-branches that would encourage experimentation in writing and staging.

Eventually the Federal Theatre had branches in forty states and published its own journal, *Federal Theatre Magazine*. It maintained a play and research bureau to assist school, church, and community theatres throughout the country. But above all, it produced plays. In its four seasons, the Federal Theatre financed over 1,200 productions of 830 major works, 105 of which were performed for the first time. At the height of its activity, it employed 1,200 people, of whom nine-tenths had been on federal relief rolls. During the four years, Congress appropriated $46 million to support the project. Most of the money went for wages, for in other respects the Federal Theatre was financed by admissions, even though 65 percent of the performances were free and no more than one dollar was ever charged for entrance.

Predictably, in the context of a conservative U.S., the project ran into difficulties. The great concentration of its work in New York (where unemployment among theatre workers was the greatest) led to many complaints from those in other parts of the country, as did the apparent incompetence of many who found their way onto the government payroll. But it was the liberal political views (sometimes labeled as Communist), especially those expressed in the *living newspapers* that aroused the suspicions of conservative legislators; and, following an investigation, Congress in 1939

refused to appropriate further funds for the project.

Nonetheless, the Federal Theatre accomplished much. It helped to revive theatre in parts of the country from which professional productions had almost wholly disappeared. It provided ambitious programs of classical and modern works, children's plays, religious dramas, outdoor productions, musical comedies, dance plays, and works by both distinguished and unknown authors. But the most significant contribution of the Federal Theatre was the *living newspaper* form of theatrical performance. The living newspaper explored major contemporary social, economic, and political issues. The principal writer was Arthur Arents, but most living newspapers included segments by many different authors. The first, *Ethiopia* (1935–1936), was never produced because, dealing with the Italian invasion of Ethiopia, it included among its characters several living foreign rulers, whom officials thought it unwise to offend. Most subsequent works centered specifically on American problems rather than those of international import: *Triple-A Plowed Under* (1936) treated the plight of farmers; *Power* (1937) dealt with electrical utilities and the Tennessee Valley Authority; *One-Third of a Nation* (1938) explored the problem of housing. (President Roosevelt had suggested during the Depression that "one-third of a nation" was ill-housed and ill-fed.) Most used the "little man" as a unifying character, an average citizen whose curiosity has been aroused by controversy over a problem. He begins to ask questions and is then led through the background of the problem, its human consequences, and possible solutions. Much of the dialogue was extracted from speeches, newspaper stories, and public documents. Dramatic scenes, often showing the desperate plight of individuals affected by the problem, alternated with film clips and projections of statistical data. Many of the tech-

FIG. 11.20
Setting by Howard Bay for *One-Third of a Nation* in 1938 at the Federal Theatre. (From *Theatre Arts*, 1938.)

niques resembled those used earlier by the Blue Blouses, Meyerhold, and Piscator. Although most of the plays advocated strong governmental action to solve problems, their solutions never exceeded the positions taken by the Roosevelt administration. Nonetheless this partisanship was enough to outrage opponents in Congress and to bring about the downfall of the Federal Theatre Project. By far the most extensive involvement ever of the American government with the theatre, the project has been used ever since as an example both of what might be accomplished with government assistance and the dangers of federal involvement in the arts.

BLACK THEATRE

The Federal Theatre also gave rise to other groups, the most important of which was the Mercury Theatre, established in 1937 by John

Houseman (1902–1989) and Orson Welles (1915–1988). Houseman headed the Negro People's Theatre, a unit of the Federal Theatre, housed at the Lafayette Theatre in Harlem. Here in 1935–1936, Welles had staged an all-black version of *Macbeth,* in which the setting had been changed to Haiti and in which the witches were transformed into voodoo witch doctors. It starred Edna Thomas as Lady Macbeth, Jack Carter as Macbeth, and Canada Lee as Banquo. It was one of the most successful productions of the Federal Theatre. Welles won additional fame with a production of *Doctor Faustus* (1937), in which he played the title role and the black actor Jack Carter played Mephistopheles. Later in 1937, when Houseman and Welles mounted Marc Blitzstein's *The Cradle Will Rock,* a prounion, witty, and derisive musical play about steel company opposition to unionization, the WPA ordered postponement on the grounds that the production was too explosive. Welles and Houseman defied the order, and out of the conflict emerged the Mercury Theatre.

With the Mercury, Welles and Houseman sought to develop a repertory of classical plays having some relevance to contemporary issues. The most famous production was of *Julius Caesar,* done in modern military uniforms to suggest parallels with the rise of Hitler and Mussolini. The text was cut, rearranged, and changed in various ways to accommodate the contemporary implications. The production was both highly controversial and popular. Later Welles and Houseman moved to Hollywood, where they intended to continue the Mercury. But in 1940, after presenting Richard Wright's and Paul Green's *Native Son* in New York, the Mercury came to an end. Although Welles and Houseman had intended to form a permanent repertory company and most of the original actors were made shareholders and promised long-term engagements, the venture eventually failed, in part because the managers, particularly Welles, would not plan sufficiently far in advance to anticipate potential difficulties.

The Federal Theatre, Welles, and Houseman also promoted black theatre, which although not widespread during the interwar years, was laying the foundations for later and more extensive developments. Despite the importance of blacks in American life from the beginning, they were long permitted little part in the theatre, except to be depicted in drama from time to time as servants or as comic caricatures.

The first serious plays on Broadway for black actors began to appear after World War I with Ridgely Torrence's *Three Plays for a Negro Theatre* (1917), designed and directed by Robert Edmond Jones. Even though this production did not have a long run, it marked a turning away from stereotypical treatments of blacks and, equally important, blacks were for the first time welcomed as part of a Broadway audience. There followed a number of sympathetic treatments of blacks: among them were O'Neill's *The Emperor Jones* (in which a black actor played the leading role in a serious American play for the first time), *The Dreamy Kid,* and *All God's Chillun Got Wings;* DuBose and Dorothy Heyward's *Porgy* (later adapted into Gershwin's opera *Porgy and Bess*) and *Mamba's Daughters;* Marc Connelly's *The Green Pastures;* Paul Green's *In Abraham's Bosom;* Paul Peters' and George Sklar's *Stevedore;* and John Wexley's *They Shall Not Die.* All these plays were written by white dramatists, but they indicate that there were at least some whites who understood something of the plight of blacks in the United States. But because such authors were not black, their plays presented only a limited perspective on the realities of the black experience in the United States.

There were a number of black authors and theatre artists, on the other hand, whose work, with few exceptions, achieved little if any national recognition. Such artists were given little encouragement by white producers, and most had their works presented under circumstances that permitted only brief runs. Among the best of these plays were Willis Richardson's *The Chipwoman's Fortune,* Frank Wilson's *Sugar Cane,* Ernest Culbertson's *Goat Alley,* Mary Hoyt Wiborg's *Taboo* (in which Paul Robeson made his debut as an actor), Hall Johnson's *Run Little Chillun,* and Langston Hughes' *Mulatto.* There were a number of musical plays, among the most successful being Noble Sissle's and Eubie Blake's *Shuffle Along, Chocolate Dandies,* and *Runnin' Wild.* But most black theatres had difficulty in remaining open, and consequently both black playwrights and black actors seldom at this time had the real opportunity, as did whites, to perfect their art. Charles Gilpin, for example, who starred as Brutus Jones in O'Neill's *The Emperor Jones,* had to take a job as an elevator operator after the play closed on Broadway. For the most part, it was only those black performers who were singers, dancers, or comedians who found real acceptance in major theatres and then only in vaudeville or musical comedy. Nevertheless, Richard Harrison, Frank Wilson, Rose McClendon, and Abbie Mitchell demonstrated that they could compete with the best actors of the period.

Black theatre received a major boost from the Federal Theatre Project, for in several cities it established so-called Negro units which in four years presented seventy-five plays. Some productions, such as Welles' *Macbeth* and *The Swing Mikado* (adapted from Gilbert and Sullivan), became nationally famous. There were as well a number of original works by black writers, such as Frank Wilson's *Walk Together Children* (a detective story), J. A. Smith's and Peter Morrell's *Turpentine* (about labor troubles in Florida), and W. E. B. Du Bois' *Haiti* (about Toussaint L'Ouverture). Unfortunately, most of the hopes raised for black theatre were dashed when the project ended in 1939.

By World War II, a number of plays about black life had found their way to the stage, but few showed the ugly side. By far the most disturbing, however, was *Native Son*, Paul Green's and Richard Wright's adaptation of Wright's novel, which showed the terrible effects of social evils on the life of the protagonist. Furthermore, only a few black actors—most notably Ethel Waters, Paul Robeson, and Canada Lee—won true fame. But the situation for blacks in the theatre had improved since 1915. Black theatre artists had made their presence felt, even if they were not yet permitted to demonstrate their full potential.

THE WORKERS' THEATRE MOVEMENT

The social consciousness seen in the Group Theatre, the Federal Theatre, and the Mercury Theatre was even more evident in the *workers' theatre* movement, which began in the 1920s and flourished after the Depression began in 1929. The movement had its beginnings in 1926 with the Workers' Drama League, but it was not until the following year with the New Playwrights' Theatre, organized by John Howard Lawson, John Dos Passos, and others, that real notice began to be taken. Seeking to advance the cause of the working class, the group presented such plays as Lawson's *Loud Speaker* (a farce on political themes) and *International* (a history of Communism). But the New Playwrights' Theatre tended to offend more than it attracted working-class audiences, for it was overly intellectual and depended heavily on unusual dramatic and theatrical techniques.

A number of foreign-language groups— German, Hungarian, Finnish, Yugoslavian, Swedish, and Yiddish—were also performing in New York generally in isolation from each other, but in 1929 twelve such groups formed the Workers' Dramatic Council. In 1932, the first National Workers' Theatre Festival and Conference was held in New York and at that time a national League of Workers' Theatres was formed. Thereafter the movement grew rapidly, and by 1934 there were an estimated four hundred such groups in the United States. The most important of all the groups was the Theatre Union, founded in 1933, which performed at the Fourteenth Street Theatre, just vacated by Le Gallienne. It sought to attract working-class audiences with admission prices ranging from fifty cents to $1.50. Its major successes were won with George Sklar's and Albert Maltz's *Peace on Earth* (1933), about the interconnections of big business and war, and Sklar's and Paul Peters' *Stevedore* (1934), a stirring plea for justice for and unionization among Southern blacks. The workers' theatre movement reached its peak between 1935 and 1937. In 1935, the League of Workers' Theatres was reconstituted as the New Theatre League, ostensibly to indicate its growing professional stance. But with professionalism came troubles, and with the beginning of World War II, the movement virtually collapsed.

ECONOMIC DEPRESSION, COMMERCIALISM, AND UNIONISM

The economic forces that motivated the workers' theatre movement affected the whole of American theatre in the interwar years. While the theatre in New York expanded until 1929, the Depression brought immediate decline in both the number of theatres and productions staged. In 1920 there were still approximately 1,500 theatres across the country; in 1930, the number had been reduced to about 500; by 1940, there were no more than 200 theatres in the entire nation. While the economy played a major part in the decline, other factors were significant: spectator sports increased steadily in popularity during the twentieth century and siphoned off many former theatregoers; motion pictures (low admissions) and radio (free) played an even more significant role in the decline of interest in the theatre. Unfortunately, just when theatres needed most to lower admissions, they were driven to raise them, chiefly by the increased union demands by Actors' Equity, United Scenic Artists, the Dramatists' Guild, the International Alliance of Theatrical Stage Employees, and the Association of Theatrical Press Agents and Managers. All these organizations provided important services for members and helped correct legitimate grievances. Nonetheless, each also contributed to rising production costs.

Another factor adversely affecting theatre specifically in New York was the building code. Because of several disastrous theatre fires in the early twentieth century, a number of restrictive laws designed to protect the public were passed and remained in force until the 1960s. One law required every theatre to be able to cut off the stage from the auditorium by means of a fireproof curtain, a major deterrent to changes in theatre architecture and thus to the alteration of the actor/audience relationship. Similarly, the law forbade any structure above a theatre (a law never extended to motion picture theatres), and in New York, where land values have always been astronomical, a theatre had to justify space that might be occupied by a skyscraper, thus causing theatre rents to be extremely high. As a consequence, most managers too often were forced to cater to the lowest common denominator of popular taste in order to survive. Hence theatrical experimentation was minimal in American theatre. If the commercial theatre shrank after 1930, the amateur theatre prospered, however. The community theatre movement mushroomed after World War I, and by 1925 there were some 1,900 groups registered with the Drama League of America. Similarly theatre was increasingly introduced into the curricula of colleges and universities (something begun in Europe on essentially a small scale only since the 1960s). In the United States, outstanding academic theatre programs developed between the wars at North Carolina, Cornell, Yale, Iowa, and others. The University of Washington, for example, introduced the first American theatre-in-the-round in 1932. Nonetheless, amateurs do not compensate for a lack of true professionalism and by 1940 there were vast reaches of the United States that were wholly devoid of professional theatre.

O'NEILL

The interwar American theatre successfully borrowed many techniques and approaches already well established in Europe, but it did not make any major innovations. Thus, it was derivative more than original. Much the same might be said of American playwrights of the period. They borrowed freely from almost every European artistic movement but paid true allegiance to none. A writer might mingle diverse elements in a single play or write successive works in contrasting styles. Except for the left-wing playwrights, few set out to change the attitudes of the American public. Most seemed content merely to explore commonly held views and their effects upon characters. If audiences objected to plays, it was usually because of unfamiliar techniques rather than because of startlingly new ideas. But the increased interest in excellence was indicated by the establishment in 1918 of the Pulitzer Prize for the best new American drama performed in New York and in 1936 of the Drama Critics Circle Award for the best American play of the season.

Between the wars, America produced a number of excellent playwrights, though few today seem as important as they once did. Ultimately the most significant was Eugene O'Neill (1888–1953), son of the popular actor James O'Neill and the first and only American dramatist to be awarded the Nobel Prize for Literature (in 1936). A problem child, O'Neill dropped out of Princeton University after one year and then worked at various odd jobs between bouts of prolonged drunkenness and debauchery. In 1912, a brush with tuberculosis marked a turning point, for during his illness he developed a consuming interest in playwriting. In 1914, five of his one-act plays were published at his father's expense, and in the same year he began attending Baker's classes in playwriting at Harvard. In 1915, he met members of the Provincetown Players, who gave him his first production and induced him to go to New York, where others of his one-acts were produced before his first full-length work,

Beyond the Horizon (1920), was presented on Broadway and won that year's Pulitzer Prize. Shortly afterward The Emperor Jones was moved from the Provincetown Playhouse to a Broadway theatre, and in 1921, Hopkins presented Anna Christie. Soon O'Neill was viewed as the leader of a new school of American playwrights, a position accorded him until the mid-1930s when American critics began to find flaws in his work.

O'Neill was a prolific writer, eventually turning out about twenty-five full-length plays. In addition to those noted above, the best-known of the early plays are The Hairy Ape (1922), Desire Under the Elms (1924), The Great God Brown (1926), Marco Millions (1928), Strange Interlude (1928), and Mourning Becomes Electra (1931). His most light-hearted play, Ah, Wilderness! (1933), an autobiographical comedy about teenage love and rebellion, was followed almost immediately by one of his most difficult and opaque works, Days Without End (1934). After 1934, O'Neill withheld his works from production, though he continued to write regularly, devoting himself to a cycle of plays that was never completed. Although he won the Nobel Prize in 1936, his reputation declined steadily under critical attack. It suffered further when in the 1940s his plays A Moon for the Misbegotten (1943) and The Iceman Cometh (1939, but produced in 1946) both failed. It was not until after O'Neill's death, when The Iceman Cometh was revived by director José Quintero, in 1956, followed soon afterward by Long Day's Journey Into Night (1939–1941), that O'Neill's reputation was revived. Thereafter, posthumously, he regained his earlier position as America's foremost dramatist.

The changes in critical opinion of O'Neill's work are explained partially by the uneven quality of his plays. Though all seem concerned with humanity's search for faith and a set of values upon which to build a meaningful life, inevitably his characters are adrift in a materi-

FIG. 11.21
O'Neill's *Desire
Under the Elms,* as
designed by Robert
Edmond Jones.
(Photo by Bruguiere;
courtesy Theatre
Collection, New York
Public Library at
Lincoln Center;
Astor, Lenox, and
Tilden Foundations.)

alist world, lost creatures searching for a way to escape despair. Critics suggest that O'Neill's language is his weakest point, though actors often consider his dialogue to be rhythmic and easily spoken. O'Neill's great strength lies in the creation of characters and situations. His faults are perhaps most evident in the plays of his middle period (approximately from 1924 to 1934), the same period when he was experimenting with novel devices such as masks, extended asides, excessive length, and expressionistic techniques. His strengths are most apparent in his late plays, especially *Long Day's Journey Into Night,* where he returns to something of the realistic base that first gained notice in his earliest works.

O'Neill's early one-acts, most of them about the sea, are well-constructed realistic pieces that create a strong sense of character and mood. Much the same approach is used in *Beyond the Horizon,* which deals with Robert Mayo, a dreamer and idealist who longs for the sea and what lies "beyond the horizon," though he is frustrated as a land-bound farmer while his brother goes to sea. With *The Emperor Jones,* O'Neill turned to expressionist techniques. Brutus Jones, a black former Pullman porter who has escaped from prison, has made himself through "Yankee bluff" emperor of an island in the West Indies. He has nothing but contempt for the natives, "ign'rent bush niggers," as he refers to them. When they rise up against his tyranny, Jones flees into the forest. There his hallucinatory fears gradually drive him deeper and deeper into his racial past. (He encounters, for example, a slave auction, a slave ship, and a Congo witch doctor.) Eventually Jones is killed at dawn by the natives on the edge of the sandy plain. Throughout, there is the steady beat of a tom-tom, which accelerates with Jones' rising pulse rate; when he is shot, the tom-tom stops abruptly.

The Hairy Ape is similar in technique and focuses on Yank, a stoker on a luxury liner who feels a strange physical and psychological unity with the steel of the ship. He makes the ship run, and, as he says, he "belongs." His confidence, however, is shattered by a rich girl who, horrified by Yank's appearance, calls him a "hairy ape." As in the plays of the German expressionists, the rest of *The Hairy Ape* is a series of scenes in which Yank's quest to regain his sense of unity is frustrated. At the end, at the zoo, he releases an ape from its cage and is crushed to death by it.

Thereafter O'Neill experimented. In *The Great God Brown,* he used masks to distinguish the characters' public and private roles, their external appearance and their inner reality. In *Strange Interlude,* O'Neill used lengthy asides or "interior monologues" in which characters reveal their inner feelings, which contrast strongly with their public statements and external manner. In *Mourning Becomes Electra,* O'Neill reshapes Aeschylus' *Oresteia* trilogy into three connected plays with a total of fourteen acts requiring six hours to perform. He transfers the action to New England at the end of the Civil War. The gods and the supernatural have been eliminated, and human motivations (conceived entirely in Freudian terms) are invested with a fatalistic aura. The blood curse of Aeschylus is finally resolved when Lavinia (the Electra figure), after the death of her brother Orin (Orestes), turns away the young man whom she had intended to marry. She will now live alone till her death in the boarded-up family home. Without newborn children, the family curse will end.

Days Without End was from the beginning a critical failure, concerned with a protagonist

FIG. 11.22
O'Neill's *Strange Interlude,* produced by the Theatre Guild in 1928. Left to right are Glenn Anders, Lynn Fontanne, Tom Powers, and Earle Larimore. (From *Theatre Arts,* 1929.)

whose perennial search for significance in life ends at the foot of the cross. The play marked an eclipse in O'Neill's fame. Though he eventually overcame his personal doubts and wrote the plays upon which his revived fame rests, they were not produced successfully until after his death in 1953. They include *A Moon for the Misbegotten, A Touch of the Poet* (1935–1942), the unfinished *More Stately Mansions* (1935–1941), *The Iceman Cometh,* and *Long Day's Journey Into Night.*

Most critics consider O'Neill's *Long Day's Journey Into Night* his finest work, not only because of its excellent dramaturgy but, at least in part, its autobiographical revelations about O'Neill, his father, mother, and brother. Again, it is a long play, and realism, though the fundamental style, is permeated by a mood and poetic sensibility that escapes realism per se. (The play is perhaps reminiscent of the last works of Sophocles, Shakespeare, and Ibsen, traditionally labeled as "visionary" by critics.) The action is confined within a very restricted framework, taking place in a single room on one day in 1912 with the focus on four characters (James and Mary Tyrone, a famous aging actor and his drug-addicted wife, and their two sons, Jamie and Edmund). In the course of the day, there is much drinking among the men and a number of ugly confrontations. Jamie, unlike his matinee-idol father, is an unsuccessful actor, while Edmund, the younger at twenty-three, learns that he must go to a sanatorium. It was the birth of Edmund which, because of a quack doctor, caused Mary to become a drug addict. At night and at the end of the play, Mary, now lost in her memories, appears almost like an apparition carrying her wedding gown. Among this group of men, now in a state of stupor after a long day of drinking, she remembers the winter of her senior year at a Catholic girls' school, when she had told Mother Elizabeth she wanted to be a nun: "Then in the spring

something happened to me. Yes, I remember. I fell in love with James Tyrone and was so happy for a time." As O'Neill suggests in his stage directions: "She stares before her in a sad dream. Tyrone stirs in his chair. Edmund and Jamie remain motionless." Then the final curtain falls.

O'Neill wrote many other plays and left several unfinished. All are variations on similar themes of the human being's struggle to find meaning in a meaningless world. In some ways, O'Neill presages the philosophical concerns of the existentialists, Beckett, and the absurd after World War II. More has been written about O'Neill internationally than any other American playwright.

OTHER AMERICAN PLAYWRIGHTS BETWEEN THE WARS

O'Neill was surrounded by a number of lesser figures, among them Rice, Howard, Kaufman, Anderson, Hellman, Lawson, and Odets. Elmer Rice (1892–1967) is primarily noted for two works, *The Adding Machine* (1923) and *Street Scene* (1929). The first, produced by the Theatre Guild, is one of several American plays of the 1920s to adopt expressionist techniques. It is a commentary on materialism, symbolized by the adding machine and its dehumanizing effects on its protagonist. An accountant named Mr. Zero is little more than an automaton (reminiscent of Kaiser's Cashier in *From Morn to Midnight*). *Street Scene* is the stylistic antithesis, for it is strongly naturalistic in tone and treatment. The setting is the sidewalk, steps, and facade of a tenement, while sound effects evoke the life of the street itself.

Sidney Howard (1891–1931) won critical fame in 1924 with *They Knew What They Wanted,* which centers on the love triangle of an aging Italian-American vineyard owner, a lonely waitress, and a young itinerant farm

worker. In the 1950s, the play became the basis for the musical *The Most Happy Fella*. Other plays by Howard include *The Silver Cord* (1927), about a mother's excessive attachment to her two sons, and *Yellow Jack* (1934), a semidocumentary about yellow fever set in Panama during the building of the canal.

George S. Kaufman (1889–1961), noted primarily for his farces, won considerable applause with *Beggar on Horseback* (1924), one of a number of plays written in collaboration with Marc Connolly. In the expressionist mode, *Beggar on Horseback* treats a young musician who views his impending marriage to a wealthy woman as a prelude to the serious pursuit of his art. When he falls asleep, there follows a series of dream episodes in which he finds himself enslaved to the materialist system epitomized by his fiancée's father and even placed in a cage and forced to turn out popular songs to meet the never-ending demand. Now realizing the danger of selling his soul for financial security, upon awakening he decides to marry the poor girl across the hall, whom he has loved all along. Later Kaufman collaborated with Moss Hart (1904–1960) between 1930 and 1941. Their best play is *You Can't Take It With You* (1936), which treats an eccentric household and celebrates the joys of nonconformity. While Kaufman after 1941 was never able to form another truly productive partnership, he won occasional success, particularly with *The Solid Gold Cadillac* (1953), written with Howard Teichmann. Nonetheless, for thirty years Kaufman, through his mastery of topical humor and comic dialogue, was considered America's leading farceur.

In the 1930s, most of these playwrights continued to be productive and others came to the fore. The most significant of the new writers was Maxwell Anderson (1888–1959); for as O'Neill's reputation declined, Anderson was often touted as his successor. Anderson actually had won fame earlier as Laurence Stallings' collaborator on *What Price Glory?* (1924), an antiromantic treatment of war noted for its then liberal use of profanity. The enormous success of the play initiated a trend toward greater freedom in language and subject matter, which reached its peak around 1927 when a number of works treating homosexuality and other previously forbidden subjects led to demands for censorship.

Despite his initial success, Anderson wrote

FIG. 11.24

Setting designed by Jo Mielziner for Elmer Rice's *Street Scene* in 1929. (Photo by Vandamm; courtesy Theatre Collection, New York Public Library at Lincoln Center; Astor, Lenox, and Tilden Foundations.)

no other important works until the 1930s, when he sought to revive poetic drama with such plays as *Elizabeth the Queen* (1930) and *Mary of Scotland* (1933). Though written in blank verse and Shakespearean in construction, such plays attracted a wide audience. Anderson is most adventurous in a work such as *Winterset* (1935), for here he abandons historical for contemporary subject matter but retains poetic dialogue. Most critics consider *Winterset* Anderson's greatest achievement. Based on the Sacco-Vanzetti case of the 1920s, the play keeps the actual events at a distance by focusing on Mio, the son of a man executed for a crime he did not commit. Though Anderson continued to write until 1958, his postwar plays added little to his reputation. Just as his fame had risen as O'Neill's declined, so in turn did it wane as O'Neill's revived in the 1950s. Between 1935 and 1955, however, Anderson was considered to be America's leading playwright.

Lillian Hellman (1905–1984) was primarily a moralist preoccupied with human evil. Her work came to prominence in 1934 with *The Children's Hour,* in which a girls' school is destroyed by malicious stories spread by a young student of a homosexual relationship between the two women who run the school.

Eventually one of the women breaks off her engagement to a young doctor, and the other commits suicide. Hellman's best-known play, however, is *The Little Foxes* (1938), which exposes the greed of the rising industrial class in the South at the turn of the century. In the 1960s, Hellman gained considerable success with *Toys in the Attic,* in which a sister deliberately seeks to destroy her brother when his business success threatens to end his dependence on her. Overall, Hellman's plays tend to be melodramas without the traditional melodramatic ending. Rather than showing virtue rewarded and villainy punished, they depict goodness so weak that it is trodden underfoot by evil.

A number of other playwrights in this period deserve at least brief mention. George Kelly (1887–1974) is best remembered for *Craig's Wife* (1925), about a neurotic woman who destroys her marriage through her obsession with neatness, while Philip Barry (1896–1949) gained acclaim for his sophisticated comedy *The Philadelphia Story,* about a rich, spoiled socialite who realizes on the eve of her second marriage that she still loves her first husband. Robert E. Sherwood (1896–1955) won fame with *The Petrified Forest* (1935), a suspenseful, realistic melodrama, and *Idiot's Delight* (1936), an almost farcical treatment of travelers in prewar fascist Europe. S. N. Behrman (1893–1973) was considered a leading exponent of high comedy in works such as *Biography* (1932), about a successful woman painter who becomes involved with two men (a politician and a revolutionary). Paul Green (1894–1981) wrote *The House of Connelly* (1931), in which a Southern aristocratic family gains new strength through a marital alliance with "poor white trash." Sidney Kingsley (1906–   ) wrote *Dead End* (1935), a naturalistic play about the kind of environment that leads to gangsterism. And the novelist William Saroyan (1900–1981) gained considerable fame

through such essentially sentimental works as *My Heart's in the Highlands* (1939), *The Time of Your Life* (1939), and *The Beautiful People* (1941), all of which celebrate the simple joys of poor but eccentric characters.

Most American playwrights of the interwar years were focused chiefly on the individual's psychological or familial relationships or on rather generalized social conditions. Though many denounced conformity or tradition, few suggested any need for revolutionary change in American society at large. Those who did received little encouragement.

Of the politically conscious dramatists, one of the best was John Howard Lawson (1895–1977), who made his debut in 1923 with *Roger Bloomer,* an expressionist evocation of the problems of an adolescent growing up in an insensitive environment. His first major work was *Processional* (1925), hailed by some critics of the time as the most important drama of the post–World War I period because its approach—a combination of expressionist devices, vaudeville techniques, and jazz music with serious, comic, and burlesque episodes—seemed so innovative. Based on the conflict between workers and owners in the West Virginia coal mines, it treats only the protagonist realistically and reduces the other characters to caricature. After the late 1930s, Lawson spent most of his time in Hollywood. Nevertheless, his plays received a much fuller hearing than did the work of such left-wing dramatists as Sophie Treadwell, Albert Maltz, George Sklar, Paul Peters, Albert Bein, Emjo Basshe, John Wexley, Michael Gold, and the novelist John Dos Passos. These playwrights for the most part were dismissed as mere propagandists and were encouraged only by workers' theatre groups. Their plays, like Lawson's, tended to disappear after the disbanding of the Theatre Union in the late 1930s as economic stability returned to America.

The drama of political and social consciousness found its finest expression in the work of Clifford Odets (1906–1963). Following a path opposite to that of Lawson, Odets became steadily less interested in propaganda as Lawson was becoming increasingly propagandistic. Odets began as an apprentice actor with the Group Theatre before writing *Waiting for Lefty* (1935), one of America's most effective agit-prop plays. Set on a bare platform of a union hall, it ostensibly begins in the midst of a meeting during which taxi drivers will decide whether to strike. Speakers rise to present their views, and vignettes of life among the taxi drivers and their families illustrate the workers' plight. But since union leadership has been taken over by racketeers in league with the owners, the drivers believe they can depend only on Lefty, whose arrival they await before making a decision. When word arrives that Lefty has been treacherously murdered, the workers rise as one with shouts of "Strike, Strike!"

Odets soon became resident playwright for the Group Theatre, for which he wrote such plays as *Awake and Sing!* (1935), *Golden Boy* (1937), and *Rocket to the Moon* (1938). *Awake and Sing!*, concerned with a close-knit Jewish family whose dreams of happiness are gradually shattered, develops a number of fully dimensional characterizations. In general approach, the play has been compared with those of Chekhov and O'Casey, for it is rich in the texture of life that undermines bright hopes. *Golden Boy* is the story of Joe Bonaparte, who dreams of being a successful violinist but becomes a prize fighter instead because the world values brute force more than it does music. Increasingly involved with gangsters, who represent the corrupting forces of capitalism, Joe grows disillusioned, particularly after he kills a man in the ring. At the end, he wrecks his automobile, killing both himself and the woman he loves. In the late 1930s, Odets like Lawson succumbed to the financial lure of

FIG. 11.25
Odets' *Golden Boy*, produced by the Group Theatre in 1937, with Luther Adler (center). (Courtesy Alfredo Valente.)

Hollywood. Most of his plays thereafter lacked the vitality of his early work, though *The Country Girl* (1950), depicting the conflicts of a wife and her alcoholic husband (a has-been actor), is a powerful psychological drama.

WILDER

Perhaps with the exception of O'Neill, the American playwright of the interwar years enjoying the greatest international reputation was Thornton Wilder (1897–1975). His work remains popular in America and Europe. Post-World War II playwrights such as Frisch and Duerrenmatt cited Wilder's work as a major influence on their own. Wilder's first play, *The Trumpet Shall Sound* (1919–1920) was produced in 1927 by the American Laboratory Theatre. Later, after his first novels had aroused wide interest in the early 1930s, Wilder wrote a number of one-act plays that strongly revealed his unwillingness to be confined by the conventions of realistic staging. In both *Pullman Car Hiawatha* and *The Happy Journey to Trenton*

and Camden, for example, a character called the Stage Manager, using a few chairs, sets a bare stage and supervises the performance.

The techniques used in the short plays were further refined in *Our Town* (1938), still one of the best-known and most popular of all American dramas. Set in a small town in New Hampshire between 1901 and 1913, *Our Town* tells the simple story of a girl who falls in love, marries a young man who lives next door, and dies while giving birth to their child. The first act, which re-creates the small-town milieu, is titled "The Daily Life," the second "Love and Marriage," and the third "Death." On a bare stage, the Stage Manager manipulates a few chairs, a ladder, and two trellises as needed by the episodes, which his narration introduces and links. He also assumes numerous roles, ranging from small children to aging adults, and comments on the events and their significance. On one level, *Our Town* treats a very specific time and place, but it does so in order to capture the archetypal patterns and life cycles in miniature that underlie human experience. (While too often the play is produced to

FIG. 11.26
The wedding scene of Thornton Wilder's *Our Town* as produced originally in 1938. (Photo by Vandamm; courtesy Theatre Collection, New York Public Library at Lincoln Center; Astor, Lenox, and Tilden Foundations.)

underscore what seem to be its sentimental values, Wilder with his minimalist staging techniques reflects a vision similar to Brechtian *Verfremdung* or distancing.)

Though Wilder's *The Merchant of Yonkers* (1938), directed by Max Reinhardt in New York, was a dismal failure, he revised the play in 1954 with a new title, *The Matchmaker*. This time, directed by Tyrone Guthrie, the play was a resounding success both in Great Britain and the United States. In 1964, as *Hello, Dolly,* the play would become one of America's longest-running musicals. Concerned with the aging but rich merchant Horace Vandergelder who hires the matchmaker Dolly Levi to find him a wife, the play is an archetypal farce with its disguises, artificial complications, surprise encounters, and asides, all of which are fully exploited and called to the attention of the audience.

In *The Skin of Our Teeth* (1943), Wilder summarizes the experience of the human race in the face of disaster (the ice age, the flood, and war) to show how each time we have escaped by "the skin of our teeth." Produced in the midst of World War II, the play was intended as a reminder of human resilience. Wilder uses broad theatricalist devices: performers step out of their roles to speak to the audience, and backstage personnel comment to the audience on the play and its ideas. Anachronisms abound: in the ice age, Mr. Antrobus lives in New Jersey and commutes to his office; at the time of the flood, the characters are on the boardwalk in Atlantic City. Wilder here seeks to emphasize the continuity of human experience.

After 1943, Wilder wrote only occasionally for the theatre and with little success. He made his impact through a theatricalism compounded of devices taken from many sources, including vaudeville, expressionism, futurism, and surrealism. Much of his approach resembles that of André Obey, particularly in a play such as *Noah*. Unlike most of his nonrealist contemporaries, Wilder was able to make his theatricalism acceptable to ordinary theatregoers, for he coupled it with subject matter clearly understandable to the most unsophisticated spectator. Although Wilder telescoped both time and space more drastically than perhaps any other playwright, he always was careful to point out dramatically that he was doing so, thus making it clear and justifiable to the audience. Such simplicity and clarity, coupled with an optimistic faith in humanity, has caused some critics to describe Wilder as a mere purveyor of clichés while at the same time causing others to praise him for cutting through the bewildering surface of experience to reveal its eternal patterns.

OVERVIEW OF THE INTERWAR YEARS

During the interwar period, theatre and drama in the British Isles and America lagged behind the innovative tendencies of the Continent and the Soviet Union. While the Americans were perhaps more willing than their British and Irish counterparts to experiment with expressionistic techniques in writing and production, realism nonetheless pervaded most theatre performed in English. Although strong directors such as Guthrie, Gielgud, and Hopkins, and significant playwrights such as O'Casey, O'Neill, and Wilder experimented with new methods, their efforts often were more imitative of Continental and Soviet techniques than in themselves original. While the interwar theatre in the British Isles was, for the most part, more competent than adventurous, the American theatre in this period for the first time came to maturity and hence to some measure of international recognition.

Chapter 12

War, Recovery, Absurdity, and Anger

Like the First, the Second World War interrupted or slowed theatrical activity everywhere. In some places performances virtually ceased, and elsewhere they emphasized patriotism and sought to build morale or provide diversion. In the immediate postwar years, the major goal was to rebuild. In many instances this meant a continuation of prewar conditions and standards. But the war had also raised serious questions about a world that had produced the Holocaust and the atomic bomb. Altered views of the human condition became evident first through the existentialist vision as set forth by Sartre and Camus and extended in the work of the absurdists. In England, a more socially conscious outlook gave rise to a new generation of "angry" writers. Thus, not only did the theatre recover from the ravages of war but it also took significant new directions.

FRANCE

In France, practically all entertainment was interrupted briefly in 1939–1940 during conflict with Germany, but after France's capitulation, the theatre in Paris, under the German occupation between 1940 and 1944, was relatively prosperous. It was never deprived of materials, and some productions were truly sumptuous.

During the war, Jean-Louis Barrault came to the fore as a director at the Comédie Française, where between 1940 and 1946 he and his wife, Madeleine Renaud, were leading performers. Here he mounted some of the most admired and influential productions of the decade: Racine's *Phèdre,* Corneille's *Le Cid,* Claudel's *The Satin Slipper* and Montherlant's *The Dead Queen.* With these, he established himself as a major force in the theatre. Barrault synthesized most of the major interwar trends. He had studied with Dullin and Decroux and had worked with Artaud. From the Cartel he learned respect for text and precision of detail, from Decroux the power of mime, and from Artaud the importance of unconscious impulses

and nonverbal means. He sought to synthesize these lessons both in his directing and in his acting. He believed that the "script is like the upper and visible part of an iceberg, representing only about one-eighth of the whole; the other seven-eighths are the invisible roots, that is to say, that which creates poetry or the signification of reality."

Barrault's greatest wartime trumph came in 1943 with Claudel's *The Satin Slipper,* designed by Lucien Coutaud, and acted by Marie Bell, Madeleine Renaud, Aimé Clairond, and Barrault, among others. *The Satin Slipper* dramatizes the conflict between human and divine love, sensuality and spirituality. Set against the background of Spain's American empire, the action is spread over a century in time and much of the globe. Barrault's success with a work that had previously been considered unstageable established his reputation. It also confirmed Claudel's theatricality and led to many subsequent productions of his plays.

At the end of the war, the Comédie Française entered a period of stress. When Pierre Dux, the administrator, attempted to

FIG. 12.1
Barrault's production of Claudel's *The Satin Slipper* in 1943. Design by Lucien Coutaud. (Photo by Pic.)

restrict the outside activities of the actors, a large number resigned. Among those who left were Barrault and Renaud, who in 1946 established their own troupe, the Compagnie Madeleine Renaud-Jean-Louis Barrault, into which they took many of those who had left the Comédie Française, including André Brunot, Jacques Dacqmine, Pierre Brasseur, and Edwige Feuillère. Until 1956, the company performed at the Théâtre Marigny in a repertory that included the *Oresteia* (as adapted by Obey), *Hamlet* (in Gide's translation), Kafka's *The Trial* (adapted by Barrault and Gide), Molière's *Scapin,* Marivaux's *False Confessions,* and Claudel's *Break of Noon* and *Christophe Colomb.* In the *Cahiers* (*Notebooks*) published by the troupe, the problems posed by each production were explored at length, providing valuable insights into the company's working methods. Forced to give up the Marigny in 1956, the troupe toured widely until 1959, when Barrault became director of the state-subsidized Théâtre de France. By that time he was considered France's most important director.

At the end of the war, the Ministry of Fine Arts took a number of actions designed to strengthen the theatre. In 1946 it established an annual festival at which substantial prizes were awarded the best production by a new company and the best work of a new director. It also began to subsidize the first productions of promising new playwrights. Furthermore, it granted subsidies to several small Parisian studio theatres to help them cope with rising production costs. But the most important government program sought to decentralize the theatre. Between the wars the provincial theatre had dwindled steadily, so that the theatre had become primarily a Parisian institution. To remedy this situation, the central government, in cooperation with departmental and municipal authorities, began in 1947 to establish "dramatic centers" throughout France.

Each of these had its headquarters in a town where it performed for several weeks at a time and then toured to others within an approximate radius of 100 miles. The first of the centers was the Théâtre de l'Est in Strasbourg, founded in 1947. Originally headed by Roland Pietri and André Clavé, it passed to Michel Saint-Denis from 1953 to 1958. There in 1957 the first new theatre built in postwar France was opened. In 1954 it also founded a training school with Saint-Denis as its head and following methods that extend back to Copeau. A second center was created in 1947 at St.-Etienne from a troupe begun in 1942 by Jean Dasté, Copeau's son-in-law. In 1949 a third center was created in Toulouse from a troupe begun in 1945 by Maurice Sarrazin, Daniel Sorano, and Jacques Duby. Also in 1949 a center was created in Rennes to serve Brittany and western France. Another was founded at Aix-en-Provence in 1952 under the direction of Gaston Baty, who died on the day of its first production. He was succeeded by Georges Douking. Still others were created later.

National and local governments also encouraged and subsidized the many annual festivals that sprang up. The first were created at Avignon and Strasbourg in 1947. Others soon followed at Besancon, Aix-en-Provence, Bordeaux, and elsewhere. Eventually there would be more than fifty each year. Of these, the most prestigious was the one at Avignon, directed by Jean Vilar (1912–1971), who during the 1950s was second only to Barrault as a force in the French theatre. A fellow student of Barrault's in Dullin's school, he had worked in a series of small companies prior to his appointment at Avignon. There he was so successful that in 1951 he was named head of the Théâtre National Populaire (TNP), then an insignificant organization but one which the government wanted to encourage and expand. Under Vilar, the company was expected to give a minimum of 150 performances in Paris each year and then to tour throughout France. It grew steadily in stature. The company included the enormously popular film star Gerard Philipe, along with other outstanding performers, among them Vilar, Maria Casarès, Philippe Noiret, Geneviève Page, and Georges Wilson. With such productions as *Le Cid*, Büchner's *Danton's Death*, Kleist's *The Prince of Homburg*, Brecht's *Mother Courage*, and Molière's *The Miser*, the TNP soon became the most popular of all the state-subsidized troupes. Its accomplishments were recognized in 1959 when it was placed on an equal footing with the Comédie Française.

Even more so than Barrault, Vilar was the heir of the Cartel and was the first French

FIG. 12.2
Jean Vilar (foreground) as Robespierre in his 1953 production of Büchner's *Danton's Death* by the TNP. (Photo by Agnès Varda.)

director to gain a wide popular following utilizing its principles. He believed in the integrity of the text and placed primary emphasis on clarity of interpretation, diction, and movement. Most typically, he used a near-bare stage without a front curtain. Scenic pieces were used sparingly, although as time went by they increased in number. Vilar's principal designer was Léon Gischia, who often used platforms to model the floor but gained most of his effects through lighting, costumes, and carefully selected furniture, properties, and projections. Vilar was especially concerned with making the theatre appealing to the masses. He used a price scale that could compete with the movies and did away with such practices as tipping ushers. Vilar resigned from the TNP in 1963 but continued to manage the Avignon Festival until his death.

The war years brought to the fore two major playwrights—Montherlant and Anouilh. Henry de Montherlant (1896–1972) had been a novelist since the 1920s but had done no playwriting before the Comédie Française asked him to translate a Spanish play. Instead, Montherlant decided to write his own. The result was *The Dead Queen* (1942), which in Barrault's production was considered a major artistic triumph. Subsequently, Montherlant wrote plays regularly, among the best of which are *The Master of Santiago* (1948), *Port-Royal* (1954), and *The Civil War* (1965). *The Master of Santiago* is often considered Montherlant's most characteristic work because of its simple external action, complex psychology and elevated style. Set in Spain in 1519, it focuses on Alvaro, head of the Order of Santiago, and his daughter Mariana. Members of the order are scheduled to go to the New World where fortunes are assured; this will permit Mariana to marry the man she loves. Mariana then learns that all this has been arranged to undercut her father's opposition to the evils of Spanish incursions in America; she reveals the truth to her father,

FIG. 12.3
Montherlant's *The Master of Santiago* at the Théâtre Hébertot in 1948. Directed by Paul Oettly, designed by Mariano Andreu. (Photo by Bernand.)

although it condemns her to a life in a convent. Through it all runs the motif of sacrifice: Mariana's of happiness out of love for her father, and his sacrifice of wealth to his conception of integrity. In his ascetic and harsh rejection of all mediocrity, Alvaro is often considered a reflection of Montherlant himself, whose work as a whole illustrates the large role played by philosophical concerns in postwar French drama.

Jean Anouilh (1910–1987) had worked for a time as Jouvet's secretary before having his first play produced in 1932. He achieved his first success in 1937 with the Pitoëffs' production of *Traveler Without Baggage*. He then formed an association with Barsacq, who between 1939 and 1948 produced Anouilh's plays at the Atelier. The production there of *Antigone* in the midst of war raised Anouilh to the forefront of living French dramatists. Altogether Anouilh wrote about forty plays, of which the best known are *Antigone* (1943), *Waltz of the Toreadors* (1952), *The Lark* (1953), and *Becket* (1959), although he continued to

write up to the time of his death. He divided his plays into *pièces noires* (black or serious) and *pièces roses* (pink or happy). Nevertheless, all pursue the same basic theme—the conflict between integrity and compromise. The action of his plays usually focuses on the protagonist's struggle to maintain purity, even as it becomes clear that compromise can be avoided only in death. *Antigone* illustrates the pattern. Unlike Sophocles, Anouilh is not concerned with the gods or the supernatural. When asked why she has buried her brother, Antigone replies, "For myself." Her adherence to self-imposed standards contrasts with Creon's views of what is best for others. Antigone dies rather than accept Creon's accommodations with a morally corrupt world. In the "happy plays," Anouilh suspends final judgment to permit happy endings, although most of the plays suggest that ultimately betrayals are inevitable. Anouilh also often mingled the serious and the comic, as in *Waltz of the Toreadors*.

There was in Anouilh's work an element of romanticism, especially in his protagonists'

FIG. 12.4
Anouilh's *Antigone*,
directed and
designed by André
Barsacq at the
Théâtre d' Atelier
in 1943. (Photo by
Bernand.)

rejection of compromise. In his late works, youthful rebellion was pushed to the background and disillusionment brought to the fore. Anouilh also had a classical bent in his development of simple, clear actions involving only a few characters. Anouilh's wide appeal is perhaps due to his skillful blending of so many modes. His disgust with life and its compromises served as a bridge between the older school and the absurdists.

Although much of the French theatre's postwar strength rested on the policies, persons, and practices already discussed, its international reputation depended above all on the existentialists and absurdists, whose work seemed a logical response to the horrors of World War II, especially the systematic extermination of

millions of persons and the destructive power of the atomic bomb. Traditional values seemed inadequate to cope with such issues and, more important, to rest on no solid foundation.

The most compelling force in immediate postwar thought was existentialism. Historically, philosophy has been primarily *essentialist*—that is, concerned with defining norms and essences. Existentialism, contrarily, sees existence as prior to essence. Modern existentialists argue that individuals are responsible for making themselves what they are, since their being is defined by their choices and actions, and that unless people act only after choosing consciously and freely, they cannot be said truly to "exist." Existentialism struck a responsive chord, since the world seemingly had gone mad through abdication of personal choice in favor of blindly following national leaders and ideologies, even when it led to unbelievable cruelties. In part, then, existentialism posed fundamental moral questions—about the source of one's standards (internal or external) and about freedom versus conformity. It argued strongly that people must define their own values and find within themselves the bases for choice and action.

The most prominent of the existentialists was Jean-Paul Sartre (1905–1980). Beginning in 1936 he wrote a number of philosophical treatises, of which the best-known is *Being and Nothingness* (1943), and fiction, such as *Nausea* (1938). In 1943 he wrote his first play, *The Flies,* and thereafter used the dramatic medium often. Among his plays probably the best-known are *No Exit* (1944), *Dirty Hands* (1948), *The Devil and the Good Lord* (1951), and *The Condemned of Altona* (1959). He also made several adaptations and wrote a number of screen plays. Sartre declared that all of his work is an attempt to draw logical conclusions from a consistent atheism. Since God does not exist, "all possibility of finding values in an intelligible heaven" disappears. Similarly, neither the state nor any other human institution can provide absolutes. Therefore, "[m]an is condemned to be free." Many cannot face the consequences, but those who can come to recognize the necessity of creating their own "being" through choice and action; ultimately "man is only what he does. Man becomes what he chooses to be." In accepting freedom, each person must find a set of values by which to live and becomes moral by adhering to those standards despite all opposition. People must also accept the necessity of "engagement" in social, moral, and political action, since, just as they must define themselves, they must also help to define their world.

These are the principal ideas that Sartre's plays illustrate. In *The Flies,* based on the *Oresteia,* Sartre shows Orestes asserting his independence both of Jupiter (god) and Egisthus (the state). Orestes demands that the Argives rid themselves of the sense of guilt through which they have been kept down so they can be free to create their own order. *No Exit*

FIG. 12.5
Sartre's *The Devil and the Good Lord* in its original production of 1951. (Photo by Pic.)

depicts the results of failing to choose properly. So long as people are alive, they may choose to change, but death fixes identity. Hell is the torture of looking back on one's failure to choose when one was able to do so.

Sartre's influence was reinforced by that of Albert Camus (1913–1960). He began writing in the late 1930s, but it was not until 1942 that he made a strong impact with a novel, *The Stranger*. Camus wrote only a few plays: *The Misunderstanding* (1944), *Caligula* (written in 1938, produced in 1945), *State of Siege* (1948), and *The Just Assassins* (1949). He subsequently made a number of adaptations, among them William Faulkner's *Requiem for a Nun* and Dostoevsky's *The Possessed*. He published as well a number of essays and novels before his death in an automobile accident.

Although Camus disliked being called an existentialist, his thought parallels that of Sartre. In "The Myth of Sisyphus" (1942), Camus states: "A world that can be explained even with bad reasons is a familiar world. But, on the other hand, in a universe suddenly divested of illusions and lights, man feels an alien, a stranger. His exile is without remedy since he is deprived of the memory of a lost home or the hope of a promised land. This divorce between man and his life . . . is properly the feeling of absurdity." He goes on to say that absurdity results from a gap between an inborn human desire for clarity and order, on the one hand, and the irrationality of the world into which people are thrown, on the other. "What is absurd is the confrontation of this irrational and wild longing for clarity whose call echoes in the human heart. . . . The absurd is born of the confrontation between the human need and the unreasonable silence of the world." Camus eventually concludes that although there are no certainties, humans must shape their own destinies through choice and action.

Like Sartre, Camus embodied his ideas in dramatic form. After Caligula discovers that "men die and they are not happy," he becomes obsessed with the need for some absolute and seeks it in unlimited power. He systematically tyrannizes his subjects in an attempt to make them recognize the world's absurdity. Eventually he is assassinated, but "he forces everyone to think. Insecurity, that is what leads to thought," and only through thoughtful evaluation of their existence can people decide what is worth living and dying for. Camus' ideas about the limits of action form the basis of *The Just Assassins*, in which the principal characters are Russian terrorists. When the protagonist fails to throw a bomb into the carriage of the Grand Duke because he would also have killed two small children, he is severely chastised by a fanatical revolutionary and told that the cause is more important than such murders. The protagonist declares that a just cause is defined by just means as well as just ends. Eventually he does kill the Grand Duke but does so openly and insists upon accepting responsibility for his deed.

Sartre and Camus defined the human condition for a postwar generation whose faith in a logical universe had been destroyed. Their influence was more ideological than artistic, for both still employed traditional forms and a dialectical process that led through logical argument to a definite conclusion. Even though they depicted humanity as adrift in an unfriendly universe, they still retained their faith in the capacity of the human mind to find a way out of the chaos.

The influence of Camus and Sartre was strengthened by another postwar event—the Nuremberg war crimes trials in which German officials were tried and convicted for obeying the laws and policies of Hitler's state. Prosecutors argued that there is a higher law—a kind of natural moral law—that takes precedence over human laws. While on the surface this position may seem to contradict the existentialists' rejection of absolutes, it nevertheless insists that each person should decide which laws to obey and which to defy and that private conscience should determine choice and action. Such concepts were to undergird the protest and civil disobedience of the 1960s.

During the 1950s, as a new school of dramatists—the *absurdists*—came to the fore, Sartre and Camus came to seem somewhat romantic in their vision of the individual standing alone against the world, as well as somewhat tainted by their implication that individuals could find values quite independent of external influences, especially since the values they found for themselves seemed remarkably similar to those of humanists throughout the ages. The absurdists—of whom the most important were Samuel Beckett,

Eugène Ionesco, Jean Genet, and Arthur Adamov—tended to accept the existentialist view of the human condition while rejecting the idea that there is any way out of the chaos. As Ionesco put it: "Cut off from his religious, metaphysical, and transcendental roots, man is lost, all his actions become senseless, absurd, useless."

This vision led to several results in drama. Cause-to-effect relationships among incidents were abandoned or reduced to a minimum. Rather than developing linearly, action tended to be circular or spiral, exploring a condition rather than telling a story. Characters tended toward the typical or archetypal rather than the individual. Time and place were generalized. Most of the plays occurred in some symbolic location or in a void cut off from the

FIG. 12.6
Camus' *The Just Assassins* as originally produced at the Théâtre Hébertot in 1949. Directed by Paul Oettly, setting and costumes by Rosnay. (Photo by Bernand.)

concrete world. Time was flexible. Language was for the most part downgraded. Although characters sometimes talked volubly, they usually recognized that they were playing with speech. Spectacle was used symbolically or metaphorically to compensate for the devaluation of language. Distinctions between dramatic forms disappeared. The serious, comic, pathetic, and ironic were intermingled, making clearcut formal categories impossible. The plays were ultimately conceptual, for they sought to project a conviction about the nature of the human condition. Many of these characteristics can be found in varying combinations in earlier drama from symbolism onward. The absurdists were especially attuned to the work of Jarry, Apollinaire, Pirandello, and the surrealists. What distinguished the absurdists from their predecessors was more a matter of vision than conventions. Their subject was human entrapment in an illogical, hostile, impersonal, and indifferent universe. Each of the major absurdists conceived this subject somewhat differently, but all came to the same conclusion: the world is irrational and truth unknowable.

Samuel Beckett (1906–1989) was the first of the absurdists to win international fame. Born and educated in Ireland, he was a friend and translator for James Joyce for a time and eventually settled permanently in France. He began writing around 1930 and published his first novel in 1938. Not until 1950 did he complete his first play, *Waiting for Godot,* which in Roger Blin's production in 1953 became a sensation. It also brought absurdism to international attention. Beckett went on to write *Endgame* (1957), *Krapp's Last Tape* (1958), *Happy Days* (1961), *Play* (1963), and several short plays. As time went by, Beckett's work seemed to become increasingly minimalist. In many ways, Beckett was the quintessential dramatist of the 1950s, a decade under the threat of the Cold War and atomic holocaust. In fact, Beckett's characters often seem to live in

FIG. 12.7
Original Paris production of Beckett's *Waiting for Godot* in 1953, directed by Roger Blin at the Théâtre de Babylone. (Photo by Pic.)

a world that has already undergone the ravages of disaster. His plays are not so much concerned with human beings as social or political creatures as with the nature of human existence itself.

Waiting for Godot is usually considered to be Beckett's best and most characteristic work. The two acts are virtually identical in structure. Vladimir and Estragon improvise diversions to pass the time while they wait in a desolate place for Godot to arrive. In each act, two other men—Pozzo and Lucky—appear briefly. Each act ends with a message, delivered by a boy, saying that Godot cannot come today but may come tomorrow. The action seems to end much where it began. There are no true climaxes or resolutions. Rather than telling a story, the play explores a condition. It depicts

FIG. 12.8

Nell and Nagg, Hamm's senile parents, in Beckett's *Endgame*, directed by Roger Blin. (Photo by Pic.)

humans as derelicts adrift in an impersonal world, improvising dialectical exchanges and other diversions to pass the time while waiting for something or someone who will give meaning or direction to life, and enduring despite disappointment. *Endgame* seems to occur in a still more advanced stage in the world's decay. It occurs in a cell-like room from which one may glimpse the outside world only by climbing a ladder. Of the four characters, only one is able to move about. The senile parents are kept in garbage cans, from which they peek out occasionally to demand attention or to mumble a few remembered phrases. All the characters cling to life even though there seems to be little to hope for. In *Happy Days*, Winnie sits buried up to her waist in the first act and up to her chin in the second in a landscape that is empty and stretches as far as the eye can see. Winnie's condition seems a visualization of the statement in *Waiting for Godot:* "We give birth astride the grave...." But throughout, Winnie remains cheerful, busying herself with her daily routine and declaring this to be another happy day. It may be interpreted as unwillingness to face up to disaster, as a comment on human endurance, or both. All of Beckett's plays depict human beings in much the same way: as isolated, accepting, enduring, hoping, improvising. He was awarded the Nobel Prize for Literature in 1969.

Eugène Ionesco (1912–) was born in Romania but grew up in France. He has said that the inspiration for his first play came from a phrase book he was using to study English. Its simple statements of the most commonplace facts struck his imagination and from them he fashioned *The Bald Soprano* (1950). He went on to write *The Lesson* (1951) and *The Chairs* (1952). But it was not until 1953, when Anouilh wrote glowingly of *Victims of Duty*, that Ionesco began to be recognized as a major new dramatist. His many subsequent works include *Amedée* (1954), *Exit the King* (1962), and *Macbett* (1972). By 1960 Ionesco's work began to appear in major theatres as Barrault presented *Rhinoceros* (1960) and *A Stroll in the Air* (1962) and

the Comédie Française presented *Hunger and Thirst* (1966). In 1970 Ionesco was elected to the French Academy.

Unlike Beckett, Ionesco is concerned with social relationships, typically those of middle-class characters. Two themes run through most of his work: the deadening nature of material-istic, bourgeois society, and the isolation of the individual. Perhaps ultimately his vision differs little from Beckett's but it is couched in more domestic terms. All of the plays seek to discredit clichés, ideologies, and materialism; indirectly they argue the need for each person to live life free from tyranny and without vain hopes. His characters are for the most part victims of a conformity imposed from without; often they are dominated by material objects. Thus, his people tend to be unthinking autom-atons, oblivious to their own mechanical be-havior and speech, just as material objects tend to proliferate and take over the space that should be occupied by people, elements that

FIG. 12.9
Ionesco's *The Chairs* at the Studio des Champs-Elysées in 1956. Directed by Jacques Mauclair, who played the Old Man. (Photo by Pic.)

FIG. 12.10

Ionesco's *Rhinoceros* at the Odéon in 1960. Barrault, second from left, played Berenger and directed the production. (Photo by Pic.)

suggest a strong link between Ionesco and the surrealists. Ionesco was especially antipathetic to the notion that drama should be didactic, and his greatest scorn was reserved for Brecht. To Ionesco, truth means the absence of commitment, either ideologically or aesthetically, for commitment is the first step toward conformity.

Jean Genet (1910–1986) spent most of his years until the late 1940s either in prison or as an itinerant criminal. He began writing around 1940—at first poems, then prose poems (or novels), and finally drama. *The Maids* (in Jouvet's production in 1947), his first work to reach the stage, was followed in 1949 by

Deathwatch (written before *The Maids*). Both plays won considerable critical favor but were generally thought scandalous. Genet then declared his intention of giving up drama but returned in 1957 with *The Balcony* and then went on to write *The Blacks* (1959) and *The Screens* (1961). Though his output was small, he is usually considered one of France's major postwar dramatists.

Genet invests evil with metaphysical significance, seeing in it total negation; any attempt to give it rational explanation merely makes evil an aspect of some structure that has been created to give life a sense of direction. He sees society as being created and given an

FIG. 12.11
Genet's *The Screens,*
directed by Roger
Blin at the Théâtre de
France in 1966.
(Photo by Pic.)

appearance of order through sets of ritualized ceremonies, most of them concerned with dominance-submission and oppressors-oppressed, in which the weaker are treated as valueless or criminal, although in actuality each is equally essential, each category depending on its opposite for its meaning. Thus, what we perceive as reality is merely a set of relationships. Characters may assume roles or put on disguises, but when one is abandoned or removed, another is revealed, a pattern that is endlessly repeatable since there is no objective, fixed reality. Genet also suggested that the theatre is like a hall of mirrors in which humans are "inexorably trapped by an endless progression of images. . . ." Thus, Genet combined subjects usually considered perverse with ritualized action.

The Balcony may be taken as representative. As it opens, a Bishop dressed in ceremonial robes delivers an elevated speech; but it soon becomes clear that this bishop is a gasman and that he is in a brothel where Mme. Irma caters to men's fantasies by letting them dress up and act out their dreams of power and sex (always

intertwined in Genet's world). Everywhere there are mirrors so the participants can watch themselves reflect those they impersonate. Outside the brothel a real revolution is underway, and when the Queen, Bishop, and other authorities are killed, their impersonators in the brothel are asked to take their places until the revolution is put down. The manipulator of the events, the Chief of Police, believing that no one has won real acceptance until someone comes to the brothel to assume that role, anxiously hopes for acknowledgment. His wish is granted when the leader of the revolutionaries arrives; once dressed, however, the man castrates himself, thus symbolically punishing the Chief of Police as an authoritarian figure and himself for wishing to break into the magic circle of power.

Arthur Adamov (1908–1971) was born in Russia but was educated in western Europe. After moving to Paris, he was associated with several of the surrealists, including Artaud. He began to write in the 1920s but then stopped because of a psychological crisis. About 1945 he began to write plays as a way of coping with

FIG. 12.12
Adamov's *Ping Pong,*
produced originally
at the Théâtre des
Noctambules in 1955.
(Photo by Bernand.)

his own anxieties. These early works (by dates of production) include *The Large and the Small Maneuver* (1950), *Parody* (1952), and *Professor Taranne* (1953). They are divided into numerous short tableaux, the characters often have generic (or letter) names, are condemned to eternal failure by their inability to communicate, and are often persecuted by authority figures; time and place are indefinite, as in dreams. They show several influences: the violent imagery of Artaud; the symbols and multiple identities of Strindberg; the nightmarish world and the search motif of expressionism.

A change became evident in Adamov's work with *Ping Pong* (1955), with its fully developed characters and their unquestioning pursuit of false ideals. Although the absurdist

mode is still perceptible, the play tends toward social commentary. Shortly afterwards, Adamov disavowed all of his earlier work, adopted the Brechtian mode, and embraced communism. His first play in the new mode was *Paolo Paoli* (1957), which examined the relationship between a materialistic society and destructiveness as evidenced in the years 1900–1914. One of the best-known of his late plays is *Spring '71* (1961) which traces the rise and suppression of the Paris Commune of 1871. Adamov continued in this Brechtian mode thereafter. Adamov's career is often said to sum up the direction of French drama following World War II: a period dominated by philosophical introspection and personal anxieties followed by social commitment and the demand for change. He bridges the Artaudian and Brechtian modes which were to dominate much of theatrical practice after 1960.

Absurdism was never a conscious movement. The label was popularized by Martin Esslin's *The Theatre of the Absurd* (1961). Because it was not a conscious school, it is difficult to specify those who should be included in it. Still, a number of dramatists of the 1950s shared certain outlooks or techniques with the major absurdists. Of these, Tardieu and Vian were perhaps the best. Jean Tardieu (1903–   ) wrote primarily short plays, a large number of which were produced after 1951. He was constantly exploring new means, and consequently his plays reflect most of the trends of his time. One of his best-known plays, *The Information Window* (1956), evokes a nightmare world when a man, seeking information about train schedules, is forced first to fill out lengthy forms. The attendant then casts the man's horoscope and predicts that he has only a few minutes to live. Disgusted, the man rushes away only to be killed by a train. Boris Vian (1920–1959) wrote his first original play, *Horsebutchering for Everyone,* in 1950. He is best remembered for *The Empire Builders* (1959), which suggests that human beings vainly try to construct a future even as they are hemmed in by the approach of death or disaster.

Other innovative dramatists departed markedly from earlier approaches without accepting the philosophical views of the existentialists or absurdists. One of the most important of these was Jacques Audiberti (1899–1965), whose first play was produced in 1946. Audiberti often resembles Ghelderode in his mixture of the saintly and the blasphemous, fantasy and realism, the serious and the farcical. He had most in common with the absurdists in his defiance of traditional notions of drama and his view of humanity as alienated. His plays include *Quoat-Quoat* (1946), *Black Festival* (1948), *The Hobby* (1956), and *Knight Alone* (1963). In the last of these, the frustrations of an attractive but somehow unlovable man give rise to a monster who ravishes women. The men of the region set out to kill the monster, but unwilling to acknowledge that they are seeking something within man, they kill a goat and name it the monster. Audiberti seems to have in mind the conflict between sexual instinct and purity; inability to reconcile humanity to its natural instincts leads to alienation and disaster. His is a pagan and sensual world in which human beings are still in touch with the supernatural.

The triumph of postwar avant-garde French drama owed much to a few studio theatres, among them Les Noctambules, Théâtre de la Huchette, Théâtre de Babylone, Théâtre de la Bruyère, and Théâtre de Poche, that could mount plays economically and perform them for restricted audiences. It owes perhaps even more to a few directors, perhaps most of all to Roger Blin (1907–1984). Originally a film critic, Blin was closely associated with Artaud, through whom he met Barrault. He did not begin directing until 1949. His fame dates from 1953 when he staged Beckett's *Waiting for Godot.* He subsequently directed most of Beckett's works, as well as Genet's *The Blacks* and *The Screens.* Blin was also Artaud's most devoted disciple, and through his work many of Artaud's ideas were brought into the French theatre.

Other important directors include: Jean-Marie Serreau (1915–1973), who did the first postwar production of Brecht in France, the first production of a play by Adamov, and, in association with Blin, plays by Beckett, Genet, Arrabal, and others, at first working in small theatres but eventually at the Comédie Française and the TNP; Georges Vitaly (1917–   ), who directed plays by Audiberti and headed consecutively the Théâtre de la Huchette and Théâtre de la Bruyère, major homes of avant-garde drama; André Reybaz (1922–   ), who directed the first productions of Ghelderode,

Audiberti, and Vian in Paris before being named director of the Dramatic Center at Tourcoing in 1950; Nicolas Bataille(1926–   ), the first to stage Ionesco; and Michel de Re (1925–   ), known especially for his productions of Tardieu's plays.

In the years between 1940 and 1960, the ferment created by the existentialist, absurdist, and other avant-garde dramatists, along with the adventurous staging of plays by innovative directors, made Paris the major theatrical center of the Western world.

GREAT BRITAIN

Of all European countries, England was perhaps the hardest hit during the early years of the war. Subjected to heavy German bombing, London during 1940–1941 had only one theatre in operation—the Windmill, which specialized in variety entertainment. Except for some lunchtime performances of Shakespeare by Donald Wolfit, regular drama almost completely disappeared in London. But this situation motivated a significant development: the British government for the first time ever provided direct financial support for the arts. In 1940, Parliament appropriated 50,000 pounds to support the Council for the Encouragement of Music and the Arts (CEMA). Originally in cooperation with the Pilgrim Trust and after 1942 alone, CEMA sponsored entertainment for the wartime population. Between 1942 and 1946, it regularly sent theatrical productions (among them *Medea, Twelfth Night,* and *The Importance of Being Earnest)* to the many hostels that had been established throughout Britain to house factory workers.

In 1946, CEMA was reorganized and renamed the Arts Council. To avoid direct government involvement and interference in the arts, the Council was made an independent body with full authority to allocate the funds received from Parliament. It was (and continues to be) composed of representatives of all artistic fields, some appointed by the government and others by organizations representing the various arts. This changed attitude toward subsidies for the arts was further manifested in 1948 when Parliament authorized local governments to allot a portion of their revenue for this purpose. Although not all did so, many local authorities began and continue to subsidize the arts. The central government also gave indirect support to theatres by exempting from the then-heavy entertainment tax those concerned with more than mere diversion.

One of the first organizations to benefit from the change in government policy was the Old Vic. When the war began, the company moved its headquarters to Burnley (and later to Liverpool). In 1940, in association with CEMA, it undertook its first wartime tour. Subsequently it sent productions ranging from Greek and Shakespearean tragedy to Victorian drama and modern plays to all parts of Britain.

In the fall of 1944, the Old Vic returned to London but to the New Theatre, since its own home had been partially bombed. It now entered its period of greatest glory. The management passed from Tyrone Guthrie to Laurence Olivier (1907–1989), Ralph Richardson (1902–1983), and John Burrell, who presented a series of brilliant productions, among them *Richard III, Love for Love, Oedipus Rex, The Critic, Peer Gynt,* and *King Lear.* By 1950, the Old Vic was among the most admired theatre companies in the world. In 1946, the Old Vic established a theatre school under the direction of Michel Saint-Denis, assisted by George Devine and Glen Byam Shaw. Here Saint-Denis applied the concepts (many derived from Copeau) that he had followed in his London Theatre Studio before the war. It soon became the best acting school in the country. Closely allied with it was the Young Vic, directed by George Devine, which performed

FIG. 12.13
Laurence Olivier as
Richard III in the Old
Vic production of
1945. (Photo by John
Vickers.)

for children and youth and bridged the gap between training and professional work. Both were housed in the patched-up Old Vic Theatre. After 1946 the Old Vic also had a second branch. In 1942, CEMA had acquired the Theatre Royal, Bristol (built in 1766 and the oldest surviving theatre building in England), then in danger of being converted into a warehouse. After the war, the Arts Council requested the Old Vic to assume control of the theatre and to establish a company there—the Bristol Old Vic. Thus, by the late 1940s the Old Vic, with its two branches, school, and Young Vic, reached its peak of activity and excellence.

Unfortunately, it soon began to decline. Olivier and Richardson, now much in demand, devoted increasing time to films and other outside engagements. Amidst considerable conflict, they were replaced in 1949. The management passed to Hugh Hunt (1911–   ), who had headed the Bristol Old Vic since its formation. In London, Hunt mounted a number of fine

FIG. 12.14

Zeffirelli's production of *Romeo and Juliet* at the Old Vic in 1959. (Photo by Houston Rogers.)

productions, the best with Michael Redgrave, but new troubles arose when in 1950 the company returned to its home theatre, now repaired. The work of the school and Young Vic was now seriously hampered by lack of space, and in 1952 Saint-Denis and Devine resigned, and both the school and the Young Vic were dissolved. From 1953 to 1958 the Old Vic was headed by Michael Benthall (1919–1974), during which all of Shakespeare's plays except *Pericles* were staged. The company was by now relatively young. Some critics welcomed the change, arguing that it had returned to its true mission which had been subverted during the Guthrie-Olivier-Richardson man-

agements. The company declined rather steadily after 1958, although it momentarily regained some of its popularity in 1960 with Franco Zeffirelli's brawling, lusty production of *Romeo and Juliet*. In 1963, the Old Vic was dissolved and its theatre became the temporary home of the newly established National Theatre.

As the Old Vic declined, the Stratford Festival Company gained prestige. During the war, the seasons at Stratford had continued, though on a much reduced scale. Then, between 1946 and 1948, under the direction of Barry Jackson, truly major changes were made in the festival. Jackson insisted on having control over both the productions and scheduling,

FIG. 12.15
Laurence Olivier (at right) in the 1955 Stratford production of *Titus Andronicus*. (Angus McBean photograph, Harvard Theatre Collection.)

which permitted him to change many of the practices that previously had made it impossible to maintain high standards. Perhaps most important, he staggered openings and used a different director for each play, thus permitting each production to be rehearsed adequately. Furthermore, he was able to make the theatre self-contained with its own workshops and storage spaces for scenery and costumes. He imported young and vigorous personnel, perhaps most notably Peter Brook (1925–   ) as a director and Paul Scofield (1922–   ) as an actor.

Once his reforms were accepted, Jackson resigned. He was replaced in 1949 by Anthony Quayle (1913–1989), joined between 1953 and 1956 by Glen Byam Shaw (1904–   ), who then managed the company alone until 1959. It was during the Quayle-Shaw decade that the festival attained its considerable international reputation, largely because, beginning in 1950, actors, directors, and designers of the first rank began to work there. Among them were John Gielgud, Peggy Ashcroft, Michael Redgrave, Laurence Olivier, Ralph Richardson, Vivien Leigh, Edith Evans, Tyrone Guthrie, and Tanya Moiseiwitsch. For the first time, London's critics attended the performances regularly and began to elevate Stratford above the Old Vic.

In the immediate postwar years, Britain suffered most from the lack of important new dramatists. The most successful writer was Terence Rattigan (1911–1977) with such works as *The Winslow Boy* (1946)—based on an actual case in which a schoolboy is unjustly accused of stealing—and *Separate Tables* (1954)—two linked short plays about women dominated by their mothers. In such plays, all in the realistic mode, Rattigan proved himself one of the best craftsmen of the age, although one without any strong vision. In the 1950s, Graham Greene (1904–   ), already an established novelist, came to the fore with plays—among them *The Living Room* (1953), *The Potting Shed* (1957), and *The Complaisant Lover* (1959)—dealing with the consequences of loss of faith. For the most part, postwar English drama seemed bent on continuing the earlier tradition of drawing-room comedy and realistic drama.

The most promising development appeared to be the rejuvenation of poetic drama by Fry and Eliot. Christopher Fry (1907–   ) had been an actor, director, and librettist before turning to playwriting in 1938. He first attracted wide favorable attention in 1946 with *A Phoenix Too Frequent,* a one-act comedy about a widow whose interest in life is reawakened by a soldier who guards her husband's tomb. He was catapulted to fame in 1949 with *The Lady's Not for Burning,* a story of witchcraft set in the middle ages and made comic through a twentieth-century perspective on superstition. When the heroine, Jennet Jourdemayne, is accused of being a witch and causing a death, Thomas Mendip, a soldier of fortune, weary of life, demands that he be hanged as the murderer. Fry's subsequent plays—among them *Venus Observed* (1950) and *The Dark Is Light Enough* (1954)—were less successful, although Fry continued to be admired for some time.

Poetic drama was strengthened by T. S. Eliot's return to playwriting in 1949 with *The Cocktail Party,* first presented at the Edinburgh Festival and later in London and New York. Ostensibly a comedy of manners about contemporary sophisticates, it concerns the search for spiritual fulfillment in a world lacking in faith. In it, Eliot uses a psychiatrist as the modern equivalent of the priest-confessor. The fusion of worldly surface detail with religious concerns characterized Eliot's subsequent dramas as well—*The Confidential Clerk* (1954) and *The Elder Statesman* (1958). In all of these works Eliot sought enlarged dimensions by recasting Greek plays in modern genres. Thus *The Cocktail Party* disguises Euripides' *Alcestis* as drawing-room comedy, just as *The Confidential Clerk* reshapes Euripides' *Ion* as brittle farce, and *The Elder Statesman* recasts Sophocles' *Oedipus at Colonus* as modern realistic drama. But, as with Fry, Eliot's popularity declined with each play. By 1955 what had seemed a renaissance in poetic drama had faded and the English theatre seemed at a standstill.

This malaise was interrupted in 1956 with

FIG. 12.16 Christopher Fry's *The Lady's Not for Burning* in 1949. At center are Pamela Brown as Jennet and John Gielgud as Thomas. (Angus McBean photograph, Harvard Theatre Collection.)

FIG. 12.17
Eliot's *The Cocktail Party*, produced at the Edinburgh Festival in 1949. Rex Harrison, center, played Sir Henry Harcourt-Reilly. (Photo by Anthony Buckley.)

FIG. 12.18
John Osborne's *Look Back in Anger* in 1956 at the Royal Court Theatre, London. Performers, left to right, are Mary Ure, Alan Bates, Helena Hughs, and Kenneth Haigh as Jimmy Porter. (Photo by Houston Rogers.)

the production of Osborne's *Look Back in Anger* by the English Stage Company (ESC), of which George Devine, who had worked with Saint-Denis at the London Theatre Studio, the Old Vic School, and the Young Vic, was the artistic director. Housed in the Royal Court Theatre, which earlier in the century had been the home of the Barker-Vedrenne company, its goal was to provide a hearing for new English works or foreign plays not yet seen in London. Like Grein in the 1890s, Devine soon found that there was no great backlog of good but unproduced plays. It was in response to an ad in *The Stage* that Osborne submitted *Look Back in Anger,* the production of which in May 1956 (the company's third) came to be looked upon as the turning point in postwar English theatre. The play was not an instant hit, but within a few months it found its audience. It came at a crucial time—when many were voicing discontent with social and political realities wholly ignored by Rattigan, Fry, and Eliot.

John Osborne (1929–   ) began his career as an actor and had written a number of plays before 1956, but none had been produced. Consequently, it was as a wholly unknown writer that he burst on the scene. *Look Back in Anger* is conventionally structured, has only five actors, and takes place in a single room. Thus, it was not technical innovations but point of view that made its mark. The protagonist, Jimmy Porter, has taken advantage of the postwar opportunity for a university education offered by the Labor government to working class students previously excluded from higher education. But upon graduation, Jimmy found himself still excluded from suitable employment because of continuing class prejudice. He is wholly disaffected, seeing Britain as held back by the inertia of all classes. Because his wife Alison comes from the upper-middle class (his primary target), Jimmy rather sadistically baits her throughout the play. He seems to have no positive solution to suggest and contents himself with angry denunciations of moral, social, and political betrayals. Although the play is essentially negative, it captured the growing rebellious mood so well that Jimmy became a symbol of all the "angry young men" of the time.

Of Osborne's plays, *The Entertainer* (1957) is probably second in importance only to *Look Back in Anger*. It suggests England's progressive decline in vigor and values as seen in three generations of the Rice family of entertainers: Billy, the respected figure of the preceding era; Archie, the tasteless failure of today; and Archie's children, one dead at Suez, the others no longer interested in the profession. It is significant not only for its own worth but also because Laurence Olivier played Archie, marking a major transition of England's classically trained actors into the new drama. Thereafter, other major performers followed suit, not only enriching the stage but also bringing new dimensions to the actors.

Osborne wrote regularly after 1956 but never recaptured the appeal of these early plays. He was most successful with *Luther* (1961), in which the great church reformer became another version of the angry young man, and *Inadmissible Evidence* (1965), a moving evocation of the wasted life of an outwardly successful lawyer.

Next to Osborne, the ESC's most important dramatist of the early years was John Arden (1930–   ). His first play to receive full production was *Live Like Pigs* (1958), which develops the conflict between gypsies forced to move into a welfare-state housing project and their narrow-minded neighbors. Like most of Arden's plays, it shows individuals seeking to define their own way of being in the face of a rapacious society. Arden's best-known work is *Sergeant Musgrave's Dance* (1959), in which the title character and his companions arrive in a town with the intention of teaching the residents a lesson about the wastefulness of aggression by taking twenty-five lives for those they were forced to take in the colonies. But Musgrave's idealism is ultimately no match for the complacent society. Arden's theme is developed further in *Armstrong's Last Goodnight* (1964), in which the Scottish chieftain Armstrong seeks to retain his freedom from the strong central government being sought by James I. After 1965, Arden collaborated with Margaretta D'Arcy on plays that typically draw startling new pictures of such heroic figures as Admiral Nelson (*The Hero Rises Up,* 1968) and King Arthur (*The Island of the Mighty,* 1972) to support a Marxist view.

Arnold Wesker (1932–   ) followed a path almost opposite to that taken by Arden, beginning his career as a politically committed writer and moving on to more personal concerns. His first major works were a trilogy—*Chicken Soup With Barley* (1958), *Roots* (1959), and *I'm Talking About Jerusalem* (1960)—centering around the Kahn family as they seek to achieve a socialist ideal. As a whole, the trilogy traces the declining sense of purpose in the socialist movement and suggests that workers have settled for too little and have chosen the wrong paths in seeking a remedy for ills. This theme is pursued further in *Chips With Everything* (1962), in which the military setting exemplifies the English class system. The protagonist argues that the lower classes are systematically deprived of all that is best in entertainment, art, and living conditions.

Shortly after completing *Chips With Everything* Wesker became head of a working-class arts organization, Center 42, which sought to popularize the arts among workers. After a brief burst of energy in 1962, the movement receded to the Roundhouse, a converted railroad shop in northern London, which after 1966 became increasingly a venue for avant-garde productions. Wesker then severed his connections with it.

Wesker's later plays, increasingly psychological and introspective, had little success. He complained that critics had pigeonholed him as a socialist writer and were unwilling to accept him on any other terms. Whatever the reason, Wesker was to be noted primarily for his early work.

Several other dramatists—among them Ann

Jellicoe, N. F. Simpson, Henry Livings, and Bernard Kops—helped to establish the reputation of the ESC as a playwright's theatre, although most later receded in critical estimation. Because the ESC nurtured new British playwrights, it is often forgotten that it mingled the new with classic and foreign works. Among its productions were *Lysistrata, The Country Wife, Major Barbara, The Good Woman of Setzuan, Endgame, The Blacks,* and *Rhinoceros.* As the company's importance was established, its original small subsidy from the Arts Council was gradually increased and augmented by the Greater London Council. By the time Devine retired in 1965, the ESC had become one of the most potent forces in the British theatre.

Another company, the Theatre Workshop, also played a significant role in the English renaissance. This company's guiding spirit was Joan Littlewood (1914–   ), who began her career in Manchester in the 1930s when she and Ewan MacColl ran the politically committed Theatre of Action. In 1945 they founded the Theatre Workshop with the goal of producing plays with contemporary relevance to working-class audiences. At first the company toured in a repertory made up primarily of MacColl's plays, but in 1953 it settled permanently in the east London suburb, Stratford, a working-class district. There it produced *The Good Soldier Schweik, Volpone,* and *Edward II,* a repertory with which it won its first (and considerable) international reputation at the Théâtre des Nations in Paris in 1955 and 1956.

Littlewood's primary goal was to create a theatre to which the working classes would go with the same regularity and enthusiasm as to fun palaces and penny arcades. In a framework of devices borrowed from popular-entertainment forms, she sought to imbed some lasting message or significant content. She wished her productions to be "grand, vulgar, simple, pathetic—but not genteel, not poetical." Her work with actors drew heavily on Stanislavsky to establish through-lines of action and character objectives. She also drew on Brecht in her concern for creating social and political awareness in audiences. Her actors were also encouraged to improve scenes through cooperative improvisation. The company was one of the first postwar groups to work directly with writers in developing scripts.

The Theatre Workshop contributed to the dramatic renaissance primarily through its work with two playwrights—Behan and Delaney. Brendan Behan (1923–1964) spent much of the time between 1939 and 1948 in prison because of his involvement with the Irish Republican Army (IRA), experiences that are evident in his plays. When *The Quare Fellow* was presented by the Theatre Workshop in 1956, it aroused almost as much excitement as *Look Back in Anger* with its cross-section of prison life on the eve of an execution (treated as legalized murder). *The Hostage* (1958), reputed to have begun as an outline fleshed out in Workshop improvisations, is set in a brothel where a young British soldier is held hostage with the threat of death if a convicted IRA agent is executed. The whole scheme is ultimately a wasted gesture, as the soldier is killed in a raid by secret agents and the execution proceeds. Much of the play is taken up with various diversions—primarily music-hall entertainment—used to pass the time while waiting. The play was successful throughout the world. Behan never completed another play, but these two exerted a tonic effect on the theatre.

Shelagh Delaney (1939–   ) made her impact almost entirely with *A Taste of Honey* (1958), said to have been written in reaction against Rattigan's dramas. Its protagonist is a teenage girl who, virtually abandoned by her slatternly mother, has an affair with a black sailor and becomes pregnant. Taken in by a young homosexual man, they establish a familial relationship until the mother reappears and

forces the man to leave. There is no anger; each character accepts life without complaint. Its strength lies in the sense of immediacy and compassion. Perhaps to counteract the somewhat naturalistic style, Littlewood used an onstage jazz combo to provide appropriate music.

Like many of its predecessors, the Theatre Workshop was weakened by its success when it succumbed to the temptation of moving hits to London's West End, thereby beginning the disintegration of what had been a close-knit company. In 1961, Littlewood resigned in protest. She returned in 1963 to stage *Oh, What a Lovely War!*, the Workshop's greatest popular success, an evocation and bitingly satirical commentary on World War I that used numerous music-hall devices. Although the Theatre Workshop continued, it was never again a truly vital force.

In postwar Britain, the dominant production mode was a simplified realism, although Guthrie's penchant for novel interpretation of the classics gained ground as it was taken up by Brook and others. An important innovation came in 1948 at the Edinburgh Festival (established in 1947) when an open stage was erected in a hall for Guthrie's production of the sixteenth-century *Satire of the Three Estates*. Guthrie found this arrangement so satisfying that thereafter he promoted it throughout the English-speaking world.

GERMAN-LANGUAGE THEATRE AND DRAMA

The wartime German theatre followed a path almost opposite to that of Britain, for at first it remained active and prosperous, and then, after 1942, rapidly declined as almost 100 theatre buildings (about 85 percent of the total) were destroyed. In 1944 all theatres were closed, and in 1945 the Ministry of Education and Propaganda, which under Hitler's regime had controlled all cultural activities, was abolished.

At the end of the war, Germany was divided into two parts, but in both, the reestablishment of resident companies was given high priority, and in both theatrical activity resumed almost immediately after peace came. Since the prewar pattern (under which each sizable city subsidized one or more permanent troupes) was revived, the theatre continued to be distributed throughout the country rather than being concentrated in a few cities. Beginning around 1950, West Germany embarked on a vast program of rebuilding. As a result, no other country has so many new theatre complexes. Most of them included a large house for operas, ballets, and traditional drama, and a small theatre for productions not expected to attract large audiences. The large houses were relatively traditional in design, with stages framed by proscenium arches and with complex machinery (revolving, elevator, and rolling platform stages). Most of the stages had aprons that were adjustable in depth, and some had prosceniums that could be varied in width. But for the most part, tradition reigned. The small houses were more flexible, many being completely adjustable in terms of audience-performer spatial relationships. By the 1960s,

FIG. 12.19
Wagner's *Götterdämmerung* as produced at Bayreuth in 1964. (Photo by Festspiele Bayreuth/Wilhelm Rauh. Copyright by Festspielleitung Bayreuth.)

there were about 175 professional theatres in West Germany, of which 120 were publicly funded either by municipal or state governments. East Germany did much less new building, and many of its companies were housed in converted structures. Its new theatres tended to be even more conservative than those in West Germany. In East Germany by the 1960s, there were about 135 companies, all operating in state-owned buildings.

In the subsidized theatres, both East and West, the government, as owner of the facilities, appointed a managing director (*intendant*), who was assisted by a chief *dramaturg*, who recommended plays, provided translations and adaptations, and encouraged high artistic standards. In East Germany, there was as well an advisory board (composed of representatives from each branch of theatrical personnel and the audience) that helped to establish policy and repertory. This arrangement (taken over from Russia) served, through manipulation of the board's composition, to keep theatres within the bounds favored by the government.

In West Germany, the *Volksbühnen*, outlawed by Hitler, were revived after the war. By the late 1960s there were more than 150 local groups with over a half million members. West Germany also had a few privately owned and operated theatres, most of them devoted to long runs of popular works. But for the most part, the German theatre (both East and West) was a subsidized institution that each season presented a diverse program of plays drawn from many periods and styles.

Festivals were also revived after the war and increased in number. In Austria, the Salzburg Festival reopened in 1946 and thereafter produced a host of attractions each summer. In 1960, it inaugurated a new theatre seating 2,158 and with one of the world's largest and best-equipped stages. At Bayreuth, the Wagnerian festival was reestablished in 1951 under the direction of Wieland Wagner

FIG. 12.20

The Theater am Schiffbauerdamm, which after 1954 housed the Berliner Ensemble. (Courtesy Berliner Ensemble.)

(1917–1966), who outraged traditionalists with his simple settings composed primarily of a few set pieces, projections, and atmospheric lighting. For the first time at Bayreuth, the operas were staged in symbolic settings reminiscent of the plans Appia had championed as early as the 1890s, and thus for the first time they were brought into touch with modern theatrical developments.

The best-known of postwar German companies was the Berliner Ensemble, established in 1949 by Bertolt Brecht. After Brecht returned to Germany in 1948, he worked for a time at the Deutsches Theater (Reinhardt's former headquarters, in East Berlin) where in 1949 he staged *Mother Courage* with the assistance of Erich Engel as director, Teo Otto as designer, and Helene Weigel in the title role. Later that year the Berliner Ensemble came into being. Helene Weigel was officially the company's head, Brecht being listed modestly as a member of the artistic advisory board. At first it shared the Deutsches Theater with another troupe. Not until 1954 did it get its own permanent home, the Theater am Schiffbauerdamm (in which *The Threepenny Opera* was originally staged in 1928).

The troupe's first production in its permanent home—*The Caucasian Chalk Circle,* directed by Brecht—was significant in many ways. Its simplified settings epitomized the company's emphasis both on functionalism and beauty. It also catapulted the ensemble to international fame when it was seen (and named the best production of the year) at the Théâtre des Nations in Paris in 1954. By the time Brecht died in 1956, he was recognized as one of the truly important figures of the modern theatre, recognition gained not only through his plays and theoretical writings but through the work of the Berliner Ensemble, which validated his ideas.

The Berliner Ensemble's excellence owed much to its care in staging. Rehearsals for a production lasted from two to six months. A large mirror was placed at the front of the stage so the actors might observe themselves, and photographers took numerous pictures so the company might study what it was doing. (These photographs, 600–800 for a production, were published in *Theaterarbeit*—which in 1952 described the first six productions—and later in the *Modellbücher* of several productions; they served both as records of productions and as inspiration for many who had never seen the troupe perform.) During the first ten years, the troupe staged only about twenty-five plays, most of them by Brecht, but a few works by East German writers. As its prestige grew, the Berliner Ensemble (with about 300 total personnel) became one of East Germany's most heavily subsidized theatres.

The Berliner Ensemble also exerted considerable influence on European scenic design. Under the Nazi regime, a grandiose realism had dominated design. After the war, material shortages curtailed design, but the power of the Brechtian productions helped to convert what had been necessity into choice. The shift is associated especially with Otto and Neher, designers who had worked with Brecht and were attuned to his ideas. Teo Otto (1904–1968) was educated at the Bauhaus and in 1931 became chief designer at the Berlin State Theater but fled to Zurich in 1933. He subsequently worked with many of the great directors of the time, among them Brecht, Gründgens, and Strehler. He was a master of selective decor, using scanty means to create impressive, unostentatious settings. More than any other designer, Otto shaped the new style. Caspar Neher (1897–1962) began his career in 1923 and worked for Jessner and the Berlin Volksbühne before becoming principal designer at the Deutsches Theater from 1934 to 1944. He was a childhood friend and lifetime collaborator of Brecht, working closely with him both before and after the Nazi period. After the war, both Otto and Neher developed a scenic theatricalism, an undisguised manipulation of stage means. They suggested place through a few architectural elements, decorative screens, projections, and lighting. Their settings were both functional and beautiful, often commenting on the drama in the epic manner. During the 1950s, their style came to dominate not only the German stage but the stages of Western Europe.

Many thought that the Berliner Ensemble would disintegrate after Brecht died, but it was held together by persons steeped in Brecht's practices. Brecht's wife, Helene Weigel (1900–1971), and Erich Engel (1891–1966), both of whom had worked with Brecht since the 1920s, provided the principal leadership, assisted by Manfred Wekwerth, Joachim Tenschert, and Peter Palitzsch.

In West Germany, postwar directors, reacting strongly against the Nazi era, sought to avoid political biases and insisted on strictly cultural goals. One of the most influential of these postwar directors, Gustav Gründgens (1899–1963), who had served as intendant of the Berlin National Theater from 1934 to 1944 and was often called Hitler's favorite actor, insisted that his motive in retaining his post under the Nazis had been to preserve theatrical culture in a time of barbarism. In postwar Germany, as intendant of theatres in Dusseldorf and Hamburg from 1947 to 1962, he was considered a major champion of the German theatrical tradition. He was also one of Germany's major actors, being especially noted for his Mephistopheles in Goethe's *Faust*. Thus, despite his Nazi connections, he was one of the most respected and influential of West German directors. Equal or greater prestige was granted Fritz Kortner (1892–1970), who had been the leading expressionist actor of the 1920s and had spent the Nazi years in exile. After returning to Germany in 1949, he worked as a director, principally in Munich and Berlin. He insisted on long rehearsals, total dedication from actors, and detailed attention to characters' emotional lives. Many consider him the most important of postwar German directors. He strongly influenced many young directors, perhaps most notably Peter Stein. Because of his political biases, Erwin Piscator had difficulty reestablishing himself after he returned to West Germany in 1951. Not until 1962, when commitment began to be acceptable once more, was he given a major post—as director of the Freie Volksbühne in West Berlin. Other major postwar directors included Heinz Hilpert, Harry Buchwitz, Hans Schalla, Gunther Rennert, Boleslaw Barlog, Rudolf Sellner, and Karlheinz Stroux.

If the theatre recovered rapidly, drama did not. Those writers who had remained in Germany during the Nazi era were no longer considered acceptable, and only a few major writers who had gone into exile returned. Georg Kaiser's last play, *The Raft of Medusa,* was a considerable hit when produced in 1945, as was Carl Zuckmayer's *The Devil's General* in 1948. Dealing with personal and social morality, these plays helped establish the tone of postwar German drama. The major figure was to be Brecht, whose popularity grew relatively quickly. By 1957–1958 he was surpassed only by Shakespeare, Schiller, and Goethe in numbers of performances in German-language theatres. Nevertheless, Brecht wrote no new works of importance after returning to Germany.

The first new dramatist to attract wide attention was Wolfgang Borchert (1921–1947) whose *The Man Outside* (1947) treated a returning soldier's difficulty in adjusting to civilian life. For several years it was among the most popular works in the repertory. Fritz Höchwalder (1911–1986), an Austrian dramatist, also came to prominence. His most famous play, *The Holy Experiment* (1943), deals with the church's demand in 1767 that the Jesuits abandon their mission in Paraguay; the protagonist is faced with a dilemma—to obey orders he considers immoral or to resist through violence. No doubt it was the moral question that appealed to post-Hitler Germans. Most of Höchwalder's subsequent plays—among them *The Public Prosecutor* (1949), in which the title character prosecutes "enemies of the people" during the French Revolution—deal with historical subjects chosen to illuminate timeless moral issues.

The postwar vacuum in German-language drama was partially filled by two Swiss playwrights, Frisch and Duerrenmatt, both of whom had come to the fore in the 1940s through productions at the Zurich Schauspielhaus, which under Oskar Walterlin (1895–

1961) and Kurt Hirschfeld (1902–1964) was then the leading German-language, anti-Nazi theatre. Max Frisch (1911–   ), trained as an architect, turned to playwriting in 1945 and wrote regularly thereafter. He became best known for *The Great Wall of China* (1946), *Biedermann and the Firebugs* (1958), and *Andorra* (1961). All of his plays suggest that human beings do not learn from the past and are unwilling to accept responsibility for their own errors. Technically, he was strongly influenced by both Wilder and Brecht. *The Great Wall of China* is set in China as the Great Wall is being celebrated as a device that will outmode war. To the celebration come real and fictional persons from many historical periods when developments were thought to make war unthinkable. Frisch's immediate concern was the atomic bomb, which he believed would be as useless as the Great Wall in putting an end to war. *Biedermann and the Firebugs* has a protagonist who takes arsonists into his home in the belief that they will spare him if he does not oppose them, but ultimately he, as well as his family and city, are destroyed. *Andorra* concerns the killing of a supposed Jewish boy as pressures from a neighboring state grow. Years later at an inquiry, most of those involved excuse themselves on the grounds that they thought the boy actually was Jewish, thereby illustrating Frisch's contention that people do not learn from their errors.

Friedrich Duerrenmatt (1921–   ) was a theology student before turning to drama in 1947. Thereafter he wrote regularly, but his international reputation rests primarily on two plays, *The Visit* (1955) and *The Physicists* (1962). *The Visit* deals with the corrupting power of materialism and unwillingness to accept moral responsibility. In it, the richest woman in the world returns to her native and bankrupt village and offers the townspeople $1 billion, half to go to the town and half to be divided among the residents if they will kill the man who seduced and disgraced her when she was a girl. Outraged, the people reject her offer, but gradually they begin to buy on credit things they cannot afford, and eventually they kill the man and rationalize their deed as an act of justice. *The Physicists* deals with the problem of potentially destructive scientific knowledge under political control. Set in an asylum, it focuses on three ostensibly insane men who have assumed the identities of world-famous physicists. Gradually it becomes clear that all are sane, that one has made a discovery with such destructive potential that he has decided to conceal his discovery behind a mask of insanity, and that the other two are agents of world powers seeking to learn his secret. The three eventually agree that all must continue their masquerade for the good of humanity, only to find that the keeper of the asylum has discovered the secret and intends to use it to control the world.

Duerrenmatt sees power as having been so diffused that the bureaucrat has become its principal sign, thereby making it easy for everyone to deny responsibility. Both he and Frisch seem to have in mind the kind of mentality that made Naziism possible—the claim that one did not know about immoral acts or that one was merely following orders, even when no one would acknowledge having originated the orders. This concern for questions of guilt and responsibility and the role of the individual in the body politic was to be the characteristic feature of practically all postwar German-language drama until the late 1960s.

THE UNITED STATES

As elsewhere, wartime America emphasized diversionary entertainment, although occasionally higher levels were achieved in such productions as Margaret Webster's staging of *Othello* with Paul Robeson, Uta Hagen, and

José Ferrer. Following the war, when price controls that had been in effect were removed, production costs skyrocketed. At the beginning of the war, staging a spoken drama required about $25,000 and a musical about $100,000 on Broadway. By 1960 these costs had risen to $150,000 and $600,000. Ticket prices increased, but not proportionately. In 1944 the maximum price at dramas was $3.50 and at musicals $4.85; by 1960 they were $7.15 and $8.60. By 1960, 75 percent of all productions were failing to regain their initial investments. Perhaps not surprisingly, Broadway theatre declined in volume. In 1940 there were about forty-three Broadway theatres; by 1960 there were thirty. New productions reached a low in 1949–1950, when there were fifty-nine. Between 1950 and 1960 the average number was sixty-two. These problems were compounded by the introduction of free entertainment on television, which in some areas began as early as 1945. By 1958 there were 512 stations and over 50 million receivers.

In this atmosphere, musicals still exerted the greatest appeal. It is often said that the musical reached maturity during World War II with *Oklahoma!* (1943) by Oscar Hammerstein II (1895–1960) and Richard Rodgers (1902–1979), which thoroughly integrated all the theatrical elements in ways that helped tell the story. Its success (2,248 performances) and that of subsequent works by Rodgers and Hammerstein—among them *Carousel* (1945), *South Pacific* (1949), and *The King and I* (1951)—established the form that dominated musicals until around 1970. The period between 1943 and 1968 was something of a golden age of musicals, encompassing as it did such works as *Brigadoon* (1947) and *My Fair Lady* (1956) by Alan Jay Lerner and Frederick Loewe; *Guys and Dolls* (1950) and *The Most Happy Fella* (1956) by Frank Loesser; *Gentlemen Prefer Blondes* (1950) and *Funny Girl* (1964) by Jule Styne; *Hello, Dolly* (1964) and *Mame* (1966) by Jerry Herman;

and *West Side Story* (1957) by Leonard Bernstein and Arthur Laurents.

In spoken drama, several prewar dramatists—among them Maxwell Anderson, Clifford Odets, Lillian Hellman, Thornton Wilder, and William Saroyan—continued to be productive. Perhaps most important, O'Neill's works returned to the stage. Although *The Iceman Cometh* failed when first presented in 1946, it was a great success in 1956 (in an off-Broadway theatre) and led to the production of previously unknown works, *Long Day's Journey Into Night* in 1956 and *A Touch of the Poet* in 1957. Thereafter, O'Neill's reputation steadily revived.

Fortunately, two major new dramatists—Williams and Miller—appeared. Tennessee Williams (1911–1983) had his first production in 1940, and his first success with *The Glass Menagerie* (1945). He confirmed his talent with *A Streetcar Named Desire* (1947), *The Rose Tattoo* (1951), *Cat on a Hot Tin Roof* (1954), *Orpheus Descending* (1957), *Sweet Bird of Youth* (1959), and *Night of the Iguana* (1961). But by 1960 Williams was being accused of merely repeating himself, and thereafter both his critical stature and his output declined, though he continued to write throughout his life.

The Glass Menagerie is both one of Williams' most popular and least characteristic works. A "memory" play in which Tom recalls scenes from his youth, it shows his mother Amanda seeking in the midst of poverty to maintain a past gentility and cajole her children into happiness. Most concern is paid to Laura, a shy girl who for comfort turns to her menagerie of glass animals. After one abortive attempt to find Laura a suitor, Tom runs away from home but not from his sense of guilt. This play did not provide any clue to the violence and sex—rape, promiscuity, drug addiction, cannibalism, castration, and homosexuality—which were to figure so prominently in many subsequent plays. It did, however, introduce a recurring

FIG. 12.21
Williams' *A Streetcar Named Desire* in 1947, with Kim Hunter, Marlon Brando, and Jessica Tandy. (Photo by Eileen Darby.)

major theme: "what place can be found in the modern world for 'lost souls'—the artist, the natural man, the aristocrat, the non-conformist?" His protagonists are almost always out of tune with accepted norms: the dull and vulgar; the hypocritical and complacent; or the ugly and violent. Williams' sympathy lay with sensitive and imaginative misfits who use sex, drugs, or alcohol to escape an unfriendly present or to recover a dead past. The action usually shows the protagonist forced to face the truth—often after being subjected to physical or psychological degradation. In a few plays (such as *The Rose Tattoo* and *Cat on a Hot*

Tin Roof) the protagonists are able to come to terms with themselves or society, but most often they end in death, violence, or insanity. Williams used theatrical means imaginatively (especially highly evocative, imagistic language), manipulating them, sometimes quite obviously, to focus attention on the inner truth of character or situation. No American playwright commanded so wide an audience as Williams between 1945 and 1960.

Arthur Miller (1915–   ) began to write plays in the 1930s but did not win success until 1947 with *All My Sons*, a well-made play about a manufacturer whose defective airplane engines have caused the death of many wartime pilots, perhaps even his own son; during the course of the play he comes to recognize that he should have considered all the pilots to be his sons. The moral concerns that inform this and most of Miller's subsequent plays echoes that of postwar German drama.

Death of a Salesman (1949) is usually considered Miller's best work. As in *All My Sons,* the protagonist, Willy Loman, is a businessman, but an unsuccessful one, who believes he is not worthy of love if he is not materially successful. Only when he recognizes that his son loves him, despite his failure, is change possible though never fully realized, since Willy commits suicide so his family will receive his insurance. In this play, Miller abandons the well-made-play form for a flexible structure that permits the action to move freely between past and present. *The Crucible* (1953) explores the hysteria that surrounded and made possible the seventeenth-century Salem witch trials and suggests parallels with Senator Joseph McCarthy's communist witch-hunts, in which accusation was often accepted as guilt.

Miller continued to write—*A View From the Bridge* (1955), *After the Fall* (1964), *The Price* (1968), and several others—but none gained acceptance comparable to that accorded *Death of a Salesman* and *The Crucible.* Through all of the plays runs the same basic theme: the ease with which people are led astray through false

FIG. 12.22
Jo Mielziner's design for Miller's *Death of a Salesman* in 1949. (Courtesy Jo Mielziner; photo by Peter A. Juley and Son.)

(often materialistic or selfish) values, and the capacity of the "common man" to recognize and accept true moral values when faced with the necessity of choosing. While he may see society as the source of false values, Miller makes individuals responsible for their own choices and for correcting society.

Among Williams' and Miller's contemporaries, one of the most successful was William Inge (1913–1973), author of such plays as *Come Back, Little Sheba* (1950), *Picnic* (1953), and *Bus Stop* (1955). Inge's resemblance to Williams stemmed primarily from his predilection for misfit characters and sexual themes, but Inge was a sentimentalist, implying that all problems can be solved merely by facing them. Thus, once characters understand themselves, happiness seems to lie ahead. Other successful dramatists included Robert Anderson (1917–) with *Tea and Sympathy* (1953), about the tensions in a boys' school after one is accused of homosexuality, and *I Never Sang for My Father* (1968), concerning the relationship between a father and son, and Paddy Chayefsky (1923–1981) with *Middle of the Night* (1956), about the relationship between a young woman and an

FIG. 12.23
Ralph Meeker and Janice Rule (at center) in Inge's *Picnic* in 1953. (Courtesy Alfredo Valente.)

aging manufacturer, and *The Tenth Man* (1959) which tells in comic terms much the same story as *The Dybbuk*. Until the late 1950s, American drama seemed dynamic, but by 1960 it was losing its vigor.

The dominant production style in the American theatre from the late 1940s until the 1960s was a theatricalized realism compounded of acting that emphasized intense psychological truth and visual elements that eliminated nonessentials but retained realistic elements. It combined near-naturalism in performance with stylization in settings. This mode was popularized by director Elia Kazan and designer Jo Mielziner through such productions as *A Streetcar Named Desire* in 1947 and *Death of a Salesman* in 1949. As this approach gained wide acceptance in the 1950s, settings increasingly moved away from full-stage representation to a few pieces that suggested the whole. The style of acting derived from Stanislavsky and the Group Theatre as embodied in the productions of Kazan, and to a lesser extent those of Harold Clurman and Robert Lewis (1909–). Above all, it was associated with the Actors Studio, founded in 1947 by Kazan, Lewis, and Cheryl Crawford (though Lee Strasberg became the dominant figure). The goal of the studio was to develop talent in isolation from public criticism by freeing actors from psychological inhibitions and by encouraging imagination through "emotion memory," improvisation, and other exercises based on Stanislavsky. It apparently placed primary emphasis on the actor's self-understanding, and consequently was often accused of encouraging self-indulgence at the expense of technical skill. Much of the public's conception of the Actors Studio was based on the performances of Marlon Brando (1924–), who first gained recognition with his performance as Stanley Kowalski in *A Streetcar Named Desire*. The novelty of serious acting based on substandard speech, untidy dress, and boorish behavior captured the public fancy. Kazan's subsequent productions also directed attention to the Studio and its methods.

The Actors Studio eventually included a number of programs. In 1956 it added a Playwrights Unit, in 1960 a Directors Unit, and in 1962 a Production Unit. For a time it staged its own productions, among them O'Neill's *Strange Interlude*. But by the early 1960s the American theatre was changing and the psychological realism favored by the Studio began to seem too limiting. Thereafter its influence waned somewhat, although the Studio continued to command a devoted following. Nevertheless, during the 1950s it was perhaps the most potent force in the American theatre.

As in France, in the United States there was concern about diversifying the theatre. Perhaps the most important result was the emergence of off-Broadway, descendant of the independent and little theatre movements. Like their predecessors, off-Broadway producers rented quarters removed from the midtown theatrical center so that production and ticket costs could be kept low. Since many operated in buildings never intended for theatrical purposes, experimentation with such audience-actor spatial arrangements as arena and thrust stages were inevitable. Perhaps most important, they could be sustained by a limited audience interested in a more eclectic repertory than that offered by Broadway. These theatres began to appear during but especially following the war. By 1949 they had become sufficiently numerous to motivate formation of the League of Off-Broadway Theatres to deal with common problems.

A major turn in the critical fortunes of off-Broadway came in 1952 when Williams' *Summer and Smoke,* a failure on Broadway, achieved enormous success at the Circle in the Square. Not only did this production bring José Quintero (1924–) to prominence as a director and raise Geraldine Page (1924–1987) to stardom, it suggested that some off-Broadway theatres might be superior to their commercial rivals. It also drew attention to the fact that off-Broadway was outdistancing Broadway in the number and diversity of its offerings.

During the 1950s the most influential of the off-Broadway theatres were the Circle in the Square and the Phoenix Theatre. The Circle in the Square was opened in 1951 by Quintero and Theodore Mann (1924–   ). As a former nightclub, the theatre's actor-audience relationship was entirely flexible, although spectators usually sat around three sides of a rectangular playing area. Here such performers as Page, Jason Robards, Jr. (1922–   ), George C. Scott (1927–   ), and Colleen Dewhurst (1926–   ) came to prominence. After his triumph with *The Iceman Cometh* in 1956, Quintero was asked to direct the Broadway production of *Long Day's Journey Into Night*. Its cumulative record made the Circle in the Square one of the most respected theatres of the 1950s.

The Phoenix Theatre was founded in 1953 by Norris Houghton (1909–   ) and T. Edward Hambleton (1911–   ). In an out-of-the-way but well-equipped proscenium theatre seating 1,172, the Phoenix presented a diverse program of plays by such authors as Aristophanes, Shakespeare, Turgenev, Ibsen, Shaw, and Pirandello, as well as the first American productions of works by Ionesco and several other European dramatists. In seeking to use a different director for each production, it turned to Tyrone Guthrie, Michael Redgrave, John Houseman, and others; it also frequently attracted well-known actors, including Joan Plowright, Robert Ryan, and Siobhan McKenna. Beginning in the late 1950s, the Phoenix employed a permanent acting company, which under the direction of Stuart Vaughan presented a series of plays each season.

For the most part, off-Broadway theatres in the 1950s were little concerned with innovative staging (except for the use of arena or thrust stages). They were most concerned with repertory. Thus, although their goal was essentially artistic, their production style differed little from Broadway's.

Outside of New York, the goal of decentralization made limited progress and depended almost wholly on the work of a few dedicated individuals. Among the first to attract wide attention was Margo Jones (1913–1955), who in 1947 established in Dallas her Theatre 47 (the name changed with the year), where she mounted a series of varied plays each season. After her death, the venture was kept alive until 1959. Other pioneering regional companies included the Alley Theatre, founded in Houston in 1947 by Nina Vance (1913–1979); the Arena Stage, founded in Washington, D.C., in 1949 by Zelda Fichandler (1924–   ), Thomas C. Fichandler, and Edward Mangum; and the Actors Workshop, founded in San Francisco in 1952 by Jules Irving (1924–1979) and Herbert Blau (1926–   ). A turning point came in 1959 when the Ford Foundation began to make large grants to those troupes that seemed most likely to survive and grow. Thus, even though the accomplishments of the 1950s were not great, the foundations were laid for more ambitious projects in the 1960s.

Summer festivals also added diversity. At Stratford, Ontario, a Shakespeare Festival was inaugurated in 1953. Here Tyrone Guthrie, the first artistic director, introduced the kind of open stage he had originally used in Edinburgh. This festival soon developed into a major cultural institution. In 1955 an American Shakespeare Festival was inaugurated in Stratford, Connecticut, but was never able to achieve stability and discontinued productions in 1982. In 1954, Joseph Papp created the New York Shakespeare Festival, which was to develop into New York's most prolific and diverse theatrical organization. Other enduring Shakespeare festivals were held annually in San

Diego, Ashland (Oregon), and elsewhere. Summer theatres, most of them in resort areas, also increased in numbers, as did amateur community theatres. In addition, by 1960 approximately 1,500 colleges and universities were offering courses in theatre and presenting plays. Thus, various groups helped to compensate for the concentration of professional theatre in New York. Nevertheless, between 1940 and 1960, for most Americans theatre meant Broadway. Unlike European countries, the United States, despite its vast resources, provided no government support for the arts.

RUSSIA, ITALY, AND SPAIN

Activities elsewhere between 1940 and 1960 can be summarized briefly. In wartime Russia, troupes were dispatched throughout the country to perform for members of the armed forces and for workers. Of the approximately 950 theatres at the beginning of the war, 450 were destroyed during the conflict. After the war the number decreased further as the government phased out most subsidies. By the time of Stalin's death in 1953 only about 250 were left.

Because censorship was relaxed during the conflict, many thought the end of the war would bring further freedom. Instead, political control was strengthened in 1949 when a party-appointed administrative director was placed in complete charge of each theatre. Many plays, among them Constantin Simonov's *Under the Chestnut Trees of Prague* (1945), sought to justify Soviet hegemony over Eastern Europe. Socialist realism was imposed on Eastern European countries as well. As the Cold War developed, most Western plays were removed from the repertory, and numerous anti-American plays, such as Simonov's *Alien Shadow* (1949) and Nikolai Pogodin's *The Missouri Waltz* (1950), were added. Stalin's role in the triumph of Communism was also greatly exaggerated in a number of plays, among them

Vsevolod Vishnevsky's *1919—The Unforgettable Year* (1949) and A. Stein's *Prologue* (1952). Following Stalin's death in 1953, a number of "thaw" plays were written, in which corruption in high places was the common theme. Among them, Viktor Rozov's (1913–   ) *Good Luck!* (1954) is representative. Krushchev's denunciation of Stalin in 1956 promised more significant changes, but the Hungarian revolt and its suppression in that year made theatrical personnel cautious. Censorship prior to production lessened, but restraints continued to be applied, though less conspicuously, through the governing councils of theatres, most of whose members had Communist party approval.

In Italy, where there were few permanent theatre companies, the war brought few changes. After the war, attempts were made to create a more stable theatre. The most important result came in 1947 with the foundation of the Piccolo Teatro in Milan by Giorgio Strehler (1921–   ) and Paolo Grassi (1919–1981), the first dramatic company in Italy to receive a government subsidy. It was a self-contained organization with its own company of actors, directors, and designers, plus technical and maintenance personnel. It also operated a school for actors and theatre personnel. Strehler directed about three-quarters of the productions, but imported a number of outstanding directors from other countries to diversify the company's work. The repertory originally ranged through European classical and modern works. After 1956, Strehler was heavily influenced by Brecht, many of whose plays he staged both in Italy and elsewhere. His principal designer, Luciano Damiani (1923–   ), was also much influenced by Brecht. Another of Strehler's favorite dramatists was Shakespeare, several of whose plays he staged in a Brechtian mode. Perhaps Strehler's most popular production was Goldoni's *Servant of Two Masters,* in which *commedia dell'arte* conventions were exploited. By 1960 the Piccolo Teatro was considered not only Italy's finest troupe but also one of the world's best.

In the postwar period, two Italian playwrights—Betti and de Filippo—achieved international recognition. Ugo Betti (1892–1953) began writing in 1927 but his major works came after the war: *Corruption in the Palace of Justice* (1948), *The Queen and the Rebels* (1951), and *The Burnt Flower Bed* (1953). All of Betti's plays treat crises of conscience among the powerful, who usually have gained their positions through party or government influence. In the beginning his protagonists usually set themselves up as arbiters of morality (his representative heroes are judges, like Betti himself), but gradually they are forced to reassess their values. No doubt it was his preoccupation with guilt and responsibility that won Betti his wide following throughout the world. His plays are traditional in structure and ultimately came to seem more derivative than original.

Eduardo de Filippo (1900–1984) was born into a Neapolitan theatrical family; with its members, he ran a troupe from the late 1920s until 1946. He began writing around 1930. Among his numerous works, some of the best are *Naples' Millionaires* (1946), *Filumena* (1955), and *Saturday, Sunday, and Monday* (1959). Most of his plays are firmly rooted in the Neapolitan background, mingling pathos and humor with closely observed local color, and are written in the dialect of the region. But his characters, who manage to survive by adapting to circumstances, are universal in their concern with the pressures of poverty, disease, war, and strained family relationships. *Naples' Millionaires* may be taken as typical: upon his return from a wartime prison camp, a man discovers that his family has prospered through prostitution and black-marketeering; after his initial shock and protestations, he settles down to enjoy the fruits of wealth. The warmth, humor, and deep human understanding of flawed humanity

as seen in his many plays and film scripts endeared de Filippo to audiences both at home and abroad.

In Spain, theatrical activity had been seriously interrupted during the civil war of the 1930s and was subsequently kept isolated from the rest of the world by heavy censorship which permitted nothing likely to conflict with "the fundamental principle of the State." Most of the censors were priests and, since there were no fixed guidelines, they often made capricious or contradictory decisions. Nevertheless, around 1950 there was a revival in Spanish drama. The turning point is usually dated from the production of *The Story of a Stairway* by Antonio Buero Vallejo (1916–) in 1949, the first time after the civil war that a new play was judged worthy of the prestigious Lope de Vega Prize. The drama traces the friendships, conflicts, and marriages over a period of twenty-eight years of four lower-class families who live on the same floor of an apartment house; most of all, it creates a sense of tragic waste as the illusions and hopes of youth are eroded. Until 1958 Buero Vallejo wrote about contemporary subjects and primarily in the realistic vein, although occasionally, as in *The Weaver of Dreams* (1952), he made forays into fantasy and symbolism. He then turned to historical subjects, often inspired by paintings. Of these later works, one of the best is *The Concert at Saint Ovide* (1962), based on an eighteenth-century engraving of the Parisian fair of St. Ovide where untrained, blind musicians were made to play for a public who came to be amused by this ridiculous spectacle. Buero Vallejo turns this into a parable about the human struggle to overcome the forces of darkness, cruelty, and prejudice.

Alfonso Sastre (1926–) made his impact as much through his essays about the theatre as through his dramas. He objected to Spain's propensity for escapist drama even as the world moves toward destruction and the working classes cry out for improved living conditions. *The Condemned Squad* (1953) is an antiwar play in which a squad of killers come to accept their guilt; it also implies that people in general must recognize their responsibility for the kind of world in which they live. Because of his concern for such social, moral, and political issues, many of Sastre's plays could not pass censorship. Among the best of these are *Gored* (1960) and *In the Net* (1961).

During the 1950s, Spain gradually became more aware of the drama of other countries. As censorship eased somewhat, works by such writers as Williams, Wilder, O'Neill, Claudel, Anouilh, and Montherlant began to be seen in the theatre, but the Spanish theatre remained conservative until well after 1960.

INTERNATIONAL ORGANIZATIONS

One other aspect of the postwar period—the formation of international organizations—is significant. Most of these organizations were affiliated with the United Nations and its subsidiaries, especially the United Nations Educational, Scientific, and Cultural Organization (UNESCO), which in 1947 sponsored the International Theatre Institute (ITI). Under ITI, each member country maintains its own center which undertakes activities of four kinds: collection and dissemination of information; publication; exchange of persons; and exchange of companies. The ITI also holds congresses every four years. Beginning in 1954 it sponsored the Théâtre des Nations in Paris, which annually presented a season of plays drawn from all over the world and offered prizes to the best productions and companies. The ITI assisted in the creation of other organizations, among them the International Association of Theatre Technicians, the International Association of Theatre Critics, and the International Federation for Theatre Research. Together these groups did much to promote greater understanding and cooperation among theatrical personnel throughout the world.

FROM ABSURDITY TO ANGER

During the war, the theatre in most countries struggled to survive and accepted as its mission to provide diversion from anxieties or to build national morale. Following the war, the primary task became to rebuild the theatre, and in pursuing this task the governments of most countries assisted, seeking at the same time to make the theatre more readily accessible to their populaces. As the theatre recovered, new directions gradually became apparent. At first, the most prominent of the innovative strands was absurdism, which in retrospect seems the most characteristic response of the 1950s, when the Cold War and the fear of atomic catastrophe created the sense of a hostile universe in which human existence itself was threatened. Action came to seem useless, even when possible. By the late 1950s, however, the mood began to shift, as anger at the state of the world grew. The advice of Sartre and Camus which the absurdists had ignored—not to be paralyzed by the world's absurdity but to establish one's own standards and to act forcefully on them—came to the surface once more. Passive contemplation of the human condition was replaced by the desire to bring about change. Martin Luther King, Jr., and others would demonstrate that passionate commitment and group effort can make people active instruments rather than passive victims. Thus, although absurdity and anger existed simultaneously during the 1950s, their results were more nearly linear—moving from absurdity to anger. The ultimate effect on the theatre would be more far-reaching than could be foreseen in 1960.

Chapter 13

Toward Commitment

*Theatre
in the 1960s*

In general, the 1960s was a time of prosperity and expansion for the theatre. In many places, the theatre, seemingly content with the status quo, underwent little change. France and England tended to strengthen the foundations they had built in the 1950s, primarily through increased government support. In other places, there were significant innovations. In Eastern Europe, especially Poland and Czechoslovakia, theatre found new creative energy as it broke with the socialist realism imposed during the Stalinist years, and in Germany documentary drama brought renewed vitality. In the United States, the primary innovations came from the establishment of off-off-Broadway and regional theatres. It was, nevertheless, a period during which social awareness steadily grew. The launching of Sputnik by the Soviets in 1957 not only catapulted the world into the space age, it aroused both new enthusiasm for and fear of technology; it also made Americans take stock, since they had long viewed the Soviets as technologically backward. Questioning soon passed over into other areas. Civil rights and involvement in Vietnam became the focus of discontent, stimulating acts of civil disobedience and other forms of protest. This American unrest, in turn, served as stimulus for European dissidence. The pressures built steadily throughout the 1960s, but not until 1968 did they come to a point of near-rebellion almost everywhere.

THE SOVIET UNION

In the Soviet Union the theatre remained conservative throughout the 1960s, although restrictions had loosened after Krushchev's denunciation of Stalin in 1956. Playwrights began to depart somewhat from socialist realism and to suggest that true communist ideals had been distorted under Stalin. In *The*

Factory Girl (1956), Alexander Volodin (1919–) treats the unjust firing of a girl from and eventual reinstatement to a factory job. In this and other plays—among them *The Elder Sister* (1961) and *The Appointment* (1963)—Volodin treats characters seeking to find personal fulfillment in the face of an impersonal system. Alexander Pogodin, for a long time one of the most orthodox of Soviet playwrights, departed drastically from his usual conformity in *Sonnet of Petrarch* (1957), which shows a middle-aged married man, after being harassed by a Party official because he has fallen in love with a young girl, accusing the system of trying to regulate everything, including love; at the end, the man seems to be victorious and headed for happiness. A new direction is probably best illustrated by the work of Viktor Rozov (1913–), one of Meyerhold's students who turned to playwriting about 1949. His plays—among them *Alive Forever* (1956), *The Reunion* (1967), and *From Night to Noon* (1969)—stress the necessity of coming to terms with one's life and

FIG. 13.1
Pogodin's *The Sonnet of Petrarch* at the Mayakovsky Theatre in 1957, directed by Y. Zotova. (From Komissarzhevsky, *Moscow Theatres*, 1959.)

placing personal integrity and fulfillment above success gained through adherence to Party ideology.

Nevertheless, playwrights did not give up reflecting current official policy. Constantin Simonov's *The Fourth* (1963) defends East-West coexistence as necessary in an atomic age, just as Alexander Korniechuk's *Over the Dneiper* (1963) reflects the demand for higher agricultural productivity. As under Stalin, the plays end on an optimistic note, either in reconciliation or pointing toward a future solution. The plays differ from their predecessors primarily in greater independence of thought. Still, by Western standards the plays seem overly didactic.

Foreign works also returned to the repertory, although they were primarily ones with political implications or ones illustrating Western decadence. In 1960, a play by Brecht was given for the first time, and soon works by Miller, Osborne, and Williams were being performed frequently. Absurdist drama was virtually ignored.

A number of Soviet dramatists and directors formerly out of favor were "rehabilitated" as well. Mayakovsky's plays were revived for the first time since the early 1930s by Valentin Pluchek at the Moscow Theatre of Satire in a style not unlike that of Meyerhold's original stagings. Soon afterwards, the Theatre of the Revolution was renamed the Mayakovsky Theatre. Meyerhold's significance also began to be acknowledged; during the 1960s a complete edition of his writings was issued, and exhibits showing his and Tairov's work were organized. Vakhtangov's prestige also rose, perhaps because his methods seemed to offer a compromise between the extremes of realism and formalism. In 1962, on the occasion of its fortieth anniversary, Vakhtangov's *Turandot* was faithfully recreated. In addition, directors who had been associated with Vakhtangov—Alexei Popov, Yuri Zavadsky, Reuben Simonov, and Nikolai Akimov—headed major theatres and helped to reassert his influence. Several survivors from the prewar era of experimentation also revived some of their own earlier productions. Okhlopkov revived Pogodin's *Aristocrats* with the audience surrounding the playing area as in the early 1930s. There was as well a trend away from doctrinaire interpretations of the classics. A considerable furore was created in 1965 when Chekhov's *The Cherry Orchard* was presented without the Soviet emphases on decaying aristocracy and the promise of future progress. Visual style also moved away from detailed representationalism

FIG. 13.2
Setting by Nisson Chifrine for a dramatization of a novel by Sholokhov at the Central Theatre of the Soviet Army, Moscow, in 1957. (From *Scene Design Throughout the World Since 1950.*)

toward suggestion or simplified realism. In place of a full stage setting for each locale, one fixed background, representative of the play's overall mood, was supplemented with small set pieces as needed.

The lot of theatrical personnel improved after 1956 with the abandonment of the policy of fixed companies, under which since the 1930s the wages and ranks of actors had been set and under which all personnel changes had to be approved by a centralized authority. The new regulations permitted transfers of personnel among troupes and lessened a major source of unhappiness—the difficulty of younger actors to rise in rank or try new roles because of the privileges of older players. All these changes served primarily to liberalize rather than to fundamentally change the Soviet theatre.

By the late 1960s there were about five hundred troupes, as well as about a hundred that played exclusively for children and youth. The Moscow Art Theatre (MAT) continued to be treated as the flagship theatre, receiving the highest subsidy and paying the highest salaries. Nevertheless, many had come to consider it Russia's most old-fashioned company. In Moscow, the Maly Theatre ranked only slightly lower than the Moscow Art Theatre and was equally conservative. Among Moscow's twenty other theatres, some of the most adventurous were the Vakhtangov, Mayakovsky, Mossoviet, Moscow Theatre of Satire, and the Central Theatre of the Soviet Army. In Leningrad, the Pushkin Theatre occupied a position comparable to that of the Maly in Moscow. The best theatre in Leningrad after 1956 was the Gorky, under the direction of Georgi Tovstonogov (1915–1989), with its mixed repertory of Russian classics, foreign, and Soviet plays. Rather than radically reinterpreting scripts, Tovstonogov seemed to find in them new values which he emphasized through a lavish pictorialism.

Two Moscow companies—the Contempo-rary and the Taganka—were the major champions of change. The Contemporary Theatre, founded in 1957, was the first new troupe to be authorized since the 1930s. Headed by Oleg Efremov (1927–   ), its personnel was drawn primarily from young actors in various theatres and students from the Moscow Art Theatre's school. Until 1961 it had no home of its own. Its work was Stanislavsky-based, while seeking to avoid the heavy-handed realism into which the MAT had fallen. It made its impact primarily by presenting plays relevant to post-thaw Russia, especially as depicted in the plays of Rozov and Volodin, who served as company dramatists. Official approval was validated in 1972 when Efremov was made artistic director of the Moscow Art Theatre.

In 1964, Yuri Lyubimov (1917–   ), then a teacher at the Shchukin Theatre Institute, became head of the Moscow Theatre of Drama and Comedy (usually called the Taganka after the square where it is located). This company soon became Russia's most adventurous troupe with its presentational style, which made use of mime, masks, puppets, direct address to the audience, and projections. Its production of Gorky's *Mother* was highly praised for its crowd scenes and brilliant use of about twenty soldiers: sometimes as living scenery (such as surrounding characters to create a prison), as a scene-changing device (sweeping a disorderly crowd offstage), or as themselves. In 1969, Lyubimov's production of *Tartuffe* was publicly attacked, and in 1970 Voznesenski's *Save Your Face* was closed for "ideological inadequacy." In that year, the Taganka was the only theatre singled out for censure at the All-Union Society of Theatre Workers. During the 1960s, Lyubimov was certainly the most adventurous, controversial, and ideologically questioning of Soviet directors.

Another director often in trouble with the authorities and moved frequently was Anatoly

Efros (1925–1987). From 1963 to 1967 he was artistic director of the Lenin Komsomol Theatre, but was removed for "ideological deficiencies"—emphasizing his individual interpretations of scripts over collective ideology. He also developed a highly physical performance style. Between 1967 and 1985 he worked most often with the Maloi Bronnoi Theatre. In 1967, his production of *The Three Sisters* was so controversial, because he played up the sexual relationships and treated ironically the prophecies of a glorious future for Russia, that it was removed from the repertory. Such arbitrary actions served as reminders that the theatre was still subordinate to the state. Nevertheless, officials seemed more interested in controlling than forbidding such work. Despite its gains, the Soviet theatre remained one of the most conservative in the world during the 1960s.

CZECHOSLOVAKIA

Following World War II, most of Eastern Europe came under Soviet domination and its demand for socialist realism. After 1956, however, the theatre in most of these countries quickly became far more adventurous than that in Russia. Of these Eastern European countries, two—Czechoslovakia and Poland—were to exert the greatest influence outside their own borders.

In Czechoslovakia in the 1960s there were about a hundred theatre groups. The most prestigious of all the companies was the Prague National Theatre, in part because its chief designer was Josef Svoboda (1920–   ), the world's best-known scenographer during the 1960s. After graduating from the School of Applied Arts, Svoboda worked as a designer at the Fifth of May Opera House before moving to the Prague National Theatre, where he became head of design in 1950. Restricted by

socialist realism until 1956, thereafter he began to experiment in collaboration with the Prague Institute of Scenography, founded in 1957. This Institute, headed by Miroslav Kouril (who before the war had worked with E. F. Burian) had four divisions, each devoted to a different range of problems: theory and history, theatrical space, sound and light, and stage means. Its experiments with new materials, equipment, and techniques was to make Czechoslovakia preeminent in theatre technology.

The crucial change in Svoboda's career came in 1958 when, in collaboration with the director Alfred Radok, he worked on two projects: *Polyekran* and *Laterna Magika*. Polyekran (multiple screens) used filmed images projected onto screens of varying sizes and hung at varying distances from the audience. The projected images (some still, others moving at differing rates, some closeup, others distant) were intended to overcome the "visual paralysis" of traditional theatre by giving the spectator a choice of what to watch. Laterna Magika was also begun in 1958. It combined live actors with moving filmed images. One sequence showed a skater on film and then the same live skater seeming to come out of the film onto the stage. It was first shown at the Brussels World Fair in 1958, where it became the major attraction. Svoboda soon decided that Laterna Magika was not suited to the stage since the inflexible filmed portion enslaved the live actors. In 1959 Svoboda began to adapt this earlier work to the stage. The first attempt, for Josef Topol's *Their Day,* used nine screens mounted on overhead tracks coordinated with movable stage wagons carrying plastic elements. Most scenes were accompanied by still projections of visual images (some closeups, others distant views, all suggesting places, associations, or moods); other scenes incorporated moving pictures.

Throughout the 1960s, Svoboda continued these experiments. He worked with extremely diverse projection surfaces: lengths of rope hung side by side, fishnet, wire, plastic. In 1966, for an adaptation of Gorky's novel, *The Last Ones,* staged by Alfred Radok, three live scenes were played on stage simultaneously at varying depths, while other scenes were shown on screens, thus creating a collage of a disintegrating society.

Although Svoboda became best-known for such multimedia designs, they make up only a small portion of his work. Like Craig, he was seeking to create a completely flexible stage. Consequently, in addition to projected images, he experimented with making three-dimensional elements mobile and quickly adjustable. Since stage machinery, such as the revolving stage, was too inflexible, he replaced it with treadmills, platforms that could move vertically, horizontally, or diagonally, and screens or panels that could be shifted in any direction

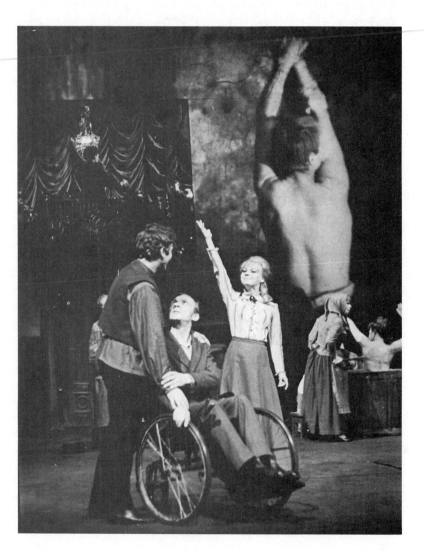

FIG. 13.3
Adaptation of Gorky's novel *The Last Ones* at the Prague National Theatre in 1966. Designed by Svoboda, directed by Alfred Radok. (Photo copyright by Jaromír Svoboda.)

without any pause in the play's action. This dynamicism is perhaps seen at its best in Svoboda's sets (in 1963) for *Romeo and Juliet*. Even in sets that did not make use of dynamic elements or innovative materials, he found some means of making them seem original. For *Oedipus Rex,* broad steps extended upward from the front of the stage out of sight overhead. Overall, Svoboda was very eclectic, believing that style is merely the solution of the problem posed by a production. He did not consider himself committed to any approach and, although he became known for innovative uses of technology, he insisted that one must be wary of letting technology become an end rather than a means. Beginning in the 1960s, Svoboda was (and continued to be thereafter) in demand as a designer throughout the world. No designer was so well-known internationally.

Despite his diversity, Svoboda's influence was probably greatest in multimedia, which was especially popular during the 1960s, as electronic means assumed ever-increasing importance. The reasons for this development were several. First, wartime and space research led to significant new technology which could be adapted to stage needs. Second, the rapid development of television played a key role in changing audience perception and sensibility. It speeded the rate at which stimuli are absorbed, and it conditioned audiences to expect instant transformations in time and place. Third, as costs escalated, the need for more economical means increased. For these and other reasons, including the influence of Brecht and Artaud, the three-dimensionality on which Appia and Craig had insisted came to seem as outmoded as nineteenth-century painted drops had to those earlier reformers. Con-

FIG. 13.4
Svoboda's setting for Shakespeare's *Romeo and Juliet* at the Prague National Theatre, directed by Otomar Krejča, in 1963. (Photo copyright by Jaromír Svoboda.)

FIG. 13.5
Svoboda's setting for *The Insect Comedy* by Čapek in 1965 at the Prague National Theatre. (Photo copyright by Jaromír Svoboda.)

sequently, settings began to depend more on electronic means than on constructed sets. A minimalist approach to furniture, properties, and set pieces came to be accepted as realistic representation, and instant transferability became a major demand. In these developments, Svoboda played a major role, although he was by no means alone.

During the 1960s, some of the most influential of Czechoslovakia's theatres were small studios. Theatre on the Balustrade, subsidized by the city of Prague, operated in a house seating only two hundred. It was headed from 1962 to 1969 by Jan Grossman, the principal champion of absurdist drama, with Václav Havel (1936–), the leading postwar Czech dramatist, as resident playwright. *The Garden Party* (1963), which turns on a struggle between the Department of Inauguration and the Department of Liquidation, introduced the traits for which Havel's drama is best-known— biting political satire, grotesque humor, and nightmarish atmosphere, all directed against attempts to bureaucratize society. In *The Memorandum* (1965), usually considered Havel's best work, the government has prescribed a new language intended to be so precise that there can be no misunderstandings. But when the first memorandum arrives, no one can translate it. Much of the remainder of the play concerns the opportunistic struggle for power precipitated by this impasse. In addition to new works, the Balustrade was also noted for productions of *Ubu Roi,* an adaptation of Kafka's *The Trial,* and similar works. It shared its theatre with the mime company headed by Ladislav Fialka, who, with a company of ten, staged silent plays of considerable complexity. This company developed an international following through tours in Europe and America.

Two other studio theatres—the Gate and Činoherní—were also outstanding. The Theatre Behind the Gate, founded in 1965 by Otomar Krejča (who had been director of the Prague National Theatre from 1956 until 1961), shared its 435-seat theatre with the Laterna Magika, for both of which Svoboda served as designer. Because of Krejča's meticulous staging, the Gate rapidly won an enviable reputation with works by Nestroy, Schnitzler, Chekhov, and its resident dramatist Josef Topol (1935–   ). It was Topol's *Their Day* in Krejča's production at the Prague National Theatre that marked Svoboda's first use of multimedia for spoken drama. Topol's most popular work was *Cat on the Rails* (1967), about a couple who, while waiting for a train, argue over their future as they sit on parallel rails that can never meet. One of Czechoslovakia's most popular dramatists, Topol never became widely known outside his own country.

The Činoherní (Actors' Club), founded in

FIG. 13.6
Topol's *Their Day* in 1959, as designed by Svoboda. (Photo copyright by Jaromír Svoboda.)

1965 and performing in a theatre seating only 220, was headed by Jaroslav Vostry. It served primarily to provide opportunities for young actors, many of whom also worked in films. It came to be considered the best ensemble in Czechoslovakia. It performed a wide range of foreign classics but also new Czech plays, especially those of Ladislav Smoček. *The Labyrinth* (1967), Smoček's best-known play, treats characters who, with fun and jollity, enter a maze only to discover that no one is permitted to leave. It suggests that bureaucratic systems swallow those who come into contact with them.

Among the dramatists not attached to specific theatres, Ivan Klíma (1931–) was perhaps the best-known. His major work, *The Castle* (1966), was inspired by Kafka's novel of the same name. It concerns a group permitted to live and work in a feudal castle; then one of the group demands an investigation of mysterious murders in the castle; although the inspector discovers that the crimes have been committed, he concludes that those responsible are too powerful to arrest, and when he leaves the informer is killed.

During the 1960s, Czechoslovakia instituted many reforms that seemed to undo much of the Soviet influence. But this "Prague Spring" was cut short in 1968 when the Warsaw Pact nations invaded Czechoslovakia and installed one of the most repressive regimes in Eastern Europe. In 1969, strict censorship was imposed, especially on all works with political implications. Grossman and Havel left the Balustrade; Havel was subsequently imprisoned, and his works were forbidden publication and production. In 1969, the Činoherní, charged with decadence, was forced to change its artistic policies, and in 1971 Krejča was removed as director of the Gate. The Institute of Scenography was disbanded, but Svoboda, perhaps because of his international standing, was otherwise little affected and continued to work both at home and abroad. Except in the area of scenography, Czechoslovakia played little role in international theatre after 1969.

POLAND

Poland was the first of the satellite countries to ease restrictions, and from 1956 until 1968 political ideology interfered little with the theatre. The major change was signalled in 1956 when Tadeusz Kantor (1915–) began to revive Witkiewicz's plays. Kantor had graduated from the School of Fine Arts in Kraków where he had studied painting and scenography with Karol Frycz, one of Poland's major interwar designers. From 1945 to 1955, Kantor was a designer for official state theatres before founding his own company, Cricot 2, in 1955. Cricot 2 was consistently one of the most experimental theatres in Poland, and beginning in the 1970s it enjoyed an international reputation (about which more will be said later).

Another prewar figure—Witold Gombrowicz (1904–1969)—also returned to prominence. Influenced by Witkiewicz, Gombrowicz was a major figure of the Polish avant-garde during the 1930s, but fled to Argentina in 1939. In 1957 his collected works were published in Poland and began to be produced once more. They were soon translated into other languages. In 1964, Gombrowicz settled in France, where he lived until his death. Two of his plays, *Ivona, Princess of Burgundy* (1935) and *The Marriage* (1946), preceded any of the French absurdist plays, with which they are often compared. After returning to Europe, he wrote only one play, *Operetta* (1966). Gombrowicz was preoccupied with interacting deformations: "People impose upon one another this or that manner of being, speaking, behaving. . . . Each person deforms other persons while being at the same time deformed by them." He saw people as constantly adapting to what is expected of them, for even if they rebel they merely fall

FIG. 13.7
Gombrowicz's
Operetta at the TNP,
Paris, in 1966. (Photo
by Pic.)

into another pattern. These ideas run through all of Gombrowicz's plays. In *Ivona*, when the prince decides to defy accepted forms by marrying the ugly Ivona, this disruption leads to so many others that a decision is made that Ivona must be killed discreetly; after her death, the royal family proclaims a suitable period of mourning and the accepted conventions are restored.

The already-existing native avant-garde tradition, represented by Witkiewicz and Gombrowicz, seems to have won absurdist drama ready acceptance in Poland. Not only were Beckett's and Ionesco's plays often produced, the major new dramatists wrote in a style resembling absurdism. Of these new writers, the best were Różewicz and Mrożek.

Tadeusz Różewicz (1921–   ), a leading poet since the late 1940s, did not turn to playwriting until 1960, by which time his vision of a chaotic world in search of order had established him as the Polish writer most attuned to Sartre and Camus, although he considered those authors overly optimistic about the human condition. In his first play, *The Card Index* (also translated as *Personal File* or *The Dossier,* 1960), the protagonist searches for a self (filed away somewhere in the records of his life contained in his card index) even as he recognizes that life is so fluid that fixed being and fixed standards are impossible. Like many subsequent Polish plays, it combines the search for a lost order with rejection of the possibility of absolutes. *He Left Home* (1964) treats a man who, through amnesia, has escaped a meaningless world, but is being forced to recall everything. Once more aware of life's absurdity, he bandages his head and leaves the room. Although it is unclear whether the man now accepts or is fleeing life, it is clear that Różewicz considers both the past and the present unsatisfactory. Różewicz writes in an open form and encourages directors and actors to collaborate in completing his fragmented dramaturgy. Różewicz's later plays include *White Marriage* (1974) and *The Trap* (1982).

Sławomir Mrożek (1932–   ) began his career as a cartoonist, an influence evident in

FIG. 13.8
A scene from Różewicz's *The Card Index*, produced at the Theatre Studio, Warsaw, in 1989. (Photo by Zygmunt Rytka.)

his early dramas. In his first play, *The Police* (1958), the secret police have been so successful in wiping out dissent that they order one of their members to assume the role of enemy agent so their jobs will not be lost. Mrożek's long plays are parables about humanity adrift in a moral vacuum. His most famous work, *Tango* (1965), shows a son's attempt to impose order at gunpoint on his bohemian family. But, too humane to believe in naked power, he eventually is killed by a boorish family hanger-on, Edek. As the play ends, the family submits to Edek as he dances the tango around the dead body. The tango of the title is a symbol of the older generation's prewar revolt, which has destroyed all traditional standards, leaving nothing to fill the vacuum but power; consequently, those most willing to exercise power, ruthlessly and without regard for humanitarian principles, become the rulers of the world. Between 1965 and 1970, this was one of the most frequently produced plays throughout Europe, probably because it was perceived as a parable of twentieth-century

history. Mrożek's later plays include *Emigrés* (1974) and *Alpha* (1984).

Poland's theatre also won an enviable reputation. By 1966 it had sixty-nine dramatic theatres scattered throughout the country. Internationally, its best-known director was Jerzy Grotowski (whose work will be discussed in a later chapter). Within Poland, perhaps the most admired directors were Axer, Kreczmar, Swinarski, and Dejmek. Erwin Axer (1917–   ) began his career just before the war but had little chance to pursue it until 1945, when he established the Chamber Theatre in Łódź. In 1949 he took most of his actors to Warsaw to open the Contemporary Theatre. Axer sought extreme simplicity in staging, discarding all irrelevant detail and shaping what remained with extreme care to create what was often called neorealism. His repertory, chosen to reflect current ethical and philosophical issues, included the first production of *Tango,* and plays by Brecht, Frisch, Witkiewicz, and many others. Jerzy Kreczmar (1902–   ) worked in a vein quite contrary to that of Axer. Attuned

FIG. 13.9
Mrożek's *Tango*, directed by Kazimierz Dejmek at the Theatre Polski, Warsaw, in 1990. (Photo by Leon Myszkowski.)

to the avant-garde, he directed the first production in Poland of *Waiting for Godot* as well as plays by Ionesco, Pinter, Albee, and other dramatists. Konrad Swinarski (1929–1975) received much of his training in Brecht's company and introduced Brecht's methods into the Polish theatre. Although he tended to use more opulent means than Brecht, he nevertheless always underlined a theatricality that compelled the spectator to adopt a critical stance. Swinarski achieved international prominence when he directed the premiere production of Weiss' *Marat/Sade* in West Berlin in 1964, after which he was in wide demand throughout Europe. Kazimierz Dejmek (1924–   ) was

noted especially for his attempts to revivify a repertory composed primarily of major Polish plays ranging from the great romantic plays of the nineteenth century through the works of Witkiewicz to those of Różewicz.

In 1968 the theatre underwent a crisis when Poland joined in the invasion of Czechoslovakia. Participation in public protests led to expulsion from the country or from positions of prominence for leading dramatists, critics, and directors. Mrożek lost his citizenship; Jan Kott, Poland's leading critic, went to teach in America; Adam Tarn, editor of the dramatic journal *Dialog*, was removed from his post and emigrated to Canada; Dejmek was forced to resign his position as head of the National Theatre in Warsaw. Much of the vigor of the period between 1956 and 1968 was lost thereafter for some time.

GERMAN-LANGUAGE THEATRE AND DRAMA

By the 1960s, the shortage of German-language dramatists had been overcome. During the 1960s Brecht became the most popular of all modern dramatists, and several playwrights of the 1950s—among them Frisch, Duerrenmatt, and Hochwälder—continued to write. With new dramatists, the most characteristic form was *documentary drama* or the *theatre of fact*.

Documentary drama took much of its inspiration from Piscator, who after returning to Germany in 1951 was for many years unable to secure a permanent position, perhaps because he was looked upon as a prewar relic. In 1962 he was named intendant of the Freie Volksbühne in West Berlin, where, in collaboration with his designer Hans Ulrich Schmuckle, he revived many of the techniques he had used in the 1920s. Piscator did much to establish documentary drama when in rapid succession he presented Hochhuth's *The Deputy*, Kipphardt's

In the Case of J. Robert Oppenheimer, and Weiss'
The Investigation. In them, Piscator found the
kind of drama he had sought in vain in the
1920s. In a tribute published shortly after
Piscator's death, Kipphardt wrote, "We all
stem from your Political Theater." This drama
seemingly came into existence because Germans
were unwilling to confront the Nazi era. As
Piscator put it: "By refusing to confront this
past, [Germans] are evading the necessary
consequence, that is: learning a lesson from the
past."

Rolf Hochhuth (1931–   ) was the first of
the documentary writers to win prominence—
with *The Deputy,* produced by Piscator in 1963.
It charges Pope Pius XII with culpability in the
extermination of the Jews because he did not
take a decisive stand. This accusation made the
play so controversial that only eight theatres in
Germany were willing to produce it. (It
became the focus of protest wherever it was
presented but ultimately was seen in twenty-
seven countries.) A diffuse, rambling, and
repetitious work, it would take some ten hours
to present in its entirety, and consequently was
considerably adapted in performance. The
play did nothing that numerous historical plays
had not already done in assigning motives to
and inventing speeches for persons who had
actually lived, but many argued that Hochhuth
had passed over into libel in his treatment of a
contemporary person and charged that, by
calling his play documentary, he sought to give
fictional work factual credibility. Hochhuth
aroused almost as much controversy with *The
Soldiers* (1967), in which Winston Churchill is
accused of having acquiesced to the death of
General Sikorski, President of the Polish gov-
ernment-in-exile, in a staged plane crash
because Sikorski threatened the Anglo-Soviet
alliance. Hochhuth went on to write other
plays—including *Guerrillas* (1970) and *Death of
a Hunter* (1982)— but none was as popular as
these two.

FIG. 13.10

Piscator's production of Hochhuth's *The
Deputy,* at the Theater am Kufüstendamm,
Berlin, in 1963. Design by Leo Kerz. (Photo by
Ilse Buhs.)

Peter Weiss (1916–1982) won wider acceptance. As a Jew, Weiss left Germany in 1934 and
lived successively in England, Czechoslovakia,
and Sweden. Originally a graphic artist, his
early plays—among them *The Tower* (1948)
and *How Mr. Mackinpott Was Cured of Suffering*
(1963)—show an affinity with surrealism. They
are quite unlike the play that catapulted Weiss
to fame—*The Persecution and Assassination of Jean-
Paul Marat as Performed by the Inmates of the
Asylum of Charenton Under the Direction of the
Marquis de Sade,* first presented in 1964 at the
Schiller Theater in West Berlin under the
direction of Konrad Swinarski and in settings

FIG. 13.11
Weiss' *Marat/Sade* at
the Schiller Theater,
Berlin, in 1964. (Photo
by Ilse Buhs.)

by Weiss. A play within a play, *Marat/Sade* is set in the Asylum of Charenton, where in 1808 the Marquis de Sade is confined and composes plays which are presented by the inmates for the amusement of a fashionable audience from nearby Paris. On this occasion, de Sade presents his play about Charlotte Corday's assassination in 1793 of Jean-Paul Marat, a leader of the French Revolution. The inmates, attendants, and the director of the asylum and his family are on stage, while the audience is separated from them by bars. A presenter introduces the scenes in de Sade's production, and Brecht-like songs are used to comment on the action. At the end of the play, the inmates get out of hand, overcome the attendants, and reduce everything to chaos. The heart of the play is the dialectic exchanges between de Sade, the sensual individualist, and Marat, the revolutionist seeking a just social order. Weiss seems to use the asylum as a metaphor for the world; the ending suggests the results of accepting de Sade's anarchistic vision. Later in 1964 Peter

Brook's production of the play, produced by the Royal Shakespeare Company, was the sensation of the London (and later, the New York) season. Audiences were most impressed by Brook's use of devices borrowed from Artaud's theatre of cruelty, especially in the stage business of the inmates. Although Weiss was greatly displeased because the dialectical exchanges were obscured, Brook's production was in many ways a watershed, since it called wide attention for the first time to Artaud's theories and since it influenced many subsequent productions through the way it imbedded social and political argument within compelling visual and aural effects.

While *Marat/Sade* mingled fact and fiction, Weiss' next play, *The Investigation,* was a fully developed documentary play, which in 1965 was produced simultaneously in seventeen theatres in East and West Germany. Composed entirely of excerpts from official hearings into the Auschwitz extermination camp, it nevertheless employs much selectivity since only a small part of the total testimony is used. With this play, Weiss seems to have committed himself both to the documentary and to Marxism, for Weiss argued that genocide is the logical extension of capitalism, whose values still dominated much of the postwar world. In 1968 he published "Fourteen Propositions for a Documentary Theatre," in which he set forth his position on this type of drama and made clear that, even though he might begin with factual material, he shaped it to fit his own ideological position; he wrote of editing and selecting material so as to cut through the camouflages erected by official sources of information and of the ultimate necessity of taking sides: "the only possible epilogue of many . . . themes is a condemnation." He also denounced the absurdist vision: "the documentary theatre affirms that reality, whatever the obscurity in which it masks itself, can be explained in minute detail."

Weiss wrote other documentary plays, although none was as successful as *The Investigation*. In *The Song of the Lusitanian Bogey* (1967), he treated the suppression of native Africans in Angola by the Portuguese, and the Vietnam war in *A Discourse on the Previous History and Development of the Long War of Liberation in Vietnam as an Example of the Necessity for the Armed Fight of the Suppressed Against the Suppressors as Well as on the Attempt of the United States of America to Destroy the Foundations of the Revolution* (1968). Around 1970, Weiss seemed to lose interest in the documentary, although his subsequent works treated political themes. In *Trotsky in Exile* (1970), he explores the role of the revolutionary thinker, and in *Hölderlin* (1971), the artist as the conscience of revolution. Weiss continued to write until 1981, but never regained the popularity he enjoyed during the 1960s.

Heinar Kipphardt (1922–   ) wrote a number of plays between 1951 and 1959 while dramaturg at the Deutsches Theater in East Berlin, but he is known almost entirely for those written after he moved to West Berlin and above all for *In the Case of J. Robert Oppenheimer*, produced by Piscator in 1964. Based on the official records of an inquiry made during the early 1950s into the loyalty of Oppenheimer when he resisted development of the hydrogen bomb, the play is, according to Kipphardt, entirely faithful to fact: "The author deliberately confined himself to drawing only upon historical data for all the facts presented in the play. The author exercised his freedom only in the selection, the arrangement,

FIG. 13.12
Kipphardt's *In the Case of J. Robert Oppenheimer*, directed by Piscator at the Freie Volksbühne, Berlin, in 1964. (Photo by Heinz Koster.)

formulation, and condensation of the material" (a statement that might have been written by Zola). Kipphardt was most interested in the conflict between a scientist's responsibility to his country and his responsibility to humanity in general—issues similar to those that pervaded postwar German drama. The play was presented simultaneously by twenty-seven theatres. Kipphardt's next play, *Joel Brand* (1965), about wartime negotiations to save Jews, had little success. After serving for a time as dramaturg of the Munich Kammerspiele, he retired, but during the 1980s wrote a few new plays, of which the most successful was *Brother Eichmann* (1983), which draws parallels between the Holocaust and present–day nuclear strategy.

The kind of documentary drama popularized by Hochhuth, Weiss, and Kipphardt soon gained currency elsewhere. In France in 1965, Jean Vilar, unhappy with Kipphardt's play, countered with *The Oppenheimer Dossier;* in England in 1967 Peter Brook produced *US,* about Vietnam; in America in 1970 Donald Freed's *Inquest* treated the Rosenberg treason trial of the early 1950s; in 1971 Daniel Berrigan's *The Trial of the Catonsville Nine* depicted a group that, opposed to the Vietnam conflict, destroyed draft records. Other examples could be listed. Overall, there was a trend toward using actual events to argue a partisan point of view. Thus documentary drama blended with political and social activism.

Not all German playwrights of the 1960s wrote documentary plays. Two of the most prominent who did not were Dorst and Walser. Tankred Dorst (1925–) began writing plays in the 1950s and subsequently won several literary prizes. Although his plays include social and political ideas, Dorst believed that such commentary should arise from the demands of the play rather than from the author's own attitudes. His *Freedom for Clemens* (1961), an allegory about human freedom told with great theatricality, concerns a man who,

while imprisoned, discovers that freedom is within. His first major play, *Toller* (1968), treats a brief period in 1919 when the twenty-six-year-old playwright Ernst Toller became head of the commune set up in Munich. Somewhat similarly, in *Ice Age* (1973), Dorst, using the novelist Knut Hamsun as protagonist, questions the relationship between art and politics. His most ambitious work has been a still-uncompleted cycle of works in several media, which seeks to explore the German consciousness from the 1920s to the present.

Martin Walser (1927–) was already well-known as a novelist when he wrote his first play in 1961. Like most contemporary German dramatists, his early plays dealt with themes of guilt and responsibility, but he did so in a style he labeled "Realismus X," a mixture of realism and symbolism which avoided Brechtian parable without being mere reproduction of external reality. *Oak and Angora* (1962) dramatizes contrasting reactions to changes in German life between 1945 and 1960, while *The Black Swan* (1964) contrasts the guilt felt by an emotionally disturbed young man, who imagines that he was an assassin for the Gestapo, with the quiet, guilt-free lives of his father and doctor, who actually were involved in such activities. In *Home Front* (1967), a Strindbergian treatment of marriage under the stresses of boredom, routine, deception, and marital infidelity is used to reflect an absence of values.

Few East German dramatists won wide renown. Most adhered to socialist realism, but a few attempted to follow in Brecht's footsteps. Perhaps the best was Peter Hacks (1928–), who moved from West Germany to East Berlin in 1955 so he might work with the Berliner Ensemble, on whose governing board he served for a time. At first he wrote satirical works in the Brechtian vein, and then socialist realist pieces about topical issues before finding his own distinctive mode—poetic comedy which uses traditional forms borrowed from Aristophanes, Shakespeare, and others to reflect contemporary problems, often more personal than political. Among his best-known plays are *Amphitryon* (1967), which explores concepts of love and marriage, and *Omphale* (1970), in which Heracles seeks to transcend the role assigned him by myth and find his own true identity. Hacks has frequently been accused of escapism because of his subjects and methods of distancing them. Although his were among the most dramatically effective German works of their time, their complexity made them difficult to translate, and consequently Hacks was little-known outside of Germany.

Until the late 1960s, the basic patterns of the German theatre continued to be those reinstituted following World War II: a network of heavily subsidized companies producing balanced seasons of new and old, foreign and domestic plays. During the 1960s, some of the most influential directors, among them Gustav Gründgens, Erwin Piscator, and Fritz Kortner, died or retired, but for the most part those directors who had become heads of major West German theatres in the postwar period continued through the 1960s. These included Heinz Hilpert in Göttingen, Karleinz Stroux in Dusseldorf, Boleslaw Barlog in Berlin, Rudolf Sellner in Darmstadt, Hans Schweikart in Munich, Hans Schalla in Bochum, and Harry Buchwitz in Frankfurt. For the most part, these directors discouraged "political" theatre and sought instead to present the playwright's work free of tendentiousness. Buchwitz was almost alone in championing Brecht's plays. (Brecht himself supervised the final rehearsals of Buchwitz's production of *The Caucasian Chalk Circle*.) Younger directors who would change this situation after 1968 were able to do innovative productions occasionally, but, without being heads of theatres, they could make little impact on theatrical policy. Nevertheless, one intendant, Kurt

Hübner at Bremen between 1962 and 1970, was very important in shaping subsequent practice, for, though he himself did not do highly innovative productions, he permitted others the leeway to do so. Consequently, many of the major directors of the 1970s gained much of their most formative experiences in his theatre during the 1960s. In East Germany, the Berliner Ensemble remained the most prestigious theatre, continuing Brecht's practices under the direction of Helene Weigel (until her death in 1971), assisted by Erich Engel (until his death in 1966), Manfred Wekwerth, and Joachim Tenschert.

FRANCE

When General Charles de Gaulle came to power in France in the late 1950s, his minister of culture, André Malraux, sought to revitalize the arts. In 1959 he removed the Odéon from the control of the Comédie Française, renamed it the Théâtre de France, and installed Barrault and his company there. The Théâtre National Populaire (TNP) was elevated to equality with the other national theatres. Under the rules established for these two theatres, directors were appointed for a limited period, although they might be reappointed so long as their work was satisfactory. Barrault headed the Théâtre de France until 1968, but Vilar resigned his post at the TNP in 1963. He was succeeded by Georges Wilson, a member of the troupe throughout Vilar's directorship. Malraux also authorized the creation of two experimental theatres, one to be headed by Albert Camus, the other by Vilar. Camus died before his theatre got underway and Vilar's never thrived. Both the Théâtre de France and the TNP, however, did create small "studio" theatres. The Théâtre de France became the focus of much innovation, in part because it served as the host each spring to the Théâtre des Nations (to which leading companies came from throughout the world for limited engagements) and to provincial theatres from within France.

The Gaullist government also extended decentralization by funding municipal cultural centers (*maisons de la culture*), the first of which was opened in 1962. These centers included facilities for films, music, dance, the visual arts, and lectures, as well as theatrical productions. After 1965, cultural centers also began to be built in the suburbs of Paris, as it became clear that many residents were too far removed from the center of Paris to benefit from its cultural resources.

Many directors from earlier years continued during the 1960s—Barrault, Vilar, Blin, Serreau, Dasté, Reybaz, Bataille, Ré, and others. Among new figures, one of the most noteworthy was Antoine Bourseiller (1930–   ) who was named head of the Studio des Champs-Elysées when Maurice Jacquemont

retired in 1960. There between 1960 and 1963 Bourseiller mounted several critically acclaimed productions of plays by Pirandello, Brecht, and others. He then staged an adaptation of Kafka's *America* for Barrault's company, and eventually was named head of the Dramatic Center at Aix-en-Provence. His greatest recognition came through an extremely controversial production of Molière's *Don Juan* at the Comédie Française in 1967, epitomizing his view that a director should provoke the audience into reassessing its preconceptions of scripts. Overall, he mingled elements drawn from Artaud, the surrealists, and Brecht.

By far the most influential new director was Roger Planchon (1931–   ) who was much influenced in his early work by Artaud, films, and mime. He began his directing career in the early 1950s as director of the 110-seat avantgarde Théâtre de la Comédie in Lyons. During these years his interest in working-class issues

FIG. 13.13
Bourseiller's controversial production of Molière's *Don Juan* at the Comédie Française in 1967. Georges Descruères is Don Juan. (Photo by Bernard.)

increased, and in 1957 he founded the Théâtre de la Cité in the industrial town of Villeurbanne, a suburb of Lyons. Taking over a 1,300-seat theatre, he set out to create a company that would attract a working-class audience. He spent much time building friendly relations with various workers' organizations and surveying potential audiences to find out what they would like to see. When Dumas *père's The Three Musketeers,* a novel, received the most support, Planchon had an adaptation made. It became one of the company's most popular productions, both in Villeurbanne and elsewhere. But Planchon did not patronize his audience. The majority of the repertory was by such dramatists as Molière, Marivaux, Shakespeare, Kleist, Marlowe, Racine, and Brecht. He also persuaded Adamov to become

resident playwright, and it was for Planchon's company that Adamov wrote most of his postabsurdist plays.

Planchon, viewing the director as an equal of the author, often described directing as "scenic writing." He thought the four essential requirements for a director were scenic inventiveness, feeling for three-dimensional images, ability to work with actors, and a world view. Because he catered to a theatrically unsophisticated audience, Planchon used devices intended to provide a clear context. Many of them—such as captions, projected commentary, and complex stage business—were influenced by Brecht, whose productions at the Théâtre des Nations in 1955 made an indelible impression on Planchon and motivated him to develop his own version of Brecht's approach. Planchon's

FIG. 13.14
Planchon's production of *The Three Musketeers* at the Théâtre de la Cité, Villeurbanne, in 1957. (Photo by Pic.)

principal designers, René Allio and André Acquart, were also admirers of Brecht, and their scenic conventions reflected many of those used at the Berliner Ensemble. Planchon's Marxist interpretations of the classics frequently aroused heated controversy, but the liveliness, richness, and clarity of his productions won him a large following, both at home and abroad. Despite many offers of prestigious posts in Paris and elsewhere, Planchon remained in Villeurbanne. The significance of his work there was acknowledged in 1963 when his company was made a dramatic center and awarded a subsidy by the central government.

Planchon also began writing plays in 1961 and subsequently wrote some dozen. The best-known are *The Deposition* (1961), *Infamy* (1969), *The Black Pig* (1972), and *Gilles de Rais* (1976). All are based on some violent actual event in a basically peasant society, although the event itself is not shown. Rather, each play attempts to reconstruct what happened so as to find an explanation for it. This search, by juxtaposing contradictory responses, reveals much about the social and ideological context, as well as illuminating events from other times or places. Planchon was especially interested in how people respond to political and social circumstances. His plays were difficult for audiences, although often powerful because of Planchon's dynamic visual imagery and Brechtian staging.

During the 1960s, the Dramatic Centers thrived. Their repertories, reflecting the Gaullist desire to preserve and make readily available the cultural heritage, emphasized the classics. The Ministry of Culture also regularly sent representatives to visit theatres throughout the country, and if a company was judged worthy it was awarded the status of "permanent troupe," which made it eligible for government assistance.

French theatre was also enlarged by the injection of drama about its colonies and the third world. In 1958, Serreau's attempt to stage the Algerian playwright Kateb Yacine's (1929-) *The Encircled Corpse* (dealing with the French struggle to maintain its hold on Algeria) created such controversy that the production was moved to Brussels (not till 1964 was it seen in Paris). Yacine's *The Man With Rubber Sandals,* about Ho Chi Minh, was considered so subversive that when it was produced in 1971 the theatre had its subsidy reduced.

Serreau also staged all of the plays of Aimé Cesaire (1913–), a native of Martinique and one of France's major playwrights of the 1960s. Cesaire said that his primary concern was to liberate black minds from the image of themselves implanted by centuries of white imperialism. Adopting many of Brecht's devices, he called his work "epic." His first major play, *The Tragedy of King Christophe* (1964), was so controversial that it had its premiere at the Salzburg Festival and only later in 1965 toured the French dramatic centers. Set in Haiti, 1811-1820, when Christophe ruled there, it also mirrors attitudes about African liberation in the postwar period. In it, Cesaire presents a number of conflicting views of events, which he leaves the audience to reconcile. His *A Season in the Congo* (1967) also had its first production outside of France before being transferred to Paris. It deals with Patrice Lumumba's attempts to establish an independent republic and his failure owing both to outside interference and to his own efforts to do too much too quickly. Despite Lumumba's failure, the play is essentially celebratory, suggesting that his vision will triumph someday. *A Tempest* (1969) is Cesaire's adaptation of Shakespeare's play. In it, Prospero, unable to leave the island, remains locked in a struggle with Caliban, which he is doomed to lose. In his productions of plays by Cesaire and others, Serreau, working tirelessly until his death in 1973, sought to convince the French that the emergence of the third world was the most important development of that time and demanded a reevaluation of Western culture.

During the 1960s, Armand Gatti (1924–) was the leading political dramatist. After surviving a German concentration camp, he came to believe that the world's problems are ones that can only be solved by collective action, and, seeing the theatre as a collective art, he sought to use it as an instrument to change consciousness. *The Imaginary Life of the Garbage-Collector Auguste Geai* (1962) shows the title character, as he is dying at the age of forty-six, recalling widely separated crucial moments in his life and imagining a future. The contradictions and interactions among these times illuminate each other and the revolutionary consciousness. Others of Gatti's plays treat, in a variation on Brecht's epic mode, the concentration-camp experience and the ravages of atomic war. During the 1960s, twelve of his plays, of which he directed six, were produced in dramatic centers. A turning point in his career came with *V Like Vietnam* (1967), difficulties over which led Gatti to conclude that establishment theatres were unsuitable to political drama. He was confirmed in his belief in 1968 when *The Passion of General Franco* at the TNP was forbidden by the French government because it threatened trade negotiations with Spain. For the most part thereafter, Gatti went to different locales, selected a topic of pertinence to that area, sought volunteers, and then worked with them to develop and perform works. His emphasis became helping people express their views so as to reveal the hidden class wars in capitalist society.

Plays of a quite different sort were written by Obaldia and Duras. René Obaldia (1918–) carried on the whimsical tradition of the 1950s. His subject, in such works as *The Agricultural Cosmonaut* (1965) and *The Wind in the Sassafras Branches* (1965), was the inanities and concealed lies of life, which he brought to the surface and treated as wholly logical. In *In the End the Bang* (1968) a man, depressed by the atomic threat, decides to imitate St. Simeon the Stylite by retreating to the top of a column, but, rather than recalling the world to its senses, he becomes a tourist attraction and eventually he and his column are disintegrated by the sonic boom of an aircraft. Obaldia suggests that it is not apocalyptic disasters we have to fear as much as jaded sensibilities and modern technology. Marguerite Duras (1914–) minutely dissected internal anxieties and attempts to make meaningful contact with other in such plays as *Entire Days in the Trees* (1965) and *The Eden Cinema* (1977). She was the most effective of the first wave of postwar French feminist dramatists.

The playwright who gained the greatest international reputation was Fernando Arrabal (1932–), who emigrated to France from Spain in 1955. He began writing plays in 1952 but did not gain wide fame until the 1960s. His early plays, such as *Picnic on the Battlefield* (1952), *The Automobile Graveyard* (1958), and *Fando and Lis* (1958), are closely related to the work of the absurdists in their childish, thoughtless cruelty. *The Automobile Graveyard* is set in a junkyard run as though it were a luxury hotel. The principal character is eventually beaten and spread on a bicycle as though it were a cross, but his sacrifice has no meaning in a world that is merely the rusty remains of a technological nightmare. Around 1962, Arrabal announced his intention to create a *théâtre panique:* "a ceremony—partly sacrilegious, partly sacred, erotic and mystic, a putting to death and exaltation of life. . . ." He also stated that he could not conceive of love without violence, both of which are always linked in his plays. His later works include *Solemn Communion* (1966), *The Architect and the Emperor of Assyria* (1968), and *And They Handcuffed the Flowers* (1970). In the second of these, two men enact a series of ritualized relationships: master and slave, judge and criminal, parent and child, male and female, sadist and masochist, and others. Finally one eats the other, but a new figure appears and the rituals begin again. Arrabal's work has been compared to both Artaud's and Genet's.

The director most successful in staging Arrabal's work was Victor García (1934–1982), an Argentinian who had come to Paris in 1961 as a television director. He first won recognition by staging Spanish plays for Serreau's company from 1962 to 1964. In 1966 he combined four of Arrabal's plays under the title of *The Automobile Graveyard,* the spatial arrangement and unusual theatrical imagery of which were to be very influential. In 1969, he directed the first production of a play by Genet to be seen in Spain—*The Maids* for the Nuria Espert company—and later it toured throughout Europe. In 1970 in São Paulo (Brazil), García staged Genet's *The Balcony* in a theatre that had been rearranged into seven circular balconies inside a 60-foot-high tubular struc-

FIG. 13.15

Arrabal's *The Automobile Graveyard* at the Théâtre des Arts, Paris, in 1967. Directed by Victor García. (Photo by Bernand.)

ture with the action taking place on transparent circular platforms and spiral constructions, an arrangement that recalled Dante's *Inferno.* It was one of the most radical restructurings of theatrical space attempted up to that time. Such productions were to make García a significant influence on the French theatre of the 1970s.

ENGLAND

The vitality of the English theatre was sustained during the 1960s by three organizations: the Royal Shakespeare Company, the National Theatre, and the English Stage Company.

After World War II, the Stratford Memorial Theatre had gradually grown in estimation, but it remained a seasonal festival until it was transformed into a diverse, year-round company by Peter Hall (1930–   ), who became its head in 1960. Educated at Cambridge University, Hall first gained recognition at the Arts Theatre in London where in 1955–1956 he staged plays by Ionesco and Beckett. After beginning his association with Stratford in 1957, he soon became one of its most effective directors. At the time he took control of the company in 1960, its major problems were lack of continuity in personnel and restriction of the repertory to works by a single author. Since the season at Stratford lasted only about six months, actors had to find employment elsewhere during the remaining time and often were not free at the beginning of a new festival season. Consequently, it was difficult to create an ensemble. To overcome these difficulties, Hall took a lease on the Aldwych Theatre in London, put actors under contract for the entire year, and varied the repertory by offering non-Shakespearean plays at the Aldwych alongside productions transferred from Stratford. In 1961, the troupe received a new government charter and name: the Royal

Shakespeare Company (RSC). Instead of five productions, the company began presenting about twenty-five each season. Because Hall found it difficult to handle all of these increased responsibilities, he brought Peter Brook and Michel Saint-Denis into the management in 1962.

The RSC then expanded its activities further. In 1962 it took over the Arts Theatre for a season of experimental works, and in 1963–1964, under the direction of Brook and Charles Marowitz, it created a series entitled "Theatre of Cruelty," consisting of Artaud's *Spurt of Blood,* scenes from Genet's *The Screens,* "collages" by Brook and Marowitz, and several improvisations. Out of this experience came Brook's production of Weiss' *Marat/Sade* in 1964—one of the company's most successful productions and the primary popularizer of Artaud's concepts in England and the U.S. By the time it produced Pinter's *The Homecoming* in 1965, the RSC was considered not only the foremost producer of Shakespearean drama but one of the world's leading purveyors of modern plays by such authors as Hochhuth, Brecht, Chekhov, and Giraudoux, as well as old and new English writers. After 1964, the

Aldwych also became host, in collaboration with Peter Daubeny (1921–1975), to the World Theatre Season which, each spring until 1973, hosted major companies from throughout the world for short engagements.

During the 1960s the RSC included in its company some of England's finest actors: Paul Scofield, Peggy Ashcroft, Ian Richardson, Ian Holm, Judy Dench, David Warner, and many others. But the true stars of the RSC were its directors, since the company's reputation depended in large part on the way scripts were shaped by directorial concepts. In addition to Hall and Brook, other important directors included Clifford Williams and John Barton. Hall favored a simplified "rough" realism that owed much to Brecht and in which verse was spoken in a measured beat. Hall's principal designer was John Bury (1925–   ) whose settings typically were functional, skeletal structures. Costumes and props usually looked long-used. This style was probably seen at its best in the cycle of Shakespeare's history plays presented in 1963–1964 under the overall title "The War of the Roses."

Peter Brook (1925–   ) was the best known of the RSC's directors. He began

FIG. 13.16 Peter Brook's production of Weiss' *Marat/Sade* at the RSC in 1964. Glenda Jackson (left) is Charlotte Corday, Patrick Magee (center) is the Marquis de Sade, and Ian Richardson (lower right) is Marat. (Photo by Morris Newcombe.)

directing while still in his teens and was first brought to Stratford in 1946 by Barry Jackson. In the late 1940s he was director of productions at the Covent Garden opera, where his *Salome,* with designs by Salvador Dali, created a sensation. During the 1950s his reputation for novel and forceful work steadily grew through such productions as *Titus Andronicus* (with Olivier and Vivien Leigh), *Hamlet* (with Paul Scofield), and *The Visit* (with the Lunts). In 1956 he directed his first play in Paris, where he worked often thereafter (among others, he directed the premiere of Genet's *The Balcony*) and developed an interest in Artaud, which was to find its fullest expression in his production of *Marat/Sade* for the RSC in 1964. This interest was also to influence his production in 1962 of *King Lear,* with its emphasis on a crude and cruel world dominated by images of barrenness, animals, and death. Brook resigned from the RSC in 1968 but returned in 1970 to direct his best-known production, *A Midsummer Night's Dream,* the most radical reinterpretation of the play since Granville Barker's in 1914. Brook wished to divest the play of the romantic aura of fairies and haunted woodlands so as to make it immediately relevant to audiences of his time. His designer, Sally Jacobs, enclosed the stage on three sides with white, unadorned walls broken only by two nearly invisible doors at the rear. A catwalk, on which musicians and actors appeared, ran around the top of the walls, and trapezes served as perches for Oberon and Puck. The forest was suggested by loosely coiled metal springs manipulated by fishing rods. The performers wore costumes that hinted at circus or *commedia dell'arte.* Overall, the production recalled Meyerhold's experiments. Brook interpreted the text as an exploration of love, in which the fairyland scenes became a series of dream-like illustrations for the royal lovers of how love can go awry. To underscore this interpretation, Brook cast the same actor as Theseus and Oberon and

FIG. 13.17

Peter Brook's production of *A Midsummer Night's Dream* at Stratford in 1970. Design by Sally Jacobs. Allen Howard as Oberon and John Kane as Puck are on the trapezes. Below are Sara Kestelman as Titania and David Waller as Bottom. (Courtesy the Royal Shakespeare Company.)

the same actress as Hippolyta and Titania. Despite the emphasis on acrobatic feats and innovative spectacle, the production remained true to Shakespeare's text and gave its verse full value. By stripping the play of encrusted tradition, Brook made the audience see it anew. It became one of the most admired and influential productions of its time. Brook's influence was further enhanced by his book, *The Empty Space* (1968), a description of four types of theatre—deadly (traditional commercial fare), holy (Artaud and Grotowski), rough (Brecht), and immediate (his own)—and a plea for a vital theatre.

By 1968, Hall apparently felt that he had accomplished all that he could with the RSC. He, Brook, and Saint-Denis resigned, and in 1969 were succeeded by Trevor Nunn, who would head the company for the next twenty years.

The strength of British theatre in the 1960s also depended on the National Theatre, which began operation in 1963. With the exception of Italy, Great Britain was the last major European country to create a national theatre. The company was authorized in 1949, but its implementation was made contingent on financial resources, and not until 1962 was final approval forthcoming. Some favored making the RSC the nucleus of the new company, but eventually the choice fell on the Old Vic, whose troupe was liquidated and its building leased. Only the Bristol branch, ownership of which passed to the city of Bristol, survived. It remained one of the best of provincial troupes.

Laurence Olivier was named director of the National Theatre with Kenneth Tynan (1927–1980) as literary advisor. A troupe was assembled and given a trial run at the Chichester Festival (begun by Leslie Evershed-Martin in 1962) during the summer before the formal opening of the National Theatre in October 1963 with *Hamlet* (a new production) followed by the four productions from Chichester. Plays for the first season ranged through Sophocles' *Philoctetes,* Shaw's *Saint Joan,* and Beckett's *Play.* This eclecticism also extended to production, for which Olivier sought to secure the best directors and designers from England or abroad. Consequently, the company favored no distinguishable approach and instead sought excellence in a broad range of styles. Several of the directors in the early years had made their reputations at the Royal Court (George Devine, Lindsay Anderson, Peter Wood, William Gas-

FIG. 13.18

All-male cast for the National Theatre's production of *As You Like It* in the late 1960s. (Photo by Dominic.)

kill, and John Dexter). Other English directors included Brook, Guthrie, Clifford Williams, Anthony Quayle, and Jonathan Miller. Outstanding foreign directors included Franco Zeffirelli, Ingmar Bergman, and Victor García. Designers also were varied: Motley, Jocelyn Herbert, Sean Kenny, Ralph Koltai, Josef Svoboda, René Allio, Rudolf Heinrich, and Lila de Nobili. Nevertheless, it was often said that the National was an actors' theatre. It built a reasonably stable ensemble but permitted outside work in films, television, and with other troupes. Its company included Olivier, Maggie Smith, Michael Redgrave, Robert Stephens, Albert Finney, Joan Plowright, Derek Jacobi, and Paul Scofield, among many others.

The heart of the National's repertory was classics, but it included recent continental plays and new English plays (such as Stoppard's *Rosencrantz and Guildenstern Are Dead,* Shaffer's *The Royal Hunt of the Sun,* and Arden's *Armstrong's Last Goodnight,* plays by writers who had already made their mark elsewhere). But during the 1960s, perhaps because of the need to establish itself, the National showed little interest in the kind of innovation that marked the RSC. Nevertheless, within a very few years it took its place among the best of European companies.

The English Stage Company (ESC) at the Royal Court continued to play an important role, especially in assisting new playwrights, but it suffered a loss of prestige in part because both the RSC and the National tended to woo its better playwrights away. Osborne was one of the few who remained faithful to the ESC. Upon George Devine's retirement in 1965, management of the company passed to William Gaskill (1930–   ), who had been its associate director from 1959 to 1963, when he took a similar post at the National. An acknowledged admirer of Brecht, Gaskill also favored a strong sense of tradition and mingled classics with new works in the repertory. The emphasis, however, continued to be on new plays, although not till the late 1960s did the ESC find a new group of significant writers. (Their work will be discussed in a later chapter.)

Outside of London, the number of resident companies increased from twenty-eight to fifty-two during the 1960s. Perhaps the best were those at Bristol, Birmingham, Manchester, Nottingham, Coventry, and Glasgow. Subsidized by local governments, most provided a varied repertory of old and recent plays and an occasional premiere. During the same period, the commercial theatre venues outside of London decreased from 130 to 33.

English companies were able to attract a substantial audience in part because of low admission fees. In the provinces the maximum admission price was about $1.80, and in London the maximum seldom rose above $4.00. These low prices were made possible in large part by low wages, for actors in the provinces were paid only about $25.00 per week. Except for a few companies, the English theatre of the 1960s remained relatively conservative until 1968, when the removal of strict censorship set off a wave of innovation.

English playwriting remained vigorous during the 1960s, in large part because writers who had begun their careers earlier continued to be productive. These included Terence Rattigan, Christopher Fry, John Osborne, John Arden, and Arnold Wesker. The most admired dramatist of the 1960s was Harold Pinter (1930–   ), who turned to playwriting in 1957 after beginning his career as an actor. His reputation rests primarily on *The Dumb Waiter* (1957), *The Birthday Party* (1958), *The Caretaker* (1960), *The Homecoming* (1965), *Old Times* (1971), *No Man's Land* (1975), and *Betrayal* (1978). Although Pinter continued to write for the stage (primarily short plays) and films, and to direct and act, his most admired pieces are those up to and including *Old Times.* Most of these plays share a number of characteristics: everyday situations that take on an air of mystery or menace; unexplained, unrevealed, or ambiguous motivations; and seemingly natural, though carefully controlled, dialogue. Pinter has stated that to him traditional drama seems strange because it assumes that everything can be known, whereas in actuality little can ever be certain. He rejected the idea that as an author he should know and reveal everything about his characters. He places his characters in a confined space (usually a room) and confronts them with a crisis, brought about by seemingly ordinary events, which forces them to question the very nature of their being. He treats all speech as a stratagem used by characters to hide their psychological nakedness

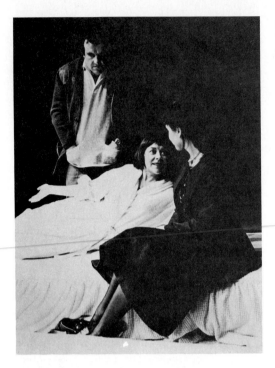

FIG. 13.19
Pinter's *Old Times*, staged by Peter Hall at the RSC in 1971. Left to right, Colin Blakely as Deeley, Dorothy Tutin as Kate, and Vivien Merchant as Anna. (Courtesy the Royal Shakespeare Company.)

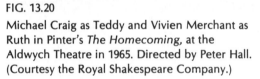

FIG. 13.20
Michael Craig as Teddy and Vivien Merchant as Ruth in Pinter's *The Homecoming*, at the Aldwych Theatre in 1965. Directed by Peter Hall. (Courtesy the Royal Shakespeare Company.)

and to avoid revealing too much about themselves. Thus for Pinter both silence and subtext are as important as what is spoken.

The Homecoming is usually considered to be Pinter's best play. In it, Teddy, a philosophy professor in an American university, returns with his wife Ruth to visit his family in London: his father, Max; two brothers—Joey (a prizefighter) and Lenny (a pimp); and his uncle Sam (a limousine driver). Eventually Lenny suggests that Ruth stay in London and let him set her up as a prostitute; she calmly acquiesces and Teddy returns to America without her. At the end, Sam collapses after revealing that the boys' mother used his

limousine for adulterous affairs, and Max grovels before Ruth begging for sexual favors. Critics have argued endlessly over the meaning of this play, probably because it is so ambiguous (even contradictory) in its treatment of the characters' motivations and about past events. It has been interpreted as a wish-fulfillment of the Oedipus complex (with the sons taking possession of their surrogate mother); as a conflict between various human instincts, with the physical the victor; as Ruth's acceptance that women must play many and contradictory roles and the discovery of all these possibilities within herself; as a variation on the parable of the prodigal son; as an adaptation of the biblical story of Ruth; and many others. So much controversy and such varied interpretations are indications of the allusive richness of the text.

As a dramatist, Pinter seems to fall somewhere between Beckett and Chekhov. Like the former, he isolates characters and lets them wrestle with their anxieties in an unverifiable universe; like Chekhov, he creates a realistic texture of background and dialogue in which surface act and speech are merely evasions or disguises of deeper conflicts and anxieties.

Among English dramatists of the 1960s, one of the most controversial was Joe Orton (1933–1967), who wrote only three works for the stage—*Entertaining Mr. Sloane* (1964), *Loot* (1966), and *What the Butler Saw* (produced in 1969)—comedies that invert traditional moral standards. In the first of these plays, a seemingly respectable brother and sister insinuate to a young man, who considers them easy prey to his manipulations, that they would like to be rid of their elderly father; but after the murder, the brother and sister, by threatening to reveal his crime, force him into a sexual slavery, dividing his time between them. *Loot* parodies the conventions of the detective thriller through a story in which the money from a bank robbery is hidden in the casket of one robber's mother. It is eventually resolved when the robbers and the police inspector agree to share the loot. *What the Butler Saw*, set in a psychiatric hospital, travesties the conventions of farce in a complex set of misunderstandings, especially about sexual relationships.

Two other playwrights—Shaffer and Bolt—achieved considerable success in the theatre, although critics often expressed doubts about the significance of their work. Peter Shaffer (1926–   ) wrote in a variety of modes. His first success came in 1958 with *Five Finger Exercise,* a conventionally structured play about a German tutor's effect on an English household engaged in psychological

warfare. He then moved on to plays in the absurdist vein in *The Private Ear* and *The Public Eye* (1962), and into pure farce with *Black Comedy* (1965), in which most of the action supposedly transpires in darkness (caused by a power failure) as a young man juggles his complex personal relationships. But Shaffer's best-known plays—*The Royal Hunt of the Sun* (1964), *Equus* (1973), and *Amadeus* (1979)—use a narrative framework, which allows a protagonist to recall a puzzling experience and try to understand it. This framework permits time and place to be handled fluidly and with frank theatricality. The plays also employ the same basic pattern: a sophisticated, disillusioned character, much to his chagrin, comes to envy a naive, unquestioning character and ultimately becomes the instrument through which that other character's faith or life is destroyed. Though he considers the other person unprepared to exist in the perilous world of intrigue and doubt, he nevertheless envies and would like to achieve comparable faith and certainty, while recognizing his own inability to do so. Shaffer, among the most commercially successful dramatists of his time, was often downgraded for what some critics saw as his romantic longing for a return to a state of innocence.

Robert Bolt (1924–   ), originally a teacher, had his first production in London in 1957 with *The Flowering Cherry,* a Chekhovian study of self-deception and failure. His most successful play, *A Man for All Seasons* (1960), based on the life and martyrdom of Sir Thomas More, is ultimately concerned with the moral and personal conflicts of all ages. To link More's ideas to the twentieth century, Bolt uses the Common Man, a chorus-like figure who addresses the audience, introduces characters, assumes different roles, and comments on the action. Bolt described his approach as a "bastardized version of . . . Brecht." He never repeated the success of *A Man for All Seasons,* although his *Vivat! Vivat Regina!* (1970), a sympathetic treatment of Elizabeth I's conflict with Mary of Scotland, achieved considerable popularity.

THE UNITED STATES

In the United States, the cost of producing plays on Broadway continued to escalate during the 1960s, intensifying a long-standing pattern of smash hit or dismal failure. The number of new productions each season declined from about sixty at the beginning of the decade to thirty-eight in 1970. At the same time, ticket prices moved upward from $7.50 to $9.50 for dramatic pieces and from $6.60 to $15.00 for musicals. The type of musical that had dominated the stage since World War II continued to be the most popular form, and composers continued to be prolific and successful through the 1960s. Among the most popular new works were *Funny Girl* (1964) by Jule Styne, *Fiddler on the Roof* (1964) by Jerry Bock, *Hello, Dolly* (1964) and *Mame* (1965) by Jerry Herman, and *Cabaret* (1966) and *Zorba* (1968) by John Kander.

During the 1960s, New York made an attempt to overcome its lack of a permanent resident company like those found in most major European cities. About 1960 plans were announced for the Lincoln Center for the Performing Arts, with facilities for ballet, opera, concerts, and drama. In 1963, a repertory company was formed, with Elia Kazan and Robert Whitehead as directors and Harold Clurman as "executive consultant." Since its permanent home was not yet completed, it opened its first season in 1964 in a temporary building erected in Greenwich Village. Because Kazan was still considered America's finest director and because Arthur Miller and S. N. Behrman had been commissioned to write new plays for the company, expectations were

high. But Behrman's *But for Whom, Charlie* and Miller's *Incident at Vichy* received lukewarm receptions, and Miller's *After the Fall* drew attention largely because it was thought to deal with Miller's marriage to Marilyn Monroe. Disappointment reached a peak with Kazan's production of the Jacobean play *The Changeling*. No doubt expectations were too high, since an ensemble cannot be created instantly, but *The Changeling* was thought to pinpoint the weakness of the "method" as then taught at the Actors Studio, where the focus was almost entirely on modern realistic plays. The failure of Kazan's production was crucial in the growing disenchantment with the method during the 1960s. In the wake of critical attacks, Kazan and Whitehead resigned.

They were replaced by Herbert Blau and Jules Irving who had achieved great success at the Actors Workshop in San Francisco. In 1965, Blau's production of Büchner's *Danton's Death* inaugurated the newly completed Vivian Beaumont Theatre at Lincoln Center. Seating about 1,100, this theatre had a proscenium-arch stage that could be extended to form a thrust stage. The first season in the new theatre, which included works by Wycherley, Sartre, and Brecht, was only marginally successful, and when the second season encountered serious difficulties, Blau resigned in 1967. Irving struggled on until 1973 but could never solve the theatre's considerable financial and artistic problems.

Lincoln Center was also home to the Juilliard School's actor-training program, inaugurated in 1969 under the direction of John Houseman and Michel Saint-Denis and following the basic plan that Saint-Denis had used in other theatre schools in France, England, and Canada, thereby creating a line from Copeau into the American theatre. As at the Old Vic School following World War II, a company, called simply the Acting Company, was formed to create a bridge for graduates of the school into the professional theatre. From the beginning, it toured regularly throughout the United States.

For a time, New York also had a second permanent company in the Association of Producing Artists (APA). Founded in 1960 by Ellis Rabb (1930–   ), the APA gave its first performances in Bermuda and toured widely before appearing in New York in 1962. In 1964 it formed an alliance with the Phoenix Theatre, which after that time acted as its producer; in 1965 the Phoenix abandoned its off-Broadway house to present the APA on Broadway and on tour. Unlike the Lincoln Center company, the APA was highly praised from the beginning, especially for the excellent acting of such performers as Helen Hayes, Rosemary Harris, Nancy Marchand, Donald Moffat, Will Geer, Rabb, and others. Its repertory was also impressive, ranging through works by Shaw, Chekhov, Pirandello, Giraudoux, Sheridan, Ibsen, Shakespeare, Molière, Ghelderode, Ionesco, and Eliot. Although it was sometimes accused of being concerned only with preserving past tradition (it did not present any new plays), it offered the most impressive cross-section of drama to be seen in America. Unfortunately, in the late 1960s it ran into trouble as its grants expired and as major actors defected. In 1969 it ceased performing in New York and in 1970 was dissolved.

Perhaps the greatest lack of the Broadway theatre in the 1960s was significant drama. Despite a steady stream of diverting productions, few of the scripts were of lasting quality. The most popular writer was Neil Simon (1927–   ), who, after a tentative beginning with *Come Blow Your Horn* (1961), hit his stride with a stream of hits, among them *Barefoot in the Park* (1963), *The Odd Couple* (1965), and *Plaza Suite* (1968). They were followed by still others, such as *The Sunshine Boys* (1972), *Biloxi Blues* (1985), and *Rumors* (1988). All made use of eccentric characters

and zany humor, although the later plays tended to acquire serious overtones.

The most critically acclaimed American dramatist of the 1960s was Edward Albee (1928–   ), whose first four plays, all short— *The Zoo Story* (1958), *The Death of Bessie Smith* (1960), *The Sandbox* (1960), and *The American Dream* (1961)—were produced off-Broadway in 1960–1961. Some of them show affinities with absurdism, and all deal with characters who are cut off from meaningful human contact by a society which indifferently discards its rejects. Albee's first full-length and most successful play was *Who's Afraid of Virginia Woolf?* (1962), which, in the vein of Strindberg and O'Neill, explores the destructive psychological relationship of its principal characters, George and Martha, who are held together by an intense love-hate relationship which is painfully abrasive both to themselves and to those around them. During a night of drinking and sadomasochistic games, they strip each other of their illusions but perhaps achieve a more realistic view of themselves as they come to accept each other's shortcomings and the awareness that life will not give them what they had hoped for. Albee's subsequent plays— *Tiny Alice* (1964), *A Delicate Balance* (1966), *All Over* (1971), *Seascape* (1975), and *The Lady From Dubuque* (1980)—were received with respect but more often with puzzlement, since their surface stories often were unsatisfying and the messages of their parables remained unclear. All seem to imply that human beings have lost the ability to cope with their problems and anxieties because they refuse to accept responsibility for their lives and invent rationalizations or project responsibility onto others for their own and the world's inadequacies.

Arthur Kopit (1937–   ) first attracted attention with *Oh, Dad, Poor Dad, Mama's Hung You in the Closet and I'm Feeling So Sad* (1960). Subtitled "A Pseudoclassical Tragifarce in a Bastard French Tradition," the play

FIG. 13.21
Albee's *Who's Afraid of Virginia Woolf?* in 1962 with Uta Hagen as Martha, George Grizzard as Nick, and Arthur Hill as George. (Photo by A. Jeffry.)

derives from absurdism but also parodies the more bizarre and decadent aspects of Williams' dramas, as a young man frees himself from his emasculating mother, who keeps her dead husband's stuffed body hanging in a closet and has piranhas and Venus' flytraps as pets. Kopit was not able to repeat his success until *Indians* (1968), a depiction of America's relations with Native Americans as seen through the distorting lens of Buffalo Bill's Wild West Show as it moves freely backward in time to show the dignity of the Native Americans and the duplicity of whites. It was another variation on the then-popular theme of the American dream gone awry. Kopit wrote only sporadically for the stage thereafter, his most important works being *Wings* (1978), which shows a woman, following a severe stroke, battling to regain the power of speech and all it entails; and *End of the World* (1984), about the specter of nuclear war.

During the 1960s, off-Broadway was plagued by the same problems as Broadway as costs of production rose. Unions withdrew many of the concessions they had made during the 1950s, and raised their minimum wage scales. This led to greater caution in choice of plays and to higher ticket prices. Therefore, although off-Broadway continued to play an important role, the distinctions between it and Broadway eroded.

The role played by off-Broadway in the 1950s passed during the 1960s to off-off-Broadway, usually dated from 1958 when Joe Cino opened the Café Cino, a coffeehouse which served also as an art gallery and as a place for poetry readings and dramatic presentations. At first, plays were given only occasionally, but from 1961 on they formed a regular part of the program. Soon Cino was besieged by young playwrights seeking a hearing for their plays. By the time Cino died in 1967, his willingness to assist young artists had made him one of the most beloved figures of Greenwich Village. As the kind of program instituted by Cino was taken up by others,

FIG. 13.22
The original production of Kopit's *Indians,*
performed by the RSC in 1968. (Courtesy the
Royal Shakespeare Company.)

fire safety regulations), Stewart established her LaMama Experimental Theatre Club (ostensibly a private organization free from many regulations), where by 1967 she had presented some 175 plays by 130 writers, as well as serving as host to other groups. After moving several times, LaMama in 1969 acquired its own building with two theatres that met all fire regulations. By that time it was also one of the most potent forces in the New York theatre, during the 1969–1970 season producing more plays than were seen on Broadway that year. The influence of LaMama was not restricted to the United States. In 1964, Stewart began taking her groups abroad, where they were greeted with such enthusiasm that she agreed to establish branches in such cities as Copenhagen, Bogotá, and Tokyo. Her companies performed so frequently at festivals that LaMama became a source of inspiration throughout Europe for young groups seeking to escape established patterns.

During the 1960s, LaMama was a playwright's theatre where talent was nourished. Some of the plays were good, many amateurish; often novelty seemed to be valued over effectiveness (or perhaps criteria for judging effectiveness were absent). Nevertheless, no organization did so much to encourage new writers. Because many of LaMama's writers were Artaudian (in approaching the brain through the nerves and sinews), a comparable directorial approach seemed to be needed. It was perfected by Tom O'Horgan (1926–   ), who emphasized frenetic physical activity, tableaux, bold anti-illusionistic devices, amplified music and sound, strobe lighting, and gimmickry of various sorts. Probably because his productions gradually came to obscure the scripts, O'Horgan came into conflict with Stewart and left the company. Nevertheless, his directorial style, probably seen at its best in the Broadway production of *Hair,* popularized a physicalization that was appropriate to many

plays were soon being presented almost anywhere. Essentially an amateur movement in its early years, off-off-Broadway had minimal budgets and depended on passing the hat for receipts. Nevertheless, between 1960 and 1965 it presented some four hundred new plays by over two hundred new playwrights.

By far the most influential of the off-off-Broadway producers was Ellen Stewart (1931–   ), who, without any previous theatrical experience, began in 1961 to present plays in a converted basement room. After encountering setbacks from municipal authorities (such theatres were often closed on charges of violating verbally inarticulate scripts, although perhaps less useful when applied to other types.

LaMama was merely the most important of numerous off-off-Broadway groups. Some, after precarious beginnings, would, like LaMama, achieve something approaching institutional status. Two of them were the American Place Theatre and the New York Shakespeare Festival. The American Place Theatre, founded in 1964 by Wynn Handman and Sidney Lanier, was housed in St. Clement's Church. Its goal was to rejuvenate the American theatre by encouraging writers with proven talent to write for the stage. Most of those it encouraged, among them Robert Lowell, Paul Goodman, and Joyce Carol Oates, were novelists or poets, although it did from time to time turn to such dramatists as Sam Shepard and Ed Bullins. Its mission won ongoing support from subscribers and foundations, and in 1971 it moved into one of the several new theatres included in mid-Manhattan skyscrapers because of tax incentives offered builders by the city. Despite its admirable goal, its success was limited, perhaps because it failed to recognize that dramatic and novelistic sensibilities differ.

Joseph Papp (1921–   ) founded the New York Shakespeare Festival in 1954. Beginning in 1957, he offered city-subsidized free performances of Shakespeare in Central Park, where in 1962 the city built the Delacorte Theatre, an outdoor amphitheatre seating 2,236, to accommodate the productions. In 1964 Papp began to tour some productions to New York neighborhoods, giving free performances for local residents. He consistently argued that, if the theatre is to escape the middle-class biases that had created most of its problems, it had to attract a new audience. Thus, he sought to show those who had not attended the theatre that it was both relevant and entertaining. In 1967, Papp further enlarged his activities when he persuaded the city to buy the Astor Library and lease it to him for

virtually no rent. The building was transformed into the Public Theatre with five auditoriums. It was inaugurated with a production of *Hair*, which after its initial run was restaged by O'Horgan. That musical's phenomenal success on Broadway (from which his company reaped no financial benefits) provided a lesson that Papp would exploit many times thereafter as in the post-1968 period when he transferred several productions to Broadway.

Other important off-off-Broadway groups of the 1960s included Judson Poets' Theatre and Theatre Genesis. The former came into existence in 1961 when the Judson Memorial Church on Washington Square began to subsidize arts programs, including dance and theatre. The assistant pastor and director of arts programs, Al Carmines, directed about half of the productions and Lawrence Kornfeld the others. Carmines came to be especially well-known as the composer of small-scale musicals, among them *Promenade*. The theatre's offerings ranged through works by Strindberg and Gertrude Stein to happenings and new plays. Theatre Genesis, housed in St. Mark's Church in the Bowery, was established in 1964. Headed by Ralph Cook, who staged most of the productions, it sought to assist new playwrights, and was the first to present plays by Sam Shepard.

The playwrights of the off-off-Broadway theatre were numerous indeed and together did much to shift American drama toward experimentation with form and disaffection from the mores and values of the past. Some of the writers who attracted the greatest attention during the 1960s failed to develop thereafter. Among these, two—Owens and Foster—may be taken as representative. Rochelle Owens (1936–   ) achieved considerable notoriety with *Futz* (1961, first staged in 1965 and restaged by O'Horgan in 1967). It treats rural characters near-mad from repressed sexual longings, who, seeking to maintain their inhibitions, destroy Cyrus Futz when he develops a passion for his sow. Owens suggests that Futz's passion is more natural than that of the local puritans, one of whom strangles a girl in a fit of passion when he hears Futz making love to his sow. The play demonstrates a considerable gift for imagery and surrealistic devices. Owens' subsequent plays—among them *Beclch* (1969) and *Queen of Greece* (1969)—develop conflicts between polar adversaries, blending cruelty and supplication. Owens was concerned with the never-ending conflict between simple and repressive people. Often disturbing and violent, the plays were among the most imaginative and imagistic of the decade. Paul Foster (1931–   ) was for a time very prolific but is best known for *Balls* (1964) and *Tom Paine* (1968). In the first, the audience sees only two moving pingpong balls while amplified voices evoke memories which suggest that life is too fleeting to be wasted in unnecessary repressions. *Tom Paine* (in O'Horgan's production) became one of New York's hits of

1968. In it, actors introduced themselves to the audience and then elected to enact the story of Tom Paine; to differentiate between Paine the man (arrogant, conceited, drunken) and Paine's ideal (equality for all humankind), the protagonist was played by two different actors, around whom the rest of the scarcely differentiated cast swirled, depicting Paine's distress. Many sections were left for the actors to improvise. Other playwrights who began their careers in off-off-Broadway in the 1960s—among them Sam Shepard, Lanford Wilson, and Maria Irene Fornes—would become far more important after 1970. (They will be discussed later.)

During the 1960s an African-American theatre movement also emerged. The promising advances of the interwar years had largely faded after 1939 with the demise of the Federal Theatre Project. A few efforts in the late 1940s—such as the Manhattan Arts Theatre and the American Negro Theatre—were abortive. The "black arts movement" of the

FIG. 13.23
Kevin O'Connor in the title role of *Tom Paine* by Paul Foster. Directed by Tom O'Horgan for Ellen Stewart's LaMama Experimental Theatre Club. (Photo by Friedman-Abeles.)

1960s differed from its predecessors in accepting the integrity and dignity of the African-American experience and in its unwillingness to compromise with white sensibilities as the price for success. Ultimately, the difference lay in a change in African-American consciousness—toward firm belief in the worth of "blackness" and all it entailed. Many African-Americans took their inspiration from Maulana Ron Karenga, who suggested seven requisites for a black culture: unity, self-determination, collective work and responsibility, cooperative economic policies, sense of common purpose, creativity, and faith.

The African-American theatre movement received its first important impetus from the Black Arts Repertoire Theatre, founded in New York in 1964 by LeRoi Jones (Imamu Baraka), Clarence Reed, Johnny Moore, Charles and William Patterson, and others. This group produced a number of plays, with support from the Office of Economic Opportunity, but it came to an end when Congress became concerned about the radical tone of its work. By that time other groups were springing up throughout the country. By 1968 there were about forty groups scattered throughout the United States. The most important of these were Black Arts/West (in San Francisco), Concept East (in Detroit), Spirit House (in Newark), the New Lafayette Theatre and the Negro Ensemble Company (both in New York). The last three were the most influential.

Spirit House was founded by LeRoi Jones, who, wholly rejecting white culture and changing his name to Imamu Baraka, left New York for Newark and sought to create a black arts movement completely removed from the white context. It served as a model for more radical African-American groups but eventually lost its power as militancy declined in the 1970s. The New Lafayette Theatre, founded in 1967, was headed by Robert Macbeth and served as a cultural center for Harlem. It received several grants from the Ford Foundation to support both a company and a workshop devoted to developing plays about African-American life. It also provided a focus for African-American groups throughout the country through an information service and *Black Theatre Magazine*. Unfortunately, dissension within the company brought its dissolution in 1973. The Negro Ensemble Company (NEC) was established in 1968 with financial support from the Ford Foundation. Douglas Turner Ward was artistic director, Robert Hooks executive director, and Gerald S. Krone administrative director. In addition to a permanent company, it included a training program for actors, directors, and playwrights. Housed in St. Marks Playhouse on the Lower East Side, it performed a varied repertory of works considered meaningful to African-Americans. It was among the least militant of African-American organizations and was often accused by more radical groups of fearing to offend whites or established middle-class African-Americans. Nevertheless, it is the only one of the major companies that still survives.

African-American theatre created a demand for African-American performers, and these not only were accepted in African-American theatres but also gained increasing acceptance in integrated companies. Among the best-known were James Earl Jones, Sidney Poitier, Ruby Dee, Claudia McNeil, Ossie Davis, Roscoe Lee Brown, Moses Gunn, Robert Hooks, and John O'Neal.

African-American theatre also created a demand for plays by African-American dramatists. Two—Baldwin and Hansberry—had gained recognition before the African-American theatre movement was fully underway. James Baldwin (1924–1987) began his career as a novelist during the 1950s. His first play, *The Amen Corner* (1955), depicts a son who, torn between his revivalist mother and jazz-musician father, eventually breaks free from his family.

Blues for Mister Charlie (1964) reflected Baldwin's rage over the Emmet Till case (in which a white man in Mississippi was acquitted of killing a young African-American whose sole offense was whistling at a white woman). It moves freely in time and place while tracing several intertwined stories relating to racism.

Lorraine Hansberry (1930–1965) completed only two plays, *A Raisin in the Sun* (1959) and *The Sign in Sidney Brustein's Window* (1964). The former has proved an enduring work. A warm, rich, moving study of family relationships and maturing values, it deals with the dreams and setbacks of an African-American family in Chicago and with the integrity and pride they affirm in the face of racism. Although conventional in its structure, it treated most of the themes that would be developed in subsequent African-American drama: integration versus separation of the races, American versus African values, the necessity of African-Americans to define their own goals, equality versus discrimination. The first play by an African-American woman to be presented on Broadway, it won the New York Drama Critics Circle Award. The second play treats a well-meaning Greenwich Village idealist, too busy campaigning for reform to recognize the problems that exist within his own family until he is forced to reassess his values. After Hansberry's death two other works were produced. *Les Blancs,* concerning the impossibility of two men from different races maintaining a friendship in an age of racial conflict, was presented in 1970 in an adaptation by Robert Nemiroff (Hansberry's husband), who also compiled *To Be Young, Gifted, and Black* (1971) from Hansberry's letters, diaries, notebooks, and plays.

The increasing militancy of African-American drama during the 1960s probably owes most to Imamu Baraka (LeRoi Jones, 1934–

FIG. 13.24
Lorraine Hansberry's *A Raisin in the Sun* in 1959. The cast included Sidney Poitier, Claudia McNeil, Ruby Dee, and Diana Sands. (Photo by Friedman-Abeles.)

). His early plays deal with love-hate relationships among African-Americans and whites which seem not beyond resolution. In *The Toilet* (1964) a group of African-American students round up a white boy, Jimmy, and beat him unmercifully because he allegedly has shown an attraction to an African-American boy, Ray. After the attackers leave, Ray returns stealthily and cradles Jimmy in his arms. Here the fear of homosexuality serves as a metaphor for the fears that keep the races apart. A far less sympathetic view is seen in *Dutchman* (1964), probably Baraka's most admired play. Set in a subway car, it shows a young white woman, Lulu, accosting a young middle-class African-American, Clay, and provoking him into a show of violence, thereby giving her an excuse for killing him. With Clay dead, Lulu is ready for her next victim. Lulu seems to represent whites who resent African-Americans escaping the stereotypes into which they have been placed and using any show of resentment as an excuse for destroying them. The play's title echoes Wagner's *The Flying Dutchman,* with the subway replacing the ship on which the protagonist is doomed to relive a pattern of behavior forever.

As the 1960s progressed, Baraka argued that African-Americans should separate themselves wholly from whites, whom he came to see as devils. The most powerful of his later plays is *Slave Ship* (1967), a montage of scenes tracing the African-American experience in America—beginning with transportation on a slave ship (which serves as a metaphor for the treatment of African-Americans by whites), then the substitution of a debased white culture for African language and religion and the betrayal of African-Americans by traitors of their own race, and the eventual rebellion against whites in the 1960s and the killing of African-American traitors. Influenced by African tribal ceremonies, the play emphasizes music, spectacle, and sound rather than language. As in several others of his plays, Baraka here champions a simple, separatist, near-tribal experience.

One of the best and most prolific African-American dramatist of the 1960s was Ed Bullins (1935–   ), resident playwright at the New Lafayette Theatre and editor of *Black Theatre Magazine*. Several of Bullins' plays are concerned with detached (or pseudo) intellectuals, as in *The Electronic Nigger* (1968), with its protagonist who is more interested in big words and parroted ideas than in the problems of the world around him. In *The Pig Pen* (1970), the protagonist, married to a white woman, discusses ideas and recommends books to his

FIG. 13.25
Ed Bullins' *Clara's Old Man* at the American Place Theatre, New York, in 1968. (Photo by Martha Holmes.)

integrated group but remains politically aloof until the news of Malcolm X's assassination precipitates a crisis that shatters relations between whites and African-Americans and suggests that African-Americans can no longer remain uncommitted. In the late 1960s, Bullins also began work on a projected cycle of twenty plays about the life of African-American people in the industrial North and West, of which only *In the Wine Time* (1968) and *In New England Winter* (1970) apparently were completed. After the collapse of the New Lafayette Theatre, Bullins' productivity diminished greatly, although he did go on to write other plays, among them *The Taking of Miss Jamie* (1975) and *Daddy* (1977).

Two playwrights are known for single, powerful works. Lonne Elder III's (1932–   ) *Ceremonies in Dark Old Men* (1969) is a compassionate picture of a Harlem family seeking to attain a sense of accomplishment through the only means that seem open to it—various illegal activities—but ending in disaster. Charles Gordone's (1925–   ) *No Place to Be Somebody* (1967), the first play by an African-American author to win the Pulitzer Prize, shows an illiterate African-American owner of a bar trying to start his own version of the Mafia as a way of getting back at the white world. It, too, ends in disaster and death. The main interest lies in the characters, imaginative dialogue, and casual air that unexpectedly bursts into violence.

Other African-American playwrights of the 1960s include Douglas Turner Ward (artistic director of the Negro Ensemble Company), Ron Milner, Ossie Davis, Adrienne Kennedy, and Melvin van Peebles. Despite great diversity, African-American playwrights were united in their aim of building racial pride. For a time, this seemed to dictate denunciation of whites, to such an extent that few whites felt comfortable at African-American performances. Not until the 1970s would African-American writers

gradually abandon this preoccupation to concentrate on the great variety to be found in the African-American experience.

Increased social and political awareness in the 1960s led to the formation of several radical companies that sought to use theatre as a weapon for change. Among the most important of these were the Bread and Puppet Theatre, the San Francisco Mime Troupe, El Teatro Campesino, and the Free Southern Theatre.

The Bread and Puppet Theatre was founded in 1961 by Peter Schumann, who had come to New York from Germany with the intention of forming a dance company. The theatre's name reflects both its philosophy and primary productional device. Schumann stated, "Theatre . . . is more like bread, more like a necessity" and at most performances this idea was reaffirmed by the ritual offering of bread to the audience. The group's productions used puppets or "moving sculptures" of various sizes, some as large as 12 feet tall and requiring several operators. Building on fairy tales, myths, biblical, and other familiar material, Schumann sought to create actions larger, simpler, and more profound than would be possible with the human figure. The company made all of its puppets and properties from "found" materials—old clothes, newspapers, and scrap wood. By 1970 the Bread and Puppet Theatre had presented about seventy shows of various kinds in New York and on tour in the U.S. and abroad. It began each performance with a parade of puppet figures and players. Then came a parable-like drama, such as *The Cry of the People for Meat,* in which capitalism sires violence (illustrated through Greek and biblical figures). Contemporary events are then interwoven with biblical events as when the Massacre of the Innocents is treated as an air raid in Vietnam. At the end, a tableau of the Last Supper is shattered by warplanes that destroy the participants. It seeks to provoke rejection of capitalism and violence and to win

FIG. 13.26
Outdoor performance in 1970 by the Bread and Puppet Theatre at the University of Kansas. (Photo courtesy Ronald A. Willis.)

acceptance of Christian values. Schumann subsequently moved his company to a farm in Vermont, where after 1974 it performed much less frequently and reduced the radical tone of its message. It has continued to the present, being best-known for its annual performances of *Domestic Resurrection Circus,* which seeks to show the banality of evil and to build hope. It continues to draw participants and spectators from all over the world.

The San Francisco Mime Troupe was founded in 1959 by R. G. Davis, a member of the Actors Workshop, under whose auspices its first performances were given. Originally it did silent plays but later introduced speech because silence dampened audience response. In 1962 it began to perform in parks and similar locations. In its early years, the company was influenced by *commedia dell'arte.* Not until 1966, with *A Minstrel Show, or, Civil Rights in a Cracker Barrel* (an attack on racism and naive integrationism) did the troupe commit itself to radical politics and agit-prop plays. At that time, it also began to tour widely in the United

States and Canada in productions using a broad acting style which ridiculed everything it disliked and reinforced everything it favored. In 1970, after Davis left the company, it was collectivized, and all important decisions were made by the group as a whole. Its principal writer thereafter was Joan Holden. In 1984, on its twenty-fifth anniversary, it for the first time applied for and received a federal subsidy for its work. Nevertheless, its plays continued to be political and agitational, as can be seen from *Steeltown* (1985), which dealt with the decline of the labor movement and the suppression of the Left. Although it has been accused of reaching an accommodation with the status quo, it vigorously denies the charge.

El Teatro Campesino was founded in 1965 by Luis Valdez (1940–   ) in conjunction with the National Farm Workers Association to dramatize, through satirical agit-prop skits, the issues of the grape pickers' strike in California and to urge workers to join the union. After 1969, having accomplished its original objectives, it developed into a bilingual

FIG. 13.27
The San Francisco
Mime Troupe giving a
puppet show at
Colorado State
University in 1969.
(Photo courtesy
Ronald A. Willis.)

troupe, based in San Juan Bautista (California), and sought to create pride in the heritage and accomplishments of Mexican-Americans. Valdez wrote not only plays that drew on Mexican myths but also works about discrimination against Mexican-American citizens of the United States—most notably *Zoot Suit* (1976) and *I Don't Have to Show You No Stinking Badges* (1987). His film *La Bamba* won a following that reached far beyond the Hispanic community.

The Free Southern Theatre was founded in Mississippi in 1963 by John O'Neal and Gil Moses but moved to New Orleans in 1964, where for a time Richard Schechner was associated with it. Growing out of the civil rights movement, it was originally concerned primarily with promoting integration. Its first production, *In White America,* used an integrated company. But as it toured through the South, it became clear that many of the audiences it wished to reach had little interest in the standard plays that made up most of the repertory. Friction over the relative importance

of art and social change developed, and in 1968–1969 the company became all-African-American. Its financial problems were continuous, and it was reorganized more than once. By 1980 it was largely a one-person theatre—John O'Neal's. It was disbanded in 1983.

There were many other radical theatre groups in America. In 1967 several joined together to create the Radical Theatre Repertory, headed by Oda Jurges and Saul Gottlieb, and in 1968 it hosted the first radical theatre festival. Although few of these groups are now remembered, collectively they played an important role in helping to create the demand for change that was so characteristic of the time.

The 1960s also saw the greatest decentralization of the theatre since the nineteenth century. In addition to the numerous off-Broadway and off-off-Broadway companies, resident troupes were established throughout the country. The major impetus came in 1959 when the Ford Foundation made sizable grants to a number of existing troupes that had already managed to establish a foothold and seemed likely to survive. The grants permitted many of these organizations to become fully professional for the first time. Among the most important of these pioneering groups were the Actors Workshop in San Francisco, the Arena Stage in Washington, and the Alley Theatre in Houston. As new companies began to be formed, the Ford Foundation also provided funds in 1961 to establish the Theatre Communications Group (TCG) to serve as a focal point, source of information, and forum. The regional theatre movement was strengthened when Tyrone Guthrie, then considered one of the world's major directors, decided to found a theatre in Minneapolis. In 1963, the Minneapolis Theatre Company opened its Tyrone Guthrie Theatre, based architecturally on the Stratford (Canada) Festival Theatre, with a 1,400-seat auditorium wrapped around the three sides of a thrust stage. Guthrie served as artistic director for the first three years, and then was succeeded first by Douglas Campbell and later by Michael Langham.

The favorable publicity received by Minneapolis helped to convince other cities that they needed resident companies. By 1966, there were about thirty-five permanent companies, and for the first time in the twentieth century there were more actors working outside of than in New York. Practically all of these companies were presenting seasons of plays (part classics, part new or recent works) for limited runs. They resembled European subsidized troupes more than Broadway theatres. All of these companies, however, were haunted by the same problem—lack of assured continuing support—for, unlike their European counterparts, who could depend on continued government subsidies, the American companies were dependent on grants from foundations and private donors to make up their inevitable deficits. There was no assurance that grants

would be renewed. Therefore, companies lived in a state of uncertainty, wary of planning far ahead.

A major step toward government subsidy was taken in 1965 when federal legislation authorized the National Endowment for the Arts (NEA) and the first-ever direct subsidization of the arts by the federal government. In its first year of operation, 1966, the NEA had a pittance—$2.5 million—to distribute among all the arts. Subsequently, its funding grew but it was never large in relation to the country's population. Nevertheless, it served as an important catalyst. The NEA offered state governments incentives to establish arts agencies, and the states, in turn, encouraged the formation of community arts agencies. Eventually, every population center of any size had an arts agency. Nevertheless, there was still no recognition, as there was in Europe, that an enlightened government should commit itself to ongoing assistance to the arts rather than making commitments on a year-to-year basis.

The legitimization of the nonprofit theatre that came with foundation, government, and private support had important consequences. Perhaps most obviously, it led to the largest boom in public buildings for performing arts the United States had seen, as major cities sought to avoid being considered culturally backward because they did not have a performing arts or cultural center. In turn, new buildings demanded activities to justify them. The result was a strong thrust toward decentralization of the arts.

THE MOVE TOWARD COMMITMENT

During the 1960s, the theatre, for the most part, continued to be prosperous. It also tended to continue along paths first made evident in the 1950s. But, at the same time, questioning of values and standards, fueled by social and political tensions associated with the struggle for civil rights, American involvement in Vietnam, East European attempts to be free from Russian domination, and other developments, was creating unrest which was reflected in playwriting and dramatic production. The goals of objectivity and neutrality gradually gave way to demands for commitment. All of these forces were to come to a head in 1968 and create upheavals that would seriously affect the theatre of the 1970s.

Chapter 14

Reshaping
the Theatre

*1968 and
Its Aftermath*

By 1968 enormous societal stresses were evident in Europe and the U.S. Public demonstrations and group protests (often leading to disruptions and violence) became an increasingly common part of daily life. These developments were symptomatic of deep-seated doubts about national policies and the willingness of governments to acknowledge the need for change. Individuals and groups began to insist that their convictions took precedence over laws they disapproved of and to demand the alteration or destruction of anything contrary to their views. The resulting fragmentation sometimes threatened to become anarchy.

The theatre could not remain aloof from these stresses. Its very nature and function became major subjects of controversy as the conception that art is concerned with contemplation, beauty, and insight was challenged by demands that it reflect immediate social issues and serve as an instrument of reform.

Both social and theatrical discontents reached a crisis in 1968. Demonstrators and police clashed in near-riots at the Democratic Party Convention in Chicago in full view of an international television audience; student rebels and workers in France paralyzed the de Gaulle government and brought its downfall; Russian troops invaded Czechoslovakia to end the reforms that threatened Soviet domination there; in England, censorship of plays, in effect since 1737, was abolished; nudity and obscenity appeared for the first time on Broadway; the Living Theatre, both in Europe and the U.S., virtually erased distinctions between theatrical performance and political stance. The decade that followed was one of frenetic innovation. But by the late 1970s a reaction had set in, and many of the groups and practices that had been so popular were coming to seem irrelevant.

THE IDEATIONAL CONTEXT

Much that happened in the late 1960s and the 1970s reflected ideas that had been taking shape since World War II. Among the most important of these influences was a network of concerns comprehended under "the New Left" (so-called because of its disenchantment with the "old" Left). In England it was triggered in 1956 by the Suez crisis and the crushing of the Hungarian uprising, events that called into question the imperialism of both East and West. In the United States it was brought into focus by the civil rights movement, especially such groups as Students for a Democratic Society (SDS) and the Student Nonviolent Coordinating Committee (SNCC), and was intensified as the war in Vietnam escalated after 1964. Disenchantment with the old Left

was further fueled throughout Europe by the Soviet invasion of Czechoslovakia in 1968.

The New Left was much influenced by neo-Marxism, especially as set forth by György Lukács (1885–1971), Jürgen Habermas (1929–), and Herbert Marcuse (1898–1979). The neo-Marxists were opposed to Stalinist dogmatic Marxism and sought to replace it with an open-ended, self-critical approach. They placed great emphasis on Marx's early concern for "alienation" as the central process in an emerging self-consciousness stemming from awareness that workers had lost control over the process of work, over the product of their labor, and over their own being, having themselves become things. The neo-Marxists redefined the proletariat, arguing that in modern society workers may also be technicians and engineers. In the United States, the neo-Marxist position was expressed most fully in Marcuse's writings, especially *Eros and Civilization* (1955), *One-Dimensional Man* (1964), and *An Essay on Liberation* (1969). Marcuse did not envision the new proletariat demanding change, but rather argued that social evils would be overcome only through the efforts of student and minority groups. He also added that true revolution is seldom possible in sated societies; instead, utopian thought, with its demand for instant fulfillment, is acted out in such rituals as demonstrations and sit-ins. Not all members of the New Left were Marxists, but they shared a rejection of technocratic society, whether Western or Soviet, and a belief that only the "alienated" see clearly the problems of society and have the incentive to insist on change.

Neo-Freudian thought also influenced the New Left. Many postwar psychologists sought to amend Freud's view that individuals are motivated by inborn instinctual drives that control the libido. They argued that environmental forces and social contexts are equally important. Neo-Freudians included Karen

Horney, Erich Fromm, and others, but the most influential in the years immediately after 1966 was probably R. D. Laing (1927–1989), an "existential psychoanalyst." In such books as *The Divided Self* (1960) and *The Politics of Experience* (1967), Laing argued that sexually based anxieties are relatively minor problems. He stated that what we label mental illness is merely a form of role-playing in which a "self" is constructed in order to cope with disturbing realities. He went on to say that Freudian psychology assumes that society represents the norm to which the individual is to be adjusted, whereas in actuality it may be society that needs alteration. Laing's views were easily converted into demands for changes in social mores and for acceptance of alternative life styles, demands that increasingly strengthened during the 1960s and 1970s. These demands were further supported by the writings of Norman O. Brown (1913–   ), among them *Life Against Death* (1959) and *Love's Body* (1966), which opposed technocratic society, competitive activity, tradition, and rationality. Brown rejected the idea that "character" requires the acceptance of restraints which delay gratification of desires; rather, he argued, happiness depends on freedom from restraints. In his world, there was little room for family, monogamy, or discrete sexual preference since they placed restraints on feeling, impulse, and pleasure. Brown's writings were extremely popular, and his vision of noncompetitive, communal activity (both private and public) influenced both lifestyles and performance modes.

Brown's views were compatible with another interest of the 1960s: "sensitivity" training—urging the members of a group to reveal their repressed (often extremely intimate) impulses, desires, and hostilities, thereby making themselves vulnerable but laying the foundations for trust and openness (as a means of overcoming the secretiveness and hypocrisy

thought to characterize a corrupted society). Such techniques came to be used not only therapeutically but also for ridding actors of inhibitions and building a spirit of ensemble in a company.

Social psychologists also began to describe personality not as fixed but as a series of roles which are assumed and discarded according to the situation and the participants, one role flowing into another in a series of transformations. (These views easily dovetailed with sensitivity training, since understanding how and why oneself and others adopt or change roles made it possible to choose or refuse the roles demanded by social conventions.) These perceptions form the basis for Erving Goffman's *The Presentation of Self in Everyday Life* (1959) and Eric Berne's *Games People Play* (1964). They also undergird Viola Spolin's *Improvisation for the Theatre* (1963), the work that popularized "theatre games" and transformational role playing in actor training and performance. They further served as basis for the improvisational company, Second City, founded in 1959 in Chicago by Spolin's son, Paul Sills.

Many of these developments were related as well to the increased acceptance, in practically all fields, of structuralism with its insistence on the precedence of underlying hidden patterns over surface messages. At first concerned only with linguistics, structuralism originated in Ferdinand de Saussure's *Course in General Linguistics* (1916), which argued that language is arbitrary rather than logical and that with any given language the overall system (*langue*)—the scheme of relationships among its elements—must be internalized (imprinted in the brain below the level of consciousness) before one can either speak or understand what another is saying. This master system is sometimes referred to as the *deep structure* of language which undergirds the *surface structure* or individual utterance (*parole*). *Langue* is analogous to the rules of a game, whereas *parole* is analogous to an individual's application of the rules in a particular situation. Since for them deep structure (*langue*) always takes precedence over surface structure (*parole*), structuralists are not so much interested in individual utterance as in the underlying set of relationships which makes communication possible.

Theatre practitioners were attracted to structuralism primarily by way of the writings of the French anthropologist Claude Lévi-Strauss (1908–   ), especially *The Elementary Structures of Kinship* (1949, revised 1967), *Structural Anthropology* (1963), and *The Savage Mind* (1966). Lévi-Strauss studied tribal customs, totems, and myths as analogues of language and therefore as modes of communication; to modern eyes, these alternative systems may seem chaotic, but, Lévi-Strauss argues, any system is arbitrary and functions only because it is composed of a societally accepted set of perceived categories, relationships, and contrasts that make up a "grid" which determines how that society perceives the world and how its members communicate with each other. Primitive societies use different modes of conceptual understanding than we do, but ones no less complex and abstract than ours. No communication grid is natural; each society creates its own grid, which it imprints on the minds of its members (as a part of the socializing process through which infants and children go) and which must be imprinted before they can communicate with each other. Lévi-Strauss also argues that myths (the focus of much of his work on primitive societies), when properly analyzed, reveal beneath their surface content the structural patterns (comparable to *langue*) that constitute that society's communication grid. Myth, then, is another way of thinking which, like language, decenters individual experience and privileges deep, archetypal structures.

Structuralists (including Lévi-Strauss) suggest that whatever grid is imposed by a society also incorporates certain basic assumptions that unconsciously influence how its users perceive and think about the world. Altering the grid, therefore, requires realigning all its parts, including the assumptions on which they are based. Thus, structuralism was compatible with the New Left, neo-Marxism, and neo-Freudianism, since the desires of all to reshape society depended on the simultaneous acceptance of new assumptions.

Structuralism influenced theatre primarily through its insistence that behind any surface action lies some far more fundamental, archetypal pattern, and that it is this hidden pattern that should be brought out and examined. This was the approach adopted by the Polish critic Jan Kott (1914–   ), whose highly influential *Shakespeare Our Contemporary* (1962), rather than concentrating on their surface stories and characters (which often link them to some past age), sought in Shakespeare's plays those underlying patterns, themes, and motifs which make the plays relevant to our time. Kott's book set forth an approach to scripts that was to be especially common from the 1960s on. This approach, essentially ahistorical, diverted concern from period-specific elements to those independent of time and place.

Another significant influence came from critics and theorists of electronic media, among whom the most prominent was Marshall McLuhan (1911–1980), author of *The Gutenberg Galaxy* (1963) and *The Medium is the Message* (1967). According to McLuhan, the invention of movable type in the fifteenth century made the printed page (with its linear arrangement) the primary medium of communication, and this linearity, in turn, encouraged serial thinking and sequential organization. With the coming of electronic media, communication became multisensory, and the human perceptual apparatus was conditioned by the new media to assimilate multiple and concurrent stimuli. McLuhan provided a rationale for downgrading language, for accepting multimedia, multiple focus, and means that involve the entire sensory apparatus rather than merely the eye and the ear. McLuhan also argued that the rapidity of electronic communication has converted the world into a global village, thereby speeding up the dissemination of ideas and encouraging cross-cultural interminglings of all sorts, including artistic.

THE LIVING THEATRE

Of all the groups dedicated to altering society and theatre, probably the most militant was the Living Theatre. Furthermore, its influence on young people in Europe and America made it especially significant in shaping change after 1960. The Living Theatre, though not originally under that name, was founded in 1946 by Judith Malina (1926–   ), one of Piscator's students, and Julian Beck (1925–1985). Their first production was given in their living room, and

subsequently they moved from one space to another, usually after difficulties with fire inspectors. Not until 1959 were they able to find a satisfactory home. Up until that time, they were interested primarily in poetic drama and nonrealistic production. They had performed works by Lorca, Gertrude Stein, Paul Goodman, Eliot, Picasso, Jarry, Kenneth Rexroth, and Brecht. They had also discovered Artaud and had become interested in applying his theories.

The turning point in the Living Theatre's work came in 1959 with *The Connection* by Jack Gelber (1932–   ), in which supposed drug addicts have agreed to be the subject of a documentary film, parts of which are being shot as the audience watches. While the addicts await their drug connection, they pass the time in small talk, arguments, performance of jazz music, all frequently interrupted by the producer; the connection finally arrives and one of the addicts nearly dies. The overall effect was that of a spontaneous, naturalistic slice of life. With it, the Living Theatre won a number of awards in New York, and in Paris it

FIG. 14.1
The Living Theatre's production of Jack Gelber's *The Connection* in 1959. Directed by Judith Malina, designed by Julian Beck, music by Cecil Payne and Kenny Drew. (Courtesy Mark Hall Amitin.)

won the prestigious Critics Circle Award at the Théâtre des Nations in 1961.

After 1959 the Living Theatre became increasingly interested in improvisation and chance. In 1960 it presented Jackson MacLow's *The Marrying Maiden,* for which the author chose a text and five hundred verbs relating to action and delivery of lines. At each performance the order of the lines and their combination with the verbs were determined by chance (using *I Ching*). Thus, the play differed each time. In 1963 the company presented Kenneth Brown's *The Brig,* which follows the inmates of a Marine prison through one day. There was virtually no story; most of the business was improvised. Seemingly a documentary, its primary emphasis was on repetitive and repressive ritual. *The Connection* and *The Brig* were crucial influences on the Living Theatre's subsequent work, in which its actors did not pretend to be characters so much as to present archetypal societal conditions. Furthermore, they moved away from scripted performance toward improvisations based on scenarios. All except two productions after 1963 would be collective creations of the company.

In 1963 the theatre was closed once more, this time for failure to pay taxes. By this time it was one of the best off-Broadway companies. Nevertheless, had it ceased to exist at that time it would have made little lasting impact. But in 1964 it left for Europe where it moved steadily toward a radical political stance while living a nomadic and communal existence and implementing its program of collective creation. Both its lifestyle and working methods exerted a powerful attraction for the young of Europe. It developed a new repertory consisting at first of Genet's *The Maids* and *Antigone* (an amalgamation of Sophocles' and Brecht's versions), but increasingly of the works for which it is now best known, its own *Frankenstein, Mysteries and Smaller Pieces,* and *Paradise Now. Frankenstein*

presents a view of history in which each generation seeks to recreate humanity, but in which the product is always so deformed as to be a monster. When the faults of the past are finally recognized and rejected, a new human can be created, no longer a monster but a vital being. In performance, this basic outline was filled out with variations and improvisations lasting some three hours. *Mysteries and Smaller Pieces* was composed of seven ritualized or archetypal segments, in each of which freedom emerged as good, conformity as evil. Mysticism, derived from Zen Buddhism, and a generalized notion of love among all people, alternated with frenetic, violent, or hate-filled scenes.

Paradise Now (first performed in 1968) was by far the Living Theatre's most radical work. It was divided into eight triads, each focusing on an obstacle that had to be overcome before the next level on the way to revolution could be reached. The distinctions between audience and performer were almost totally abolished, since both roamed the stage and auditorium indiscriminately. Furthermore, the company cast spectators (especially those who by dress and behavior seemed most conservative) as opposers of change, confronted them directly, met objections with insults and obscenities until they overrode opposition, and then proceeded triumphantly on to the next level of revolutionary development. At the end, the audience was urged to move into the streets and continue there the revolution begun in the theatre. The overall effect was more that of a disorderly, inflammatory, and violent political gathering than a theatrical performance.

In all of these late works, the group performed in everyday work clothing. Scenery was reduced to scaffolding and essential properties; there was little dialogue but much vocal and other sound, with occasional moments of quiet spirituality. The dominant effect was of aggressiveness. Although the company professed interest in direct audience participation, it strongly rejected any response that differed from its own point of view.

The Living Theatre reached the peak of its influence in 1968–1969 when its production of *Paradise Now* reinforced student agitation throughout Europe and especially the May uprisings in France. Wherever it went, it stirred up controversy (perhaps most notably at the Avignon Festival in 1968) and gained additional notoriety. Consequently, it was almost as a legend that it returned to the United States in late 1968. It played in various cities, always accompanied by enormous publicity and conflict, partly fueled by its refusal to differentiate between lifestyle and theatrical performance, since it insisted that theatre and life should not be separate. But this tour also marked the end of the company's widespread acceptance. Many radical groups accused it of being self-indulgent, out of touch with reality, and counterproductive in its aggressively insulting approach.

After leaving America in 1969, the troupe returned to Europe before splitting into three groups in 1970. The Becks took their contingent to Brazil where they were arrested and deported in 1971. The company continued, mostly in Europe, but with greatly diminished effect. In 1984, when it presented a repertory of four works in New York, critics thought its work amateurish and lacking in significant content. It has continued to perform, although sporadically.

Despite this decline in popularity after 1970, the Living Theatre's importance in the 1960s cannot be questioned. It provided an example of work quite unlike that of established groups, and it became a rallying point for the disaffected, who were indeed numerous around 1968. To many, the Living Theatre came to personify commitment and change through its denigration of any text that could not be transformed into an argument for radical change, its downgrading of language in favor of Artaudian techniques, its physicality, its insistence upon confronting and overriding audiences, its evangelical tone, and its lifestyle.

Many characteristics of the Living Theatre's productions were adapted around 1968 to what came to be called *guerilla theatre,* a term that had

FIG. 14.2
"The Plague" section of the Living Theatre's *Mysteries and Smaller Pieces* at Avignon in 1968. The image of piled bodies relates to Artaud's statements on "The Theatre and the Plague." (Courtesy Mark Hall Amitin.)

been proposed by R. G. Davis in 1966 in pointing out how the theatre might be adapted for uses analogous to guerilla warfare. As political and social stresses increased after 1968, many groups began to seize the opportunities offered by gatherings to present brief, pithy, unscheduled dramatizations of some issue. Most frequently the issues involved Vietnam or some aspect of civil rights. A good example is *Military Execution of the Bill of Rights,* performed by the American Playground, in which, as each provision of the Bill of Rights was read, it was executed by a military firing squad.

THE OPEN THEATRE

A far less controversial group than the Living Theatre, the Open Theatre, was founded in New York in 1963 by Joseph Chaikin (1935–) and Peter Feldman. Chaikin, who had acted with the Living Theatre, was always the dominant figure, and Feldman soon dropped out. With a membership composed of actors and playwrights (and occasionally choreographers and musicians), the Open Theatre was more nearly a workshop than a producing theatre, showing the results of its work only at irregular intervals.

Chaikin began the Open Theatre out of dissatisfaction with established approaches to acting, especially the Stanislavsky method as it was then being taught in New York. He wished to explore ensemble acting without the pressures involved in a commercial theatre. He also sought to concentrate on those aspects that are peculiar to theatre as a medium: "the only thing that makes the theatre different from movies and TV is this encounter with mortality. . . . The sense of being alive now in this room, in this place." Chaikin was also attuned to the New Left, and most of his work was an indirect comment on political and social issues. He rejected naturalism: "it corresponds to

social order . . . and certain kinds of repression. . . . To accept naturalism is to collaborate, to accept society's limits." Instead, the Open Theatre worked from the "games" and "role-playing" theories of human behavior—a constantly transforming set of relationships. Feldman stated: "The transformation, besides questioning our notion of reality in a very graphic way, also raises certain questions about the nature of identity and the finitude of character."

The Open Theatre abandoned all nonessential theatrical elements. In performance, the actors wore rehearsal or street clothing and never changed costumes during the course of the performance. They used no makeup and often no properties. Scenery was usually nonexistent and lighting simple. The emphasis was almost entirely on the actor. Because most of its scripts were evolved with transformations in mind, the Open Theatre used a small company to play a multitude of roles through which they moved without leaving the stage.

The Open Theatre performed some already existing plays, but most of its work was based on its own improvisations or the work of playwrights with whom it established close relationships. Eventually, the company participated in the evolution of scripts. The writer supplied an outline, scenes, situations, or themes; working from this base, the actors began exploratory improvisations and discussions, through which they sought to discover the multiple possibilities imbedded in the conception. Gradually movement, dialogue, and sound emerged, from among which the dramatist selected those which seemed most effective. The most successful collaborations were those with Megan Terry (1932–) whose *Viet Rock* (1966), through a series of transformational scenes, questions war in general and the Vietnam conflict in particular, and Jean-Claude van Itallie (1936–) whose *The Serpent* (1969) was the basis for one of the company's finest productions. In the production

FIG. 14.3

"Eve and the Serpent" in the Open Theatre's production of *The Serpent*. The script was developed by Jean-Claude van Itallie from actor improvisations. (Photo by Henri Dauman.)

of *The Serpent* the actors warmed up in all parts of the theatre and on stage while the audience assembled. The play began with a procession accompanied by percussive rhythms beaten out by the actors on their own bodies. This procession transformed into a pantomime recalling the assassinations of John F. Kennedy and Martin Luther King, Jr. The place then became the Garden of Eden where the temptation, fall, and expulsion were enacted. This was followed by a series of statements, many of them highly personal, others philosophic. Then came the Cain and Abel story, followed by

Blind Man's Hell, during which the actors groped their way about the stage while delivering a second set of statements. Next came a reading from Genesis (enumerating all the generations that followed Adam) accompanied by pantomimes of meetings, matings, births, child rearing, and so on. Eventually all grow old and line up across the front of the stage, where each undergoes a kind of death. Eventually as themselves, the actors sing a song as they leave through the audience.

In this production, there were no scenery or props and each actor played many roles. But the actors did not pretend to be characters so much as to present the essence of roles without losing their own identities. Primary emphasis was on significant human experience rather than on the personal stories of individuals. Ultimately *The Serpent* is a parable in which the serpent is that impulse in humans that makes them violate the limits set on them, whereas God is an idea that people have invented in order to set limits on themselves. Thus, God equals conformity, the serpent freedom. The play as a whole suggests that since existing rules have led to so much violence, we need to break those limits and make new and better choices. The same basic approach was followed in *Terminal* (1969–1970), all the scenes of which related in some way to death, including death-in-life, to which most people consent. Special emphasis was placed on those moments when different choices were possible.

In 1970 the Open Theatre was reorganized as a collective and thereafter performed primarily for prison and university audiences. It was dissolved in 1973. Chaikin subsequently established a workshop with Meredith Monk and directed and acted elsewhere until 1984 when a stroke forced him to cease performing. In the late 1980s he resumed limited performance activity.

The Open Theatre usually avoided attempts to involve the audience or to be confrontational.

Unlike most other similar groups, it often struck an optimistic note in its productions, probably because its transformational techniques implied that, since reality is constantly changing, it can be altered for the better if the right choices are made. It also contributed to the ideal of collective creation and the consequent deemphasis on virtuoso performers. During its ten-year existence, the Open Theatre became one of the most admired of companies. Through its performances (both at home and abroad) and its approach to acting, it exerted considerable influence both in the United States and Europe.

THE POLISH LABORATORY THEATRE

Some of the goals and practices of the Open Theatre paralleled those of the far better-known and more influential Polish Laboratory Theatre, founded in 1959 by Jerzy Grotowski (1933–   ) with the critic Ludwik Flaszen (1930–   ) as literary advisor. At first located in Opole, it moved in 1965 to Wrocław, where it also eventually was given the title Institute for Research into Acting. Thus, it was not so much a performing company as a laboratory devoted to experimentation out of which productions (ultimately about ten) evolved.

During the first few years of its existence, the Polish Laboratory Theatre worked in relative isolation. Grotowski's work was first championed abroad by Eugenio Barba (1936–   ), an Italian who worked with Grotowski during the early years of the Laboratory and who wrote the first book about his work, *In Search of the Lost Theatre* (1965). In 1964, Barba founded his own troupe, the Odin Teatret, modeled on Grotowski's. In 1966 this company was invited to settle in a municipally owned and subsidized theatre in Holstebro (Denmark), where it has continued its experimental work

to the present. Barba was also responsible for the publication of *Towards a Poor Theatre* (1968), a collection of essays by and about Grotowski. It has been translated into more than a dozen languages.

Around 1965 Grotowski and his company began to be invited abroad. In 1966 his production of *The Constant Prince* was seen at the Théâtre des Nations in Paris, and in the same year he and his principal actor, Ryszard Cieślak (1937–1990), worked with members of the Royal Shakespeare Company. Peter Brook became one of Grotowski's most ardent admirers. In the late 1960s, the Polish Laboratory began to perform in London, New York, and elsewhere. By 1970, Grotowski was probably second only to Stanislavsky in renown as a theorist of acting.

Grotowski began his work rather conventionally but came to believe that the theatre can survive only if it ceases competing with film and television to concentrate on what makes it unique—the "collective introspection" created by the direct and immediate interaction between actor and audience. Two concepts dominated Grotowski's theory: theatre as ritualized, communal experience, and the "poor theatre."

Grotowski viewed the theatre as the modern equivalent of the primitive tribal ceremony that liberated the spiritual energy of the congregation or tribe. Recognizing that the community of belief which underlay ancient ritual is now missing, he sought to replace it with archetypal human experiences, actions, and images—deeply imbedded in the human psyche quite independent of religion or faith. Consequently, in working with a script, he first searched for its archetypes and then reshaped the original text around them and eliminated whatever did not apply. The ultimate goal was not so much to interpret a text as to confront both it and ourselves through a psychospiritual experience which brings order and meaning to existence, leading to "total acceptance of one human being by another."

To achieve these ends, Grotowski adopted means that he labeled the *poor theatre*. Unlike technologically rich cinema and television, the poor theatre grew from "a *via negativa*—not a collection of skills but an eradication of blocks." Everything not essential was eliminated. The proscenium arch theatre was abandoned in favor of a completely flexible space that could be rearranged to create the spectator-actor relationship appropriate to each production. Elaborate lighting effects were avoided in favor of fixed sources, although there might be bright or dark areas, candlelight or glaring floodlights, depending on the production's needs. Usually, both actors and spectators were lighted. Makeup was forbidden. Actors had to transform themselves as needed through posture, movement, and facial expression. Costume was entirely functional, and actors were not permitted to change clothing in order to indicate a change of role or change in the character's state, although actors could adjust whatever they were wearing. Properties were treated as extensions of the actors' movements and gestures; they were chosen for their functionalism and multiple symbolic potential. Traditional scenery was not used. A few functional props—wheelbarrows, platforms, metal pipes—might be rearranged but were never treated representationally. All music had to be produced by the actors. Occasionally a musical instrument was employed, but more typically music was created by vocal sound or the rhythmic clash of objects. All this meant that actors were thrown back on their own resources, since external means were reduced to the minimum. The actor was the heart of Grotowski's theatre. He admitted his indebtedness to many influences, among them Stanislavsky, Meyerhold, Vakhtangov, Delsarte, Dullin, Jung, Lévi-Strauss, Kathakali, Yoga, and others.

In his program, physical training played a large role. But he insisted that such training was useless unless it extended into the psychological realm so that, through a process of association, inner impulses were released. The goal was the elimination of all blocks, physical and psychic, so that in performance the actors gave themselves totally without exhibitionism or narcissism. Grotowski also believed that the magic of the theatre consists in the actors doing what is normally considered impossible. Therefore, his actors were trained to transform their bodies and voices to the fullest extent. He did not permit improvisation during performances, although much of the performance developed from improvisational rehearsal techniques. Each moment had to be executed with precision. The ultimate goal was absolute control of capabilities that exceed those of the audience so far as to create a sense of awe.

The second essential ingredient in Grotowski's theatre was the audience, which he treated as privileged participants in a ritual. He did not believe in direct audience participation. He thought the kind of involvement sought by the Living Theatre only made the audience self-conscious. Thus, for each production the audience space was designed to permit the audience to play its role unself-consciously. His productions were most often designed for a specific number of spectators, ranging from forty to one hundred, and he would not permit a larger number to attend.

Among the Laboratory's public performances, the best-known are adaptations of Słowacki's *Kordian*, Wyspiański's *Akropolis*, Marlowe's *Doctor Faustus*, Calderón's *The Constant Prince*, and an original work, *Apocalypsis cum figuris*, with passages drawn from the Bible, Eliot, Dostoevsky, and Simone Weil. In *Doctor Faustus*, Marlowe's text was reworked so that the audience became guests invited by Faustus to a banquet on the night that his soul is to be claimed by the Devil. The spectators were seated at two long tables and Faustus at a third. Thus, the audience was cast as friendly listeners for whom scenes are conjured up as Faustus tells his story. Images of the Last Supper run throughout, as does the notion of Faustus as martyr accepting damnation as the price of seeking knowledge.

Akropolis was one of the Laboratory's best-known and most controversial productions. Wyspiański's original text was set in the Royal Palace at Kraków (the Polish equivalent of the Greek Acropolis) on the night of the Feast of the Resurrection. Figures from tapestries on the walls come to life and enact a history of Europe, at the end of which the resurrected Christ leads them in a mission to liberate Europe from its past errors. Grotowski saw *Akropolis* as the cemetery of our civilization and set it in the extermination camp at Auschwitz (approximately thirty-five miles west of Kraków), where the characters are inmates building the ovens in which prisoners are cremated. Their work is interrupted by

these tortured souls' fantasies—the equivalents of the tapestry figures—and at the end of the play a rag-doll figure (a fantasy Christ) leads them into the ovens.

The Constant Prince was based on Calderón's play about a nobleman who transcends bodily suffering and overcomes all the tortures of temporality. Grotowski abandoned the Christian framework and presented a hero who suffers as a direct result of the evil in human beings, but who through suffering is made sacred. The performance required such physical and psychological endurance by the Prince (played by Cieślak) that Grotowski treated the space as a medical operating theatre where spectators looked down into a pit where psychic surgery was taking place.

Despite the success of his company, Grotowski decided around 1970 that he would create no new productions. He came to consider the theatre as an intermediary between the audience and its direct experience of wholeness and communion. Therefore, he

FIG. 14.4
Scene from Grotowski's production of *The Constant Prince*—the Pietà—in which the Prince, played by Ryszard Cieślak, is embraced by Fenixana, played by Rena Mirecka. (Courtesy Jerzy Grotowski.)

concluded that those who had been spectators should participate directly by leaving their daily lives behind and come to a place where they could experience the elemental connections between their bodies, imagination, and the natural world. The first major revelation of this new direction came in 1975 when approximately five hundred people from around the world attended a "research university" organized by Grotowski under the auspices of the Théâtre des Nations. The group included students, teachers, journalists, and a number of famous directors, including Brook, Barrault, and Chaikin. Everyone who attended had to participate. The activities included taking groups into the woods for twenty-four hours where they participated in improvisatory re-enactments of basic myths, archetypes, and symbols involving fire, air, earth, water, eating, dancing, playing, planting, and bathing. Through this process, participants were led to rediscover the roots of the theatre in pure ritualized experience, as well as to discover, in some ways, their own true being.

After 1975 Grotowski began studying the diverse ritual performances of Japan, India, Haiti, Mexico, Africa, and elsewhere, and used these experiences to enhance the work he had started in 1970. He called this new phase the *Theatre of Sources*. In 1983, Grotowski became head of an institute at the University of California at Irvine, where he sought to develop

FIG. 14.5
The crucifixion scene from the Laboratory Theatre's *Apocalypsis cum figuris*. The actors are, left to right standing, Zygmunt Molik, Antoni Jahołkowski, Stanisław Scierski, and Elizabeth Albahaca. Kneeling is Zbigniew Cynkutis; foreground is Ryszard Cieślak. (Courtesy Jerzy Grotowski.)

these explorations more systematically in what he called *Objective Drama* (to be discussed in Chapter 15).

In 1984 the group's members dissolved the Polish Laboratory Theatre. Perhaps because Grotowski's recent work is difficult to understand by those who have not participated in it directly, it is primarily on the theatre work done during the 1960s that Grotowski's reputation rests. Without question, that work stimulated theatre workers almost everywhere who were seeking to reassess theatre and its potential.

HAPPENINGS AND ENVIRONMENTAL THEATRE

In 1968, Richard Schechner (1934–   ), then editor of *The Drama Review (TDR),* finding common features in the work of the Living Theatre, the Open Theatre, the Polish Laboratory Theatre, the Bread and Puppet Theatre, and other similar groups, labeled their approach *environmental theatre,* which he saw as rebelling against the kind of theatre that is scenically characterized by (1) segregation of audience and performers; (2) fixed and regular seating of audiences; (3) construction of scenery situated in one part of the theatre only. He set forth six "axioms" that define and limit environmental theatre.

1. The events can be placed on a continuum, with Pure/Art at one end and Impure/Life at the other, and with traditional theatre at one pole and public events and demonstrations at the other. He located environmental theatre somewhere between traditional theatre and "happenings."

2. All the space can be used by both performers and audience. Spectators become a part of the total event and thus are both "scene makers" and "scene watchers."

3. The event can take place either in a "found" space or a transformed space. In other words, a flexible space may be converted into an environment appropriate to the event, or a place may be found and the event shaped to fit it.

4. Focus is both flexible and variable. Several parts of an event may occur simultaneously and in different parts of the total space.

5. All the production elements can serve as "language" and need not be thought of merely as words.

6. A text need not be thought of as the starting point or the product of performance; a text is not necessary and there may be none.

Schechner's environmental theatre is an extension of developments reaching back to the futurists, dadaists, and surrealists, some aspects of which had resurfaced during the 1950s, especially in happenings. The key figure in the development that led to happenings was John Cage (1912–   ), a composer and theorist of the arts. In 1952 at Black Mountain College (North Carolina)—a haven for innovative artists, among them several former members of the Bauhaus—he arranged what many consider to have been the first happening: a forty-five-minute program that included, either at intervals or simultaneously, visual art by Robert Rauschenberg, dance by Merce Cunningham, poetry by Charles Olson and Mary C. Richards (the American translator of Artaud) read from the top of ladders, music by David Tudor, films, slides, phonograph records, and a lecture by Cage. Much of this was improvised but controlled by time brackets. (For instance, during a given time period Cunningham would dance but no one knew what he would be dancing.) Cage subsequently taught in New York, where many of those who would be major creators of happenings were his students.

Cage was not concerned with linear structure. He imposed order primarily through time frames. One of his most controversial pieces was entitled *4' 33"* (1952), in which a pianist came on stage and sat at the piano for four minutes and thirty-three seconds without ever striking a note. According to Cage, the piece is made up of all the sounds heard by the audience during that time, no matter what the source. His goal was to "intensify, alter perceptual awareness and hence consciousness . . . of the real, material world," rather than to convey some predetermined intention or to arouse some predetermined response. He labeled any attempt to make a hearer respond in a specific way or perceive a specific intention "police work," since what each person experiences is no one else's business. The only legitimate criticism is what one is stimulated to do after experiencing an art work. Cage also argued that one distinguishing feature of contemporary performance is the breaking down of the traditional distinctions between creator, performer, and spectator. In the art he advocated, the composer or writer supplied an outline or general instructions based on time frames but left many decisions about the order in which things would be done within those time frames up to the performers (often the order was determined by chance). Thus, the performer became part-composer while the composer, like the audience, did not know what the piece would be until it was performed; and the audience had also to become part-composer, since it was forced to assemble discontinuous, seemingly aleatoric sound into patterns. Cage served as music director for the dance company of Merce Cunningham (1922–   ), who approached movement much as Cage did sound—exploring its possibilities, usually by letting both the many aspects of particular movements and the order of those movements be determined by chance operations based on *I Ching*. Furthermore, the dance was not set to music, nor was music fitted to the dance; rather, dance and music proceeded simul-taneously but independently. The only element they shared was agreed-upon time frames.

Although the events called happenings owed much to Cage, they were popularized by visual artists, the most important of whom—Allan Kaprow, Robert Rauschenberg, Jim Dine, and several others—had been students of Cage or had worked with him. (Rauschenberg was the principal designer for the Cunningham dance company.) These artists had become dissatisfied with the two-dimensionality of painting and had experimented with ways of transcending these limitations. Rauschenberg began attaching three-dimensional objects (such as a radio or a goat's head) to his canvases. "Action painters" and "abstract expressionists" sought to capture in brush strokes the feeling and sense of movement at the moment of creation.

The name *happening* and the first self-conscious example of a happening came from Allan Kaprow (1927–   ), a painter and art historian who was especially interested in "environments" (that is, the extension of the concept of art to include the surroundings in which it is seen). The dadaists had championed this idea, but it was used to greatest effect in the Parisian retrospective exhibit of surrealist art in 1938. Kaprow came to believe that all those who attend an exhibit are a part of the total environment; consequently, he began to give them things to do. In 1959 he published an outline of an artistic event he called a "happening" because he considered the term neutral. In the same year he gave the first public showing of the form he had proposed—*18 Happenings in 6 Parts*—at the Reuben Gallery in New York.

For this happening, the gallery was divided by transparent plastic into three compartments, each of which was decorated differently and contained a number of chairs. Those attending were given directions telling them which compartment to sit in during each of the parts;

each person was in at least two different compartments during the event. The instructions also included directions about things to do during particular time frames. The activities were different in each compartment and were accompanied by tapes of sound, music, voices, and abstract noise—often several, simultaneously but dissynchronously. Slides of paintings, familiar objects, and collages were projected onto screens, the walls, and people. A number of performers carried out prescribed tasks: painting on canvas; slicing oranges, squeezing them and drinking the juice; rolling and unrolling trouser legs; bouncing a ball. Several of these things occurred simultaneously. Everything was carefully planned and the non-audience performers carefully rehearsed. Audience members were also given specific tasks to do within clearly defined time spans, though precisely when or how was left open. (Cage left because he felt it too prescriptive.)

As the vogue for happenings spread, the form lost definition. Eventually the label was used for any event in which improvisation or chance played a significant part—even demon-strations and sit-ins. This probably accounts for the decline in popularity of happenings in the late 1960s. Later, the concept would be revived and reshaped into "performance art."

Happenings were not specifically theatrical. Nevertheless, several characteristics were carried over into theatre during the 1960s. First, as "institutionalized" art came under attack, performance spaces other than museums, concert halls, and theatres were sought. There were also attempts to enlarge the audience for art by removing it from the confining atmosphere of fixed places and fixed attitudes that had made it the preserve of a privileged class. Second, emphasis was shifted from watching to participating, from product to process. Often audience and performers were the same. Third, emphasis shifted to audience awareness and away from artistic intention. Guideposts suggesting meaning were correspondingly scarce. Fourth, simultaneity and multiple focus tended to replace orderly sequence and cause-to-effect arrangement. Usually there was no pretense that everyone could see the same thing at the same time. Fifth, since happenings were essentially nonverbal, they promoted the

FIG. 14.6
Eat, an "environment" by Allan Kaprow, presented in 1964 in a cave in the Bronx, New York. A performer, seated at left, served fried bananas to visitors. (Courtesy Allan Kaprow.)

retreat from the conceptual to the perceptual. They tended to be multimedia events appealing to the total sensory apparatus. Sixth, happenings largely ignored characterization and story. Participants carried out tasks rather than assuming roles; in most instances, they did not pretend to be someone else, but remained themselves involved in a novel experience. Thus, they did not require trained performers; everyone could participate on an equal level.

Schechner's conception of environmental theatre was in many ways the adaptation of happenings to a more theatrical framework. Thus, when he created his continuum, he located environmental theatre somewhere between traditional theatre and happenings. Those companies labeled environmental by Schechner had some shared characteristics, the most common being the replacement of traditional performance spaces with adaptable and transformable spaces. Many made use of multiple focus and simultaneity; the amount of direct audience participation varied widely; most treated scripts as "found" objects to be reshaped as desired. In almost every instance, the environmental groups radically reshaped received ideas about theatrical space and theatrical conventions.

Schechner was not content merely to write about the theatre. In 1968 he founded his own company, the Performance Group, which had as its home a converted garage without any conventional seating. Rather, the audience sat or stood on the floor or on the wooden platforms and towers scattered around the space. The first production, *Dionysus in 69,* a reworking of Euripides' *The Bacchae,* was a series of ritualistic scenes, most relating to sexuality, repression, and freedom. Dionysus was equated with a total lack of conflicting impulses, whereas Pentheus was eventually destroyed by violence-begetting repressions. Overall the production reflected the issues of the moment in its plea for greater freedom

FIG. 14.7
The Performance Group in *Commune.* (Photo by Fred Eberstadt.)

coupled with a warning against the dangers of blindly throwing off restraints. The production underwent many changes during its run, one being the adoption of total nudity for some of the orgiastic scenes, a feature which brought it considerable notoriety. *Commune* (1970) was a montage of events from the American past and present, in which the force behind the emerging youth culture was seen as a continuation of those motives that brought the U.S. into being: evasion of the past and rejection of boundaries. It depicts the American dream of community and love being subverted by competition and

hatred. During performances, actors borrowed articles of clothing or used spectators as victims in massacres, and invited them to write slogans on the walls or to assist in other ways. Subsequently, the company presented Sam Shepard's *The Tooth of Crime* (1973), a play about rivalries in the pop music world seen through the lens of gangsterism, and in 1975 Brecht's *Mother Courage,* which many critics thought the best of all the Performance Group's productions. In 1980 Schechner left the company and it soon ceased to exist.

OTHER AMERICAN DEVELOPMENTS

The growing demand during the 1960s for the relaxation of strictures led to ever-greater freedom of subject matter, behavior, and language in the theatre. Perhaps the greatest impact was made by the introduction of nudity and obscenity. The first notable use of obscenity and nudity came in 1968 in the Broadway production of *Hair,* a revised version of the work with which Papp had opened the Public Theatre. Subtitled "An American Tribal Love-Rock Musical," its book and lyrics were by Gerome Ragni and James Rado and its music by Galt MacDermot. Its story was slight. Primary emphasis was on themes and anxieties (the military draft, war in Vietnam, mismatched couples, the conflict between generations). Most of all it was a good-natured attempt to justify an alternative lifestyle, ending in a plea for understanding and for happiness and peace. Throughout the work, obscenity was introduced freely, and at the end of the first part the performers briefly removed all their clothing. Both innovations created a furore and continued to do so as *Hair* was produced in France, Japan, England, and elsewhere.

Other productions soon followed *Hair*'s

FIG. 14.8
Tom O'Horgan's production of *Hair* (1968), the American Tribal Love-Rock Musical by Gerome Ragni, James Rado, and Galt MacDermot. (© 1990 Martha Swope.)

example. In late 1968, Terrence McNally's *Sweet Eros,* in which a nude actress remained on stage throughout, was produced off-Broadway. In 1969, *Che!* by Lenox Raphael had as its hero Che Guevara, who seemingly was sexually irresistible to all the other characters. The actors and production staff were prosecuted and convicted on charges of obscene behavior. The court concluded: "The stage directions permitted actual sex on stage," both heterosexual and homosexual; "standards of public acceptance and morality so sharply different and shocking" cannot be permitted. Nevertheless, producers continued to make use of both nudity and obscenity. In 1969, *Oh! Calcutta!,* a revue devised by Kenneth Tynan (Literary Advisor of England's National Theatre) and with scenes by famous playwrights all involving sex and many performed by nude actors, considerably extended the use of nudity. The revue rapidly won a following and continued to play in New York until 1989. By the early 1970s, although the limits of permissibility were still vague, almost any sexual theme or obscenity had become potentially usable on stage. Actors' unions laid down conditions (clear notice to the actor about what would be required, and indemnification in case of public prosecution) to protect its members. Perhaps nothing so clearly defined the differences between old and new standards than the acceptance of nudity and obscenity on the stage.

Hair also marked a significant change in the musical. Almost all of its elements were derived from the youth-oriented culture of the 1960s: its anti-establishment stance, lifestyle, and dress; its highly amplified rock music; and its popular dance forms. It paved the way for such successors as Stephen Schwartz's *Pippin* (1972) and *Godspell* (1974). The older form continued in such works as Charles Strouse's *Annie* (1977) and Jerry Herman's *La Cage aux Folles* (1983), but the musical after 1970 seemed

to lose a sense of direction, and it could no longer be counted on as the mainstay of Broadway.

By far the most successful and innovative writer of musicals after 1968 was Stephen Sondheim (1930–   ), who began his career as lyricist for *West Side Story* (1957) and wrote his first score for *A Funny Thing Happened on the Way to the Forum* (1962). Not until 1970 with *Company* did his originality become clearly evident. Rather than a developed story, *Company* explores the concept of marriage through the bachelor Robert and five married couples who are his friends but who make him wonder if marriage is for him. There is no chorus; the work's effectiveness depends on the ensemble. Sondheim continued his innovations in such works as *Pacific Overtures* (1976), which incorporated conventions drawn from the Japanese theatre; *Sweeney Todd* (1979), which approached opera in its use of music throughout; *Sunday in the Park With George* (1984), which took its inspiration from Georges Seurat's paintings and raised significant questions about the nature of art; and *Into the Woods* (1987), which explored the dark side of fairy tales. More than anyone, Sondheim established the direction that the musical would take during the 1970s. His lead was followed by *A Chorus Line,* (1975), a "concept" musical about auditions for a chorus. The book was by James Kirkwood and Nicholas Dante and the music by Marvin Hamlisch and Edward Kleban, but the most crucial figure was Michael Bennett (1943–1987), who gathered the material for the book through tape-recorded sessions with dancers, as well as directing and choreographing the production. *A Chorus Line* became the most successful musical of the 1970s in the U.S. and internationally and was the longest-running production in Broadway's history.

The post-1968 attacks on traditional values and artistic forms strengthened the role of off-off-Broadway, since it offered the most sym-

FIG. 14.9
Stephen Sondheim's *A Little Night Music* on Broadway. (Photo by Van Williams.)

pathetic home to new modes of writing and staging. LaMama and Papp's Public Theatre perhaps benefited most, becoming virtually institutionalized supporters of innovation. LaMama continued to encourage new playwrights, but it also hosted other companies and developed ensembles of special interest to ethnic and minority groups (Puerto Rican, black, Native American, feminist, gay and lesbian). Papp continued to enlarge the scope of his organization, and from 1973 to 1978 added the Lincoln Center theatre to his responsibilities (though success there eluded him as it had his predecessors). During the 1970s probably no one played a larger role in New York's theatrical life.

Among the numerous off-off-Broadway companies, a few were of special importance. Between 1965 and 1980, the Chelsea Theatre Center, headed by Robert Kalfin and housed at the Brooklyn Academy of Music, did much to acquaint American audiences with innovative European works—among them Genet's *The Screens,* Witkiewicz's *The Water Hen,* Bond's *Saved,* and Handke's *Kaspar*—and controversial American plays—such as Baraka's *Slave Ship.* One of the most original groups was the Ridiculous Theatrical Company, founded by Charles Ludlam (1943–1987) in 1967, which parodied familiar genres—such as the gothic novel, film noir, opera, science fiction, and melodrama—and the absurdities of modern life and art—such as psychoanalysis, artistic fads, superstars, and popular culture icons—

through what Ludlam described as a synthesis of "wit, parody, vaudeville, farce, melodrama and satire." Ludlam wrote and acted in most of the pieces (often playing several roles, many of them female). The numerous productions included *The Enchanted Pig* (which combined elements of *King Lear* and *Cinderella*), *Le Bourgeois Avant-garde* (a parody of artistic minimalism), *Camille* (in which Ludlam played a hairy-chested heroine), *The Mystery of Irma Vep* (a horror comedy which drew on such gothic novels as *Wuthering Heights*), and *The Artificial Jungle* (which combined elements of such films as *Double Indemnity* and *The Little Shop of Horrors*). In these and other pieces, Ludlam used imaginative comic invention to deconstruct popular culture and artistic pretension. After Ludlam's death, the company was continued by Everett Quinton, who had long been integrally associated with it.

The Circle Repertory Theatre Company was founded in 1969 by Marshall Mason, Lanford Wilson, Rob Thirkield, and Tanya Berezin. Mason served as artistic director until 1986, when he left the company; he was succeeded by Berezin. Offering a season of plays each year, the Circle Rep sought to encourage young artists. A major part of its work was done through its Lab, modeled on Café Cino, where (within the protected environment of workshops) actors, directors, and playwrights could develop. Under Mason, the company came to be associated with a Chekhovian "lyric realism" epitomized in the work of its major writer, Lanford Wilson (1937–   ), whose *Hot L Baltimore* (1973) established the company's reputation. A prolific writer, Wilson is concerned only minimally with story. In such plays as *Balm in Gilead* (1965), *The Fifth of July* (1978), *Talley's Folly* (1979), and *Burn This* (1987), the focus is on character relationships and the revelation of hidden feelings, disappointments, and hopes. Wilson's compassionate treatment of lonely and displaced misfits mark him as one of the most humane of contemporary playwrights.

After 1968, Broadway became increasingly less significant in American theatrical life as off-off-Broadway theatres became the major outlet for young dramatists, while regional theatres (which continued to increase in numbers) provided a steady diet of classics intermingled with new or recent plays. More and more, Broadway imported productions already seen elsewhere. The opportunity to develop scripts without the commercial pressures of Broadway led most writers to take their plays to non-Broadway groups; some achieved international reputations without ever having a work seen on Broadway.

Such was the case with Sam Shepard (1943–   ) who by 1980 was considered by many to be America's finest playwright. Shepard began his playwriting career in 1964 with short plays presented off-off-Broadway by Theatre Genesis. Until the mid-1970s Shepard wrote without revising his work because, he says, he thought it dishonest to alter what he had originally set down. His extremely prolific output includes *Cowboys* (1964), *Mad Dog Blues* (1971), *The Tooth of Crime* (1972), *Curse of the Starving Class* (1977), *Buried Child* (1978), *True West* (1980), *Fool for Love* (1983), and *A Lie of the Mind* (1985). Although there is much variety in Shepard's work, a number of themes recur: attempts to escape or deny the past; the cowboy and the West as basic American myths; the family as a battleground; and characters caught between empty dreams and an insubstantial reality. His images, rhythms, and allusions rely most heavily on popular culture and mass media. He is not interested in developing and resolving an action so much as with the collision of characters' only partially understood motivations and intuitions.

Unlike Shepard, David Rabe (1940–   ) has had plays on Broadway but only after they were first performed elsewhere. Most of his early pieces were written in response to the Vietnam war. These include *The Basic Training of Pavlo Hummel* (1971), which traces the gradual dehumanization of a naive and patriotic young soldier, and *Sticks and Bones* (1971), which concerns a veteran blinded in Vietnam and the effect on his family of his return home. Both of these plays make considerable use of expressionistic devices and symbolism. *Streamers* (1976), a more realistic piece which takes place just as the Vietnam war is beginning, derives much of its power from the veteran soldiers who, in recalling the Korean conflict, make us recognize the price exacted by any war. Others of Rabe's plays are concerned with contemporary American values. *Hurlyburly* (1984), set in Hollywood, treats characters who practice casual cruelties on each other within the moral wasteland they inhabit. Overall, Rabe's plays present protagonists whose longing for order and spiritual fulfillment is frustrated by others' complacent acceptance of empty rituals and failed values.

FRANCE

In 1968, France was virtually paralyzed by student demonstrations and workers' strikes. Attuned to the New Left, the alienated students were not so much concerned with economic as with cultural issues. They declared that established theatres treated art as a product to be marketed to a consumer society, and in Paris they occupied the state-owned Odéon (the home of Barrault's Théâtre de France) and urged others to take similar action elsewhere. In place of "establishment" theatre—which they found embodied in traditional theatre architecture (with its formalized separation of spectators from performers), scripts written by individuals, and long-accepted production conventions—they urged a return to popular forms (such as *commedia dell'arte,* circus, and vaudeville) or collectively created pieces performed in the streets, parks, and other spaces that made theatre readily available to everyone and encouraged interaction among performers and audiences.

Collective creation became common in the wake of the uprising. Even before the uprising began, Armand Gatti was experimenting with collective creation. At the Théâtre de l'Est Parisien (located in a working-class suburb of Paris and under the artistic direction of Guy Rétoré), Gatti asked thirty adults to imagine what would replace their street were it to be demolished. Out of these discussions came *The Thirty Suns of the Rue Saint-Blaise* (1968). This experience led Gatti to champion a *theatre without spectators,* since everyone would be directly involved. Disillusioned with France, he left to work in Germany and then in Belgium, where in 1974 he created *The Durruti Column* with factory workers and, subsequently, a piece about farm conditions that eventually involved some three thousand people. He later returned to France where he continued this collective work, creating, among others, a play with and about immigrant workers.

In eastern France, Jacques Kraemer, director of the Théâtre Populaire de Lorraine, used different methods to accomplish goals similar to those of Gatti by creating plays immediately related to the concerns of working-class people in his area. Following research which included discussions with numerous iron workers in this economically depressed region, Kraemer wrote *The Splendor and Misery of Minette, the Maid of Lorraine,* which used a surface story about gangsters and prostitution to satirize mine owners and their treatment of workers. Kraemer went on to create pieces about bankruptcy, immigrant workers, the corruption of local newspapers, and other topics. Kraemer's theatre gained strong support from workers but was continuously at odds with those in power. Somewhat similarly, the Nouvelle Compagnie d'Avignon, headed by André Benedetto, used a small core-group of actors to work with local people in creating and performing works intended to provoke insight into local conditions and to encourage a revolutionary attitude among those who have been displaced or oppressed by the dominant group. Perhaps the best-known of these pieces is *Our Lady of the Garbage Heap* (1973).

The integration of social commentary with popular entertainment forms is best exemplified in the Grand Magic Circus headed by Jerome Savary (1942–   ), who, like many of his contemporaries, came in the late 1960s to reject text-based theatre and to proclaim that bourgeois "high culture" must be replaced by "low culture." The group's collectively created pieces satirized established theatre forms even as they sought to shock middle-class audiences through the use of nudity and various other devices borrowed from popular entertainment. Its first major piece, *Zartan* (1970), was originally performed in English (in Toronto) and only after presentation at LaMama in New York moved on to France and elsewhere in Europe. "The story of Tarzan's deprived brother," it was described by Savary as the "marvelous story of colonialism from the Middle Ages to the present." Other pieces included *Robinson Crusoe* (1972), *From Moses to Mao* (1973), and *Adventures in Love* (1976). Savary described his pieces as a pretext for people to come together in joyous celebration. The company played on beaches, in hospitals, parks, and elsewhere—except in traditional theatres. Using improvisations, acrobatic feats, outrageous props, trick stage effects, clowning, song, dance, and extended comic routines, the Grand Magic Circus gained a very wide following.

The most important of the collective companies was the Théâtre du Soleil, formed in 1964 by Ariane Mnouchkine (1940–   ), who has said that one of the company's goals was to create a form of theatre "where it will be possible for everyone to collaborate without there being directors, technicians, and so on in the old sense." The company made its first impact in 1967 with Arnold Wesker's *The Kitchen* and Shakespeare's *A Midsummer Night's Dream.* During the 1968 uprising, it performed *The Kitchen* in factories, where it engendered lively discussions of working conditions and what could be done about them. Beginning at this time, all members of the company were paid the same salary. They also began to reconsider the political function of theatre and the role of the playwright. Their next work, *The Clowns* (1969), was based on the premise that the clown is the most representative artist. The result was not entirely successful, however, for it was made up of essentially improvisatory individual creations rather than being a collective creation. Building on what they had learned, their next piece, *1789* (1970), was one of their most satisfactory. About the French revolution, it ultimately argued that the Revolution served merely to replace an aristocracy of the nobility with an aristocracy of the rich. It was staged in the Cartoucherie (an abandoned cartridge factory) in the Parisian suburb of Vincennes, which thereafter served as the company's home. The performance style, which created a sense of festival or celebration, impressed audiences with its marked contrast to the sense of alienation emphasized by the then-dominant absurdist mode. The carnival atmosphere of *1789* incorporated puppets, farce, acrobats, music, and dance. Costumes and makeup were put on in full view of the audience. Although some bleacher seats were available, most of the audience stood and moved around five raised platforms. At times, alternative versions of the same event were presented. The production was enormously

FIG. 14.10
Ariane Mnouchkine's production of *1789* for the Théâtre du Soleil, staged in an old cartridge factory just outside Paris in 1970. (Photo by Bernand.)

successful and for the first time aroused widespread interest in collective creation among the French public. *1789* was followed by a sequel, *1793* (1972), which, though popular with theatregoers, was faulted by many critics. By this time the company was so destitute that between 1973 and 1975 most of its members went on unemployment. It began to recover in 1975 with *The Age of Gold,* which explored contemporary society and the interrelationships of exploiters and exploited as brought to focus through the character of Abdallah, an immi-

grant worker. For this production, the playing space within the Cartoucherie was shaped into four large hollows created by mounds of earth covered with matting on which the audience sat; there was no scenery in the usual sense. Overhead there were reflecting panels and innumerable colored lights. The atmosphere was that of a fair or picnic. The "golden age" of the title was pursued through contrast between the materialistic present and a future utopia (for which everyone yearns). By 1975, the Théâtre du Soleil had become sufficiently well-established that it was receiving a sizable subsidy from the French government and had become financially stable. But by the late 1970s, it was also giving up collective creation and would subsequently be better-known for productions of scripted works.

The 1970s were not kind to French playwrights, who, because of their working methods, were often labeled "bourgeois individualists" by the New Left. Many actors thought that being asked to repeat a writer's lines was an oppressive remnant of the old authoritarian system, unlike collective creation in which they had a part in the development of scripts.

Of the playwrights who did gain prominence, the most notable was Jean-Claude Grumberg (1939–   ). The son of Jewish immigrant parents, Grumberg began to write for the stage in the mid-1960s, mostly on themes of racial and other forms of intolerance. His first commercial success came in 1971 with *Amorphe d'Ottenberg,* a black farce which indirectly mirrors the Nazi rise to power through support from industry and church. One of his best-known plays is *Dreyfus* (1974), set in a Jewish ghetto in a Polish town around 1930 where amateurs, while rehearsing a play about the Dreyfus affair, explore the phenomenon of anti-semitism. It won the critics' award as the best play of the 1974–1975 season. *Comings and Goings at the Expo* (1975) takes place in 1900 at the time of the Universal Exposition, which serves as an appropriate meeting ground for both the frivolity and idealism that would eventually lead to World War I. Scenes alternate between the *café concert,* with its clichéd songs that stir up militaristic sentiment, and union halls, where ideas of peace through international cooperation among workers are ineffectually promoted. *The Workshop* (1979) shows Jewish survivors of the Occupation, now workers in a small tailor shop, coping with their pain as survivors when

so many others have perished. Staged wholly naturalistically, suits of clothing were actually made during the performance.

The 1968 uprisings affected the government's relationship to the arts in various ways, as it sought both to contain the dissatisfaction and respond to criticism. After de Gaulle retired in 1969, the government reorganized the national theatre system. Because Barrault was accused of cooperating with the rebels, he was dismissed as director of the Odéon, but, because the troupe there was under contract to him, the Odéon was left without a company. In 1970, the Odéon was assigned to the Comédie Française, which sought to broaden its appeal by reserving the Odéon for new and avant-garde pieces or for visiting companies. In 1975 the rules governing the actors at the Comédie Française also were altered in an attempt to attract more major performers. The number of *sociétaires* was increased, and the length of contracts was reduced from twenty to ten years.

The government also for the first time designated some companies outside of Paris as "national" theatres. These included the Théâtre National de Strasbourg (a former dramatic center), the Théâtre de l'Est Parisien (a company in a working-class suburb of Paris), and Planchon's company in Villeurbanne (which was given the title Théâtre National Populaire after Planchon refused to move to Paris; the Parisian-based company that had held that title was retained but renamed the Théâtre National de Chaillot). Decentralization also continued. By the mid-1970s there were eighteen dramatic centers, fifteen *maisons de la culture,* and about twenty-five other provincial companies. But because so many theatres had responded favorably to the 1968 rebels, the government viewed most of them with suspicion. In 1973 the Minister of Culture declared that he could not subsidize any group that came to him "with a beggar's bowl in one hand and a Molotov cocktail in the other." This statement, interpreted as a threat of reprisal and a demand for acceptance of the government's conservative views, provoked an enormous demonstration.

Although subsidies did not diminish, rampant inflation meant that most of the money went to pay administrative costs. Many companies reduced the number of their own productions and booked in touring groups, a practice referred to as "garaging." By the late 1970s, many were declaring decentralization dead. Nevertheless, this was the period when great numbers of new companies were formed, many in reaction to the conservatism of established theatres.

For some older directors, the 1970s was a period of renewal. In the midst of the student uprisings in 1968, Planchon's theatre in Villeurbanne hosted a meeting of theatre workers from throughout France. Over an extended period they discussed cultural policy and concluded that they had become too far removed from the common people. It was also pointed out that, despite Brecht's great popularity in France, his essential rationality had seemed to fail. There followed a call to combine Brecht and Artaud, Marxism and surrealism—a call heeded by many directors, among them Planchon.

Planchon also reenforced the demand for a popular theatre, then being championed, by refusing to move to Paris and instead gaining the transfer of the Théâtre National Populaire to Villeurbanne. Planchon appointed Patrice Chereau (1944–   ), who had run a theatre in a Communist suburb of Paris from 1966 to 1969, co-artistic director of the TNP. Chereau's first production for the TNP, in 1972, was of Marlowe's *The Massacre at Paris,* in which the stage gradually filled with a red liquid that made the characters seem to wade in blood. Most of Chereau's productions were contro-

versial, but together Planchon and Chereau set a standard for a people's theatre in France during the 1970s and the 1980s.

While working with Planchon, Chereau gained international recognition in 1976 when he staged Wagner's *Ring* cycle for Bayreuth's one-hundredth anniversary. This was the most controversial staging at Bayreuth since 1951 when Wieland Wagner had abandoned the conventions that had prevailed there since the festival was established. Chereau, working with his usual designer, Richard Peduzzi, set the cycle in a capitalistic, industrialized world where materialism, selfishness, and betrayal lead inexorably toward destruction; ultimately the gods themselves are destroyed, leaving human beings to discover values that will make survival possible. Initially disliked by many, Chereau's staging, filmed and shown throughout the world, subsequently came to be seen as a standard against which to judge other *Ring* productions. From 1982 to 1989 Chereau was director of the Théâtre des Amandiers in Nanterre, a working-class suburb of Paris. There he continued his reinterpretations of well-known scripts, perhaps most notably with Genet's *The Screens,* staged to reflect the racial tensions created in France by the influx of North African workers, and *Hamlet.*

Barrault also seemed to find renewal. In 1968, he conceived and staged *Rabelais,* a three-hour adaptation of material from Rabelais' writings that stressed repression and revolution. Originally staged in a sports arena in Paris, it drew on practically all recent theatrical trends. It subsequently played in London, New York, and elsewhere. Barrault then staged *Jarry sur la Butte* (1970) in a wrestling arena, and between 1972 and 1980 presented pieces based on the works of Nietzsche, Diderot, and others at his theatre in the former d'Orsay railway station and later at his Théâtre du Rond Pont. In 1971, Barrault was reap-

FIG. 14.11
Barrault's production
of *Rabelais,* first
performed at the
Elysée-Montmartre in
1968. (Photo by
Bernand.)

pointed director of the Théâtre des Nations, which was based in Paris until 1976. (Subsequently, it has moved to a different country each year.)

GERMAN-LANGUAGE THEATRE AND DRAMA

In West Germany, the theatre, which had been determinedly apolitical throughout the 1950s, began to move toward the left during the 1960s. This trend owed much to Piscator's staging of the documentary dramas of Hochhuth, Weiss, and Kipphardt. Brecht was also crucial, although until the 1960s his influence was felt primarily on staging techniques (especially simplified settings) rather than on ideological interpretation or the need for social change. Instead of seeking the alienation that Brecht prescribed, West German directors of Brecht's plays sought to insure the audience's emotional involvement. Because most of the intendants of the 1950s remained in their posts through the 1960s, the majority of subsidized theatres continued to emphasize "text-true," apolitical productions, and to consider themselves preservers of culture rather than instruments of social change. The leftward trend of the 1970s owed most to universities, in which New Left ideas gained a strong foothold, and to student theatre groups, on which the influence of Brecht and the Living Theatre was strong. When members of this new group began to enter the mainstream theatres, they brought with them the demand for change.

The dissatisfaction of young actors and directors over the almost unlimited power of intendants came to a head in 1968–1969, when in several theatres actors interrupted performances to discuss (or read statements about) the role of theatre in society and the implications of their own status in the theatre. Out of this crisis came a number of experiments in management. Cologne appointed a triumvirate of directors, each with his own group of performers; Wuppertal adopted a six-person directorate; Frankfurt, Kiel, and West Berlin attempted participatory directorates, in which every member in the company was involved. Some of these organizational schemes proved too cumbersome and were either abandoned or altered. The tensions were eased after 1972, when many older intendants retired and were replaced by younger men more sensitive to the issues that had been raised.

By 1972, Brecht had become the most produced playwright in West Germany. By that time, young directors, influenced by Brecht but extending or reinterpreting his theories, had begun to reshape interpretational modes. Peter Palitzsch (1918–   ), who had been Brecht's chief dramaturg, was in West Germany in 1961 when the Berlin wall was begun; he refused to return to East Germany and became one of West Germany's most respected and influential directors. His production of Brecht's *The Resistible Rise of Arturo Ui,* designed by Luciano Damiani, at Bremen in 1964 made an enormous impact and helped move the staging of the plays toward what Brecht had desired. But Brecht's more significant influence came through the way young directors adapted his methods to the staging of German classics.

Hansgunther Heyme (1935–   ), once an assistant to Piscator, became head of the Cologne company in 1968. His production there in 1969 of Schiller's *Wallenstein* became something of a watershed. Heyme reduced Schiller's trilogy to a single play, cutting and rearranging the order of scenes, eliminating characters, and making other changes that deemphasized Schiller's idealist emphasis on moral transcendence. Instead he pointed up the ideologies (of social class, political power, economic system) that Schiller had glossed over. The production also echoed concern for the Vietnam conflict. These changes made audiences look at one of Germany's major classics with a fresh eye and examine Schiller's own ideological biases.

Perhaps an even more influential production was that of Goethe's *Tasso,* as staged by Peter Stein (1937–   ) at Bremen in 1969. Goethe's play is a revered classic about the Renaissance Italian poet Torquato Tasso, who, although from the middle class, enjoys the patronage of the court until he oversteps the unstated bounds and is exiled. Stein radically altered the play's structure (rearranging the five acts into a prologue, ten episodes, and two interludes) so as to clarify the social forces implied by the play. The setting, by Wilfried Minks (1931–   ), became an integral part of Stein's interpretation. The stage floor was covered from front to back with green carpeting and enclosed with plexiglass. On stage the only objects were the Duke's chair, Tasso's desk, and a bust of Goethe. The overall effect was that of tamed nature, a kind of enclosure in which the poet was kept and expected to perform for the court on demand. The production became, then, not merely a staging of the play but a critique of the ideology which informed the play (much of it unconscious on Goethe's part). It was ultimately a comment on present-day artists and their dependence on state subsidies and public patronage, which is offered as long as the bounds are not overstepped. The last point became concrete when

FIG. 14.12
Peter Stein's production of Chekhov's *Three Sisters* in 1984, with Jutta Lampe as Masha, Edith Clever as Olga, Corinna Kirchoff as Irina, and Wolf Redl as Chebutykin. (Photo courtesy Story Press— Jochen Clauss.)

Stein and others were fired because the actors, despite being forbidden to do so, read political statements to the audience at intermission. Stein and a number of other actors—including Bruno Ganz, Edith Clever, Jutta Lampe, and Michael König—subsequently formed a collective and settled in the Schaubühne am Halleschen Ufer in West Berlin, where it became the most respected company in West Germany.

Stein and his company also were influential in enlarging views of dramaturgy. In most theatres, dramaturgs had been somewhat peripheral to actual production work, serving primarily as artistic consultants, but Stein involved not only his dramaturgs but everyone else in the dramaturgical process. In cooperation with the company's official dramaturgs, Dieter Sturm and Botho Strauss, each member of a play's cast was asked to research some aspect of the play or its context, especially its historical and ideological foundations, and to share information with the rest of the company.

Thus, everyone was involved in the process and could work from a common understanding. (This concept of "production dramaturgy," or some variation on it, soon became common in Germany theatres.) Scripts were reshaped to reveal the ideological assumptions obscured by the text's form and to clarify those assumptions by revealing the determinants that had shaped them. Stein did not believe that the theatre can change society, but he thought it could work indirectly through esthetically satisfying, ideologically revealing illustrations, based on thorough dramaturgical explorations. Stein's productions often showed characters escaping from unsatisfying reality into some utopian dream, or fantasy realm, but ultimately returning to the real world, the problems of which have been revealed to the audience (and often the characters) by the detour. Such productions as Ibsen's *Peer Gynt,* Kleist's *Prince of Homburg,* and Shakespeare's *As You Like It* were among the most praised in West Germany between 1970 and 1984 (Stein's years with the company). Eight of Stein's first twelve productions were invited to the West Berlin Theatertreffen, inaugurated in 1963 to give focus to the current state of German theatre by inviting to the festival each May the ten most significant, provocative, or innovative productions of that season. The choices have often been controversial, but they have offered a fair measure of theatrical trends in Germany.

Although the new approach to production popularized by Heyme and Stein emphasized the need to examine social realities critically, it did not rely on illusionistic staging. Minks' sets established the approach most usually adopted: the stage as stage, emphasized by calling attention to its frame (the proscenium) through the use of painted panels or lighting instruments; on the stage a few seemingly unrelated objects that remained unchanged throughout and that created emotionally expressive, metaphorical images. Thus, the stage was used to stimulate the imagination of the audience rather than to provide it with images of actual places. The stage was conceived of as a space not where reality occurs but where it may be examined, where the dialectical nature of social reality can be explored and the possibility of change revealed.

Not all directors were attuned to the New Left. Peter Zadek (1926–   ) certainly was not. The son of Jewish parents who emigrated to England in 1933, he attended Oxford University and the Old Vic Theatre School, and directed a number of productions (including the English premiere of Genet's *The Balcony,* which so enraged Genet that he disrupted performances) before returning to Germany in 1958. He served as artistic director at Bremen (1964–1967) and at Bochum (1972–1975). In Germany, he directed many English plays by O'Casey, Behan, Shakespeare, Bond, and others and was often accused of being more British than German in his tastes. Zadek emphasized entertainment, often incorporating

music-hall and revue elements, in a desire to make his productions accessible to everyone and not just intellectuals, but at times his productions also were greeted with charges of sensationalism or bad taste. He also seemed at times deliberately provocative, as in *The Merchant of Venice,* with its malicious and petty Shylock, and in Dorst's *Ice Age,* with its sympathetic Nazi collaborator, productions meant deliberately to question whether official anti-fascism is merely a disguise for anti-semitism. His production of *Othello* (1976), with its vaudeville black-face Othello, "hippie" Desdemona, and homoerotic implications was especially controversial.

In East Germany, the Berliner Ensemble continued to maintain the Brecht repertory but, by the time of Helene Weigel's death in 1971, was considered to have become a museum. Ruth Berghaus succeeded Weigel and attempted to revitalize the company through highly experimental productions of Wedekind's *Spring Awakening,* Strindberg's *Miss Julie,* and others, but they were greeted with charges of "self-indulgent formalism." She was succeeded in 1977 by Manfred Wekwerth (1929–   ), who had worked closely with Brecht. Under his direction the Berliner Ensemble regained some of its former stature.

From all the controversies, the Bayreuth Festival remained relatively aloof. In 1973 the Wagner family ostensibly relinquished much of its control over the festival and archival materials when the Richard Wagner Foundation was formed. This foundation is to maintain, but not run, the festival, and a member of the Wagner family is to direct future festivals "if no better qualified applicants come forward." In 1976, the festival celebrated its centennial with great fanfare and with a new staging by Patrice Chereau of the *Ring* cycle, which made the operas commentaries on the Industrial Revolution and capitalism. These productions eventually would seem conservative alongside those of Harry Kupfer (of East Berlin's Komische Oper) in 1988. Kupfer's *Ring* seemed to suggest a technological world nearing its end, in which the gods resembled gangsters.

German-language playwriting also changed during the late 1960s. Peter Handke (1942–   ) turned away from postwar concern for themes of guilt and responsibility to concern for language as ideology and controller of behavior. He began his playwriting career in 1966 with a group of short "speech plays" in which he abandoned plot, character, and environment. One of them, *Offending the Audience,* uses four unnamed and undifferentiated speakers to make, attack, and reformulate statements concerning theatre-going and the nature of theatrical illusion. In *Kaspar* (1968), probably Handke's best-known play, a young man who has been brought up in isolation is gradually reduced to conformity by making him learn and accept a linguistic code. *My Foot, My Tutor* (1969) extends Handke's theme to another type of language, learned physical behavior. In a kind of slave-master relationship, one character accepts a code and manner of behavior—an archetypal tyranny—imposed by the other without words. The title of *The Ride Across Lake Constance* (1971) is taken from a ballad about a knight who, after riding a horse across the frozen lake, is told that the ice is only one inch thick, whereupon he dies of fright. The five principal characters of the play, who have the names of actual German film stars, are disoriented through most of the play, seeking to find coherence between thought and event and panic-stricken at their inability to do so. A difficult play to interpret, it is perhaps concerned with twentieth-century disjunctures in perception created by rapid technological developments (here represented by cinema). *They Are Dying Out* (1974) is concerned with alienation and doubt about the possibility of any "free play" in thought or life. After the early 1970s Handke devoted most of his writing to novels, long dramatic poems, and film scripts for Wim Wenders.

Other German writers had more conventional social concerns. Martin Sperr (1944–   ) is best-known for a trilogy of plays (the first of a genre that has come to be called contemporary "folk plays") that provide a cross-section of German life: peasants, small-town residents, and city dwellers. *Hunting Scenes From Lower Bavaria* (1966) depicts peasant life within the framework of a manhunt and shows characters who are vital but hate-filled in their thoughtless cruelty to a homosexual man. *Tales of Landshut* (1967) centers around the pigheaded struggle of two businessmen for supremacy in a small town. *Munich Freedom* (1971) uses a building scandal to reveal the flagrant disregard by authorities of the rights of the majority, but the protestors, after occupying a brewery for a time, give up as everyone gradually becomes corrupted. In all these plays, Sperr depicts humans as selfish, corruptible, and cruel. *Koralle Meier* (1970), set in Nazi Germany, shows a prostitute, after helping a Jew, being sent to a concentration camp where, in desperation, she agrees to become an informer; eventually, repelled by herself, she denounces the system and is shot. After an illness of several years, Sperr returned to the theatre in 1977 with *Spitzeder,* a street-ballad entertainment about an actual nineteenth-century trickster. Sperr's moral and social questioning, combined with his directness, made him one of the most popular writers of the 1960s and 1970s.

Franz Xaver Kroetz (1946–   ), another author of folk plays, wrote seemingly simple dramas that recreated the speech and behavior patterns of subproletarians, working-class, and middle-class characters from his native Bavaria, through which he hoped to make his audiences assess their own place in society and take the steps needed for change. *Request Concert* (1971) has no dialogue. It shows a lonely, middle-aged, working-class woman going through her evening routine, then spreading out pills and taking them in an act of suicide. *Dairy Farm* (1972) and its sequel *Ghost Train* (1972) develop the relationship of two misfits—an older farmworker, Sepp, and the farmowners' mentally retarded adolescent daughter, Beppi. There are many naturalistic details, including Sepp's first helping Beppi clean herself up, when she suffers from diarrhea at an amusement park, and then raping her. Beppi's resulting pregnancy leads to a botched abortion, and eventually Beppi and Sepp go away together. After Sepp dies of pneumonia and social workers threaten to take her child, Beppi kills the child and leaves it on the "ghost train" at the amusement park. Among Kroetz's many later plays, probably the best-known is *Mensch Meier* (1978), a work in which the disintegration of a family reflects a disintegrating society. The father, Otto, is a worker who does nothing except insert screws into cars on an assembly line, although his hobbies and fantasies indicate that he has the imagination and skill to do much more; his wife Martha and son Ludwig are as financially dependent on him (being forced to perform menial tasks in return for handouts) as he is on his company. Both Ludwig and Martha leave home seeking greater independence, although both end up in jobs that enslave them to someone else as much as they were to Otto. By 1980 Kroetz was the most popular of all contemporary German-language dramatists.

Botho Strauss (1944–   ), one of Stein's dramaturgs, also became one of Germany's leading playwrights during the 1970s. He began writing plays in 1972 with *The Hypochondriacs*. Subsequent works included *Familiar Faces, Mixed Feelings* (1975), and *Big and Little* (1978). In all of these, Strauss treated alienation, the inability to feel emotion honestly and fully, and the disparity between everyday reality and a desired (often fantasized) state. Of these

plays, *Big and Little* was the most successful. In it, the characters are isolated in something like cells (an image captured by the set of white cubicles used in the original production). The principal character, Lotte, an alienated woman approaching middle age, seeks to make contact with others somewhat in the way expressionist protagonists did, but with Strauss the very search seems a delusion. It was awarded the critics' prize as the best play of 1978.

Thomas Bernhard (1931–1989) began as a novelist and did not have his first play produced until 1970. All of his work is about the ultimate futility of human striving. He places no hope in change or progress; he is constantly concerned with the gulf between characters' perceptions of their capabilities and their actual circumstances. In Bernhard's first play, *A Feast for Boris,* a woman gives a birthday party for her legless husband at which his principal presents are long underwear and a pair of boots; thus, what at first seemed to be love turns into sadism. Because Bernhard's plays are written with virtually no punctuation or stage directions, they require special actors, one of whom, Bernhard Minetti, acted in several, even in one entitled *Minetti* (1976). In this play, the first scene shows an elderly actor waiting to be interviewed for the role of Lear; the director never arrives and in the second scene the actor is sitting on a park bench as snow falls on him. Bernhard's general misanthropy, sometimes taking the form of attacks on his fellow beings, often led to protests against his plays, as it did with his final work, *Heroes' Square* (1988), which accused Austria of still being antisemitic, as well as "a nation of 6.5 million idiots living in a country that is rotting away, falling apart, run by the political parties in an unholy alliance with the Catholic Church." Nevertheless, the public seemed fascinated by Bernhard's plays, a fact explained by some as the German middle class' inherent self-critical masochism.

The desire to reshape society, which came

to a focus after 1968, led many to use theatre to reach children and youth. The best-known of these companies was West Berlin's Grips. Beginning in 1968, Grips abandoned fairy tales (long the preferred source) for material related directly to the children's lives. The resulting *emancipatory theatre,* which dealt with a wide variety of topics, sought to free its audiences from the tyranny of stereotypical ideas and behavior. *Stokkerlod and Millipilli* (1969) shows a girl demonstrating that she can use her talents as well as a boy can, and then uniting with a boy to oppose an unjust authoritarian figure. *Rhinoceroses Don't Shoot* (1974) is about children discovering the differences between real needs and the artificial needs created by advertising. *The Best Years of Your Life* (1978) concerns the intertwined lives of eight working-class teenagers who are striving to find some satisfaction in a system that neither permits creativity nor recognizes their human potential; it chronicles their battles with such problems as sexuality, delinquency, unemployment, exploitation of teen labor, and the use of alcohol and drugs. Not surprisingly, Grips was frequently accused of encouraging children to rebel against parents, teachers, and other adults, and of indoctrinating children with leftist ideas. Germany had many other children's theatres. In 1976 the Alliance for Children's and Young People's Theatre was formed to help companies deal with common problems. An annual festival of children's theatre was also established.

GREAT BRITAIN

Many changes in British theatre after 1968 can be traced to the abolishment of censorship in that year. This change was provoked primarily by the English Stage Company (ESC) which, using a private club to evade censorship, had presented plays denied licenses by the Lord Chamberlain. Although the use of "private"

performances to get around the censor was a long-established practice in England, the plays performed by the ESC—Bond's *Saved* (in which a baby is stoned to death on stage) and Osborne's *A Patriot for Me* (in which there was overt onstage homosexuality)—provoked the Lord Chamberlain to bring a lawsuit, which he won. The resulting controversy led to Parliamentary hearings and the eventual abolition of the censorship that had been in effect since 1737. The first result was the immediate production of works—among them *Hair* and Hochhuth's *The Soldiers*—that had previously been forbidden.

More important, the lifting of censorship removed the principal deterrent to what had been called *underground* theatres (groups comparable to the off-off-Broadway or radical theatre companies of the United States), most of which, because of their anti-establishment stance, found it difficult to get scripts licensed and many of which preferred to work improvisationally. After 1968, these companies proliferated rapidly and soon came to be known as "fringe" groups. They performed at universities, in meeting halls and pubs, on playgrounds, or almost anywhere an audience could be assembled. Some performed at lunchtime and others late at night. Their great variety (in ideology, targeted audiences, performance style, times and places of performance) did much to broaden the British theatre.

Americans played a key role in the English fringe. LaMama had appeared in London more than once, and in 1967 the Open Theatre first performed there. Both served as catalysts for the new movement. In addition, Jim Haynes, a charismatic American who after 1963 had headed the Traverse Theatre in Edinburgh, in 1968 founded the Arts Lab in London, which spawned several fringe companies. Beginning in 1968, another American, Ed Berman, gradually built Interaction into one of the most complex community arts services in Europe.

His organization operated a lunchtime theatre (Ambiance); a mobile theatre (the Fun Art Bus); a children's theatre (Dogg's Troupe); a professional company (the Other Company) which, with Ambiance, performed at the Almost Free Theatre; a theatre for senior citizens; and other related activities. As the title of his organization suggests, he was concerned about how theatre can interact with a community, its interests, and problems. Nancy Meckler, another American, headed Freehold, which was consciously based on American models and, through its emphasis upon physicality, did much to move the British theatre away from its dependency on voice and speech. Charles Marowitz, who had worked with Peter Brook on his season of Theatre of Cruelty in 1963–1964 and had reworked *Hamlet* into a twenty-minute collage at that time, established the Open Space in 1968, where he favored experimental theatre writing and production, especially those using Artaudian techniques. He was often very critical of what he considered to be unprofessional work by many fringe theatres.

The English fringe was extremely varied. The Pip Simmons Group followed American models but combined the physicality of LaMama with cartoon-like characters and abundant music to create biting social commentary. The People Show, run by Jeff Nuttall, Mark Long, and Roland Miller, was essentially improvisational, developing its performances according to the reactions of the audience. Using a melange of conflicting images and styles once described as a cross between dada and happenings, its productions influenced many other groups. The Portable Theatre, founded by David Hare and Tony Bicat in 1968, attracted a group of new playwrights, among them Howard Brenton, Snoo Wilson, and Hare himself, many of whom would become increasingly important in the British theatre. Visually the Portable's performances were usually quite spartan because of the troupe's insistence on minimal scenery and props so as to be as mobile as possible. In content, the plays almost invariably depicted English society in a state of extreme moral decay.

Not all of the fringe groups were based in London. Welfare State, founded by John Fox in 1968, began in Leeds, but it performed at various places in England, often choosing a town and then creating a play based on local history or legend and performed in or near the supposed location of the events being dramatized. Thus, it promoted an environmental concept of theatre. It also made use of rock culture, music, and pagan ritual, fused with the local material to create archetypal patterns that showed human beings liberated from a hypocritical and repressive society. The Traverse Theatre Workshop was established by Max Stafford-Clark in Edinburgh in 1969. More than any other group, it popularized in England the idea of collective creation, with its company of actors working directly with playwrights to create pieces through a cooperative process of research and company improvisation. This method would be exploited especially well after 1974 by the Joint Stock Theatre Company, which worked with such playwrights as David Hare and Caryl Churchill and which developed a special relationship with the ESC, where many of its works were performed.

The fringe grew quickly. In late 1969 the ESC hosted at the Royal Court Theatre an event called *Come Together,* in which fringe groups were invited to participate. It lasted for twenty days and twenty nights and provided a summation of the fringe as it existed at that time. Like such movements elsewhere, the groups involved had quite checkered histories. Many disappeared quickly, others underwent metamorphoses. But the fringe greatly expanded the range and accessibility of British theatre. In 1969–1970, the Arts Council for the first time provided subsidy to a fringe company, and thereafter the struggle (and often animosity) between established and fringe companies increased.

Ironically, it was the ESC that suffered most from the lifting of censorship, for with the growth of the fringe theatres many of the playwrights who previously would have brought their work to the ESC now found more opportunity and freedom elsewhere. When George Devine retired in 1965, management of the ESC had passed to William Gaskill. Noted for his clear but restrained directing, Gaskill acknowledged Brecht as the greatest influence on his work. He continued to champion new plays, and in 1969 enlarged this commitment by opening the Theatre Upstairs, in the attic of the Royal Court, to give short runs to plays by new playwrights. In 1975 Gaskill resigned to devote more time to the Joint Stock Theatre Company, which he ran with Max Stafford-Clark and David Hare. During Gaskill's tenure, the ESC introduced many new writers, but two—Bond and Storey—were of special importance.

Edward Bond (1935–   ) made his debut as a playwright with *The Pope's Wedding* on one of the ESC's Sunday evening programs in 1962. He achieved overnight notoriety in 1965 when *Saved* was given "privately" by the ESC. It treats the absence of humanity in a generation without hope for the future. Its most shocking scene shows a baby being stoned to death in its pram by a group of young men, one of them the child's father. *Early Morning* (1968), a surrealistic farce about the cannibalism of a class-dominated capitalist system inherited from the Victorian era, became notorious more for the lesbian relationship it depicted between Queen Victoria and Florence Nightingale than for its ultimate theme: "Souls die first and bodies live." These plays were among those most responsible for the controversy over and ultimate removal of censorship. Bond's subsequent plays tended to be less sensational but no less political. *Lear* (1971) is a reworking of Shakespeare's play in which the thematic focus is shifted to show how harsh social restrictions lead to an ongoing cycle of aggression. This

FIG. 14.13
"Private" production of Edward Bond's *Saved* at the Royal Court in 1965. This is the scene in which a baby is stoned to death. (Photo by Dominic.)

theme is summed up in the wall, which Lear originally built but which serves both to defend and entrap those who control it. Unlike Shakespeare's, Bond's play has no sympathetic character; Cordelia fights more viciously than anyone to preserve the wall, which she defends as necessary until threats to order are eliminated. At the end, Lear takes one small step toward breaking the cycle by attacking the wall, even though he knows he will be shot for doing so.

Bond returns to Shakespeare once more in *Bingo* (1974), a play about the role of the artist in society with Shakespeare as its protagonist. It shows Shakespeare in his retirement acquiescing to the enclosure of lands which will deprive many people of livelihood. Ultimately his anguish over the disparity between the humanity of his plays and the inhumanity of the immediate situation leads him to suicide. *The Bundle* (1978) is a reworking of Bond's earlier play, *Narrow Road to the Deep North* (1968), in which characters seek to avoid any responsibility for an abandoned baby. The Ferryman's generosity in taking the baby is treated as the kind of patchwork solution that delays the

major change that the revolutionary Wang champions. Wang argues that one may save the first child but what about the hundredth? "You saints who crucify the world so that you can be good! You keep us in dirt and ignorance! Force us into the mud with your dirty morality!" He (and apparently Bond) argues that rifles offer a better solution, since now "only the evil can afford to do good." Bond has continued to write plays, but his later works have seldom aroused the enthusiasm that greeted the early ones.

David Storey (1933–   ) began his career as a teacher and novelist and turned to playwriting in 1967 with *The Restoration of Arnold Middleton*, staged at the Royal Court by Lindsay Anderson, who also directed Storey's subsequent plays. *The Contractor* (1970) displays concern for psychological pressures, in addition to its considerable concern for class divisions. On the surface little happens. The rhythm of the action is largely controlled by the physical process of erecting (during the first part) and taking down (during the second part) of a tent, used for the wedding of Ewbank's daughter (which takes place between the two parts).

FIG. 14.14
Storey's *The Contractor*, produced at the Royal Court in 1970. (Photo by Tom Murray.)

The characters are divided into two groups: Ewbank's family and the workmen. From the first group there emanates a sense of lost illusions and shattered ideals, from the second an undercurrent of hostility and potential violence. Much is revealed, nothing resolved. The alienation of *The Contractor* is translated in *Home* (1970) into a metaphor—the insane asylum. Here alienation exists on several planes: England from its former glory; class from class; men from women; individuals from themselves. The title (which may mean one's country, one's dwelling, or one's sense of belonging) strengthens the allusions. In the opening scene, two apparently refined gentlemen meet on a terrace furnished only with two chairs and an empty flagpole. They converse pleasantly but reveal little. When they leave, two rather bawdy women, obviously from a lower class, take their place. Gradually it becomes clear that all are inmates in some kind of asylum. In the second part, one of the men is said to have molested young girls, the other to be a pyromaniac; one of the women cannot control her kidneys, the other is sexually promiscuous. The overpowering effect is of loneliness, of people on parallel paths that never converge. Like Beckett, Storey here treats the existential plight of humanity. His method, however, more nearly resembles Pinter's, since everything that happens might occur in real life. Ultimately, the play's power resides in its multiple implications and deep compassion. In *The Changing Room* (1971) members of a semi-professional rugby team (all of whom have other jobs during the week) change into their uniforms in the first act and back to their street clothes in the final act; class, social distinctions, and purposelessness are similarly divested and reassumed after a short period of community achieved during a harsh ritual. The play gained some notoriety because of the male nudity during the changes. Storey wrote other plays but none achieved the

power of these. Few writers have so precisely recreated the detail of real-life situations or used them to imply so much about contemporary society.

The Royal Shakespeare Company continued to play a major role after 1968, the year in which its management passed to Trevor Nunn (1940–   ). At the time, Nunn seemed a strange choice. Having joined the RSC in 1965, his early work was thought little short of disastrous, but in 1966 he staged the work that would change his career—Tourneur's *The Revenger's Tragedy*. Not only was it hailed as one of the best productions of the decade but also as one that marked a significant break with what had become RSC's dominant production mode (neo-Brechtian). Designed by Christopher Morley, it was determinedly theatrical, shaped around an image of moths drawn to a flame (suggested by a silver circle painted on the floor and black and silver costuming). It also featured a new generation of actors who were to become mainstays under Nunn's regime: Alan Howard, Norman Rodway, Patrick Stewart, and Helen Mirren. Nevertheless, when Nunn assumed the directorship of RSC two years later, he had had practically no managerial experience.

Hall left Nunn many problems to cope with and, not surprisingly, the company went through a series of ups and downs during the first years of Nunn's leadership. Nunn reduced actors' contracts from three to two years and alternated their residency each year between Stratford and London. He also virtually eliminated the production of new plays at the Aldwych and instead shifted to revivals of little-known or rarely performed classics. He also transferred all of Stratford's successful Shakespearean productions to London. At Stratford, Hall's reputation rested primarily on his productions of Shakespeare's history plays; Nunn turned to the late plays in scaled-down productions in Morley's minimal settings that resembled empty boxes. The style that developed was given its fullest expression in Brook's 1970 production of *A Midsummer Night's Dream*, one of the most influential Shakespearean productions of the century. This production also did more than any other to restore the RSC's shaky financial position.

The forces that encouraged the growth of fringe theatres also influenced the RSC as it was attacked for the amount of subsidy it received in relation to that given fringe companies, especially considering its restricted repertory, its failure to serve the country as a whole, its large expenditures on a limited number of productions, and its lack of commitment to new playwrights and contemporary issues. Erratic changes in policies resulted in part from attempts to deal with these issues. To recoup the expenditures, a greater number of productions were moved to London and sent on international tours. Beginning in 1974, the season at Stratford was extended into January, and the abandonment of the World Theatre Seasons made the rotation of companies between London and Stratford more fully practicable.

The RSC also developed its small company work. Theatregoround, which had taken small-scale productions on tour in Britain, had to be abandoned in 1971 because of finances. The company had no ongoing small group until 1974, when it opened The Other Place, an adjustable space seating 140, in Stratford. It was headed by Buzz Goodbody (1947–1975), the company's first female director and one with strong connections to the fringe theatres. (After Goodbody's death, it was run by Ron Daniels.) There Shakespearean and other classics, along with new plays, were done on minimal budgets. One of its most highly acclaimed productions came in 1976 when Nunn directed *Macbeth* there. The playing area was outlined as a black circle on the floor, creating a magic area within which the action

occurred and intensifying the psychological, almost ritualized elements by reducing the production's scale. In 1977, the RSC opened a similar small theatre—the Warehouse—in London under the direction of Howard Davies. Its first season included four works moved from Stratford and five new plays by dramatists who had become associated with the fringe. These small theatres did much to bridge the former gulf between the RSC and the fringe.

The season of 1977–1978, during which it mounted thirty-one productions, marked a high point for the RSC. During that season it also won practically all the awards that normally went to West End productions. By then, the program had become so complex that in 1978 Terry Hands (1941–   ), one of the company's most effective directors, was named joint artistic director. Thus despite ongoing financial problems, the RSC maintained its position as one of the world's most respected theatres.

After leaving the RSC, Hall served as director of the Royal Covent Garden Opera Company before being appointed to succeed Laurence Olivier as head of the National Theatre in 1973. (Olivier's service to the theatre was recognized in 1970 when he became the first English actor to be made a lifetime peer.) In addition to administering a complex organization, Hall had to cope with numerous problems related to the company's new home. Scheduled to open in 1974, the building was not ready until 1976, by which time its cost had escalated to some $32 million. When completed, it included three performance spaces: the 1,160-seat Olivier open-stage theatre with a revolving stage 40 feet in diameter divided into two parts that could be lowered to workshops 45 feet below; the 890-seat Lyttleton proscenium theatre; and the 400-seat Cottesloe laboratory theatre. There were more than 100 dressing rooms, several stage-sized rehearsal rooms, and numerous workshops.

Because of the building's cost and the anticipated expense of running it, the National became a target, especially for fringe groups, who argued that the great sums spent on the National could more productively be assigned to the many small theatres that constituted the country's true "national" theatre, unlike the National which seemed destined to perform in one city for an elite few. The hostility increased in 1975–1976, when one-quarter of the Arts Council's drama budget went to the National; the controversy was not quieted by the explanation that the largest percentage of the funds went for operating and maintenance costs. Thus, Hall found himself besieged, with much of his energy spent in justifying the national role of his company. Nevertheless, the National was to remain a ready target, especially for those who wished to reshape the theatre into a more democratic institution.

The stated goal of the National was to present a diverse repertory of classic, new, and neglected plays from the whole range of world drama. Its repertory ranged from *The Oresteia* to new scripts by such authors as Peter Shaffer, Tom Stoppard, and David Hare. Membership in its acting company changed frequently but always included some of England's most outstanding performers, among them Maggie Smith, Joan Plowright, Irene Worth, Laurence Olivier, Alan Bates, Albert Finney, and many others. Not only did the National pay considerably higher salaries but it was also considered more hospitable to actors than the RSC, where directorial concept usually took precedence. Hall, as at the RSC, appointed John Bury as head of design. Throughout the 1970s, the National maintained its reputation as one of the major theatres of the world, but much of its energy was expended on transition in management, completing and adjusting to a new building, and controversy over funding.

Both the RSC and the National promoted the careers of several British playwrights, especially Stoppard and Nichols. Tom Stoppard (1937–   ), born in Czechoslovakia but reared in England, began writing plays in 1960 and achieved his first major success in 1967 when the National Theatre presented his *Rosencrantz and Guildenstern Are Dead,* a play resembling Beckett's dramas, in which the two attendant lords in *Hamlet* become the protagonists, although they die without ever understanding the events of which they have been a part. In this and many of his other numerous plays, Stoppard draws on familiar literary works, dramatic forms, actual or fictional persons, and philosophical concepts. He also makes use of linguistic virtuosity and dazzling theatricality to create engaging and entertaining plays which are ultimately concerned with the ways in which contemporary behavior is dominated by pragmatism, moral blindness, and self-interest. *Jumpers* (1972) opens with the onstage murder by some unseen person of one member of a gymnastic team (composed of a university's philosophy faculty). Much of the remainder of the play concerns attempts to conceal or solve the murder, but the larger concern is the "acrobatics" of contemporary philosophy and its inability to make any meaningful connection with life because of relativist values. *Travesties* (1974) is set in Zurich during World War I when James Joyce, Lenin, and Tristan Tzara were resident there and when a seedy Englishman stages a production of Wilde's *The Importance of Being Earnest.* These juxtapositions permit Stoppard to comment on the relationship between revolutionary art and revolutionary politics. *The Real Thing* (1982) draws on the conventions of drawing-room comedy to juxtapose scenes from a play written by the protagonist with scenes from his real life to explore the nature of truth, art, and love. *Hapgood* (1988) recalls *Jumpers* in its intermingling of quantum physics and spy thriller.

Peter Nichols (1929–   ) achieved his first stage success with *A Day in the Death of Joe Egg*

(1967), which deals with the attempts of a school teacher and his wife to cope with their spastic child, whom they view as a joke played on them by life but who ultimately serves as a catalyst to bring to the surface their suppressed anxieties and frustrations. This mixture of humor, compassion, and astringent observation marks most of Nichols' subsequent work. *The National Health* (1969) juxtaposes life in a hospital ward (where elderly patients drag out their lives) with the romanticized television soap operas the patients eagerly watch on television. This use of popular-culture forms to illuminate social and political issues was further developed by Nichols in *Privates on Parade* (1977), in which a Song and Dance Unit, entertaining troops in Singapore in 1948, performs unconscious travesties of the very culture they supposedly wish to save, just as army personnel are shown undermining high-minded British goals through their moral anarchy and violence. Popular-culture forms also played a prominent role in *Poppy* (1982), which used the conventions of British pantomime to expose the imperialist platitudes used in the nineteenth century to justify England's exploitation of the Opium Wars in order to acquire territorial rights in China.

English dramatists after 1968 were numerous and most embodied in varying degrees left-wing protests against then-current sociopolitical conditions. Two examples suffice. Heathcote Williams' *AC/DC* (1970) made considerable impact with its attack on the "psychic capitalism" imposed by media standards and personalities. In Trevor Griffith's *Comedians* (1975) a training course for would-be comedians is used to comment on class relationships and the way in which most comedy caters to the audience's prejudices; the protagonist ultimately defies the proferred advice and reveals in his own comic turn the class hatred usually glossed over in daily life. These examples could be extended many times over; they illustrate a strain that would dominate English theatre throughout the 1970s and 1980s.

FIG. 14.15
Peter Nichols' *The National Health* at the National Theatre in 1969. (Photo by Reg Wilson.)

ITALY

In Italy after 1968, Dario Fo (1926–   ) was the dramatist most attuned to the new directions, probably because he had anticipated most of them in his own earlier work. Fo had begun to write and perform in the late 1940s, and first gained recognition as a radio performer who retold well-known legends and plays, turning them upside down to make the underdogs triumphant. He then moved into revue as a performer and writer before forming a company with his wife, Franca Rame. At first this company produced short, satirical, topical plays, most of them by Fo, who drew extensively on earlier popular entertainment forms. The first of Fo's full-length plays, *Archangels Don't Play Pinball* (1959), was also his first to abandon the revue-sketch format for an approach that showed the influence of Brecht. Like his early radio sketches, these full-length plays ended in the besting of established authority (usually depicted as fascistic) by ingenious subproletarians. For a time, Fo also wrote and performed pieces for television but, although these were extremely popular, he ultimately quit in protest against censorship of his work.

Following the events of 1968, Fo decided that he could not achieve his goals by performing in theatres or media controlled by bourgeois and government authorities and, seeking an alliance with the Italian Communist party, began to perform primarily in workers' halls and similar spaces. But Fo soon ran afoul of the Communists, and in 1970 he formed the Colletivo Teatrale 'La Commune,' a company which ultimately offended almost every political faction in Italy through its wide-ranging satirical thrusts. For it, Fo wrote *Accidental Death of an Anarchist* (1970), in which he performed the role of a man who assumes numerous disguises in his effort to prove that the police have covered up their culpability in

FIG. 14.16
Dario Fo's *Accidental Death of an Anarchist* at the Arena Stage, Washington, D.C., in 1984. Directed by Douglas C. Wager. (Photo by Joan Marcus, courtesy Arena Stage.)

the death of a left-wing agitator whom they wish to blame for a bombing (actually done by right-wing extremists). Fo's subsequent plays include *We're All in the Same Boat, but That Man Over There, Isn't He the Boss?* (1971), which traces the Italian working-class struggle from 1911 to 1922, when the fascists came to power; and *Can't Pay? Won't Pay!* (1974), about women who "appropriate" food from the supermarket in protest against rampant inflation. Probably his most representative piece is *Mistero Buffo,* a solo piece that Fo has performed throughout much of his career. In it he recounts how the medieval story teller (*guillare*) first came into being and then goes on to give his version of biblical stories and church history, recreating events from various points of view, demystifying the stories, and suggesting parallels with contemporary events. In this and most of his other plays, Fo makes extensive use of *grammelot*, his own made-up language which is rendered comprehensible largely by Fo's imaginative and expressive pantomime.

By 1977, times had sufficiently changed that Fo was invited to present some of his plays on Italian state television. Fo also wrote a number of feminist plays for his wife, later published under the collective title *Female Parts*, indicting the traditional Italian male view of women. Franca Rame subsequently performed these throughout Europe and in the U.S. By the late 1970s, then, Fo had achieved sufficient acceptance to be reintegrated into mainstream theatre, even though he continued his satirical thrusts at authority, capitalism, antifeminism, and hypocrisy. By that time, he had also become one of the few contemporary Italian playwrights to gain international fame.

Like Fo (and Barrault in France), Giorgio Strehler, Italy's foremost director, also decided in 1968 that he could not continue within the context of establishment theatre. Consequently, he resigned as director of Milan's Teatro Piccolo and created the Gruppo Teatro e Azione to explore politically engaged theatre. In 1972, he resumed his former post at the Teatro Piccolo, where he remained thereafter, although continuing to direct elsewhere frequently. Among his productions during the 1970s, probably the best-known was Shakespeare's *The Tempest*, seen in Milan in 1978 and subsequently in major cities throughout the world. Long recognized as a major director of Brecht's plays, Strehler was heavily influenced by Brecht in this production, mounted on a stage erected on the theatre's stage to emphasize the theatricality of the piece. At the end, when Prospero breaks his staff, the onstage platform collapses, and Prospero, standing in the auditorium, seems to suggest that the lessons learned from the play must now be applied in the spectators' world.

Luca Ronconi (1933–   ), although he had been directing for many years, gained international recognition in 1969 with his production of *Orlando Furioso*, presented at the Spoleto festival and subsequently in major cities throughout Europe and in New York. The text was adapted by Eduardo Sanguineti from Lodovico Ariosto's sixteenth-century epic poem about chivalric adventures involving mythical creatures, enchanted castles, sorcerers, and other fanciful beings. About fifty tall platforms,

FIG. 14.17
Ronconi's and Sanguineti's *Orlando Furioso* at the Festival of Two Worlds, Spoleto, in 1969. (Photo by Pic.)

some surmounted by such mythical creatures as hippogriffs, were wheeled about a large open central space, at each end of which was a platform stage where other scenes progressed. The open area was occupied both by the mobile wagons and spectators, who moved about, choosing what they wished to see. The overall effect was a mixture of street parade, pageant, a happening, and several playlets proceeding simultaneously.

Ronconi's subsequent productions attracted less attention but were equally imaginative. In *XX* (1971), he divided the audience into groups and placed each in separate rooms, the walls between which were gradually removed. Each group saw only a few disturbing events but heard voices and sounds elsewhere. When all the walls were gone, a *coup d'état* was announced and the audience was ordered to disperse. Ronconi stated that he wished to show how dictatorial power can be assumed almost unnoticed until it is too late.

TOWARD POSTMODERNISM

The period between 1968 and 1980, then, brought rebellion against accepted modes of thought and artistic expression. It was a time of frantic experimentation in which almost any innovation could find support. But by the late 1970s, the public had become sated with the variety and unimpressed by the latest trend. To many, the possibility of truly new ideas seemed exhausted and a new age—of postmodernism—was said to have arrived.

Chapter 15

Postmodernism, Deconstruction, and the 1980s

The dynamic ferment that characterized theatrical activity after 1968 stemmed in part from the optimistic sense of the disaffected that they, after discrediting hypocritical values and outmoded artistic conventions, could create both a more equitable society and a more relevant theatre. The heady sense of accomplishment derived from defying taboos and creating new artistic modes had encouraged the notion of unlimited possibilities. But by the 1980s, as this sense of mission faded, other theoretical concerns, fostered by the 1960s but largely ignored except by intellectuals, came to the fore and exerted increasing, though often unacknowledged, influence on theatre. These concerns were probably best exemplified in postmodernism and poststructuralism (or deconstruction), along with other growing voices, perhaps most notably feminism and New Historicism.

THEORETICAL CONTEXTS

A sense of belatedness (or, alternatively, of having entered a new age)—exemplified in such terms as *postindustrial* and *posthumanist*—was characteristic of the 1980s. Among such terms, *postmodernism* came to be the one most frequently used as a label for certain characteristic tendencies in art. As a term, postmodernism implies a discernible break with modernism, the blanket term typically applied to early twentieth-century art. Under modernism, a variety of styles had flourished, but within any one, the artist usually sought unity by adhering consistently to a set of conventions associated with that mode (expressionism, surrealism, epic theatre, and so on). If there were disparate elements, they were ultimately harmonized into a unified whole. Contrarily, postmodernists were undisturbed by lack of consistency and continuity. They allowed disparities to exist without seeking to mask them and juxtaposed various styles and moods that previously would have been considered incompatible or unacceptably inconsistent. They collapsed categories considered distinct under modernism; boundaries were breached between the arts, between styles and periods, between dramatic forms, between cultures. Postmodern art often was reflexive, calling attention to the fact that it was being made and how it was being made. It might include overt references to other works. It tended to value popular and high culture equally and to intermingle them. Some postmodernists suggested that the possibilities of significant new insights had been exhausted and that therefore one could only recycle the past. But if, as many contended, postmodernism was a sign of malaise, much of the work that came out of it seemed innovative because, although it might recycle and combine familiar elements, it did so in unfamiliar ways.

Many aspects of postmodernism were supported or supplemented by poststructuralism (or deconstruction). *Poststructuralism* was associated especially with Jacques Derrida (1930–), author of such works as *Of Grammatology* (1967, tr. into English 1977) and *Writing and Difference* (1967, tr. into English 1978). Other key figures in poststructuralist thought were Roland Barthes, Jacques Lacan, Michel Foucault, Louis Althusser, Gilles Deleuze, Felix Guattari, and Julia Kristeva. Deconstruction was promoted in the United States by such literary critics as Paul DeMan, Geoffrey Hartman, J. Hillis Miller, and Harold Bloom.

Derrida did not reject structuralism as much as seek to correct what he saw as its serious flaws. One of these was structuralism's tendency to give precedence to face-to-face speech as more authentic than written discourse, thereby suggesting that meaning is more fully present in speech than in writing. Derrida reversed these tenets by arguing that writing must be conceived as something like an archetypal precondition of language (whether spoken or physically recorded)—an unconscious grasp of relationships that must be present before linguistic communication of any kind is possible. This argument is part of a larger one that constitutes Derrida's critique of all Western philosophy, which he sees as based on the premise that reality and truth are independent of language—that they have an objective existence which philosophers can perceive, and that language is merely a neutral medium used to transmit those perceptions. Instead, Derrida argues, all statements about truth and reality are linguistic constructs, and it is impossible ever to reach a point in thought that precedes language. Consciousness does not precede and give birth to language, but rather language makes consciousness possible. Therefore, any language predisposes its users to see the world in particular ways, and thus invalidates (or seriously compromises) any claim to objectivity. In addition, meaning can never be fully present because, in the process of communication, it is always being modified by what has gone before and *deferred* by what is yet to come.

Structuralism tended to describe linguistic relationships in binary terms—parallelisms, oppositions, inversions—but, as Derrida pointed out, one in any set of binary terms is almost always privileged over its opposite (for example, male over female) and eventually, because it has been linguistically infused into our thought processes, this privileging comes to be unthinkingly accepted. Thus, all language has ideology imbedded in it, and consequently statements are haunted by what they suppress or ignore. In any statement or category, a supplement of meaning is always left over, and as we examine the supplement it begins to call into question the adequacy of the original statement (or the boundaries of the category) and to suggest modifications which lead to still other modifications in an endless chain of deferred and differing meanings. This analytical process has come to be known as deconstruction. On the one hand, deconstruction uncovers the unstated ideological premises and assumptions that undergird any statement (or work of art) and allows us to see what has been privileged and what has been ignored or suppressed. On the other hand, it demonstrates that there can be no closure of meaning, since the deconstructive process is always uncovering additional possible readings (or "misreadings") of a text, often ones of which an author may have been unaware or did not intend. Ultimately, deconstruction leads to the conclusion that all statements are reflections of ideological stances and that one can never arrive at a single, "correct" reading or interpretation of any work (although some readings may be more defensible than others).

Poststructuralists stated a number of other influential ideas. Barthes sought to distinguish between a "work" (what an author wrote—the physical document) and a "text" (what individual readers find when they "interrogate" the work). He argued that the author has no more right than anyone else in the text, since no one can dictate how it can be "read." In effect, readers become at least partial writers of the text they perceive in a work. This view, combined with the principle of no closure of meaning, provides justification, if any were needed, for directorial interpretations (or "misreadings") that depart drastically from dramatists' instructions within their works.

Other statements by poststructuralists reinforce postmodernism. Kristeva has argued that the notion of artistic originality is greatly exaggerated since all works are absorptions and transformations of those that have gone before and are, in effect, mosaics of citations. Bloom has stated that most artists and critics suffer from a sense of belatedness, which leads them to misrepresent ("misread") the work of their predecessors in order to exaggerate their own originality.

Poststructuralism also reinforced feminism, one of the major forces in the 1980s, although it had been gaining strength for some time. Feminism has a long history and has gone through many stages but was especially strong beginning in the 1960s when it gained renewed strength from the civil rights movement. Feminism was not monolithic. In the United States, three types of feminism were most evident. "Liberal" feminism, probably the most widely known type, sought to achieve full equality for women within the existing system. "Cultural" or "radical" feminism saw a clear difference between men and women and claimed superiority for women as being instinctively connected with others and the cycles of nature, and as nurturing, pacifistic, and life-affirming as opposed to men, who were seen as self-serving, competitive, violent, aggressive, and death-affirming. The goal, then, was a reorientation that would substitute female for male values. "Materialist" feminism viewed women as a suppressed group not merely on the basis of gender but also class, race, and other factors that linked them with other groups, both male and female.

Feminism made especially effective use of deconstructionist analysis to show how a dominant set of values becomes so completely imbedded in language as to pass for nonideology (normality) and how this is transformed into social structures that privilege white male, heterosexual, capitalist values and subordinate others. In addition, it deconstructed art works (especially films), aesthetic theory, and critical commentary to uncover the unstated ideological stances that had shaped them. Feminism, in its several shapes, was one of the most potent and productive forces during the 1980s.

Another consequence of deconstruction was to rehistorify much critical thinking. Structuralism had been ahistorical in its concern for the fixed, basic sets of relationships that undergird language quite independent of time and place. Poststructuralism, on the other hand, in pursuing the suppressed and privileged aspects of discourse, moved inevitably toward examining the historical conditions reflected in language. Althusser and Foucault were especially concerned with such issues. The approach that emerged from these concerns is usually referred to as New Historicism. Basically, New Historicists seek to read a work in relation to the cultural context in which it was written in order to uncover unstated or unacknowledged power relationships by analyzing what groups or values are "marginalized" on the one hand or "empowered" on the other, how a work reflects the "dominant order" (often a "patriarchal authority"), and how the work supports such dominance through "culturally determined ways of seeing," or calls it into question through "emancipatory" or "transgressive discourse." Just as Freudian criticism seeks to uncover what has been suppressed or privileged by the individual

writer's unconscious, New Historicism seeks to uncover what has been suppressed or privileged by a culture. It argues that we should look beneath and beyond the surface if we are to comprehend the interaction between a work and the culture of its time, as well as what it implies about our own culture's assumptions and values.

AMERICAN POSTMODERNISM

In the United States, a few individuals and groups clearly show the influence of postmodernism or poststructuralism. They include Robert Wilson, Mabou Mines, Richard Foreman, and the Wooster Group, along with a number of directors and performance artists.

Robert Wilson (1941–   ) was trained as a graphic designer and sculptor and came to the theatre primarily through his work as a therapist with the handicapped. (He himself had suffered from a speech impediment, which he overcame with the help of a movement teacher, Byrd Hoffman, for whom Wilson subsequently named the foundation that managed much of his work.) Wilson began to create theatre pieces in the late 1960s, and until 1975 all grew out of workshops, most of which included either Raymond Andrews, a profoundly deaf, black adolescent, or Christopher Knowles, a seemingly autistic young man. It was partially out of these experiences that Wilson developed his belief that everyone experiences the world in two different ways: on an exterior screen (the way we perceive the external world) and on an interior screen (which we usually suppress except in dreams). Believing that the blind, deaf, and handicapped depend more fully on the interior screen, Wilson sought their help in understanding and activating this screen in others. This helps to explain why Wilson's early pieces, such as *Deafman Glance* (1970), *The Life and Times of Joseph Stalin*

(1973), and *A Letter to Queen Victoria* (1974), depend little on speech and show a marked affinity with surrealism in their juxtaposed, apparently unrelated visual images and in their use of movement that creates a hypnotic state through its slow pace (crossing the stage might take an hour). Most of the pieces were long—from four to twelve hours—and one (*KA MOUNTAIN,* 1972) continued through seven days and nights. In subsequent works, among them *Einstein on the Beach* (1976) and *Death, Destruction and Detroit* (1979), Wilson allowed speech a larger role, although visual imagery continued to be primary.

In all of his works, Wilson usually began with some striking image or insight, which he then allowed to expand through a chain of associations. Eventually he ordered the images by creating a story-board (rather than a traditional dramatic script) which he meticulously elaborated on stage as precise visual images in which light, composition, and movement were the principal elements. Visual metaphors, gradually metamorphosing into others, were created somewhat in the manner of the surrealists. (Louis Aragon hailed Wilson's as the art he and other surrealists had sought in vain in the 1920s.) In his use of light, Wilson was seen by many critics as Appia's heir, while in his creation of an autonomous theatre—"scenic writing" rather than staged script—he was viewed by others as the successor to Craig and Artaud.

Wilson's most ambitious work, *CIVIL warS,* was intended for the Olympic Arts Festival in Los Angeles in 1984. Segments were created and performed in different countries—West Germany, the Netherlands, France, Italy, Japan, and the United States—but it was never performed as a whole because of lack of funds. As in Wilson's other pieces, here there was an overarching theme—conflict among human beings, ranging from armed combat to domestic disturbance (and an ultimate vision) breaking down barriers between people and cultures. These were pursued not through linear storytelling but through multiple evocations of archetypal images and cultural icons. Thus, Wilson mingled disparate historical and fictional characters, including King Lear, Abraham Lincoln, Karl Marx, Voltaire, Frederick the Great, and an American Indian tribe; the spoken portions (though brief) utilized twelve languages. About this and his other works, Wilson has stated: "[T]here's nothing to understand. It's something one experiences. I try to give a certain space or dimension that allows you to see, where one doesn't think so much, but can more freely associate, dream, and see one's own pictures in one's own mind." Thus, spectators must become partially their own dramatists, creating their own piece out of an associative processing of sensory stimuli.

While continuing to devise his own works—among them *Death, Destruction and Detroit II* (1987) and *The Forest* (1988)—Wilson began about 1986 to stage works by others. They included Euripides' *Alcestis* for the American Repertory Theatre in 1986, Müller's *Hamletmachine* in 1986, and Strauss' *Salome* at LaScala in 1987. In staging these pieces, Wilson did not seek a Wagnerian unity of production. Rather, he wished to "reinforce the text, but with another event that may have nothing to do with it." The visual and aural were almost independent of each other, and, as in Wilson's autonomous pieces, audiences were permitted to make their own syntheses. His *Alcestis* began with Heiner Müller's *Description of a Picture* as a prologue and then went on to a rewritten and reassembled version of the Fitts-Fitzgerald translation of Euripides' play, stripped of psychological motivation and most of the choral passages. Wilson also wove into Euripides' play excerpts from Müller's prologue and from Rilke's poem on Alcestis. As an interlude that divided Euripides' work into two parts, a Japanese Kyogen play which parodies many of

FIG. 15.1
A scene from Robert Wilson's *CIVIL warS*. (Photo by Richard Feldman.)

Alcestis' themes was performed to music by Laurie Anderson. Despite the seeming disparities among these elements, all were linked by thematic concerns related to death and rebirth.

Because his productions, with their complex and precise visual spectacle, were so expensive to mount, Wilson worked most often in the subsidized theatres of Europe, where he was considered by many to be the most significant theatre artist of his generation. His works were seen far less often in America, usually in productions imported for festivals. Probably no other theatre artist embodied so fully the postmodern vision.

Mabou Mines is a theatre collective of nine persons. The best-known member was Lee Breuer (1937–   ), who worked with the San Francisco Actors Workshop and spent some time in Europe before joining with others to create the Mabou Mines (named for a mining town in Canada near which the group first worked together in 1969). Other members included Ruth Maleczech, JoAnne Akalaitis, David Warrilow, Fred Neumann, Bill Raymond, and Philip Glass. Until 1976, Mabou Mines sought to work through collaborative equality in creation, but eventually, deciding that too much energy was being spent on discussion and compromise, it moved to an arrangement under which members took turns directing and which allowed them to work both within and outside the group. By the late 1980s, the group had presented some thirty works in the United States, and had toured in Europe, Asia, and Australia. Some of its best productions were of Beckett's plays (or adaptations of his nondramatic works), but most of its productions were created by company members, often using existing works by other authors as a starting point—as in Akalaitis' *Dressed Like an Egg* (1977), based on the writings of Collette.

Breuer's early pieces—among them *Red Horse Animation* (1970), *B-Beaver Animation* (1974), and *Shaggy Dog Animation* (1978)—were explorations of personal concerns and anxieties, using the horse as symbolic of the search for self-awareness and identity, the beaver of self-protectiveness, and the dog of loyalty and devotion. These pieces replaced dialogue and plot with emotional narratives about the passage of life and physical setting with personal space. They also drew on popular-culture conventions of comic books and film. They embodied ideas then prevalent in avant-garde circles that works reflecting personal experience are more authentic than those purely fictional (ideas that reflected the structuralist assumption that face-to-face discourse is more authentic than writing). *Prelude to Death in Venice* (1979), a further elaboration on one section of *Shaggy Dog Animation,* was written, according to Breuer, to help him understand why he was clinging to youth; it used a puppet as alter ego to the only onstage character; other characters were represented by a recorded voice that metamorphosed from girlfriend to mother to father to agent; quotations from Thomas Mann's *Death in Venice* and images from Dracula films were also interjected. All of these seemingly disjointed elements were ultimately linked through their Oedipal associations.

During the 1980s, Breuer turned to more universal and cross-cultural concerns. His most popular work, *The Gospel at Colonus* (1983), blended the tragic vision of Sophocles' *Oedipus at Colonus* with a present-day black gospel concert and sermon on mystical religious experience. *The Warrior Ant,* from which three of the projected twelve episodes were presented in 1988, concerns the birth, life, and death of an archetypal ant as it seeks the meaning of its existence. In the opening section, set to Latino carnival music and using some one hundred singing and dancing "ants," a 28-foot-tall puppet version of the queen ant gives birth. The later sections make use of Japanese Bunraku and Chinese glove puppets, belly dancers, computers, and a philosophical tone which contrasts sharply with the opening section. As in his "animations," Breuer, in this still-incomplete work, explores through nonhuman characters questions about how human existence achieves meaning.

In the late 1980s Breuer began work on *Lear,* a transposition of Shakespeare's play to Georgia in the 1950s, in which the gender of characters is reversed, races are intermingled, and wars are fought by gangs. Breuer has said that his version is concerned with the relationship between power and behavior and with whether women can have power and love at the same time. Breuer has also directed for other companies.

Another member of Mabou Mines, JoAnne Akalaitis (1937–   ), became well-known for experimental pieces performed in the United States, Italy, France, and Germany, and as a director. Her production of Beckett's *Endgame* for the American Repertory Theatre in 1984 became especially controversial because Beckett denounced it for altering his prescribed setting. In 1989, she staged a highly praised production of Genet's *The Screens* for the Guthrie Theatre in Minneapolis.

Richard Foreman (1937–   ) began by

trying to write conventionally structured plays but subsequently, under the influence of Gertrude Stein and the underground film movement of the 1960s, he radically altered his approach. In 1968 he founded his own group, the Ontological-Hysteric Theatre, where he directed and designed his own pieces. These included *Dr. Selavy's Magic Theatre* (1972), *Pandering to the Masses* (1974), *Rhoda in Potatoland* (1974), *Miss Universal Happiness* (1985), *Film Is Evil: Radio Is Good* (1987), and several others.

Foreman has described in some detail his writing process. He begins with random jottings which accrue over months; when he is ready to create a text, he thumbs through his jottings until he settles on a key passage; next, he looks for other passages that have some associational relationship with the key passage; he then assembles them into a text. Instead of telling linearly arranged stories or developing complex characters, Foreman's plays are essentially his meditations on art and existence. During performances, Foreman often sat in the front row of the auditorium, where he was both audience member and operator of a sound system from which his own tape-recorded or amplified voice called attention to the play's ideas and to the characters' actions and thoughts; many of the characters' speeches were also recorded. All functioned as aspects of the dialectical process of thought, usually atomized in order to focus attention on specific moments.

The processes of thought were also illustrated through precise visual images. Foreman's actors, in creating a series of tableaus, had to execute his directions accurately and without deviation. Foreman also used cords, painted with alternating black and white dashes and stretched diagonally or horizontally, to divide the picture into segments as points of reference for his analytical commentaries. The actress Kate Manheim, often nude, appeared in most of Foreman's pieces as an embodiment of the interplay between the sensual and the intellectual, one of Foreman's preoccupations. Foreman's ultimate purpose was to make his

FIG. 15.2
Richard Foreman's Ontological-Hysteric Theatre in *Rhoda in Potatoland*. (Photo by Arnold Aronson.)

audience aware of how it actually sees (as well as making it aware of how it has been conditioned to see).

In the late 1980s, Foreman changed his approach somewhat in a series of new pieces—among them *Symphony of Rats* (1988) and *What Did He See?* (1988)—which, although they continued his concern for the processes of thought, abandoned many of his earlier staging devices, such as the recorded voices, stretched cords, and continual reminders of the author's presence.

Beginning in the late 1970s, Foreman also directed plays for others, among them Brecht's *The Threepenny Opera* for the New York Shakespeare Festival, Molière's *Don Juan* for the Guthrie Theatre, and an operatic version of Poe's *The Fall of the House of Usher* for the American Repertory Theatre. All, but especially *Don Juan,* were controversial.

As his overall body of work indicates, no one used theatre as extensively as Foreman to deconstruct the processes of thought and to call attention to the fact that art is being made, how art is being made, and how the spectator is responding to these complex processes.

The Wooster Group developed out of Schechner's Performance Group. While working with the Performance Group, Elizabeth LeCompte (1944–   ), Spalding Gray (1941–   ), and others began about 1975 to do their own pieces. Although owing much to Schechner, they were also influenced by Robert Wilson, Mabou Mines, Richard Foreman, and a number of performance artists. In 1980, when the Performance Group dissolved, the Wooster Group was formally established. Its core membership included LeCompte, Gray, Willem Dafoe, Ron Vawter, Kate Valk, Peyton Smith, and Jim Clayburgh. Elizabeth LeCompte was the major artistic force as director and primary shaper of the group's pieces.

Several of the Wooster Group's early productions—*Sakonnet Point* (1975), *Rumstick Road*

(1977), *Nyatt School* (1978), and *Point Judith* (1979)—were based on Spalding Gray's recollections of growing up in Rhode Island. But its most significant work was done with its deconstructive pieces *Route 1 & 9* (1981) and *L.S.D. (. . . Just the High Points . . .)* (1985).

Route 1 & 9 works off of Wilder's *Our Town,* long considered the archetypal play of American family life. The Wooster Group's production began with a videotaped lecture on *Our Town* in which humanistic criticism's clichés about universal values freed from time, place, and political realities were reiterated. The production then deconstructed *Our Town* by showing what it has suppressed and that, rather than being universal, it expresses the ideology of a particular group. The crucial elements were a Pigmeat Markham black-face vaudeville routine and a film of sexually explicit behavior during a van ride on highways 1 and 9 (which run through the industrial wasteland of New Jersey and from which the piece takes its title). This process thereby introduced elements excluded from Wilder's idyllic, small-town, preindustrial, racially pure, sexually repressed America. Thus, by "violating" Wilder's text, the Wooster Group made the spectator look at it anew by breaking through the encrusted layers of unthinking response that accumulate around many classic texts. This production, widely misunderstood, aroused intense controversy. The black-face routine was especially singled out as racially offensive and was used by some agencies as a reason for withdrawing or reducing financial support for the company.

In *L.S.D.,* the company originally made somewhat similar use of Miller's *The Crucible,* but eventually eliminated those segments when Miller threatened legal action. In an early version, both John Proctor (in Miller's play) and Timothy Leary and his drug experiments were treated as adversaries of established authority. Miller's work was seen as reflecting the "red baiting" of the 1950s and Leary's problems as emblematic of opposition to the counterculture of the 1960s. The piece opened with a playback of memories by a baby sitter in the Leary household and with readings by company members from books about that period. It then went on to scenes from Miller's play. A later section of *L.S.D.* included filmed portions of an actual debate between Leary and Gordon Liddy, at the end of which a blind Vietnam veteran charged that Leary was responsible for the tolerance of drugs that had victimized him and others. The ultimate purpose of the piece was in part to demonstrate that both fiction and history are fabrications created from sources that ideology has determined sufficiently important to preserve and use.

The issue raised by the Wooster Group's experience with Miller epitomized Barthes' argument about the relationship of authors to their works and the distinction between work and text. Miller sought (and copyright law supported his right) to control how his text could be used. Thus, it brought into focus a major issue of the 1980s: the director's right to interpret a script however he/she sees fit versus the author's right to restrict interpretational latitude. Although the Wooster Group lost this battle, no other company demonstrated so thoroughly the goals and means of theatrical deconstruction.

All of these groups showed some affinities with performance art, which gained new strength after the demise of happenings. During the 1970s, performance pieces usually were brief, minimally rehearsed, and given one time only. They tended to be based on personal experience or conviction and excluded spectators from any active part in the performance. Because they thought performance pieces should avoid impersonation and emphasize the personal and near-improvisatory, most champions of performance art were bitter opponents

of theatre. But in the 1980s, performance art and theatre moved closer together and frequently overlapped to create *interarts* or *new theatre*. Increased acceptance of this new theatre was encouraged by the National Performance Network, a nationwide organization of performing spaces, theatres, and museums (with financial support from the National Endowment for the Arts and the Ford Foundation), and from inclusion in such festivals as Pepsico Summerfare and the Brooklyn Academy of Music's Next Wave, both of which presented groups from throughout the world that seemed on the innovative cutting edge of the performing arts.

Among the most successful creators of new theatre was Martha Clarke (1944–   ), a member of Pilobolus Dance Theatre for seven years before establishing her own company. She made her first major impact with *The Garden of Earthly Delights* (1984), and then went on to *Vienna:Lusthaus* (1986) and *Miracolo d'Amore* (1988). Of these, *Vienna:Lusthaus,* with text by Charles Mee and music by Richard Peaslee, was both characteristic and the most successful. A melding of dance, text, music, and spectacle in simultaneous or overlapping scenes, it evoked through dream imagery the multi-layered, unconscious world of Freud's Vienna (in which sex and death seemed ever-present). Other significant practitioners of this new theatre were Meredith Monk, Eric Bogosian, Laurie Anderson, and Ping Chong.

Another aspect of new theatre was its renewed interest in popular culture and its integration with "high" culture. A number of performers, including Bill Irwin, the Flying Karamazov Brothers, Bob Berky and Michael Moschen, and Avner the Eccentric, came to be called *new vaudevillians* because they included (in varying degrees) clowning, juggling, acrobatics, dance, and magic in their performances. Several also appeared in productions of plays from the standard repertory. In 1987, the

Flying Karamazov Brothers and Avner (the Eccentric) Eisenberg had leading roles in Shakespeare's *Comedy of Errors,* directed by Robert Woodruff at Lincoln Center's Vivian Beaumont Theatre. The best-known of such performers was Bill Irwin (1950–   ), who, in addition to acting with several repertory companies, perhaps most notably in Lincoln Center's production of *Waiting for Godot* in 1988, also created his own highly praised theatrical pieces, *The Regard of Flight* (1982) and *Largely New York* (1989), in the last of which he played "the Post-modern Hoofer" seeking to cope with a high-tech world.

Postmodernism and poststructuralism were also reflected in directing practice as the primacy of text and the goal of achieving "text-true" productions weakened. Many directors already accepted the notion that classic texts need to be revitalized by transposing the action to another time or place more familiar to the audience, an approach relatively common after World War II, especially with Shakespeare. Others took from film the concept of director as *auteur,* assuming the right to use the text as a "found" object to be rearranged or used however they chose. Some undertook deconstructions of texts in an attempt to expose the submerged (or overriding) themes or ideologies. Among the best-known of such deconstructive directors are Andrei Serban (1943–   ), Liviu Ciulei (1923–   ), and Peter Sellars (1957–   ), as well as Robert Wilson, Richard Foreman, Lee Breuer, and JoAnne Akalaitis.

Most deconstructive productions have been of works by authors long dead, but during the 1980s the long-simmering issue of authorial versus directorial rights was brought to a crisis by two events: the Wooster Group's negotiations with Arthur Miller, and JoAnne Akalaitis' production of Beckett's *Endgame* at the American Repertory Theatre (rights for which Beckett threatened to cancel, even though no lines had been altered, because the director, contrary to his text, had set the action in a subway station). The issue—which generated more argument than agreement—was framed at one end by Miller's statement that he did not want his play produced "except in total agreement with the way I wrote it," and at the other end by Barthes' argument that once a work is published the author has no more right than anyone else in how it can be interpreted.

OTHER AMERICAN DEVELOPMENTS

During the 1980s, Broadway was primarily an importer of productions that had been successful elsewhere—London, off-Broadway, or in regional theatres. As costs continued to escalate, it became increasingly difficult to recover investments, and the number of new productions declined. In 1956 it had cost $400,000 to produce *My Fair Lady* and the top ticket price was $6; in 1988 it cost $8,000,000 to produce *Phantom of the Opera* and the top ticket price had risen to $50. In 1987–1988 only thirty-one new productions, a twentieth-century low, opened on Broadway.

Off-Broadway underwent many of the same stresses. The approximately fifty-four off-Broadway theatres reported that between 1985 and 1989 the rent on their performance spaces had risen 75 percent, and that the cost of producing a musical off-Broadway was approximately twice as much as it had been for such works on Broadway thirty years earlier.

Financial stresses also affected not-for-profit theatres. During the 1980s, although the federal government's support of the arts (approximately $170 million annually) remained relatively constant in dollar amount, inflation effectively reduced the support by some 24 percent. Of these appropriated funds, only about 18 percent went to theatre and opera combined. (By comparison, West Germany's subsidy of theatre alone was about $1 billion annually.) In addition, changes in tax laws reduced the incentives for private and corporate giving to the arts. By the late 1980s slightly more than half of not-for-profit theatres were running deficits. The response of many theatres was more small-cast, small-budget pieces or more crowd-pleasing fare. These retrenchments came to be called "artistic deficits"—reducing artistic standards to avoid financial deficits.

Nevertheless, most of the significant work in the American theatre during the 1980s took place in not-for-profit organizations. In New York, the Lincoln Center company seemed at last to find stability. After Joseph Papp gave up its management in 1977, the theatre remained dark most of the subsequent eight seasons, the years under Richmond Crinkley's management, 1980–1984, being spent primarily in controversy over whether the stage should be remodeled. In 1985 Gregory Mosher (1952–   ), previously head of Chicago's Goodman Theatre, was named director, with Bernard Gersten as executive director. Within a short time, the company had gained critical acceptance, and by 1988 had 36,000 subscribers. Because several of its productions became hits—among them John Guare's *The House of Blue Leaves,* Wilder's *Our Town,* Mamet's *Speed-the-Plow,* and the musicals *Sarafina* and *Anything Goes*—it was by 1989 performing both at Lincoln Center and in Broadway houses. Perhaps its most controversial production (because not all subscribers could see it) was *Waiting for Godot* with Robin Williams, Steve Martin, Bill Irwin, and F. Murray Abraham.

Many other older organizations continued to play a significant role in New York's theatre. The New York Shakespeare Festival remained one of the most prolific groups, producing both its own plays—at the Public Theatre, in Central Park, and on Broadway—

and providing performance space for many others. In 1987, it announced a "marathon" under which, over a period of six years, it would mount all of Shakespeare's plays with well-known actors (many of them film stars) in leading roles. LaMama and the Circle Repertory Theatre Company also continued to be significant producers of new plays, as did the Manhattan Theatre Club under the direction of Lynne Meadow, Playwrights Horizons under the direction of André Bishop, and Second Stage Theatre under Carole Rothman. In addition to these (and many other) off-Broadway theatres, there were approximately 150 off-off-Broadway groups.

Outside of New York, there were more than 200 not-for-profit theatres, which together mounted about 2,500 productions a year. They varied considerably in size, facilities, total program, and quality, but they offered live performances in almost all parts of the United States. Several played a major role in American theatrical life.

The American Repertory Theatre in Cambridge, Massachusetts, founded in 1979 by Robert Brustein (1927–   ), was probably the most adventurous of the resident companies, with its wide-ranging repertory of old and new plays in innovative and imaginative productions directed by Andrei Serban, Liviu Ciulei, Lee Breuer, JoAnne Akalaitis, Robert Wilson, and others. It achieved international stature through its participation in numerous festivals at home and abroad. The Yale Repertory Theatre, which Brustein founded and headed from 1966 to 1978 and which continued thereafter under Lloyd Richards, owed much of its distinction to its close affiliation with the Yale Drama School, the most influential of America's theatre training programs. In addition to producing an eclectic repertory, the company promoted new playwrights through a Winterfest of new works. Richards also served as artistic director of the Eugene

O'Neill Theatre Center, which each summer after 1964 hosted the National Playwrights Conference, where writers were assisted in developing their plays. The Guthrie Theatre in Minneapolis, a leading theatre since its formation in 1963, was especially innovative from 1981 to 1985 under the direction of Liviu Ciulei, a Romanian director noted for his provocative, deconstructive treatments of standard works, and again in the late 1980s under Garland Wright. Other outstanding regional companies during the 1980s included the Arena Stage in Washington, D.C., under the direction of Zelda Finchandler; the Mark Taper Forum in Los Angeles under the direction of Gordon Davidson; the La Jolla Playhouse under Des McAnuff; the Seattle Repertory Theatre under Dan Sullivan; the Trinity Square Repertory Company (in Providence, Rhode Island) under Adrian Hall and later Anne Bogart; the Hartford Stage under Mark Lamos; and the Actors Theatre of Louisville under Jon Jory.

During the 1980s, several American playwrights from earlier decades—Sam Shepard, David Rabe, Lanford Wilson, Neil Simon, and many others—continued to write. Newer dramatists were numerous, although few gained wide recognition. Among those who achieved critical success during the 1980s, perhaps the best-known was David Mamet (1947–   ). He first gained recognition in 1974 with *Sexual Perversity in Chicago,* an episodic play about a love affair that falls apart under pressures that stem primarily from stereotyped cultural and sexual attitudes or expectations. His reputation grew when in 1977 *A Life in the Theatre* (about the vicissitudes of two actors in regional theatre) and *American Buffalo* (about a junkstore owner and his two pals who plan—and fail—to steal a coin collection) opened in New York. Mamet wrote a number of other dramas and screenplays before winning the Pulitzer Prize in 1984 for *Glengarry Glen Ross,* about men who sell out-of-state real estate of questionable value to unwary customers and use or betray each other. Still other film work preceded and followed *Speed-the-Plow* (1988), about business deals and betrayals in Hollywood. Mamet's plays have been characterized as displaying a "comic impulse, a heightened social conscience, and a sense of moral decay," to which might be added a sensitivity to language. Mamet's characters have been infected by cultural values that make them strive for material or sexual success even as these values are shown to be inauthentic and insubstantial. Reiterative speech (often obscene) reveals characters trapped by stereotyped attitudes, which they seek to articulate and sometimes succeed in recognizing and breaking through. More often they become victims of their own attempts to live up to the expectations of others like themselves.

African-American dramatists continued to make significant contributions. Of these, perhaps the best was August Wilson (1945–   ) who worked closely with the director Lloyd Richards. His first success came with *Ma Rainey's Black Bottom* (1984), about the humiliations, small victories, and defeats of African-American musicians who must work for exploitative whites in Chicago in the 1920s. *Fences* (1985), set in Pittsburgh in the 1950s just before the civil rights movement gained force, reveals the psychological and economic wounds inflicted on an African-American family by social and employment barriers. It contained a powerful portrait of Troy Maxson, a role played by James Earl Jones, a talented and energetic man whose potential has been subverted by crime, low-paying jobs, and philandering. It was awarded the Pulitzer Prize. *Joe Turner's Come and Gone* (1986) takes place in Pittsburgh in 1911 in a boarding house peopled with characters for whom slavery is still a strong memory and who, having been disconnected from their past, are searching for reconnections that will rebuild shattered lives and dreams. Wilson's plays, unlike those of

FIG. 15.3

August Wilson's *The Piano Lesson* as staged in New York in 1990 by the Yale Repertory Theatre. The actors are Tommy Hollis (left) and Charles S. Dutton (right). (Photo by Gerry Goodstein.)

African-American sergeant in an Army camp in Louisiana in 1944 to illuminate how white prejudice induces in African-Americans a loathing of themselves. It won the Pulitzer Prize and was subsequently made into a film. After viewing with indignation D. W. Griffith's 1915 film *Birth of a Nation,* Fuller decided to write a cycle of plays that would chronicle African-American experience since the freeing of slaves in the 1860s. The first two, *Sally* (1987) and *Prince* (1988), show how the freed slaves continue to be exploited by their supposed liberators, who pay them lower wages than they do whites and who fail to fulfill their pledges of benefits that will permit African-Americans to function effectively as free persons.

In 1988, the inaugural National Black Arts Festival, entitled "A Celebration of Artistic Achievement," was held in Atlanta to provide a panoramic overview through art of the African-American experience in America. Included in the festival were most of those who had made African-American theatre vital since the 1960s. It was followed in 1989 by what was billed as the first National Black Theatre Festival, held in Winston-Salem with attendance by representatives of nearly two hundred African-American theatre companies from throughout the United States.

Other minority groups also gained increased acceptance in mainstream theatres. Among Asian-American dramatists, the most successful was David Henry Hwang (1957–   ), who intermingled Asian and Western conventions and attitudes. *FOB* (1979), developed in part at the O'Neill Center's National Playwrights Conference and presented in New York by Joseph Papp, concerns a "fresh-off-the-boat" Chinese immigrant caught between assimilated Chinese-Americans and the society from which he has come (symbolized by legendary Chinese figures who invade the action) and combining conventions of the well-made play with those

some earlier African-American writers, do not exploit themes of African-American rage or white oppression as much as concentrating on African-American identity and quests for fulfillment and dignity.

Charles Fuller (1939–   ) had a number of plays produced off-Broadway in the 1970s and began to gain recognition with *The Brownsville Raid* (1976), about the framing of African-American soldiers falsely accused of shooting up a Texas town in 1906. His greatest success was won with *A Soldier's Play* (1982), which uses an investigation into the murder of an of Oriental theatre. Hwang continued this mingling of East and West in *The Dance and the Railroad* (1981), set in America in 1867, with two Chinese seeking to maintain or learn the skills needed for Beijing Opera while working on the transcontinental railroad. Hwang achieved his greatest success with *M. Butterfly* (1988), one of the few recent plays to open on Broadway without having first been produced elsewhere. *M. Butterfly* is based on an actual story—of a French diplomat who declared that he did not know that the Chinese star of Beijing Opera with whom he had lived for twenty years was actually a man. Through a series of flashbacks that intermingle Western and Oriental conventions, Hwang not only tells this story but uses it to suggest much about other types of East-West relationships, especially how the West has always looked upon the East as the submissive female accepting domination from a macho male West. In addition to intertwining Eastern and Western conventions, Hwang has also been involved in such postmodern productions as *1000 Airplanes on the Roof* (1988), a ninety-minute monologue-text by Hwang, music by Philip Glass, and complex visual imagery by designer Jerome Sirlin. Other Asian-American playwrights include Frank Chin, Paul Lim, Philip Kan Gotanda, and James Yoshimura. Asian-American theatre has been nourished most consistently by the Pan Asian Repertory Theatre in New York and the East-West Players in Los Angeles.

During the 1980s, Hispanic-American theatres gained new strength. A survey made in 1985 found 101 theatre groups: 29 Chicano, 24 Cuban, 28 Puerto Rican, and 20 with a variety of other backgrounds. Some performed only in Spanish, some were bilingual, and some performed only in English. Most were based in New York, Florida, Puerto Rico, the Southwest, or California. El Teatro Campesino remained the best-known of the organizations, but in California the Bilingual Foundation of the Arts (founded in Los Angeles in 1973 by Carmen Zapata and Margarita Galban) offered the most stable repertory. In New York, the best-known groups were: INTAR (International Arts Relations), founded in 1972, which did a variety of plays in English, including at least one new play a year developed in its playwrights workshop; Repertorio Español (founded by Gilberto Zaldivar and René Buch in 1968), which emphasized Spanish classics, although it did other types of plays, all in Spanish; and the Puerto Rican Traveling Theatre (founded by Miriam Colon in 1967), which performed contemporary Latin American, Spanish, and Hispanic-American plays in both English and Spanish. Festival Latino, begun in 1972 and after 1985 an annual event under the sponsorship of the New York Shakespeare Festival, was the largest presenter of Latin American and U.S. Hispanic theatre. Despite the totality of these activities in the United States, few Hispanic-American playwrights gained wide recognition.

One of the most noteworthy developments was the increased number of women playwrights. Many of them had begun writing earlier but seemed to make their major impact during the 1980s. Among the best-known were Marsha Norman, Maria Irene Fornes, Beth Henley, and Wendy Wasserstein. Marsha Norman (1947–   ) wrote primarily about defining oneself and making choices. She first gained recognition with *Getting Out* (1977), about a woman just released from prison; the protagonist is represented as two persons, her before and after prison personae, both on stage at the same time, to show how she remakes her life. Norman became best known for *'night, Mother* (1981), winner of the Pulitzer Prize in 1983, in which a woman, having lost all desire to live, matter-of-factly and without self-pity announces and carries through her plan to commit suicide, while at the same time preparing her mother so she can go on living without any sense of guilt.

Maria Irene Fornes (1930–   ) was born in Cuba and emigrated to the United States in 1945. A prolific dramatist, she wrote her first play, *Tango Palace,* in 1963, and went on to collaborate with Al Carmines on a number of small-scale musicals, among them *Promenade* (1965). During the 1970s she virtually gave up writing for six years while administering the New York Theatre Strategy—an organization of avant-garde writers. She returned to writing with *Fefu and Her Friends* (1977), a play about the reunion of eight women who look back over their lives as women and seek to understand themselves in a patriarchal society. Among her many subsequent plays, a few stand out. *Mud* (1983) has as its protagonist a subproletarian woman striving to enlarge her understanding of the world and who, upon seeking to escape her present situation, is killed by one of the two men with whom her life is entangled. *The Conduct of Life* (1985), set in Latin America, draws telling parallels between the treatment of women and political subjugation. Fornes never achieved wide popular recognition (although she won six Obie awards for her work in off-Broadway theatres). From early on, she insisted on directing her own plays, and devoted much time to workshops formed to develop other writers (perhaps most notably at INTAR and California's Padua Hills Playhouse during the 1980s).

Beth Henley (1952–   ) wrote primarily about colorful characters caught in bizarre situations in small Southern towns. She made her first impact with *Crimes of the Heart* (1979), a play about three sisters who, faced with charges of attempted murder and the death of their grandfather, eventually recognize the ways in which they have shortchanged themselves. It won the Pulitzer Prize in 1981. Henley's subsequent plays—among them *The Miss Firecracker Contest* (1981), *The Wake of Jamie Foster* (1982), and *The Lucky Spot* (1986)—developed themes about attempts to overcome the past by some accomplishment that will validate one's worth.

Wendy Wasserstein (1950–   ) made her

FIG. 15.4
Wendy Wasserstein's *The Heidi Chronicles* at Playwrights Horizons, New York, in 1989. Performers, left to right, are Sarah Jessica Parker, Alma Cuervo, Joan Allen, and Anne Lange. (Photo by Gerry Goodstein.)

first impact with *Uncommon Women and Others* (1977), a collage about the struggles of bright, promising, confused young college women, and went on to *Isn't It Romantic?* (1981) about the difficulty of growing up and freeing oneself from stereotypical expectations. Her reputation depended above all on *The Heidi Chronicles* (1988), winner of the 1989 Pulitzer Prize. Divided into thirteen scenes, the action, which begins in the mid-1960s and ends in the present, traces changes in the political, artistic, and personal sensibility of its protagonist, art historian Heidi Holland, as she develops a feminist consciousness and gains professional acceptance but fails to achieve personal fulfillment. Eventually she comes to feel "stranded" by the failure of possibilities that once seemed so bright. A number of other playwrights—among them Alice Childress, Adrienne Kennedy, Emily Mann, Tina Howe, and Ntozake Shange—also deserve mention.

In addition to female playwrights, the number of feminist theatres grew during the 1980s. Among the most important of them were: Women's Experimental Theatre, WOW Cafe, Spiderwoman Theatre, and Split Britches, all in New York; Double Edge in Cambridge, Massachusetts; the Rhode Island Feminist Theatre; At the Foot of the Mountain in Minneapolis; and Omaha Magic Theatre. During the 1980s, there were more than ten national festivals of women's theatre. The most important and extensive was Boston's Women in Theatre Festival.

ENGLAND

In England during the 1980s, there was a continual struggle to maintain excellence in the face of financial stresses. Although the government did not decrease its contributions to the Arts Council, inflation seriously eroded its value. At the end of the 1980s, the Arts Council was being given approximately $700 million for all the arts (a per capita amount far in excess of the $170 million provided the NEA by the United States) of which about $282 million went to performing arts. Theatre companies (even the Royal Shakespeare Company and the National Theatre) were encouraged to (and did) turn to corporations and banks to underwrite productions. In the late 1980s, in order to facilitate the transfer of successful productions to the West End, the RSC and National theatres also altered the repertory schedule they had used since the 1960s. Ticket prices, long among the lowest anywhere, steadily rose until they approached Broadway levels.

Perhaps the institution that suffered most was the English Stage Company (under the management of Max Stafford-Clark after 1980), in part because its controversial offerings made it less attractive to private sponsors. During the 1980s, it reluctantly reduced its offerings from sixteen each year (eight in the main theatre and eight in the Theatre Upstairs) to eight (four in each), although it tried to make up for this loss by exchanging productions with other theatres, among them New York's Public Theatre. But in 1989, continuing problems forced the closure of the Theatre Upstairs, leaving the ESC with only four productions annually. Since no theatre had been so hospitable to women writers—among them Caryl Churchill—or to plays about such controversial subjects as Northern Ireland, its decline had major implications for the future of playwriting in Britain.

Like Broadway, the West End came to acquire most of its productions from other sources, especially the subsidized houses. A large proportion of its offerings were revivals of classics that had been transferred from the Royal Shakespeare Company, the National Theatre, Britain's regional theatres, or New York. Among its most successful productions was a series of spectacular musicals, many subsequently exported to New York, where they theatened the supremacy of the U.S. in this form. By far the most successful composer of musicals was Andrew Lloyd-Webber (1948–) with *Jesus Christ Superstar* (1971), *Evita* (1976), *Cats* (1981), *Starlight Express* (1984), *Phantom of the Opera* (1986), and *Aspects of Love* (1989). These were joined in popularity by *Les Misérables* (1985) by the Frenchmen Alain Boublil and Claude Michel Schonberg as adapted and directed by Trevor Nunn and John Caird. Nunn's involvement with this musical (which was presented by the Royal Shakespeare Company) and his direction of some of Andrew Lloyd-Webber's musicals not only blurred the boundaries between the commercial and subsidized theatres but aroused considerable controversy over the extent to which Nunn used his position as director of the RSC to do work from which he profited financially, charges that contributed to Nunn's resignation as director of the RSC in 1987.

Despite ongoing complaints of financial difficulties, the RSC continued to expand its activities during the 1980s. In 1982, it at last moved into its long-awaited new London home with its two theatres: the Pit, a flexible space seating approximately 200; and the Barbican, seating 1,166, with a stage 73 feet wide by 48 feet deep and a 30-foot-high opening with, above the stage, 109 feet of flyspace which permitted the storage of scenery at two levels, thereby facilitating the presentation of a rotating repertory. In 1986, the RSC opened another new theatre in Stratford, the Swan, a 400-seat open-stage theatre intended primarily for non-Shakespearean plays written between 1570 and 1750. In 1987, to accommodate transfers from the Swan, it leased the Mermaid Theatre in London. Thus, it was presenting plays on six stages divided between Stratford and London and was employing some 700 persons.

The RSC began the 1980s with two remarkable productions: *The Greeks,* John Barton's adaptation, amalgamation, and production of ten plays that treat the Orestes legends; and Trevor Nunn and John Caird's production of David Edgar's eight-hour adaptation of Charles Dickens' *Nicholas Nickleby.* The latter was especially one of the company's most successful ventures, both in England and abroad. Throughout the 1980s, the RSC, in addition to a steady stream of Shakespearean productions, offered diverse fare ranging from new scripts to revivals of non-Shakespearean plays to adaptations of nondramatic pieces, of which the most popular were *Les Misérables* and *Les Liaisons Dangereuses* (Christopher Hampton's 1985 adaptation of Laclos' 1782 novel).

When Trevor Nunn resigned in 1987, Terry Hands became artistic director of the RSC. At first, he continued Nunn's policies, but in 1989 he reduced the actors' two-year contracts to a sixty-week contract, one half to be spent in Stratford, the other in London, a change made in an attempt to attract top actors who were reluctant to commit themselves for two years. In 1989 the RSC produced a total of twenty-seven productions.

The RSC's great strength continued to be its directors, among them John Barton, Howard Davies, Barry Kyle, Nicholas Hytner, and Bill Alexander, in addition to Hands and Nunn. In the late 1980s, the RSC's first major female director, Deborah Warner (1959–), emerged. In 1988, she won England's Laurence Olivier Award as the year's best director for an uncut version of Shakespeare's *Titus Andronicus,* a production that toured throughout Europe to enormous critical acclaim. Her productions of *King John* and Sophocles' *Electra* were similarly praised. Another of the RSC's major directors, Adrian Noble (1951–), was named to take over the directorship of the company when Hands relinquishes it in 1991.

In some ways, developments at the National

Theatre during the 1980s paralleled those at the RSC. It, too, mounted a number of lengthy, ambitious productions, among them *The Oresteia,* done with full-face masks and an all-male cast; *The Mystery Plays,* a highly successful, three-part amalgamation of medieval cycle plays; and Ben Jonson's seldom-produced *Bartholomew Fair.* Like the RSC, the National also produced some musicals, the best-known example being *Guys and Dolls.* The National continued to range widely through the Western repertory and to present new plays by such writers as Harold Pinter, Tom Stoppard, David Hare, and Alan Ayckbourn.

Throughout the 1980s, the National remained a target for those who resented the amount of its subsidy (by far the largest of any theatre in Britain). It sought to counteract this criticism in part by sending productions on tour for an average of twenty weeks each year. It was also plagued by internal dissatisfactions and, in response to them, Hall in the mid-1980s set up five relatively autonomous production groups, each with its own director and priorities. Like Nunn at the RSC, Hall, after being strongly criticized for the amount of time he spent on noncompany productions, resigned. In 1988, leadership of the company passed to Richard Eyre (1943–), who had worked in both the fringe and regional theatres before coming to the National in 1981. Although he continued some of Hall's policies, he reinvigorated the company by appointing several young associate directors noted for their innovative staging (among them Howard Davies, Nicholas Hytner, and Deborah Warner) and by abandoning Hall's division of the company into separate production groups. He retained several of Hall's associate directors (among them David Hare, Bill Bryden, Peter Gill, and Ian McKellan) and increased the number and length of the company's tours. He also enlarged the theatre's programs by inviting regional and foreign companies to perform at the National.

In 1988, to honor its twenty-fifth anniversary, the company was renamed the Royal National Theatre. By that time it had presented more than three hundred productions and was acknowledged to be one of the world's major theatrical companies.

Upon leaving the National, Peter Hall founded his own company designed to bridge the gap between the British and American theatres. The intention was to present plays in London and then move them to New York— or to reverse this process. The first production, Tennessee Williams' *Orpheus Descending* with Vanessa Redgrave, opened in late 1988 to critical acclaim, as did its second production, *The Merchant of Venice,* starring Dustin Hoffman, in 1989. Both then played limited engagements in New York beginning in late 1989.

Among English directors, Peter Brook remained the best-known. With his Paris-based International Center for Theatre Research, he continued his explorations of cross-cultural conventions, working with actors from all over the world in productions drawn from disparate sources. One of his best-known productions in the 1980s was *The Tragedy of Carmen* (1982), based partially on Merimée's novel and partially on Bizet's opera. The story was reduced to its essential elements, the characters to six, and the setting to a sand-covered circle (supplemented by a few props) which suggested a bull ring. The goal was to eliminate everything that in the opera tends to distract from the sense of tragic inevitability. During the 1980s Brook also staged Chekhov's *The Cherry Orchard* twice, in 1981 and in 1988. The second of these, at the Brooklyn Academy of Music's Majestic Theatre, used a virtually bare stage. The floor of the acting area was covered with Persian carpets on which there was little more than a large cabinet and a screen. The cast was primarily English and American, but also included a Swedish and a

Czech actor. This production was subsequently taken to the Soviet Union.

The production with which Brook made his greatest impact in the 1980s was *The Mahabharata,* first performed in a quarry as part of the Avignon Festival in 1985 and subsequently in Paris, New York, and elsewhere. Based on the Sanskrit epic poem (the longest in the world, being fifteen times the length of the Bible), the adaptation by Jean-Claude Carrière evolved over a period of several years. Requiring more than nine hours to perform, its tangle of intertwined myths was essentially concerned with the loss of innocence and the catastrophes that stem from pride and love of power. The extremely large cast (which included Ryszard Cieślak, Grotowski's principal actor) represented sixteen countries, among them Italy, France, Japan, India, Jamaica, Senegal, Germany, and Britain. When moved indoors, it was performed on a sand-covered stage, with a stream of water across the back and a small pool near the front. The production emphasized images of earth, air, fire, and water and the repeated violation and reassertion of nature (both human and nonhuman). The music, costumes, and colors suggested but did not attempt to recreate those of India. Brook stated, "Our costumes look Indian, but . . . are variations on Indian colors and designs . . . the music is . . . our way of interpreting [Indian music]. What we are doing is refracting the Indian work through the many nationalities of our company." It was one of the prime examples of cross-cultural influences in the 1980s.

In Britain, festivals also continued to be important. The Edinburgh Festival (forty-four years old in 1990) offered by far the greatest number of productions (422 in 1989) representing many countries. To give some focus and variety, it adopted a different theme each year (in 1989, it was Spain and the Spanish repertory). The London International Theatre Festival (LIFT), biennial since its founding in 1981, won growing respect during the 1980s. In the beginning, LIFT emphasized visual theatre and performance art as a counterbalance to the British theatre's long-standing emphasis on text. But by the late 1980s the festival had relaxed its guidelines in order to include more text-based productions by innovative companies from Russia, Hungary, Poland, and elsewhere.

British playwriting continued to be vital, although many critics claimed to detect a decline in quality. Many writers whose careers had begun much earlier—among them Harold Pinter, Edward Bond, Peter Shaffer, and Tom Stoppard—continued to write. Others achieved prominence during the 1980s. Alan Ayckbourn (1939–   ) began writing plays in 1959 for a theatre in Scarborough and thereafter was one of England's most prolific dramatists. His first London production came in 1970. Although long considered merely a successful writer of farcical comedy, his early plays—among them *How the Other Half Loves* (1970), *Absurd Person Singular* (1973), and *The Norman Conquests* (1974)—while making use of the traditional techniques of farce, were already suggesting the direction his work would take in the future: the examination of characters who fall into questionable behavior out of a desperate need to escape a shallow, unsatisfying existence. As time went by, Ayckbourn increasingly blurred the distinctions among comic forms, and by the 1980s he had come to be recognized as a serious writer who used comedy to make penetrating comments on contemporary life. In 1977 the National Theatre began to include his plays in its repertory, and in 1986 it appointed him head of one of its production groups. His later plays include: *A Chorus of Disapproval* (1985), which uses an amateur production of Gay's *The Beggar's Opera* to illuminate contemporary behavior through parallels with Gay's world; *A Small Family*

Business (1987), which shows a network of petty graft within a small business gradually growing into arrangements with an international crime ring, implying that these are the consequences of England's governmental policies; and *Henceforward* (1988), in which an electronic composer becomes so alienated from his chaotic society that he seeks to replace even the women in his life with programmable robots.

Many of the principal dramatists of the 1980s had their roots in the fringe theatre and in anti-establishment, New Left attitudes. Of these, perhaps the most successful was David Hare (1947–   ), who began his career with the Portable Theatre and whose early plays introduced the themes that dominated his work thereafter: how the desire to gain and maintain power and wealth undermine and destroy personal integrity, shared values, and concern for the common good. In a characteristic early play, *Knuckle* (1974), a young man who has turned detective in order to investigate a murder and expose the corruption of his father's world of brokers and bankers ultimately capitulates to that world's values because he concludes that capitalism itself is the murderer and that, though he could bring about his father's downfall, nothing would change—his father would merely be replaced by someone more skillful at hiding the corruption. Among Hare's later plays, two of the best-known were *Plenty* (1978) and *Secret Rapture* (1988). The first of these, through a flexible treatment of time and place, moves through the two decades that follow World War II, during which the British empire disintegrates. As the stakes become less, the scramble for "plenty" in a world where "everything is up for grabs" intensifies, displacing the heroine's vision of collective endeavor for the common good. In protecting her inner sense of moral integrity as her disillusionment grows, she disrupts the lives of all those around her, and she eventually drifts into drug-induced oblivion. In *Secret Rapture,* a junior minister in the Thatcher government declares that it is irresponsible not to make money, and in an attempt to help her artist sister (who runs a small design firm with her lover), has her husband persuade the lover to let him take over the firm, an action which leads to both a moral and domestic crisis and the death of the artist, who is killed by the lover when she leaves him. Most of all the play concerns the inability of humanistic, moral values to survive in a world in which greed has become the most potent force. Other plays by Hare include *Fanshen* (1975), *Teeth 'n' Smiles* (1975), and *A Map of the World* (1983). Like Ayckbourn, Hare's plays began to be produced by the National Theatre during the 1970s, and, again like Ayckbourn, during the 1980s he became head of one of the National Theatre's producing groups and one of the company's major directors.

Hare also collaborated on a number of plays with Howard Brenton (1942–   ), who began his career in fringe theatres. Their two major collaborative works were *Brassneck* (1973) and *Pravda* (1985). The first of these traces the fluctuations and manipulation of power by a family through three generations. Originally, it is Alfred Bagley who perceives that worming oneself into the power structure depends on acceptance into the society's rituals, here embodied by the Masonic lodge; when Bagley eventually sits on the lodge's throne, the scene mirrors the investiture of a Renaissance pope. Subsequent acts trace the fall of the family and then its rise again through drug trafficking. *Pravda* shows a newspaper tycoon gaining almost unchallengeable control over the sources of public information through his manipulation of language and morality and his appeals to the weaknesses of others. He is successful because, unlike those who oppose him, he knows exactly what he wants and has no scruples about how to obtain it.

Brenton also wrote a number of plays alone, most of them deconstructions of popular heroes or of conventional behavior and beliefs. *The Churchill Play* (1974) opens with a scene that seems to show Churchill's body lying in state but is revealed to be part of a play being staged in a concentration camp some time in the future. Churchill's wartime rallying speeches are eventually depicted as no more than political propaganda used to dupe the working classes, who are always used and betrayed by those in power. Probably Brenton's most controversial play was *The Romans in Britain* (1980), which related the contemporary British military presence in Northern Ireland to the Roman occupation of England, and deconstructed numerous myths about England and its relations with Ireland. The play was especially controversial, not only for its use of humor in violent scenes (including murder and homosexual rape) but also because it was performed at the National Theatre at a time when Britain was trying to resolve the crisis in Northern Ireland.

The 1980s brought a number of female British playwrights to prominence, among them Pam Gems, Louise Page, and Sarah Daniels. But by far the best-known was Caryl Churchill (1938–   ), whose political and moral stances were related to those of Hare and Brenton but with a strongly feminist perspective. She declared that her plays were primarily about "power, powerlessness, and exploitation." She began by writing radio plays but turned to full-length works for the stage in the early 1970s. Several of her plays evolved cooperatively with the Joint Stock Theatre Company or Monstrous Regiment (a feminist company). One of these, *Vinegar Tom* (1976), shows how the seventeenth century used charges of witchcraft to rid society of women who did not or would not conform to the expectations of that male-dominated society. Churchill's best-known play, *Cloud 9*

(1979), explores the relationship between sexual and social roles. The first act is set in colonial Africa, the second in present-day London (though supposedly only twenty-five years have passed for those characters who appear in both acts). Cross-gender casting is used to indicate the relationship between social stereotyping and sexual roles. In the first act, Victorian mores that demand social conformity make the characters feel guilty about any expression of sexual feelings. In the second act, contemporary mores encourage the open discussion of sexual behavior, but the characters now feel guilty about their inability to achieve social cohesion. Like *Cloud 9*, *Top Girls* (1982) also uses an historical dimension. An opening fantasy scene brings together women from several eras (including a present-day managing director, Marlene) who defied the stereotypes of their time to achieve positions of prominence. Thereafter, the scenes involve women associated with Marlene's life or her business firm. Marlene, who considers herself superior because she has succeeded in stereotypically male terms, even though it has been at great personal cost, is contrasted with her sister Joyce, who has stayed in her working-class environment at great economic cost and therefore sees the need for a radical change, one that makes her Marlene's class enemy. *Fen* (1983) looks at the exploitation of frustrated and despairing female farm workers caught in a life of drudgery. In contrast, *Serious Money* (1987) shows the dominant roles played by greed, self-interest, and corruption in the lives of stock brokers. Written primarily in rhymed couplets which, in performance, were often spoken as rapid-fire overlapping speeches, it creates a frenzied, obsessional focus on money-making no matter the cost. As one character sums up, "Sexy greed *is* the late 80's." Deconstructing capitalist greed or male ideology is the principal focus of Churchill's plays, but she is seldom didactic, preferring instead to entertain her audiences and trust them to reach their own conclusions.

FRANCE

In France during the 1980s the theatre was dominated by directors more than by playwrights. Most made their major impact with reinterpretations of classics rather than with productions of new works. Several of the most influential directors—among them Planchon, Chereau, Mnouchkine, and Savary—had begun their careers much earlier. While Planchon and Chereau for the most part continued along paths already established in their work, Mnouchkine and Savary explored new paths during the 1980s.

In the early 1980s, Ariane Mnouchkine and the Théâtre du Soleil took a new direction when, instead of creating its own pieces through a collaborative process, the group turned to Shakespeare—*Richard II* (1981), *Twelfth Night* (1982), and *Henry IV, Pt. I* (1984). Seeing these plays as images of social structures steeped in ritual, Mnouchkine sought to distance and mythologize the action by adapting and transforming Eastern theatrical conventions—primarily Japanese (Kabuki and Noh) for the two history plays, Indian (Sanskrit and Kathakali) for *Twelfth Night*—and intermingling them with Western conventions. Characters were defined more by movement, gesture, costume, and mask than by realistic psychological detail. The stories, which seemed mythical, timeless, and patterned, were performed with great vitality and rhythmic precision. The plays became ritualizations: the history of power, the comedy of love's ambiguities. These productions achieved international recognition, in part through their presentation at the Olympic Arts Festival in Los Angeles in 1984. In 1985, the company presented *The Terrible but Unfinished History of Norodom Sihanouk, King of Cambodia,* a text by the feminist writer Hélène Cixous based on improvisations by the company. It traced the history of Cambodia from the accession of Sihanouk in 1955 to the overthrow of Pol Pot and the Khmer Rouge in 1979. In two parts, each four hours long, it was performed in a large, open space surrounded by six hundred Cambodian ancestor figures. A contemporary version of the Shakespearean chronicle play, it juxtaposed various styles and mingled elements borrowed from several cultures. Ultimately the emphasis was upon the political machinations of world leaders rather than on the Cambodian populace. This production was followed by a somewhat similar work also written by Cixous, *The Indiade, or The India of Their Dreams* (1987), about the efforts of Indian leaders to create a nation by overcoming the legacy of British colonialism.

Although Mnouchkine sought to maintain the communal principle on which the company had been founded, by the 1980s it had become increasingly clear that she was the only indispensable member. Nevertheless, the entire company continued to do everything from sweeping floors to painting scenery and setting lights. Productions were rehearsed for five to six months, much of that time being devoted to improvisational explorations of a text. Roles were not assigned to specific actors until it became obvious who was best-suited to each. Productions, therefore, were communal up to a point, after which Mnouchkine took over and shaped the final product. By the late 1980s, Mnouchkine's company, which included actors from twenty-one countries, was even more multicultural than Brook's.

Jerome Savary also broadened his approach in the 1980s, as he began to direct classical scripts, while continuing his more typical work with the Grand Magic Circus. The first of his scripted productions was of Büchner's *Leonce and Lena,* done at the invitation of the Hamburg

Schauspielhaus. This new direction was first unveiled in France in 1981 with his production of Molière's *Le Bourgeois Gentilhomme* at the Théâtre de l'Est Parisien. Although he retained Molière's text, he added acrobats, belly dancers, jugglers, clowns, rock, and classical chamber music. The overall effect was to reverse the usual interpretation (which has usually treated M. Jourdain as a *nouveau-riche*, boorish upstart) by calling into question the culture Jourdain aspires to and by glorifying the popular sources of Molière's theatre. Savary subsequently applied this approach to other classics, including *Cyrano de Bergerac*, at the Maison de la Culture in Béziers, of which he had been named director in 1982. Savary's success in fusing elitist and popular culture forms was further recognized in 1989 when he was named head of the Théâtre National de Chaillot.

Other major directors included Vincent and Vitez. Jean-Pierre Vincent (1942–   ) was a classmate of Chereau and worked with him early in his theatrical career. He began to attract notice around 1970 through productions of Brecht's minor works—among them *The Private Life of the Master Race* and *In the Jungle of Cities*—at Avignon, the TNP, and at various dramatic centers. He achieved a major triumph in 1973 at Avignon (and later in 1975 in Paris) with his production of Grumberg's *Comings and Goings at the Expo*. In 1975 he was named head of the Théâtre National de Strasbourg and its theatre school, both of which he raised considerably in critical estimation. With this major permanent company, he was able to practice and perfect his characteristic mode, derived in part from Brecht and Stein, in which works were deconstructed to reveal their underlying ideology and to comment not only on the play being performed but also on its relationship to the present. He appointed two dramaturgs, the playwrights Bernard Chartreux and Michel Deutsch, whose primary role was to do research as a basis for creating scripts and material that examined French history. Some of Vincent's most successful early productions at Strasbourg were an adaptation of Zola's novel *Germinal* (about a miners' strike in the nineteenth century) and Molière's *The Misanthrope*. He then moved on to original work created for the company by Chartreux and Deutsch on the Vichy government of Marshal Pétain during the German occupation, *Vichy Fictions*. By 1983, Vincent's reputation was sufficient to justify naming him head of the Comédie Française, France's most prestigious theatre. There he sought to continue the kind of work he had done in Strasbourg, but the organizational structure of the theatre and its essentially conservative stance as the conservator of French culture was not wholly compatible with his goals and he left the post in 1986. In 1989 Vincent succeeded Chereau as head of the Théâtre des Amandiers in Nanterre.

Antoine Vitez (1930–1990) began acting at the age of eighteen and subsequently became an influential teacher of acting. He also served for a time as secretary to the surrealist writer, Louis Aragon. A Marxist, he became one of France's most respected directors as head (from 1971 to 1980) of the Théâtre des Quartiers d'Ivry, located in one of Paris' working-class suburbs. From 1981 until 1988 he was artistic director of the Théâtre National de Chaillot and in 1988 became director of the Comédie Française. Probably no director commanded so much respect in France during the 1980s. He was also one of the directors most attuned to poststructuralism. His most notable productions were radical reinterpretations of such classics as Racine's *Britannicus*, Molière's *Tartuffe* and *The Misanthrope*, Hugo's *Hernani*, and Claudel's *The Satin Slipper*. In staging these plays, he worked closely with his designer Yannis Kokkos and his actors to break down and reorient realistic conventions. Settings were usually composed of a few elements which could be moved about by the actors; perspective was often used but reversed by placing smaller elements downstage and larger ones upstage, thereby enhancing the sense of characters looming larger as they moved toward the audience; elements treated in the script as scenery—such as sailing ships on which the characters supposedly were located—were sometimes small models which could be picked up and moved about like toys; a portrait of a dead ancestor was reduced to a giant hand that seemed to press down on the living; strong lateral lighting often divided the stage into planes of action; the actors sometimes shifted abruptly from a naturalistic to a nonnaturalistic mode, emphasized discontinuities, or inexplicably shifted moods; units of action were often detached from the narrative flow and given special emphasis. Vitez did not seek to impose meaning and unity as much as to call attention to the overlapping realities, time frames, and varying textures so the spectator would become aware of the complexities, contradictions, incongruities, and multiple possibilities of the action.

The best-known of the French playwrights attuned to deconstructionism was Michel Vinaver (1926–), who as early as the 1950s had written two plays that anticipated aspects of poststructuralism. In *The Koreans* (1956), a lost French soldier taken in by Korean villagers becomes so integrated into his new world that the ideology which had previously shaped his experience of life loses its meaning. It received a number of productions, but *Hotel Iphigènie* (1959), about French tourists in a Greek hotel trying to make sense of the snatches of information they get via radio about a crisis back home, was not produced until 1977 (by Vitez, the director probably most attuned to Vinaver's method). Director of a multinational corporation, Vinaver wrote little during the 1960s, but after Roger Planchon produced his *Overboard* in 1973, he was quickly recognized as

a major playwright and wrote regularly thereafter. Nevertheless, Planchon's production, which severely cut the script and imposed an orderly narrative on it, was not adequate to the play's total conception. Vinaver's original text would require some eight hours to perform and ranges through almost every performance style. Its primary concern is how American marketing strategies have altered European business, but, by introducing numerous discontinuous and seemingly unrelated scenes, it ultimately suggests that everything from board-room politics to mythology interconnects. One plot strand concerns a toilet paper company and its attempts to keep up with the changing market. Another includes lectures on old Norse legends and a group of dancers who try to perform the myths. The "languages" of various classes and professions not only compete but also serve as running commentaries on each other and the ways in which the corporate world displaces the world of myth and personal integrity. Significantly, Vinaver saw his text as a basis for many and quite disparate productions. But apparently no other director wanted to risk comparison with Planchon, and consequently the script did not receive the variety of treatments Vinaver had hoped for.

Vinaver's subsequent plays—among them *Bending Over Backwards* (1980) and *The Ordinary* (1983)—went even further in the demands they made on (or opportunities they offered) directors. They included no punctuation (except question marks) and almost no stage directions, thus remaining open to multiple interpretations, since both what the characters are doing and what they mean by what they say remain ambiguous. Vinaver's plays are discontinuous, fragmented, and immediate; each possible meaning leads to still other possibilities, thereby defying closure of meaning and interpretation.

During the 1980s, the French government continued to support its national theatres and its network of dramatic centers, but its official policy varied according to which political party was in power. Party politics also influenced who was appointed as heads of theatres and how money was distributed. The socialists, in power from 1981 to 1986 and again after 1988, were far more generous to the arts than were their opposition. In 1989, they allocated some $1.6 billion to the arts, of which about one-third went to the performing arts. They also sought to make the arts more accessible to everyone by supporting groups that sought to mesh elitist and popular culture. Jack Lang, Minister of Culture and a former director of the Théâtre National de Chaillot, appointed such innovative directors as Vitez, Vincent, and Savary to head major theatres, and Robert Wilson to stage the ceremony marking the two-hundredth anniversary of the French Revolution in 1989.

The Avignon Festival, which celebrated its fortieth anniversary in 1987, had by that time been accepted as a cross-section of French theatrical activity. The most ambitious and serious work was presented there alongside a vast range of popular entertainment and avant-garde experimentation—adding up to a total of more than three hundred productions during the one-month annual event. By the late 1980s, the Avignon Festival had become the premiere cultural event of France.

ITALY

In Italy, Giorgio Strehler had by the late 1980s done more than any other person to restore the Italian theatrical tradition. By that time, he had directed more than two hundred productions which demonstrated his commanding theatrical flair in an extremely wide range of drama. While continuing his work at Milan's Piccolo Teatro during the 1980s, he also helped to create (in 1983) the Théâtre de l'Europe, under the patronage of and with financial support

from the Council of the European Community and the French government. For this organization, based at the Odéon in Paris, Strehler not only directed productions—among them Shakespeare's *The Tempest* and Brecht's *The Threepenny Opera*—but also brought there the best work being done throughout Europe. It marked the fulfillment of Strehler's international vision of the theatre as a way of seeing how we function in society and of transcending cultural, national, and ideological barriers. In 1986 Strehler opened a conservatory in Milan to train persons for this supranational theatre. In the late 1980s, he also had under construction a new building for his Milan company (with a 1,200-seat auditorium along with scene and technical shops) and was at work on a production of *Faust* (in collaboration with Josef Svoboda) which he did not expect to be fully completed until 1995, although portions began to be performed in 1989.

Luca Ronconi also continued his innovative stagings, most of them after 1977 developed in his Prato Theatre Workshop. He tended to concentrate on reinterpretations of plays from the standard repertory rather than on adaptations of nondramatic works (with which he had gained his international reputation). In many of his productions, scenography played a key interpretational role. In Ibsen's *The Wild Duck*, photography (Hjalmar's profession) became a central interpretive device. Not only were the sets black and white, they were divided into compartments that seemed photocopies of each other, and characters conversed with each other through the walls that separated the compartments. Only in the final act, when the characters' programmed emotional responses were shattered, did the set become a single unit without dividing walls. In 1982, Ronconi staged Ibsen's *Ghosts* at the Spoleto festival in the crypt of a church which had been converted into a glass-covered conservatory that encompassed both acting and audience space. This use of a hothouse to enclose tombs became a metaphor for Mrs. Alving's attempt to prolong a society already dead and whose members are themselves ghosts. Others of Ronconi's productions were concerned primarily with uncovering the ideologies embedded within the texts. In 1987 his staging of Goldoni's *The Loving Servant* concentrated on how attitudes about money, class, and gender operate within the society depicted in the play. Somewhat similarly, Shakespeare's *The Merchant of Venice* was staged to emphasize symbolic exchanges of sex and money within the play's action.

The Italian director most attuned to deconstruction was Carmelo Bene (1937–   ), who began his career as an actor in traditional theatre but soon turned to directing productions in which he also acted. Believing strongly in the autonomy of the theatre and the right of the director to use scripts to explore significant issues, Bene was especially attracted to Shakespeare because the plays were sufficiently well-known to provide a point of reference for his "interrogations" of those texts. Beginning in the 1970s, he staged deconstructions of a number of Shakespeare's plays: *Hamlet, Romeo and Juliet, Richard III,* and *Othello.* Of these, his treatment of *Othello* made the greatest impact, perhaps because he continued to work on it for several years, presenting one version in 1979 and another in 1985. In this second version, there were only eight characters, all dressed uniformly in white robes. The action unfolded as a series of tableaux on a large white bed. Othello was played by a white actor in blackface, whereas Iago was played by a black actor in whiteface. Ultimately the concern was thematic: the nature of jealousy and how it encompasses other desires, especially to possess and control others, and how this in turn is related to male rivalries and bondings which place women on the periphery and exclude them from power. Other Italian directors noted for deconstructing classical texts include Leo de Berardinis and Carlo Cecchi.

In the late 1970s, Dario Fo began to be valued as a director not merely of his own

FIG. 15.5
Dario Fo's *Elisabetta* as produced by the Berliner Ensemble. Directed by Manfred Wekwerth and Alejandro Quintana; setting and costumes by Klaus Noack. (Photo by Vera Tenschert, courtesy Berliner Ensemble.)

works but also those of others. He was invited to stage Stravinsky's *Tale of a Soldier* at LaScala and Brecht's *The Threepenny Opera* at the Berliner Ensemble, but he made these works so thoroughly his own that LaScala soon withdrew its production and the Berliner Ensemble never permitted its to be seen. Nevertheless, Fo was scheduled to direct two of Molière's farces at the Comédie Française in 1990.

Fo remained Italy's only living dramatist to achieve a significant international following. By the early 1980s, Fo's plays were being more frequently produced throughout the world than those of any other living playwright. Not until 1985 was Fo permitted to enter the United States, being considered politically dangerous; in 1986 he performed *Mistero Buffo* in four American cities. Fo also continued to write new pieces. *Elisabetta* (1984) concerns Queen Elizabeth's relationship with Shakespeare, much of it seen from the perspective of the Queen's maid, played by Fo. A prologue compares the Queen's methods with those of today's Italian police. One of the highlights is a two-minute condensation of *Hamlet,* with all parts taken by the maid. The script also makes much of the complexities involving a man playing a woman who serves a woman who must act like a man in order to rule. *Hellequin, Arlekin, Arlechino* (1986) seeks to recapture the bawdy, convention-breaking, epic clown that Harlequin was before being polished and regulated by late *commedia dell'arte.*

During the 1970s, a number of persons became disenchanted with theatre as it was then being practiced in Italy and set out to create alternative forms. They drew on new technologies, electronic and mixed media, and explored modes of communication, perception, and response, as well as relationships between stage and audience and between theatrical space and the larger environment. They also privileged pantomime, music, and surrealistic visual imagery over speech. Among the best-known of these new groups were Falso Movimento, La Gaia Scienza, Krypton, Out and Off, Dark Camera, and Il Marchingegno. Their work tended to resemble American performance art or new theatre.

GERMANY

In the late 1980s, West Germany had approximately 280 legitimate theatres. Of these, the majority were owned by state or local governments, which granted subsidies amounting to approximately 83 percent of their theatre's expenses. There were also numerous "free" (privately owned) theatres, many of which also received some subsidy. Theatre was more readily available in Germany than almost anywhere else in the world, although critics often charged that German theatre catered primarily to the middle class.

By the 1980s, Berlin's Schaubühne under Peter Stein was widely considered West Germany's most preeminent theatre. Its status was further confirmed in 1981 by the completion of its new home, the Schaubühne am Lehniner Platz, built at a cost of $30 million by West Berlin to Stein's specifications. Departing from the proscenium-arch mode that had dominated postwar German theatre and architecture, it was a long open space which could be divided by activating two revolving metal walls, into three separate performance spaces. Its seventy-six floor sections could also be raised, lowered, or pivoted to create almost any configuration, both for staging and seating.

By the 1980s, Stein had altered his previous approach to staging—reshaping scripts so as to reveal and comment on their hidden ideologies. Instead, he began to undertake meticulous, "text-true" productions of such older works as the *Oresteia* (1980), Genet's *The Blacks* (1983), and Chekhov's *The Three Sisters* (1984), along with new plays by Botho Strauss. *The Three*

Sisters (designed by Karl-Ernst Herrmann) with its astonishing realism became perhaps the Schaubühne's most popular production. (In 1989, it was performed at the Moscow Art Theatre on the stage where the play had had its premiere; Russian critics considered it a revelation of what the play must have been in its original Stanislavskian staging.) Although many Germans charged Stein with having retreated from his earlier, Marxian stance, he saw his work in the 1980s as a continuance of what he had been doing all along—investigating the history and consequences of bourgeois consciousness—although less overtly.

In 1985 Stein resigned as director of the Schaubühne, although he returned to direct regularly, perhaps most notably O'Neill's *The Hairy Ape* in 1986. He also began to direct opera, earning especially strong praise for his meticulously staged and acted productions of Verdi's *Otello* (1986) and *Falstaff* (1988) for the Welsh National Opera. Although several of the key actors also left the Schaubühne, continuity was assured through the directorial work of Stein's protegés, Klaus Michael Gruber and Luc Bondy. In 1988 Jürgen Grosch, an East German who after emigrating had directed in Hamburg and elsewhere, was named artistic director. At the end of the 1980s, the Schaubühne was still a major force even if its preeminence no longer seemed as evident as it once had.

Peter Zadek continued to be Germany's most provocative director. After leaving Bochum in 1977, he free-lanced until 1985 when he became artistic director of the Deutsches Schauspielhaus in Hamburg. Wherever he directed, he used the same core group of actors (Ulrich Wildgruber, Heinrich Giskes, Barbara Sukowa, Hans Michael Rehberg) and designers (Johannes Grutzke and Wilfried Minks) and stirred up controversy. Among his productions during the 1980s, two of the most notable were Webster's *The Duchess of Malfi*

(1985) and Wedekind's *Lulu* (1987). Webster's play, set by Zadek in the present with characters who drive Ferraris and talk on telephones, was interpreted as a work about personal and political betrayal in contemporary high society. *Lulu* was set in the ruins of Berlin in the 1950s. A victim of machismo, false morality, and her own sexuality, this naive Lulu searched for love but found only abuse and death. Zadek's status as one of the most innovative directors of the time was confirmed by the inclusion during the 1980s of several of his productions in the Berlin Theatertreffen.

Jürgen Flimm emerged as a major director in the 1980s, winning recognition first for productions at the Cologne Schauspielhaus and then as intendant of the Thalia Theater in Hamburg. His *Uncle Vanya* at Cologne in 1980 (with settings by Erich Wonder) made no attempt to evoke Russia, concentrating instead on time as the destroyer of hopes and visions. This emphasis on time was concretized in the set's back wall, which moved slowly but continuously—three centimeters per second—gradually revealing other views beyond the neutral room in which the action passed. In 1988, Flimm's staging of Hebbel's *The Niebelungen* in Hamburg gave the action a twentieth-century framework by using newsreel footage of the World War II German attack on Stalingrad, while Erich Wonder's set reflected the world after the destruction of battle. Flimm sought through this production to show the need for Germany to learn and remember the lessons of the past. In 1989, Flimm directed his own adaptation of Chekhov's *Platonov*. Concentrating on Platonov's disgust with himself and his society, the production suggested that we cannot begin a new life because we do not know what to do with the one we have. It was one of two productions from the Thalia Theater included in the 1989 Berlin Theatertreffen. Flimm's standing was also enhanced when in 1987 he became the first

German director to be invited to direct a production (of Büchner's *Woyzeck*) in China.

Robert Wilson might also be considered a German director, since most of his major works of the 1980s originated in West Germany and were supported by government subsidies. The German section of *CIVIL warS* was mounted in Cologne, both parts of *Death, Destruction and Detroit* were created at the Berlin Schaubühne, and *The Forest* was produced at the Berlin Freie Volksbühne. Thus, Wilson's work is better-known and more influential in Germany than in the United States.

Wilson also allied himself with Germany's leading playwright, Heiner Müller (1929–), who wrote portions of the texts of *CIVIL warS* and *The Forest* and some of whose plays Wilson directed or incorporated into other productions. Their affinity is probably explained by Müller's uses of discontinuity, juxtaposition, and indeterminancy, qualities that make his textual writing analogous to Wilson's scenic writing.

An East German, Müller began his play-writing career with *The Scab* (1958), which, in the tradition of socialist realism, concerns the problem of meeting production quotas in a factory and the difficulty of building socialism in a society corrupted by the Nazis, all of which is finally resolved on a positive note. Although this play introduced themes that would remain central to Müller's plays (such as the subversion and distortion of ideals by bureaucrats and ideologues), it gave few clues about the directions his work would take (the intermingling of contemporary with mythic or literary subjects, the liberal use of borrowings from and transformations of other works, the juxtaposition of disparate styles) to become the most multilayered, provocative, and controversial in the contemporary repertory. Much the same might also be said about *Philoktetes* (1966), one of Müller's most popular pieces, in which Odysseus persuades the naive Neoptol-

emus that, for the good of the state, he should kill Philoktetes by stabbing him in the back; then, while Neoptolemus deals with the corpse, Odysseus takes possession of Philoktetes' bow. In performance, the universality of Odysseus' deceptive manipulation was reinforced by the projected images of war from the earliest to present times that accompanied the action. With *Cement* (1972), a dramatization of a Soviet novel about building a cement factory, Müller began to juxtapose disparate styles and subjects by inserting into his dramatization long narrative passages about the labors of Hercules; not only did these additions serve a distancing function, they also became commentaries on how revolutionary ideals are subverted by those who have gained power. Müller's subsequent plays became increasingly indirect and allusive. *Hamletmachine* (1977), a short work without dialogue or designated characters, uses Shakespeare's play only as a point of reference. Müller's concern is primarily for the thematic implications of *Hamlet* today; he calls *Hamletmachine* a "self critique of the intellectual's position" in the contemporary world. Subsequently he wrote a trilogy of pieces—*Despoiled Shore, Medeamaterial,* and *Landscape With Argonauts*—which used the Medea myth in much the same way *Hamletmachine* had used Hamlet. All of Müller's subsequent pieces are similar "explosions of memory." *Description of a Picture* (1985) is a single sentence extending over some ten pages without any concern for plot, character or conflict. Müller described it as a "synthetic fragment of a landscape beyond death," where resurrection becomes a source of terror. He listed as sources on which he had drawn as a Noh play, the *Odyssey,* Alfred Hitchcock's *The Birds,* and a drawing. (Robert Wilson used this play as prologue to Euripides' *Alcestis* at the American Repertory Theatre in 1986.) The open structure and indeterminate meaning of these pieces invite multiple approaches to

FIG. 15.6
Heiner Müller's
Hamletmachine at the
Thalia Theater,
Hamburg, in 1987.
Directed and
designed by Robert
Wilson. (Photo
courtesy Story Press—
Jochen Clauss.)

staging; posing questions but evading solutions, they suggest that there can be no "correct" interpretation.

Müller was the only East German playwright to win a large following in West Germany. Not only were his plays performed there frequently but also in 1985 he was awarded the coveted Georg Büchner Award. As if in response, in 1986 East Germany gave him the GDR National Prize. Furthermore, in 1988 as one of the programs related to Berlin's designation as European Cultural City for that year (a different city is designated each year), a "Presentation of Heiner Müller's Work" brought together productions from Amsterdam, Paris, Warsaw, Sofia, and various cities of East and West Germany. A colloquium on his plays by scholars and critics was also held.

In 1988, Müller directed a production at the Deutsches Theater in East Berlin of *The Scab*, not seen since 1958, which in many ways pulled together the many strands of his work. Instead of the socialist realist settings of the original,

the play was performed in Erich Wonder's simplified, timeless sets, which created a near-mythic quality. Furthermore, Müller inserted into the text two of his own more recent works. One, *The Horatians,* inspired by an incident in Roman history, concerns the need to recall the past truthfully; the other, one part of *Wolokolamsker Highway,* shows a bureaucrat becoming fused with his desk only to hear termites eating the wood. Müller also eliminated *The Scab*'s final scene of optimistic reconciliation, thereby leaving the characters estranged (as in all his late plays). The production was judged the best East German production of the year and was one of two East German productions included in the Berlin Theatertreffen in 1989—the first time that East Germany had been permitted to participate.

In the late 1980s *glasnost* eased restrictions in East Germany and made possible the production of many works that had previously been forbidden. Volker Braun (1939–   ) was one beneficiary, for even though he had been a

FIG. 15.7

Volker Braun's *Lenin's Death* as performed at the Berliner Ensemble. Directed by Christoph Schroth, setting by Lothar Scharsich, costumes by Christine Stromberg. (Photo by Ute Eichel, courtesy Berliner Ensemble.)

Gorky Theater under the direction of Thomas Langhoff). It asks what Chekhov's three sisters would be like if they were living in a contemporary East Germany, a daring question since Chekhov's play had long been interpreted as looking forward to fulfillment and happiness under Communism. But in Braun's play, though the characters all work and have their basic needs met, they have not found happiness, since the state cannot regulate or meet the individual's private needs. As in his other plays, Braun ultimately suggests that, despite its shortcomings, East Germany is the best of countries though still in a transitional state. Braun also seems to satirize Heiner Müller in the person of a writer who views himself as "a destroyer and demolition worker" who stands outside his society, tearing it down but putting nothing in its place. This was the second East German production (along with Müller's staging of *The Scab*) to be invited to the Berlin Theatertreffen in 1989.

By the late 1980s, Botho Strauss, who had come to prominence in the 1970s as a playwright and dramaturg at the Berlin Schaubühne, was the most produced living West German dramatist. In 1989, he premiered three new plays, two of which were included in the Berlin Theatertreffen. In *Visitor,* one sees actors rehearsing a scene and later mingling with the audience in the theatre lobby. Using rehearsal as a metaphor for role-playing and theatre for the world, the play suggests that, like actors playing roles they know are fictional, we live like visitors to a fictional world because we will not face up to the reality of problems and commit ourselves to dealing with them. *Seven Doors,* eleven short scenes about the banalities of everyday life, sums up most of Strauss' common themes: loneliness, loss of reality, and the failures of marriage, theatre, and television. In *Time and the Room,* all the characters who enter the room are seeking to discover their identities (although they claim to be looking

respected playwright since the 1960s, several of his works had never been performed. His *Lenin's Death,* written in 1970 and first performed in 1988 at the Berliner Ensemble, concerns Lenin's realization, as he slowly dies, that Soviet Communism needs to be democratized, even as Trotsky and Stalin struggle to gather power into their own hands. Although by Western standards, there is little controversial in this play, it had not been considered politically acceptable prior to Gorbachev's call for openness. Braun's *The Transitory Society* (1982, premiered in Bremen in 1987) was produced in East Berlin in 1988 (at the Maxim for a watch, a lover, or some other object or person), and all want, but fail to get, support from those they meet there. Time, which fluctuates among past, present, and future, becomes as uncertain as human fulfillment. These variations on longing, loneliness, frustration, and lack of self-knowledge were orchestrated into a comic melange that often bordered on the slapstick in the production (directed by Luc Bondy and designed by Richard Peduzzi) at the Berlin Schaubühne.

Female playwrights also began to gain recognition in Germany during the 1970s and 1980s, although none was accorded the recognition given to several male dramatists. In Elfriede Jelinek's *Illness, or Modern Women* (1987), blood is the central image. The play contrasts the blood men have spilled on battlefields since the beginning of time with the blood that women have shed as part of their nature. The women turn into lesbian vampires, since it is useless to bite men, for they are totally bloodless in the sphere that matters to women. Ursula Krechel began her playwriting career in 1974 with *Erika,* since translated into several languages. It deals with a woman breaking away from the patriarchal milieu in which she has been reared. Most of the action occurs between scenes while onstage the concern is for the multilayered contradictions and questions that have been raised by the offstage action. Krechel stated that she was not interested in dramaturgy that emphasized the kind of confrontations and logic that had characterized male notions of effective writing. In *Out of the Sun* (1985), the protagonist moves back and forth in time, examining the lies she has been told, and creating her own new reality, which remains open to still further modifications. Krechel believes that the theatre, as the art form most suited to transformation, is especially adaptable to reshaping female consciousness.

A number of groups in West Germany have created Dance Theatre. Among these, the best known is the one headed by Pina Bausch (1940-), the Wuppertal Dance Theater. Trained in Europe and the United States as a dancer and especially influenced by Kurt Jooss and Anthony Tudor, she began to choreograph in 1968. In 1973 she was named head of the Wuppertal Opera Ballet, which she transformed into her present company. Although thereafter movement remained central in her work, Bausch broke down the barriers between dance and spoken or musical theatre by combining movement, speech, singing, properties, theatrical design, and elements of psychoanalysis into a nonlinear, nonliterary drama capable of expressing human anxieties, obsessions, conflicts, and hopes ranging through the everyday and comic to the epic and terrifying. At first she found little support for her work, because most dance groups and performance artists were at that time seeking to escape the influence of theatre. But by the 1980s, the Wuppertal Dance Theater had become one of the most honored companies in the world with myriad imitators. A representative work is *Carnations* (1983). When the piece opens, a romantic world is invoked through the pristine, upright carnations that cover the stage. During the full-length dance-drama that follows, disparate dances, songs, and vignettes (of varying moods) are presented, and individual performers come forward to make highly personal confessions to the audience; these elements are punctuated by police dogs and their handlers, who patrol in the background, and by a master of ceremonies who repeatedly requires the performers to show their passports. By the end, the carnations (and their implied romantic vision) have been trampled underfoot. Although the elements that make up the piece are so discontinuous as often to seem unrelated, they ultimately create an emotional texture that raises questions about the possibility of love in an alienated, legalistic, and dehumanized world.

FIG. 15.8
An untitled
production in 1985 by
Pina Bausch's
Wuppertal Dance
Theater. (Photo by
Gert Weigelt, courtesy
German Information
Center, New York.)

During the 1980s, Germany's leading designers, especially Wilfried Minks, Erich Wonder, Karl-Ernst Hermann, Johannes Grutzke, and Achim Freyer, sought to have stage design recognized as an autonomous art, which equally with, and more or less independently of, the director's interpretation provides its own vision of the drama. They treated settings more as metaphors of existential conditions than as external environments in which characters lived, although at times they fused these functions. The characteristic features of such settings included: spatial dislocations, large empty spaces, enclosed spaces without visible exits, spaces in which isolated objects or pieces of furniture were juxtaposed surrealistically, and abstract technological landscapes. As some directors returned to a "text-true" mode, the challenge for designers became how to provide both text-true settings and metaphorical interpretations. In many instances, the foreground was treated repre-sentationally while images (for example, of a garbage heap or a burned-out urban landscape) seen through openings commented on the foreground and the world of the action. In general, scenography, like directing, manifested a strongly evocative bent even when text-true.

SOVIET AND EAST EUROPEAN THEATRE IN THE GORBACHEV ERA

After 1985, the Soviet Union, under the leadership of Mikhail Gorbachev, experienced the most profound political changes since the Revolution of 1917. Gorbachev sought these changes in three specific areas: *glasnost* (a new openness both domestically and internationally), *demokratizatsiya* (democratizing the Soviet political system), and *perestroika* (a restructuring of Soviet economy and the heavy and inefficient governmental bureaucracy). Although faced with domestic strife and frequently opposed by conservative old-guard Party members and sometimes opposite-extreme radicals, Gorbachev, who represented the first of a new generation of Russian leadership born after the Revolution, served as a dominant force in easing Cold War tensions between East and West. Such political changes in the Soviet Union had positive effects in other countries of the so-called Eastern bloc, although some, such as Czechoslovakia, continued almost to the end of the 1980s to be dominated by Stalinist-like repressions. Ironically, when Czechoslovakia freed itself from repressive rule in 1989, it chose dissident avant-garde playwright Vaclav Havel as its new president.

The growing freedom in the Soviet Union and Eastern Europe was reflected in the theatre. From the 1950s through the 1970s, Western plays (particularly those by Americans) were not often seen on Soviet stages. In the 1980s, however, a number of works by Williams, Miller, and Albee, plus productions of *West Side Story, Oklahoma!, Hello, Dolly,* and *My Fair Lady* began to appear. No longer were such productions staged as indictments of capitalism, and their production styles showed a variety of directing approaches, often reflecting the traditions of Meyerhold, Tairov, and Vakhtangov as much as of Stanislavsky. Soviet directors also began to stage perceptive adaptations of such American novels as Hemingway's *The Sun Also Rises* and *For Whom the Bell Tolls.*

In the late 1980s, American directors such as Mark Lamos of the Hartford (CT) Stage Company and Nagle Jackson of the McCarter Theatre (Princeton, NJ) directed Soviet professional companies in Moscow and Leningrad, respectively, in productions of O'Neill's *Desire Under the Elms* and Williams' *The Glass Menagerie.* In exchange, Soviet directors from the Pushkin Drama Theatre in Moscow and the Gorky Theatre in Leningrad staged pro-

ductions at the Hartford and McCarter with American actors. Russian critics were generally cool to these two quickly developed productions directed by Americans, but that they occurred at all was a positive result of *glasnost* and of lessening tensions between East and West. In addition to language difficulties between directors and performers, such exchanges pointed to the vast differences between the American box-office-oriented free-enterprise system and the Soviet state-subsidized system. While American actors and directors, by financial necessity, were used to short but intensive rehearsal periods of four to five weeks, Soviet counterparts traditionally were used to lengthier, more leisurely, and ultimately more in-depth periods of development.

With the exception of the controversial work of such directors as Lyubimov and Efros in the 1960s and early 1970s, few other Soviet directors or playwrights were willing to risk offending Party officials. For the most part grounded in realism and Stanislavskian practice, Soviet theatre and drama was conservative. By the mid-1970s, however, there was evidence of a growing tendency toward artistic experimentation with newer methods and deconstructive performances, at least partly inspired by theatrical innovations in Eastern Europe (Grotowski and others) and the West (Chaikin, Brook, Strehler, Planchon, Wilson, Foreman, and others). Lyubimov was, for a time, in the forefront of this movement. His earlier productions of Brecht, Molière, Shakespeare, and Bulgakov at the Taganka had always been artistically and often politically provocative. His methods challenged and confronted texts and often rendered them in very personalized "readings." His first staging of Dostoevsky's novel *Crime and Punishment* in 1976, however, marked a distinct breakthrough artistically. Using five white doors as the basic scenic element against an otherwise empty black

FIG. 15.9
Lyubimov's production of *Crime and Punishment* at the Taganka Theatre in 1979; design by David Borovsky. (Courtesy Alma Law Archive.)

space, Lyubimov stressed the image of a door smeared with fresh blood as a central metaphor (the word *door* appears more than two hundred times in the novel). While the traditional Marxist explanation for Dostoevsky's Raskolnikov always had been that his murders of the old pawnbroker and his sister were acts of protest against the injustices of capitalist society, Lyubimov saw Raskolnikov more precisely as a despicable terrorist, a killer with no moral ethic. The production was staged not only at the Taganka in Moscow but in a number of other cities (Budapest, London, Vienna, Bologna, and Washington, D.C.) with a variety of casts and in different languages.

Always resisting pressures to do "politically correct" productions, and functioning as "the theatrical conscience of his nation," Lyubimov in 1984 was dismissed from his post after twenty years as head of the Taganka Theatre and was stripped of his Soviet citizenship. Continuing to direct productions in the West, Lyubimov eventually became an Israeli citizen, serving as a director at the Habima Theatre. Although he returned to the Soviet Union for short periods both in 1987 and 1989 and his Soviet citizenship was restored, Lyubimov

faced an uncertain future in the USSR, where his work was now considered by some as out-of-date.

Perhaps the most innovative and controversial Soviet director in the 1980s was Anatoly Vasilyev (1942–). Sometimes designated as the Soviet Union's "slowest director," Vasilyev sometimes took as long as three years to develop a production. Although he first began directing professionally in the 1960s, it was not until 1987 that his work was acknowledged internationally with Viktor Slavkin's *Cerceau*, which he took to the World Theatre Festival in Stuttgart and later to London. Slavkin's lengthy post-Chekhovian epic, about a group of acquaintances who gather at a half-ruined country house for a weekend of games and confessions, was developed by Vasilyev through improvisational techniques reminiscent of those used by Grotowski in his final major works. Based on a juxtaposing of styles, Vasilyev's production in Act I used music and dance as a prime motif, underscoring the characters' actions with a jazz beat; Act II developed the ironic Chekhovian atmosphere, where the characters (all dressed in white garments found in the attic) gathered at the dining table to read old love letters aloud; Act III, in rainy autumnal light, had the characters delivering extended monologues on their inherent incapacities to change their lives.

Even more innovative was Vasilyev's production of Pirandello's *Six Characters in Search of an Author,* first performed at his own School of Dramatic Art in Moscow in 1987. (The production eventually won enthusiastic responses at festivals in Avignon, Berlin, Milan, and in 1989 at the Pepsico Summerfare Festival in Purchase, New York.) Unlike *Cerceau,* which featured an all-star professional cast that rehearsed for three years, *Six Characters* brought together twenty-two fifth-year students from Vasilyev's newly opened School of Dramatic Art in a short and divided rehearsal period, though all performers worked alone for many months before coming together to develop the production. In Moscow, the play was produced in a basement room in a white, rectangular performing space designed by Igor Popov, Vasilyev's long-time collaborator. Approximately eighty numbered chairs were desig-

nated for the audience; a dozen more chairs were for the Actors plus a table for the Director; there was a stylized Greek-columned partition, and a canvas curtain was hung diagonally in one corner.

Central to Vasilyev's conception of *Six Characters* was the constantly changing relationship between performers and spectators. While in Act I, the configuration was a conventional proscenium arrangement (without the actual proscenium), the audience was deliberately disoriented in Act II by having the numbered chairs arranged in a rough circle (the actors' chairs now mixed in with those of the spectators). In Act III, the chairs were again rearranged to split the audience into sections with the acting space between them. The mixing of life and art is central to Pirandello's play, and Vasilyev played strongly on this image: at the opening, as the Director and Actors enter, improvisational lines and actions were blended with Pirandello's text, and later Actors were assigned more than one role (the Director becoming the Father; the

FIG. 15.10
Performers and audience members mingle in Vasilyev's production of Pirandello's *Six Characters in Search of an Author* at the School of Dramatic Art, Moscow, in 1987; design by Igor Popov. (Courtesy Alma Law Archive.)

Stepdaughter playing the Mother; the Mother performing Madam Pace); in Act II, the Stepdaughter, a prostitute for Madam Pace, directly solicited men in the audience.

Some critics have suggested that Vasilyev's production of Pirandello's play was something of a theatrical manifesto. He has said that he sees himself and his actors as wanderers in the world of theatre searching for a home: "[The production is] about that lack of faith in the existing theatre. . . . It's our attempt to figure out—Just what is theatre? What is art? What is the borderline between life and art?" Though sometimes maligned by more conventional Soviet critics as "arrogant," Vasilyev was designated by critic Marina Stroeva as "our only hope."

Somewhat similar to Vasilyev in deconstructive outlook and approach though not as well-known in the 1980s were two Georgian directors, Robert Sturua of the Rustaveli Theatre in Tbilisi and Temur Chkheidze of the nearby Mardzhanishvili Theatre, both in their early fifties. Sturua and Chkheidze gained international reputations in the 1980s for their radical productions of Shakespeare. As pupils of Mikhail Tumanishvili, who himself studied with Georgi Tovstonogov, Sturua and Chkheidze were well-grounded in the Stanislavsky system even though eventually both moved toward, respectively, a *theatre of spectacle* and a *theatre of intimacy and psychology*.

Sturua's unconventional production of *Richard III* in the late 1970s and early 1980s made of Shakespeare's play a grotesque farce. The title role was played without a hump by Ramaz Chkhikvadze, a well-known Georgian comic actor. Sturua saw Richard not so much as a tyrant and monster but as a scheming politician who acts the role of a cripple to mollify his rivals. Richard's costume was a Nazi SS coat, and he clicked his heels like a Nazi officer as he limped across the stage. Another touch by Sturua was to have Queen Margaret, dressed in black with white makeup, serve as prompter and stage manager. Throughout the performance, the actor who would eventually play Richmond (who kills Richard and takes over the kingdom) was the understudy of Richard, observing his every move and even taking notes.

Even more startling was Sturua's production of *King Lear,* finally performed publicly in 1987 after nearly eight years of preparations and rehearsals. With a musical score by Gia Kancheli (who had also developed the music for *Richard III*) and setting (a classic theatre in ruins) by Mirian Shvelidze, Sturua's *Lear* emphasized that its action was taking place in a police state. A chorus at one side of the stage sings a musical accompaniment to the terrible events, and from time to time sang extended, mournful chords. Cordelia was dressed punkstyle in black satin shorts and net stockings, while the Fool was a drunk who hated Lear but could not leave him. Lear, played by Chkhikvadze in a cruel manner vastly different from his grotesque Richard, divided his kingdom as a gamey, self-indulgent amusement. A greedy Goneril and Regan in the first scene groveled on all fours, seeking to grab from each other the pieces of the torn map that Lear had crumpled and thrown on the floor. At the end, Shvelidze's setting literally began to fall apart to the sounds of crashing thunder (or nuclear explosions?) as Lear, doomed to live on, dragged the limp, grotesque corpse of Cordelia behind him. His final words—"Pray you, undo this button"—were said into a void, for there was no one left to hear him.

Director Chkheidze's *Othello,* first performed in 1982, showed a vastly different approach to Shakespeare than Sturua's *Richard III* or *Lear*. While Sturua's works were eminently theatrical and spectacular, Chkheidze sought a subtly intimate psychological portrait of the embattled Othello. The original text was cut by at least one-third, with the entire first act dropped, except for Othello's speech to the Senate, later delivered simply as a soliloquy. The performance opened and closed with the final scene—Othello's arrest and captivity—with the events leading to the ending played between. In the opening scene, Otar Megvinetukhutsesi as Othello was seen in traditional dark makeup, but in the course of the action, he used a corner of his shirt to wipe his face clean, thus remaining light-skinned until the end, when, after murdering Desdemona, he again smeared his face with dark makeup. As Chkheidze explained: "The question here isn't one of whether Othello is white or black. Of course, he's black. But the makeup gets in the way and distances us from him. What happens to him can happen to anyone. That's what I wanted to emphasize."

A more traditional Soviet director was Lev Dodin (1944–   ), who was appointed in 1983 as chief director of the Maly Dramatic Theatre in Leningrad. His production in 1985 of Fedor Abramov's epic *Brother and Sisters,* concerned with the lives of villagers in northern Russia during the Stalinist years following World War II, won fame both at home and abroad and was seen at the New York International Festival of the Arts in 1988. The performance ran for over seven hours and was played in two evenings. Dodin also staged Aleksandr Galin's *Stars in the Morning* in 1987, a documentary drama about prostitutes expelled from Moscow during the 1984 Olympics. Much in the tradition of Stanislavsky, Dodin, when adapting Golding's *Lord of the Flies* to the stage in 1987, took his cast to the Caspian Sea, where the group lived for a month in conditions similar to those encountered in the novel. Dodin often spent up to two years working on a production before presenting it publicly: "I couldn't possibly bring to life a production in as short a period of time as American directors do."

Other Soviet directors who gained recognition in the 1980s included Getta Yanovskaya

of the Moscow Young People's Theatre; Yuri Eremin of the Pushkin Drama Theatre; Nikolai Gubenko (1941–   ), who took over the Taganka Theatre upon the death of Efros in 1987 and eventually was named Soviet Minister of Culture; Mikhail Mokeev of the Theatre-Studio Chelovek; and Mark Rozovsky of the Nikitsky Gate People's Studio Theatre.

Despite the frequent experimental tendencies among directors such as Lyubimov, Vasilyev, Sturua, and Chkheidze, few Soviet playwrights of the mid-1970s and 1980s seemed so boldly theatrical. Like many of their Western counterparts, Soviet playwrights remained firmly tied to the realist tradition that has influenced Russian drama since the time of Turgenev, Tolstoy, Chekhov, and Gorky. Although socialist realism had been generally rejected even as long ago as the Krushchev era, occasional vague reminders of the melodramatic sentimentalism of that form, if not the politics, were still to be found in more recent Russian drama. Many truly innovative Soviet directors seemed little interested in plays written by their contemporaries, preferring instead to develop deconstructive productions based on plays from the past (thus following the example of earlier directors such as Meyerhold, Vakhtangov, and Tairov). Occasionally, however, a true unity of director and contemporary playwright occurred, as in the case of Vasilyev and Viktor Slavkin with *The Grown-up Daughter of a Young Man* in 1978 and *Cerceau* in 1987.

One of the best dramatists writing in the period of the 1970s and 1980s was Edvard Radzinsky (1936–   ), whose historical-philosophical trilogy comprised of *Conversations With Socrates* (1971), *I, Mikhail Sergeevich Lunin* (1977), and *Theatre in the Time of Nero and Seneca* (1981) deals with the theme of oppressive authority and its ultimate incapacity to enslave the human spirit. In the first play, for example, Radzinsky bases his action on Plato's account of the final days of Socrates, but in Radzinsky's treatment, Socrates becomes more humanized in his suffering. Sentenced to death for heresy and the corrupting of Athenian youth, Socrates' followers plot his escape, but he chooses to remain imprisoned and accept the "freedom of death." In *Lunin,* Radzinsky deals with the abortive Decembrist uprising in 1825 and the Russian aristocrat and imprisoned martyr, Mikhail Lunin. *Theatre in the Time of Nero and Seneca* is a highly theatrical work which explores the relationship between Seneca and his pupil Nero and the sources of evil in the world.

Others of Radzinsky's plays such as *Don Juan Continued* (1979) and *Jogging* (1986) show clearly the playwright's stylistic versatility. The first play, staged effectively by Efros as the premiere production in the Maloi Bronnoi's arena theatre, is a satiric comedy which poses the question: what would happen if Don Juan was to return to today's Moscow? In *Jogging,* Radzinsky presents a four-character battle of the sexes, somewhat reminiscent of Albee's *Who's Afraid of Virginia Woolf?,* which Radzinsky admitted to admiring. The play, however, is a subtle exposé of the dissolute lives of the privileged children and grandchildren of the Kremlin elite. In a society unused to gossip columns or magazine exposés, Radzinsky's play shocked (but also titillated) most Soviet audience members.

Another playwright whose works began to win favor in the 1980s was Ludmilla Petrushevskaya (1938–). Trained as a journalist, Petrushevskaya worked for a number of years as a radio reporter, tape-recording interviews and conversations, many of which came to serve as raw material for her future writing of short stories and plays. (Petrushevskaya's keen sense of the intonations of Moscow slang, for example, is one of her greatest strengths as a playwright.) Though filled with wry humor, the plays, usually short, are startlingly realistic

FIG. 15.11

Edvard Radzinsky's *Don Juan Continued* as staged by Anatoly Efros at the Maloi Bronnoi arena theatre, Moscow, in 1979. (Courtesy Alma Law Archive.)

and seemingly plotless. Each, however, possesses a theatrical "twist" which makes it inherently stageable.

Two short companion plays, *Cinzano* and *Smirnova's Birthday* (both first produced in 1978), are simple "slices of life." In the first, three young men—Pasha, Valia, and Kostia— meet in an essentially vacant apartment on the outskirts of Moscow to settle their debts. In the process, they get drunk on several bottles of expensive Cinzano, newly imported from the West. As the action proceeds, the discussion turns increasingly to the situation of Pasha's mother, presumed ill in the hospital. By the

FIG. 15.12
Ludmilla Petrushevskaya's *Smirnova's Birthday* as staged in Moscow at "Creative Workshops" in 1988; directed by Roman Viktiuk; design by Georgy Krutinsky. (Courtesy Alma Law Archive.)

end of the play, however, it becomes clear that Pasha's mother has actually died and that the money intended to cover her funeral expenses has been spent on the expensive Western Cinzano. The action of *Smirnova's Birthday* takes place at the same time as the encounter of the men and treats their female counterparts: Smirnova, a fellow worker with the three men; Kostia's wife, Polina; and Rita, Kostia's former girlfriend. They, too, drink several bottles of the newly imported Western Cinzano, birthday gifts for Smirnova, and discuss and argue (with increasing incoherence) issues of marriage and children. At the end, the uninvited Valia from *Cinzano* arrives with another bottle and says: "Girls, don't cry, your little boy has come to you." Others of Petrushevskaya's plays are *Come Into the Kitchen* (1979), *Love* (1979), and *Three Girls in Blue* (1984), similar in tone to *Cinzano* and *Smirnova's Birthday*.

Vasilyev's production of *Cerceau* by Viktor Slavkin (1935–   ) has already been noted. Slavkin's *The Grown-up Daughter of a Young Man* (1979), also directed by Vasilyev, is a work with a similar nostalgic atmosphere. A number of friends gather at the Kuprianov apartment for a reunion twenty years after their graduation in the late 1950s from the university. The three men twenty years before all had been in love with Lucy, Kuprianov's wife, who had been a singer at a local movie house. Lucy now seems simply disenchanted. In the 1950s, Kuprianov and Prokup had been enamored of American jazz and had dressed in extravagant styles. Now both are somewhat dull engineers, though Prokup is the more successful. The conformist Ivchenko is now dean at the university. Suddenly the underlying conflicts between the men are punctuated by the arrival of Ella, Kuprianov's and Lucy's daughter, with her young friends. She tells the older generation that she hates all of them. At dawn, all peer and generational conflicts are resolved, however, when the whole group leaves to see a movie together.

Mikhail Roshchin (1933–   ) gained popularity with such plays as *Valentin and Valentina* (1971) and *Echelon* (1975). The first concerns a pair of teenagers who are in love and wish to marry, though they are opposed by Valentina's mother, a divorcée, and Valentin's friends, who suggest to him that love turns men into monkeys and blinds them to everything else in the world. But Valentin's mother, and particularly his sister Zhenya, are more encouraging. Zhenya tells Valentina to follow her own heart and not make a mess of her life. *Echelon* takes place on a Russian evacuation train during the German advance on Moscow in 1941. The passengers, mostly women and children, squabble over food and the attentions of their commanding officer. When a bomb strikes the train and kills several, the survivors realize that their strength lies in their unity. While Roshchin cannot be accused of writing socialist realism per se, his plays sometimes are reminiscent of that form.

Among other playwrights of the period were Chingiz Aitmatov (1928–   ) and Kaltai Mukhamedzhanov (1928–   ) whose *The Ascent of Mount Fuji* is an exploration of one's ethical responsibilities to friends or to society in general. In *Last Summer in Chulimsk* (1972), Aleksandr Vampilov (1937–1972) presents a gallery of character portraits in a Siberian village and the story of a young provincial girl who falls in love with an aging displaced court investigator who has come to Siberia to retire from bureaucracy. He cruelly rejects her; she then loses her virginity to a boy of the village; finally the court investigator goes back to the city, suddenly aware of the girl's love and his own failure. She is condemned to stay in the village.

POLAND IN THE AGE OF SOLIDARITY

Of all the countries of Eastern Europe, Poland in the 1980s experienced the most gradual though sweeping political changes. Such changes occurred over the entire decade, while in other countries of the Eastern bloc the dynamic revolution became apparent only in the closing months of 1989. Poland's trade union Solidarity was born in August 1980 with the strike of shipyard workers in Gdańsk, but in December 1981 General Wojciech Jaruzelski, under pressure from the Soviets, declared Poland in a state of martial law, thus outlawing Solidarity and what had become a national movement. Though the government under domestic pressure from Solidarity eventually restored some normalcy to the country, Poland continued throughout the 1980s to suffer severe economic crises. In 1989, however, a national election overwhelmingly swept Communist Party representatives from power, and a new government was formed with formerly jailed Solidarity leader Tadeusz Mazowiecki as Poland's Prime Minister. Nonetheless, faced by continuing economic problems, Poland's future remained uncertain at the end of the 1980s.

The Polish propensity toward myth, ritual, and tradition continued in the 1980s. Such national images as those of "Bleeding Poland," Poland under occupation, and Polish leaders and artists jailed or forced into exile (images resonant of early nineteenth-century romantic plays by Mickiewicz, Słowacki, and Krasiński) were sometimes invoked by members of Solidarity, Poland's activist Catholic Church, and indirectly by theatre artists, particularly in the period of martial law. (In Polish significantly the term for martial law is *stan wojenny* or "state of war".)

During martial law, Grotowski and various members of his company left Poland. While other members of the group remained in Wrocław during this crisis, developing a performance titled *Thanatos Polski* (or *Polish Death*), directed by Ryszard Cieślak, by 1984, after twenty-five years of operation, the group officially disbanded. Though a new group comprised of younger performers from various countries (called the Second Studio of Wrocław) was formed in 1984 under the leadership of former Laboratory Theatre actor Zbigniew Cynkutis (1938–1987), shortly after his death that group too was dissolved.

Grotowski went to the United States in 1982, developing after 1983 a new continuing project titled *Objective Drama* at the University of California at Irvine. This work reflected not only his earlier theatrical work and paratheatrical explorations from the 1970s and early 1980s in such projects as *The Mountain of Flame, Tree of People,* and *Theatre of Sources* but also a renewed concern with physical, vocal, and psychological discipline and precision for the performer. In 1985, Carla Pollastrelli and Roberto Bacci established the European Center for the Work of Jerzy Grotowski in Pontedera, Italy, and it was here that Grotowski devoted most of his energies as the 1980s came to a close.

Though granted honorary degrees from many universities and his continuing work supported by many foundations internationally, Grotowski remained at the end of the 1980s essentially an exile, much in the Polish tradition of Mickiewicz, Słowacki, and Krasiński, who had found it necessary to leave Poland in the period of Partition. While insisting in the 1960s and thereafter that his work was apolitical, Grotowski, upon leaving Poland, declared that his work had always been political: "I had to say I was not political in order to *be* political. *The Constant Prince,* for example, was a very political work." Such a statement eventually may cause political "readings" and reevaluations of such productions as *Tragical History of Doctor Faustus* and *Apocalypsis cum figuris.*

Still not fully acknowledged in the 1980s for his theatrical innovations (Grotowski directed no theatrical productions after *Apocalypsis cum figuris,* which premiered in 1968 and continued to be performed internationally until 1981), his influence and example persisted. In his various projects, he continued to train performers, developing numerous "meetings" of theatre and nontheatre people, as in *Objective Drama,* and introduced them to his latest discoveries about performance and the actor-audience relationship. Such "meetings," which often included many outside participants, depended heavily upon improvisation and the process of finding form, basic cornerstones of the Grotowski method.

Often designated as the most significant theatrical figure since Stanislavsky and Brecht, Grotowski continued to influence developments in the 1980s. It was he who had first popularized in the contemporary period the necessity of a lengthy preparation period as essential to the development of a true theatrical work. It was he, too, who first developed a new method of improvisational work with the actor, which, in various forms, became in the 1980s almost a commonplace in most advanced actor-training programs throughout the world. The example of a "poor theatre," which used minimalist setting, lighting, and costumes (and was extremely mobile for touring), eventually came to seem more artistically viable to theatrical practitioners in the 1980s, faced as they were with diminishing economic support. And it was Grotowski's conscious strategy to first gain "international resonance outside Poland," as actor Zbigniew Cynkutis once described it, that often guided the similar strategies among significant Eastern bloc directors and their companies to show their work worldwide in a similar manner.

Though long acclaimed in the West (since 1965) and much of the rest of the world, Grotowski's influence upon theatrical work in the Soviet Union and Eastern Europe generally became apparent internationally only in the 1980s. Though Soviet directors such as Vasilyev, Sturua, and Chkheidze were probably not directly influenced by Grotowski's work, their productions and developmental methods were clearly reminiscent of those employed in Grotowski's productions during his so-called "theatrical period" with the Laboratory The-atre (1959–1971). Grotowski's greatest contribution to the 1980s was essentially as a teacher. As such, he inspired directly many who came to his projects by insisting on the ethical and artistic integrity of the actor/participant, the demand for rhythmic precision, and the articulation and demonstration of clear methods to achieve such results.

It is noteworthy that *Towards a Poor Theatre* (1968, and since published in many languages) was scheduled for publication for the first time in Polish in 1990. Now printed in a Slavic language, the book opens up the possibility of the continued dissemination of Grotowski's early ideas and methods in the Eastern bloc. Also in Wrocław in 1987, an archive and museum devoted to the work of Grotowski and the Laboratory Theatre were established.

A Polish director who in the 1980s achieved an international reputation almost comparable to Grotowski's (in the 1960s and early 1970s) was Tadeusz Kantor, whose earliest work as a director of Witkiewicz's plays has already been mentioned. Kantor's distinctive reputation, however, came after the mid-1970s when his production titled *The Dead Class* (1975) began to be performed internationally. (The company henceforth was seldom in Kraków, spending most of its time abroad performing at world theatre festivals.) Using an amalgamation of his own text plus parts of texts taken from Witkiewicz, Gombrowicz, and Bruno Schultz, Kantor subtitled *The Dead Class* "a dramatic seance." The setting was a long rectangular playing area with four rows of wooden school desks vintage early twentieth century. The audience sat on two sides of the playing area. The students were not children but old people with corpselike faces and dressed in black school uniforms. Sometimes they carried dummies, effigies of their younger selves. Sometimes the old people sat at the desks; sometimes only the dummies. Throughout the performance at various moments, the dynamic *Waltz François* was played over loudspeakers.

FIG. 15.13
The dummies seated at the desks in Tadeusz Kantor's *The Dead Class*, first performed in 1975, but played internationally for many years. (Courtesy Authors' Agency, Ltd., Warsaw.)

The teacher was the director himself, Kantor, who remained onstage throughout the ninety-minute production, intently conducting the actors, the music, the pace of the performance. (Kantor was a presence in all his performances, usually wearing a dark suit and an open-collared white shirt.) The playing area was constantly alive with motion, verbal sound, recorded music, precise movement. As critic Jan Klassowicz has said of the actors: "They walk with gusto, but they are still bent, awkward, rickety, carrying their own child-hoods on their backs [the dummies]."

At the same time that *The Dead Class* was first produced, Kantor formulated his manifesto titled "The Theatre of Death." Here he focused on the idea of using dummies: "I do not think that a DUMMY . . . could replace a LIVE ACTOR, as Kleist and Craig wished. . . . Its appearance falls in with my steadily increasing conviction that *life* can be expressed in art only through the *absence of life,* by reference to DEATH, through APPEARANCES, through the VOID and the absence of a MESSAGE. In my theatre the dummy is to become a MODEL through which a feeling of DEATH and a strong feeling of the condition of the Dead emanate: the model for a LIVE ACTOR."

In 1980, Cricot 2 presented a new original work, *Wielopole, Wielopole,* the title based on the name of the town in which Kantor was born, and the performance itself an almost hallucinatory evocation of his childhood at the time of World War I. Here, too, Kantor dealt with the living dead. This time, however, the characters were Kantor's family and seven World War I conscripted soldiers. The performance was inspired by Kantor's having seen a faded photograph of his own father in uniform, taken on the day of his father's departure for the front lines, never to return. Thus in the performance the seven conscripts had faded uniforms and moved like puppets. Kantor says, in seeing the photograph of his father, that he was "fascinated by the very person of a conscript as someone marked with death."

In his performance of *Let the Artists Die* (1985), a work subtitled "a revue," Kantor staged a comic-burlesque of his own obituary. At one point, a clownish doctor ran back and forth between a bed-ridden man and Kantor himself, taking their pulses, predicting the imminent death of the author. Kantor's appearances with his performers in the works just mentioned were always as an observer signaling to them, sometimes disapprovingly. As one critic has put it: "Watching him try vainly to orchestrate the unruly images of the production is like watching a man engaged in mortal combat with his memory." Kantor's imagination has always been that of the visual artist, the painter, and, like directors such as Wilson and Foreman, he has always exploited that element of his talent.

In *I Shall Never Return* (1988), however, Kantor, for the first time, became a speaking presence, still appearing as himself, but now the central character of the performance. As Kantor himself suggested, *I Shall Never Return* was a resumé of his own career: "Everything I have done so far is in the nature of a confession. The confession grew more and more personal." The work contained a collage of allusions and images reminiscent of numerous of his productions ranging from Wyspiański's *The Return of Odysseus,* which he had staged in a clandestine theatre during the Nazi occupation (the image of an elegantly dressed group of Nazi officers with violins rather than guns dance a tango), through *The Dead Class* (the image of the school desks), to *Let the Artists Die* (the image of a "gang" of ruffians and prostitutes invading a barroom).

On the occasion of Kantor's seventieth birthday in 1985, he was presented with a number of awards, medals, and state honors for his more than forty years of work as a creative artist in the Polish theatre. In addition to opening a new performance space for Cricot 2 near Wawel Castle in Kraków, a special museum and archive devoted to Kantor's work were also established.

Internationally renowned cinema director Andrzej Wajda (1926–   ), whose films such as *Ashes and Diamonds* (1959), Wyspiański's *The Wedding* (1973), *Man of Marble* (1976), *Man of Iron* (1981), and *Danton* (1985) had won numerous prizes, was generally unknown before the mid-1970s outside Poland for his equally strong work as a theatre director. But at approximately the time Wajda directed a theatrical production based upon Dostoevsky's *The Possessed* with American actors at Yale (1976), his international reputation as a theatre director began to equal that of his work in film. After 1969, Wajda was the major director at Kraków's Stary (or Old) Theatre, and in the late 1980s he also became director of Warsaw's Contemporary Theatre. In 1989, as well, Wajda was elected as a Solidarity representative to the Sejm (Poland's congress) in the sweeping victory of his party at the polls.

Despite his work in both film and theatre,

Wajda always made clear distinctions between the two media: "Film is an imitation of life, whereas theatre is artistic transposition. . . . [T]heatre has taught me to tell the difference between what is natural and what is true. Theatre is the art of form." Some of his most distinctive productions at the Stary Theatre were of Dostoevsky's *The Possessed* (1971, later restaged at Yale), Wyspiański's *November Night* (1974), Mrożek's *The Emigrés* (1976), and Sophocles' *Antigone* (1984). Typically Wajda's wife, Krystyna Zachwatowicz, designed the costumes and sometimes the settings for his productions, though occasionally Wajda himself designed his own settings.

In 1988, Wajda staged a distinctive production of *The Dybbuk*, the first time since World War II that Ansky's play had been seen in Poland. Later in the same year, the production was taken to Israel and performed at the Habima Theatre. But perhaps even more interesting was Wajda's *Hamlet IV* (1989), the title indicating the director's fourth staging of Shakespeare's classic. What made this production so distinctive was that Hamlet was played by a woman, Teresa Budzisz-Krzy-

FIG. 15.14 Andrzej Wajda's *Hamlet IV*, as performed at the Stary Theatre, Kraków, in 1989; design by Krystyna Zach- watowicz. Hamlet was played by a woman, Teresa Budzisz- Krzyzanowska. (Photo by Wojciech Plewiński.)

zanowska, and the performance took place backstage and focused on the idea of an actor preparing to play the Danish prince. In discussing the question of why he cast a female Hamlet, Wajda said: "Since it's *about* an actor, I felt the gender didn't matter. . . . It's not just Hamlet dying, but the actor putting his [/her] soul into the character—attempting to maintain stamina until the last breath—and dying every night." As Wajda has suggested, he sees *Hamlet* as dealing with "how to approach the end of your life."

When both *The Dybbuk* and *Hamlet IV* were performed at the Pepsico Summerfare Festival in 1989, the audience for *Hamlet IV* sat at the extreme rear of an empty stage facing the footlights and looking out into the empty auditorium where the audience would sit for the next performance of *The Dybbuk*. The production stressed the differences between public acts and behind-the-scenes machinations. When "The Death of Gonzago" was staged for the benefit of Claudius and Gertrude, Hamlet told Horatio to watch Claudius's expression on a backstage video monitor also in view of the audience. Thus the audience had two simultaneous views of Claudius.

Though somewhat older than Wajda, Józef Szajna (1922–   ) continued in the late 1970s and 1980s to direct at his own Studio Theatre in Warsaw outstanding and original productions of works which he titled *Dante* (1974) and *Cervantes* (1976). Like Kantor, Szajna began his work as a painter, the visual element being a strong feature in all his productions. As a young man during the Nazi occupation, Szajna was confined to the prison camps at both Auschwitz and Buchenwald, and it was this experience that inspired his setting and costume designs for Grotowski's production of Wyspiański's *Akropolis* in 1962. (Szajna later used the basic costume design again in his own production of *Replika* [1973].) Szajna's company at the Studio Theatre, which he has headed

since 1971, has toured widely, chiefly in Western Europe but also in the United States and Mexico.

Other Polish directors whose work came to prominence internationally in the 1980s were Jerzy Jarocki (1929-   ), whose productions often were labeled "neonaturalistic"; Zygmunt Hübner (1930–1988), director of the Powszechny Theatre in Warsaw, who staged many productions of foreign works; Helmut Kajzar (1941–1982), chiefly responsible for introducing Różewicz's plays; Kazimierz Braun (1936–   ), also important for his various stagings of Różewicz's works before being fired from his directorship of Wrocław's Contemporary Theatre during the period of martial law; Alina Obidniak, an organizer of international street theatre festivals in Jelenia Góra; and Jerzy Grzegorzewski (1939–   ), who, in directing and designing productions based upon literary works by Kafka and Joyce, revealed his strong background in the visual arts.

While the work of most directors discussed above was decidedly avant-garde, all, with the exception of Grotowski, worked within the organizational parameters of the traditional theatre. Some younger Polish directors, however—notably Lech Raczak of the Theatre of the 8th Day and Włodzimierz Staniewski of the Gardzienice—chose to work in what might best be described as alternative theatre. Both the 8th Day and the Gardzienice were at least partially inspired by the work of Grotowski, though both in the 1970s and 1980s took divergent paths not only from Grotowski but from each other.

The Theatre of the 8th Day was founded in 1964 at Poznań University as part of the student theatre movement that thrived chiefly in the 1960s. The group never included trained actors, since, according to its present director, Raczak, graduates of Polish theatre schools cannot act with their "whole self." Almost from the beginning, the group was devoted to political engagement, and, despite almost perpetual harassments and arrests, the 8th Day persisted. While numerous street productions such as *In One Breath* (1971), *Paradise on Earth* (1975), *More Than One Life* (1981), *Absinthe* (1984), and *Auto de Fé* (1985) grew from collective improvisational work in the manner of the Laboratory Theatre, Raczak precisely stated his disagreement with Grotowski: [W]hat I object to in Grotowski is that he insists that the emerging actor must shake off all the weights and burdens that are placed on the individual by civilization and cultural inhibitions. . . . We felt it was indispensible to continue the work inspired by Grotowski on the Self, but a new desire was born—a kind of duty—to cut ourselves free from those mythical concerns and move toward our contemporary problems."

Staniewski in 1971 had been for three years a member of another student theatre, STU, in Kraków when Grotowski invited him to become a member of the Laboratory Theatre (just at the time the group was moving from theatrical toward paratheatrical work). Staniewski became involved with a number of projects with the Laboratory Theatre but in 1976 left the company, eventually to found the Gardzienice in 1977. The Gardzienice, named after a village near Lublin in southeastern Poland and comprised of approximately ten performers, traveled to isolated rural regions of Poland to perform and interact culturally with people who had never seen a conventional theatrical performance. In these "expeditions," the Gardzienice played such collectively developed works as *Evening Performance, Sorcery, Avvakum,* and *Gathering.* In the process, typically an "exchange" occurred between those performing and those watching. Often the village people watching a performance would be encouraged after the performance to sing songs from Ukrainian, Belorussian, or Lemko traditions and to teach these songs to members of the Gardzienice. For a short time the group would remain in the village, exchanging food, talk, songs, stories, and performances. In the 1980s, the group toured internationally, going, for example, to the United States in 1986 for

FIG. 15.15
The Gardzienice in performance in a Polish peasant village. (Courtesy Halina Filipowicz.)

the Theatre of Nations in Baltimore. Staniewski has stated that he rejects folklorist and anthropological methods as "intrusive" and "fascist": "We don't study the people. We learn from them. It's necessary to have mutuality when two different cultures meet. And to understand someone else's life, you have to plunge into it."

Already mentioned in an earlier chapter is the Italian director Eugenio Barba, who served a lengthy apprenticeship under Grotowski in the early 1960s when the Laboratory Theatre was preparing *Akropolis*. As the leader of the Odin Teatret in Holstebro, Denmark since 1964, Barba and his group in the late 1970s and 1980s visited many international locales to do street performances. The actors often walked on stilts and wore imaginative costumes and masks. Barba is a foremost expert in the field of theatre anthropology and has written extensively on the subject in such books as *The Stranger Who Dances* (1977) and *The Floating Islands* (1979) in addition to many individual articles in various journals.

Throughout the late 1970s and 1980s, Mrożek and Różewicz continued to be the major dramatists writing in Polish, but the work of two other important writers—Iredyński and Głowacki—plus a host of other lesser figures deserve at least some notice.

Ireneusz Iredyński (1939–1985) began his career as a poet but in the early 1960s started to write plays. It was not, however, until the early 1970s that his work began to gain some popularity. Aside from the plays of Różewicz, eventually those by Iredyński were the most frequently staged in the 1980s. *Nativity-Moderne* (1962) occurs on the eve of the liberation of a World War II prison camp, and the inmates rehearse a nativity play written by one of their guards. The action occurs on a variety of planes: the camp itself, the play-within-a-play, and a focus on the motives of the guard who has written the play. Ultimately all the actors, except the one who plays Herod, are killed before they are liberated, and the guard himself commits suicide.

In a more ironic style is *The Third Breast* (1973), which is set in a religious commune in the jungle. Two men, George and Thomas, are in love with Eva, the beautiful founder of the commune. While she is the sexual partner of both men, among others, Eva recently has grown a third breast and persuades George to kill two members who know about the third breast "for the good of the commune." Thomas is one of those whom George kills, and in the final act, when Eva has gone to the city to have the third breast removed, George rules the commune despotically in her absence. When Eva returns, now "normalized," George finds her dull.

Iredyński's *A Nice Quiet Evening* (1981), set in the aftermath of the rise of Solidarity, deals with a father whose loyalty to the Party would not allow him to join his striking fellow workers at the factory. While the father has resolved to put his private life in order, his son turns against him, accusing the father of blind loyalty to the Communist regime. Disgusted by the political passivity of his father, the son at the conclusion announces his decision to enter a seminary.

Janusz Głowacki (1938–   ) for many years was a filmscript, short story, and editorial writer before turning to playwriting in the late 1970s. His weekly editorials in the Warsaw-based *Kultura* frequently were considered inflammatory by Party officials and were often suppressed. With the rise of the Solidarity movement followed eventually by martial law, Głowacki found himself under attack and eventually fled to the United States. His play *Sluterella* (or *Cinders*, 1979) deals with a film crew that goes to a girls' reformatory to shoot a documentary on the girls and their production of *Cinderella*. The girls are a tough lot, including the girl who plays Cinderella, and yet she reveals a sensitivity and resistance to the situation in which she finds herself. At the end, unwilling to submit to the repressive circumstances, the girl slashes her wrists.

In the wake of martial law in Poland, four short plays by Głowacki—*Journey to Gdańsk, Tea With Milk, A Walk Before Dawn,* and *Flashback*—were given their world premiere at the Westside Mainstage Theatre in New York in 1982. Both *Journey to Gdańsk* and *Flashback* deal specifically with the period of the rise of Solidarity In August 1980. In the first, an extremely nervous journalist debates with his combative wife whether he should go to Gdańsk to cover the strike and the meetings of the Solidarity union workers. He could lie and do an interview with a famous actor and not go to Gdańsk. If he goes to Gdańsk and the strike fails, he will lose his job; but if the strike succeeds, he has missed the story and sacrificed his journalistic integrity. In *Flashback,* an aging famous writer catching a night train for Warsaw encounters a man, probably a former member of the secret police, who once had intensively investigated the writer for subversive activities. Głowacki's *Hunting Cockroaches* (1985), deals with the semicomic plight of a Polish emigré couple living in a squalid, shabby apartment in New York City. Uprooted from his homeland, Głowacki at the end of the 1980s adjusted his writing to the new American environment, though still, as in Poland, critical of the idiosyncracies of that environment.

In *From Here to America* (1988, thus written before the election victory of Solidarity), Władysław Zawistowski deals with life among intellectuals, artists, and scientists in the Polish crisis period of the 1980s. Although the characters are inspired by the courage of the Gdańsk shipyard workers and the rise of Solidarity, they seem distinctly disenchanted as the 1980s draw to a close.

Some of the most successful of Polish plays written in the 1980s often treated materials from the past. Joanna Kulmowa's *Seeking* (1988) has the past merging with the present in the nightmarish memories of an elderly Jewish woman who was a child and teenager during World War II. Similarly, Jerzy Sito's *Listen, Israel* (1986) is a long, two-part play that treats the history of the Warsaw Ghetto. *The Cyclops* (1988) by Władysław Terlecki returns to nineteenth-century Dresden and the controversial historical Polish figure Aleksander Wielopolski. Often thought to be a traitor and tsarist official during the period of Polish Partition, the aging Wielopolski confronts his past in a series of flashbacks. Sometimes the return to the past has taken the form of contemporary treatments of biblical materials, as in Stanisław Brejdygant's *Golgotha* (1987), which deals with the Jerusalem terrorist Barabbas, his hatred of the Romans, and his persuasion of Judas to betray Christ. Though Barabbas begins to come under the influence of the teachings of the so-called New Messiah, it is he who is pardoned while Christ is executed.

Though his plays were generally unknown before he became pope, Karol Wojtyła (1920–) was revealed as a dramatist of some talent, though his works are generally static by comparison with most contemporary Polish playwrights. A number of Wojtyła's plays were produced in the 1980s and include *The Jeweler's Shop* (1960), a poetic drama concerned with past and contemporary love and marriage, in which a young woman seeks to sell her wedding ring but cannot, and *Radiation of Fatherhood* (1964), which, also partly in poetry, has a long monologue by Adam in which he analyzes his self-awareness and loneliness.

CZECH THEATRE AND DRAMA

As the 1980s came to a close, the repressive government of Party leader Milos Jakes was overthrown and avant-garde playwright Václav Havel became President of Czechoslovakia. Imprisoned as a dissident six times for a total of five years (the most recent period being in February 1989), Havel's plays such as *The Garden Party* and *The Memorandum* were denied production for many years. Nonetheless, Havel's determined stance as the major Czech dissident won him admiration not only among his own people but throughout the world. (Samuel Beckett, for example, had dedicated a play to Havel, and Harold Pinter sought throughout Havel's numerous confinements to maintain contact with him.) In August 1989, before the December overthrow of the Jakeš government, Havel had publicly warned fellow dissidents that demonstrations in Prague's Wenceslas Square on the twenty-first anniversary of the 1968 Soviet invasion might produce another Tiananmen Square-style massacre by government troops.

Such a political environment throughout the 1980s continued to have its negative effects in the theatre. Like the plays of Havel, those by writers such as Ivan Klíma, Josef Topol, Milan Kundera, and Pavel Kohout were banned from the stage. (Kundera had fled to France and Kohout to Vienna during the 1980s.) Although Ladislav Smoček remained in Czechoslovakia, he did not produce a new play after 1970.

One sign of continuing theatrical vitality during the 1980s was in a number of provincial theatres rather than in Prague, the traditional theatrical capitol, where governmental surveillance was the most strenuous. Such theatres as the Ypsilon of Liberec, the Drama Studio of Ustí had Labem, Theatre on a String in Brno, and the Ha-theatre of Prostějov often depended upon irregular, unorthodox forms and sometimes elements such as mime, puppetry, and song. A number of productions in such theatres were devised by the companies themselves.

In Prague, owing to the repressive censorship, productions often were of plays dealing with past historical events, as in the case of Oldřich Danek's *You Are Jan* (1987), which treats the story of Jan Hus, the fifteenth-century Czech Protestant who was burned at the stake, and Jan Vedralls *Urmefisto* (1987), based on the career of German actor/director Gustaf Gründgens, who found success under the Nazis. Daniela Fischerová's (1948–) *Princess T* (1986) resurrects the fantasy story of Princess Turandot and her innumerable suitors, while Karel Stiegerwald's (1945–) *The Neopolitan Disease* (1984) treats the survivors of a future nuclear war.

Inevitably, the major Czech contribution theatrically continued to be in scenography. While the work of Svoboda remained acknowledged internationally, he, along with a new generation of designers that included Jaroslav Malina, Jan Dušek, Albert Pražák, and Miroslav Melena, formulated in the late 1970s and 1980s a new aesthetic referred to as *Action Design*. Partly growing out of economic necessity (Svoboda has acknowledged that his famous design for *Romeo and Juliet* at the National Theatre in 1963 would have been too expensive for the 1980s), Action Design nonetheless defined a legitimate minimalist aesthetic.

Based upon the presence of the three-dimensional actor, Action Design defines space visually rather than pictorially and thus more fully integrates the design into the performance. The entire stage, auditorium, lobby, foyer, and street become a part of the total theatrical space, and the design emerges collaboratively, piece by piece, as every element is scrutinized for its functional necessity. Unlike earlier scenographic beliefs that the design alone evokes the atmosphere of the drama, Action Design is closely dependent upon the presence of the actor, who becomes an integral part of the design itself. Inevitably, examples of Action Design viewed in isolation seem spare, abstract, nondecorative; but, when inhabited by actors, the dramatic action takes on an immediacy not

FIG. 15.16
Action Design by Josef Svoboda for a production of *Hamlet* at the Smetana Theatre, Prague, in 1982. Directed by M. Macháĉhek. (Photo by Jaromír Svoboda, courtesy Delbert Unruh.)

often possible in a traditionally elaborate setting under atmospheric lighting.

As in the rest of Eastern Europe and the Soviet Union, where the close of the 1980s brought many internal revolutions and overthrows of repressive regimes, the political situation in Czechoslovakia remained uncertain. Such startling images as the dismantling of the Berlin Wall and the numerous almost theatricalized demonstrations for freedom seemed to promise a renewed creative vitality in the Eastern bloc, but only the future can affirm if that will occur. At the end of the decade, most Western governments, in their surprise, seemed generally uncertain about how to respond to the seeming end of the Cold War.

LOOKING TOWARD THE 1990s

During the 1980s, theatrical production (particularly by innovative directors, actors, and designers) generally outdistanced the work of playwrights. A number of theatre artists such as Wilson, Foreman, Fo, and Kantor took to writing and directing their own works. Owing to the basic conventionality of many playwrights' scripts, few truly innovative directors were much interested in producing plays by their contemporaries, preferring instead the development of deconstructive performances focused upon works from the past. Like the great tradition of Soviet directors after the Revolution, contemporary directors inter-

FIG. 15.17
Action Design by Jaroslav Malina for a production of *A Midsummer Night's Dream*, A.B.C. Theatre, Prague, 1984. Directed by Karl Kříž. (Courtesy Delbert Unruh.)

rogated older plays for their immediate values in the present. This does not suggest that in the 1980s the playwright became unimportant, for many significant scripts continued to be written, even though often plays remained more in the modern, realistic style than in the newer, postmodern, deconstructive mode that many theatre directors favored. Clearly the director in the 1980s was the chief force in the shaping of theatre. With such directorial imaginativeness coupled with the increased dissemination of more recent actor-training and scenographic methods, the theatre in Europe and America continued to be a viable artistic form as it approached the twenty-first century.

Bibliography

GENERAL

Allen, John. *History of the Theatre in Europe.* Totowa, NJ, 1983.

Altman, George et al. *Theatre Pictorial.* Berkeley, 1953.

Banham, Martin, ed. *The Cambridge Guide to World Theatre.* Cambridge, 1988.

Bentley, Eric, ed. *The Theory of the Modern Stage.* Baltimore, 1968.

Bradbury, Malcolm and McFarlane, James, eds. *Modernism, 1890-1930.* New York, 1976.

Braun, Edward. *The Director and the Stage: From Naturalism to Grotowski.* London, 1982.

Brockett, Oscar G. *History of the Theatre.* 6th ed., Boston, 1991.

Carlson, Marvin. *Theories of the Theatre.* Ithaca, NY, 1984.

Cole, Toby, ed. *Playwrights on Playwriting.* New York, 1960.

Cole, Toby and Chinoy, Helen K., eds. *Actors on Acting.* rev. ed. New York, 1970.

————. *Directors on Directing.* Indianapolis, 1963.

Enciclopedia dello Spettacolo. 9 vols. Rome, 1953–1965.

Melchinger, Siegfried. *The Concise Encyclopedia of Modern Drama.* Transl. by George Wellwarth. New York, 1964.

Rischbieter, Henning. *Art and the Stage in the Twentieth Century.* Greenwich, CT, 1968.

Seltzer, Daniel (ed.). *The Modern Theatre: Readings and Documents.* Boston, 1967.

Styan, J. L. *Modern Drama in Theory and Practice.* 3 vols. Cambridge, 1980.

CHAPTER 1

Arvin, Neil. *Eugène Scribe and the French Theatre, 1815-1860.* Cambridge, MA, 1924.

Bancroft, Marie Effie. *The Bancrofts.* New York, 1909.

Barzun, Jacques. *Darwin, Marx, Wagner.* Boston, 1941.

Carlson, Marvin. *The French Stage in the Nineteenth Century.* Metuchen, NJ, 1972.

————. *The German Stage in the Nineteenth Century.* Metuchen, NJ, 1972.

Cole, J. W. *The Life and Theatrical Times of Charles Kean.* London, 1859.

Downer, Alan. S. *The Eminent Tragedian: William Charles Macready.* Cambridge, MA, 1966.

Fitzgerald, Percy. *The World Behind the Scenes.* London, 1881.

Hazelton, Nancy. *Historical Consciousness in Nineteenth Century Shakespearean Staging.* Ann Arbor, 1987.

Hopkins, A. A. *Magic: Stage Illusions and Scientific Diversions.* New York, 1897.

Kindermann, Heinz. *Theatergeschichte das Europas.* Vol. 7: *Realismus.* Salzburg, 1965.

Klenze, Camillo von. *From Goethe to Hauptmann.* New York, 1926.

Lacey, Alexander. *Pixérécourt and the French Romantic Drama.* Toronto, 1928.

Mammen, Edward W. *The Old Stock Company School of Acting.* Boston, 1945.

Matthews, Brander. *French Dramatists of the Nineteenth Century.* 5th ed. New York, 1914.

Meisel, Martin. *Realizations: Narrative, Pictorial, and Theatrical Arts in Nineteenth-Century England.* Princeton, NJ, 1983.

Melcher, Edith. *Stage Realism in France Between Diderot and*

Antoine. Bryn Mawr, PA, 1928.

Rowell, George. *The Victorian Theatre, 1792-1914.* 2nd ed. London, 1979.

Savin, Maynard. *Thomas William Robertson: His Plays and His Stagecraft.* Providence, RI, 1950.

Southern, Richard. *Changeable Scenery: Its Origins and Development in the British Theatre.* London, 1952.

Talmon, Jacob L. *Romanticism and Revolt: Europe, 1815-1848.* New York, 1967.

Taylor, Frank. A. *The Theatre of Alexander Dumas fils.* Oxford, 1937.

Vardac, A. N. *Stage to Screen: Theatrical Method from Garrick to Griffith.* Cambridge, MA, 1949.

Watson, Ernest B. *Sheridan to Robertson: A Study of the Nineteenth-Century London Stage.* Cambridge, MA, 1926.

CHAPTER 2

Bentley Eric. *The Playwright as Thinker: A Study of Drama in Modern Times.* New York, 1946.

Brereton, Austin. *The Life of Henry Irving.* 2 vols. London, 1908.

Brustein, Robert. *The Theatre of Revolt.* New York, 1964.

Carter, Lawson A. *Zola and the Theatre.* New Haven, 1963.

Downs, Brian W. *Ibsen: The Intellectual Background.* Cambridge, 1946.

Felheim, Marvin. *The Theater of Augustin Daly.* Cambridge, MA, 1956.

Grant, Elliott M. *Emile Zola.* New York, 1966.

Grube, Max. *The Story of the Meiningen.* Transl. by Ann Marie Koller. Coral Gables, FL, 1963.

Gutzman, Robert W. *Richard Wagner: The Man, His Mind, and His Music.* New York, 1968.

Hart, Jerome A. *Sardou and the Sardou Plays.* London, 1913.

Hemmings, Frederic. *Emile Zola.* Oxford, 1953.

Huneker, James G. *Iconoclasts.* London, 1905.

Irving, Laurence. *Henry Irving.* London, 1951.

Josephson, Matthew. *Zola and His Time.* Garden City, NY, 1928.

Kindermann, Heinz. See Chapter 1.

—————. *Theatergeschichte das Europas.* Vol. 8: *Naturalismus und Expressionismus.* Salzburg, 1968.

Koht, Halvdan. *The Life of Ibsen.* 2 vols. New York, 1931.

Koller, Ann Marie. *The Theatre Duke: Georg II of Saxe-Meiningen and the German Stage.* Stanford, CA, 1984.

Mackaye, Percy. *Epoch: The Life of Steele Mackaye.* 2 vols. New York, 1927.

Marker, Frederick J. and Marker, Lise-Lone. *Ibsen's Lively Art: A Performance Study of the Major Plays.* Cambridge, 1989.

McFarlane, James W. *Ibsen and the Temper of Norwegian Literature.* London, 1960.

Melcher, Edith. See Chapter 1.

Newman, Ernest. *The Life of Richard Wagner.* 4 vols. New York, 1933–1960.

Northam, John. *Ibsen's Dramatic Method.* London, 1953.

Odell, G. C. D. *Annals of the New York Stage.* Vols. 8–15. New York, 1936–1949.

Osborne, John. *The Meiningen Court Theatre, 1866-1890.* Cambridge, 1988.

Quinn, Arthur H. *A History of American Drama from the Civil War to the Present Day.* 2nd ed. New York, 1949.

Rowell, George. See Chapter 1.

Sanderson, Michael. *From Irving to Olivier: A Social History of the Acting Profession in England, 1880-1983.* London, 1984.

Shaw, George Bernard. *The Quintessence of Ibsenism.* London, 1913.

Skelton, Geoffrey. *Wagner at Bayreuth.* New York, 1965.

Smith, Hugh A. *Main Currents in Modern French Drama.* New York, 1925.

Southern, Richard. See Chapter 1.

Stebbins, G. *The Delsarte System of Expression.* 5th ed. New York, 1894.

Stein, Jack M. *Richard Wagner and the Synthesis of the Arts.* Detroit, 1960.

Valency, Maurice. *The Flower and the Castle: An Introduction to Modern Drama.* New York, 1963.

Vardac, A. N. See Chapter 1.

Wagner, Richard. *Opera and Drama.* Transl. by Edwin Evans. London, 1913.

—————. *Richard Wagner on Music and Drama.* Ed. by Albert Goldman and Evert Sprinchorn. New York, 1964.

Antoine, André. *Memories of the Théâtre Libre.* Transl. by Marvin Carlson. Carol Gables, FL, 1964.

Bablet, Denis. *Esthétique Générale du Décor de Théâtre de 1870 à 1914.* Paris, 1965.

Bentley, Eric. See Chapter 2.

Borras, F. M. *Maxim Gorky the Writer.* Oxford, 1967.

Bruford, W. H. *Chekhov.* London, 1957.

————. *Stanislavsky.* New York, 1951.

Carpenter, Charles A. *Bernard Shaw and the Art of Destroying Ideals: The Early Plays.* Madison, WI, 1969.

Chandler, Frank W. *The Contemporary Drama of France.* Boston, 1920.

Clark, B. H. *The British and American Drama of Today.* New York, 1921.

Claus, Horst. *The Theater Director Otto Brahm.* Ann Arbor, 1981.

Cordell, Richard. *Henry Arthur Jones and the Modern Drama.* New York, 1932.

Crompton, Louis. *Shaw the Dramatist.* Lincoln, NE, 1969.

Dickinson, T. H. *The Contemporary Drama in England.* Boston, 1931.

Ervine, St. John. *Bernard Shaw.* New York, 1956.

Fyfe, H. Hamilton. *Sir Arthur Pinero's Plays and Players.* London, 1930.

Garten, Hugh F. *Gerhart Hauptmann.* New Haven, 1954.

————. *Modern German Drama.* New York, 1959.

Hudson, L. A. *The English Stage, 1850-1950.* London, 1951.

Incorporated Stage Society. *Ten Years: 1899 to 1909.* London, 1909.

Jones, Henry Arthur. *The Renascence of the English Drama.* London, 1895.

Kaun. Alexander. *Maxim Gorky and His Russia.* New York, 1931.

Knight, K. G. and Norman, F., eds. *Hauptmann Centenary Lectures.* London, 1964.

Koteliansky, S. S. *The Life and Letters of Anton Tchekov.* New York, 1925.

Lavrin, Janko. *Pushkin to Mayakovsky.* London, 1948.

Levin, Don. *Stormy Petrel: The Life and Work of Maxim Gorky.* New York, 1965.

Magarschack, David. *Chekhov the Dramatist.* London, 1952.

Mason, A. E. W. *Sir George Alexander and the St. James' Theatre.* London, 1935.

Meisel, Martin. *Shaw and the Nineteenth Century Drama.* Cambridge, 1963.

Melcher, Edith. See Chapter 1.

Melik–Zakharov, S. and Solntsev, N. *Konstantin Stanislavsky, 1863-1963.* Moscow, 1963.

Miller, Anna Irene. *The Independent Theatre in Europe, 1887 to the Present.* New York, 1931.

Nemirovich-Danchenko, Vladimir. *My Life in the Russian Theatre.* Transl. by John Cournos. Boston, 1936.

Newmark, Maxim. *Otto Brahm: The Man and the Critic.* New York, 1938.

Nicoll, Allardyce. *A History of Late Nineteenth Century Drama.* Cambridge, 1946.

Orme, Michael. *J. T. Grein: The Story of a Pioneer.* London, 1936.

Schiefley, W. H. *Brieux and Contemporary French Society.* New York, 1917.

Segel, Harold B. *Twentieth Century Russian Drama: From Gorky to the Present.* New York, 1979.

Shaw, George Bernard. *Our Theatre in the Nineties.* London, 1932.

————. *Shaw on Theatre.* Ed. by E. J. West. New York, 1958.

Shaw, Leroy R. *Witness of Deceit: Gerhart Hauptmann as Critic of Society.* Berkeley, 1958.

Sinden, Margaret. *Gerhart Hauptmann: The Prose Plays.* Toronto, 1957.

Slonim, Marc. *Russian Theatre from the Empire to the Soviets.* Cleveland, 1961.

Smith, Hugh A. See Chapter 1.

Smith, Joseph P. *The Unrepentant Pilgrim: A Study of the Development of Bernard Shaw.* Boston, 1965.

Stanislavsky, Konstantin. *An Actor Prepares.* Transl. by Elizabeth R. Hapgood. New York, 1936.

————. *Building a Character.* Transl. by Elizabeth R. Hapgood. New York, 1949.

————. *Creating a Role.* Transl. by Elizabeth R. Hapgood. New York, 1961.

————. *My Life in Art.* Transl. by J. J. Robbins. New York, 1924.

————. *Stanislavsky on the Art of the Stage.* Transl. by David Magarschack. New York, 1952.

————. *Stanislavsky's Legacy.* Transl. by Elizabeth R. Hapgood. New York, 1958.

Styan, J. L. *Chekhov in Performance.* Cambridge, 1971.

Valency, Maurice. *The Breaking String: The Plays of Anton Chekhov.* New York, 1966.

Varneke, Boris. *History of Russian Theatre, Seventeenth*

through Nineteenth Centuries. Transl. by Boris Brasol. New York, 1951.

Waxman, Samuel. *Antoine and the Théâtre Libre.* Cambridge, MA, 1926.

Whitton, David. *Stage Directors in Modern France* [Antoine to Mnouchkine]. Manchester, Eng., 1987.

Wilson, Colin. *Bernard Shaw: A Reassessment.* New York, 1969.

CHAPTER 4

Beaumont, Keith. *Alfred Jarry: A Critical and Biographical Study.* New York, 1985.

Beckson, Karl E., ed. *Oscar Wilde: The Critical Heritage.* London, 1970.

Bennett, Benjamin. *Hugo von Hofmannsthal: The Theatre of Consciousness.* Cambridge, 1988.

Bithell, Jethro. *The Life and Writings of Maurice Maeterlinck.* London, 1913.

Block, Haskell. *Mallarmé and the Symbolist Drama.* Detroit, 1963.

Brown, J. A. C. *Freud and the Post-Freudians.* Baltimore, 1961.

Chandler, Frank. W. See Chapter 3.

——————. *Aspects of Modern Drama.* New York, 1914.

Chiari, Joseph. *The Poetic Drama of Paul Claudel.* New York, 1954.

——————. *Symbolism from Poe to Mallarmé.* 2nd ed. New York, 1970.

Claudel, Paul. *Claudel on Theatre.* Coral Gables, FL, 1971.

Cornell, Kenneth. *The Symbolist Movement.* New Haven, 1951.

Cooperman, Hayes. *The Aesthetics of Stephane Mallarmé.* New York, 1933.

Dahlstrom, C. E. W. L. *Strindberg's Dramatic Expressionism.* Ann Arbor, MI, 1930.

Ellmann, Richard, ed. *Oscar Wilde: A Collection of Critical Essays.* Englewood Cliffs, NJ, 1969.

Fowlie, Wallace. *Mallarmé.* Chicago, 1953.

——————. *Paul Claudel.* New York, 1957.

Gray, Ronald D. *The German Tradition in Literature, 1871-1945.* Cambridge, 1965.

Halls, W. D. *Maurice Maeterlinck: A Study of His Life and Thought.* Oxford, 1960.

Hammelmann, Hanns A. *Hugo von Hofmannsthal.* New Haven, 1957.

Heller, Otto. *Prophets of Dissent: Essays on Maeterlinck, Strindberg, Nietzsche, and Tolstoy.* New York, 1918.

Hollingdale, R. J. *Nietzsche: The Man and His Philosophy.* London, 1965.

Jasper, Gertrude. *Adventure in the Theatre: Lugné-Poë and the Théâtre de l'Oeuvre to 1899.* New Brunswick, NJ, 1947.

Johnson, Walter. *Strindberg and the Historical Drama.* Seattle, 1963.

Jones, Ernest. *The Life and Work of Sigmund Freud.* 3 vols. New York, 1953–1960.

Knapp, Bettina. *Paul Claudel.* New York, 1982.

Lamm, Martin. *August Strindberg.* Transl. and ed. by Harry G. Carlson. New York, 1971.

Lehmann, Andrew. *The Symbolist Aesthetic in France, 1885-1895.* Oxford, 1950.

Love, Frederick R. *Young Nietzsche and the Wagnerian Experience.* Chapel Hill, NC, 1963.

Madsen, Borge G. *Strindberg's Naturalistic Theatre: Its Relation to French Naturalism.* Copenhagen, 1962.

McGill, V. J. *August Strindberg: The Bedeviled Viking.* London, 1930.

Mortensen, B. M. E. and Downs, B. W. *Strindberg: An Introduction to His Life and Works.* Cambridge, 1949.

Ojala, Aatos. *Aestheticism and Oscar Wilde.* 2 vols. Helsinki, 1954–1955.

Quennell, Peter. *Baudelaire and the Symbolists.* New York, 1929.

San Juan, Epifanio. *The Art of Oscar Wilde.* Princeton, 1967.

Shattuck, Roger. *The Banquet Years: The Arts in France, 1885-1918.* New York, 1961.

Sprigge, Elizabeth. *The Strange Life of August Strindberg.* New York, 1949.

Stockenström, Gören, ed. *Strindberg's Dramaturgy.* Minneapolis, 1988.

Strindberg, August. *Open Letters to the Intimate Theatre.* Transl. by Walter Johnson. Seattle, 1966.

Symons, Arthur. *The Symbolist Movement in Literature.* rev. ed. New York, 1919.

Weintraub, Stanley. *The Literary Criticism of Oscar Wilde.* Lincoln, NE, 1968.

Whyte, Lancelot. L. *The Unconscious Before Freud.* Garden City, NY, 1962.

Wolman, Benjamin. B. *The Unconscious Mind: The Meaning of Freudian Psychology.* Englewood Cliffs, NJ, 1968.

Worth, Katherine. *Oscar Wilde.* New York, 1984.

CHAPTER 5

Agate, James. *A Short View of the English Stage, 1900-1926.* London, 1926.

Belasco, David. *The Theatre Through Its Stage Door.* New York, 1919.

Bernheim, Alfred L. *The Business of the Theatre.* New York, 1932.

Blake, Ben. *The Awakening of the American Theatre.* New York, 1935.

Bourgeois, Maurice. *J. M. Synge and the Irish Theatre.* New York, 1965.

Brustein, Robert. See Chapter 2.

Byrne, Dawson. *The Story of Ireland's National Theatre: The Abbey.* Dublin, 1929.

Buckley, Reginald R. *The Shakespeare Revival and the Stratford-upon-Avon Movement.* London, 1911.

Chandler, Frank W. See Chapter 4.

Cheney, Sheldon. *The Open Air Theatre.* New York, 1918.

Clark, B. H. See Chapter 3.

————. *Contemporary French Dramatists.* Cincinnati, 1915.

Coxhead, Elizabeth. *Lady Gregory: A Literary Portrait.* New York, 1961.

Dickinson, T. H. See Chapter 3.

Downer, Alan S. *Fifty Years of American Drama, 1900-1950.* Chicago, 1950.

Dunbar, Janet. *J. M. Barrie.* New York, 1970.

Ellis, Ruth. *The Shakespeare Memorial Theatre.* London, 1948.

Ellis-Fermor, Una. *The Irish Dramatic Movement.* London, 1939.

Fay, Gerard. *The Abbey Theatre.* London, 1958.

Garten, Hugh F. *Modern German Drama.* London, 1959.

Gittelman, Sol. *Frank Wedekind.* New York, 1969.

Greene, David H., and Stephens, E. M. *J. M. Synge, 1871-1909.* New York, 1959.

Gregory, (Lady) Isabella Augusta. *Our Irish Theatre.* New York, 1913.

Hudson, L. A. See Chapter 3.

Ishibashi, Hiro. *Yeats and the Noh.* Ed. by Anthony Kerrigan. Dublin, 1966.

Jameson, Storm. *Modern Drama in Europe.* London, 1920.

Jourdain, Eleanor F. *The Drama of Europe in Theory and Practice.* New York, 1924.

Lamm, Martin. See Chapter 4.

Le Gallienne, Eva. *Mystic in the Theatre: Eleanora Duse.* New York, 1966.

Liptzin, Sol. *Arthur Schnitzler.* New York, 1932.

Lucas, F. L. *The Drama of Chekhov, Synge, Yeats, and Pirandello.* London, 1963.

MacClintock, Lander. *The Contemporary Drama of Italy.* Boston, 1920.

Mackaye, Percy. *The Civic Theatre and Its Relation to the Redemption of Leisure.* New York, 1912.

————. *Community Drama.* Boston, 1917.

March, Harold. *Romain Rolland.* New York, 1971.

Marker, Lise-Lone. *David Belasco: Naturalism in the American Theatre.* Princeton, NJ, 1974.

Maxwell, C. E. W. *A Critical History of Modern Irish Drama, 1891-1980.* New York, 1985.

McLeod, Addison. *Plays and Players in Modern Italy.* London, 1912.

Moore, James R. *Masks of Love and Death: Yeats as a Dramatist.* Ithaca, NY, 1971.

Morgan, Margery M. *Drama of Political Man: A Study of the Plays of Granville Barker.* London, 1961.

Nathan, Leonard E. *The Tragic Drama of William Butler Yeats.* New York, 1965.

O'Neill, Michael J. *Lennox Robinson.* New York, 1964.

Peak, J. Hunter. *Social Drama in Nineteenth-Century Spain.* Chapel Hill, NC, 1965.

Pearson, Hesketh. *The Last Actor-Managers.* London, 1950.

Penuelas, Marcelino. *Jacinto Benavente.* New York, 1968.

Poel, William. *Shakespeare in the Theatre.* London, 1913.

Poggi, Jack. *Theater in America: The Impact of Economic Forces, 1870-1967.* Ithaca, NY, 1968.

Prevots, Naima. *American Pageantry: A Movement for Art and Democracy.* Ann Arbor, 1990.

Purdom, Charles B. *Harley Granville Barker: Man of the Theatre, Dramatist, and Scholar.* London, 1955.

Quinn, Arthur H. See Chapter 2.

Rabey, David I. *British and Irish Political Drama in the Twentieth Century.* London, 1986.

Reichert, H. W. and Salinger, H., eds. *Studies in Arthur Schnitzler.* Chapel Hill, NC, 1963.

Robinson, Lennox, ed. *Ireland's Abbey Theatre: A History, 1899-1951.* London, 1951.

Rolland, Romain. *The People's Theatre.* Transl. by B. H. Clark. New York, 1918.

Rowell, George. See Chapter 1.

──────. *The Repertory Movement: A History of Regional Theatre in Britain.* Cambridge, 1984.

Salmon, Eric, ed. *Bernhardt and the Theatre of Her Time.* Westport, CT, 1984.

Skelton, Robin. *J. M. Synge and His World.* London, 1971.

Skinner, Cornelia Otis. *Madame Sarah.* Boston, 1967.

Speaight, Robert. *William Poel and the Elizabethan Revival.* London, 1954.

Stokes, John et al. *Bernhardt, Terry, Duse: The Actress in Her Time.* Cambridge, 1988.

Trewin, J. C. *Benson and the Bensonians.* London, 1960.

──────. *Shakespeare on the English Stage, 1900-1964.* London, 1964.

Trewin, J. C. and Kemp, T. C. *The Stratford Festival: A History of the Shakespeare Memorial Theatre.* Birmingham, 1953.

Ure, Peter. *Yeats the Playwright.* London, 1963.

Valency, Maurice. See Chapter 2.

Vendler, Helen H. *Yeats' Vision and the Later Plays.* Cambridge, MA, 1963.

Walbrook, Henry M. *J. M. Barrie and the Theatre.* London, 1922.

Weaver, William. *Duse: A Biography.* New York, 1984.

Winter, William. *The Life of David Belasco.* 2 vols. New York, 1918.

Winwar, Frances. *Wingless Victory: A Biography of Gabriele D'Annunzio and Eleanora Duse.* New York, 1956.

Yeats, William Butler. *Autobiography.* New York, 1938.

──────. *Plays and Controversies.* London, 1923.

CHAPTER 6

Alexandre, Arsène. *The Decorative Art of Leon Bakst.* Transl. by Harry Melville. New York, 1971.

Appia, Adolphe. *Essays, Scenarios and Designs.* Transl. by Walther R. Volbach. Ed. by Richard C. Beacham. Ann Arbor, 1989.

──────. *Music and the Art of the Theatre.* Transl. by R. W. Corrigan and M. D. Dirks. Coral Gables, FL, 1962.

──────. *The Work of Living Art* and *Man is the Measure of All Things.* Transl. by H. D. Albright and Barnard Hewitt. Coral Gables, Fl, 1960.

Bablet, Denis. *Edward Gordon Craig.* Transl. by Daphne Woodward. New York, 1966.

──────. *The Revolution of Stage Design in the Twentieth Century.* Paris, 1977.

Bakshy, Alexander. *The Path of the Modern Russian Stage.* Boston, 1918.

Beacham, Richard C. *Adolphe Appia: Theatre Artist.* Cambridge, 1987.

Blake, Ben. See Chapter 5.

Bowlt, John. *Russian Stage Design: Scenic Innovation, 1900-1930.* Jackson, MS, 1982.

Braun, Edward. *Meyerhold on Theatre.* New York, 1969.

──────. *The Theatre of Meyerhold: Revolution on the Modern Stage.* New York, 1979.

Carter, Huntly. *The Theatre of Max Reinhardt.* New York, 1914.

Cheney, Sheldon. *The Art Theatre.* New York, 1917.

──────. *The New Movement in the Theatre.* New York, 1914.

Craig, Edward Gordon. *Index to the Story of My Days.* New York, 1957.

──────. *On the Art of the Theatre.* Chicago, 1911.

──────. *The Theatre—Advancing.* Boston, 1921.

Downer, Alan. S. See Chapter 5.

Dukore, Bernard F. *Bernard Shaw, Director.* London, 1971.

Evreinov, Nikolai. *The Theatre in Life.* Transl. by A. I. Nazaroff. New York, 1927.

Frank, Waldo. *The Art of the Vieux-Colombier.* New York, 1918.

Fuchs, Georg. *Revolution in the Theatre.* Translated by C. C. Kuhn. Ithaca, NY, 1959.

Fuchs, Theodore. *Stage Lighting.* Boston, 1929.

Fuerst, René and Hume, S. J. *Twentieth Century Stage*

Decoration. 2 vols. London, 1928.

Goldie, Grace. *The Liverpool Repertory Theatre.* London, 1922.

Golub, Spencer. *Evreinov: The Theatre of Paradox and Transformation.* Ann Arbor, 1984.

Gorelik, Mordecai. *New Theatres for Old.* New York, 1940.

Granville Barker, Harley. *The Exemplary Theatre.* London, 1922.

Green, Michael, ed. *The Russian Symbolist Theatre.* Ann Arbor, 1986.

Gregor, Joseph and Fülop-Miller, René. *The Russian Theatre.* Transl. by Paul England. Philadelphia, 1930.

Grigoriev. S. L. *The Diaghilev Ballet, 1909–1929.* Harmondsworth, England, 1960.

Hansen, Robert C. *Scenic and Costume Design for the Ballets Russes.* Ann Arbor, 1985.

Hudson, L. A. See Chapter 3.

Innes, Christopher D. *Edward Gordon Craig.* Cambridge, 1983.

Jaques-Dalcroze, Emile. *Rhythm, Music, and Education.* London, 1921.

Jelavich, Peter. *Munich and Theatrical Modernism: Politics, Playwriting, and Performance, 1890-1914.* Cambridge, MA, 1985.

Kinne, W. P. *George Pierce Baker and the American Theatre.* Cambridge, MA, 1954.

Knapp, Bettina L. *Louis Jouvet, Man of the Theatre.* New York, 1958.

Knight Arthur. *The Liveliest Art: A Panoramic History of the Movies.* New York, 1957.

Kochno, Boris. *Diaghilev and the Ballets Russes.* Transl. by Adrienne Foulke. New York, 1970.

Kommisarjevsky, Theodore. *Myself and the Theatre.* New York, 1930.

Komissarzhevskii, V. *Moscow Theatres.* Moscow, 1959.

Leach, Robert. *Vsevelod Meyerhold.* Cambridge, 1989.

Leeper, Janet E. *Gordon Craig: Designs for the Theatre.* Harmondsworth, England, 1948.

Levinson, André I. *Bakst: The Story of the Artist's Life.* New York, 1971.

MacCarthy, Desmond. *The Court Theatre, 1904-1907.* London, 1907.

Macgowan, Kenneth. *The Theatre of Tomorrow.* New York, 1921.

Mackay, Constance D. *The Little Theatre in the United States.* New York, 1917.

Marker, Frederick J. and Marker, Lise-Lone. *Edward Gordon Craig and The Pretenders: A Production Revisited.* Carbondale, IL, 1981.

Moderwell, Hiram. *The Theatre of Today.* New York, 1914.

Pearson, Hesketh. See Chapter 5.

Pichel, Irving. *Modern Theatres.* New York, 1925.

Pogson, Rex. *Miss Horniman and the Gaiety Theatre. Manchester.* London, 1952.

Purdom, Charles B. See Chapter 5.

Quinn, Arthur H. See Chapter 2.

Roose-Evans, James. *Experimental Theatre: From Stanislavsky to Peter Brook.* rev. ed. London, 1984.

Rudlin, John. *Jacques Copeau.* Cambridge, 1986.

Rudnitsky, Konstantin. *Meyerhold the Director.* Ann Arbor, 1981.

————. *Russian and Soviet Theatre: Tradition and the Avant-Garde.* London, 1988.

Sayler, Oliver M. *Max Reinhardt and His Theatre.* New York, 1936.

Shaw, G. B. *Letters to Granville Barker.* Ed. by C. B. Purdom. New York, 1957.

Stern, Ernst. *My Life, My Stage,* London, 1951.

Styan, J. L. *Max Reinhardt.* Cambridge, 1982.

Tairov, Alexander. *Notes of a Director.* Transl. by William Kuhlke. Coral Gables, FL, 1969.

Volbach, Walther R. *Adolphe Appia, Prophet of the Modern Theatre.* Middletown, CT, 1968.

Walton, J. Michael, ed. *Craig on Theatre.* London, 1983.

Whitton, David. *Stage Directors in Modern France* [Antoine to Mnouchkine]. Manchester, Eng., 1987.

CHAPTER 7

Balakian, Anna. *André Breton, Magus of Surrealism.* New York, 1971.

Ball, Hugo. *Flight Out of Time: A Dada Diary.* New York, 1974.

Bates, Scott. *Guillaume Apollinaire.* New York, 1967.

Benson, Renate. *German Expressionist Drama: Ernst Toller and Georg Kaiser.* New York, 1985.

Bigsby, C. W. E. *Dada and Surrealism.* London, 1972.

Breton, André. *Manifestoes of Surrealism*. Translated by Richard Seaver and Helen R. Lane. Ann Arbor, MI, 1969.

——————. *What is Surrealism?* Transl. by David Gascoyne. London, 1936.

Carrieri, Raffaele. *Futurism*. Milan, 1963.

Carter. Huntly. *The New Spirit in the European Theatre, 1914-1924*. New York, 1926.

Cheney, Sheldon. *Expressionism in Art*. rev. ed. New York, 1948.

Clough, Rosa T. *Futurism—The Story of a Modern Art Movement*. New York, 1961.

Cocteau, Jean. *Journals*. Ed. and transl. by Wallace Fowlie. Bloomington, IN, 1964.

Davies, Margaret. *Apollinaire*. Edinburgh, 1964.

Dry, Avis M. *The Psychology of Jung*. New York, 1961.

Duran, Manuel, ed. *Lorca: A Collection of Critical Essays*. Englewood Cliffs, NJ, 1962.

Eisner, Lotte. *The Haunted Screen*. London, 1969.

Fowlie, Wallace. *The Age of Surrealism*. Bloomington, IN, 1960.

Fuerst, René and Hume, S. J. See Chapter 6.

Garten, Hugh F. See Chapter 5.

Glover, Joseph G. *The Cubist Theatre*. Ann Arbor, 1980.

Goldberg, Roselee. *Performance Art: From Futurism to the Present*. rev. ed. New York, 1988.

Golding, John. *Cubism: A History and an Analysis, 1907-1914*. 2nd ed. London, 1968.

Gordon, Mel, ed. *Dada Performance*. New York, 1987.

Gorelik, Mordecai. See Chapter 6.

Grossman, Manuel L. *Dada: Paradox, Mystification, and Ambiguity in European Literature*. New York, 1971.

Honig, Edwin. *Federico García Lorca*. Norfolk, CT, 1944.

Hulsenbeck, Richard. *Memoirs of a Dada Drummer*. New York, 1969.

Ilie, Paul. *The Surrealist Mode in Spanish Literature*. Ann Arbor, 1968.

Infeld, Leopold. *Albert Einstein: His Work and Its Influence on our World*. New York, 1950.

Jacobi, Jolande. *Complex, Archetype, and Symbol in the Psychology of C. G. Jung*. Transl. by Ralph Manheim. New York, 1959.

Kenworthy, B. J. *Georg Kaiser*. Oxford, 1957.

Kirby, Michael. *Futurist Performance*. New York, 1971.

Krakauer, Siegfried. *From Caligari to Hitler*. London, 1947.

Krispyn, Egbert. *Style and Society in German Literary Expressionism*. Gainesville, FL, 1964.

Leavens, Ileana B. *From "291" to Zurich: The Birth of Dada*. Ann Arbor, 1983.

Lemaître, Georges. *From Cubism to Surrealism in French Literature*. Cambridge, MA, 1941.

Levy, Julian. *Surrealism*. New York, 1936.

Lima, Robert. *The Theatre of Garcia Lorca*. New York, 1963.

Macgowan, Kenneth and Jones, R. E. *Continental Stagecraft*. New York, 1922.

Mackworth, Cecily. *Guillaume Apollinaire and the Cubist Life*. London, 1961.

Matthews, J. H. *Theatre in Dada and Surrealism*. Syracuse, 1974.

Melzer, Annabelle. *Latest Rage the Big Drum: Dada and Surrealist Performance*. Ann Arbor, 1980.

Miesel, Victor H., ed. *Voices of German Expressionism*. Englewood Cliffs, NJ, 1970.

Moussinac, Leon. *The New Movement in the Theatre*. London, 1931.

Nadeau, Maurice. *The History of Surrealism*. New York, 1965.

Orenstein, Gloria. *The Theatre of the Marvelous: Surrealism and the Contemporary Stage*. New York, 1975.

Oxenhandler, Neal. *Scandal and Parade: The Theatre of Jean Cocteau*. New Brunswick, NJ, 1957.

Patterson, Michael. *Revolution in the German Theatre, 1900-1933*. Boston, 1981.

Peterson, Elmer. *Tristan Tzara: Dada and Surrealist Theorist*. New Brunswick, NJ, 1971.

Reichenbach, Hans. *From Copernicus to Einstein*. Transl. by Ralph B. Winn. New York, 1942.

Richter, Hans. *Dada: Art and Anti-Art*. New York, 1966.

Samuel, Richard and Thomas, R. Hinton. *Expressionism in German Life, Literature, and the Theatre*. Cambridge, 1939.

Sandrow, Nahma. *Surrealism: Theatre, Arts, Ideas*. New York, 1972.

Schvey, Henry I. *Oskar Kokoschka: the Painter as Playwright*. Detroit, 1982.

Shattuck, Roger. See Chapter 4.

Sokel, Walter H. *The Writer in Extremis: Expressionism in Twentieth Century German Literature*. New York, 1964.

Steinke, G. E. *The Life and Work of Hugo Ball, Founder of Dadaism*. The Hague, 1963.

Toller, Ernst. *I Was a German*. New York, 1934.

Tzara, Tristan. *Seven Dada Manifestoes and Lampesteries*. London, 1977.

Verkauf, Willy et al. *Dada: Monograph of a Movement.* New York, 1957.

Willett, John. *Expressionism.* New York, 1970.

CHAPTER 8

Black, Lendley C. *Mikhail Chekhov as Actor, Director and Teacher.* Ann Arbor, 1987.

Bradshaw, Martha. *Soviet Theatres, 1917-1941.* New York, 1954.

Braun, Edward. See Chapter 6.

Carter, Huntly. *The New Spirit in the Russian Theatre, 1917-1928.* London, 1929.

Chekhov, Michael. *To the Actor.* New York, 1953.

Csato, Edward. *The Polish Theatre.* Warsaw, 1963.

Dana, H. W. L. *Handbook of Soviet Drama.* New York, 1938.

Erlich, Victor. *Russian Formalism.* The Hague, 1955.

Fencl, Otakar. *The Czechoslovak Theatre Today.* Prague, 1963.

Fuerst, René and Hume, S. J. See Chapter 6.

Gerould, Daniel. *Witkacy: Stanislaw Ignacy Witkiewicz as an Imaginative Writer.* Seattle, 1981.

Gorchakov, Nikolai A. *The Theatre in Soviet Russia.* Transl. by Edgar Lehman. New York, 1957.

Gorchakov, Nikolai M. *The Vakhtangov School of Stage Art.* Moscow, 1961.

Gorelik, Mordecai. See Chapter 6.

Gregor, Joseph and Fülop-Miller, René. See Chapter 6.

Hoover, Marjorie. *Meyerhold: The Art of Conscious Theatre.* Amherst, 1974.

Houghton, Norris. *Moscow Rehearsals.* New York, 1936.

Kiebuzinska, Christine. *Revolutionaries in the Theatre: Meyerhold, Brecht, and Witkiewicz.* Ann Arbor, 1988.

Kohansky, Mendel. *The Hebrew Theatre: Its First Fifty Years.* New York, 1969.

Komissarzhevskii, V. See Chapter 6.

Lavrin, Janko. See Chapter 3.

Leach, Robert. *Vsevelod Meyerhold.* Cambridge, 1989.

Magarschack, David. *Stanislavsky.* New York, 1951.

Markov, P. A. *The Soviet Theatre.* London, 1934.

Markov, Vladimir. *Russian Futurism.* Berkeley, 1968.

Melik-Zakharov, S. and Solntsev. N. See Chapter 3.

Miłosz, Czesław. *The History of Polish Literature.* New York, 1969.

Moussinac, Leon. See Chapter 7.

Nemirovich-Dantchenko, Vladimir. See Chapter 3.

Rudnitsky, Konstantin. See Chapter 6.

Sayler, Oliver M. *Inside the Moscow Art Theatre.* New York, 1925.

————. *The Russian Theatre.* New York, 1922.

Schmidt, Paul, ed. *Meyerhold at Work.* Austin, TX, 1980.

Segel, Harold G. See Chapter 3.

Seton, Marie. *Sergei M. Eisenstein.* New York, 1952.

Simonov, Reuben. *Stanislavsky's Protégé, Eugene Vakhtangov.* Transl. by Miriam Goldina. New York, 1969.

Slonim, Marc. See Chapter 3.

Stanislavsky, Konstantin. See Chapter 3.

Symons, James. *Meyerhold's Theatre of the Grotesque: The Post-Revolutionary Productions, 1920-1932.* Coral Gables, FL, 1971.

Tairov, Alexander. See Chapter 3.

Van Gyseghem, André. *Theatre in Soviet Russia.* London, 1944.

Weil, Irwin. *Gorky: His Literary Development and Influence on Soviet Intellectual Life.* New York, 1966.

Wolfe, Bertram D. *The Bridge and the Abyss: The Troubled Friendship of Maxim Gorky and V. I. Lenin.* New York, 1967.

Worozylski, Wiktor. *The Life of Mayakovsky.* Transl. by Boleslaw Doborski. New York, 1970.

Worrall, Nick. *Modernism to Realism on the Soviet Stage: Tairov, Vakhtangov, Okhlopkov.* Cambridge, 1989.

Yershov, Peter. *Comedy in Soviet Russia.* New York, 1956.

CHAPTER 9

Artaud, Antonin. *The Theatre and Its Double.* Transl. by M. C. Richards. New York, 1958.

Bassnett-McGuire, Susan. *Luigi Pirandello.* New York, 1984.

Bishop, Thomas. *Pirandello and the French Theatre.* New York, 1960.

Bredel, Oscar. *Pirandello.* New York, 1966.

Brustein, Robert. See Chapter 2.

Chandler, Frank. *Modern Continental Playwrights*. New York, 1931.

Chiari, Joseph. *The Contemporary French Theatre: Flight from Naturalism*. New York, 1958.

Cohen, Robert G. *Giraudoux: Three Faces of Destiny*. Chicago, 1968.

Daniels, May. *The French Drama of the Unspoken*. Edinburgh, 1953.

Dickinson, T. H. *The Theatre in a Changing Europe*. New York, 1937.

Fuerst, René and Hume, S. J. See Chapter 6.

Greene, Naomi. *Antonin Artaud: Poet Without Words*. New York, 1970.

Guicharnaud, Jacques. *Modern French Theatre from Giraudoux to Beckett*. New Haven, 1961.

Inskip, Donald. P. *Jean Giraudoux: The Making of a Dramatist*. London, 1958.

Knapp, Bettina L. *Antonin Artaud, Man of Vision*. New York, 1969.

——————. *Louis Jouvet, Man of the Theatre*. New York, 1958.

Knowles, Dorothy. *French Drama of the Inter-war Years, 1918-1939*. New York, 1967.

LeSage, Laurence. *Jean Giraudoux, Surrealism and the German Romantic Ideal*. Urbana, IL, 1952.

MacClintock, Lander. *The Age of Pirandello*. Bloomington, IN, 1951.

Moussinac, Leon. See Chapter 7.

Palmer, John. *Studies in Contemporary French Theatre*. New York, 1927.

Pronko, Leonard. *Avant-Garde: The Experimental Theatre in France*. Berkeley, 1962.

Pucciani, Oreste F. *The French Theatre Since 1930*. Boston, 1954.

Rudlin, John. *Jacques Copeau*. Cambridge, 1986.

Saint-Denis, Michel. *Theatre: The Rediscovery of Style*. New York, 1960.

Sellin, Eric. *The Dramatic Concepts of Antonin Artaud*. Chicago, 1968.

Starkie, Walter F. *Luigi Pirandello*. New York, 1926.

Vittorini, Domenico. *The Drama of Luigi Pirandello*. New York, 1957.

Whitton, David. See Chapter 6.

CHAPTER 10

Braun, Hanns. *The Theatre in Germany*. Munich, 1952.

Bertolt Brecht on Stage. Frankfort-am-Main, 1968.

Brecht, Bertolt. *Brecht on Theatre*. Transl. by John Willett. New York, 1964.

Demetz, Peter, ed. *Brecht: A Collection of Critical Essays*. Englewood Cliffs, NJ, 1962.

Esslin, Martin. *Brecht: A Choice of Evils*. New York, 1984.

Fuerst, René and Hume, S. J. See Chapter 6.

Garten, Hugh F. See Chapter 5.

Gropius, Walter, ed. *The Theatre of the Bauhaus*. Middletown, CT, 1961.

Haas, Willy. *Bertolt Brecht*. Transl. by Max Knight and Joseph Fabry. New York, 1970.

Hayman, Ronald. *Brecht: A Biography*. New York, 1983.

Innes, C. D. *Erwin Piscator's Political Theatre*. New York, 1972.

——————. *Modern German Drama: A Study in Form*. Cambridge, 1979.

Jones, David Richard. *Great Directors at Work: Stanislavsky, Brecht, Kazan, Brook*. Berkeley, 1986.

Kiebuzinska, Christine. See Chapter 8.

Ley-Piscator, Maria. *The Piscator Experiment*. New York, 1967.

Lyons, Charles R. *Bertolt Brecht: The Despair and the Polemic*. Carbondale, IL, 1968.

Moholy-Nagy, Laszlo. *Vision in Motion*. Chicago, 1947.

Patterson, Michael. *The Revolution in German Theatre, 1900-1933*. Boston, 1981.

Piscator, Erwin. *The Political Theatre: A History, 1914-1929*. Transl. Hugh Rorison, New York, 1978.

Sayler, Oliver M. See Chapter 6.

Spalter, Max. *Brecht's Tradition*. Baltimore, 1967.

Weideli, Walter. *The Art of Bertolt Brecht*. New York, 1963.

Wengler, Hans M. *Bauhaus*. Cambridge, MA, 1969.

Whitford, Frank. *Bauhaus*. London, 1984.

Willett, John. *Art and Politics in the Weimar Period: The New Sobriety, 1917-1933*. New York, 1978.

——————. *The Theatre of Bertolt Brecht*. New York, 1959.

——————. *The Theatre of Erwin Piscator*. New York, 1979.

—————. *The Theatre of the Weimar Republic.* New York, 1988.

Zortman, Bruce. *Hitler's Theatre: Ideological Drama in Nazi Germany.* El Paso, 1984.

CHAPTER 11

Alexander, Doris. *The Tempering of Eugene O'Neill.* New York, 1962.

Atkinson, Brooks. *Broadway Scrapbook.* New York, 1947.

Bailey, Mabel D. *Maxwell Anderson: The Playwright as Prophet.* New York, 1957.

Benstock, Bernard. *Sean O'Casey.* Lewisburg, PA, 1970.

Bernheim, Alfred L. See Chapter 5.

Bigsby, C. W. E. *A Critical Introduction to Twentieth-Century American Drama.* Vol. I: 1900–1940. New York, 1983.

Bishop, G. W. *Barry Jackson and the London Theatre.* London, 1933.

Bogard, Travis. *Contours in Time: The Plays of Eugene O'Neill.* New York, 1972.

Bond, Frederick. *The Negro and the Drama.* Washington, DC, 1940.

Bordman, Gerald. *American Musical Comedy: From Adonis to Dreamgirls.* New York, 1982.

—————. *American Musical Revue: From The Passing Show to Sugar Babies.* New York, 1985.

Bridges-Adams. W. *The Irresistible Theatre.* London, 1957.

Bronssard, Louis. *American Drama: Contemporary Allegory From Eugene O'Neill to Tennessee Williams.* Norman, OK, 1962.

Brustein, Robert. See Chapter 2.

Burbank, Rex. *Thornton Wilder.* New York, 1961.

Browne, E. Martin. *The Making of T. S. Eliot's Plays.* London, 1969.

Cargill, Oscar et al. *O'Neill and His Plays: Four Decades of Criticism.* New York, 1961.

Cheney, Sheldon. *The Art Theatre.* rev. ed. New York, 1925.

—————. *Stage Decoration.* New York, 1928.

Clunes, Alec. *The British Theatre.* London, 1964.

Clurman, Harold. *The Fervent Years: The Story of the Group Theatre in the Thirties.* New York, 1957.

Davis, Hallie Flanagan. *Arena.* New York, 1940.

Dent, Edward J. *A Theatre for Everybody: The Story of the Old Vic and Sadlers Wells.* London, 1946.

Deutsch, Helen and Hanau, Stella. *The Provincetown.* New York, 1931.

Donoghue, Denis. *The Third Voice: Modern British and American Verse Drama.* Princeton, 1959.

Downer, Alan S. *Fifty Years of American Drama, 1900–1950.* Chicago, 1951.

Eaton, Walter P., ed. *The Theatre Guild: The First Ten Years.* New York, 1929.

Ellis, Ruth. See Chapter 5.

Engel, Edwin. *The Haunted Heroes of Eugene O'Neill.* Cambridge, MA, 1953.

Evans, Gareth L. *J. B. Priestley: The Dramatist.* London, 1964.

Falk, Doris V. *Eugene O'Neill and the Tragic Tension.* New Brunswick, NJ, 1958.

Findlater, Richard. *Lilian Baylis: The Lady of the Old Vic.* London, 1975.

Geddes, Norman Bel. *Miracle in the Evening.* Garden City, NY, 1960.

Gelb, Arthur and Gelb, Barbara. *O'Neill.* New York, 1962.

Gielgud, John. *Early Stages.* New York, 1939.

Gorelik, Mordecai. See Chapter 6.

Grebanier, Bernard. *Thornton Wilder.* Minneapolis, 1964.

Guthrie, Tyrone. *A Life in the Theatre.* London, 1960.

—————. *In Various Directions.* New York, 1965.

Himmelstein, Morgan Y. *Drama was a Weapon: The Left-wing Theatre in New York, 1929-1941.* New Brunswick, NJ, 1963.

Hinchliffe, Arnold. *Modern Verse Drama.* London, 1977.

Hogan, Robert G. *After the Irish Renaissance: A Critical History of the Irish Drama Since "The Plough and the Stars."* Minneapolis, 1967.

—————. *The Experiments of Sean O'Casey.* New York, 1960.

Hopkins, Arthur. *Reference Point.* New York, 1948.

Hudson, L. A. See Chapter 3.

Isaacs, Edith J. R. *The Negro in the American Theatre.* New York, 1947.

Krause, David. *Sean O'Casey: The Man and His Work.* New York, 1960.

Krutch, Joseph W. *The American Drama Since 1918.* rev. ed. New York, 1957.

Levin, Milton. *Noel Coward.* New York, 1968.

McFall, Haldane. *The Book of Claud Lovat Fraser.* London, 1923.

Macgowan, Kenneth. *Footlights Across America.* New York, 1925.

MacLiammoir, Michael. *Theatre in Ireland.* Dublin, 1950.

Marshall, Norman. *The Other Theatre.* London, 1949.

Mersand, Joseph. *The American Drama, 1930-1940.* New York, 1941.

Meserve, Walter J. *Robert E. Sherwood: Reluctant Moralist.* New York, 1970.

Miller, Jordan Y. *Playwright's Progress: O'Neill and the Critics.* Chicago, 1965.

Moussinac, Leon. See Chapter 7.

O'Connor, Garry. *Sean O'Casey: A Life.* New York, 1988.

O'Connor, John and Lorraine Brown, eds. *Free, Adult, Uncensored: The Living History of the Federal Theatre Project.* Washington, DC, 1978.

Peacock, Ronald. *The Poet in the Theatre.* New York, 1946.

Pendleton, Ralph. *The Theatre of Robert E. Jones.* Middletown, CT, 1958.

Playfair, Nigel. *Story of the Lyric Theatre, Hammersmith.* London, 1925.

Poggi, Jack. See Chapter 5.

Quinn, Arthur H. See Chapter 2.

Rabey, David Ian. *British and Irish Political Drama in the Twentieth Century.* London, 1986.

Rabkin, Gerald. *Drama and Commitment: Politics in the American Theatre of the Thirties.* Bloomington, IN, 1964.

Robinson, Lennox. See Chapter 5.

Sanders, Leslie Catherine. *The Development of Black Theater in America.* Baton Rouge, 1988.

Sanderson, Michael. See Chapter 2.

Sarlos, Robert. *Jig Cook and the Provincetown Players.* Amherst, MA, 1982.

Simmons, James. *Sean O'Casey.* New York, 1984.

Simonson, Lee. *Part of a Lifetime.* New York, 1943.

Tornqvist, Egil. *A Drama of Souls: Studies in O'Neill's Supernaturalistic Technique.* New Haven, 1968.

Trewin, J. C. See Chapter 5.

————. *The Birmingham Repertory Theatre, 1913-1963.* London, 1963.

Tuisanen, Timo. *O'Neill's Scenic Images.* Princeton, 1968.

Wainscott, Ronald H. *Staging O'Neill: The Experimental Years, 1920-1934.* New Haven, 1988.

Weales, Gerald. *Clifford Odets, Playwright.* New York, 1971.

Whitworth, G. A. *The Making of a National Theatre.* London, 1951.

Williams, E. Harcourt. *Old Vic Saga.* London, 1949.

Young, Stark. *The Theatre.* New York, 1927.

CHAPTER 12

Allsop, Kenneth. *The Angry Decade: A Survey of the Cultural Revolt of the 1950s.* London, 1958.

Andrews, John. *International Theatre.* London, 1949.

Armstrong, William A., ed. *Experimental Drama.* London, 1963.

Aslan, Odette. *Roger Blin and Twentieth Century Playwrights.* Cambridge, 1988.

Bair, Dierdre. *Samuel Beckett: A Biography.* New York, 1978.

Barrault, Jean-Louis. *Reflections on the Theatre.* London, 1951.

————. *The Theatre of Jean-Louis Barrault.* Transl. by J. Chiari. New York, 1961.

Bentley, Eric. *In Search of Theatre.* New York, 1954.

————. *What is Theatre? Incorporating the Dramatic Event and Other Reviews, 1944-1967.* New York, 1968.

Bigsby, C. W. E. *A Critical Introduction to Twentieth-Century American Drama.* Vol. 2. Cambridge, 1984.

Bordman, Gerald. See Chapter 11.

Bowers, Faubion. *Broadway USSR: Theatre, Ballet and Entertainment in Russia Today.* New York, 1959.

Bradby, David. *Modern French Drama, 1940-1980.* Cambridge, 1984.

Braun, Hans. See Chapter 10.

Brecht, Bertolt. See Chapter 10.

Bree, Germaine. *Camus.* New Brunswick, NJ. 1961.

Bronssard, Louis. See Chapter 11.

Brown, Ivor. *Shakespeare Memorial Theatre.* 4 vols. London, 1951–1959.

Brown, John Russell, ed. *Modern British Dramatists: A Collection of Critical Essays.* Englewood Cliffs, NJ, 1968.

Browne, E. Martin. *The Making of T. S. Eliot's Plays.* London, 1969.

Browne, Terry W. *Playwrights' Theatre: The English Stage Company at the Royal Court Theatre.* London, 1975.

Brustein, Robert. See Chapter 2.

Champigny, Robert. *Stages on Sartre's Way, 1938-1952.* Bloomington, IN, 1959.

Chiari, Joseph. See Chapter 9.

Clunes, Alec. See Chapter 11.

Clurman, Harold. *Lies Like Truth.* New York, 1958.

Coe, Richard. *Ionesco.* Edinburgh, 1961.

Cohn, Ruby. *Currents in Contemporary Drama.* Bloomington, IN, 1969.

—————. *From Desire to Godot: Pocket Theatre of Postwar Paris.* Berkeley, 1987.

Donoghue, Denis. See Chapter 11.

Driver, Tom. *Jean Genet.* New York, 1966.

Edwards, Christine. *The Stanislavsky Heritage.* New York, 1965.

Elsom, John. *Post-War British Theatre.* London, 1976.

English Stage Company. *Ten Years at the Royal Court, 1956-1966.* London, 1966.

Esslin, Martin. *The Theatre of the Absurd.* rev. ed. London, 1968.

Five Seasons of the Old Vic Theatre Company . . . , 1944-1949. London, 1949.

Fowlie, Wallace. *Dionysus in Paris: A Guide to Contemporary French Theatre.* New York, 1960.

Freeman, E. *The Theatre of Albert Camus.* London, 1971.

Gardner, R. H. *The Splintered Stage: The Decline of the American Theatre.* New York, 1965.

Garten, Hugh F. See Chapter 5.

Goorney, Howard. *The Theatre Workshop.* London, 1980.

Gorchakov, Nikolai A. See Chapter 8.

Grossvogel, David. *Four Playwrights and a Postscript: Brecht, Ionesco, Beckett, Genet.* Ithaca, NY, 1963.

—————. *The Self-conscious Stage in Modern French Drama.* Athens, GA, 1958.

Guicharnaud, Jacques. See Chapter 9.

Hainaux, René, ed. *Stage Design Throughout the World Since 1935.* New York, 1956.

—————. *Scene Design Throughout the World Since 1950.* New York, 1964.

Harvey, John E. *Anouilh: A Study in Theatrics.* New Haven, 1964.

Hayman, Ronald. *Arnold Wesker.* 3d ed. New York, 1979.

—————. *Sartre: A Life.* New York, 1987.

Hinchliffe, Arnold. *British Theatre, 1950-1970.* Oxford, 1974.

—————. *John Osborne.* Boston, 1984.

—————. *Modern Verse Drama.* London, 1977.

Hirsch, Foster. *A Method to Their Madness: The History of the Actors Studio.* New York, 1984.

Hobson, Harold. *The French Theatre of Today.* London, 1953.

Innes, C. D. *Modern German Drama.* New York, 1979.

Ionesco, Eugene. *Notes and Counter Notes.* Transl. by Donald Watson. New York, 1964.

Jackson, Esther. *The Broken World of Tennessee Williams.* Madison, WI, 1965.

Jacobsen, Josephine and Mueller, William R. *Ionesco and Genet: Playwrights of Silence.* New York, 1968.

Jameson, Frederic. *Sartre: The Origins of a Style.* New Haven, 1961.

Jeffs, Rae. *Brendan Behan : Man and Showman.* London, 1966.

Jones, David Richard. *Great Directors at Work: Stanislavsky, Brecht, Kazan, Brook.* Berkeley, 1986.

Jones, Robert Emmett. *The Alienated Hero in Modern French Drama.* Athens, GA, 1962.

Kenner, Hugh. *Samuel Beckett.* Carbondale, IL, 1961.

Kernan, Alvin B., ed. *The Modern American Theatre: A Collection of Critical Essays.* Englewood Cliffs, NJ, 1967.

Kienzle, Siegfried. *Modern World Theatre: A Guide to Productions in Europe and the United States Since 1945.* New York, 1970.

Kitchin, Laurence. *Mid-Century Drama.* 2nd ed. London, 1962.

Kolin, Philip. C., ed. *American Playwrights Since 1945; A Guide to Scholarship, Criticism, and Performance.* Westport, CT, 1989.

Lewis, Allan. *American Plays and Playwrights of the Contemporary Theatre.* New York, 1965.

Londré, Felicia H. *Tennessee Williams.* New York, 1983.

Lyons, Charles. *Samuel Beckett.* New York, 1984.

McMahon, Joseph H. *The Imagination of Jean Genet.* New Haven, 1963.

McMillan, Dougald and Martha Felsenfeld. *Beckett in the Theatre: The Author as Practical Playwright and Director.* Vol. 1. London, 1988.

Mielziner, J. *Designing for the Theatre.* New York, 1965.

Moss, Leonard. *Arthur Miller.* New York, 1967.

Nelson, Benjamin. *Arthur Miller.* New York, 1970.

—————. *Tennessee Williams.* New York, 1961.

Olivier, Laurence. *Confessions of an Actor: an Autobiography.* New York, 1982.

Peppard, Murray. *Friedrich Duerrenmatt.* New York, 1969.

Price, Julia. *The Off-Broadway Theatre.* New York, 1962.

Pronko, Leonard. *The World of Jean Anouilh.* Berkeley, 1968.

—————. *Eugene Ionesco.* New York, 1965.

—————. See Chapter 9.

Pucciani, Oreste F. See Chapter 9.

Rabey, David Ian. See Chapter 11.

Ribalow, Harold U. *Arnold Wesker.* New York, 1965.

Roose-Evans, James. See Chapter 6.

Roy, Emil. *Christopher Fry.* Carbondale, IL, 1968.

Sartre, Jean-Paul. *Literary and Philosophical Essays.* London, 1955.

—————. *Saint Genet, Actor and Martyr.* Transl. by Bernard Frechtman. New York, 1964.

Savona, Jeanette L. *Jean Genet.* New York, 1985.

Segel, Harold B. See Chapter 3.

Shaw, Leroy. *The German Theatre Today.* Austin, TX, 1963.

Simpson, Alan. *Beckett, Behan, and a Theatre in Dublin.* London, 1962.

Speaight, Robert. *Drama Since 1939.* London, 1947.

Strasberg, Lee. *Strasberg at the Actor's Studio.* New York, 1965.

Styan, J. L. *The Dark Comedy.* 2nd ed. Cambridge, 1968.

Taylor, John Russell. *The Angry Theatre: New British Drama.* New York, 1969.

Tischler, Nancy. *Tennessee Williams: Rebellious Puritan.* New York, 1961.

Trewin, J. C. *Dramatists of Today.* London, 1953.

Trussler, Simon. *The Plays of John Osborne.* London, 1969.

Tynan, Kenneth. *Curtains: Selections from Drama Criticism.* London, 1961.

Weales, Gerald. *American Drama Since World War I.* New York, 1962.

Weisstein, Ulrich. *Max Frisch.* New York, 1967.

Welland, Dennis. *Arthur Miller.* Edinburgh, 1961.

Wellwarth, George E. *The Theatre of Protest and Paradox.* New York, 1964.

Whitton, David. See Chapter 6.

Willett, John. *Caspar Neher: Brecht's Designer.* London, 1986.

CHAPTER 13

Addenbrooke, David. *The Royal Shakespeare Company: The Peter Hall Years.* London, 1974.

Bigsby, C. W. E. *Confrontation and Commitment: A Study of Contemporary American Drama, 1959-1966.* Columbia, MO, 1967.

Brook, Peter. *The Empty Space.* New York, 1968.

—————. *The Shifting Point: Forty Years of Theatrical Exploration, 1946-1987.* London, 1988.

Burian, Jarka. *The Scenography of Josef Svoboda.* Middletown, CT, 1971.

Burkman, Katherine H. *The Dramatic World of Harold Pinter.* Columbus, OH, 1970.

Cheney, Anne. *Lorraine Hansberry.* Boston, 1984.

Cohn, Ruby. *New American Dramatist, 1960-1980.* New York, 1982.

Corballis, Robert. *Stoppard: The Mystery and the Clockwork.* New York, 1984.

Csato, Edward. See Chapter 8.

Debusscher, Gilbert. *Edward Albee.* Brussels, 1967.

Dent, Thomas O. et al. *The Free Southern Theatre.* Indianapolis, 1969.

Esslin, Martin. *The Peopled Wound: The Work of Harold Pinter.* New York, 1970.

—————. See Chapter 12.

Fairweather, Virginia. *Cry God for Larry: An Intimate Memoir of Sir Laurence Olivier.* London, 1969.

Fencl, Otakar. See Chapter 8.

Goodwin, John, ed. *Royal Shakespeare Theatre Company, 1960-1963.* New York, 1964.

Grotowski, Jerzy. *Towards a Poor Theatre.* New York, 1968.

Hainaux, René. *Stage Design Throughout the World Since 1960.* New York, 1973.

Hansen, Al. *A Primer of Happenings and Space/Time Art.* New York, 1966.

Hinchliffe, Arnold. *Harold Pinter.* rev. ed. Boston, 1981.

Houghton, Norris. *Return Engagement: A Postscript to "Moscow Rehearsals."* New York, 1962.

Kernan, Alvin B. See Chapter 12.

Kitchin, Laurence. *Drama in the Sixties.* London, 1966.

Kostelanetz. Richard. *The Theatre of Mixed Means.* New York, 1968.

Little, Stuart. *Enter Joseph Papp: In Search of a New American Theatre.* New York, 1974.

—————. *Off-Broadway: The Prophetic Theatre.* New York, 1972.

Marowitz, Charles and Trussler, Simon. *Theatre at Work: Playwrights and Productions in the Modern British Theatre.* New York, 1968.

Miłosz, Czesław. See Chapter 8.

Mitchell, Loften. *Black Drama: The Story of the American Negro in the Theatre.* New York, 1967.

National Theatre (Great Britain). *Some Facts and Figures, 1963-1967.* London, 1968.

Neff, Renfreu. *The Living Theatre USA.* Indianapolis, 1970.

Novick, Julius. *Beyond Broadway.* New York, 1968.

O'Connor, Garry. *Ralph Richardson: An Actor's Life.* New York, 1979.

Osiński, Zbigniew. *Grotowski and His Laboratory.* Transl. Lillian Vallee and Robert Findlay. New York, 1986.

Pasolli, Robert. *A Book on the Open Theatre.* New York, 1970.

Poggi, Jack. See Chapter 5.

Roose-Evans, James. See Chapter 6.

Rostagno, Aldo. *We, the Living Theatre.* New York, 1970.

Rutenberg, Michael. *Edward Albee.* New York, 1969.

Scharine, Richard. *The Plays of Edward Bond.* Lewisburg, PA, 1976.

Schechner, Richard. *Public Domain: Essays on the Theatre.* Indianapolis, 1969.

Slonim, Marc. See Chapter 3.

Taylor, John Russell. See Chapter 12.

Trensky, Paul. *Czech Drama Since World War II.* White Plains, NY, 1978.

Weales, Gerald. *The Jumping Off Place: American Drama in the 1960s.* New York. 1969.

CHAPTERS 14 AND 15

Ansorge, Peter. *Disrupting the Spectacle: Five Years of Experimental and Fringe Theatre in Britain.* London, 1975.

Aronson, Arnold. *American Set Design.* New York, 1985.

—————. *The History and Theory of Environmental Scenography.* Ann Arbor, 1981.

Barba, Eugenio. *Beyond the Floating Islands.* New York, 1986.

Bartow, Arthur. *The Director's Voice: 21 Interviews [with American Directors].* New York, 1988.

Betsko, Kathleen and Koenig, Rachel. *Interviews with Contemporary Women Playwrights.* New York, 1987.

Bigsby, C. W. E. *A Critical Introduction to Twentieth Century American Drama.* Vol. 3. Cambridge, 1985.

Biner, Pierre. *The Living Theatre.* New York, 1972.

Blau, Herbert. *The Eye of Prey: Subversion of the Postmodern.* Urbana, IL, 1987.

Blumenthal, Eileen. *Joseph Chaikin: Exploring at the Boundaries of Theatre.* Cambridge, 1984.

Bordman, Gerald. See Chapter. 11.

Bradby, David. See Chapter 12.

Bradby, David and Williams, David. *Director's Theatre.* [Littlewood, Planchon, Mnouchkine, Grotowski, Brook, Stein, Wilson]. New York, 1988.

Brecht, Stefan. *The Bread and Puppet Theatre.* 2 vols. London, 1988.

—————. *The Theatre of Visions: Robert Wilson.* Frankfurt am Main, 1978.

Breines, Paul, ed. *Critical Interruptions: New Left Perspectives on Herbert Marcuse.* New York, 1970.

Brustein, Robert. *Revolution as Theatre: Notes on the New Radical Style.* New York, 1971.

Bull, John. *New British Political Dramatists: Howard Brenton, David Hare, Trevor Griffiths, and David Edgar.* London, 1984.

Byrd Hoffman Foundation. *Robert Wilson: The Theatre of Images.* 2nd ed. New York, 1984.

Cage, John. *Silence.* Middletown, CT, 1961.

Calandra, Denis. *New German Dramatists: A Study of Peter Handke, Franz Xaver Kroetz, Rainer Werner Fassbinder, Heiner Müller, Thomas Bernhard.* New York, 1983.

Case, Sue-Ellen. *Feminism and Theatre.* New York, 1988.

Cave, Richard Allen. *New British Drama in Performance on the London Stage, 1970-1985.* New York, 1988.

Champagne, Lenora. *French Theatre Experiment Since 1968.* Ann Arbor, 1984.

Chinoy, Helen K. and Jenkins, Linda W. *Women in*

American Theatre. rev. ed. New York, 1987.

Cook, Judith. *Directors' Theatre.* London, 1974.

————. *The National Theatre.* London, 1976.

Cranston, Maurice, ed. *The New Left: Six Critical Essays.* New York, 1970.

Croyden, Margaret. *Lunatics, Lovers, and Poets: The Contemporary Experimental Theatre.* New York, 1974.

Davy, Kate. *Richard Foreman and the Ontological-Hysteric Theatre.* Ann Arbor, 1981.

Day, Barry. *The Message of Marshall McLuhan.* London, 1967.

Dolan, Jill. *The Feminist Spectator as Critic.* Ann Arbor, 1988.

Eagleton, Terry. *Literary Theory.* Minneapolis, 1983.

Ellis, Roger. *Peter Weiss in Exile: A Critical Study of His Works.* Ann Arbor, 1987.

Etherton, Michael. *Contemporary Irish Dramatists.* New York, 1989.

Feral, Josette. *Theatre in France: Ten Years of Research.* Madison, WI, 1978.

Filler, Withold. *Contemporary Polish Theatre.* Warsaw, 1977.

Findlater, Richard, ed. *At the Royal Court: 25 Years of the English Stage Company.* New York, 1981.

Finkelstein, Sidney W. *Sense and Nonsense of McLuhan.* New York, 1968.

Foster, Stephen. *"Event" Arts and Art Events.* Ann Arbor, 1988.

Goldberg, Roselee. *Performance Art: From Futurism to the Present.* rev. ed. New York, 1988.

Grodzicki, August. *Polish Theatre Today.* Warsaw, 1978.

Hainaux, René. *Stage Design Throughout the World, 1970–1975.* New York, 1976.

Hall, Peter. *Peter Hall's Diaries.* London, 1983.

Harland, Richard. *Superstructuralism: The Philosophy of Structuralism and Post-Structuralism.* London, 1987.

Hart, Lynda, ed. *Making a Spectacle: Essays on Contemporary Women's Theatre.* Ann Arbor, 1989.

Hayes, Eugene N., ed. *Claude Lévi-Strauss: The Anthropologist as Hero.* Cambridge, MA, 1970.

Hayman, Ronald, ed. *The German Theatre.* London, 1975.

————. *Theatre and Anti-theatre: New Movements Since Beckett.* London, 1979.

————. *Tom Stoppard.* 4th ed. London, 1982.

Hill, Errol. *The Theatre of Black Americans.* 2 vols. Englewood Cliffs, NJ, 1980.

Hutchings, William. *The Plays of David Storey.* Carbondale, IL, 1988.

Innes, Christopher. *Holy Theatre: Ritual and the Avant-Garde.* Cambridge, 1981.

Itzin, Catherine. *Stages in the Revolution: Political Theatre in Britain Since 1968.* London, 1980.

Jenkins, Anthony. *The Theatre of Tom Stoppard.* 2nd ed. Cambridge, 1989.

Jenkins, Ron. *Acrobats of the Soul: Comedy and Virtuosity in Contemporary American Theatre.* New York, 1988.

Kaprow, Allan. *Assemblage, Environments, and Happenings.* New York, 1966.

————. *Some Recent Happenings.* New York, 1966.

Karpiński, Maciej. *The Theatre of Andrej Wajda.* Cambridge, 1989.

Kerensky, Oleg. *The New British Drama: Fourteen Playwrights Since Osborne and Pinter.* New York, 1979.

Kirby, Michael. *Happenings.* New York, 1966.

Kolin, Philip. C., ed. See Chapter 12.

Kostelanetz, Richard. *The Theatre of Mixed Means.* New York, 1968.

Kumiega, Jennifer. *The Theatre of Grotowski.* London, 1985.

Lahr, John. *Up Against the Fourth Wall: Essays on Modern Theater.* New York, 1970.

Leach, Edmund R. *Claude Lévi-Strauss.* New York, 1970.

Lesnick, Henry. *Guerrilla Street Theatre.* New York, 1973.

Lyotard, Jean-Francois. *The Postmodern Condition.* Minneapolis, 1984.

Marranca, Bonnie. *The Theatre of Images.* New York, 1977.

Mitchell, Tony. *Dario Fo: People's Jester.* London, 1984.

Mottram, Ron. *Inner Landscapes: The Theatre of Sam Shepard.* Columbia, MO, 1984.

O'Connor, Garry. *French Theatre Today.* London, 1975.

Oliva, Judy L. *David Hare: Theatricalizing Politics.* Ann Arbor, 1990.

Osinski, Zbigniew. See Chapter 13.

Pasolli, Robert. *A Book on the Open Theatre.* New York, 1970.

Patterson, Michael. *German Theatre Today: Postwar Theatre in West and East Germany, Austria, and Northern Switzerland.* London, 1976.

————. *Peter Stein: Germany's Leading Theatre Director.* Cambridge, 1982.

Pottlitzer, Joanne. *Hispanic Theatre in the United States and Puerto Rico.* New York, 1988.

Roberts, Philip. *The Royal Court Theatre, 1965–1972.* London, 1986.

Robinson, Paul A. *The Freudian Left.* New York, 1969.

Roose-Evans, James. See Chapter 6.

Rouse, John. *Brecht and the West German Theatre: The Practice and Politics of Interpretation.* Ann Arbor, 1989.

Rowell, George. See Chapter 5.

Sanders, Leslie C. *The Development of Black Theatre in America: From Shadows to Selves.* Baton Rouge, 1988.

Savran, David. *In Their Own Words: Contemporary American Playwrights.* New York, 1988.

——————. *The Wooster Group, 1975-1985: Breaking the Rules.* Ann Arbor, 1986.

Schechner, Richard. *The End of Humanism: Writings on Performance.* New York, 1982.

——————. *Environmental Theatre.* New York, 1973.

Schechter, Joel. *Durov's Pig: Clowns, Politics, and Theatre.* New York, 1985.

Schevill, James. *Breakout! In Search of New Theatrical Environments.* Chicago, 1972.

Segel, Harold B. See Chapter 3.

Sellner, Maxine S., ed. *Ethnic Theatre in the United States.* Westport, CT, 1983.

Servos, Norbert. *Pina Bausch—Wuppertal Dance Theatre.* Cologne, 1984.

Shank, Theodore. *American Alternative Theatre.* New York, 1982.

Shyer, Laurence. *Robert Wilson and His Collaborators.* New York, 1989.

Taylor, John Russell. *Second Wave: British Dramatists for the Seventies.* New York, 1971.

Valency, Maurice. *The End of the World: An Introduction to Contemporary Drama.* New York, 1980.

Van Erven, Eugene. *Radical People's Theatre.* Bloomington, IN, 1988.

Wandor, Michelene. *Look Back in Gender: Sexuality and the Family in Post 1956 British Drama.* London, 1987.

Whitton, David. See Chapter 6.

Williams, Mance. *Black Theatre in the 1960s and 1970s.* Westport, CT, 1985.

Zeigler, Joseph. *Regional Theatre: The Revolutionary Stage.* Minneapolis, 1973.

Information about recent developments must still be sought primarily in periodicals. Some of the most helpful are:

American Theatre
Comparative Drama
Drama Survey
Journal of Dramatic Theory and Criticism
Modern Drama
New Theatre Quarterly
The New York Times
PAJ (Performing Arts Journal)
Plays and Players
Shakespeare Quarterly
TDR (The Drama Review)
Theater der Zeit
Theater Heute

Theater Week
Theatre
Theatre Crafts
Theatre Design and Technology
Theatre in Poland
Theatre Journal
Theatre Survey
Theatre Three
Travail Théâtral
Variety
The Village Voice
Women and Performance

Index